McGraw-Hill's ACT

McGraw-Hill's ACT

Steven W. Dulan
and the faculty of
Advantage Education

McGraw-Hill

New York   Chicago   San Francisco   Lisbon   London   Madrid   Mexico City
Milan   New Delhi   San Juan   Seoul   Singapore   Sydney   Toronto

CONTENTS

ACKNOWLEDGMENTS

The author would like to acknowledge the contribution of the faculty and staff of Advantage Education. You are not only the smartest, but also the best. Special thanks to Jennifer Kostamo, a quiet genius who almost always keeps her composure no matter how often she is rudely interrupted by me; Josh Singer and Stephanie Price, our math whizzes; and, Pamela Chamberlain, our brilliant, versatile, and hard-working contributor/editor. All of you put in extra effort to make this book a success.

I would also like to specifically acknowledge the students, faculty, and staff of Steamboat Springs High School, in Steamboat Springs, Colorado, and Coral Shores High School, in Tavernier, Florida, who have made me feel like a part of their schools for many years now. (I told you that you were my favorites!) Special thanks are due to Dan Kratish of the Upper Keys Rotary Club and to Mike Campbell of Steamboat Springs High School.

Most importantly, I would like to acknowledge the single biggest contributor to this work: my wife, colleague, co-author, editor, typist, employee, boss, and friend: Amy Dulan. None of this would have been possible without your hard work and dedication. Thanks for stickin' with me.

ABOUT THE AUTHOR

Steve Dulan has been involved with the ACT since 1982 when he received a score of 32 on his own test as a high school junior at Iron Mountain High School. That score qualified him for the State of Michigan Competitive Scholarship in 1983. In 1989, after serving as a U.S. Army Infantry Sergeant, and during his time as an undergraduate at Michigan State University, Steve became an ACT instructor. He has been helping students to prepare for success on the ACT and other standardized exams ever since. Steve attended The Thomas M. Cooley Law School on a full Honors Scholarship after achieving a 99th percentile score on his Law School Admission Test (LSAT). In fact, Steve scored in the 99th percentile on every standardized test he has ever taken. While attending law school, Steve continued to teach standardized test prep classes (including ACT, SAT, PSAT, GRE, GMAT, and LSAT) an average of thirty hours each week, and tutored some of his fellow law students in a variety of subjects and in essay exam writing techniques. Professor Dulan has also served as an instructor at the college and law school levels.

Thousands of students have benefited from his instruction, coaching, and admissions consulting and have gone on to their colleges of choice. Steve's students have gained admission to some of the most prestigious institutions in the world, and received many scholarships of their own. A few of them even beat his ACT score! Since 1997, Steve has served as the President of Advantage Education (www.study-smart.com), a company dedicated to providing effective and affordable test prep education in a variety of settings, including classes and seminars at high schools and colleges around the country, summer College Prep Camps at The University of Michigan, and one-on-one via the Internet worldwide. The techniques included in this book are the result of Steve's experiences with students at all ability and motivation levels over the years.

INTRODUCTION: USING THIS BOOK

This book contains general information about the ACT and chapters on each of the test sections. It also contains a Diagnostic Assessment and four Practice Tests. If you have the version with the CD-ROM, you also have access to three more simulated ACT tests. At the end of the book you'll also find a discussion of related topics such as choosing a college.

In a perfect situation, you will be reading this at least several weeks before you take your actual ACT exam. If that is not the case, you can still benefit from this book. You should read Chapter 2, which covers test-taking strategies, and then get through at least some of the questions on each section of the Diagnostic Test. Even just a few hours of study and practice can have a beneficial impact on your ACT score.

If you are reading this only days before your ACT exam, you should not pre-order any ACT score reports. ACT, Inc. allows you to pick and choose which scores you send out to colleges. So you should send scores only after you have a chance to review them yourself. If your score is not acceptable, you can always retake the ACT and only send the scores from your best testing day to your schools of choice. This option is especially important if you are unsure of how you will score and if you are going in with only minimum preparation.

At the end of this section you'll find scheduling hints to help you to plan out your preparation. You should count backward from your ACT test day and try to complete as many of the suggested activities as you can. If you have enough time between now and your ACT (at least three weeks but preferably twelve to eighteen weeks), you should work through this entire book. Some of the material should be used as practice and some should be used as "dress rehearsal" material to get you ready for the whole experience of taking an ACT exam. If you have less than three weeks, go to the ACT Emergency Plan on page xvi.

In our experience, the students who increase their scores the most are the ones who put in consistent effort over time. Try to keep your frustration to a minimum when you aren't doing as well as you had hoped. Similarly, try to keep yourself from becoming overconfident when you have a great testing day.

HOW TO USE THE PRACTICE TESTS

The Diagnostic Assessment in Part II of this book is a simulated full-length ACT. Take it as the first step in your test-preparation program. It will help you to pinpoint areas of strength and weakness in your knowledge base and your skill set. Take it under realistic conditions. Time yourself strictly. You need to have an accurate picture of what your performance would be like if test day were today. When you take the real ACT, you will be given about a ten-minute break after the Mathematics Test, so give yourself a similar break during the Diagnostic Assessment. A good place to take the test is a library; there will be other people around but they will be relatively quiet, just like at a testing center. After you have scored the Diagnostic Assessment, you should review the parts of the chapters that cover any content areas that you found difficult.

When you have finished your review, start tackling the Practice Tests in Part IV of this book. Like the Diagnostic Assessment, each one is a full-length simulated ACT. These tests are fairly accurate simulations written by experienced experts. They contain some variations in style and mix of question types. This approach is intentional so that you can get a taste of all of the various formats and styles that can appear on an ACT exam. If you work through all of the material provided, you can rest assured that there won't be any surprises on test day. However, you should keep your score results in perspective. Generally, students tend to score slightly higher on each successive practice test. But the truth is that ACT exams are sensitive to factors such as fatigue and stress. So the time of the day that you take the exams, your surroundings, and other things going on in your life can have an impact on your scores. Don't get worried if you see some variations due to an off day or because the practice test exposed a weakness in your knowledge base or skill set. Just use the information that you gather as a tool to help you improve.

Use the suggestions in the Training Schedule at the end of this section to plan your study program. There will be times when you will want to work through some material without a time limit. The Training Schedule can help you decide when to switch the focus of your training from studying knowledge to practicing skills and when to make the shift to working on your timing.

There is an explanation for each of the practice questions in this book. You will probably not need to read absolutely all of them. Sometimes you can tell right away why you got a particular question wrong. We have seen countless students smack themselves on the forehead and say "stupid mistake." We try to refer to these errors as "concentration errors." Everyone makes them from time to time, and you should not worry when they occur. There is a good chance that your focus will be a little better on the real test as long as you train yourself properly with the aid of this book. You should distinguish between those concentration errors and any understanding issues or holes in your knowledge base. If you have the time, it is worth reading the explanations for any of the questions that were at all challenging for you. Sometimes, students get questions correct but for the wrong reason, or because they guessed correctly. While you are practicing, you should mark any questions that you want to revisit and be sure to read the explanations for those questions.

A NOTE ON SCORING THE PRACTICE TESTS

The tests in this book are simulations created by experts to replicate the question types, difficulty level, and content areas that you will find on your real ACT. The scoring worksheets provided for each test are guides to computing approximate scores. Actual ACT exams are scored from tables that are unique to each test. The actual scaled scores depend on a number of factors, which include the number of students who take the test, the difficulty level of the items (questions and answer choices), and the performance of all of the students who take the test. This means that "your mileage may vary." Do not get too hung up on your test scores; the idea is to learn something from each practice experience and to get used to the "look and feel" of the ACT.

Each Scoring Worksheet has formulas for you to work out an approximate scaled score for each section, as well as an overall Composite Score. Each computation includes a "correction factor," which is an average correction derived from analysis of recent ACT exams. The correction factor is most valid for students whose scores are in the middle 50% of all scores. The correction factor starts to lose a bit of its effectiveness at the top and bottom of the scoring scale. This is not a major flaw in the practice tests; your actual ACT score report will include a "band" around each score. ACT, Inc. says, right on each student's score report, that they do this to highlight the fact that all test scores are just estimates.

ACT Training Schedule

At least eight weeks before your ACT

Take the Diagnostic Assessment under actual test conditions. Time yourself strictly. Take the test in a place that approximates actual test conditions, such as a library. Evaluate your results and pinpoint your areas of strength and weakness. Register for your ACT exam following the procedures set out at www.act.org.

The first four to six weeks of training

Don't worry about timing. Work through the first two ACT Practice Tests in this book at your leisure. Think about how the questions and passages are put together and study whatever other sources you need to so that you can fill any holes in your knowledge base.

Two or three weeks before your ACT

Using another of the Practice Tests in this book, take your first "dress rehearsal" exam on a Saturday morning at 8:00 a.m. Time yourself strictly as you did on your Diagnostic Assessment. Use the results to fine-tune the last part of your training. If you don't have your admission ticket yet, follow up with ACT and make sure that your registration was processed properly. Purchase a Mozart CD if you don't already have one.

One or two weeks before your ACT

Take your second "dress rehearsal" exam. If it doesn't go well, don't get too worried. Try to figure out what went wrong and review the explanations provided and the other relevant portions of this book. If it does go well, don't rest on your laurels. There is still time to consolidate your gains and continue to improve. Start planning a fun event for after your ACT exam! (Remember that there is a pretty good chance that you will want a nap after your ACT.)

Two to five days before your ACT

Make a practice run to the testing center. Figure out what you are going to wear on test day. Gather your materials together. (Ticket, ID, pencils, calculator). Adjust your sleep schedule, if necessary, so that you are able to wake up by 7:00 a.m. and be thinking clearly by 8:00 a.m. Confirm your plans for fun after the exam!

The day before your ACT

Do little or no practice or studying. Get some physical activity in so that you are better able to sleep, and because the endorphins that you release in your brain will help with stress management. Rest and relaxation are the order of the day. Make sure that you take care of your transportation issues and wake-up plan.

Test Day!

Get up early. Eat breakfast. Read something to get you "warmed up." Bring your materials. Listen to your Mozart. Be on time. Follow the instructions of the proctors. Avoid any fellow test takers who are "stress monsters." Remember your game plan for each section. Don't forget to breathe deeply and evenly, and don't tire yourself out with needless physical exertion like tensing up your muscles while taking your ACT. When the test is finished, relax and try not to think about it until you get your score report.

Good luck!

ACT Emergency Plan

If you have only a day or two before your ACT exam, you should take the following steps. They are listed in order or priority so you should do as many of them as you can before your test.

1. **Seriously consider rescheduling.** The ACT is given several times each year at various locations. Rather than taking your exam with little or no preparation, you should look at the calendar and the ACT Web site and wait to take your ACT if you can do so and still get the information to your schools of choice before their deadlines.

2. **Relax.** Even if you don't have enough time to reschedule, you can get some useful information out of this book that will help you to pick up a few points that you might not have gotten otherwise.

3. **Take the Diagnostic Assessment.** There is a psychological theory called "Test Re-Test" that says that you should do a little bit better on a second ACT than a first ACT, even if you don't do any preparation in between. So make the Diagnostic Assessment your first ACT. Time yourself strictly and do it all in one sitting. Take a 5- to 10-minute break after the Mathematics Test.

4. **Review the strategies in Chapter 2.** Those are the high-yield test-taking strategies that will get you the most extra points on test day.

5. **Read through the content chapters.** The order should be:

   a. Reading (These are the least intuitive strategies.)
   b. English (This is the weirdest format of the ACT tests.)
   c. Mathematics (Skim through the stuff that you already know. Focus on the material that tends to confuse you. Don't worry about Trig at all if you haven't had it in school yet.)
   d. Do the Science Reasoning chapter last.

6. **Do as many practice questions as you can in your weakest area.** Look at the explanations to gain a better understanding of how to approach the questions.

7. **Get some sleep.** Being well rested will have a bigger impact on your score than staying up all night "cramming." There is a significant skill component on this test. It is not all about knowledge. So you can't learn enough information to guarantee a higher score.

PART I

GETTING STARTED

CHAPTER 1

UNDERSTANDING THE ACT

WHAT IS THE ACT?

The authors of the ACT insist that the ACT is an achievement test, meaning that it is designed to measure your readiness for college instruction. There is ongoing debate about how well the ACT accomplishes that mission. What is not debated is that the ACT is not a direct measure of abilities. It is not an IQ test. The ACT is certainly not a measure of your worth as a human being. It is not even a perfect measure of how well you will do in college. Theoretically, each of us has a specific potential to learn and acquire skills. The ACT doesn't measure your natural, inborn ability. If it did, we wouldn't be as successful as we are at raising students' scores on ACT exams.

The ACT actually measures a certain knowledge base and skill set. It is "trainable," meaning that you can do better on your ACT if you work on learning the knowledge and gaining the skills that are tested.

The ACT is broken up into four multiple-choice tests and one optional essay. The multiple-choice tests are called English, Mathematics, Reading, and Science Reasoning, respectively. They are always given in the same order. In fact, there is a lot of predictability when it comes to the ACT. The current exam still has very much in common with ACT exams from past years. This means that we basically know what is going to be on your ACT in terms of question types and content. The following chart provides more information on the structure of the ACT.

ACT Structure

English	
75 Questions 45 Minutes	
Content/Skills	**Number of Questions**
Usage/Mechanics	**40**
Punctuation	10
Grammar/Usage	12
Sentence Structure	18
Rhetorical Skills	**35**
Strategy	12
Organization	11
Style	12

Mathematics	
60 Questions 60 Minutes	
Content	**Number of Questions**
Pre-Algebra and Elementary Algebra	24
Intermediate Algebra and Coordinate Geometry	18
Plane Geometry	14
Trigonometry	4
Reading	
40 Questions 35 Minutes	
Passage Type	**Number of Questions**
Prose Fiction	10
Humanities	10
Social Studies	10
Natural Sciences	10
Science Reasoning	
40 Questions 35 Minutes	
Format	**Number of Questions**
Data Representation	15
Research Summaries	18
Conflicting Viewpoints	7
Content Areas: Biology, Physical Sciences, Chemistry, Physics	

ACT offers a thirty-minute Writing Test as an optional component to the ACT for students testing within the United States who are applying to college for the fall of 2006 or later.

WHO WRITES THE ACT?

There is a company called ACT, Inc. that decides exactly what is going to be on your ACT exam. This group of experts consults with classroom teachers at the high school and college level. They look at high school and college curricula and they employ educators and specialized psychologists called "psychometricians" (measurers of the mind), who know a lot about the human brain and how it operates under various conditions. We picture them as "evil genius" researchers in white coats somewhere, gleefully rubbing their hands together and trying to think up ways to keep you out of college. Don't fear, however, we are the "good geniuses" trying to get you into the college of your choice. We'll lay out the details of how you will be tested so that you can get yourself ready for the "contest" on test day.

■ REGISTERING FOR THE ACT

You must register for the ACT in advance. You can't just show up on test day with a number 2 pencil and dive right in. The best source of information for all things ACT is, not surprisingly, the ACT Web site: **www.act.org**. There is also a very good chance that a guidance counselor, and/or pre-college counselor at your school has an *ACT Registration Book*, which includes all of the information that you need for your test registration.

■ WHY DO ACT EXAMS EXIST?

Back in the mid-twentieth century, some people noticed that there was a disturbing trend in college admissions. Most of the people who were entering college came from a fairly small group of people who went to a limited number of high schools. Many had parents who had attended the same colleges. There wasn't much opportunity for students from new families to "break into" the higher education system. Standardized entrance exams were an attempt to democratize the situation and create a *meritocracy* where admissions decisions were based on achievement and not just social status. The ACT was not the first standardized college entrance exam. It came a little later as an attempt at improving on the older SAT.

Colleges use the ACT for admissions decisions and, sometimes, for advanced placement. It is also used to make scholarship decisions. Since there are variations among high schools around the country, the admissions departments at colleges use the ACT, in part, to help provide a standard for comparison. There are studies that reveal a fair amount of "grade inflation" at some schools. So, colleges cannot simply rely upon grade point averages when evaluating academic performance.

The ACT also measures a certain skill set that is not necessarily measured as part of a GPA. We'll dig a little more into that in the individual test chapters.

■ ACT SCORES

Each of the multiple-choice sections of the ACT is called a Test. (English Test, Mathematics Test, Reading Test, Science Reasoning Test) Each test is given a score on a scale of 1 to 36. These four "scaled scores" are then averaged and rounded according to normal rounding rules to yield a Composite Score. It is this Composite Score that is most often meant when someone refers to your ACT score.

Your actual score report will also refer to "subscores," which are reported for your English, Mathematics, and Reading tests. These are based on your performance on a subset of the questions on each of these tests. We'll discuss them briefly in each of their respective chapters. Our experience has been that there is nothing to be gained from discussing them in detail with students. Reports from the field indicate that many college admissions professionals don't even glance at them or have the faintest idea how to utilize them when making admissions decisions.

The most important thing that can be said about scores is that you don't have to be perfect to get a good score on the ACT. The truth is that you can miss a fair number of questions and still get a score that places you in the top 1% of all test takers. In fact, this test is so hard and the time limit is so unrealistic for most test takers that you can get a score that is at the national average (about a 21) even if you get almost half of the questions wrong.

BIAS ON THE ACT

Some research suggests that members of different ethnic groups, and residents of different states, have different average scores on the ACT. The reasons for the different scores are beyond the scope of this book. However, we would like to point out that the differences are small and that the variations among different members of any group are far more substantial than the differences in averages among groups. In other words, if you are a member of a group that does well on the ACT, don't rely on that group membership to guarantee a good score. Conversely, if you are a member of a group with a slightly lower average, don't turn that group membership into a self-fulfilling prophecy. Those students who take the exam seriously and put time and effort into their preparation are the ones who succeed, regardless of ethnicity or state of residence.

The sexes, overall, score about the same as each other. Males tend to do slightly better on Math and Science Reasoning and females tend to do better on English, Reading, and, it is predicted, Writing. The gender differences are not significant enough to allow anyone to make score predictions for any one individual. So, as with ethnicity and state of residence, disregard your gender and work hard if you want to maximize your scores.

DISABILITIES AND THE ACT

Some students identify learning disabilities for the first time when they begin to prep for the ACT. Factors to look out for include extreme anxiety or panic, a marked inability to focus, and major differences in scores between timed and untimed exams.

If any of these warning signs apply to you, it is recommended that you seek assistance from your parents, school counselors, and other professionals who can advise you regarding the screening process for learning disabilities.

If you have a diagnosis from a qualified professional, a law called the Americans with Disabilities Act (ADA) states that reasonable accommodations must be granted that will allow you a level playing field. No discrimination is allowed against anyone who has a legitimate medical condition that affects performance on the ACT.

The most common accommodation is to allow extra time for completion of the exam. Previously, ACT, Inc. would flag score reports of students who were granted extra time. Such is no longer the case. Students with accommodations are not identified to the colleges anymore. Most people see this as a great step forward in fairness under the ADA.

Of course, accommodations are also allowed for physical disabilities. For more information on accommodations for disabilities, contact ACT directly. Be sure to contact ACT very early in the process. You must allow a reasonable length of time for ACT to confirm your diagnosis and for some back and forth discussion regarding proposed accommodations.

TESTING IRREGULARITIES

A "testing irregularity" is basically an accusation of cheating. You can avoid this situation by following all instructions and only working on the section on which you are supposed to be working. This includes marking the answer sheets. Don't go back to a previous section, or forward to a later section, either in the test book, or on the answer sheet. Do write in the test booklet. We are aware of one student who could have saved himself the time, inconvenience, and expense of a testing irregularity accusation if he had merely showed some work in his test book. If you are accused of a testing irregularity, don't panic. You have certain due process rights. Discuss the matter with your parents and perhaps an attorney as soon as possible so that you can react appropriately.

■■■ SAT DIFFERENCES AND SIMILARITIES

The SAT is another standardized college admissions examination. It includes multiple-choice sections and a mandatory writing test. Some of the material tends to be the same as on the ACT. For instance, the reading comprehension passages are often very similar in structure and content, and some of the math questions are very similar as well.

Perhaps the most significant difference is the fact that the SAT has a "guessing penalty." This means that SAT takers lose an extra fraction of a point when they mark a question incorrectly. If you leave a question blank on the SAT, you basically lose 1 raw point. If you mark it incorrectly, you lose an extra ¼ point. So, you have to worry about whether or not to guess. Additional stress makes the SAT seem harder than it actually is.

The SAT is also a longer exam overall and includes an "experimental" section that does not count toward your score. The SAT math section doesn't have any trigonometry questions at all, whereas the ACT does include four such questions. But the SAT math section has more problems that are really logic questions and less like what you probably learned in your high school math classes.

The SAT also tests vocabulary directly. The ACT only has a few vocabulary questions, as such. However, a solid vocabulary can really help you to understand the passages and questions on the ACT. See Appendix 2: "ACT Vocabulary List" for a list of words that are typical of the words that you will encounter on your ACT.

The vast majority of colleges and universities accept both SAT scores and ACT scores. There are persistent myths that say that schools in certain states either all require the ACT or all require the SAT. These myths simply are not true. Rather than relying upon generalities, you should investigate the colleges in which you are interested and find out for yourself which entrance exams they will accept and whether they have a preference for one or the other.

CHAPTER 2
STRATEGIES TO GET YOUR BEST SCORE

THE PSYCHOLOGY OF TESTING

Cognitive psychologists, the ones who study learning and thinking, use the letters KSA to refer to the basic components of human performance in any activity, from academics to athletics, music to video games. The letters stand for Knowledge, Skills, and Abilities. The ACT measures certain predictable areas of knowledge, and it measures a specific set of skills. You probably already understand this since you are reading this book. In fact, thousands and thousands of students have successfully raised their ACT scores through study and practice.

There is a difference between the ways that humans learn knowledge and the way they learn skills. Knowledge can be learned fairly quickly and is fairly durable, even under stress. For example, when military trainees are asked to repeat their names and social security numbers while standing in a room filled with tear gas, they can usually do it. However, when asked to perform complicated physical or mental tasks under the same conditions, they often cannot, even when they are highly motivated to do so.

Skills, on the other hand, require repetition in order to perfect. There is an old joke about a tourist in New York City who jumps into the back of a taxicab and asks the driver if he knows how to get to Carnegie Hall. The driver says, "Sure. Practice! Practice! Practice!"

The cabbie's answer was, of course, meant to be humorous. But, he was basically correct. Psychologists speak of something called a "perfectly internalized skill," which means that the skill is executed automatically, without any conscious thought.

In our training classes, we often use the example of shoe tying. If you tied your shoes this morning, it is highly unlikely that you can remember the exact moment of tying them, unless something significant occurred, like a broken shoelace. The reason that you probably cannot remember actually doing the tying is because, as an adult shoe tier, you have, by now, perfectly internalized the skill of shoe tying through thousands and thousands of repetitions.

Ideally, you will internalize your response to the stimuli on the ACT, so that you do not have to spend time and energy devising plans during the exam. We are hoping that you will just dig right in and be well into your work on each section while some of your less-prepared classmates are still reading the directions and trying to figure out what, exactly, they are supposed to be doing.

We have included so many practice exams in this book for a reason. We want you to do sufficient practice that you will develop good test-taking skills, and, specifically, good ACT-taking skills. As you practice, you should distinguish between practice that is meant to serve as a learning experience and practice that is meant to be a realistic "dress-rehearsal" for your actual ACT.

During practice that is meant to be a learning device, it is okay to "cheat." You should feel free to turn off the timer and just think about how the questions are put together and even stop to look up information in schoolbooks or on the Internet, or examine the explanations in the back of the book. It is even okay to talk to someone about what you are working on during your "learning practice." But, you need to do some "dry runs" or "dress-rehearsal" type practice. This is the stage where you time yourself strictly and make sure that you control as many variables as possible in your environment. Some research shows that you will have an easier time repeating your acquired skills and retrieving information from the storage part of your brain if the environment in which you are testing is similar to the environment where you learned the information or acquired the skill.

So, you learn factual information by studying and you acquire skills through practice. Of course there is some overlap between these activities and, it is hoped, you will do some learning while you practice, and vice-versa. In fact, research shows that repetition is important for both information storage and skills acquisition in human beings.

But there is a huge difference between knowledge and skills: *Knowing* about a skill, even understanding the skill, is not the same as actually *having* that skill. For example, you may be told all about a skill such as driving a car with a standard (stick-shift) transmission, or playing the piano, or typing on a computer keyboard. You could have the best teacher in the world, possess spectacular learning tools, and pay attention very carefully so that you take in all of the information that is imparted. You might *understand* everything perfectly. But the first few times that you actually attempt the skill, you will probably execute that skill less than perfectly. In fact, the odds are that you will experience some frustration at that point because of the lag between your *understanding* of the skill and your actual ability to *perform* the skill.

Perfecting skills takes practice. You need to do repetitions to "wear in" the pathways in your brain that control each skill. So don't be satisfied with merely reading through this book and saying to yourself, "I get it." You will not reach your full ACT potential unless you put in sufficient time practicing as well as understanding and learning.

Ideally, you will have several weeks between now and test day. If so, you can use the Training Schedule at the beginning of this book to schedule your preparation. If not, you should use the "ACT Emergency Plan" on page xvi.

Later in this book, we'll go into great detail about the facts that make up the "knowledge base" that is essential for ACT success. First, you need to learn about the skills and strategies.

STRATEGIC THINKING

In college, you are likely to experience stress from things such as family expectations, fear of failure, a heavy workload, increased competition, and difficult material. The ACT tries to mimic this stress. The psychometricians (specialized psychologists who study the measurement of various aspects of the mind) who help design standardized tests, use what they call "artificial stressors" to help determine how you will respond to that test.

The main stressor that the test makers use is the time limit. The time limits are set up on the ACT so that most students cannot finish all of the questions in the time allowed.

Another stressor is the element of surprise. If you have practiced sufficiently, there will be no surprises on test day. The ACT is a very predictable exam. In fact, the chart in Chapter 1, tells you *exactly* how many questions of each type there are.

▇▇▇ RELAX TO SUCCEED

One of the worst things that can happen to a test taker is to panic before or during an exam. Research has shown that there are very predictable and specific results when a person panics for any reason. To panic is to have a set of recognizable symptoms. These symptoms include sweating, shortness of breath, muscle tension, increased heart rate, tunnel vision, nausea, light-headedness, and even loss of consciousness.

These symptoms are the result of chemical changes in the brain that are brought on by some stimulus. Interestingly, the stimulus does not have to be external. That means that we can panic ourselves simply by thinking about certain things in certain ways. You could prove this to yourself by closing your eyes and carefully recalling as many details as you could about a past car accident or near miss. Almost everyone has had at least one close call. If you were able to recreate a vivid memory, you would probably start to notice the onset of some of the symptoms mentioned above. You would likely feel some mild symptoms when remembering the event — for example, you might feel some tingling and hairs standing up instead of actual sweating.

The stress chemical, *epinephrine*, which is more commonly known as *adrenaline*, brings about the symptoms. Adrenaline actually shifts the priorities in your brain. It diverts blood and electrical energy away from some parts of the brain in favor of others. Specifically, it moves the center of your brain activity to the areas that control your body, and away from the parts of your brain that are involved in complex thinking and fine muscle skills.

One theory hypothesizes that this ability to shift the brain's activities around on a moment's notice was very beneficial to our remote ancestors, providing a higher likelihood of survival and procreation. The set of physical and emotional responses that result from adrenaline's impact on the brain is known as the "fight-or-flight response." It means that you become temporarily more ready to confront physical threats like a wild animal attack or run fast to avoid danger. The side effect of this change is that you also temporarily are less able to think clearly. In fact, true stories are told of people under the influence of adrenaline performing amazing feats of strength and speed, which they would probably not have even attempted otherwise. So, panic makes a person stronger and faster — and also less able to perform the type of thinking that is rewarded on an ACT exam.

Adrenaline can be useful and even pleasurable in some situations. In fact, it is not a bad thing to have a small amount of adrenaline in your bloodstream while testing due to a healthy amount of excitement about the exam. But, it is something that you should control as much as possible before and during an exam.

The worst situation involving adrenaline arises when a person knows that he is suffering from its effects, and that knowledge, itself, causes more panic, and therefore, more adrenaline release. This is often referred to as the "panic spiral." In extreme cases, the panic spiral can lead to such rapid heartbeat and shallow breathing that the subject is unable to remain conscious. Obviously, an "overdose" of adrenaline can seriously hurt your chances of scoring well on an exam.

Two of the most important stimuli for the release of adrenaline into the bloodstream are suspense and surprise. This fact is well known to those who design haunted houses and horror movies. Suspense involves the stress that is present during the anticipation phase before an event that involves unknowns. Surprise occurs when you actually experience the unknowns. The speculation and wondering "what if?" that you do before a big event can significantly increase stress and its effects on thinking patterns. There is also a sharper rise in adrenaline levels when you experience surprise, such as when someone yells "Boo!" behind you when you thought that you were home alone, or, when you find a question on an exam that looks unlike anything that you have ever seen before.

You can control both suspense and surprise by minimizing the unknown factors. The biggest stress-inducing questions involving the ACT are: What do the ACT writers expect of me? Am I prepared? How will I respond to the ACT on test day? If you spend some time and effort answering these questions by studying and practicing under realistic conditions before test day, you'll have a much better chance of controlling your adrenaline levels and handling the exam with no panic.

The goals of your preparation should be to learn about the test, acquire the knowledge and skills that are being measured by the test, and learn about yourself and how you respond to the different aspects of the exam.

The psychometricians, and other experts who work on the design of ACT exams, refer to certain parts of the ACT as "artificial stressors." In other words, they are actually trying to create a certain level of stress in the test taker. They are doing this because the ACT is supposed to tell admissions professionals something about how you will respond to the stress of college exams.

The time limit is usually the biggest stressor for test takers. The first thing to consider is whether you even need to attempt all of the questions within the time allowed. On the ACT, a score of 75% correct is considered significantly above average. In fact, if you can get 75% of the questions correct across the board, you'll get about a 27 composite score, which would put you in the top 10% of all scores nationwide. Therefore, you should not feel extra stress if the time limit doesn't allow you to get to all of the questions.

The next thing to consider is which question types you will attempt and on which ones you will guess. You need to be familiar with the subject matter that is tested on each section of your test and, at the beginning of your training period, first work on filling any gaps in your knowledge base. If you know for a fact that a certain topic, like trigonometry, is consistently tested with only a few questions (there are exactly four trigonometry questions on every ACT Mathematics Test), you may decide to focus your study and practice elsewhere. As you work through this book, you should make a realistic assessment of the best use of your time and energy so that you are concentrating on the areas that will yield the highest score that you can achieve in the amount of time that you have remaining until the exam. This will result in a feeling of confidence on test day, even when you are facing very challenging questions.

Specific Relaxation Techniques

Before the ACT

- **Be prepared.** The old Boy Scout motto has been repeated for generations for a good reason: It works. The more prepared you feel, the less likely it is that you'll be stressed on test day. Do your studying and practice consistently during your training period. Be organized. Have your supplies and wardrobe ready in advance. Make a practice trip to the test center before your test day.

- **Know yourself.** This means knowing your strengths and weaknesses on the ACT as well as the ways that help you to relax. Some test takers like to have a bit of an anxious feeling that helps them to focus. Others are best off when they are so relaxed that they are almost asleep. You will learn about yourself through practice.

- **Rest.** Shakespeare described sleep as the thing that "knits the wraveled sleeve of care," meaning that the better rested you are, the better things seem. As you get fatigued, you are more likely to look on the dark side of things and worry more.

- **Nutrition.** Sugar is bad for stress and for brain function in general. Pouring tons of refined sugar into your system creates biological stress that has an impact on your brain chemistry. Add in some caffeine, as many soda manufacturers do, and you are only magnifying the problem. If you are actually addicted to caffeine, (you get headaches when you skip a day), then get your normal dosage but no extra.

- **Music.** Some types of music increase measured brain stress and interfere with clear thinking. Specifically, some rock, hip-hop, and dance rhythms, while great for certain occasions, can have detrimental effects on certain types of brain waves that have been measured in labs. Other music seems to help to organize brain waves and create a relaxed state that is conducive to learning and skills acquisition.

- **The Mozart effect.** There is a great debate raging among scientists and educators about a study that was done some years ago, which seemed to show that listening to Mozart made students temporarily more intelligent. While not everyone agrees that it helps, no one has ever seriously argued that it hurts. So, get yourself a Mozart CD and listen to it before practice and before your real test. It might help. In the worst-case scenario, you will have listened to some good music and maybe broadened your horizons a bit. You cannot listen to music *during* your ACT exam, so do not listen to it during your practice tests.

During the ACT

- **Breathe.** When humans get stressed, our breathing tends to get quick and shallow. If you feel yourself tensing up, slow down and take deeper breaths. This will relax you and probably get more oxygen to your brain so that you can think more clearly.

- **Take breaks.** You cannot stay focused intently on your ACT for the entire time that you are in the testing center. You are bound to have distracting thoughts pop into your head or times when you simply cannot process the information at which you are looking. These occurrences are normal. What you should do is close your eyes, clear your mind, and then dig back in to the test. This procedure can be accomplished in less than a minute. You could pray, meditate, or simply picture a place or person that helps you to relax. Try visualizing something fun that you have planned for right after your ACT.

- **Stay calm.** Taking an important exam can certainly lead to stress. As part of the process of preparing thousands of students for standardized entrance exams, we have seen a variety of stress reactions. These reactions range from a mild form of nervousness to extreme anxiety that has led to vomiting and fainting in a few cases. Most students deal fairly well with the stress of taking a test. Some students could even be said to be too relaxed in that they don't take the test seriously enough. On very rare occasions, a student may even fall asleep during an ACT exam! (Since you are reading this book, we will assume that you are taking the ACT seriously and that there is no danger of you falling asleep during the exam.)

- **Have a plan of attack.** The directions printed in this book (both in the chapters and on the Practice Tests) are very similar to the directions that you will find on your ACT. You need to know how you are going to move through each portion of the exam. No time is available to formulate a plan of attack on test day. In fact, you should do enough practice so that you have internalized the skills necessary to do your best on each section and don't have to stop to think about what to do next.

GETTING READY TO TAKE THE TEST

- **Do some recon.** Make sure that you know how long it will take to drive to the testing center and where you will park if you are driving yourself. If you are testing in a place that is new to you, try to get into the building between now and test day so that you can get used to the sounds and smells and know where the bathrooms are, and so on.
- **Rest.** You'll need to get some sleep the night before the big day. We recommend exercise the day before so that you can get some good, quality sleep. Research has shown that there is really no such thing as getting too much sleep. So, don't be afraid to go to bed early the night before the test.
- **Wake up early.** Set an alarm and have someone on wake-up duty — either a family member in your house, or someone who can call you on the telephone as a back-up plan in case your alarm doesn't go off. You have to be at the testing center by 8:00 a.m.
- **Dress comfortably.** Loose, comfortable, layered clothing is best. That way, you can adjust to the temperature of the room. Don't forget your watch. The proctor will probably give you a five-minute warning but that is all the timing help you can count on. There may not even be a clock in your testing room.
- **Eat something.** Breakfast may not always be the most important meal of the day but it is a good idea to eat something without too much sugar on the morning of your test. Get your normal dose of caffeine, if any.
- **Bring stuff.** You will need your driver's license (or passport), your admission ticket, number 2 pencils, a good eraser or two, and your calculator. You can check the ACT Web site for up-to-date information about which calculators are acceptable. Bring your glasses or contact lenses if you need them. You can bring a snack for the break, but you won't be able to eat or drink while the ACT is in progress.
- **Read something.** "Warm up" your brain by reading a newspaper or something similar so that the ACT isn't the first thing that you read on test day.

▮▮▮ TAKING THE TEST

- **Do the easy stuff first.** You will have to get familiar with the format of each section of the ACT so that you can recognize passages and questions that are likely to give you trouble. We suggest that you bypass "pockets of resistance" and go around those trouble spots rather than through them. It is a much better use of your time and energy to pick up all of the correct answers that you can early on, and then go back and work on the tougher questions that you actually have a legitimate shot at answering correctly. Remember that you don't have to get all of the questions right in order to get a great score on the ACT. So, you should learn to recognize the ones that are likely to give you trouble and be sure not to get goaded into a fight with them.

  All of the questions on an ACT test are weighted exactly equally to one another. Some of the questions are harder than others. You don't have to get all of the questions right to get a great ACT score. So you are foolish if you get sucked into a battle with a hard question while there are still other, probably less difficult questions waiting for you. We often tell students that they should picture their ACT test booklets sitting in a stack in a locked closet somewhere. Your book is there, waiting patiently for you. Within it are some questions that you are probably going to get wrong on test day. So, when you see them, don't be surprised. Just recognize them and work on the easier material first. If time permits, you can always come back and work on the challenging problems in the final minutes before the proctor calls, "Time!"

  This strategy is both a time management and a stress reduction strategy. The idea is to make three or four passes through the test section, always being sure to work on the easiest of whatever material remains.

- **Manage the answer grid.** You should be certain to avoid the common mistake of marking the answer to each question on your answer document as you finish the question. In other words, you should *not* go to your "bubble sheet" after each question. This is dangerous and wastes time. It is dangerous because you run an increased risk of marking your answer grid incorrectly and perhaps not catching your error on time. It wastes time because you have to find your place on the answer sheet and then find your place back in the test booklet. The amount of time that is "wasted" is not large as you mark each question. But it adds up over the course of an entire test section and could cost you the amount of time you need to get a few more questions done correctly.

  Instead, you should mark your answers in the test booklet and transfer your answers from the test booklet to the answer sheet in groups. Doing this after each passage on English, Reading, and Science Reasoning is an obvious idea and has the added benefit of helping you to clear your head between passages so that it is easier to concentrate on the passage at hand rather than possibly still processing memories of the previous passage. On the Mathematics test, you should fill in some "bubbles" on your answer sheet every two pages or so. On any of the sections, filling in bubbles can be a good activity to keep you busy when you simply need a break to clear your head.

  There is a dangerous, and dishonest, strategy that we have heard of from some students. Apparently, some so-called ACT prep experts are telling students simply to put a little pencil dot in the answer oval on the answer sheet and then come back to fill them in later. Specifically, some students are taught to do this on the sections that they have trouble finishing on time.

Then they are told to come back to the section later and fill in the ovals while they are supposed to be working on another section. The idea is dangerous because of the directions for the ACT, which clearly state that a test taker is not to work on any other section than the one being timed by the proctor. This rule means that you may *not* go back to fill in the ovals that you marked with a dot. If you are tempted to cheat in this manner, remember that ACT will not hesitate to report confirmed instances of cheating to colleges and universities.

- **You own the test booklet.** An ACT test booklet is meant to be used by one test taker only. You will not have any scratch paper on test day. You are expected to do all note taking and figuring on the booklet, itself. Generally, no one ever bothers to look at the test booklet, since you cannot receive credit for anything that is written there. Your score comes only from the answers that you mark on the answer sheet.

- **Be aware of time.** You really don't want it to be a surprise when the proctor yells "Time!" on test day. Therefore, you are going to want to time yourself on test day. You should time yourself during at least some of your practice exams so that you get used to the process, and to your timepiece. We suggest that you use an analog (dial face) watch. They generally are not set up to give off any annoying beeps that could get you in trouble with your fellow test takers and your proctor on test day. If you want to avoid the subtracting that comes along with checking the board at the front of the testing room for the time that the proctor wrote down as start and stop times (who wants to do *more* math on ACT day?), you can turn the hands on your watch back from noon to allow enough time for the section that you are working on. For instance, if you are working on an ACT Mathematics section, which is sixty minutes long, you can turn your watch back to 11:00 and set it on the desk in front of you. You will be finished when your watch points to 12:00. Similarly, if you are working on a Science Reasoning section or a Reading section, which is thirty-five minutes long, set your watch to 11:25 and, again, you will be done at noon. This method has the added benefit of helping you to forget about the outside world while you are testing.

  All that matters during the test is your test. All of life's other issues will have to be dealt with after your test is finished. You might find this mind-set easier to attain if you lose track of what time it is in the "outside world."

- **Changing answers.** You need to find out whether you are an answer changer or not. In other words, if you change an answer, are you more likely to change it *to* the correct answer or *from* the correct answer? You can only learn this fact about yourself by doing practice exams and paying attention to your tendencies.

GUESSING

Since there is no added scoring penalty for incorrect answers on the ACT, you should never leave a bubble blank on your answer sheet. We counted all of the correct answers on three recent, released ACT exams. We found that the distribution of answers by position on the answer sheet was almost exactly even. This means that there is no position that is more likely to be correct than any other. We use the term "position" when referring to the answer sheet because the letter assigned to the positions change depending on whether you are working on an odd or even question. The odd-numbered questions have answer choices labeled A through D (or A through E on the Mathematics Test), and the even-numbered questions have answer choices that are labeled F through J (or F through K on the Mathematics Test). This system allows you to stay on track on your answer sheet.

Since the answers are distributed fairly evenly across the positions, you should always guess the same position if you are guessing at random. Of course, if you can eliminate a choice or two, or if you have a hunch, then this advice doesn't apply.

Note: Some students worry if they notice long strings of same-position answers on their answer sheets. This arrangement does not necessarily indcate a problem. While analyzing actual, released ACT exams, we counted strings of up to six questions long, all marked in the same position on the answer sheet, and all correct.

AFTER THE TEST

Most students find it easier to concentrate on their exam preparation and on their ACT exams if they have a plan for fun right after the test. You should plan something that you can look forward to as a reward to yourself for all of the hard work and effort that you'll be putting into the test. Then, when the going gets tough, you can say to yourself, "If I push through and do my work now, I'll have so much fun right after the exam."

PART II

ACT DIAGNOSTIC ASSESSMENT

ACT DIAGNOSTIC ASSESSMENT TEST

This test will help you to assess your strengths and weakness. Take the test under realistic conditions (preferably early in the morning in a quiet location), and allow approximately 3.5 hours for the entire test. Each of the test sections should be taken in the time indicated at the beginning of the sections, and in the order in which they appear. Fill in the bubbles on your answer sheet once you have made your selections.

When you have finished the entire test, check your answers against the Answer Key. Follow the directions on how to score your test, and calculate your score using the Scoring Guide that appears on pages 75 to 78. Then, read the Answers and Explanations, paying close attention to the explanations for the questions that you missed.

Your scores should indicate your performance on the individual test sections, as well as your overall performance on the Diagnostic Test. Once you have identified your areas of strength and weakness, you should review those particular chapters in the book.

1 ■ ■ ■ ■ ■ ■ ■ ■ 1

ENGLISH TEST

45 Minutes – 75 Questions

DIRECTIONS: In the passages that follow, some words and phrases are underlined and numbered. In the answer column, you will find alternatives for the words and phrases that are underlined. Choose the alternative that you think is best and fill in the corresponding bubble on your answer sheet. If you think that the original version is best, choose "NO CHANGE," which will always be either answer choice A or F. You will also find questions about a particular section of the passage, or about the entire passage. These questions will be identified by either an underlined portion or by a number in a box. Look for the answer that clearly expresses the idea, is consistent with the style and tone of the passage, and makes the correct use of standard written English. Read the passage through once before answering the questions. For some questions, you should read beyond the indicated portion before you answer.

PASSAGE I

> The following paragraphs may or may not be in the most logical order. You may be asked questions about the logical order of the paragraphs, as well as where to place sentences logically within any given paragraph.

Helen Keller's Light in the Darkness

[1]

Helen Keller was born in 1880. Her life begun as any
₁

other. She was happy, and healthy learning to walk and
₂

talk like her toddler peers. It was not until a high fever
₂

robbed her of sight and hearing that her life began its

remarkable journey. The illness plunged Helen into a dark

silence such as most people cannot even imagine. ⒊ The

Kellers' beloved first-born was blind and deaf.

[2]

④ Helen wandered around the family's property,

1. **A.** NO CHANGE
   B. had began
   C. begins
   D. began

2. **F.** NO CHANGE
   G. happy and healthy, learning to walk and talk
   H. happy, and healthy, learning to walk, and talk,
   J. happy and healthy learning to walk and talk

3. At this point, the writer would like to contrast the relief over Helen's positive progress with the realization that her illness had resulted in long-lasting effects. Which of the following sentences, if added here, would best accomplish this goal?
   A. Helen had probably had scarlet fever.
   B. Helen had not really progressed at all.
   C. The joy at Helen's return to health quickly changed to despair.
   D. Helen eventually went to college.

4. Which of the following sentences if added would best introduce the new subject of Paragraph 2?
   F. Helen didn't obey her parents.
   G. The next few years were frustrating for Helen, and physically and emotionally draining for her family.
   H. Annie Sullivan came to teach Helen.
   J. Helen loved plants and animals, and many different kinds could be found near her home.

GO ON TO THE NEXT PAGE.

1 ■ ■ ■ ■ ■ ■ ■ ■ 1

anxious to <u>discover new sensations</u> but unable really to
                         5
understand anything that she experienced. Her resulting

tantrums became more violent as she continued to grow.

Feeling sorry for their <u>impaired, daughter Helen's,</u>
                                    6
<u>parents</u> allowed the tantrums to occur with no con-
6
sequences. In a last-ditch effort to keep the increasingly

<u>not-to-be-managed</u> Helen from being sent to the State
       7
Insane Asylum, the Kellers contacted the Perkins Institute

in Boston, Massachusetts.

<u>Primarily a school for the blind alone,</u> the school had
                          8
once taught a child who was both blind and deaf.

[3]

Enter Annie Sullivan, who truly became the "miracle

worker" in Helen's life. <u>Only with self-discipline would</u>
                                      9
<u>Helen be</u> able to overcome her tremendous challenges.
9
Unfortunately, Helen's parents' constant coddling of their

daughter was undermining Annie's efforts.

<u>One's stubbornness is</u> exhausting, but
        10

Annie knew that, if <u>channeled; it</u> would be Helen's
                              11
salvation. In order to work her "miracle," Annie needed

to get Helen away from her parents' pampering. Annie

<u>was given</u> permission to take Helen to live in a little house
    12
on the opposite side of the Kellers' garden. Initially,

Helen continued to fight <u>Annies efforts,</u> but gradually,
                                  13
she began to behave. <u>Nevertheless,</u> with Helen's submis-
                              14
sion came her trust in Annie. Helen began to comprehend

5. **A.** NO CHANGE
   B. discover sensations that felt new
   C. feel new sensations and make discoveries
   D. make discoveries and sense new feelings

6. **F.** NO CHANGE
   G. impaired daughter, Helen's parents
   H. impaired daughter Helens' parents
   J. impaired daughter Helen's, parents

7. **A.** NO CHANGE
   B. unmanageable
   C. unmanaged
   D. not manageable

8. **F.** NO CHANGE
   G. Primarily a school for only blind students,
   H. Primarily a school for the blind,
   J. Primarily a school for only the blind alone,

9. **A.** NO CHANGE
   B. Helen, only with self-discipline, would be
   C. Only by exercising self-discipline, would be Helen
   D. Only Helen, with self-discipline, would be

10. **F.** NO CHANGE
    G. One's stubbornness was
    H. Her stubbornness is
    J. Her stubbornness was

11. **A.** NO CHANGE
    B. channeled it
    C. channeled: it
    D. channeled, it

12. **F.** NO CHANGE
    G. were given
    H. was giving
    J. gave

13. **A.** NO CHANGE
    B. Annies' efforts
    C. Annies efforts
    D. Annie's efforts,

14. **F.** NO CHANGE
    G. However,
    H. And,
    J. On the other hand,

GO ON TO THE NEXT PAGE.

1 ■ ■ ■ ■ ■ ■ ■ ■ **1**

that everything she touched had a name. Her constant darkness was suddenly illuminated by this new-found understanding, and her hunger for knowledge became insatiable. For the remainder of her life, Annie Sullivan continued to feed Helen's appetite for learning, providing a constant light in Helen's otherwise impenetrable darkness.

Question 15 asks about the passage as a whole.

15. In reviewing notes, the writer discovers that the following information has been left out of the essay:

   A former Perkins student whose vision had been restored with surgery, Annie was charged with the daunting task of teaching Helen. But how?

   If added to the essay, the sentence would most logically be placed after Sentence:
   A. 4 in Paragraph 2
   B. 5 in Paragraph 2
   C. 1 in Paragraph 3
   D. 2 in Paragraph 3

PASSAGE II

The following paragraphs may or may not be in the most logical order. You may be asked questions about the logical order of the paragraphs, as well as where to place sentences logically within any given paragraph.

Holiday Joy (and Chaos)

[1]

Why do the holidays make you feel like a kid again? I'm not talking about the wide-eyed wonder of seeing the tree at Rockefeller Center initially illuminated for the first time. No, I mean
                                     16
the tantrum-filled, "I want to do it all" attitude of a two-year-old. You begin the season with enthusiasm. Then the realistic reality sets in.
         17

[2]

A critical part of the holiday has shopped for gifts.
                                    18

Not wanting to be rushed with last-minute purchases: you
                                                        19
begin your holiday shopping early. In September, you buy the perfect gift for Aunt Susie. You compliment yourself

16. F. NO CHANGE
   G. first illuminated for the initial time.
   H. illuminated for the first time.
   J. firstly illuminated.

17. Which of the choices would be most appropriate here?
   A. NO CHANGE
   B. horrible
   C. ordinary
   D. cheerful

18. F. NO CHANGE
   G. was shopping for gifts.
   H. is shopping for gifts.
   J. shopped for gifts.

19. A. NO CHANGE
   B. purchases, you
   C. purchases you
   D. purchases; you

GO ON TO THE NEXT PAGE.

1 ■ ■ ■ ■ ■ ■ ■ ■ 1

for thinking ahead. In October, you <u>find</u> just the right
                                      20
gift for Uncle John (who collects ghost figurines).

<u>This year you're</u> holiday shopping is going to be a snap!
        21

[3]

Suddenly, it's Thanksgiving. The holiday invitations
begin to arrive. As you mark the dates on the calendar,
you vow that <u>differently this holiday is going to be</u> from
                                    22
those in

the past. You notice a <u>few overlapping events that are</u>
                                              23
<u>double-booked at the same time,</u> but you're not con-
        23
cerned. You are determined to enjoy every holiday event.

[4]

You calmly begin writing a list that includes names
of family and <u>friends placing</u> checkmarks next to those
                        24
whose gifts you've purchased. What? You've purchased
only two gifts out of fifteen relatives and twelve friends?
Suddenly, the holiday season <u>had became</u> a nightmare.
                                      25
You begin making frantic phone calls to obtain wish
lists. Instead, you hear: "I don't have any more gift
ideas for Ed, but I'll call you if I think of something."
"Fa La La, we've gone shopping. Leave a message at
the beep."

[5]

Now it's November and the radio stations are playing
Christmas carols. How silly — we have six weeks until
Christmas!

20. **F.** NO CHANGE
    G. found
    H. will find
    J. have found

21. **A.** NO CHANGE
    B. This year, your
    C. This year: your
    D. This year you're,

22. **F.** NO CHANGE
    G. this holiday will be different
    H. the differences this holiday would have
    J. a different holiday it would be

23. **A.** NO CHANGE
    B. double-booked, overlapping set of events on the
        schedule,
    C. few overlapping events,
    D. few overlapping events scheduled at the same
        time,

24. **F.** NO CHANGE
    G. friends. Placing
    H. friends: placing
    J. friends, placing

25. **A.** NO CHANGE
    B. has become
    C. becoming
    D. became

GO ON TO THE NEXT PAGE.

1 ■ ■ ■ ■ ■ ■ ■ ■ 1

[6]

[26] You rush from store to store. Your eyes dart among the displays for the perfect gift. Finally, you give up and purchase twenty-five generic gift certificates at a department store.

They are not the most inspired gifts, but you're done shopping! You trudged home exhausted to begin baking
        _____
              27

cookies. Immediately, your son asked, "What did you get
                              ____
                               28
Miss Jones?" You burst into tears, realizing you forgot not only his teacher but seven other people who somehow didn't make your list. Your son cautiously approaches and gives you a gentle hug. You feel a glimmer of joy return. You decide to skip the cookies and get some sleep. As you turn out the lights, you silently vow to start earlier next year!

26. Which of the following sentences offers the best introduction to Paragraph 6?
   F. Deciding that you must come up with your own gift ideas, you head to the mall.
   G. Christmas should not be stressful.
   H. Malls have a diverse selection of stores within steps of each other.
   J. Most stores offer gift certificates for last-minute shoppers.

27. A. NO CHANGE
   B. trudging home, exhausted, to
   C. exhaustedly trudge home to
   D. trudge home, exhausted, to

28. F. NO CHANGE
   G. had asked
   H. asks
   J. ask

Questions 29 and 30 ask about the passage as a whole.

29. What function does Paragraph 6 serve in relation to the rest of the essay?
   A. It refers back to the opening sentences of the essay, suggesting that adults act like toddlers.
   B. It indicates that the narrator will likely succeed in next year's goal of completing her holiday responsibilities early.
   C. It summarizes the essay's main point, that Christmas is the most relaxed holiday of the year.
   D. It indicates that, despite the narrator's feelings of being overwhelmed, she may eventually be able to enjoy the holiday.

30. For the sake of unity and coherence of the essay, Paragraph 5 should be placed:
   F. where it is now.
   G. after Paragraph 1.
   H. after Paragraph 2.
   J. after Paragraph 3.

PASSAGE III

Have You No Shame?

Popular opinion teaches us that "guilt is a wasted emotion." Ironically, this same culture teaches us,
                                              _____
                                                31
"No pain, no gain." Although we recognize that physical fitness may involve occasional discomfort, we are

31. Which choice would most precisely sharpen the focus of this paragraph, in keeping with the way the writer develops the argument in the rest of the essay?
   A. NO CHANGE
   B. emotion.
   C. specimen.
   D. OMIT the underlined portion

GO ON TO THE NEXT PAGE.

1 ■ ■ ■ ■ ■ ■ ■ ■ 1

unwilling to accept that <u>societal fitnesses</u> may as well.
                              32
Despite what we may have learned about pain, studies

show that if an exercise hurts, you're probably doing it

wrong. Similarly, if a course of action (or inaction) causes

pangs of guilt, <u>you should stop exercising.</u> Nature
                      33
provides our bodies with pain receptors to limit injury

to ourselves — if you place your hand on a hot stove,

pain prompts you to remove your hand. Guilt helps to

<u>stop us from causing or inflicting pain to other people.</u>
                              34
    Imagine driving through your local business district.

A car is <u>attempting a</u> turn left into your lane. Although
              35
you could safely allow the car to merge, you instead

accelerate so as not to delay your trip another second.

<u>Vehicles these days can stop much more quickly than</u>
                                                36
<u>those in the past.</u> As you drive by, you recognize your
            36
neighbor behind the wheel — the one who watched your

dog during your vacation. You feel an uncomfortable

twinge of guilt and you <u>find, yourself, driving</u> more
                                    37
courteously for the rest of your trip.

    Discounting guilt is akin to turning off conscience.

Imagine a society in which no one <u>is in</u> a manner which
                                          38
benefits another unless

failure to cooperate will result in <u>legal penalties</u>.
                                          39
Although you may joke that I've just described

rush-hour traffic,

<u>just have</u>, in fact, described sociopathic behavior.
    40
    By definition, guilt is "a feeling of being

blame-worthy." Shame is a "feeling of strong regret" or

"painful emotion caused by consciousness of guilt." Not

32. **F.** NO CHANGE
    G. societal fitness
    H. societal's fitness
    J. societal's fitnesses

33. Which choice best supports the argument that guilt
    serves a purpose?
    A. NO CHANGE
    B. you should call a psychiatrist.
    C. you should ignore it.
    D. you should change your course of action.

34. **F.** NO CHANGE
    G. stop us from causing unnecessary and grievous
        pain to other people.
    H. limit emotional injury to others.
    J. limit unnecessary and grievous injury to others.

35. **A.** NO CHANGE
    B. trying to attempt a
    C. trying to attempt to
    D. attempting to

36. **F.** NO CHANGE
    G. The faster you are traveling, the longer it will take
        you to stop.
    H. Vehicles today can stop faster than in the past.
    J. OMIT the underlined portion.

37. **A.** NO CHANGE
    B. find yourself, driving,
    C. find yourself driving
    D. find, yourselves, driving

38. **F.** NO CHANGE
    G. acts in
    H. acts as if he is in
    J. performs of and for

39. **A.** NO CHANGE
    B. penalties of a legal nature, which may include
        fines and/or imprisonment.
    C. fines, imprisonment, or other legal penalties.
    D. penalties of a legal nature.

40. **F.** NO CHANGE
    G. I, myself, just
    H. Myself, have to,
    J. I have,

GO ON TO THE NEXT PAGE.

1 ■ ■ ■ ■ ■ ■ ■ ■ 1

surprisingly, an insanity plea

stating that the criminal is criminally insane is usually
_____
                    41

sought when a criminal feels no regret for his actions. So

how did guilt get its bad reputation? First, we hate pain,

and if we can avoid it, we do. In the case of guilt, however,
                                          _____
                                                 42

it is difficult to escape the negativity.

Therefore, we decide the guilt itself is wrong — not the
_____
    43

action that prompted the guilt. Second, guilt, if

improperly managed; can lead to devastation. Guilt
         _____
            44

should not be ignored, but it should be examined (What

caused me to feel guilty?), analyzed (How can I avoid that

mistake in the future?), and then released (I move on with

new wisdom). Unfortunately, some people spend so much

time on the examination that, they never move on to the
                          _____
                             45

analysis and release. They become crippled by the guilt.

The purpose of guilt is not to cause people to withdraw

from society but to become better members of it.

41. **A.** NO CHANGE
    B. that he is criminally insane
    C. that he is not in his right mind
    D. OMIT the underlined portion

42. **F.** NO CHANGE
    G. guilt, so,
    H. guilt, then,
    J. guilt, instead,

43. **A.** NO CHANGE
    B. Conversely,
    C. However,
    D. Moreover,

44. **F.** NO CHANGE
    G. managed, which
    H. managed,
    J. managed, it

45. **A.** NO CHANGE
    B. that they,
    C. that they
    D. that; they

PASSAGE IV

> The following paragraphs may or may not be in the
> most logical order. You may be asked questions
> about the logical order of the paragraphs, as well as
> where to place sentences logically within any given
> paragraph.

A Picture of Health

[1]

President John F. Kennedy's public image

was one of enviable health. Tall and trim, he embodied
_____
          46

the tanned, athletic image other men sought. In reality,

46. **F.** NO CHANGE
    G. was enviable health, tall
    H. was one of enviable health, tall
    J. of enviable health. Tall

GO ON TO THE NEXT PAGE.

1 ■ ■ ■ ■ ■ ■ ■ ■ **1**

his "tan" was a symptom of Addison's disease.

He had been bedridden for much of
‾‾‾‾‾‾‾‾‾‾‾‾‾‾‾‾‾‾‾‾‾
47

his childhood, although he was genuinely
‾‾‾‾‾‾‾‾‾‾‾‾‾‾‾‾‾‾‾‾‾‾‾‾‾‾‾‾
47

athletic, he was forced to watch as healthier children
‾‾‾‾‾‾‾‾‾‾‾‾
47

and youth played.
‾‾‾‾‾‾‾‾
48

[2]

Kennedy's ailments began with a two-month

hospitalization for scarlet fever at age two. At age

thirteen, he developed colitis. By 1940, he had

osteoporosis and compression fractures in his lower back,

and in 1944, he had his first back surgery. In 1947, he

was officially diagnosed with Addison's disease, [49] He

underwent two more unsuccessful back surgeries in 1954

and 1955. He was taking chronic pain medication from

that point until his death in 1963.

[3]

By the time Kennedy was president, he was taking ten

to twelve pills every day, including anti-spasmodics,

muscle relaxants, various steroids, pain medications, and

Nembutal for sleep. In addition, he received anesthetic
‾‾‾‾‾‾‾‾‾‾‾‾‾‾‾‾‾‾‾‾‾
50

injections in his back up to six times a day
‾‾‾‾‾‾‾‾‾‾‾‾‾‾‾‾‾‾‾‾‾‾‾‾‾‾‾‾‾‾‾‾‾
50

[4]

How did Kennedy hide such significant health

problems from the American people without them
‾‾‾‾‾‾‾‾‾‾‾‾
51

seeing it? His best alibi was his appearance: He looked
‾‾‾‾‾‾‾‾‾
51

healthy. Questions of his health were unthinkable to

anyone, who saw him, in person, or, on television.
‾‾
52

47. **A.** NO CHANGE
B. He had been bedridden for much of his life. He was genuinely athletic. He was
C. Although genuinely athletic, he had been bed-ridden for much of his childhood,
D. He was a bedridden childhood athlete.

48. **F.** NO CHANGE
G. and youths
H. and young people
J. OMIT the underlined portion

49. The writer would like to add more detail to help the reader to understand the symptoms of Addison's disease. Assuming all are true, which of the following completions of this sentence best achieves this effect?
A. an auto-immune disorder that has numerous symptoms.
B. which is rare.
C. a rare auto-immune disorder, characterized by weight loss, muscle weakness, fatigue, low blood pressure, and, as mentioned above, darkening of the skin.
D. which causes a variety of unpleasant symptoms and can result in death, often at a very early age.

50. **F.** NO CHANGE
G. he received anesthetic injections up to six times a day in his back.
H. in his back, up to six times a day, he received anesthetic injections.
J. up to six times a day in his back, he received anesthetic injections.

51. **A.** NO CHANGE
B. without their knowledge or noticing it
C. without there knowledge
D. OMIT the underlined portion

52. **F.** NO CHANGE
G. anyone who saw him: in person, or
H. anyone who saw him; in person or
J. anyone who saw him in person or

GO ON TO THE NEXT PAGE.

1 ■ ■ ■ ■ ■ ■ ■ ■ 1

He was well-practiced at acting healthy, as, well, he was
₅₃

able to hide his crippling pain from all except his doctors
₅₄
and closest relatives. Finally, he was well-rehearsed

with answers to any questions related to his overall
₅₅
health and well-being; for example,
₅₅

he attributes his back problems to old football and war
₅₆
injuries.

[5]

Perhaps a better question is why Kennedy was sick.
₅₇
The answer is a testimony to Kennedy's incredible
strength and perseverance. A detailed, time-line
evaluation of his illnesses and treatments and his
corresponding decisions and actions resulted in the
following discovery: Neither his illness and the drugs
₅₈
seemed to have affected his performance as a president.
Despite great physical pain and excessive medication,
his judgment wasn't compromised.

[6]

By today's standards, Kennedy had medical problems
severe enough to qualify him for federal disability or
retirement. Nevertheless, he not only survived, but he
performed at the highest level.
₅₉

53. A. NO CHANGE
    B. healthy as, well, he
    C. healthy as well; he
    D. healthy as well he

54. F. NO CHANGE
    G. crippling pain from his doctors, except
    H. pain, which was crippling, from all accept his doctors
    J. doctors from his crippling pain

55. A. NO CHANGE
    B. related questions about his health;
    C. health-related questions about his healthiness;
    D. health-related questions;

56. F. NO CHANGE
    G. attributed
    H. is attributing
    J. was attributed

57. Which of the choices provides the most effective introductory sentence for Paragraph 5?
    A. NO CHANGE
    B. Perhaps a better question is whether Kennedy played football.
    C. Perhaps a better question is whether such an ill man was competent to be president.
    D. Perhaps a better question is why Kennedy had Addison's disease.

58. F. NO CHANGE
    G. and not the drugs
    H. nor the drugs
    J. and either the drugs

59. A. NO CHANGE
    B. at the highest level, performed.
    C. highly performed at his level.
    D. achieved high performance above his expected level.

GO ON TO THE NEXT PAGE.

1 ■ ■ ■ ■ ■ ■ ■ ■ 1

Question 60 asks about the passage as a whole.

60. Suppose the writer had been assigned to write a brief essay about Addison's disease and treatment of the disease. Would this essay successfully fulfill the assignment?
    F. Yes, because the essay describes the symptoms.
    G. Yes, because the essay explains that Addison's is treated with steroids.
    H. No, because the essay focuses on President Kennedy's health.
    J. No, because the essay does not describe any symptoms of the disease.

PASSAGE V

The following paragraphs may or may not be in the most logical order. You may be asked questions about the logical order of the paragraphs, as well as where to place sentences logically within any given paragraph.

Warmth in the Arctic

[1]

"We're going where?" "To the gateway to the Arctic — the Land of the Midnight Sun! We're going traveling to Tromso, Norway!" As the
                    ‾‾‾‾‾‾‾‾‾‾
                        61
school year ended, I was looking forward to going home

to Southern California, planning to lifeguard and use my
                       ‾‾‾‾‾‾‾
                         62
spare time to surf. Now my friend was proposing that we spend the summer 250 miles north of the Arctic Circle. Was he nuts? As I look back, it was the best crazy decision I ever made.

[2]

Although the weather in Tromso wasn't hot, it wasn't cold. I occasionally needed a sweater, but seldom a coat. And, although I didn't develop my usual summer

61. A. NO CHANGE
    B. go
    C. traveling
    D. went on a trip

62. F. NO CHANGE
    G. where I planned
    H. which I planned
    J. in which I planned

GO ON TO THE NEXT PAGE.

1 ■ ■ ■ ■ ■ ■ ■ ■ 1

tan, the people of Tromso more than made up for the

lack of warmth provided by the climate.

　Tromso is sometimes called, "the Paris of the North,"

but not because of the way foreigners are treated!

Everyone we encountered was eager to help us. [64]
　　　　　63

[3]

(1) My days that summer weren't spent <u>sitting</u> in a
　　　　　　　　　　　　　　　　　　　　65

lifeguard chair spinning a whistle.

(2) <u>Tromso, like other towns, may boast it never</u>
　　　　　　　　　　　　　　　　66

<u>sleeps, but in Tromso it seems to be true.</u>
　　　　　　　　66

(3) Although I feared that the time would drag, the

opposite was true. (4) I know I slept less that summer than

I ever have; yet, I didn't feel tired. (5) My days weren't

spent working — or sitting — <u>at all</u>. (6) Whether that was
　　　　　　　　　　　　　　　　67

the result of the midnight sun or the potently rich

coffee, I'm not sure. [68]

[4]

Much of our free time was spent hiking.

63. Given that all are true, which of the choices best
illustrates the "warmth" described in the previous
paragraph?
　A. NO CHANGE
　B. The food in Tromso was delicious.
　C. Most of the people wore fur hats.
　D. Tromso gets very cold in the winter.

64. The writer wishes to include an example of the
Tromso residents' eagerness to help. Which of the
following true sentences, inserted here, would best
fulfill that goal?
　F. When we asked for directions, the residents
　　usually provided them.
　G. We had only to glance up from a map to find
　　someone asking us (in nearly perfect English)
　　if they could help us find our way.
　H. My mother is Norwegian and she is very helpful.
　J. Tromso has more pubs per capita than any other
　　city in Norway, which makes the people very
　　friendly.

65. A. NO CHANGE
　B. in a reclining position
　C. occupying
　D. sitting upon the seat

66. F. NO CHANGE
　G. Other towns may boast that they never sleep,
　　but in Tromso it seems to be true.
　H. In other towns, people may boast that it never
　　sleep, but in Tromso it seems they're true.
　J. Towns other than Tromso may boast, but it isn't
　　true that they don't sleep except there.

67. A. NO CHANGE
　B. besides.
　C. regardless.
　D. OMIT the underlined portion.

68. Which of the following sequences of sentences makes
this paragraph most logical?
　F. NO CHANGE
　G. 2, 3, 1, 5, 4, 6
　H. 1, 6, 5, 3, 2, 4,
　J. 1, 6, 2, 4, 3, 5,

GO ON TO THE NEXT PAGE.

1 ■ ■ ■ ■ ■ ■ ■ ■ 1

On a long hike, good hiking boots are essential,
especially in preventing blisters. Hiking is so popular in
Norway that the government has passed regulations such
as the Friluftsleven (Outdoor Recreation Act) that allows
anyone to hike or ski across wilderness areas, 70 One of
our favorite places to hike was on Mount Storsteinen,
which is accessible from Tromso by cable car. From the
top, we would hike one of the many trails. The views were
amazing. I took

photos of many beautiful scenes.

[5]

Now that I'm home, I look forward to returning to
Tromso soon. However, next time I am determined to

see Tromsos' sights in the winter. As much as I enjoyed

the midnight sun, I am anxious to see the northern
lights from Mount Storsteinen, a view that has been
described as world class — exactly as I would

describe it's inhabitants.

---

69. **A.** NO CHANGE
B. Good hiking boots are essential to preventing blisters, especially on a long hike.
C. My favorite hiking boots are made in Maine.
D. OMIT the underlined portion.

70. The writer wishes to add a detail to the end of this sentence that will explain how the Act regularly affects hikers' rights. Given that all are true, which of the following statements would most directly accomplish this?
F. adding designated areas as demand increases.
G. even if the areas can't be reached by cable car.
H. despite the difficulties of hiking.
J. including those people who don't enjoy hiking.

71. Which of the descriptions of the photos best creates a vivid image for the reader?
A. NO CHANGE
B. high mountain lakes, birch forests, fjords, and the midnight sun.
C. lakes, forests, fjords, and the sun.
D. people and places I had never photographed before.

72. **F.** NO CHANGE
G. home, therefore,
H. home, for example,
J. home, on the other hand,

73. **A.** NO CHANGE
B. Tromsos
C. Tromso's most
D. Tromso's

74. **F.** NO CHANGE
G. sun from Tromso and Mount Storsteinen, I am anxious to see the northern lights from there too, a
H. sun, the northern lights from Mount Storsteinen I am anxious to see, a
J. view of the sun, the northern lights from Mount Storsteinen are something I am anxious to see: a

75. **A.** NO CHANGE
B. the region's
C. their
D. its

END OF THE ENGLISH TEST
STOP! IF YOU HAVE TIME LEFT OVER, CHECK YOUR WORK ON THIS SECTION ONLY.

2 △ △ △ △ △ △ △ △ **2**

MATHEMATICS TEST

60 Minutes – 60 Questions

DIRECTIONS: Solve each of the problems in the time allowed, then fill in the corresponding bubble on your answer sheet. Do not spend too much time on any one problem; skip the more difficult problems and go back to them later. You may use a calculator on this test. For this test you should assume that figures are NOT necessarily drawn to scale, that all geometric figures lie in a plane, and that the word *line* is used to indicate a straight line.

1. If $4x - 9 = 11$, then $x = ?$
   A. 5
   B. 6
   C. 6.5
   D. 9
   E. 16

DO YOUR FIGURING HERE.

$$4x - 9 = 11$$
$$9 + 9$$
$$4x = 20$$
$$x = 5$$

2. Consider the following 2 logical statements:

   If the length of $\overline{XY}$ is 4, then the length of $\overline{YZ}$ is 7.
   The length of $\overline{YZ}$ is NOT 7.
   If these statements are both true, then the length of:

   F. $\overline{XY}$ is NOT 4
   G. $\overline{XY}$ is 7
   H. $\overline{YZ}$ is 4
   J. $\overline{YZ}$ is NOT 4
   K. $\overline{YZ}$ is 7

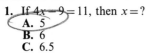

3. If the probability that Tom will go for a run is 0.6, what is the probability that he will NOT go for a run?
   A. 0.0
   B. 0.12
   C. 0.3
   D. 0.35
   E. 0.4

4. Mark bought 1 video for $12.99 and 2 others for $6.50 each. Which of the following represents the average price that Mark paid per video?

   F. $\dfrac{\$12.99 + 2(\$6.50)}{3}$

   G. $\$12.99 + \dfrac{\$6.50}{2}$

   H. $\dfrac{\$12.99}{3} + \dfrac{\$6.50}{2}$

   J. $\dfrac{\$12.99 + \$6.50}{3}$

   K. $\dfrac{\$12.99 + \$6.50}{2}$

GO ON TO THE NEXT PAGE.

2   **2**

DO YOUR FIGURING HERE.

5. On Saturday, Joan received her pay and spent $\frac{1}{4}$ of it. On Sunday she spent $\frac{1}{5}$ of the remaining money, and on Monday she spent $\frac{1}{2}$ of what remained from Sunday. If $18.00 then remained, how much pay did she receive originally?
   A. $24.00
   B. $36.00
   C. $48.00
   D. $60.00
   E. $72.00

6. If $P = 5a$ and $Q = 3b - 2a$, then what is the value of $P - Q$?
   F. $7a + 3b$
   G. $3a + 3b$
   H. $7a - 3b$
   J. $3a - 3b$
   K. $5a - 3b$

7. In the figure below, l_1 is parallel to l_2, l_3 is parallel to l_4, and the lines intersect as shown. What is the measure of angle z?

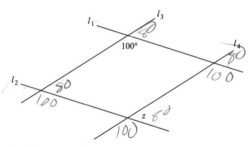

   A. 40°
   B. 50°
   C. 60°
   D. 70°
   E. 80°

8. If $x = 2$, then $-x^2 + 4x - 3 = ?$
   F. 9
   G. 5
   H. 1
   J. -1
   K. -7

9. The average of 8 numbers is 6.5. If each of the numbers is decreased by 3, what is the average of the 8 new numbers?
   A. 0.0
   B. 3.5
   C. 4.0
   D. 7.5
   E. 9.5

10. The expression $5a + 5b$ is equivalent to which of the following?
   F. $5(a - b)$
   G. $10(a + b)$
   H. $5ab$
   J. $5(a + b)$
   K. $10ab$

GO ON TO THE NEXT PAGE.

2   **2**

11. For each day at the flower shop, you receive $12.00 plus a fixed amount for each flower bouquet that you deliver. Currently you are earning $22.00 per day for delivery of 20 flower bouquets. Today you are asked to deliver 16 additional flower bouquets. How much will you earn today?
   A. $14.00
   B. $22.00
   C. $30.00
   D. $38.00
   E. $50.00

DO YOUR FIGURING HERE.

12. If $\frac{8}{x} \geq \frac{1}{4}$, what is the largest possible value for x?

   F. $\frac{1}{2}$
   G. 4
   H. 16
   J. 24
   K. 32

13. On the clock shown below, what is the number of degrees that the hour hand of the clock moves from 1:00 p.m. to 8:00 p.m.?

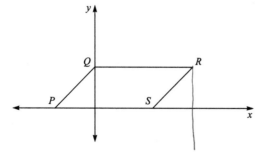

   A. 70°
   B. 150°
   C. 210°
   D. 270°
   E. 300°

14. In the standard (x, y) coordinate plane below, $PQRS$ is a parallelogram. Points P, Q, and S are located on the axes as shown. Which of the following could be the coordinates of point R?

   F. $(0, 4)$
   G. $(4, 0)$
   H. $(-3, 0)$
   J. $(6, 4)$
   K. $(6, -4)$

GO ON TO THE NEXT PAGE.

2 △ △ △ △ △ △ △ △ 2

15. Which of the following is a factored form of $3x^3y^3 + 3xy$?
- **A.** $3xy(x^2y^2 + 1)$
- **B.** $3(3x^2y^2)$
- **C.** $(3x + 3y)(3x + 3y)$
- **D.** $3x^2y^2(xy)$
- **E.** $3x(x^2y^2 + 3)$

DO YOUR FIGURING HERE.

$3x^3y^3 + 3xy$

16. A classroom has $(r + s)$ rows of seats and t seats in each row. Which of the following is an expression for the number of seats in the entire classroom?
- **F.** $r \cdot s \cdot t$
- **G.** $(r \cdot s) + (r \cdot t)$
- **H.** $t + (r \cdot s)$
- **J.** $r + s + t$
- **K.** $(t \cdot r) + (t \cdot s)$

17. If 20% of x equals 16, then $x = ?$
- **A.** 2
- **B.** 3.2
- **C.** 32
- **D.** 80
- **E.** 800

18. The cost of picking apples at a local apple orchard is $0.05 per apple for the first 30 apples picked and $0.03 per apple for each additional apple picked. What did Matt pay if he picked 75 apples?
- **F.** $2.85
- **G.** $3.25
- **H.** $3.75
- **J.** $5.10
- **K.** $6.00

19. You are standing in line at the cash register to pay for a watch priced at $12.99. A sales tax of 6% of the $12.99 will be added (rounded to the nearest cent) to the price of the watch. You have 15 one-dollar bills, but how much will you need in coins if you want to have exact change ready?
- **A.** $0.23
- **B.** $0.33
- **C.** $0.53
- **D.** $0.67
- **E.** $0.77

20. For which nonnegative value of x is the expression $\dfrac{1}{16 - x^2}$ undefined?
- **F.** 0
- **G.** 4
- **H.** 16
- **J.** 32
- **K.** 256

GO ON TO THE NEXT PAGE.

2   **2**

21. What is the correct order of π, $\frac{5}{2}$, and 4 from greatest to least?

DO YOUR FIGURING HERE.

   A. $\frac{5}{2} > \pi > 4$

   B. $\frac{5}{2} > 4 > \pi$

   C. $4 > \pi > \frac{5}{2}$

   D. $\pi > \frac{5}{2} > 4$

   E. $4 > \frac{5}{2} > \pi$

22. Two strips of tape are to be used to seal a box, as shown below. Both strips must go completely around the box. What is the minimum length of tape, in centimeters (cm), required to seal the box?

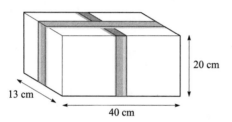

20 cm

13 cm

40 cm

   F. 73 cm
   G. 112 cm
   H. 120 cm
   J. 146 cm
   K. 186 cm

23. You have been asked to make punch for your friend's birthday party. The punch recipe calls for 9 quarts of fruit juices to 4 quarts of soda. To make 52 quarts of this punch, how many quarts of soda should you use?
   A. 4
   B. 9
   C. 13
   D. 16
   E. 36

24. Which of the following gives all the solutions of $x^2 + 2x = 8$?
   F. 4 and -2
   G. -4 and 2
   H. -8 and 1
   J. -4 only
   K. -8 only

25. If $(f+g)^2 = 81$ and $fg = 20$, then $f^2 + g^2 = ?$
   A. 1
   B. 9
   C. 41
   D. 81
   E. 100

GO ON TO THE NEXT PAGE.

2   △ △ △ △ **2**

26. If, for all x, $(x^{4a-3})^2 = x^{10}$, then $a = ?$

    F. $\dfrac{1}{2}$

    G. 1

    H. $\dfrac{13}{4}$

    J. 2

    K. $-\dfrac{15}{6}$

[handwritten: $8a-3$ over $5^{\bullet}$]

27. For the complex number i such that $i^2 = -1$, what is the value of $i^6 + 3i^4$?

    A. -2
    B. -1
    C. 0
    D. 1
    E. 2

[handwritten: $=-1$, $=-1$, $=-1$, $3(-1)(-1)$, $=-1+3$]

28. In the (x, y) coordinate plane, what is the y-intercept of the line $5x - 4y = 7$?

    F. -4

    G. $-\dfrac{7}{4}$

    H. $\dfrac{5}{4}$

    J. $\dfrac{7}{4}$

    K. 7

[handwritten: $\dfrac{-4y}{-4} = \dfrac{-5x+7}{-4}$, $y = \dfrac{-5x+7}{-4}$]

29. In the (x, y) coordinate plane, what is the radius of the circle with the equation $(x + 3)^2 + (y - 2)^2 = 10$?

    A. 2
    B. 3
    C. $\sqrt{3}$
    D. $\sqrt{10}$
    E. 10

30. In the right triangle pictured below, l, m, and n are the lengths of its sides. What is the value of $\sin \beta$?

    F. $\dfrac{l}{n}$

    G. $\dfrac{m}{n}$

    H. $\dfrac{n}{l}$

    J. $\dfrac{l}{m}$

    K. $\dfrac{n}{m}$

[handwritten: $\sin\theta = O/H$, $\cos\theta = A/H$, $\tan\theta = O/A$]

DO YOUR FIGURING HERE.

GO ON TO THE NEXT PAGE.

2   **2**

31. For all nonzero a and b, $\dfrac{(4a^3b)(-5a^5b^3)}{(10a^4b^2)} = ?$

  A. $2a^4b^2$

  B. $-2a^2b^2$

  C. $\dfrac{a^4b^4}{2}$

  D. $\dfrac{9}{b}$

  E. $-2a^4b^2$

DO YOUR FIGURING HERE.

32. In the figure below, 3 parallel lines are crossed by 2 transversals, as shown. The points of intersection and some distances, in inches, are labeled. What is the length, in inches, of x?

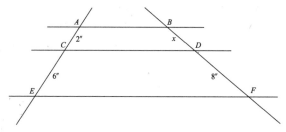

  F. 2

  G. $\dfrac{8}{3}$

  H. 3

  J. $\dfrac{4}{3}$

  K. 4

33. The figure below shows square $ABCD$ and also shows the circle centered at D with radii DC and DA. If the perimeter of the square is 28 units, what is the area of the circle, in square units?

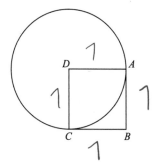

  A. 7π

  B. 14π

  C. 28π

  D. 49π

  E. 56π

GO ON TO THE NEXT PAGE.

2 △ △ △ △ △ △ △ △ **2**

34. Which of the following logical statements identifies the same set as the graph shown below?

   F. $x \le 2$ or $x \ge 4$
   G. $x \le 2$ and $x \ge 4$
   H. $x < 2$ or $x > 4$
   J. $x \le 2$ and $x > 4$
   K. $x \le 2$ or $x > 4$

DO YOUR FIGURING HERE.

35. A mailbox is 500 feet from the base of an office building, across level ground. If the office building is 400 feet tall, how many feet is it from the top of the office building to the mailbox at ground level?
   A. 900
   B. $800\sqrt{2}$
   C. $100\sqrt{41}$
   D. $\sqrt{41,000}$
   E. $500\sqrt{3}$

$\sin 500 = \dfrac{400ft}{X}$

$\dfrac{X\sin 500}{\sin 500} = \dfrac{400ft}{\sin 500 ft}$

$X =$

36. If x and y are real and $\sqrt{4\left(\dfrac{x^2}{3y}\right)} = 1$, then what must be true of the value of y?
   F. y must be negative
   G. y must be positive
   H. y must equal 4
   J. y must equal $\dfrac{1}{2}$
   K. y may have any value

37. If c is a positive integer that divides both 64 and 96 but divides neither 16 nor 20, what should you get when you add the digits in c?
   A. 3
   B. 5
   C. 7
   D. 8
   E. 10

GO ON TO THE NEXT PAGE.

2   **2**

38. What is the slope of any line parallel to the y-axis in the (x, y) coordinate plane?

- **F.** -1
- **G.** 0
- **H.** 1
- **J.** Undefined
- **K.** Cannot be determined from the given information

DO YOUR FIGURING HERE.

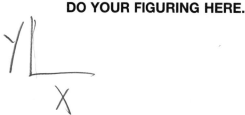

39. Which of the following lines has the largest slope?

- **A.** $y = 2x + 5$
- **B.** $y = 5x - 4$
- **C.** $y = 3x + 8$
- **D.** $3y = 9x + 6$
- **E.** $4y = 4x - 8$

40. The 2 triangles in the rectangle below share a common side. What is $\sin(a - b)$?

(Note: $\sin(a - b) = \sin a \cos b - \cos a \sin b$ for all a and b.)

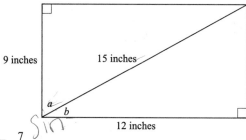

- 9 inches
- 15 inches
- 12 inches

- **F.** $\dfrac{7}{25}$
- **G.** $\dfrac{1}{2}$
- **H.** $\dfrac{3}{5}$
- **J.** 1
- **K.** $\dfrac{25}{9}$

41. Jason can walk 4 miles in j minutes. At that pace, how many minutes would it take him to walk 11 miles?

- **A.** $\dfrac{11j}{4}$
- **B.** $\dfrac{4j}{11}$
- **C.** $44j$
- **D.** $\dfrac{11}{4j}$
- **E.** $\dfrac{4}{11j}$

GO ON TO THE NEXT PAGE.

2   **2**

DO YOUR FIGURING HERE.

42. Which of the following calculations will yield an odd integer for any integer n?

F. $4n^2$

G. $3n^2 + 1$

H. $6n^2$

J. $n^2 - 1$

K. $4n^2 - 1$

43. In triangle ABC, the measure of $\angle A$ is $60°$ and the measure of $\angle B$ is $30°$. If AB is 8 units long, what is the area, in square units, of triangle ABC?

A. 4

B. $4\sqrt{3}$

C. 8

D. $8\sqrt{3}$

E. $16\sqrt{3}$

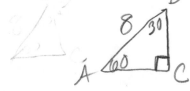

44. Trapezoid $FGHJ$ below is isosceles, with side lengths as marked. Its diagonals intersect at K. What is the ratio of the length of $\overline{GK}$ to the length of $\overline{JK}$?

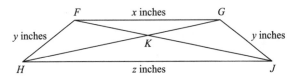

F. $\dfrac{x}{y}$

G. $\dfrac{x}{z}$

H. $\dfrac{y}{z}$

J. 1

K. $\dfrac{z}{y}$

45. A certain rectangle is 4 times as long as it is wide. Suppose the length and width are tripled. The area of the second rectangle is how many times as large as the area of the first?

A. 3

B. 4

C. 9

D. 12

E. 16

GO ON TO THE NEXT PAGE.

2   **2**

46. For what value of b would the following system of equations have an infinite number of solutions?

$$3x + 4y = 14$$
$$6x + 8y = 7b$$

DO YOUR FIGURING HERE.

   F. 2
   G. 4
   H. 7
   J. 14
   K. 28

47. If $\log_3 x = 2$, then $x = ?$

   A. $\dfrac{1}{\log_9}$
   B. 3
   C. 6
   D. 9
   E. 18^2

48. When measured from a point on the ground that is a certain distance from the base of a telephone pole, the angle of elevation to the top of the telephone pole is 37°, as shown below. The height of the telephone pole is 24 feet. What is the distance, in feet, to the telephone pole?

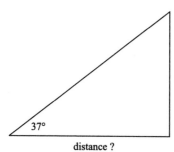

24 feet (pole)

distance ?

   F. 24 tan 37°
   G. 24 sin 37°
   H. 24 cos 37°
   J. 24 sec 37°
   K. 24 cot 37°

GO ON TO THE NEXT PAGE.

2   **2**

49. In the parallelogram below, lengths are given in inches. What is the area of the parallelogram, in square inches?

DO YOUR FIGURING HERE.

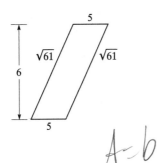

A. 15
B. $\sqrt{61}$
C. 30
D. $\sqrt{122}$
E. $2\sqrt{61}$

50. Points *A*, *B*, and *C* are 3 dist<u>inct</u> points that lie on the same li<u>ne.</u> If the length of $\overline{AB}$ is 12 meters and the length of $\overline{BC}$ is 15 meters, <u>then</u> what are all the possible lengths, in meters, for $\overline{AC}$?

F. 3 only
G. 27 only
H. 3 and 27 only
J. Any number less than 27 or greater than 3
K. Any number greater than 27 or less than 3

51. Given the vertices of parallelogram *FGHJ* in the standard (x, y) coordinate plane below, what is the area of triangle *FGH*, in square units?

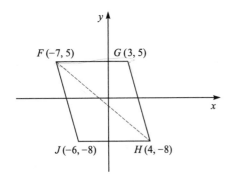

A. 12.5
B. 30.0
C. 45.0
D. 65.0
E. 130.0

GO ON TO THE NEXT PAGE.

2   **2**

52. If $6a^4b^3 < 0$, then which of the following CANNOT be true?
  F. $b < 0$
  G. $b > 0$
  H. $a = b$
  J. $a < 0$
  K. $a > 0$

DO YOUR FIGURING HERE.

53. The 1st and 2nd terms of a geometric sequence are p and sp, in that order. What is the 734th term of the sequence?
  A. $(sp)^{733}$
  B. $(sp)^{734}$
  C. $s^{733}p$
  D. $s^{734}p$
  E. sp^{733}

54. If a system of 2 linear equations in 2 variables has NO solution, and 1 of the equations is graphed in the (x, y) coordinate plane below, which of the following could be the equation of the other line?

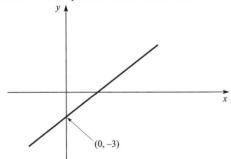

(0, −3)

  F. $y = -2$
  G. $y = -4x + 2$
  H. $y = -2x - 3$
  J. $y = 4x + 2$
  K. $y = 4x - 3$

GO ON TO THE NEXT PAGE.

2 △ △ △ △ △ △ △ △ **2**

55. If $0° \leq x \leq 90°$ and $\tan x = \dfrac{15}{8}$, then $\cos x = ?$

DO YOUR FIGURING HERE.

A. $\dfrac{8}{17}$

B. $\dfrac{15}{17}$

C. $\dfrac{17}{8}$

D. $\dfrac{17}{15}$

E. $\dfrac{8}{15}$

56. For every dollar increase in price of an admissions ticket to a professional soccer match, the soccer team sells 750 fewer tickets per month. The soccer team normally sells 2,500 tickets per month at $9.00 per ticket. Which of the following expressions represents the number of tickets sold per month if the cost is increased by x dollars per ticket?

F. $(9.00 + x)(2,500 - 750x)$
G. $2500(9.00 + x)$
H. $9.00 + x$
J. $2,500 + 750x$
K. $2,500 - 750x$

57. In a game, 75 marbles numbered 00 through 74 are placed in a box. A player draws 1 marble at random from the box. Without replacing the first marble, the player draws a second marble at random. If both marbles drawn have the same ones digit (that is, both marbles have a number ending in 0, 1, 2, 3, etc.), the player is a winner. If the first marble drawn is numbered 28, what is the probability that the player will be a winner on the next draw?

A. $\dfrac{2}{25}$

B. $\dfrac{7}{25}$

C. $\dfrac{3}{37}$

D. $\dfrac{8}{75}$

E. $\dfrac{4}{37}$

GO ON TO THE NEXT PAGE.

2   **2**

58. In order to clean her aquarium, Rana must remove half of the water. The aquarium measures 24 inches long, 12 inches wide, and 10 inches deep. The aquarium is currently completely full. What volume of water, in cubic inches, must Rana remove?

F. 288
G. 960
H. 1,440
J. 2,880
K. 5,760

59. In the figure below, line p has the equation $y = 3x$. Line q is below p, as shown, and q is parallel to p. Which of the following is an equation for q?

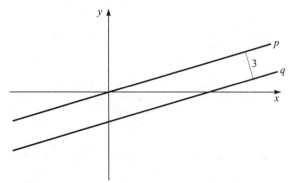

A. $y = x - 3$
B. $y = 3x - 3\sqrt{2}$
C. $y = x - 3\sqrt{2}$
D. $y = 3x - 3$
E. $y = 3x + 3$

60. What is the smallest possible value for the product of 2 real numbers that differ by 12?

F. -36
G. -27
H. -11
J. 0
K. 13

DO YOUR FIGURING HERE.

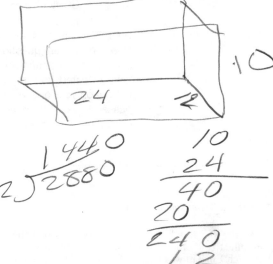

END OF THE MATH TEST
STOP! IF YOU HAVE TIME LEFT OVER, CHECK YOUR WORK ON THIS SECTION ONLY.

3 ████████████████████████████████ **3**

READING TEST

35 Minutes – 40 Questions

DIRECTIONS: This test includes four passages, each followed by ten questions. Read the passage and choose the best answer to each question. After you have selected your answer, fill in the corresponding bubble on your answer sheet. You should refer to the passages as often as necessary when answering the questions.

Passage I
PROSE FICTION: *"Assimilating in Mecca"*

Before she was born, Eui Thi's parents fled the communist rule of North Vietnam to settle in Laos. Although Eui Thi was born in Laos, her family never truly belonged there. While they spoke "the lan-
5 guage," it was with a different dialect. Her father found odd jobs that provided food and shelter for the family, but she never felt at home — and she never felt truly safe.

As the oldest child, ten-year-old Eui Thi's
10 responsibilities were many, but her parents' trust did not include the sharing of adult concerns. Nevertheless, Eui Thi recognized the worried tones of their late-night whispers. As the last U.S. troops evacuated Saigon, the communist
15 enemy was once again too close. Her parents hurriedly packed up the family and fled to Thailand. Suddenly, surrounded by thousands of other refugees, Eui Thi found herself longing for the "stability" of Laos.

20 Eui Thi now dreamed of going to America. She had heard it called a "melting pot" because people from all over the world lived there; it was the mecca where she would no longer be an outsider! America was huge, with room to run, play, and grow food.
25 She couldn't remember the last time she wasn't hungry.

And then, in October 1975, the word came. Her family was being sent to Iowa. She tried to hide her disappointment as she politely asked, "Where is
30 Iowa? I thought we might be going to America." Her parents laughed. "Oh, sweet child — Iowa is in America!" Eui Thi was too excited to feel embarrassed. She was finally going to America.

Weeks later, her family arrived in Iowa. Despite
35 the fact that they had traveled with hundreds of other refugees, her family was suddenly alone with strangers who spoke an unintelligible language. The strangers ushered Eui Thi's family into a car and drove to a house — not just any house — her
40 new home. The strangers walked her to a vast building surrounded by playground equipment. "In a few days," one said, "you will go to school

here." America was all Eui Thi had hoped it would be — and more.

45 Her zeal quickly faded. On her first day of school, many children pointed, waved, and smiled at her, but she could not understand what they were saying. The friendly strangers had given her clothes for school, but she could plainly see that her clothes
50 were older and more faded than those of the other children. When she voiced this concern to her parents, they scolded her. "We have been given a tremendous gift — a new home in a safe land, school for you children, and a job for your father — and you
55 don't like the clothes these people have provided?" Ashamed, Eui Thi vowed never to share such petty concerns again.

Eui Thi learned quickly, and occasionally wished she hadn't. As she began to understand a few words
60 and phrases, she realized that she was a topic of conversation. She overheard some of the other girls talking about "the funny smells" that wafted from her home. When a child in her brother's class was discovered to have lice, her family was blamed as the
65 source. Despite the challenges, Eui Thi did her best to dress and act like the other girls, and gradually made a few friends.

Time quickly passed, and soon it was time for Eui Thi's first Junior High dance. She was so excited.
70 Dancing was universal! How she had missed the celebratory dancing of the Tai-Dam. When Eui Thi arrived at the dance and her eyes slowly adjusted to the darkness, she realized she knew nothing of *this* kind of dance. Eui Thi silently prayed that no one
75 would ask her to dance. And then, as no one did, she reached a sudden, horrible conclusion. She was from a different world — and there were no other Asians at her school. Everyone else at the dance had fair skin and fine hair, and they had all paired up to dance
80 with each other.

She may have been able to copy the fashions and Farrah Fawcett hairstyles, and even, eventually, the slang, but she would never be the same as the other girls. Surrounded by other adolescents, Eui Thi was
85 alone. "Some 'melting pot'!" she thought. "Will I ever truly belong?"

GO ON TO THE NEXT PAGE.

3 ███████████████████████████████ **3**

1. One of the points suggested in Paragraph 2 regarding Eui Thi's longing for Laos was that:
   A. Laos was now more politically stable.
   B. the threat of communism was no longer present in Laos and it was safe to return.
   C. Thailand is plagued by earthquakes, making Laos safer by comparison.
   D. feeling like an outsider in Laos was preferable to the chaos of the refugee camp.

2. As it is used in the passage (line 45), the word *zeal* most nearly means:
   F. fear.
   G. apathy.
   H. understanding.
   J. enthusiasm.

3. The passage states that:
   A. Eui Thi was too young to be responsible.
   B. Eui Thi always had enough to eat.
   C. Eui Thi was immediately disappointed by America.
   D. Eui Thi did not feel at home in Laos.

4. It can reasonably be inferred from Paragraph 2 that Eui Thi's parents were whispering about:
   F. the military conflict in Vietnam.
   G. Eui Thi's lack of close friends.
   H. Eui Thi's lack of appreciation.
   J. an anticipated sibling for Eui Thi.

5. According to the passage, which of the following were provided for Eui Thi's family?
   I. A job for her father
   II. Hand-me-down clothes
   III. An account at the local supermarket
   A. II only
   B. I and II only
   C. II and III only
   D. I, II, and III

6. According to the passage, Eui Thi's "mecca" would include:
   I. a new car
   II. room to run
   III. the communist enemy
   IV. adequate food
   F. I and II only
   G. II and IV only
   H. I, II, and III only
   J. I, II, and IV only

7. The original homeland of Eui Thi's parents was:
   A. Laos.
   B. Vietnam.
   C. Thailand.
   D. America.

8. According to the passage, Eui Thi was able to mimic her peers in all aspects EXCEPT:
   F. language.
   G. hairstyle.
   H. culture.
   J. fashion.

9. The dancing at Eui Thi's Junior High, as compared to traditional Tai-Dam dancing, was judged in this passage to be:
   A. upbeat and celebratory.
   B. a universal style.
   C. an entirely different style.
   D. dark and exciting.

10. According to the passage, Eui Thi's American school was:
   F. on a hill.
   G. within driving distance of her home.
   H. within walking distance of her home.
   J. surrounded by trees.

GO ON TO THE NEXT PAGE.

3 ████████████████████████████████████ **3**

Passage II
SOCIAL SCIENCE: *"Mayan Dependency on Agriculture"*

Eleven thousand years ago, the Yucatán Peninsula of Mexico was home to nomadic hunters and gatherers. About 6,500 years later, these nomads abandoned their wandering ways; they started
5 cultivating *maize*, a native corn, and settling in villages surrounded by cornfields. From this early agrarian beginning grew the grand Mayan civilization.

The ancient Maya spread until they occupied
10 much of Central and South America. Although the Mayan civilization spanned from 2000 B.C. to 1500 A.D. it is most famous for its Classical Period (300–900 A.D.). During this time, the Mayas built awe-inspiring temples, pyramids, and cities and
15 formed a political and social order. They developed the most complex system of writing in the Americas. Many of their enduring ancient arts, including weaving, pottery, basket weaving, and woodcarving, are now recognized worldwide. One of the truly
20 remarkable achievements of the ancient Mayas was their complex system of calendars, which reached an accuracy of being within one day every 6,000 years — far more accurate than our modern calendar.

The reason for the Mayan civilization's collapse
25 in the tenth century is still shrouded in mystery, although many hypotheses exist. What is known is that, by the 900s, the cities were being consumed by the jungle. By the time European explorer and conqueror Hernán Cortés reached the area in the
30 1500s, the empire had been long-since abandoned and the wandering barbarian tribes could provide no recollection of its rich history.

In the 1800s, abandoned cities were discovered in Yucatán, Guatemala, and Honduras. Since then,
35 the Mayas have attracted a great deal of academic and popular attention. The living descendants of the Mayas have been studied so much that an anthropologist can now be found in or near most of today's Mayan communities. Accordingly, understanding of
40 Mayan society before European influence has grown considerably. One sure conclusion resulting from these studies is the Mayas' perpetual dependence on agriculture. Even in the present day, the inhabitants of Yucatán are almost exclusively agriculturalists.
45 They are able to earn a comfortable living by raising *maize*, their chief crop, from soil so shallow that modern farming methods cannot be used. Experts believe that the present agricultural methods are the same as those used by the ancients. Hence, through a
50 study of these methods, the ancient population can be estimated with some degree of accuracy.

Despite its lushness and moisture, a tropical rain forest can only support small human populations. As the rain falls almost without ceasing, plant
55 and animal growth sometimes seems out of control. Because growth is so rapid, the nutrients provided by dead plants and animal feces get used up very quickly. As a result, the soil is remarkably unfertile for agriculture.

60 To create arable land, the Mayas used a "slash-and-burn" technique (called *milpa* by the Mayas) to clear the forests. They quickly cut down a swath of forest, burned the felled trees and plants for fertilizer, and then cultivated the plot. They planted
65 maize and secondary crops such as beans, squash, and tobacco. Then, as now, the Mayas did not employ sophisticated fertilization techniques, so the plot of land would be exhausted in two to seven years, depending on weeding techniques. As the
70 soil nutrients were depleted, the Mayas moved their fields to new locations, allowing the old fields to lie fallow for about ten years before reusing them. One of the primary reasons for the Mayas' elaborate system of calendars was undoubtedly their singular
75 dependence on agriculture and the effects of time on the poor soil.

Because of the challenges replete in farming in the rain forest, it takes an immense amount of land to support a 100-member family group — among the
80 Maya, it probably required at least seventy acres for every five people. The population, then, throughout the Classical Period was undoubtedly very small.

Slash-and-burn agriculture is labor intensive but not all-consuming. Modern-day Native Americans
85 in Guatemala who employ this agriculture spend about 190 days every year in agricultural work, leaving at least 170 days (almost half of a year) for other types of labor. This excess time was clearly used during the Classical Period for the building and
90 maintenance of their elaborate cities as well as the extensive creation of artwork. In addition to being the root of Mayan civilization, agriculture remained at the center of all the Mayas had achieved.

---

11. It can most reasonably be inferred from the passage that the nomads abandoned their wandering because:
   A. barbarian tribes kept attacking.
   B. they had sufficiently mastered farming techniques to allow for a more stable lifestyle.
   C. their complex calendar indicated it was time to settle down.
   D. Cortés taught them European farming techniques, including *maize* cultivation.

12. In the author's view, would the assertion that Mayan civilization collapsed as a result of plagues be an expression of fact or opinion, and why?
   F. Opinion, because many viable hypotheses for the collapse exist.
   G. Opinion, because the passage argues that everything the Mayas did was because of the calendar.
   H. Fact, because historical research has already proven that plagues occurred around 900 B.C.
   J. Fact, because it is well known that plagues have caused the downfall of many great civilizations.

13. All of the following are examples of accomplishments made during the Mayan Classical Period EXCEPT:
   A. basket weaving.
   B. elaborate calendars.
   C. nomadic hunting and gathering.
   D. a complex writing system.

GO ON TO THE NEXT PAGE.

3 ████████████████████████████████████ **3**

14. According to the passage, the most likely reason the Mayas developed such an elaborate system of calendars was because:
- **F.** they had time left over after performing farm labor to develop elaborate systems.
- **G.** European explorers gave them a simple calendar and the Mayas improved on the concept.
- **H.** the agrarian lifestyle evolved from social order.
- **J.** their dependence on agriculture necessitated an understanding of seasons and time.

15. The dates referred to in the passage indicate that the height of Mayan civilization occurred:
- **A.** between 6500 B.C. and 2000 B.C.
- **B.** between 2000 B.C. and 1500 A.D.
- **C.** between 900 B.C. and 300 B.C.
- **D.** between 300 A.D. and 900 A.D.

16. As indicated in the passage, the *slash-and-burn* technique was used because:
- I. it was the most efficient way to remove trees for farmland.
- II. the burned plants provided nutrients for the soil.
- III. the Mayas worshiped a god of fire.
- IV. the blazing fire provided much needed warmth.
- **F.** I and II only
- **G.** I, II, and IV only
- **H.** II, III, and IV only
- **J.** I, II, III, and IV

17. Details in the passage suggest that modern-day farmers in Guatemala:
- **A.** are totally dependent upon nomadic hunters and gatherers.
- **B.** have not learned anything from their ancient relatives.
- **C.** still employ some of the techniques perfected by the ancient Maya.
- **D.** spend less than six months out of the year working on their farms.

18. As it is used in line 60, the word *arable* most nearly means:
- **F.** fit to be cultivated.
- **G.** controllable.
- **H.** barren and unproductive.
- **J.** technical.

19. According to the passage, *milpa* is:
- **A.** the Mayan word for calendar.
- **B.** a lost art.
- **C.** a farming technique.
- **D.** Mayan fertilizer.

20. According to the passage, anthropologists are common near Mayan communities because:
- **F.** many indigenous students of Mayan descent have received college scholarships to study anthropology in Mexico.
- **G.** anthropologists are common throughout Mexico and Central America.
- **H.** anthropology originated in Classic Mayan society.
- **J.** Modern-day descendants of the Mayas have attracted a great deal of attention since the discovery of abandoned Mayan cities.

GO ON TO THE NEXT PAGE.

3 ▮▮▮▮▮▮▮▮▮▮▮▮▮▮▮▮▮▮▮▮▮▮ **3**

Passage III
HUMANITIES: "Teen Heartthrob"

It was 1977 when I first read his name — Shaun Cassidy. I was flipping through the pages of a *Tiger Beat* magazine when my older sister came up behind me and casually pointed at his picture.

5   "He's cute. Isn't he the one who sings that 'Da Doo Ron Ron' song you like?"

"No, I don't think so," I replied. "I think he's one of the guys on *The Hardy Boys* show I watch on Sunday nights."

10   As my sister walked away, I began reading about Shaun. His older brother was David Cassidy — the one I could remember my sister swooning over in years past. I learned that Shaun Cassidy was, in fact, both the guy on the radio and the guy on *The Hardy*

15 *Boys*. I became enthralled and quickly developed my first adolescent crush. The walls of my room were soon covered with over 100 images of Shaun's big blue eyes and toothy grin. I became a card-carrying member of the Hardy Boys fan club. His sultry voice

20 serenaded me each night as I drifted off to sleep with his debut album playing on my bright-green record player.

Although part of my appreciation for Cassidy stemmed from his physical allure, my admiration of

25 his talent was not inappropriate. Like most teen pop stars, his fame as a teenage heartthrob was destined to be a short-lived. But his artistic ability was real. After his singing popularity waned and his television show was cancelled, Shaun performed in several

30 other television series and made-for-television movies. Eventually, however, he turned his attention to a new challenge — the theatre.

By this time, my pubescent crush on this "cute boy" had long-since passed. Nevertheless, his name

35 popped out to me occasionally as I scanned the news or glanced through a magazine. In this haphazard way, I casually followed his career through the years. And as I learned of each of his accomplishments, I couldn't help but be pleased for my former

40 idol.

On and off-Broadway, Cassidy continued to develop his acting skills. He soon proved his talent as a stage actor, winning a Critics Circle Award for *The Subject Was Roses* and a Dramalogue award for

45 Best Actor for *Diary of a Hunger Strike*. Although he appeared to enjoy performing, the world of television once again beckoned — but Shaun no longer performed in front of the television camera.

Throughout his television career, Cassidy had

50 been curious about the production side of the business. Despite having occasional questions for the camera crew and others on the technical end, he was especially interested in the responsibilities of the writers, directors, and producers.

55   Several years into his stage-acting career, Cassidy's early fascination with the production end of the entertainment industry beckoned and he felt compelled to learn more. His first foray into the world of television production was naively ambi-

60 tious. He worked hard as the Supervising Producer and Show Developer for a TV series that never

aired. After this rude awakening, he decided to learn more about his new craft from more experienced specialists in the entertainment industry.

65   As he wrote and co-produced the TV movie, *Strays*, Cassidy realized that writing provided a tremendous outlet for his creativity and he spent several of the following years as a television script-writer. Later, Cassidy made a second attempt at

70 producing and was far more successful. Although Cassidy occasionally performs on stage and screen (even singing the theme song for one of the television series he created), he spends most of his time now as a creator and executive producer of television shows

75 for several networks. My youthful admiration of Shaun Cassidy was naive and shallow, but his talent was real and is standing the test of time.

---

21. Which of the following descriptions most accurately and completely represents this passage?
- **A.** A thoughtful and heartfelt reminiscence of the singer, Shaun Cassidy
- **B.** A biographical overview of Shaun Cassidy's entertainment career from the 1970s to the present
- **C.** A careful and impartial critique of the singing talent of Shaun Cassidy
- **D.** A discussion of the author's own singing career in relation to that of Shaun Cassidy

22. All of the following aspects of Shaun Cassidy's life were described EXCEPT:
- **F.** his childhood.
- **G.** his singing career.
- **H.** his acting career.
- **J.** his television writing career.

23. The passage states that:
- **A.** Shaun Cassidy was more popular than his brother, David.
- **B.** Shaun Cassidy personally serenaded the author.
- **C.** Shaun Cassidy was a talented performer.
- **D.** Shaun Cassidy left the entertainment industry.

24. As it is used in the last paragraph, the word *naive* most nearly means:
- **F.** clever.
- **G.** childlike.
- **H.** inventive.
- **J.** generous.

25. It can be inferred from the passage that the writer, in her adolescence, most valued which of the following in a performer?
- **A.** Physical attractiveness
- **B.** Strong teeth
- **C.** Debut albums
- **D.** Writing ability

GO ON TO THE NEXT PAGE.

3 ▐███▌ **3**

26. It can be most reasonably concluded from the writer's reference to Cassidy's fame being "destined to be short-lived" that:
  F. most teen performers enjoy longer periods of fame and fortune.
  G. Cassidy had no talent.
  H. most teen performers who rise quickly to fame fall out of favor just as quickly.
  J. teen fans are usually very loyal.

27. According to the passage, in which order did the following events occur in the writer's life?
    I. Recovering from her adolescent crush
    II. Casually following Cassidy's career
    III. Reading about Cassidy in *Tiger Beat*
  A. I, II, III
  B. II, III, I
  C. III, II, I
  D. III, I, II

28. Which of the following best describes the writer's immediate reaction to reading about Cassidy for the first time?
  F. Envy of Cassidy's musical and acting ability
  G. Serious interest in learning about careers in entertainment
  H. Apathy toward entertainers in general
  J. Awe and admiration of the teen idol

29. According to the passage, Cassidy's achievements include all of the following EXCEPT:
  A. operating a camera.
  B. stage acting.
  C. producing TV shows.
  D. television writing.

30. The writer describes Shaun Cassidy as having:
    I. big blue eyes.
    II. a toothy grin.
    III. a green record player.
    IV. a sultry voice.
  F. I and II only
  G. I, II, and IV only
  H. II, III, and IV only
  J. I, II, III, and IV

GO ON TO THE NEXT PAGE.

3 ████████████████████████████████████ **3**

Passage IV
NATURAL SCIENCE: *"The Need to Succeed"*

After the archeological discoveries of two samples of early man — the very primitive-appearing Neanderthals and the more modern-looking Cro-Magnons — archeologists throughout
5 the world wondered about the relationship between the two. Evidence of Neanderthals is nearly 300,000 years old. Evidence of Cro-Magnon man is about 130,000 years old. Did Cro-Magnons evolve from Neanderthals? Did they co-exist? Did they
10 associate with one another? Why did evidence of Neanderthals' existence stop 30,000 years ago? Although many mysteries still surround these early humans, more is known today than previously.

Early understanding of Neanderthals was that
15 they had small brains and could not speak. In fact, their brains were as big as modern humans and they were (at least anatomically) capable of speech. Neanderthals were strong, capable of making basic tools, and, from the beginning, controlled fire. The
20 spearheads they carved were even rather appealing.

Scientists have argued over two rival theories about the relationship between Neanderthals and modern humans. One theory claimed that the descendants of Neanderthals live on to this day;
25 these scientists use the phrase, *"Homo sapiens neanderthalensis."* (*Homo sapiens* is a Latin phrase, meaning "sapient — or intelligent — mankind"). A rival theory hypothesized that Neanderthals were an evolutionary dead end — a species that became
30 extinct about 30,000 years ago; these scientists therefore use the phrase, *"Homo neanderthalensis."* The latter theory now appears to be correct. The skulls of Neanderthals and modern human beings differ too much for Neanderthals to be our relatives.
35 In addition, DNA results show that current humans share many genes with early *Homo sapiens* but very few with Neanderthals.

So, given that Cro-Magnons (an example of *Homo sapiens sapiens*) did not evolve from
40 Neanderthals, did these two species of early humans ever meet? And why did Neanderthals become extinct? Based on extensive data from sediment cores, archaeological artifacts such as fossils and tools, radiometric dating, and climate models, we
45 now have better answers to these questions.

Evidence of Cro-Magnons and Neanderthals overlaps by 100,000 years; they clearly coexisted. In fact, where geography dictated, they occasionally occupied the same cave sites. Whether their associa-
50 tions were always amicable is questionable, but archeologists have found no evidence of violence between the two groups. Instead, a combination of other factors likely conspired against Neanderthals, leading to their ultimate demise.
55 During the time of their coexistence, Neanderthals competed with anatomically modern humans for mutually required resources. This occurred at a time when the increasingly severe cold was affecting not only the early humans but
60 also the food resources on which they relied. Although Neanderthals tolerated temperatures as

cold as zero degrees Fahrenheit, winter temperatures during the last ice age dipped to well below that. To compensate for the reduced temperatures,
65 Neanderthals would have needed significantly more food than normal. Unfortunately, the severe cold and the competition of their contemporaries were negatively impacting the availability of food.

Anatomically modern humans were better at
70 dealing with the cold. Early *Homo sapiens* utilized what was then advanced technology in the pre-historic world. They wore warm clothing made of fur and woven materials and lived in enclosed dwellings. They possessed a sophisticated range of
75 weaponry, including bows, arrows, snares, traps, nets, and spears. Their spearheads were carved from a variety of materials, including flint and obsidian. Some of the spears were designed as projectile weapons (javelins), complete with spear throwers to
80 increase effective range. Finally, *Homo sapiens* exhibited the beginnings of communal activity — living, hunting, and fishing in organized groups.

Neanderthals, on the other hand, used general-purpose spears — the identical pattern they had
85 used for 100,000 years. These spears, though reasonably effective, required close-range contact with increasingly scant prey. The Neanderthals lacked the innovation skills necessary to survive in a changing world. Adapting to changing condi-
90 tions, our ancestors used technology to win the prehistoric battle for survival. In essence, the Cro-Magnons won the ultimate "Survivor" contest 30,000 years ago.

---

31. According to the passage, most scientists now believe that *Homo sapiens:*
A. evolved from *Homo sapiens neanderthalensis.*
B. evolved from *Homo neanderthalensis.*
C. killed off the *Homo neanderthalensis.*
D. is not the same species as *Homo neanderthalensis.*

32. According to the passage, during colder weather, Neanderthals needed:
F. to move to a warmer climate.
G. more food than normal.
H. flint and obsidian.
J. less clothing.

33. According to the passage, DNA testing of Neanderthal remains reveal that:
A. Neanderthals and modern-day humans share very few of the same genes.
B. Neanderthals were genetically similar to Cro-Magnons.
C. Neanderthals and modern-day humans are descended from Cro-Magnons.
D. Neanderthals' brains were as large as modern humans.

GO ON TO THE NEXT PAGE.

3   **3**

34. The passage states that *Homo neanderthalensis* is:
    F. an abbreviated form of the phrase, "*Homo sapiens neanderthalensis.*"
    G. an extinct species.
    H. a communal hunter.
    J. a rival of *Homo sapiens neanderthalensis*.

35. According to the passage, all of the following evidence led to a better understanding of Neanderthals EXCEPT:
    A. comparative femur measurements.
    B. radiometric dating.
    C. sediment cores.
    D. climate models.

36. According to the passage, the last evidence of Neanderthals is:
    F. about 100,000 years old.
    G. about 30,000 years old.
    H. 130,000 years old.
    J. 300,000 years old.

37. As it is used in line 71, the word *technology* most nearly means:
    A. technical language.
    B. living in organized groups.
    C. applied science.
    D. objects necessary for human survival.

38. According to the passage, some of the weapons used by Cro-Magnons included all of the following EXCEPT:
    F. bows and arrows.
    G. snares and traps.
    H. gill nets.
    J. javelins.

39. According to the passage, all of the following factors led to the extinction of the Neanderthals EXCEPT:
    A. increasingly cold winters.
    B. Cro-Magnons' slaughter of the Neanderthals.
    C. Neanderthals' lack of innovation.
    D. superior competitors for scarce resources.

40. Place the following events in chronological order:
    I. The first Cro-Magnon exists
    II. Neanderthals control fire
    III. The first Neanderthal exists
    IV. Cro-Magnons develop tools
    F. III, II, I, IV
    G. I, II, III, IV
    H. I, III, II, IV
    J. III, I, IV, II

END OF THE READING TEST
STOP! IF YOU HAVE TIME LEFT OVER, CHECK YOUR WORK ON THIS SECTION ONLY.

4 ○ ○ ○ ○ ○ ○ ○ ○ **4**

SCIENCE REASONING TEST

35 Minutes – 40 Questions

DIRECTIONS: This test includes seven passages, each followed by several questions. Read the passage and choose the best answer to each question. After you have selected your answer, fill in the corresponding bubble on your answer sheet. You should refer to the passages as often as necessary when answering the questions. You may NOT use a calculator on this test.

Passage I

Certain types of insects are abundant in each region of the United States. These insects have a profound impact on the indigenous (native) plant life that grows in each region. If foreign insects are introduced into a region, the plant life can be devastated. Two experiments were performed to study the effect that foreign insects can have on indigenous plants.

Experiment 1
A botanist placed indigenous plant life in a local greenhouse. For 3 weeks no insects were allowed to enter. The amount of plant growth was recorded at the end of 3 weeks. For the next 3-week period, only indigenous insects were allowed near the plants. The plants' growth was recorded again after 6 weeks. In the last 3-week period foreign insects were introduced. The growth of the plants was recorded at the end of the 9-week period. The results are shown in Table 1.

Table 1		
Plant type	Time frame	Total growth (in)
Big blue stem	0–3 weeks	0.25
	3–6 weeks	0.50
	6–9 weeks	0.25
Fragrant sumac	0–3 weeks	0.15
	3–6 weeks	0.30
	6–9 weeks	0.25
Yaupon	0–3 weeks	1.00
	3–6 weeks	2.00
	6–9 weeks	0.50

Experiment 2
A botanist studied indigenous plants in a greenhouse. This time, foreign insects were introduced from the start of the experiment. The plants' growth was recorded over the same 9-week period. The results are shown in Table 2.

Table 2		
Plant type	Time frame	Total growth (in)
Big blue stem	0–3 weeks	0.125
	3–6 weeks	0.250
	6–9 weeks	0.125
Fragrant sumac	0–3 weeks	0.025
	3–6 weeks	0.025
	6–9 weeks	0.015
Yaupon	0–3 weeks	0.500
	3–6 weeks	0.500
	6–9 weeks	0.400

Information on the insect types used is given in Table 3.

Table 3	
Insect type	Indigenous
Mosquito	Yes
Grasshopper	Yes
Aphid	Yes
Mantid	No
Dragonfly	No

1. The results of Experiment 2 indicate that all of the plants experienced a decline in growth rate during what time frame?
   A. 0–3 weeks
   B. 3–6 weeks
   C. 6–9 weeks
   D. No decline in growth rate was recorded.

GO ON TO THE NEXT PAGE.

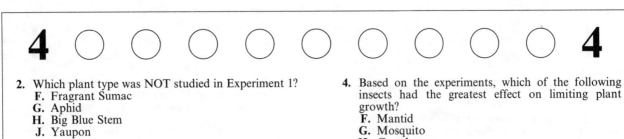

2. Which plant type was NOT studied in Experiment 1?
  F. Fragrant Sumac
  G. Aphid
  H. Big Blue Stem
  J. Yaupon

3. According to Experiments 1 and 2, which plant type experienced the most total growth during weeks 6–9?
  A. Big Blue Stem
  B. Fragrant Sumac
  C. Yaupon
  D. Each plant type experienced the same total growth.

4. Based on the experiments, which of the following insects had the greatest effect on limiting plant growth?
  F. Mantid
  G. Mosquito
  H. Grasshopper
  J. Aphid

5. Based on the results of Experiments 1 and 2, which of the following statements is most accurate?
  A. Foreign insects have little to no impact on indigenous plant growth.
  B. Native insects can help to increase growth in some plants.
  C. Indigenous plant life is most affected by native insects.
  D. Foreign insects cannot survive in local greenhouses.

GO ON TO THE NEXT PAGE.

4 ◯ ◯ ◯ ◯ ◯ ◯ ◯ ◯ **4**

Passage II

Two scientists discuss the possibility of predicting hurricanes and the paths that the hurricanes will take.

Scientist 1

Hurricane prediction can be made at the current time based on certain events. For example, there is a shift inland in wind direction and an increase in wind speed up to 2 days before the hurricane makes landfall. The tidal volume can increase by 30% one day before the hurricane makes landfall. Animals are sometimes seen exhibiting strange behavior as far ahead as weeks before the hurricane makes landfall. Certain instruments such as seismographs can detect the ground vibrations that occur while the hurricane is making its way across the ocean. The direction of the vibrations' origin allows the scientific community to predict the path that the hurricane will take. Historical evidence is also a valuable predictive tool.

Scientist 2

Hurricane prediction cannot be made at the current time. Shifts in wind direction on shore have not been proven to have any effect on the direction of or time of landfall of a hurricane. Only when the hurricane makes landfall can the seismograph be used to determine direction of the hurricane's path. Tidal volume is constantly changing for many different reasons and therefore cannot be used as a predictive tool. Previous records of hurricane patterns are a much more accurate way to predict when and where a hurricane will occur. Once enough information has been derived from past hurricanes, predictive measures can be developed.

6. Which of the following ideas about hurricane prediction is implied by Scientist 2?
   F. Present-day predictive tools are not based upon enough past data to be accurate.
   G. Hurricane prediction will never be possible.
   H. Animal behavior is proving itself to be the best possible hurricane predictor available.
   J. Scientific tools are the only things that can predict a hurricane's location and path.

7. A scientific article is published that states that the study of animal behavior is useful in predicting hurricanes. Which of the scientists' viewpoints, if any, is (are) supported by this statement?
   A. Scientist 1
   B. Scientist 2
   C. Both Scientists 1 and 2
   D. Neither Scientist 1 or 2

8. Increased seismic activity has been recorded along the coastline of Florida. With which of the following statements about the finding would Scientist 1 agree?
   F. Tidal volume is likely to decrease by 30%.
   G. A seismograph is only useful for predicting earthquake activity.
   H. Seismic activity has little to do with when or where the hurricane will travel.
   J. A hurricane could be moving across the ocean.

9. Which statement, if true, would support both scientists' viewpoints?
   A. Historical hurricane data has recently been used to predict the path a hurricane will take.
   B. Seismic activity is predictive of both when and where the hurricane will make landfall.
   C. Tidal volume cannot be used as a predictive tool because it is constantly changing.
   D. Tidal volume and wind direction are not accurate or useful predictors of hurricanes.

10. What would be the best way to test the claims made by Scientist 2?
    F. Compare current hurricane data with the past data in the same area.
    G. Monitor seismic activity along the coastline.
    H. Keep a record of the tidal volume before a hurricane makes landfall.
    J. Track animal behavior before the arrival of the hurricane.

11. Suppose a new type of tidal volume meter was created that could distinguish between a tidal increase due to a hurricane and an increase due to other weather conditions. This ability to distinguish the cause of tidal volume increase would:
    A. weaken Scientist 1's argument.
    B. strengthen Scientist 2's argument.
    C. weaken Scientist 2's argument.
    D. have no relevance to either scientist's argument.

12. According to Scientist 2, which of the following is a major flaw in Scientist 1's theory on hurricane prediction?
    F. Information gathered from past hurricanes could be useful.
    G. Seismographs are used to monitor the path that a hurricane takes.
    H. Historical data is accurate.
    J. Tidal volume increases can be used to predict hurricanes.

GO ON TO THE NEXT PAGE.

4 ◯ ◯ ◯ ◯ ◯ ◯ ◯ ◯ ◯ **4**

Passage III

One of the primary physical properties of matter is volume. Solids, liquids, and gases, which make up the 3 observed states of matter, can easily be recognized by certain physical characteristics, such as volume. The effect of compression — the ability of pressure to alter the volume of matter — is called *compressibility*.

Gases are highly compressible because the volume of a gas is very responsive to changes in pressure. A very small change in pressure can considerably alter the volume. On the other hand, most liquids and solids have a higher density and, therefore, low compressibility.

Figure 1 shows pressure and volume along an *isotherm*. An isotherm is a line of constant temperature. One can determine the compressibility by noting the relationship between the change in pressure and the change in volume. Portions of the line where large changes in pressure result in only minimal changes in volume signify low compressibility. Portions of the line where small changes in pressure result in a significant change in volume suggest high compressibility.

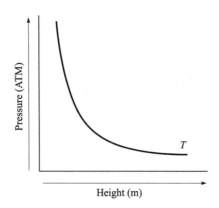

Figure 1

Figure 2 shows the air pressure (in ATM) at different depths of water.

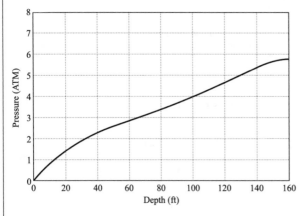

Figure 2

Underwater, pressure can be felt in certain air spaces in the body, such as the lungs, sinuses, and ear canals. Air is a gas with a low density and high compressibility. Therefore, the volume of air inside the body is dependent on the space that contains it. The volume of air in a flexible spaces, such as the lungs or sinuses, is reduced or expanded proportionate to the pressure. For example, a driver moving from 33 feet underwater to the surface will have the amount of air in his or her lungs double.

13. According to Figure 2, what is the air pressure at 100 feet below the surface?
    A. 1.5 ATM
    B. 4.0 ATM
    C. 5.0 ATM
    D. 5.5 ATM

14. According to the data provided, one could generalize that the volume of air in the lungs:
    F. increases as one moves closer to the surface.
    G. increases in proportion to the temperature.
    H. increases as the air pressure increases.
    J. increases as one moves deeper underwater.

15. According to the passage, as compared to gases, which of the following statements is true?
    A. Solids have lower compressibility because of their higher density.
    B. Liquids have lower compressibility because of their lower density.
    C. Both liquids and solids have higher compressibility because of their lower density.
    D. Both liquids and solids have lower compressibility because of their higher density.

16. The information provided indicates that compressibility is a problem when diving. Which of the following statements would best explain why this is true?
    F. Atmospheric pressure is nonexistent under the water's surface.
    G. As you descend underwater, the air in the lungs expands quickly.
    H. Moving to the surface causes the air inside the lungs to expand very quickly.
    J. Moving to the surface causes the air inside the lungs to compress very quickly.

17. According to Figure 1, compressibility is lowest where:
    A. temperature is lowest and pressure is the lowest.
    B. temperature is highest and pressure is the lowest.
    C. the change in pressure is less than the change in volume.
    D. the change in pressure is greater than the change in volume.

GO ON TO THE NEXT PAGE.

4 ◯ ◯ ◯ ◯ ◯ ◯ ◯ ◯ **4**

Passage IV

Studies have shown that acid rains damage the skin pigmentation in certain species of salamanders. This results in an inability to change color and be protected from predators. Increased predation accounts for a decrease in the percentage of salamanders that make it to adulthood. Certain species of salamander have developed weather protective behavior that has an effect on their relative ability to avoid skin damage (Table 1).

Table 1			
Species	Relative ability to avoid acid rain damage	Weather protective behavior	Exposure to acid rain
A	<0.2	seeks protection out in the open	high
B	0.2	seeks protection under small plants	moderate
C	0.2	seeks protection under tree cover	moderate
D	0.5	seeks protection inside trees	low
E	0.7	seeks protection inside buildings	none
F	1.0	seeks protection inside buildings	none
G	1.5	seeks protection inside buildings	none

Figure 1 shows the percentage of each species that generally make it to adulthood.

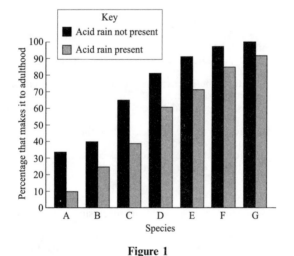

Figure 1

Figure 2 shows predicted levels of acid rain over time in 4 geographic regions with a salamander population.

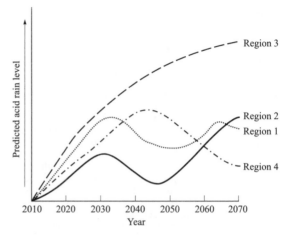

Figure 2

18. Based on the information in Figure 1, salamanders from which species are most likely to survive to adulthood despite the presence of acid rain?
 F. Species A
 G. Species D
 H. Species E
 J. Species G

19. According to the data in Figure 1, which of the following species showed the greatest difference between survival with no exposure to acid rain and survival with exposure to acid rain?
 A. Species A
 B. Species C
 C. Species E
 D. Species G

20. Researchers have recently discovered a new species of salamander that exhibits the weather protective behavior of burrowing into the ground. Based on the information in Table 1, the salamander's relative ability to avoid skin damage is most likely:
 F. <0.1.
 G. 0.1.
 H. 0.5.
 J. >1.5.

21. According to the information in Table 1, for all of the species shown, as the exposure to acid rain increases, the relative ability to avoid skin damage due to acid rain generally:
 A. increases only.
 B. decreases only.
 C. increases then decreases.
 D. decreases then increases.

22. Based on the information in Table 1 and Figure 1, the species of salamander with the lowest percentage surviving to adulthood:
 F. seeks protection inside trees.
 G. seeks protection inside buildings.
 H. seeks protection under plants.
 J. does not seek protection.

GO ON TO THE NEXT PAGE.

4 ○ ○ ○ ○ ○ ○ ○ ○ ○ **4**

Passage V

Some mountains have been shown to lose rock or sediment due to seasonal snow melting. Figure 1 shows mountain composition, mountain peak heights in meters (m), and the net change in snowcap lower levels (SCLL) in meters, from 1880–1980 along a section of the Rocky Mountains. A net negative change in the SCLL indicates a loss of rock or sediment, and a net positive change indicates a gain of sediment.

Table 1 shows the percentage of the year that a vertical section of the mountain range is exposed to snow melt erosion.

Table 1	
Mountain section height (meters)	Percentage of a year mountain section is exposed to snow melt erosion
0–5	14
5–10	22
10–15	30
15–20	38
20–25	46
25–30	54
30–35	62
35–40	70

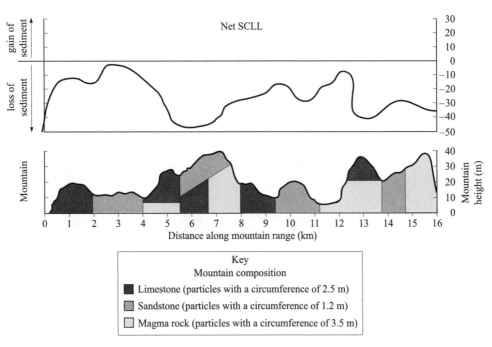

Figure 1

GO ON TO THE NEXT PAGE.

4   **4**

23. According to Figure 1, at 13 miles along the mountain range, the mountain is composed of:
A. magma rock and limestone.
B. magma rock and sandstone.
C. limestone and sandstone.
D. limestone only.

24. At a height of 20 meters, the net change in SCLL is mostly:
F. greater than 20.
G. between −10 and −30.
H. less than −50.
J. between −40 and −50.

25. Based on the information in Table 1, a mountain section with a height between 40–45 meters would be exposed to snow melt erosion approximately what percentage of the year?
A. 28%
B. 56%
C. 78%
D. 92%

26. According to Figure 1, a net negative change in SCLL or a net positive change in SCLL is most consistent with:
F. exposure to rock and sediment.
G. mountain composition.
H. distance along the mountain range.
J. mountain height.

27. According to the information in Table 1, which of the following figures best represents the relationship between the mountain's height and the percentage of the year the mountain is exposed to snow melt erosion?

A.

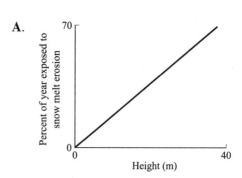

B.

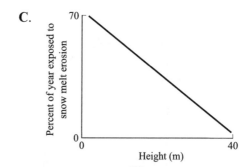

C.

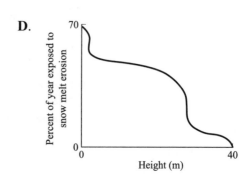

D.

GO ON TO THE NEXT PAGE.

4 ⃝ ⃝ ⃝ ⃝ ⃝ ⃝ ⃝ ⃝ ⃝ **4**

Passage VI

Microbial flora such as bacteria, play an important role in maintaining the digestive tract. Bacteria exist in the stomach, jejunum, ileum, and colon in different amounts and at different pH levels. Defecation output is a good indicator of digestive tract health — the higher the defecation output, the healthier the digestive tract. A student investigated the effects of creating a bacteria-free environment in a rat's digestive tract.

Experiment 1

The student collected 10 rats to include in the experiment. Five of the rats were given antibiotics to kill all bacteria within their digestive tracts. The remaining 5 rats were not treated with antibiotics. All of the rats were allowed to eat a normal diet. The animals' defecation amounts, measured in feces pellets, and pH levels of the defecation were measured after 5 hours. The results are shown in Table 1.

	Table 1		
Rat	Antibiotic given	Defecation output (no. of pellets)	pH level
1	Yes	3	1.2
2	Yes	2	1.7
3	Yes	3	1.6
4	Yes	4	1.7
5	Yes	5	1.5
6	No	7	3.0
7	No	9	3.0
8	No	12	3.3
9	No	11	3.5
10	No	10	3.1

Experiment 2

Each of 5 different rats was given an antibiotic to kill all bacteria in the digestive tract. The rats were then given a dose of microbial flora 1 hour later. The rats were allowed to eat a normal diet. Each rat's defecation is measured in terms of pH level at 1 hour and again at 5 hours. The pH levels are compared in Table 2.

	Table 2	
Rat	pH at 1 hour	pH at 5 hours
11	1.5	3.0
12	1.4	2.7
13	1.3	2.5
14	1.6	3.2
15	1.7	3.3

28. Based on Experiment 1, what is the relationship between defecation output and pH level?
 F. As pH level increases, defecation output decreases.
 G. As pH level increases, defecation output increases.
 H. As defecation output increases, pH level decreases.
 J. Both defecation output and pH levels remain the same.

29. In which of the following ways are the designs of Experiments 1 and 2 different?
 A. A dose of bacteria was given to the rats in Experiment 2 and not in Experiment 1.
 B. A normal diet was followed in Experiment 2 and not in Experiment 1.
 C. A control group was established in Experiment 2 and not in Experiment 1.
 D. A smaller population was used in Experiment 1 than in Experiment 2.

30. Which of the following hypotheses about the effects of a bacteria-free digestive tract in a rat is best supported by the results of Experiment 2? If all bacteria are eliminated and then reintroduced, the pH level will:
 F. remain the same.
 G. increase over time.
 H. decrease over time.
 J. increase, and then decrease rapidly.

31. Suppose that rat number 5 was given the microbial flora 1 hour after being given the antibiotics. Based on the results in Experiment 2, one would predict that the pH level after 5 hours would be approximately:
 A. 1.3
 B. 1.7
 C. 2.1
 D. 3.0

32. According to the passage, which of the following rats had the highest defecation output?
 F. Rat 3
 G. Rat 6
 H. Rat 8
 J. Rat 10

33. According to the results of both experiments, one can conclude that:
 A. antibiotics only kill bacteria that are harmful to the digestive tract.
 B. pH levels in the digestive tract cannot be tested effectively.
 C. bacteria are necessary to the normal functioning of a healthy digestive tract.
 D. the presence of bacteria in the digestive tract leads to unhealthy pH levels.

GO ON TO THE NEXT PAGE.

4 ◯ ◯ ◯ ◯ ◯ ◯ ◯ ◯ **4**

Passage VII

Students performed 3 studies to determine the following: the effect that an object's weight and wind resistance has on the rate that the object travels to the ground from a height, and the time it takes the object to settle on the ground.

In each study the students stood on top of a 12-foot bleacher inside the gymnasium and used an adjustable fan to create wind resistance at a constant rate. The fan was either positioned on the floor, pointing upward, or on the 12-foot bleacher, pointing downward. The objects included a tennis ball, a golf ball, a feather, and a piece of paper.

Study 1

When no wind was blowing, the students dropped a tennis ball and a golf ball at the same time. The times it took for each object to hit the ground and to settle on the ground were recorded. Settling on the ground was determined to be when the object did not bounce or move up anymore. The same process was followed for the tennis ball and feather, and the golf ball and piece of paper. The students performed the tests 3 times for each group of objects. The results are shown in Table 1.

Table 2			
Object	Fall time (sec)	Settle time (sec)	Total time (sec)
Trial 1:			
Tennis ball/golf ball	3/3	4/4	7/7
Tennis ball/feather	3/17	4/5	7/22
Golf ball/paper	4/25	5/10	9/35
Trial 2:			
Tennis ball/golf ball	4/5	5/5	9/10
Tennis ball/feather	4/15	5/7	9/22
Golf ball/paper	5/22	4/12	9/34
Trial 3:			
Tennis ball/golf ball	3/4	3/3	6/7
Tennis ball/feather	2/10	5/18	7/28
Golf ball/paper	4/18	4/12	8/30

Study 3

With the fan blowing downward, the students performed the experiment in the same manner. The fan was turned off when the objects reached the ground. The results are recorded in Table 3.

Table 1			
Object	Fall time (sec)	Settle time (sec)	Total time (sec)
Trial 1:			
Tennis ball/golf ball	2/2	2/3	4/5
Tennis ball/feather	2/13	3/2	5/15
Golf ball/paper	3/8	4/1	7/9
Trial 2:			
Tennis ball/golf ball	2/3	2/4	4/7
Tennis ball/feather	2/14	2/2	4/16
Golf ball/paper	2/9	3/3	5/12
Trial 3:			
Tennis ball/golf ball	1/1	3/7	4/8
Tennis ball/feather	2/17	4/2	6/19
Golf ball/paper	3/11	3/2	6/13

Table 3			
Object	Fall time (sec)	Settle time (sec)	Total time (sec)
Trial 1:			
Tennis ball/golf ball	1/1	2/2	3/3
Tennis ball/feather	1/6	2/2	3/8
Golf ball/paper	2/5	2/1	4/6
Trial 2:			
Tennis ball/golf ball	2/3	1/1	3/4
Tennis ball/feather	2/7	3/4	5/11
Golf ball/paper	2/4	2/1	4/5
Trial 3:			
Tennis ball/golf ball	4/5	2/3	6/8
Tennis ball/feather	3/6	2/2	5/8
Golf ball/paper	4/3	2/1	6/4

Study 2

With the fan blowing upward, the experiment was repeated. The fan was turned off when the objects reached the ground. The results are shown in Table 2.

34. According to Study 3, which objects differed most in Total Time?
   F. Trial 1, Tennis ball and Golf ball
   G. Trial 2, Tennis ball and Feather
   H. Trial 2, Golf ball and Paper
   J. Trial 3, Tennis ball and Feather

GO ON TO THE NEXT PAGE.

4 ○ ○ ○ ○ ○ ○ ○ ○ ○ **4**

35. The fall time of the objects was different in Studies 2 and 3. This difference is most likely due to:
  A. wind direction.
  B. settle time.
  C. wind speed.
  D. drop height.

36. Which of the following changes to all 3 studies would most likely have produced shorter fall times for all of the objects?
  F. Dropping the items from a height of 10 feet.
  G. Increasing the speed of the fan.
  H. Dropping the items at different times rather than all together.
  J. Measuring the times from an adjacent bleacher.

37. According to Study 2, which object consistently experienced the most wind resistance?
  A. Golf ball
  B. Paper
  C. Feather
  D. Tennis ball

38. In Study 2 it took the paper longer than the feather to fall and settle. Which of the following can be inferred from this data?
  F. The larger surface area of the paper is affected by the wind, resulting in longer fall times.
  G. The heavier weight of the paper causes it to fall more quickly than the feather.
  H. The lighter weight of the feather causes it to fall more slowly than the paper.
  J. The smaller surface area of the feather is affected by the wind, resulting in longer fall times.

39. In Study 1, Trial 2, it took the paper a total of 12 seconds to fall and settle on the ground. If the height from which the paper was dropped was 6 feet, how long would it probably have taken the paper to fall and settle?
  A. 2 seconds
  B. 3 seconds
  C. 6 seconds
  D. 24 seconds

40. The students conduct a fourth experiment to test the rate at which each object falls in a vacuum. What are the most likely results of this experiment?
  F. Each object falls much more slowly in a vacuum.
  G. The rate of fall will be almost the same for each object.
  H. The rate of fall will not be affected.
  J. Each object falls more quickly in a vacuum.

END OF THE SCIENCE REASONING TEST
STOP! IF YOU HAVE TIME LEFT OVER, CHECK YOUR WORK ON THIS SECTION ONLY.

5 ☆ ☆ ☆ ☆ ☆ ☆ ☆ ☆ **5**

WRITING TEST

DIRECTIONS: This test is designed to assess your writing skills. You have thirty (30) minutes to plan and write an essay based on the stimulus provided. Be sure to take a position on the issue and support your position using logical reasoning and relevant examples. Organize your ideas in a focused and logical way, and use the English language to clearly and effectively express your position.

When you have finished writing, refer to the Scoring Rubrics discussed in Chapter 7 to estimate your score.

Note: On the actual ACT you will receive approximately 2.5 pages of scratch paper on which to develop your essay, and approximately 4 pages of notebook paper on which to write your essay. We recommend that you limit yourself to this number of pages when you write your practice essays.

Essay Prompt

In some cities and towns, many citizens and government officials have proposed a curfew of 11:00 p.m. for anyone under the age of eighteen. Some officials and citizens support the idea as a way of preventing mischief and vandalism and as a way to help parents to look after the best interests of their children. Other citizens and officials do not support the idea of a curfew because they feel that teenagers should be treated as young adults and they should be trusted to act appropriately unless they demonstrate a lack of trustworthiness. In your opinion, should your cities and towns adopt curfews for teenagers?

In your essay, take a position on this question. You may write about one of the points of view mentioned above, or you may give another point of view on this issue. Use specific examples and reasons for your position.

ANSWER KEY

English Test

1. D	21. B	41. D	61. C
2. G	22. G	42. F	62. G
3. C	23. C	43. A	63. A
4. G	24. J	44. H	64. G
5. A	25. B	45. C	65. A
6. G	26. F	46. F	66. G
7. B	27. D	47. C	67. A
8. H	28. H	48. J	68. G
9. A	29. D	49. C	69. D
10. J	30. H	50. F	70. F
11. D	31. A	51. D	71. B
12. F	32. G	52. G	72. F
13. D	33. D	53. C	73. D
14. H	34. H	54. F	74. F
15. C	35. D	55. D	75. B
16. H	36. J	56. G	
17. B	37. C	57. C	
18. H	38. G	58. H	
19. B	39. A	59. A	
20. F	40. J	60. H	

Mathematics Test

1. A	21. C	41. A
2. F	22. K	42. K
3. E	23. D	43. D
4. F	24. G	44. G
5. D	25. C	45. C
6. H	26. J	46. G
7. E	27. E	47. D
8. H	28. G	48. K
9. B	29. D	49. C
10. J	30. F	50. H
11. C	31. E	51. D
12. K	32. G	52. G
13. C	33. D	53. C
14. J	34. K	54. J
15. A	35. C	55. A
16. K	36. G	56. K
17. D	37. B	57. C
18. F	38. J	58. H
19. E	39. B	59. B
20. G	40. F	60. F

Reading Test

1. D	21. B
2. J	22. F
3. D	23. D
4. F	24. G
5. B	25. A
6. J	26. H
7. B	27. D
8. H	28. J
9. C	29. C
10. H	30. G
11. B	31. D
12. F	32. G
13. C	33. C
14. J	34. J
15. D	35. A
16. F	36. G
17. C	37. D
18. F	38. H
19. C	39. B
20. J	40. F

Science Reasoning Test

1. C	21. B
2. G	22. J
3. C	23. A
4. F	24. G
5. B	25. C
6. F	26. J
7. C	27. A
8. J	28. G
9. A	29. A
10. F	30. G
11. C	31. D
12. J	32. H
13. B	33. C
14. F	34. G
15. A	35. A
16. H	36. F
17. D	37. B
18. J	38. F
19. B	39. C
20. H	40. J

▬▬ SCORING GUIDE

Your final reported score is your COMPOSITE SCORE. Your COMPOSITE SCORE is the average of all of your SCALED SCORES.

Your SCALED SCORES for the four multiple-choice sections are derived from the Scoring Table on the next page. Use your RAW SCORE, or the number of questions that you answered correctly for each section, to determine your SCALED SCORE. If you got a RAW SCORE of 60 on the English test, for example, you correctly answered 60 out of 75 questions.

Step 1 Determine your RAW SCORE for each of the four multiple-choice sections:

English	_60_
Mathematics	_37_
Reading	_____
Science Reasoning	_____

The following Raw Score Table shows the total possible points for each section.

RAW SCORE TABLE	
KNOWLEDGE AND SKILL AREAS	**RAW SCORES**
ENGLISH	75
MATHEMATICS	60
READING	40
SCIENCE REASONING	40
WRITING	12

Multiple-Choice Scoring Worksheet

Step 2 Determine your SCALED SCORE for each of the four multiple-choice sections using the following Scoring Worksheet. Each SCALED SCORE should be rounded to the nearest number according to normal rules. For example, $31.2 \approx 31$ and $31.5 \approx 32$. If you answered 61 questions correctly on the English section, for example, your SCALED SCORE would be 28.

English $\underset{\text{RAW SCORE}}{60} \times 36 = 2160 \div 75 = 28.8$

$\underline{-2}$ (*correction factor)

$\underset{\text{SCALED SCORE}}{26.8}$

Mathematics $\underset{\text{RAW SCORE}}{37} \times 36 = 1332 \div 60 = 22.2$

$\underline{+1}$ (*correction factor)

$\underset{\text{SCALED SCORE}}{23.2}$

Reading $\underset{\text{RAW SCORE}}{\underline{}} \times 36 = \underline{} \div 40 = \underline{}$

$\underline{+2}$ (*correction factor)

$\underset{\text{SCALED SCORE}}{\underline{}}$

Science Reasoning $\underset{\text{RAW SCORE}}{\underline{}} \times 36 = \underline{} \div 40 = \underline{}$

$\underline{+1.5}$ (*correction factor)

$\underset{\text{SCALED SCORE}}{\underline{}}$

*The correction factor is an approximation based on the average from several recent ACT tests. It is most valid for scores in the middle 50% (approximately 16–24 scaled composite score) of the scoring range.

The scores are all approximate. Actual ACT scoring scales vary from one administration to the next based upon several factors.

If you take the optional Writing Test, you will need to combine your English and Writing scores to obtain your final COMPOSITE SCORE. Refer to Chapter 7 for guidelines on scoring your Writing Test Essay. Once you have determined a score for your essay out of 12 possible points, you will need to determine your ENGLISH/WRITING SCALED SCORE, using both your ENGLISH SCALED SCORE and your WRITING TEST SCORE. The combination of the two scores will give you an ENGLISH/WRITING SCALED SCORE, from 1 to 36, that will be used to determine your COMPOSITE SCORE mentioned earlier.

Using the English/Writing Scoring Table, find your ENGLISH SCALED SCORE on the left or right hand side of the table and your WRITING TEST SCORE on the top of the table. Follow your ENGLISH SCALED SCORE over and your WRITING TEST SCORE down until the two columns meet at a number. This number is your ENGLISH/WRITING SCALED SCORE and will be used to determine your COMPOSITE SCORE.

Step 3 Determine your ENGLISH/WRITING SCALED SCORE using the English/Writing Scoring Table on the following page:

English _____

Writing _____

English/Writing _____

ENGLISH/WRITING SCORING TABLE

ENGLISH SCALED SCORE	WRITING TEST SCORE											ENGLISH SCALED SCORE
	2	3	4	5	6	7	8	9	10	11	12	
36	26	27	28	29	30	31	32	33	34	32	36	36
35	26	27	28	29	30	31	31	32	33	34	35	35
34	25	26	27	28	29	30	31	32	33	34	35	34
33	24	25	26	27	28	29	30	31	32	33	34	33
32	24	25	25	26	27	28	29	30	31	32	33	32
31	23	24	25	26	27	28	29	30	30	31	32	31
30	22	23	24	25	26	27	28	29	30	31	32	30
29	21	22	23	24	25	26	27	28	29	30	31	29
28	21	22	23	24	24	25	26	27	28	29	30	28
27	20	21	22	23	24	25	26	27	28	28	29	27
26	19	20	21	22	23	24	25	26	27	28	29	26
25	18	19	20	21	22	23	24	25	26	27	28	25
24	18	19	20	21	22	23	23	24	25	26	27	24
23	17	18	19	20	21	22	23	24	25	26	27	23
22	16	17	18	19	20	21	22	23	24	25	26	22
21	16	17	17	18	19	20	21	22	23	24	25	21
20	15	16	17	18	19	20	21	21	22	23	24	20
19	14	15	16	17	18	19	20	21	22	23	24	19
18	13	14	15	16	17	18	19	20	21	22	23	18
17	13	14	15	16	16	17	18	19	20	21	22	17
16	12	13	14	15	16	17	18	19	20	20	21	16
15	11	12	13	14	15	16	17	18	19	20	21	15
14	10	11	12	13	14	15	16	17	18	19	20	14
13	10	11	12	13	14	14	15	16	17	18	19	13
12	9	10	11	12	13	14	15	16	17	18	19	12
11	8	9	10	11	12	13	14	15	16	17	18	11
10	8	9	9	10	11	12	13	14	15	16	17	10
9	7	8	9	10	11	12	13	13	14	15	16	9
8	6	7	8	9	10	11	12	13	14	15	16	8
7	5	6	7	8	9	10	11	12	13	14	15	7
6	5	6	7	7	8	9	10	11	12	13	14	6
5	4	5	6	7	8	9	10	11	12	12	13	5
4	3	4	5	6	7	8	9	10	11	12	13	4
3	2	3	4	5	6	7	8	9	10	11	12	3
2	2	3	4	5	6	6	7	8	9	10	11	2
1	1	2	3	4	5	6	7	8	9	10	11	1

Step 4 Determine your COMPOSITE SCORE by finding the sum of all your SCALED SCORES for each of the four sections: English only (if you do not choose to take the optional Writing Test) *or* English/Writing (if you choose to take the optional Writing Test), Mathematics, Reading, and Science Reasoning, and divide by 4 to find the average. Round your COMPOSITE SCORE according to normal rules. For example, $31.2 \approx 31$ and $31.5 \approx 32$.

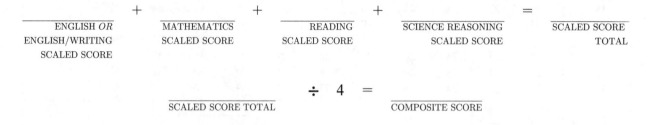

| ENGLISH *OR* ENGLISH/WRITING SCALED SCORE | + | MATHEMATICS SCALED SCORE | + | READING SCALED SCORE | + | SCIENCE REASONING SCALED SCORE | = | SCALED SCORE TOTAL |

$$\text{\underline{\hspace{3cm}}} \div 4 = \text{\underline{\hspace{3cm}}}$$

SCALED SCORE TOTAL   COMPOSITE SCORE

ANSWERS AND EXPLANATIONS

English Test Explanations

PASSAGE I

1. **The best answer is D.** To maintain parallel construction within this paragraph, you need to use the past tense of the verb *begin*. Notice that Sentences 2 and 3 use the past tense for their main verbs. Sentence 4 also has a clause with the main verb *began*. The verb forms should agree, that is, have the same tense.

2. **The best answer is G.** The question asks you to identify the correct punctuation surrounding the phrase, *happy and healthy learning to walk and talk*. The phrase contains two clauses, *she was happy and healthy* and *learning to walk and talk like her toddler peers*, that are not connected by a coordinating conjunction (e.g., *and*). Moreover, the second clause is not independent (i.e., it can't stand on its own as a complete sentence). In these situations, commas are always used to separate the clauses.

3. **The best answer is C.** You must decide which answer choice best captures the contrast between the Kellers' relief at Helen's apparent progress and their concern that she has been permanently harmed by her illness. Answer choice C focuses on her parents' initial, positive response and how it changed when they learned she had become blind and deaf.

4. **The best answer is G.** Paragraph 2 illustrates the difficulties faced by both Helen and her parents as they adapted to their new situation. Answer choice G provides the best introduction because it summarizes what is to come while providing enough detail to be complete: Helen is frustrated by her inability to understand the world around her, and her parents are overwhelmed by her resulting tantrums (they consider sending her to an asylum).

5. **The best answer is A.** The underlined phrase is a "to-infinitive clause," meaning, an infinitive form of a verb has to follow the *to*. That eliminates answer choice B, which begins with a noun. The other choices are simply restatements of the original phrase. The most concise selection is answer choice A.

6. **The best answer is G.** The possessive *Helen's* modifies *parents*. Therefore, the two words should not be separated by a comma. A comma is placed after the clause *Feeling sorry*

for their impaired daughter, to avoid misunderstanding.

7. **The best answer is B.** This question requires you to express the idea clearly and simply. The best word to use is *unmanageable*.

8. **The correct answer is H.** The words *alone*, or *only* are redundant in this context. Answer choice H gives all the necessary information.

9. **The correct answer is A.** This question requires you to express the idea clearly and simply. The main idea of the paragraph is Helen's need for self-discipline. Only the original phrase has that emphasis and is grammatically correct. The other answer choices are awkward.

10. **The correct answer is J.** The rest of the passage is in the past tense, so to maintain parallel construction, you should use the past-tense verb form *was*. Also, the stubbornness in question belongs to a particular person: Helen. Therefore, *she* is a better pronoun choice than the more general pronoun, *one*.

11. **The correct answer is D.** This question asks you to identify the correct punctuation surrounding the phrase *if channeled*. The phrase is a conditional clause that limits the possibility of Helen's salvation. It needs to be separated from the rest of the sentence with parallel punctuation. In other words, since it is introduced with a comma (following *that*), it needs to be concluded with a comma.

12. **The correct answer is F.** The phrase *was given* implies that Annie is the one who is acting. The context of the passage clearly indicates that it is Helen's parents who act; they are the ones who give permission for Annie and Helen to move to a different house. Since Annie receives the action, the verb phrase must be in the passive voice. Only the original phrase is correct.

13. **The correct answer is D.** In this context, *Annies* is possessive. Therefore, it requires the addition of an apostrophe: *Annie's*. Furthermore, the phrase *Annie's efforts* introduces another clause, *but gradually*. Since this second clause ends with a comma, it should be introduced with one to maintain parallel construction.

14. **The best answer is H.** The sentence that follows the underlined portion implies continuation. The author has told us that Helen's submission to Annie would bring positive results; this sentence describes one of those positive results, namely Helen's trust in Annie. The conjunction *and* signals continuation. The other answer choices signal contrast, or a change in expected direction. They would not be appropriate selections and should be eliminated.

15. **The best answer is C.** Annie is first mentioned in Paragraph 3, which logically eliminates answer choices A and B. The omitted sentence provides additional information about Annie herself and introduces the challenges of teaching Helen. Since the existing Sentence 2 describes those challenges, the new sentence should come before it. Therefore, the addition should be placed after Sentence 1 in Paragraph 3.

PASSAGE II

16. **The best answer is H.** The phrases *initially* and *for the first time* mean the same thing. It is not necessary to include more than one of them in the sentence. Answer choice H is correct because it avoids redundancy, and is the simplest choice.

17. **The best answer is B.** The phrase *realistic reality* is redundant, which eliminates answer choice A. More specifically, the author sets up a contrast between positive and negative, e.g., "wide-eyed wonder" is contrasted with "tantrum-filled . . . attitude." Therefore, the reader can expect another positive/negative contrast between "enthusiasm" and the adjective describing "reality." Answer choices C and D are neutral and positive, respectively, so they should be eliminated. That leaves "horrible" as the best response.

18. **The best answer is H.** To maintain parallel construction within this paragraph, you need to use a present tense form of the verb *shop*, i.e., *is shopping*. Notice that the paragraph uses the words *begin* and *buy*, both of which are present tense. The verb forms should agree, i.e., have the same tense.

19. **The best answer is B.** The phrase, *not wanting to be rushed with last-minute purchases* is a dependent clause and needs to be separated from the main clause by a comma.

20. **The best answer is F.** To maintain parallelism in the paragraph, all of the verb forms must match. The passage states that you "buy" and you "compliment." Therefore, you "find" the ghost figurine.

21. **The best answer is B.** *You're* is a contraction of *you are*. Since the sentence already has a main verb, *you're* is incorrect grammar. The correct form is the possessive pronoun *your*. Also, while in this context the qualifier *this year* could be set off by a comma or left without punctuation, it would never be followed by a colon. Therefore, answer choice is B is correct.

22. **The best answer is G.** This question requires you to express the idea clearly and simply. The word *that* introduces a relative clause. A relative clause follows standard grammar rules, which means its subject, *this holiday*, should begin the clause.

23. **The best answer is C.** The phrases *overlapping*, *double-booked*, and *at the same time* mean the same thing. To avoid redundancy, only one is needed in the sentence. Answer choice C eliminates all but "overlapping" and is the best answer.

24. **The best answer is J.** Semicolons and periods separate complete sentences. While the first half of this sentence could stand on its own, the second half could not. It does not have a finite verb. Colons, on the other hand, usually introduce lists or examples. Neither of these occur here. Therefore, a comma is the best punctuation mark for the sentence.

25. **The best answer is B.** One way to approach this question is by process of elimination. The sentence as it is written doesn't include a legitimate verbal form. So, eliminate answer choice A. The passage has consistently been in the present tense, which means the sentence requires a verb with a sense of the present. That eliminates choice D. Choice C would leave the sentence without a finite verb — it would no longer be a complete sentence. That leaves answer choice B, "has become." *Has become* is in the present perfect, which is a tense that refers to a state that began before the present time of writing and continues until that time. This awareness of time captures the developing sense of doom felt by the author.

26. **The best answer is F.** In this case, the transition is from Paragraph 4 to Paragraph 6. Paragraph 4 ends with the author discovering that she is running out of time to buy gifts and that no one is available to help her. She must solve this problem on her own and act quickly. Answer choice F best captures this sentiment. The choice is supported by the first sentence in Paragraph 6, which emphasizes her frantic shopping.

27. **The best answer is D.** To maintain parallel construction within this paragraph, you need to use a present tense form of the verb *trudge*. Notice that the paragraph uses the words *dart*, *give up* and *are*, all of which are present tense. The verb forms should agree, that is, have the same tense. Finally, answer choice D is more concise than answer choice C, which makes it stylistically the better choice.

28. **The best answer is H.** To maintain parallel construction within this paragraph, you need to use a present tense form of the verb *ask*. Because the person asking ("your son") is in the third person singular, the correct form is *asks*, answer choice H.

29. **The best answer is D.** The passage as a whole describes one person's holiday stress building as it gets closer to Christmas. In Paragraph 6, everything comes to a head and the author breaks down as she realizes that she will never finish her tasks in time. A hug from her son helps to remind her of the joy of the season, and she decides to rest instead of doing the next thing on her list. Answer choice D indicates her frustration and her ultimate decision to relax. This best captures the function of Paragraph 6 in relation to the rest of the passage.

30. **The best answer is H.** Paragraph 5 serves as a temporal marker: it tells the reader that, at this point in the narrative, it's the beginning of November with six more weeks before Christmas. Logically, it should be placed after Paragraph 2, with its reference to Halloween, and before Paragraph 3, with its reference to Thanksgiving.

PASSAGE III

31. **The best answer is A.** The paragraph starts with a reference to "popular opinion." The next sentence refers back to that by using the phrase "this same." That means the sentence needs a subject noun that is a synonym for *popular opinion*. The word *culture* captures that sense more accurately than either *emotion* or *specimen*.

32. **The best answer is G.** To answer this question, you should first recognize that *physical fitness* is a singular noun phrase. In order to maintain parallel construction within the sentence, you should use *societal fitness*, a singular noun phrase. Eliminate answer choices F and J. The word *societal* is an adjective, describing the noun *fitness*, so it should not show possession. Eliminate answer choice H.

33. **The best answer is D.** The writer is setting up a parallel construction, comparing physical exercise to social activity. In both cases, the writer argues, if it hurts, don't do it — you're probably doing something wrong. Answer choice D best completes the parallel construction.

34. **The best answer is H.** It is important to maintain parallel construction within a sentence. The author states that pain receptors exist to limit physical injury. Guilt, the writer implies, is a psychological pain receptor that helps us "limit injury to others." Repeating the phrase *limit injury* allows the author to emphasize the parallel nature of the processes. The other answer choices either fail to mark the parallel or are too wordy.

35. **The best answer is D.** The word *attempting* is modifying the verb *turn*. In this usage, *turn* needs to be in the infinitive, that is, the sentence needs to read "attempting to turn." If *attempting* were modifying a noun (*left turn*, for example), it would be correct as it stands. Since it isn't, the most concise and correct selection is answer choice D.

36. **The best answer is J.** The focus of the paragraph is social interaction. Information about the time it takes to stop a car is irrelevant and should be deleted. It is best to omit or remove the underlined portion.

37. **The best answer is C.** This question requires you to correctly punctuate the underlined portion. The sentence does not contain any clauses that need to be set apart by commas. Answer choice C is the best selection.

38. **The best answer is G.** Because *manner* describes a behavior, the sentence requires a verb that denotes action (*acts*), not a state of being (*is*). Answer choices H and J are too wordy and are grammatically incorrect.

39. **The best answer is A.** This question requires you to express the idea clearly and simply. The phrase *legal penalties* is concise and complete. Adding detailed descriptions of those penalties would only distract from the focus of the paragraph, which is social behavior.

40. **The best answer is J.** To maintain parallel construction, the verbal phrase should be *I have*. The resulting *I have... described a sociopath* would mirror the *have* implicit in the previous sentence's *I've... described rush-hour traffic*.

41. **The best answer is D.** The underlined phrase is redundant and therefore unnecessary. It should be omitted.

42. **The best answer is F.** The transition word *however* suggests a contrast between the idea contained in the preceding sentence, and the idea contained in the sentence that includes the underlined portion. This is, in fact, the case, so answer choice F is correct.

43. **The best answer is A.** The paragraph implies that it is human nature to avoid pain, including the pain of guilt. The writer suggests there are two ways to do this: avoid making mistakes, or avoid accepting responsibility for mistakes. The first is impossible. That leaves the second. The way to mark this type of logical progression is with the logical connective *therefore*, indicating that one thing is the result of another.

44. **The best answer is H.** The phrase *if improperly managed* is extra information in the sentence and should be set off by commas. The comma at the beginning of the phrase is a clue to the reader to expect a second comma at the end. A semicolon would require a complete sentence preceding it. The relative pronoun *which* would also require a complete sentence preceding it. Therefore, the best answer is H. Eliminate answer choices F and G. It is redundant to include the pronoun *it* in the sentence, so eliminate answer choice J.

45. **The best answer is C.** This question requires you to correctly punctuate the underlined portion. The relative clause *that they never move on* is one unit and should not be broken up by commas or any other punctuation.

PASSAGE IV

46. **The best answer is F.** The sentence as written implies that Kennedy's public image was of a healthy person and that Kennedy himself was tall and trim, which makes sense in the context of the paragraph.

47. **The best answer is C.** This question requires you to express the idea clearly and simply. The focus of this paragraph is the contrast between Kennedy's appearance of health and his actual state of chronic illness. Answer choice C best captures this dynamic. It starts with an acknowledgment that Kennedy naturally enjoyed sports ("Although he was genuinely athletic"), then emphasizes that he was unable to participate through much of his childhood because of his disease. Answer choice A also includes these ideas, but the order is not parallel to the rest of

the paragraph and, more importantly, it is grammatically incorrect because it connects two complete sentences with a comma instead of separating them with a period.

48. **The best answer is J.** This question requires you to express the idea clearly and simply. In this context, there is no significant difference in meaning between *children* and *youth*. Therefore, the underlined portion is redundant and should be omitted.

49. **The best answer is C.** The best way to provide more detail is to offer a better description. Paragraph 2 continues from Paragraph 1 by describing in more detail the effects of Addison's disease on Kennedy. A list of the symptoms of the disease would help the reader gain a more complete understanding of those symptoms.

50. **The best answer is F.** The sentence is best as written. The phrase begins in subject-verb-object order, which makes it clear right away what is being done to whom. The rest of the information follows in logical order. The clause *in his back* immediately comes after *anesthetic injections* because that is where the injections occurred. The frequency is last because it's not directly connected to any other clause.

51. **The best answer is D.** The phrase *without them seeing it* is already implied in the word *hide*. Therefore, it, along with answer choices B and C, is redundant and should be omitted.

52. **The best answer is G.** The sentence as it stands suffers from an overdose of punctuation. In this case, one mark would be enough. Colons are often used to introduce examples or lists. Here, the colon introduces a short list that identifies how Kennedy was seen: in person, or on television.

53. **The best answer is C.** Like the sentence before it, this one's punctuation is overly complicated. The key is to simplify it. If we read for sense, we see two complete sentences spliced together with commas. They should be separated by a semicolon, as in answer choice C.

54. **The best answer is F.** The question requires you to express the idea clearly and simply. The idea that Kennedy was able to "act healthy" is developed by the sentence, which explains exactly what that means: He was able to hide crippling pain from everyone except his doctors and relatives. These three distinct groups (doctors, relatives, and everyone else) should be kept together in the sentence because they comprise

three parts of one audience. In other words, the author implies that Kennedy is trying to fool all of them, but it only works with one group. Answer choice F includes all of that information while also being the most concise choice.

55. **The best answer is D.** This question requires you to express the idea clearly and simply. Answer choice D is complete and the most concise. The other answer choices are awkward and wordy.

56. **The best answer is G.** To maintain parallel construction within this paragraph, you need to use the past tense of the verb *attribute*, which is *attributed*. Notice the use of the verbs *was* and *looked*. The verb forms should agree, that is, have the same tense. Because Kennedy himself is doing the attributing, the verb needs to be in the active voice.

57. **The best answer is C.** The last two sentences of this paragraph clarify its focus, which is proving that Kennedy's illness did not negatively affect his ability to govern. Answer choice C asks the question that the last two sentences answer. Therefore, it is the best response.

58. **The best answer is H.** Like the positive pairing *either* and *or*, *neither* and *nor* are usually used together. Therefore, to maintain the parallelism, the phrase should be *nor the drugs*.

59. **The best answer is A.** The sentence as it stands gives us the most important information first, i.e., what he did ("performed"), followed by how he did it ("at the highest level"). This order makes logical sense and is the most concise option.

60. **The best answer is H.** This question requires you to determine the main idea of the passage. Although the passage does describe Addison's disease in some detail, its primary focus is the effect of Addison's disease on President Kennedy. For example, the reader is not told if Kennedy's experience of the disease is common among Addison's sufferers. Likewise, the reader is also not told if treatment has changed since the early 1960s. Therefore, the essay would not be a good general description of Addison's disease and its treatment. Eliminate answer choices F and G. While the essay does describe symptoms of the disease, this is not the main focus, so eliminate answer choice J.

PASSAGE V

61. **The best answer is C.** In order to maintain parallel construction, the verbal forms should

match. That means "*We're going* where?" should be followed by "*We're traveling to* Tromso."

62. **The best answer is G.** The word *planning* introduces a relative clause describing what the author intends to do in Southern California. Because the emphasis is on location, the relative clause should begin with *where*, which indicates location.

63. **The best answer is A.** The author is making a contrast between personal warmth, or genuine friendliness, and the outdoor temperature. She implies that the people of Tromso demonstrate the former. Being helpful is an excellent way to show friendliness. The other answer choices are not relevant to the question.

64. **The best answer is G.** The correct answer will focus on the residents of Tromso and will show them taking the initiative to provide help. This best matches answer choice G. While answer choice F describes polite behavior, it doesn't show people acting eager, or going out of their way to be helpful.

65. **The best answer is A.** The sentence as it stands is grammatically correct, complete, and concise. No change is necessary. Answer choices B and D are redundant, and should be eliminated.

66. **The best answer is G.** This question requires you to express the idea clearly and simply. The current sentence is wordy and redundant (it's unnecessary to repeat *Tromso* in this context). Answer choice G sets up a neat, parallel contrast between what other towns claim to do and what Tromso actually does.

67. **The best answer is A.** The paragraph that follows indicates that, instead of working or sitting, the writer spent much of his time hiking. The phrase *at all* is appropriate here, because it makes a connection between the idea that the writer thought his time in Norway would drag, and the fact that his visit was actually very enjoyable.

68. **The best answer is G.** The best introductory sentence will be one that shows a transition from Paragraph 3 to Paragraph 4. Since Paragraph 3 discusses some of Tromso's attributes (mild weather and friendly people) it makes sense that Paragraph 4 should start out with another of Tromso's characteristics. Sentence 2 does this best. Therefore, the correct sequence of sentences will begin with Sentence 2. Since only answer choice G places Sentence 2 in the first position, it must be correct.

69. **The best answer is D.** The sentence introduces the idea of boots and blisters to the paragraph. Since this is not echoed elsewhere, it is irrelevant and should be omitted. Eliminate answer choices B and C for the same reason.

70. **The best answer is F.** The first part of the sentence indicates that hiking is so popular in Norway, that the government passed regulations allowing anyone to hike across wilderness areas. Answer choice F further discusses the popularity and demand for access to these wilderness areas, so it is the most appropriate addition here.

71. **The best answer is B.** Answer choice B is the only one with descriptive adjectives that help create a vivid image of the "many beautiful scenes." The other answer choices are either too general or contain irrelevant information.

72. **The best answer is F.** The sentence is complete and concise as it stands. The addition of a transition word is not necessary, so eliminate answer choices G, H, and J.

73. **The best answer is D.** The sentence requires the possessive form of *Tromso*, a singular noun. The correct form adds an apostrophe and an *s* to create *Tromso's*. Eliminate answer choices A and B. The word *most* is unnecessary, so eliminate answer choice C.

74. **The best answer is F.** This question requires you to express the idea clearly and simply. The clause *a view that has been described as world class*, describes a singular view (i.e., not *views*). This implies that the author is referring to only one vantage point: Mount Storsteinen. This eliminates answer choice G. Answer choices H and J are wordy and grammatically confused.

75. **The best answer is B.** The answer choices ask the reader to consider various forms of the word *its*, but the pronoun itself is unclear in its reference. The word *it's* is the contraction of *it is*. Eliminate answer choice A. A better choice would be to skip the pronoun completely and simply use the noun: *the region's*. Since there is only one Tromso, you should not use the plural pronoun *their*. Eliminate answer choice C.

Mathematics Test Explanations

1. **The correct answer is A.** This is a basic Algebra problem that requires you to solve for x. Isolate the variable, x, on 1 side of the equation, as follows:

   (1) $4x - 9 = 11$

   (2) $4x = 20$

   (3) $x = 5$, answer choice A.

2. **The correct answer is F.** This kind of statement is called a "conditional." You are told that if the first part is true (XY is 4), then the second part (YZ is 7) will certainly be true. Since the second part is NOT true, you can conclude logically that the first part is also NOT true. Therefore, answer choice F is correct. If XY *were* equal to 4, then, according to the given statement, YZ would have to be 7. This is really a logic problem that just happens to be in the mathematics section.

3. **The correct answer is E.** *Probability* refers to how likely it is that something will happen. You can look at probability in this problem as a percentage. Convert the 0.6 probability that Tom will go for a run into a 60% chance that Tom will go for a run. The question asks you for the probability that Tom will NOT go for a run, which is $100\% - 60\%$, or 40%. Convert 40% into decimal form, 0.4, to arrive at answer choice E.

4. **The correct answer is F.** To find the average price that Mark paid per video, you must divide the total dollar amount that Mark paid for the videos by the number of videos that Mark bought. The total dollar amount that Mark paid for the videos can be set up like this:

   (1) 1 video for $12.99 + 2$ videos for $6.50 each

   (2) $\$12.99 + 2(\$6.50)$

   You know from information in the problem that Mark purchased a total of 3 videos. Divide the total dollar amount that he paid, $\$12.99 + 2(\$6.50)$ by 3:

   (3) $\dfrac{\$12.99 + 2(\$6.50)}{3}$, answer choice F.

5. **The correct answer is D.** The easiest way to solve this problem is to work backward. Since $18.00 was $\dfrac{1}{2}$ of what remained from Sunday, then there must have been $\$18.00 \times 2$, or $36.00 remaining

from Sunday. Since Joan spent $\dfrac{1}{5}$ of the money on Sunday and still had $36.00 remaining, $36.00 must be $\dfrac{4}{5}$ of the money that she started out with on Sunday. Calculate the amount of money that she started out with on Sunday (x):

   (1) $36 = \dfrac{4}{5x}$

   (2) $\dfrac{36}{x} = \dfrac{4}{5}$; cross multiply and solve for x.

   (3) $4x = 180$

   (4) $x = 45$

So, after spending $\dfrac{1}{4}$ of her pay on Saturday, Joan had $45.00 left. Since she spent $\dfrac{1}{4}$ of her pay on Saturday and still had $45.00 left, $45.00 must be $\dfrac{3}{4}$ of the money that she started out with on Saturday. Calculate the amount of money that she started out with on Saturday (x):

   (1) $45 = \dfrac{3}{4x}$

   (2) $\dfrac{45}{x} = \dfrac{3}{4}$; cross-multiply and solve for x.

   (3) $3x = 180$

   (4) $x = 60$

Joan received $60.00 originally, answer choice D.

6. **The correct answer is H.** This problem requires you to substitute the values given for P and Q into the equation $P - Q$. The problem states that $P = 5a$, and $Q = 3b - 2a$ Set up the equation as follows, and remember to keep track of the negative sign as you simplify the expression:

   (1) $P - Q =$

   (2) $5a - (3b - 2a) =$

   (3) $5a - (-2a) - 3b =$

   (4) $5a + 2a - 3b =$

   (5) $7a - 3b$, answer choice H.

7. **The correct answer is E.** The figure in the problem represents 2 parallel lines cut by 2 parallel transversals. The angles created as a result have special properties. Where each of the parallel lines is cut by a transversal, there are 2 pairs of vertical, or opposite angles. Each angle in the pair is congruent to, or equal to, the other angle in the pair. Therefore, where l_3 cuts l_1 and also where it cuts l_2, two 100° angles are formed; in addition, two 80° are formed that are adjacent to the 100° angles, since a straight line has 180°. The same angles are

created where l_4 cuts l_1 and l_2. This means that angle z must be equal to 80°, answer choice E.

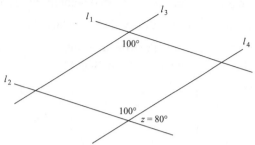

8. **The correct answer is H.** Simply plug 2 in for x wherever x appears in the equation and solve the equation. Don't forget to keep track of the negative signs!

   (1) $-(2^2) + 4(2) - 3 =$

   (2) $-(4) + 8 - 3 =$

   (3) $8 - 4 - 3 = 1$, answer choice H.

9. **The correct answer is B.** If the average of 8 numbers is 6.5, then the total of the 8 numbers is $8 \cdot 6.5$, or 52. If each of the 8 numbers is decreased by 3, then the total of the 8 new numbers is $52 - 8(3)$, or $52 - 24$, which is 28. To find the average, divide 28 by 8, to get 3.5, answer choice B.

10. **The correct answer is J.** This question tests your ability to recognize and apply the distributive property. According to the distributive property, for any numbers a, b, and c, $c(a + b) = ca + cb$. In this problem, c is 5 so you can simplify the expression $5a + 5b$ into $5(a + b)$, answer choice J.

11. **The correct answer is C.** The first step in solving this problem is to calculate the amount of money that you earn each day for delivering bouquets:

    (1) $22.00 (total amount earned per day) $-$12.00 (fixed amount earned per day) $=$ $10.00 (amount earned for bouquets delivered).

    Next, calculate the amount that you earn per bouquet:

    (2) $10.00 (amount earned for bouquets delivered) $÷$ 20 (number of bouquets delivered) $=$ $0.50 (amount earned per bouquet delivered).

    Now determine the amount that you will earn today for delivering the extra bouquets:

    (3) 16 (additional number of bouquets delivered) $\times$ $0.50 (amount earned per bouquet delivered)$=$ $8.00 (additional income for the day).

Finally, add this amount to your fixed daily earnings:

(4) $22.00 + $8.00 = 30.00, answer choice C.

12. **The correct answer is K.** The easiest way to solve this problem is to plug the answer choices into the inequality and solve. Because the question asks you for the largest possible value of x, start with the largest answer choice (note that the answer choices are in ascending order):

    (1) $\dfrac{8}{32} \geq \dfrac{1}{4}$

    (2) $\dfrac{8}{32} = \dfrac{1}{4}$

    This satisfies the inequality, so answer choice K, because it is the largest, must be correct.

13. **The correct answer is C.** In order to solve this problem you must know that there are 360° in a circle, and that the clock shown is divided into 12 segments, 1 for each hour in the day. To calculate the number of degrees that the hour hand moves from 1:00 p.m. to 8:00 p.m. perform the following operations:

    (1) $360° ÷ 12 = 30°$. Each hour in the day is equivalent to 30°.

    (2) $30° \cdot 7$ (the number of hours between 1:00 p.m. and 8:00 p.m.)$= 210°$, answer choice C.

14. **The correct answer is J.** The first step in choosing the correct answer is to locate point R in the coordinate plane. You will see that it is located in the upper right quadrant, which means that both of the coordinates must be positive. Eliminate answer choices H and K because they both include negative coordinates. You can also eliminate answer choices F and G, because neither of the coordinates of point R is zero. That leaves answer choice J as the only possible correct answer.

15. **The correct answer is A.** This problem requires you to find the Greatest Common Factor. The Greatest Common Factor is $3xy$, because each term has at least 1 factor of 3, 1 factor of x, and 1 factor of y. When you factor $3xy$ out of $3x^3y^3$ you are left with x^2y^2, and when you factor $3xy$ out of $3xy$, you are left with 1. Therefore, when factored, $3x^3y^3 + 3xy = 3xy(x^2y^2 + 1)$, answer choice A.

16. **The correct answer is K.** To find the total number of seats in the entire classroom, you must multiply the number of rows, $(r + s)$, by the number

of seats in each row, t, using the Distributive Property:

(1) $(r + s) \cdot t = (r \cdot t) + (s \cdot t)$

(2) $(r \cdot t) + (s \cdot t) = (t \cdot r) + (t \cdot s)$, answer choice K.

17. **The correct answer is D.** The first step in selecting the correct answer to this problem is to recognize that x cannot be less than 16. This means that answer choices A and B can be eliminated. If you look at answer choice C, you should notice that 16 is $\frac{1}{2}$, or 50% of 32, not 20% of 32, so answer choice C can be eliminated. It does not make sense that 20% of 800 would be 16, so by a simple process of elimination you can arrive at the correct answer, which is answer choice D. To solve this problem mathematically, follow these steps:

(1) 16 is to x as 20% is to 100%.

(2) $\frac{16}{x} = \frac{20}{100}$; cross-multiply and solve for x.

(3) $20x = 1,600$

(4) $x = 80$, answer choice D.

18. **The correct answer is F.** The first step in solving this problem is to calculate the total that Matt paid for the first 30 apples that he picked:

(1) $30 \cdot \$0.05 = \$1.50$ (cost of first 30 apples picked)

Next, you must calculate the total that Matt paid for the rest of the apples that he picked:

(2) $75 - 30 = 45$ (number of apples picked at $0.03 per apple)

(3) $45 \cdot \$0.03 = \$1.35$ (cost of next 45 apples picked)

Finally, add the two amounts together:

(4) $\$1.50 + \$1.35 = \$2.85$ (total cost for picking 75 apples), answer choice F.

19. **The correct answer is E.** In order to solve this problem you must first calculate the total cost of the watch, including tax. Since the sales tax is 6%, multiply the price of the watch ($12.99) by 0.06, the decimal equivalent of 6%:

(1) $\$12.99 \cdot 0.06 = \$0.7794$

(2) $0.7794 rounded to the nearest cent is $0.78.

Now, add the sales tax to the price of the watch:

(3) $\$12.99 + \$0.78 = \$13.77$

Based on these calculations, you will need $0.77 in exact change, answer choice E.

20. **The correct answer is G.** An expression is undefined when the denominator equals 0. Set the denominator equal to 0 and solve for x:

(1) $16 - x^2 = 0$

(2) $16 = x^2$

(3) $4 = x$, answer choice G.

21. **The correct answer is C.** In order to solve this problem you must know that π is approximately equal to 3.14. The next step is to find the value of the fraction $\frac{5}{2}$. To do this, divide the numerator (5) by the denominator (2): $5 \div 2 = 2.5$. Now, put the values in order from greatest to least: $4 > 3.14 > 2.5$, answer choice C.

22. **The correct answer is K.** The key to solving this problem is to recognize that the box has a top and a bottom, plus 4 sides. Because the tape must go completely *around* all 4 sides of the box, you must account for the sides as follows:

(1) $2(40 \, \text{cm}) = 80 \, \text{cm}$ (top and bottom, length)

(2) $2(13 \, \text{cm}) = 26 \, \text{cm}$ (top and bottom, width)

(3) $4(20 \, \text{cm}) = 80 \, \text{cm}$ (four sides, height)

(4) $80 + 26 + 80 = 186 \, \text{cm}$, answer choice K.

23. **The correct answer is D.** To solve this problem you must compare the parts of the recipe to the whole recipe. The recipe calls for 9 quarts of fruit juices to 4 quarts of soda. This means that the recipe calls for a total of $9 + 4$, or 13 quarts. The proportion of soda (the part) to punch (the whole) is 4:13. You are making 52 quarts of punch, which is 4 times what the recipe will make. Therefore, to make 52 quarts of punch, you must have $4 \cdot 4$, or 16 quarts of soda, answer choice D.

24. **The correct answer is G.** To find the solutions of the expression $x^2 + 2x = 8$, first put it in the correct quadratic form by subtracting 8 from both sides: $x^2 + 2x - 8 = 0$. Now you can factor the polynomial $x^2 + 2x - 8$:

(1) $(x + \underline{\quad})(x - \underline{\quad}) = 0$

Find 2 factors of -8 that, when added together give you 2, and plug them into the solution sets:

(2) $(x + 4)(x - 2) = 0$.

Now, solve for x:

(3) $(x + 4) = 0$, so $x = -4$

(4) $(x - 2) = 0$, so $x = 2$

The solutions of $x^2 + 2x = 8$ are -4 and 2, answer choice G.

25. The correct answer is C. The key to solving this problem is to recognize that, if $(f+g)^2 = 81$, then $f+g$ must equal 9, because 9^2 equals 81. Now, since you are given that $fg = 20$, you need to find 2 numbers that, when added together give you 9, and when multiplied together give you 20. The only 2 numbers that will satisfy both equations are 4 and 5. Substitute 4 for f and 5 for g in the final equation: $f^2 + g^2 = 4^2 + 5^2 = 16 + 25 = 41$, answer choice C.

26. The correct answer is J. When exponents are raised to an exponential power, the rules state that you must multiply the exponents by the power to which they are raised. In this problem, x is raised to the $(4a - 3)$ power. This exponent is then squared, so you should multiply $4a - 3$ by 2: $2(4a - 3) = 8a - 6$ You now have the equation $x^{8a-6} = x^{10}$. Since the coefficients are equal (x), the exponents must also be equal, so $8a - 6 = 10$. Solve for a:

(1) $8a - 6 = 10$

(2) $8a = 16$

(3) $a = 2$, answer choice J.

27. The correct answer is E. The first step in solving this problem is to determine the value of i^6 and $3i^4$. Even though this problem contains a complex number, it is actually a relatively simple exponent problem. You are given that $i^2 = -1$, which means that $i^6 = (i^2)(i^2)(i^2) = (-1)(-1)(-1)$, which equals -1. By the same token, $3i^4 = 3(i^2)(i^2) = 3(-1)(-1)$, which equals 3. Therefore, the value of $i^6 + 3i^4$ is $-1 + 3$, or 2, answer choice E.

28. The correct answer is G. The standard form for the equation of a line is $y = mx + b$, where m is the slope and b is the y-intercept. Put the given equation in the standard form as follows:

(1) $5x - 4y = 7$

(2) $-4y = -5x + 7$

(3) $y = \dfrac{5}{4x} - \dfrac{7}{4}$

Based on this solution, b, the y-intercept, is equal to $-\dfrac{7}{4}$, answer choice G.

29. The correct answer is D. A circle centered at (a, b) with a radius r, has the equation $(x - a)^2 + (y - b)^2 = r^2$. Based on this definition, a circle with the equation $(x + 3)^2 + (y - 2)^2 = 10$ would have a radius of $\sqrt{10}$. If $r^2 = 10$, then $r = \sqrt{10}$, answer choice D.

30. The correct answer is F. The sine of any acute angle is calculated by dividing the length of the side opposite the acute angle by the length of the hypotenuse $(\sin = \frac{\text{opp}}{\text{hyp}})$. In this problem, the length of the side opposite angle β is l, and the length of the hypotenuse is n. Therefore, the sin of angle β is $\dfrac{l}{n}$, answer choice F.

31. The correct answer is E. You should think of this problem as a basic fraction, where $(4a^3b) \times (-5a^5b^3)$ is the numerator and $(10a^4b^2)$ is the denominator. The first step is to multiply together the 2 elements in the numerator, as follows:

(1) When multiplying exponents, the rules state that you should add exponents with like coefficients, so $(4a^3b)(-5a^5b^3) = -20a^8b^4$

To solve a fraction, you simply divide the numerator by the denominator.

(2) When dividing exponents, the rules state that you should subtract exponents of the same coefficients in the denominator from the exponents of the same coefficients in the numerator, so $-20a^8b^4 \div 10a^4b^2 = -2a^4b^2$, answer choice E.

32. The correct answer is G. Because the 3 lines are parallel, the distances between the points of intersection of each of the transversals are directly proportional. So, the distance from point E to point C ($6''$) is directly proportional to the distance from point A to point C ($2''$), and the distance from point F to point D ($8''$) is proportional to the distance from point D to point B (x''). Set up the following proportion and solve for x:

(1) $6 : 2$ as $8 : x$

(2) $\dfrac{6}{2} = \dfrac{8}{x}$

(3) $x = \dfrac{16}{6}$, which can be simplified to $\dfrac{8}{3}$, answer choice G.

33. The correct answer is D. A square is a parallelogram with 4 right angles and 4 sides of the same length. The perimeter of a square is the distance around the square, or the sum of all 4 sides. Since the perimeter is given as 28, the length of each side of the square must be $28 \div 4$, or 7. This means that radii $\overline{DA}$ and $\overline{DC}$ are both equal to 7. The area of a circle is calculated using the formula $A = \pi r^2$. Plug 7 in for r and solve:

(1) $A = \pi r^2 = \pi^4(7)^2$

(2) $A = \pi 49$, or 49π, answer choice D.

34. **The correct answer is K.** According to the graph shown, the number 2 is included, but the number 4 is not included. This means that x must be less than or equal to $2 (x \le 2)$ and/or x must be greater than $4 (x > 4)$. You can eliminate answer choices F and G, which both say that x is greater than or equal to $4 (x \ge 4)$. You can also eliminate answer choice H, which says that x is less than, but not equal to, 2 $(x < 2)$. Now you must decide whether to use *and* or to use *or*. Since the sets do not overlap on the graph, the correct answer is $x \le 2$ *or* $x > 4$, answer choice K.

35. **The correct answer is C.** The easiest way to solve this problem is to draw a diagram, as shown:

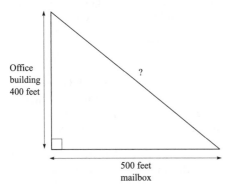

Now you simply need to apply the Pythagorean Theorem to solve for the missing length of the hypotenuse. The Pythagorean Theorem states that $a^2 + b^2 = c^2$, where a and b are the lengths of the sides of a right triangle, and c is the length of the hypotenuse. Plug in the values for a and b and solve for c:

(1) $400^2 + 500^2 = c^2$

(2) $160{,}000 + 250{,}000 = c^2$

(3) $410{,}000 = c^2$

(4) $\sqrt{410{,}000} = \left(\sqrt{10{,}000}\right)\left(\sqrt{41}\right) = 100\sqrt{41}$, answer choice C.

36. **The correct answer is G.** Because a negative number cannot have a square root, the value under a square root sign *must* be positive. In this problem, the value under the square root sign is $4\left(\dfrac{x^2}{3y}\right)$. Choose values for the answer choices and eliminate those choices that could give you a negative value under the square root sign:

(1) If y is negative, then $3y$ will be negative, so the value under the square root sign could also be negative. Eliminate answer choice F.

(2) If y is positive, then $3y$ will be positive. Since the square of a negative number is also positive, even if x is negative, as long as y is positive the value under the square root sign will be positive. This answer choice will work.

(3) Answer choices H and J are not true, because you have just determined that y must be positive, which means that, while y *could* be either 4 or $\dfrac{1}{2}$, it could also be some other positive value.

(4) Answer choice K does not work, because y must be a positive number. By process of elimination, you are left with answer choice G.

37. **The correct answer is B.** To solve this problem, first list all of the distinct factors of 96: 96, 48, 32, 24, 16, 12, 8, 6, 3, 2, 1. All of these numbers divide evenly into 96. Next, list all of the distinct factors of 64: 64, 32, 16, 8, 4, 2, 1. All of these numbers divide evenly into 64. The only factors that both 96 and 64 have in common are 1, 2, 4, 8, 16, and 32. Since you are told that c is NOT a factor of either 16 or 20, you can eliminate 1, 2, 4, 8, and 16, which factor evenly into either 16 or 20. This leaves you with a value for c of 32. When you add the digits $(3 + 2)$ you get 5, answer choice B.

38. **The correct answer is J.** The slope of a line is defined as the change in the y-values over the change in the x-values in the standard (x, y) coordinate plane. Slope can be calculated by using the following formula: $\dfrac{(y_1 - y_2)}{(x_1 - x_2)}$. Any line parallel to the y-axis is a vertical line: The x-values do not change (see diagram).

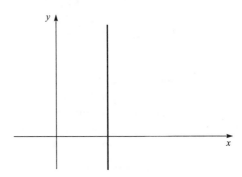

The slope of a vertical line is undefined, answer choice J, because there is no change in x, which means that the denominator $(x_1 - x_2)$ is zero.

39. **The correct answer is B.** The standard form of a line is $y = mx + b$, where m is the slope. In order to determine which line has the largest slope, you

must first put all of the answer choices into the standard form. Answer choices A, B, and C are already in the standard form. The slopes of those lines are 2, 5, and −7, respectively. Calculate the slope of answer choices D and E:

(1) $3y = 9x + 6$

(2) $y = \dfrac{9}{3x} + \dfrac{6}{3}$; $y = 3x + 2$

Answer choice D has a slope of 3.

(1) $4y = 4x − 8$

(2) $y = \dfrac{4}{4x} − \dfrac{8}{4}$; $y = x − 2$

Answer choice E has a slope of 1. Therefore, the line with the largest slope is answer choice B, with a slope of 5.

40. The correct answer is F. The first step in solving this problem is to calculate the sine and the cosine for both angle a and angle b. The sine of any acute angle is calculated by dividing the length of the side opposite the acute angle by the length of the hypotenuse ($\sin = \dfrac{\text{opp}}{\text{hyp}}$) The cosine of any acute angle is calculated by dividing the length of the side adjacent to the acute angle by the hypotenuse ($\cos = \dfrac{\text{adj}}{\text{hyp}}$). In this problem, the sin of angle a is $\dfrac{12}{15}$, which can be reduced to $\dfrac{4}{5}$, and the cos of angle a is $\dfrac{9}{15}$, which can be reduced to $\dfrac{3}{5}$. The sin of angle b is $\dfrac{9}{15}$, or $\dfrac{3}{5}$, and the cos of angle b is $\dfrac{12}{15}$, or $\dfrac{4}{5}$. Now you can plug these values into the equation given in the problem and solve for $\sin(a − b)$:

(1) $\sin(a − b) = \sin a \cos b − \cos a \sin b$

(2) $\sin(a − b) = \left(\dfrac{4}{5}\right)\left(\dfrac{4}{5}\right) − \left(\dfrac{3}{5}\right)\left(\dfrac{3}{5}\right)$

(3) $\sin(a − b) = \left(\dfrac{16}{25}\right) − \left(\dfrac{9}{25}\right) = \dfrac{7}{25}$, answer choice F.

41. The correct answer is A. This problem requires you to set up a simple proportion and solve for a variable. According to information in the problem, Jason can walk 4 miles in j minutes. This means that he can walk 4 miles per j minutes, or $\dfrac{4}{j}$. The question asks you to calculate the amount of time it will take him to walk 11 miles. In other words, Jason can walk 11 miles per x minutes, or $\dfrac{11}{x}$; what is the value of x?

(1) $\dfrac{4}{j}$ is to $\dfrac{11}{x}$

(2) $\dfrac{4}{j} = \dfrac{11}{x}$

(3) $4x = 11j$

(4) $x = \dfrac{11j}{4}$, answer choice A.

42. The correct answer is K. The best approach to this problem is to pick some numbers for n, plug them into the answer choices, and eliminate the answer choices that do not always yield an odd number.

(1) If $n = 1$, then $4n^2 = 4(1)^2 = 4$, which is not odd. Eliminate answer choice F.

(2) If $n = 1$, then $3n^2 + 1 = 3(1)^2 + 1 = 3 + 1 = 4$, which is not odd. Eliminate answer choice G.

(3) If $n = 1$, then $6n^2 = 6(1)^2 = 6$, which is not odd. Eliminate answer choice H.

(4) If $n = 1$, then $n^2 − 1 = (1)^2 − 1 = 0$, which is not odd. Eliminate answer choice J.

(5) If $n = 1$, then $4n^2 − 1 = 4(1)^2 − 1 = 4 − 1 = 3$, which is odd. Try another number: $n = 2$, then $4n^2 − 1 = 4(2)^2 − 1 = 16 − 1 = 15$, which is also odd. Answer choice K will work.

Answer choice K is the only one that will give you an odd number for any value of n.

43. The correct answer is D. The area of a triangle is calculated using the formula $A = \dfrac{1}{2}(bh)$, where b is the length of the base, and h is the height. Based on the measures of the angles given, you can draw triangle ABC as shown below:

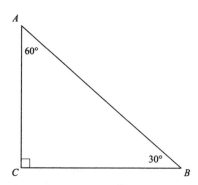

You are given that $\overline{AB}$, the hypotenuse, is 8 units long. Because this is a 30–60–90 triangle, you can calculate the lengths of the base ($\overline{BC}$) and the height ($\overline{AC}$). The relationship between the sides of a 30–60–90 triangle is as follows: The side opposite the 30° is equal to $\dfrac{1}{2}$ of the length of the hypotenuse, and the side opposite the 60° is equal to $\frac{1}{2}$ of the length of the hypotenuse times $\sqrt{3}$. Calculate the lengths of the sides:

(1) Side $\overline{BC}$ (the base) $= \frac{1}{2}(8)\sqrt{3} = 4\sqrt{3}$.

(2) Side $\overline{AC}$ (the height) $= \frac{1}{2}(8) = 4$.

Now you can plug these values into the formula for the area of a triangle:

(1) $A = \frac{1}{2}\left(4\sqrt{3}\right)(4) = \frac{1}{2}\left(16\sqrt{3}\right) = 8\sqrt{3}$, answer choice D.

44. The correct answer is G. For isosceles trapezoids, the ratio of the top part of the diagonal to the bottom part of the diagonal is equal to the ratio of the top side of the trapezoid to the bottom side of the trapezoid. Therefore, the ratio of $\overline{GK}$ (the top part of the diagonal) to $\overline{JK}$ (the bottom part of the diagonal) is equal to the ratio of $\overline{FG}$ (the top of the trapezoid) to $\overline{HJ}$ (the bottom of the trapezoid). This statement is expressed as $\overline{GK}/\overline{JK} = \overline{FG}/\overline{HJ}$. Since FG is x inches, and $\overline{HJ}$ is z inches, $\overline{GK}/\overline{JK}$ is equal to x/z, answer choice G.

45. The correct answer is C. The area of a rectangle is calculated by multiplying the length by the width ($A = w \times l$). Calculate the area of the first rectangle as follows:

(1) Set the width equal to x, and the length equal to $4x$.

(2) $A = x(4x) = 4x^2$.

Now calculate the area of the second triangle:

(1) The length and width are tripled, so the width $= 3x$ and the length $= 12x$.

(2) $A = (3x)(12x) = 36x^2$.

The area of the second triangle is $36x^2$, which is 9 times greater than the area of the first triangle ($4x^2$), answer choice C.

46. The correct answer is G. Systems of equations will have infinite solutions when the equations are equal to each other. The first step in solving this problem is to recognize that the second equation is exactly twice the value of the first equation: $6x = 2(3x)$, $8y = 2(4y)$, so $7b$ must equal $2(14)$. Solve for b:

(1) $7b = 2(14)$

(2) $7b = 28$

(3) $b = 4$, answer choice G.

47. The correct answer is D. Logarithms are used to indicate exponents of certain numbers called bases. This problem tells you that log to the base 3 of x equals 2. So, the question is, when 3 is raised to power of 2, what do you get? By definition, $\log_a b = c$ if $a^c = b$. Therefore, $\log_3 x = 2$ if $3^2 = x$. Since $3^2 = 9$, answer choice D is correct.

48. The correct answer is K. The first step in solving this problem is to recognize that the distance to the telephone pole is equal to the length of the side adjacent to the 37° angle, and the height of the telephone pole is equal to the length of the side opposite the 37° angle. The length of the side opposite to any given angle divided by the length of the side adjacent to any given angle is the tangent of that angle. So, in this problem, $\tan 37° = \frac{24}{\text{distance}}$. Solve for the distance:

(1) $\tan 37° = \frac{24}{\text{distance}}$

(2) (distance) $\tan 37° = 24$

(3) distance $= \frac{24}{\tan 37°} = 24\left(\frac{1}{\tan 37°}\right)$

By definition, cotangent is $\frac{1}{\tan}$, so the distance is equal to $24 \cot 37°$, answer choice K.

49. The correct answer is C. The area of a parallelogram is calculated by using the formula $A = (b \times h)$, where b is the base, and h is the height. The length of the sides, $(\sqrt{61})$ is not relevant in calculating the area. Plug the given values into the formula:

(1) $A = (6 \cdot 5)$

(2) $A = 30$, answer choice C.

50. The correct answer is H. The easiest way to solve this problem is to draw a line and place the given points on the line, as follows:

(1)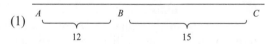

Based on the line above, one possible length of $\overline{BC}$ is 27. Eliminate answer choices F, J, and K. Since you are left with answer choices G and H, you need to determine if $\overline{AC}$ could also be 3 meters long. Draw another line, and change the order of the points:

(2)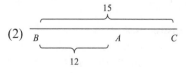

Based on this line, another possible length of $\overline{AC}$ is 3, so answer choice H must be correct.

51. **The correct answer is D.** The area of a parallelogram is calculated by using the formula $A = (bh)$, where b is the base, and h is the height. The area of a triangle is $\frac{1}{2}(bh)$. You can determine the base by measuring the distance along the x-axis, and you can determine the height by measuring the distance along the y-axis:

(1) The distance between -7 and 3 on the x-axis is 10 units; likewise, the distance between -6 and 4 on the x-axis is 10 units. The length of the base is 10.

(2) The distance between 5 and -8 on the y-axis is 13. The height is 13.

Now plug these values into the formula for the area of a triangle:

(1) $A = \frac{1}{2}(bh)$

(2) $A = \frac{1}{2}(10 \cdot 13)$

(3) $A = \frac{1}{2}(130) = 65$, answer choice D.

52. **The correct answer is G.** In this problem, the quantity $6a^4b^3$ is less than zero, which means it must be negative. Since 6 is positive, and a^4 will always be positive, b^3 must be negative. By definition, if you cube a negative number, the result will be negative. Therefore, if b^3 is negative, then b must be negative, or less than zero. This means that b CANNOT be greater than zero, so answer choice G is correct.

53. **The correct answer is C.** In a geometric sequence, the quotient of any 2 successive members or terms of the sequence is a constant. This means that the exponent is 1 larger in each successive element of the progression, because you multiply by the same number each time you move to the next element in the sequence. Here, the second term of the sequence will have an exponent of 1 (sp), the third term of the sequence will have an exponent of 2 (s^2p), the fourth term will have an exponent of 3 (s^3p), and so on. You can see that the exponent of any given term is 1 less than the number of the term. Therefore, the exponent of s of the 734th term must be 733, ($s^{733}p$), answer choice C.

54. **The correct answer is J.** If a system of 2 linear equations in 2 variables has no solution, that means that the lines do not cross each other anywhere in the (x, y) coordinate plane. If the lines do not cross each other, then they must be parallel. Parallel lines have the same slope. The line shown has a positive slope, so you can eliminate answer choice F, which has a slope of zero, and answer choices G and H which have negative slopes. Parallel lines cannot have the same y-intercept, so eliminate answer choice K, which intercepts the y-axis at -3, as does the line shown. This leaves answer choice J.

55. **The correct answer is A.** Because angle x is less than $90°$, it is an acute angle. The tangent of any acute angle is calculated by dividing the length of the side opposite of the acute angle by the length of the side adjacent to the acute angle ($\tan = \frac{\text{opp}}{\text{adj}}$). This means that the length of the side opposite angle x is 15, and the length of the side adjacent to angle x is 8. The cosine of any acute angle is calculated by dividing the length of the side adjacent to the acute angle by the hypotenuse ($\cos = \frac{\text{adj}}{\text{hyp}}$). Since you know the lengths of 2 of the sides, you can calculate the hypotenuse by using the Pythagorean Theorem:

(1) Pythagorean Theorem: $a^2 + b^2 = c^2$, where c is the hypotenuse.

(2) $8^2 + 15^2 = c^2$

(3) $64 + 225 = c^2$

(4) $289 = c^2$

(5) $\sqrt{289} = c$, so $c = 17$

The hypotenuse is 17, which means that the cos of angle x is $\frac{8}{17}$, answer choice A.

56. **The correct answer is K.** The problem asks for an expression that represents the *number* of tickets sold, not the *cost* of the tickets sold. Therefore, answer choices F, G, and H can be eliminated because they all include reference to the cost of each ticket ($9.00). The problem states that fewer tickets are sold when the price is increased, so the correct expression must be K, which shows a decrease from the 2,500 tickets that the team normally sells.

57. **The correct answer is C.** The rules of the game state that a player is a winner if 2 marbles drawn have the same 1's digit. The player has already drawn the marble numbered 28, which has an 8 in the 1's digit. In order to win, the player must draw another marble with an 8 in the 1's digit.

The possible winning marbles are 8, 18, 38, 48, 58, and 68. Therefore, the player has 6 chances to draw a winning marble. Since he has already drawn 1 of the 75 marbles and did not put it back, he has 6 chances out of 74 to draw a winning marble. $\frac{6}{74}$ can be reduced to $\frac{3}{37}$, answer choice C.

58. **The correct answer is H.** In order to determine the volume of water to remove from the aquarium, you must first calculate the total amount of water that the aquarium holds. Volume is calculated by multiplying the length (24 inches) by the width (12 inches) by the height/depth (10 inches):

(1) $24 \cdot 12 \cdot 10 = 2,880$

The total volume of the aquarium is 2,880 cubic inches. Since Rana must remove half of that volume to clean the aquarium, divide 2,880 by 2:

(2) $2,880 \div 2 = 1,440$

Rana must remove 1,440 cubic inches of water, answer choice H.

59. **The correct answer is B.** The standard form of the equation of a line is $y = mx + b$, where m is the slope and b is the y-intercept. Parallel lines have the same slope. Since line p has a slope of 3, line q must also have a slope of 3. Eliminate answer choices A and C, because the slope is not 3. Now you need to determine the y-intercept. Line q intercepts the y-axis below the origin $(0, 0)$, which means that the y-intercept must be negative. Eliminate answer choice E, which has a positive y-intercept. This leaves answer choices B and D. The distance between lines p and q is 3, as shown in the figure. If you draw a perpendicular line from the origin to line q, you will create a right triangle, with the y-axis as the hypotenuse. Since the hypotenuse is longer than either of the sides, the y-intercept of line q will be greater than 3, so answer choice B must be correct.

60. **The correct answer is F.** If 2 numbers, x and y, differ by 12, that means that $x - y = 12$. Multiplying the 2 numbers, $(x)(y)$, will yield the product. Solve the first equation for x, then substitute the result for x in the second equation, as follows:

(1) $x - y = 12$

(2) $x = y + 12$

(3) $(y + 12)y =$

Since one of the answer choices must be the solution to that equation, plug in the answer choices, starting with the smallest value (note that the answer choices are in ascending order):

(1) $(y + 12)y = -36$

(2) $(y + 12)y + 36 = 0$

(3) $y^2 + 12y + 36 = 0$

(4) $(y + 6)^2 = 0$

(5) $y = -6$

Now, substitute -6 for y in the first equation and solve for x:

(6) $x - (-6) = 12$

(7) $x = 6$

Both equations are satisfied, and -36 is the smallest value among the answer choices, so the smallest possible value for the product of 2 real numbers that differ by 12 is -36, answer choice F.

Reading Test Explanations

PASSAGE I

1. **The best answer is D.** Eui Thi's longing for Laos is triggered by the crowding of thousands of other refugees in Thailand. The vast number implies an uncomfortable chaos in the refugee camp. Answer choice D captures Eui Thi's feeling of distress. Furthermore, the paragraph emphasizes the continuing political instability and danger in Laos. The author reinforces that emphasis in line 19 by putting the word *stability* in quotation marks to show she is using the term ironically. This eliminates answer choices A and B. Earthquakes aren't mentioned in the passage, which eliminates answer choice C.

2. **The best answer is J.** The previous paragraph ends with a description of Eui Thi's hopeful excitement at the idea of living in America and going to a new school. This emotion fades when she realizes the difficulties she will face. The word *enthusiasm* is the best replacement for *zeal* to capture her initial excitement.

3. **The best answer is D.** The passage states that Eui Thi "was born in Laos ... but she never felt at home." The other answer choices are not supported by details in the passage.

4. **The best answer is F.** The description of Eui Thi's parents' "late-night whispers" is immediately followed by the military situation in Vietnam. The American army has left the Vietnamese capital, and her parents fear the influence of the communists. This information supports answer choice F.

5. **The best answer is B.** Lines 52–55 list the support given Eui Thi's family by the local community. Only a job and clothes (I and II) are mentioned.

6. **The best answer is J.** Lines 21–25 describe Eui Thi's hopes for life in America. She would not be an outsider, meaning she would feel like she belonged there. She would have room to run. And she would have enough to eat so she wouldn't be hungry all of the time. This covers I, II, and IV.

7. **The best answer is B.** Lines 1–2 tell the reader that Eui Thi's parents are from Vietnam.

8. **The best answer is H.** The passage indicates that Eui Thi's "did her best to dress and act like the other girls" and that she was able to "copy the fashions ... hairstyles, and even, eventually, the slang." But, she "was from a

different world," and would always be an outsider. This best supports answer choice H.

9. **The best answer is C.** Lines 71–74 tell the reader that the dancing at Eui Thi's school dance is completely different from the Tai-Dam dancing she was used to. This supports answer choice C. The author doesn't describe the specific differences, which eliminates the other answer choices.

10. **The best answer is H.** In lines 40–41, Eui Thi's sponsors walk her from her house to her new school. This information best matches answer choice H.

PASSAGE II

11. **The best answer is B.** The first paragraph describes the Mayas shift from nomadic wandering to settled farming. Lines 3–8 imply this was a more stable lifestyle that enabled the development of a great civilization.

12. **The best answer is F.** Lines 24–26 tell the reader directly that the reason for the collapse of the Mayan civilization is still unknown. Therefore, any specific possible cause, such as plagues, would have to be an opinion.

13. **The best answer is C.** Lines 15–21 list weaving, elaborate calendars, and complex writing systems as accomplishments of the Mayas (choices A, B, and D). Lines 3 and 4 tell the reader that the Mayas gave up nomadic wandering before the Classical Period. This information supports answer choice C.

14. **The best answer is J.** Lines 73–75 explain that the Mayas needed elaborate calendars to sustain their agriculture. This suggests that their agricultural cycle led them to develop their calendar system. This best matches answer choice J.

15. **The best answer is D.** According to lines 12–13, the Mayas achieved their most important accomplishments — in other words, the height of their civilization — during the Classical Period, 300–900 A.D.

16. **The best answer is F.** The passage indicates that the "slash-and-burn" technique allowed the Mayas to clear large areas of forest quickly, and that the burned trees and plants could be used for fertilizer. Roman Numerals III and IV are not supported by information in the passage.

17. **The best answer is C.** The passage states that early Mayas "used a slash-and-burn technique ... to clear the forests." The passage goes on to

say in the last paragraph that modern-day Native Americans in Guatemala employ slash-and burn agriculture. This best supports answer choice C.

18. The best answer is F. The last sentence in the previous paragraph states that the "soil is remarkably unfertile for agriculture." The implication is that, since the Mayas rely on agriculture, they would have to do something to prepare the soil for cultivation. Based on the context of the passage, the word *arable* must mean "fit to be cultivated," answer choice F. The other answer choices are not supported by the context of the passage.

19. The best answer is C. *Milpa* is defined in lines 60–64, but the reader is told it is still used by modern Guatamalans in lines 84–86.

20. The best answer is J. The important information here comes just before lines 36–39. The beginning of that paragraph tells the reader that it was the discovery of abandoned Mayan cities that attracted academics' attention. Since anthropologists are academics, this supports answer choice J.

PASSAGE III

21. The best answer is B. Answer choice B captures the descriptive tone of the passage (unlike choice A). The passage focuses on all aspects of Cassidy's career from its beginning to the present day, and never mentions the author's own singing career.

22. The best answer is F. While the passage highlights the author's childhood interests, it does not discuss Shaun Cassidy's childhood. However, his singing career, acting career, and television writing career are described respectively in the first, second, and third parts of the passage. This supports answer choice F.

23. The best answer is D. Answer choices A, B, and C are details describing either the author or a particular aspect of Cassidy's career. Choice D summarizes these specifics. In short, all of the answer choices are mentioned at some point in the passage, but only answer choice D is consistent with the entire passage. Therefore, the best choice is D.

24. The best answer is G. The phrases "youthful admiration" and "shallow" suggest that the author's feelings were appropriate for a child, or that they were "childlike." The

contrasting phrase "but his talent was real" suggests that the author's initial view was inaccurate or "simple." These clues support answer choice G.

25. The best answer is A. Paragraph 4 describes the author's infatuation with Shaun Cassidy. Most of her description involves his physical attractiveness. This supports answer choice A.

26. The best answer is H. The sentence states that most teen pop stars have short careers. This supports answer choice H.

27. The best answer is D. Option I is covered in lines 33–34 (where the author's crush is described as "long-since passed," or chronologically prior). Option II is covered in lines 37–38, while option III is covered in lines 1–3. So these events happen in the order III, I, II, or answer choice D.

28. The best answer is J. Lines 15–16 describe the author's immediate reaction to reading about Cassidy for the first time. Her enthusiasm and adolescent crush support answer choice J. No mention is made of envy (F) or a general interest in entertainment careers (G) — her interest is definitely focused on Cassidy.

29. The best answer is C. Lines 60–62 tell the reader that the first show Cassidy produced never aired on TV. This failure supports answer choice C.

30. The best answer is G. Cassidy's big, blue eyes, toothy grin, and sultry voice are all described in lines 17–19. The green record player (lines 21–22) belongs to the author.

PASSAGE IV

31. The best answer is D. Lines 38–40 tell the reader that our species, *Homo sapiens sapiens*, is not related to *Homo neanderthalensis*. While the last paragraph states that human beings were better able to compete for scarce resources, this does not imply that they actively killed off the Neanderthals (C). Therefore, the passage supports answer choice D.

32. The best answer is G. Lines 65–66 tell the reader that the Neanderthals needed more food to survive in colder weather.

33. The best answer is C. Lines 35–37 state that humans share no genes at all with Neanderthals. This evidence supports the conclusion that Neanderthals are extinct and did not pass on their genetic heritage (28–30) Therefore, C is the best answer choice.

34. The best answer is J. Lines 46–47 state that Neanderthals and Cro-Magnon co-existed. That means they were contemporaries.

35. The best answer is A. Lines 42–44 list data from radiometric dating (B), sediment cores (C), and climate models (D). Comparative femur measurements is the only one NOT mentioned; therefore, A is the best answer.

36. The best answer is G. Lines 10–11 state that the last evidence of Neanderthals is from about 30,000 years ago.

37. The best answer is D. The following lines list the types of innovations that helped humans survive the ice age. The wide range, from clothing to weaponry, supports answer choice D.

38. The best answer is H. Although line 76 mentions nets, the passage doesn't specify the type. All of the other answer choices are specifically mentioned in the passage.

39. The best answer is B. Cro-Magnons are defined as an early example of modern humans. While the last paragraph states that human beings were better able to compete for scarce resources, this does not imply that they actively killed off the Neanderthals. Therefore, the best answer is B.

40. The best answer is F. Lines 6–8 tell the reader that Neanderthals existed (III) approximately 180,000 years before Cro-Magnons (I). Lines 18–19 tell us that Neanderthals probably controlled fire (II) from the beginning. Therefore, the logical order is III, II, I, IV, or answer choice F.

Science Reasoning Test Explanations

PASSAGE I

1. **The correct answer is C.** The results of Experiment 2 are shown in Table 2. While all of the plants grew during each time period, the amount of growth declined after week 6. Therefore, the time frame during which all of the plants began to experience a decline in growth rate was the 6–9 week period, answer choice C.

2. **The correct answer is G.** Based on the passage, an Aphid is not a plant, but an insect. Therefore, answer choice G, since it is not a plant, must be correct.

3. **The correct answer is C.** The results of experiments 1 and 2 are shown in Tables 1 and 2. If you look at the total growth in inches for weeks 6–9, you will see that Yaupon experienced the most growth during weeks 6–9 in both studies.

4. **The correct answer is F.** Based on the results of the experiments, all of the plants experienced the least amount of growth during the time that foreign insects were present in the greenhouse. Table 3 indicates that the mosquito, the grasshopper, and the aphid are all indigenous, or native insects. Therefore, the mantid, a foreign insect, would have the greatest effect on limiting plant growth.

5. **The correct answer is B.** The results of Experiment 1 show that all of the plants experienced more growth when native insects were present. Therefore, based on these results, you can conclude that, under some circumstances, native insects can help to increase growth in some plants, answer choice B.

PASSAGE II

6. **The correct answer is F.** According to Scientist 2, predictive measures can be developed "once enough information has been derived from past hurricanes." This suggests that Scientist 2 believes that present-day predictive tools are not based on enough past data to be accurate, answer choice F.

7. **The correct answer is C.** Based on the passage, Scientist 1 believes that historical data is a valuable predictive tool. Therefore, this article would support Scientist 1's viewpoint. The passage states that, although Scientist 2 believes more historical data is needed, previous records of hurricane patterns are an accurate predictor of hurricanes. Therefore, both viewpoints are supported by this article.

8. **The correct answer is J.** According to the passage, Scientist 1 believes that hurricanes making their way across the ocean cause ground vibrations. These vibrations can be detected by seismographs. It makes sense that, if seismic activity has been recorded, Scientist 1 would agree that a hurricane could be moving across the ocean, answer choice J.

9. **The correct answer is A.** Since both scientists agree that historical data is a useful and accurate predictor of hurricanes, it makes sense that both scientists' viewpoints would be supported by the fact that historical hurricane data has recently been used to predict the path of a hurricane. The other answer choices may support one or the other viewpoint, but not both.

10. **The correct answer is F.** Scientist 2 believes that past hurricane data is an accurate way to predict when and where a hurricane will occur. Therefore, comparing current data with past data would be a good way to test whether Scientist 2's claims are realistic. The other answer choices are not supported by the discussion of Scientist 2.

11. **The correct answer is C.** Since Scientist 2 argues that tidal volume is constantly changing for many different reasons and cannot be used to predict hurricanes, any evidence or discovery to the contrary would weaken that argument. Therefore, the development of a new tidal volume meter that could distinguish the cause of tidal volume increase would weaken Scientist 2's viewpoint, answer choice C.

12. **The correct answer is J.** Scientist 1 believes that an increase in tidal volume signals the arrival of a hurricane. Scientist 2 believes that tidal volume can increase for other reasons, so an increase in tidal volume is not a good predictor of hurricanes. According to Scientist 2, then, one major flaw in Scientist 1's viewpoint is the assumption that tidal volume increases only before or during hurricanes, answer choice J.

PASSAGE III

13. **The correct answer is B.** To answer this question, look at Figure 2. Find 100 feet on the x-axis, which is depth, and follow it up until you reach the line. Follow that point on the line over to the left until you reach the y-axis, which is pressure in atm. The point on the y-axis is 4 ATM, which means that at a depth of 100 feet below the surface, the pressure is 4 ATM, answer choice B.

14. **The correct answer is F.** The passage states the volume of air in your lungs is reduced or expanded proportionate to the pressure. As one moves closer to the surface, the pressure on the air spaces in the body is decreased, meaning that the space inside the lungs increases. Since the volume of a gas, like air, is dependent on the space that contains it, then the volume of air inside the lungs will increase when the space inside the lungs increases, answer choice F.

15. **The correct answer is A.** According to the question, gases have a higher compressibility *because* of their lower densities. The passage states that solids have a higher density and a lower compressibility. If the compressibility of a gas is dependent on its density, then the higher density of a solid causes it to have a lower compressibility, answer choice A.

16. **The correct answer is H.** Compressibility is the ability of pressure to alter the volume of matter. Answer H is the only choice that could be a hazard of scuba diving. The remaining answer choices are all false based on the information given in the passage.

17. **The correct answer is D.** According to the passage, portions of the line where large changes in pressure result in only minimal changes in volume signify low compressibility. Therefore, when the change in pressure is greater than the change in volume, compressibility is low, answer choice D.

PASSAGE IV

18. **The correct answer is J.** The *y*-axis indicates the percent of salamanders that make it to adulthood. To determine which species of salamanders is most likely to make it to adulthood, find the tallest bar on the graph — the one that is closest to 100%. Species G is most likely to make it to adulthood, answer choice J.

19. **The correct answer is B.** According to Figure 1, the light gray bars represent the percent that make it to adulthood when acid rain is present, and the dark gray bars represent the percent that make it to adulthood when acid rain is not present. To answer the question, find the species that has the biggest difference between the height of the light gray bar and the dark gray bar. Species A shows a difference of about 15 percentage points; Species C shows a difference of about 30 percentage points; Species E shows a difference of about 10 percentage points. Species

G shows a difference of about 5 percentage points. Therefore, the species with the greatest difference is Species C, answer choice B.

20. **The correct answer is H.** Common sense tells you that, if a species of salamander burrows into the ground, it should be pretty well protected from rain, acid, or otherwise. Table 1 compares the weather protective behavior with the species' ability to avoid acid rain damage. It is unlikely that burrowing into the ground would provide more protection than seeking cover inside a building, so the relative ability to avoid skin damage will probably not be greater than 1.5. Eliminate answer choice J. Based on the data in Table 1, it makes the most sense that this species would have a relative ability to avoid skin damage of 0.5, answer choice H.

21. **The correct answer is B.** Information in Table 1 shows that at high levels of exposure to acid rain, the relative ability to avoid skin damage is low. As exposure decreases, damage avoidance ability increases. This supports answer choice B.

22. **The correct answer is J.** The first step in answering this question is to look at Figure 1 and notice that Species A has the lowest percentage of survival to adulthood. Next, look at Table 1 and see that Species A does not seek protection, answer choice J.

PASSAGE V

23. **The correct answer is A.** To answer this question, locate 13 miles on the "Distance along mountain range" axis of Figure 1. Then, look at the Mountain Composition Key. According to this information, at 13 miles along the mountain range, the mountain is composed of both magma rock and limestone, answer choice A.

24. **The correct answer is G.** To answer this question, locate 20 meters on the "Mountain height" axis of Figure 1. Then, notice that, wherever the mountain height is 20 meters, the net change in SCLL is somewhere between −10 and −30, answer choice G.

25. **The correct answer is C.** The data in Table 1 shows that for every increase of 5 meters in height, exposure to snow melt erosion is increased by about 8%. This means that at a height of 40–45 meters, the mountain would be exposed about 8% more during the year than it is at a height of 35–40 meters. Based on Table 1, at 35–40 meters, the mountain is exposed about

70% of the year. So, at 40–45 meters, it would be exposed approximately 78% of the year, answer choice C.

26. **The correct answer is J.** Figure 1 shows a direct relationship between net SCLL and mountain height. At lower heights, the net SCLL is lower; at greater heights, the net SCLL is higher. This information supports answer choice J.

27. **The correct answer is A.** Table 1 shows a direct relationship between the mountain's height and the percentage of the year that the mountain is exposed to snow melt erosion. As the height goes up, the exposure time goes up. The graph in answer choice A represents this direct relationship.

PASSAGE VI

28. **The correct answer is G.** The results of Experiment 1 are shown in Table 1. Based on the data in Table 1, as pH levels increase, defecation output also increases, answer choice G.

29. **The correct answer is A.** According to information in the passage, the rats in Experiment 2 were given a dose of bacteria (microbial flora) 1 hour into the experiment. No such dose was administered to the rats in Experiment 1. Normal diets were followed by rats in both experiments, so answer choice B can be eliminated. Answer choices C and D contain information that contradicts information given in the passage, so they should be eliminated.

30. **The correct answer is G.** The results of Experiment 2 are shown in Table 2. While you don't know what the pH levels were at the start of the experiment, you can see that the levels were higher after 5 hours than they were after 1 hour. Therefore, based on the results of Experiment 2, you can say that, if all bacteria are eliminated (as was done at the start of the experiment) and then reintroduced (as was done 1 hour into the experiment), the pH level will increase over time, answer choice G.

31. **The correct answer is D.** According to Table 1, Rat 5 had a pH level of 1.5 at 5 hours. This is the same pH level that Rat 11 had at 1 hour, before the bacteria were reintroduced. If Rat 5 were administered the bacteria after 1 hour, it is likely that its pH level would be the same as Rat 11's pH level at 5 hours. Table 2 shows that this level was 3.0, answer choice D.

32. **The correct answer is H.** Table 1 shows defecation output, as measured by number of pellets. The rat with the highest defecation output was Rat 8, which had a defecation output level of 12.

33. **The correct answer is C.** The passage states that, "the higher the defecation output, the healthier the digestive tract." Table 1 shows that rats with a higher defecation output also had pH levels around 3.0 to 3.5. Table 2 shows that after bacteria were reintroduced to the digestive tract the pH levels went up to around 3.0 to 3.5. These results support the conclusion that bacteria are necessary to the normal functioning of a healthy digestive tract, answer choice C.

PASSAGE VII

34. **The correct answer is G.** The results of Study 3 are shown in Table 3. Look at each answer choice and calculate the differences in Total Time:

    (1) Trial 1, Tennis ball and Golf ball: 0 seconds

    (2) Trial 2, Tennis ball and Golf ball: 6 seconds

    (3) Trial 2, Golf ball and Paper: 1 second

    (4) Trial 3, Tennis ball and Feather: 3 seconds

    The objects which differed most in Total Time were the tennis ball and feather during Trial 2, answer choice G.

35. **The correct answer is A.** Based on the passage, the only difference between Study 2 and Study 3 was the direction that the wind was blowing. This could affect the fall times.

36. **The correct answer is F.** Common sense tells you that dropping an object from a lower height would most likely result in a shorter fall time. Since the objects were dropped from a height of 12 feet, dropping them from a height of 10 feet would most likely produce shorter fall times for all of the objects, answer choice F.

37. **The correct answer is B.** Greater wind resistance is likely to lead to slower fall times. According to data in Table 2, paper consistently took the longest to fall, and therefore, registered the slowest fall times. It is most likely, then, that paper consistently experienced the most wind resistance.

38. **The correct answer is F.** Since, during Study 2, the fan was blowing up at a constant rate, and

the paper took longer than the feather to fall and settle, it makes sense that the paper was affected more by the wind from the fan. Answer choice F best reflects this conclusion.

39. **The correct answer is C.** The passage states that all of the objects were dropped from a height of 12 feet. It would probably take the paper less time to fall from a lower height, so eliminate answer choice J. Since the new height is half of the original height, it would probably take the paper about half the time to fall, so answer choice C makes the most sense.

40. **The correct answer is J.** Since a vacuum contains no air, there would be no air resistance. Therefore, the objects would most likely fall more quickly in a vacuum, answer choice J.

PART III

STRATEGIES AND REVIEW

CHAPTER 3

ACT ENGLISH TEST: STRATEGIES AND CONCEPT REVIEW

The ACT English Test is designed to measure your ability to understand and interpret Standard Written English. Each English test includes five passages, with fifteen questions each, for a total of seventy-five multiple-choice questions. The passages cover a variety of subjects, ranging from historical discussions to personal narratives. The questions are divided into two main categories: Usage/Mechanics questions and Rhetorical Skills questions. Usage/Mechanics questions test your basic English and grammar skills, while Rhetorical Skills questions test your ability to express an idea clearly and concisely. In this chapter, we'll give you useful strategies and techniques, an overview of the rules of grammar and punctuation that will be tested by Usage/Mechanics questions, and a breakdown of the writing skills tested by Rhetorical Skills questions. (You will find all of this information useful on the optional Writing Test also.) At the end of the chapter, you will find some sample practice questions and explanations.

STRATEGIES AND TECHNIQUES

Listen to Your Brain

This technique is known as "subvocalization" to psychologists. It means to sort of "read aloud silently." You can usually trust your impulses when answering many of the questions on the English Test. In other words, if it sounds right to you, it probably is. You will recognize when and how to apply basic rules of grammar, even if you don't recall what the specific rule is. You can tap into the part of your brain that controls speech and hearing as you read. That part of your brain "knows" how English is supposed to sound. Let that part of your brain work for you. Remember, the ACT English Test does NOT require you to state a specific rule, only to apply it correctly.

Brevity Is the Soul of a Good ACT English Score

If all else is equal, you should lean toward the shortest answer.

Department of Redundancy Department

On the ACT English Test, wordiness and redundancy are never rewarded. Throughout the test, you will be asked to make choices that best express an idea. Usually, the fewer words that you use, the better. Be wary of words that have the same meaning being used in the same sentence. For example, it is not necessary to say "the tiny, little girl smiled at me." Both *tiny* and *little* have the same meaning, so using one or the other is sufficient.

Skim First

Most of the ACT English Test questions are presented as underlined portions of the passages. It is helpful to read the passage through once quickly before you answer the questions. If you have a general sense of the structure and overall meaning of the passage, you will be more likely to choose the correct answers on questions that ask about a specific part of the passage.

Take OMIT Seriously

You will sometimes see the answer choice "OMIT the underlined portion." Selecting this option will remove the underlined portion from the sentence or paragraph. "OMIT" is a viable answer choice when it eliminates redundant or irrelevant statements. When "OMIT" is given as an answer choice on the ACT, it is correct more than half of the time.

There Can Be Only One

Since there can only be one correct answer for each question, you can eliminate any two choices that mean the same as each other. If you find that two of the choices are synonyms, eliminate them both.

Pause at Commas

As you read the passages and answer choices, pause an extra-long time at each comma that you come to. If the pause seems out of place and breaks the rhythm of the sentence, it is probably not needed.

Sometimes, It Helps to "Fear Change"

On the ACT English test, the first answer choice for almost every question is NO CHANGE. This answer choice should come up about as often as the others do on your answer sheet. Just because a portion of the passage is underlined doesn't mean that there is something wrong with it.

USAGE AND MECHANICS

This area of the ACT English Test address Punctuation, Grammar and Usage, and Sentence Structure. The forty Usage/Mechanics questions on the actual ACT ask you to apply the rules of Standard Written English to specific sections of the passage, which are usually underlined.

Punctuation Rules

> **Punctuation:** *Standard marks and signs in writing and printing to separate words into sentences, clauses, and phrases in order to clarify meaning.*

A properly punctuated sentence will help the reader understand the organization of the writer's ideas. The ACT English Test includes questions that address both the rules and use of punctuation. You should be able to identify and correct errors involving the following punctuation marks:

1. Commas
2. Apostrophes
3. Colons and Semicolons
4. Parentheses and Dashes
5. Periods, Question Marks, and Exclamation Points

Commas

A comma is used to indicate a separation of ideas or elements within a sentence.

Use a comma with a coordinating conjunction to separate main clauses within a sentence.

A coordinating conjunction connects words, phrases, or clauses that are of equal importance in the sentence.

1. Jenny sings in the choir, *and* she plays the guitar in a rock band.
2. Amanda enjoys her job, *but* she is looking forward to her vacation.
3. His mother doesn't eat meat, *nor* does she eat dairy products.
4. Jordan will be playing football this year, *for* he made the team.
5. Frank earned a promotion, *so* we decided to celebrate.
6. I just completed my workout, *yet* I'm not tired.

Use a comma to separate elements that introduce and modify a sentence.

1. Yesterday, I painted the entire garage.
2. Before deciding on a major at college, Rana discussed her options with her parents.

Use commas before and after a parenthetical expression.

A parenthetical expression is a phrase that is inserted into the writer's train of thought. Parenthetical expressions are most often set off with commas.

1. Stephanie's decision, in my opinion, was not in her best interest.
2. The new park, of course, is a popular tourist destination.

Use a comma to set off an appositive.

An appositive is a noun or phrase that renames the noun that precedes it.

1. My brother, a well-respected scientist, made an important discovery.
2. Mr. Smith, the fifth-grade math teacher, was a favorite among the students.

Use commas to set off interjections.

1. Well, it's about time that you got here.
2. Say, did you pass your history test?

Use commas to separate coordinate adjectives.

If two adjectives modify a noun in the same way, they are called coordinate adjectives. Coordinate adjectives can also be joined with *and* (without a comma).

1. We walked the long, dusty road to the abandoned farm.
2. *OR* — We walked the long and dusty road to the abandoned farm.
3. My cousin ordered a unique, signed copy of her favorite book.
4. *OR* — My cousin ordered a unique and signed copy of her favorite book.

Use commas to set off a nonrestrictive phrase or clause.

A nonrestrictive phrase or clause is one that can be omitted from the sentence without changing the meaning of the sentence. Nonrestrictive clauses care useful because they serve to further describe the nouns that they follow.

1. My sister's dog, a brown-and-white terrier, barks at me whenever I visit.
2. Katie celebrated her birthday, which was in June, with a party and a chocolate cake.

Use a comma to separate items in a list or series.

1. Jill decided to purchase a leash, a collar, and a water dish for her dog.
2. Skippy packed his suitcase, put on his jacket, and left the house.
3. Please bring the following items to camp: pillow, blanket, toothbrush, and other personal hygiene products.

Use commas in dates, addresses, place names, numbers, and quotations.

Commas generally separate a quotation from its source.

1. Mary is leaving for Jamaica on January 7, 2004.
2. The Library of Congress is located at 101 Independence Avenue, Washington, D.C.
3. Annual tuition is currently $42,500.
4. "My sister is a nurse," Becky said proudly.

Do *not* use a comma:

-to separate a subject from a verb.

1. The police officer walked down to the corner.
2. *NOT* — The police officer, walked down to the corner.

-to separate an adjective from the word it modifies.

1. The pretty girl sat in front of me on the bus.
2. *NOT* — The pretty, girl sat in front of me on the bus.

-before a coordinate conjunction and a phrase (unless it is an independent clause with its own subject and a verb)

1. Jeff likes to relax on his couch and listen to music.
2. *NOT* — Jeff likes to relax on his couch, and listen to music.

-to separate two independent clauses; this is known as a comma splice.

1. I plan to attend a liberal arts college. My parents want me to get a well-rounded education.
2. *NOT* — I plan to attend a liberal arts college, my parents want me to get a well-rounded education.

Apostrophes

An apostrophe is used to form possessives of nouns, to show the omission of letters, and to indicate plurals of letters and numbers.

Add an apostrophe and an s to form the possessive of singular nouns, plural nouns, or indefinite pronouns that do not end in s.

1. My friend's house is at the end of the street.
2. The Women's Society meets every Thursday at the high school.
3. Someone's bicycle is leaning against the building.

Add an apostrophe to form the possessive of plural nouns ending in s.

1. The horses' stalls were filled with straw.
2. I did not enjoy the brothers' rendition of my favorite song.

Add an apostrophe to the last noun to indicate joint possession.

Frank and Ruth's anniversary is in September.

Add an apostrophe to all nouns to indicate individual possession.

Brian's, Jason's, and Michael's computers were all stolen.

Add an apostrophe to indicate contractions.

1. It's raining outside again.
2. We're running against each other in the election.
3. If you're going to the movie with me, we should leave now.
4. My cousin should've taken the bus.
5. Didn't Kevin know that classes had begun?

Add an apostrophe to form the plural of letters and numbers.

1. Did you dot your i's and cross your t's?
2. There are a total of four 7's in my phone number.

Do not use an apostrophe with a possessive pronoun.

1. The car with the flat tire is ours.
2. *NOT* — The car with the flat tire is our's.
3. Yours is the dog that barks all night.
4. *NOT* — Your's is the dog that barks all night.

Colons and Semicolons

A colon is used before a list or after an independent clause that is followed by information that directly modifies or adds to the clause. An independent clause can stand alone as a complete sentence. A semicolon is used to join closely related independent clauses when a coordinate conjunction is not used, with conjunctive adverbs to join main clauses, to separate items in a series that contains commas, and to separate coordinate clauses when they are joined by transitional words or phrases.

Use a colon before a list.

We are required to bring the following items to camp: a sleeping bag, a pillow, an alarm clock, clothes, and personal-care items.

Use a colon after an independent clause that is followed by information that directly modifies or adds to the clause.

1. Jennifer encountered a problem that she had not anticipated: a broken Internet link.
2. My sister suggested a great location: the park down the street from our house.

Colons may also precede direct quotations and should be used in business salutations and titles.

1. Captain John Paul Jones said: "I have not yet begun to fight."
2. Dear Mr. Smith:
3. *Blaze: A Story of Courage*

Use a semicolon to join closely related independent clauses when a coordinate conjunction is not used.

1. Jane starts a new job today; she is very excited.
2. I don't understand the directions; my teacher must explain them to me.

Use a semicolon with conjunctive adverbs to join independent clauses.

1. Skippy is interested in taking the class; however, it does not fit in his schedule.
2. My brother is very tall; in fact, he is the tallest person in our family.

Use a semicolon to separate items that contain commas and are arranged in series.

1. The art museum contained some beautiful, classically designed furniture; bronze, plaster, and marble statues; and colorful, abstract modern art pieces.
2. My first meal at college consisted of cold, dry toast; runny, undercooked eggs; and very strong, acidic coffee.

Use a semicolon to separate coordinate clauses when they are joined by transitional words or phrases.

When a sentence contains more than one clause, each of which is considered to be equally as important as the other, the clauses are called "coordinate clauses." They are typically joined by a coordinating conjunction, such as *and* or *but*. When the coordinating conjunction is not used, a semicolon should be.

1. My sister and I enjoyed the play; afterward, we stopped for an ice cream cone.
2. *OR* — My sister and I enjoyed the play, and afterward, we stopped for an ice cream cone.
3. Betty often misplaces her keys; perhaps she should get a key locator.
4. *OR* — Betty often misplaces her key, so perhaps she should get a key locator.

Parentheses and Dashes

Parentheses are used to enclose supplemental information that is not essential to the meaning of the sentence. Dashes are used to place special emphasis on a certain word or phrase within a sentence.

Use parentheses to enclose explanatory or secondary supporting details.

1. In addition to serving as Class Treasurer (during her Junior year), she was also a National Merit Scholar.
2. Alan visited the Football Hall of Fame (on a guided tour) during his summer vacation.

Use dashes in place of parentheses to place special emphasis on certain words or phrases.

1. Dr. Evans — a noted scientist and educator — spoke at our commencement ceremony.
2. The Homecoming float — cobbled together with wire and nails — teetered dangerously down the street.

Periods, Question Marks, and Exclamation Points

Periods, question marks, and exclamation points are considered "end punctuation" and should be used at the end of a sentence.

Use a period to end most sentences.

Scott enrolled in classes at the university.

Use a question mark to end a direct question.

Do you think it will rain today?

Use an exclamation point to end an emphatic statement.

Please don't leave your vehicle unattended!

Grammar Rules

> **Grammar:** *The study and application of combining words to form sentences.*

A well-put-together sentence will contain a subject and a verb and will express a complete thought. The ACT English Test includes questions that will test your ability to identify and correct poorly written sentences. You should have a firm grasp of the following concepts:

1. Subject/Verb Agreement
2. Nouns and Pronouns
3. Verbs and Verb Forms

Subject/Verb Agreement

A sentence is composed of two basic parts: the subject and the verb. The subject is who or what the sentence is about. The verb tells you either what the subject is doing or what is being done to the subject. The subject and verb must agree; that is, they must share the same *person, number, voice,* and *tense.*

Person

A verb must be in the same person as the subject.

1. First Person: *I am* eating lunch.

2. Second Person: *You are* eating lunch.
3. Third Person: *She is* eating lunch.

Number

A singular subject requires a singular verb.

1. The *earth is* round.
2. *One* of the boys *has* a dog.
3. *Everyone thinks* that I will win.

A plural subject requires a plural verb.

1. The *girls are* waiting for the bus.
2. *Amy and Jill enjoy* suspense novels.

Voice

Active voice means that the subject is acting. In the following sentence, *dog* is the subject.

1. The *dog licked* my brother.

   The ACT English Test is more likely to reward answer choices that are in the active voice. The graders on the Writing Test are also more likely to award points to essays that are in the active voice.

Passive voice means that the subject is being acted upon. In the following sentence, *my brother* is the subject.

2. *My brother was licked* by the dog.

Tense

Verb tense provides you with information about when the action took place. Actions take place in the present, in the past, or in the future. The ACT English Test will not require you to recall the names of the tenses, but it will require you to recognize correct and incorrect uses of verb tense. While there are many classifications of verb tense, for the purpose of preparing for the ACT, you should remember the following tenses:

1. Present Tense — The action is taking place now: *Jenny works* at the mall after school.
2. Present Perfect Tense — The action is occurring over time: *Jenny has worked* at the mall for the last two years.
3. Past Tense — The action happened in the past: *Jenny worked* at the mall last year.
4. Past Perfect Tense — The action took place before another specified action: *Jenny had worked* at the mall before taking a job at the theater.
5. Future Tense — The action will happen in the future: *Jenny will work* at the mall this year.
6. Future Perfect Tense — The action will continue to happen until or after a certain point: *Jenny will have worked* at the mall for two years as of next week.

Nouns and Pronouns

The English language contains two forms of nouns: *proper nouns*, which name a specific person, place, or object, and *common nouns*, which name a nonspecific person, place, or object. Proper nouns begin with an uppercase letter, and common nouns do not. *Pronouns* take the place of either a proper or a common noun. Generally, a pronoun begins with an uppercase letter only if the pronoun begins a sentence. The one notable exception is the personal pronoun *I*, which is always capitalized. A pronoun should be placed so that it clearly refers to a specific noun. One of the errors that the ACT commonly tests is a pronoun with an unclear antecedent. You should be able to determine and correctly apply pronoun case, as follows:

Nominative Case (renames the subject)

I, you, he, she, it, they, we

> *Mandy* recently graduated from college; *she* now has a degree in Nursing.

Possessive Case (shows possession)

my, mine, our, ours, your, yours, his, hers, its, their, theirs

> This is *my* plane ticket.

Objective Case (acts as direct or indirect object or object of a preposition)

me, us, you, him, her, it, them

> The monkey made faces at *him* through the bars of the cage.

In addition, the ACT requires that you distinguish between *personal*, *relative*, and *indefinite* pronouns.

Personal Pronouns

Personal pronouns are used to identify a specific person or thing. The ACT English test includes questions that assess the correct use of personal pronouns.

Use the nominative case of a personal pronoun with a compound subject.

If the subject consists of one or more nouns, it is a compound subject.

1. Jason and *I* worked together on the project.
2. *She* and Pamela have been friends for a long time.

Use the nominative case of a personal pronoun with the verb form to be.

1. The person running for class president *was she*.
2. It *is we* who must stay after school today.

Use the nominative case for pronouns that are the subject of an incomplete clause.

Completing the clause will lead you to the correct pronoun case.

1. No one in the classroom was as surprised as *I*. (was)
2. He worked longer today than *she*. (worked)

Use a possessive pronoun before a gerund.

A gerund is a verb ending in *–ing* that functions as a noun.

1. *Her* singing has often been admired.
2. The class was shocked by *his* studying for the exam.

Use the objective case when the pronoun is the object of a verb.

1. A large dog chased *me* down the road.
2. The teacher gave *him* and *her* a passing grade.

Use the objective case when the pronoun is the object of a preposition.

A preposition is a word like *from* or *before* that establishes a relationship between an object and some other part of the sentence, often expressing a location in place or time.

1. Matt received the greatest support from *you* and *me*.
2. The paper fluttered to the ground before *him*.

Relative Pronouns

Relative pronouns are used to identify people, places, and objects in general. The relative pronouns *who*, *whom*, and *whose* refer to people. The relative pronouns *which*, *what*, and *that* refer to places and objects.

Indefinite Pronouns

Indefinite pronouns are used to represent an indefinite number of persons, places, or things. Following are some examples of indefinite pronouns:

1. *Everyone* gather around the campfire!
2. There will be a prize for *each* of the children.
3. *One* of my sisters always volunteers to drive me to school.

Be sure to maintain consistency in pronoun person and number.

It is not grammatically correct to use the plural pronoun *their* to represent neutral gender. This is an example of a major difference between standard written English and the English that we ordinarily use when speaking.

1. *A small child* should always be with *his or her* parent or guardian.
2. *NOT — A small child* should always be with *their* parent or guardian.
3. The anxious *students* waited for *their* grades to be posted.

Verbs and Verb Forms

A *verb* describes the action that is taking place in the sentence. All verbs have four principle forms:

Simple Present: I write.
Simple Past: I wrote.
Present Participle: I am writing.
Past Participle: I have written.

Simple Past vs. Past Participle

The simple past and past participle forms of verbs can sometimes be confusing. Most past tenses are formed by adding *–ed* to the word.

1. Present Tense — We *move* often.
2. Past Tense — We *moved* again this year.

Some verbs have special past tense forms.

1. Present Tense — I *see* my best friend every day.
2. Simple Past Tense — I *saw* my best friend yesterday.
3. *NOT* — I *seed* my best friend yesterday.
4. Present Tense — My little sister *eats* her breakfast quickly.
5. Simple Past Tense — My little sister *ate* her breakfast quickly.
6. *NOT* — My little sister *eated* her breakfast quickly.

Remember that the past participle includes *has*, *had*, or *have*, the so-called *helping verbs*.

1. Past Participle — I *had seen* my best friend the day before.
2. *NOT* — I *had saw* my best friend the day before.
3. Past Participle — My little sister *has eaten* her breakfast quickly.
4. *NOT* — My little sister *has ate* her breakfast quickly.

Be sure to maintain consistent verb form throughout a sentence.

1. We *rode* to school on the bus and *started* our first class at 9:00 a.m.
2. *NOT* — We *ride* to school on the bus and *started* our first class at 9:00 a.m.
3. His brother *walks* to school and often *arrives* ahead of us.
4. *NOT* — His brother *walks* to school and often *arrived* ahead of us.

Sentence Structure Rules

> **Sentence Structure:** *The grammatical arrangement of words and phrases in sentences.*

It is important that a sentence be arranged in such a manner that the idea is expressed completely and clearly. The ACT will test your ability to recognize and correct errors involving the following:

1. Run-On Sentences
2. Sentence Fragments
3. Misplaced Modifiers
4. Parallelism

Run-on Sentences

A run-on sentence is a sentence that is composed of more than one main idea and that does not use proper punctuation or connectors. The ACT requires you to recognize run-on sentences, as well as to avoid creating run-on sentences. The following are examples of run-on sentences along with suggested corrections:

1. Run-on Sentence — Jill is an actress she often appears in major network television shows.
2. Correct Sentence — Jill is an actress who often appears in major network television shows.
3. Run-on Sentence — My nephew loves to play football you can find him on the practice field almost every day.
4. Correct Sentence — My nephew loves to play football. You can find him on the practice field almost every day.

Run-on sentences are often created by substituting a comma for a semicolon or a period. This is called a *comma splice,* and it is incorrect. Following are examples of comma splices along with suggested corrections:

1. Comma Splice — Yesterday my mother prepared my favorite dinner, she even baked a cake.
2. Correct Sentence — Yesterday my mother prepared my favorite dinner; she even baked a cake.
3. Comma Splice — History is my favorite subject in school, I always get the highest grade.
4. Correct Sentence — History is my favorite subject in school. I always get the highest grade.

Sentence Fragments

A sentence fragment is a *dependent clause,* which typically functions as part of a complete sentence and cannot stand alone. Sentence fragments are sometimes punctuated as if they were complete sentences. The following are examples of sentence fragments along with suggested corrections:

1. Sentence Fragment — My car is difficult to start in the winter. Because of the cold weather.
2. Correct Sentence — Because of the cold weather, my car is difficult to start in the winter.
3. Sentence Fragment — Michigan State University offers a variety of courses. Such as Psychology, Biology, Physics, and Music.
4. Correct Sentence — Michigan State University offers a variety of courses, such as Psychology, Biology, Physics, and Music.

Misplaced Modifiers

Modifiers are words, phrases, or clauses that provide description in sentences. Typically, a modifier is placed near the word or phrase that it modifies. A misplaced modifier creates confusion because it appears to modify some word or phrase other than the word or phrase it was intended to modify. The following are examples of misplaced modifiers along with suggested corrections:

1. Misplaced Modifier — Josh had trouble deciding which college to attend *at first.*
2. Correct Sentence — *At first,* Josh had trouble deciding which college to attend.
3. Misplaced Modifier — The young girl was walking her dog *in a raincoat.*
4. Correct Sentence — The young girl *in a raincoat* was walking her dog.

Parallel Construction

Parallel construction enables you to show order and clarity in a sentence or a paragraph, by putting grammatical elements that have the same function in the same form. For example, when two adjectives modify the same noun, the adjectives should have similar forms. When providing a list, each element of the list should have the same form. Also, when the first half of a sentence has a certain structure, the second half should maintain that structure. Following are examples of faulty parallel construction along with suggested corrections:

1. Faulty Parallel Construction — Amy enjoyed *running* and *to ride* horses.
2. Correct Sentence — Amy enjoyed *running* and horseback *riding.*

3. Faulty Parallel Construction — Our field trip included *a visit to the art museum*, *talking to a local artist*, and *a workshop on oil-painting techniques*.
4. Correct Sentence — Our field trip included *visiting the art museum*, *talking to a local artist*, and *attending a workshop on oil-painting techniques*.

RHETORICAL SKILLS

This area of the ACT English Test addresses writing strategy, organization, and style. Rhetoric can be defined as "effective and persuasive use of language." The thirty-five Rhetorical Skills questions assess your ability to make choices about the effectiveness and clarity of a word, phrase, sentence, or paragraph. You may also be asked about the English passage as a whole. Most of the Rhetorical Skills questions are referred to by a number in a box. The following is more information on the three main categories of Rhetorical Skills questions:

> **Strategy:** *The choices made and methods used by an author when composing or revising an essay.*

The ACT English Test measures your ability to recognize several areas of writing strategy, including the flow of ideas; the appropriateness and purpose of both the passage and elements of the passage; and the effectiveness of opening, transitional, and closing sentences. Take a look at the following sample Strategy question:

Horseback riding requires less skill than many people think. Granted, not just anyone can hop onto the back of a horse and maneuver the animal around a racetrack or jumping course. But many people can sit comfortably in a saddle for a short period of time while a horse calmly walks along a wooded trail. ☐

1. The writer wishes to add information here that will further support the point made in the preceding sentence. Which of the following sentences will do that best?
   A. Saddles are designed for specific purposes, such as pleasure riding, barrel racing, and roping.
   B. Each year, thousands of people who have never before been on a horse enjoy guided, one-hour trail rides.
   C. Even experienced riders enjoy the peace and tranquility of a ride through the woods after a long day of training.
   D. Former racehorses are often used as trail horses when they retire from the track.

1. To correctly answer this question, you must first determine the point made in the preceding sentence. The main point of the sentence is that many people, even if they are not skilled at horseback riding, can ride at a slow pace for a short period of time. Answer choice B best supports that idea by providing information about the large number of first-time riders who enjoy relatively short trail rides.

> **Organization:** *Developing logical sequences, categorizing elements, ranking items in order, identifying main ideas, making connections, writing introductions and conclusions, and resolving problems within an essay.*

Organization questions on the ACT English Test are designed to test issues related to the organization of ideas within a passage, the most logical order of sentences and paragraphs, and the relevance of statements made within the context of the passage. The following is an example of an Organization question:

[1] Prior to this, my mother had stated that she and my dad would only be staying with me for three days. [2] As adults, we often have mixed feelings about a visit from our parents — while we are happy to see them, we also hope that their stay is for a definite and short period of time. [3] My parents recently planned a trip to my neck of the woods, and I prepared my humble home for their arrival. [4] They showed up on the appointed day and my mother announced that they would stay for a full week.

2. Which of the following sequences of sentences will make this paragraph most logical?
   F. NO CHANGE
   G. 1, 4, 3, 2
   H. 2, 3, 4, 1
   J. 4, 3, 2, 1

2. The best approach to this type of question is to determine which sentence should come first. The first sentence of a paragraph usually introduces the topic of the paragraph. In this case, the sentence that provides us with information about the topic of the paragraph is sentence [2]. Therefore, the first sentence in the logical sequence of this paragraph is sentence [2]. Because the only answer choice that places sentence [2] in the first position is answer choice H, that must be the correct choice. By positioning one sentence at a time you will be able to eliminate answer choices until only the correct one remains.

> **Style:** *The author's presentation of the written word, usually either formal or informal.*

Good writing involves effective word choice as well as clear and unambiguous expression. The ACT English Test requires you to recognize and eliminate redundant material, understand the tone of the passage, and make sure that the ideas are expressed clearly and succinctly. The following Style questions focus on these issues:

While <u>having the appearance</u> to be a simple game,
                          3
checkers is actually quite complicated. Mathematically there are about 500 quintillion possible ways to win

3. **A.** NO CHANGE
   B. appearing
   C. appearing that
   D. appearances show it

the game. Despite this, checkers continues to be mostly

a fun game for those who play it, even at the competitive

level. <u>Checkers was first played in the twelfth century.</u>
₄

Some of the classic moves used in competitions have

names like the Goose Walk, Duffer's Delight, and the

Boomerang.

With names like these, it seems <u>that even a serious game</u>
₅

has its own sense of humor.

4. **F.** NO CHANGE
    G. First played in the twelfth century was checkers.
    H. Checkers was originally from the twelfth century.
    J. OMIT the underlined portion.

5. **A.** NO CHANGE
    B. crucial that a serious game
    C. that such a serious game
    D. in all seriousness, a game

3. By replacing the underlined portion with each answer choice you can see that the best way to express this idea is simply with the word *appearing*, answer choice B. Remember to trust the way that things "sound," and go for the shortest, most simple way to say something.

4. Although the sentence as it is used is grammatically correct, it does not fit the context of the paragraph. In other words, it is irrelevant information and should be omitted; answer choice J is correct.

5. This question asks you to look at the choice and function of the words in the sentence. The tone of the paragraph is informational, yet informal. A word like *crucial* does not fit the context; therefore, answer choice B should be eliminated. Answer choices C and D do not really fit the context of the paragraph either. The sentence as it is written fits best within the style and tone of the passage, so answer choice A is correct.

> **Idiom:** *The common or everyday usage of a word or phrase; does not usually follow any particular grammatical rule.*

Standard Written English includes many idiomatic phrases. The strategy of "Listening to Your Brain" is especially helpful here. The following is a list of idiomatic phrases that may appear on the ACT English test:

1. *sit across from* — you would not *sit across with* someone, for example.
2. *bogged down* — most often used to mean *overwhelmed*.
3. *admit to* — while *admit of* is also correct, it is not commonly used.
4. *on each side* — this phrase has essentially replaced *on either side of*.
5. *single out* — this phrase means to *select from a group*.
6. *big break* — most often used to signify good luck.
7. *depict as* — this phrase has essentially replaced *depict to be*.
8. *eye-catching* — this phrase is often used to mean *attractive*.

9. *sympathize with* — while *sympathize in* is also correct, it is not commonly used.
10. *know the score* — this phrase is used to indicate having practical knowledge about something.

The ACT English Test will not include any "slang" words, primarily because slang often becomes quickly outdated and can be very regionalized, which means that some parts of the country use spoken English in ways that other parts of the country do not.

COMMONLY MISUSED WORDS

There are certain words and phrases in the English language that are often misused and that often show up on the ACT English Test. We've included a list of commonly misused words here, along with definitions and examples of the proper use of the words.

Accept, Except

Accept is a verb that means "to agree to receive something."
Example: Jenny did not **accept** my invitation to dinner.
Except is either a preposition that means "other than, or but," or a verb meaning "to omit or leave out."
Example: The entire family, **except** for my sister Jill, attended the reunion.

Affect, Effect

Affect is usually a verb meaning "to influence."
Example: His opinion will **affect** my decision.
Effect is usually a noun used to "indicate or achieve a result."
Example: His opinion had a great **effect** on my decision.

All ready, Already

All ready means "completely ready" or "everyone is ready."
Example: The students were **all ready** to get on the bus.
Already means "by or before a specified time."
Example: The students were **already** late for the bus.

All right, Alright: There is no such word as **alright.**

Example: It was **all right** with Carla that the dance was cancelled.
NOT: It was **alright** with Carla that the dance was cancelled.

Among, Between

Among is used with more than two items.
Example: The scientist is living **among** a group of native people.

Between is usually used with two items.
Example: The race **between** Amy and Jenny was very close.

Amount, Number

Amount is used to denote a quantity of something that cannot be divided into separate units.
Example: There was a small **amount** of water in the glass.
Number is used when the objects involved are discrete or can be counted.
Example: A large **number** of students participated in the festivities.
Example: The tank contained a large **number** of gallons of oil.

Assure, Ensure, Insure

Assure means "to convince," or "to guarantee" and usually takes a direct object.
Example: I **assure** you that I will not be late.
Ensure means "to make certain."
Example: **Ensure** that the door is locked when you leave.
Insure means "to guard against loss."
Example: Please **insure** this package for $100.

Bring, Take

Bring should be used in situations where something is being moved toward you.
Example: Please **bring** me the book.
Take should be used in situations where something is being moved away from you.
Example: Did you **take** my book with you when you left?

Capital, Capitol

Capital refers to "the official seat of government of a state or nation."
Example: The **capital** of Michigan is Lansing.
Capital can also be used to mean "wealth or money."
Example: He needed to raise investment **capital** to start his company.
Capital, when used as an adjective, means "foremost," or "excellent."
Example: "That is a **capital** idea," Steve said.
Capitol refers to the "building where government meets."
Example: Some members of the legislature have their offices in the **capitol** building downtown.

Compare to, Compare with

Compare to means "assert a likeness."
Example: My grandmother often **compares** me *to* my mother.

Compare with means "analyze for similarities and differences."
Example: The detective **compared** the photograph *with* the drawing.

Complement, Compliment

Complement implies "something that completes or adds to" something else.
Example: The tasty dessert **complemented** my meal.
A **compliment** is "flattery or praise."
Example: Pam appreciated Mike's **compliment** on her high test scores.

Eager, Anxious

Eager implies "an intense desire" and usually has a positive connotation.
Example: Carrie was **eager** to begin her new job.
Anxious indicates "worry or apprehension" and has a negative connotation.
Example: Fred waited **anxiously** for the plane to take off.

Farther, Further

Farther refers to distance.
Example: Matt traveled **farther** than all of the others.
Further indicates "additional degree, time, or quantity."
Example: The airline representative told us to expect **further** delays.

Fewer, Less

Fewer refers to units or individuals.
Example: **Fewer** students went on the class trip this year.
Example: I weigh **fewer** pounds this year than I did last year.
Less refers to mass or bulk.
Example: There is **less** air in my bicycle's front tire than in its rear tire.
Example: I weigh **less** this year than I did last year.

Imply, Infer

Imply means "to suggest." The speaker or author "implies."
Example: His pants and shirt colors **imply** that he is color blind.
Infer means "to deduce," "to guess," or "to conclude." The listener or reader "infers."
Example: He is not color blind, so we can **infer** that he simply has bad taste in clothes.

Its, It's

The possessive form of *it* is **its**.
Example: The dog lost **its** collar.
The contraction of *it is* is **it's**.
Example: **It's** too bad that your dog ran away.

Lay, Lie

Lay means "to put" or "to place," and requires a direct object to complete its meaning.
Example: Please **lay** your scarf on the back of the chair.
Lie means "to recline, rest, or stay," or "to take a position of rest." This verb cannot take a direct object.
Example: Carrie likes to **lie** down when she gets home from school.

Learn, Teach

Learn means to "gain knowledge."
Example: I have always wanted to **learn** how to cook.
Teach means to "impart, or give knowledge."
Example: My uncle agreed to **teach** me to cook.

Lend, Borrow

Lend means to "give or loan something" to someone else.
Example: Will you **lend** me your jacket for the evening?
Borrow means to "obtain or receive something" from someone else.
Example: May I **borrow** your jacket for the evening?

Precede, Proceed

Precede means "to go before."
Example: Katie **preceded** Kahla as an intern at the law office.
Proceed means "to move forward."
Example: Please **proceed** to the testing center in an orderly fashion.

Principal, Principle

Principal is a noun meaning "the head of a school or an organization."
Example: Mr. Smith is the **principal** of our high school.
Principal can also mean "a sum of money."
Example: Only part of the payment will be applied to the **principal** amount of the loan.
Principal can also be used as an adjective to mean "first," or "leading."
Example: Betty's **principal** concern was that Gary would be late.
Principle is a noun meaning "a basic truth or law."
Example: We learned the **principles** of democracy in class today.

Set, Sit

The verb **set** takes an object, while the verb **sit** does not.
Example: Please **set** the glass down on the table.
Example: Please **sit** in the chair next to mine.

Than, Then

Than is a conjunction used in comparisons.
Example: Jill would rather eat fruit **than** eat chocolate.

Then is an adverb denoting time.
Example: First, I will go for a run, **then** I will do my homework.

That, Which

That is used to introduce an essential clause in a sentence. Commas are not required before the word *that*.
Example: This is the book **that** Jenny recommended I read.
Which is best used to introduce a clause containing nonessential and descriptive information. Commas are required before the word *which*.
Example: That book, **which** is old and tattered, is a favorite of mine.

There, Their, They're

There is an adverb specifying location.
Example: My car is parked over **there**.
Their is a possessive pronoun.
Example: **Their** car is parked next to mine.
They're is a contraction of *they are*.
Example: **They're** afraid of getting a ticket if the car is not moved.

To, Too, Two

To is a preposition.
Example: **To** get a good grade in this class, you must take notes.
Too is an adverb, and means *also*.
Example: It is important that you read the textbook, **too**.
Two is a number.
Example: There are only **two** tickets remaining for the game.

Your, You're

Your is a possessive pronoun.
Example: **Your** brother is going to be late for school.
You're is a contraction of *you are*.
Example: **You're** going to be late as well.

PRACTICE QUESTIONS

DIRECTIONS: In the passages that follow, some words and phrases are underlined and numbered. In the answer column, you will find alternatives for the words and phrases that are underlined. Choose the alternative that you think is best and circle it. If you think that the original version is best, choose "NO CHANGE," which will always be either answer choices A or F. You will also find questions about a particular section of the passage or about the entire passage. These questions will be identified by a number or numbers in a box. Read the passage through once before answering the questions. An Answer Key and Detailed Explanations are included at the end of this section.

PASSAGE I

Solutions

Humans can be a remarkably optimistic — and often ingenuous — group. Each new scientific discovery has the ability to inspire hopes (and rumors) that the breakthrough will be the solution to one (or more) of society's woes. One discovery may give rise to expectations of ending cancer or world <u>hunger, while another</u> is
₁
anticipated to be a veritable fountain of youth.

1. Which of the following alternatives to the underlined portion would NOT be acceptable?
   A. hunger. Another
   B. hunger; and another
   C. hunger. Because another
   D. hunger. Meanwhile, another

A classic example is the story <u>from</u> what happened in the
₂
years following the discovery of radioactivity.

2. **F.** NO CHANGE
   G. of
   H. with
   J. to

One hundred years ago, the husband and wife team of Marie and Pierre Curie discovered the power of radioactivity. Over the course of the next several years, other scientists sought to harness this power to benefit society. Soon, the radioactive elements radium and uranium were being used to treat cancer and generate electricity, respectively. People were anxious to see what other remarkable capabilities <u>these</u> radioactive elements might
₃

3. **A.** NO CHANGE
   B. it's
   C. this
   D. that

possess, and they were especially <u>eager</u> to see how the
₄
discovery might benefit them personally. When traditional science failed to meet this immediate desire, shrewd entrepreneurs readily filled the void.

4. **F.** NO CHANGE
   G. apprehensive
   H. foreboding
   J. foolish

GO ON TO THE NEXT PAGE.

During the 1920s, an era of flappers and raccoon coats, several businesses began selling "radium water," claiming that the product had various curative powers. Some of these businesses were eventually revealed as frauds, whereas they falsely claimed their products contained radium. The money wasted by the patrons of these businesses was nothing compared to the suffering experienced by consumers of Radithor a drinkable solution which actually contained radium.

This product which was insidious in its results, was purported to help cure symptoms: of rheumatism, gout, syphilis, anemia, epilepsy, multiple sclerosis, and sexual impotence. One advertisement went as far as to claim that insanity and mental retardation could be cured, stating: "Science to Cure All the Living Dead ... the new plan to close up the insane asylums and wipe out illiteracy."

Over 400,000 bottles of Radithor were produced before the hazardous dangers of the radium water became apparent. One of the biggest fans of Radithor was a millionaire playboy named Eben M. Byers. Purchasing the product by the case, Byers consumed over 1,000 bottles of the solution between 1928 and 1930. Eventually, Byers' teeth began to fall out and which the bones of his jaws began to deteriorate. As Byers becomes increasingly ill, he was finally diagnosed with radiation poisoning. While Byers lay dying in the hospital, even his breath was found to be radioactive. At the time of Byers' death, radiation poisoning was a relatively new phenomenon, primarily seen among makers of radium dial watches who

5. **A.** NO CHANGE
   B. 1920s, when flappers and raccoon coats were both popular,
   C. 1920s (an era of flappers and raccoon coats),
   D. 1920s,

6. **F.** NO CHANGE
   G. frauds,
   H. frauds so
   J. frauds, because

7. **A.** NO CHANGE
   B. Radithor a drinkable solution,
   C. Radithor, a drinkable solution,
   D. Radithor, a drinkable, solution

8. **F.** NO CHANGE
   G. product,
   H. product was
   J. product, which

9. **A.** NO CHANGE
   B. symptoms of rheumatism,
   C. symptoms of; rheumatism
   D. symptoms of rheumatism:

10. **F.** NO CHANGE
    G. perilous
    H. risky
    J. OMIT the underlined portion.

11. **A.** NO CHANGE
    B. However,
    C. Still,
    D. Similarly,

12. **F.** NO CHANGE
    G. that
    H. and
    J. OMIT the underlined portion.

13. **A.** NO CHANGE
    B. is becoming
    C. became
    D. will be coming

GO ON TO THE NEXT PAGE.

was licking his paint brushes to exact a fine tip.
<u>   </u>
14
Nevertheless, Byers' highly publicized death swiftly led

to the laws that regulate the use and sale of radium and
  <u>   </u>
           15

other radioactive elements.

    The scientific discoveries of the past 100 years have led to a quality of life previously unknown among the world's population. Nevertheless, history has also demonstrated that with many solutions come new problems. The lesson is not to stop seeking innovation. Instead, the optimism following a scientific breakthrough must be tempered with an equal measure of skepticism.

PASSAGE II

Where's the "Play" When Children Play Sports?

    According to health experts, over the past thirty years, the childhood obesity rate in the United States has more than tripled for <u>some of them</u> aged six to eleven, and has
      16
doubled for younger children and adolescents. Over nine million children over the age of six are currently considered obese. One of the primary causes of the epidemic is <u>inactivity: but, ironically more</u> young children
          17
participate in organized sports than in the leaner days of decades past.

    This apparent paradox has two possible explanations. The first is that without all the organized sports, today's children would be even more overweight. With families eating more high-fat, less nutritious convenience foods, <u>this makes sense</u>.
18

    Another possible explanation is that organized sports inadvertently discourage children from spontaneous physical activity, or "free play." Thirty years ago, most <u>childrens'</u> first experience with organized games was in
19
school gym classes. By school age, most children had already participated in neighborhood "pick-up" games

14. **F.** NO CHANGE
    G. had licked his
    H. licked their
    J. licks his

15. **A.** NO CHANGE
    B. regulation of
    C. regulatory laws of
    D. legal regulation and laws relating to

16. **F.** NO CHANGE
    G. them
    H. children
    J. OMIT the underlined portion.

17. **A.** NO CHANGE
    B. inactivity but ironically more
    C. inactivity, but ironically more
    D. inactivity; but ironically more,

18. **F.** NO CHANGE
    G. this is most certainly a distinct possibility.
    H. this is a certain possibility.
    J. possibly, this is certain.

19. **A.** NO CHANGE
    B. children's
    C. childrens
    D. children

GO ON TO THE NEXT PAGE.

where the focus was on fun. <u>They have played</u> catch for
hours, ran until they were breathless, and developed
strategies for how to win "kick the can." They groaned
with disappointment when the streetlights came on,
indicating that it was time to run home for dinner. It never
dawned on the children that they were "practicing"
<u>skills. They</u> were just playing.

[1] By the time they were old enough to participate in
organized sports, children had learned the most critical
skills from their peers. [2] They knew how to run, throw,
catch, and hit a ball. [3] They <u>previously</u> learned that
playing fair, being a team player, and displaying good
sportsmanship were critical if they wanted to be invited to
play again. [4] Being allowed to play on a team was a new
privilege for adolescents — not a drudgery they had
"endured" for the last eight years. 23

The professionals who study the phenomenon of obese
children in the United States offer additional support for

the value of "free play." <u>Although</u> many doctors and
psychologists today are concerned that the complex rules
in organized sports may confuse a young child and a
child's bones and muscles may not be ready for what a
sport demands. <u>As</u> a final irony, one of the reasons
families are consuming so much fattening convenience

food is a result of rushing <u>their</u> young children from

one <u>planned, scheduled, and coached sport</u> to another.

20. **F.** NO CHANGE
    G. They're playing
    H. They're going to play
    J. They played

21. Which of the following alternatives to the underlined
    portion would NOT be acceptable?
    A. skills; they
    B. skills they
    C. skills, for they
    D. skills, because they

22. **F.** NO CHANGE
    G. also
    H. instead
    J. conversely

23. The writer wishes to add the following sentence in
    order to emphasize the concept already expressed in
    the paragraph:

    No one was "burned out" in a sport by the time he
    turned ten.

    The new sentence would best amplify and be placed
    before Sentence:
    A. 1
    B. 2
    C. 3
    D. 4

24. **F.** NO CHANGE
    G. However,
    H. In fact,
    J. Alternatively,

25. **A.** NO CHANGE
    B. If
    C. Whether
    D. For

26. **F.** NO CHANGE
    G. they're
    H. there
    J. this

27. **A.** NO CHANGE
    B. practices and/or games of one type of organized
    sport
    C. organized sport
    D. sport (the organized type)

GO ON TO THE NEXT PAGE.

Should parents send their children out to play
28
with the instruction to come home when the streetlights
28
come on? Of course not. Should they refuse to allow their
28
six-year-olds to learn soccer because they aren't old
enough? No. What parents can do is look for children's
sports programs that focus on fun rather than winning.
Programs for young children should be one third
instruction and two thirds free play. Rather than running
from one planned activity to another, parents should
devote part of each weekend to "family play," participating in activities the whole family can
enjoy, such as hiking, swimming, or cross-country skiing.
29
When possible, they should invite a few other families to
join in the fun and play an unorganized game of kickball
at the local park.

28. If the writer were to delete the question and answer at the beginning of the final paragraph, the paragraph would primarily lose:
   F. details about the health implications of childhood obesity.
   G. an explanation of why children become obese.
   H. a tone of nostalgia for times past.
   J. clarification of the risks twenty-first century parents should reasonably take.

29. A. NO CHANGE
   B. enjoy such as hiking swimming or
   C. enjoy; such as hiking, swimming or
   D. enjoy: such as hiking swimming, or

Question 30 asks about the passage as a whole.

30. Suppose the writer had intended to write an essay about children's health worldwide. Would this essay accomplish the writer's goal, and why?
   F. Yes, because it discusses the national epidemic of childhood obesity and encourages parents to sign up their children for organized sports.
   G. Yes, because it discusses the impact of sports on children's health.
   H. No, because it discusses two possible explanations for childhood obesity in the United States only.
   J. No, because it doesn't discuss the impact of convenience foods on obesity.

ANSWERS AND EXPLANATIONS

1. **The best answer is C.** You must be careful not to select answer choices that create incomplete sentences. *Because another is anticipated to be a veritable fountain of youth* is an incomplete sentence, so answer choice C is NOT acceptable and is, therefore, the correct answer.

2. **The best answer is G.** The word *of* is the correct preposition to use in this sentence. The other answer choices do not make sense in the context of the sentence.

3. **The best answer is A.** The plural pronoun *these* clearly refers to both radium and uranium, the elements being discussed. *It's* is the contraction of *it is*, so answer choice B should be eliminated. Both *this* and *that* are singular

pronouns, so answer choices C and D should be eliminated.

4. **The best answer is F.** Based on the context of the passage, people were "anxious" and "optimistic" about the possible uses of radioactive elements. *Eager* implies this optimism. The other answer choices have negative connotations and should be eliminated.

5. **The best answer is D.** The phrase *an era of flappers and raccoon coats* is not relevant to the context of this passage and should be omitted, or removed.

6. **The best answer is J.** The conjunction *because* implies that the rest of the sentence will explain why the businesses were revealed as frauds, which,

in fact, it does. *Whereas* suggests a contradiction, and *so* implies that the sentence will explain what happened as a result of the businesses being revealed as frauds. These answer choices are not supported by the passage and should be eliminated. If you do not use a conjunction at all, the sentence does not make sense.

7. **The best answer is C.** The phrase *a drinkable solution* is a parenthetical expression, which adds useful information to the sentence. Parenthetical expressions should always be set off by commas. The other answer choices make the sentence awkward and confusing.

8. **The best answer is G.** The phrase *insidious in its results* is a parenthetical expression, which adds useful information to the sentence. Parenthetical expressions should be set off by commas. Answer choice F can be eliminated, because it does not include a comma before *which*. The other answer choices make the sentence awkward and confusing.

9. **The best answer is B.** You only need to use commas to separate the items in this sentence. The other answer choices either create sentence fragments or include punctuation that makes the sentence awkward.

10. **The best answer is J.** The words *hazardous*, *perilous*, and *risky* all have similar meanings. They can't all be correct, so those choices should be eliminated. Since *dangerous* implies *hazard*, *peril*, and *risk*, including these words in the sentence would be redundant.

11. **The best answer is A.** The adverb *eventually* correctly implies the passage of time. This fits with the context of the passage. The other answer choices are not supported by the context of the passage.

12. **The best answer is H.** The simple conjunction *and* joins the phrase *teeth began to fall out* with the phrase *the bones of his jaw began to deteriorate*. These are two things that happened. The adjective *which* suggests that one thing caused the other, so eliminate answer choice F. The sentence will not make sense if you omit the underlined portion, so eliminate answer choice J.

13. **The best answer is C.** Since these events took place in the past, the past tense verb *became* is correct. The other answer choices suggest present or future tense, and should be eliminated.

14. **The best answer is H.** There is more than one radium dial watch maker, so you must use the plural pronoun *their*. The other answer choices

contain the singular pronoun *his* and should be eliminated.

15. **The best answer is B.** By definition, laws are used to regulate something. It is not necessary to use any form of the words *law* or *regulate* in the same sentence, because it is redundant.

16. **The best answer is H.** Using the word *children* adds clarity to this sentence. Answer choices F and G should be eliminated because they contain ambiguous pronouns — it is unclear to whom the pronoun *them* refers. Omitting the underlined portion makes the sentence awkward.

17. **The best answer is C.** It is necessary to separate the two main ideas of this sentence with a comma, because the coordinating conjunction *but* is used. Eliminate answer choice B, which does not use a comma before the coordinating conjunction *but*. Use of a colon and a semicolon is not appropriate here, so eliminate answer choices A and D.

18. **The best answer is F.** The easiest way to express the idea in this sentence is with the phrase *this makes sense*. The other answer choices are nonsensical or too wordy, and should be eliminated.

19. **The best answer is B.** Since *children* is a plural noun, it is not correct to add an *s'*. Therefore, answer choice A should be eliminated. In this sentence, the children "possess" the "first experience" — it is theirs. So, you must use the possessive form of children, which is *children's*, answer choice B.

20. **The best answer is J.** You need to maintain consistent verb tense with the sentence. Since the children "ran" and "developed," both past tense, you should use the past-tense verb *played*. By including the word *have* in answer choice F, the tense becomes future perfect, which is not consistent with the rest of the sentence. Eliminate answer choices G and H, which use the present tense and future tense, respectively.

21. **The best answer is B.** It does not make sense that children would practice "skills they were just playing" — you don't "play" skills. The only selection that would NOT be acceptable is answer choice B, so it is correct.

22. **The best answer is G.** The word *also* correctly suggests that the children learned about "playing fair, being a team player, and displaying good sportsmanship" at the same time that they were

learning "critical skills" from their peers. The other answer choices do not fit the context of the sentence, because they are signals of contrast, which is not appropriate here.

23. **The best answer is D.** It is most appropriate to mention a child getting "burned out" before beginning a discussion of how playing sports can be a "drudgery" that children "endured." It is irrelevant if placed elsewhere in the paragraph.

24. **The best answer is H.** This paragraph goes on to provide more information supporting the idea that children should engage in "free play" over organized sports. *However* and *alternatively* suggest a contrast that doesn't exist.

25. **The best answer is A.** The word *as* is used here as a pronoun to imply a fact, thereby giving the statement emphasis. It is not idiomatically correct to say *if* or *for* a final irony, so eliminate answer choices B and D. *Whether* implies that something may or may not happen, which is not supported by the context, so eliminate answer choice C.

26. **The best answer is F.** The plural pronoun *they* correctly refers to the plural noun *families*. *They're* is the conjunction of *they are*, and *there* refers to a location. These words are not appropriate in this sentence, so eliminate answer choices G and H.

27. **The best answer is C.** The best way to express the idea is with the phrase *organized sport*. The other answer choices are too wordy or awkward.

28. **The best answer is J.** The opening sentences serve to clarify what the author suggests parents should and should not do to encourage healthy activity in their children. The other answer choices are not supported by the passage and should be eliminated.

29. **The best answer is A.** Commas are an effective means to set off both the list and the items in the list. The other answer choices are not punctuated correctly. A colon can also be used to set off a list, but the colon should not be followed by connecting words, as it is in answer choice D.

30. **The best answer is H.** The first step in answering this question is to decide if the essay fulfilled the writer's goal. Since the essay is about children in the United States only, it would not fulfill the goal of writing an essay about children's health worldwide. Eliminate answer choices F and G. Now look at the remaining answer choices. The main focus of the essay is the paradox that exists regarding childhood obesity in the United States and children's participation in organized sports. This theme is best reflected in answer choice H.

CHAPTER 4

ACT MATHEMATICS TEST: STRATEGIES AND CONCEPT REVIEW

The ACT Mathematics Test is designed to test your ability to reason mathematically, to understand basic mathematical terminology, and to recall basic mathematical formulas and principles. You should be able to solve problems and apply relevant mathematics concepts in the following areas:

1. Pre-Algebra
2. Elementary Algebra
3. Intermediate Algebra
4. Coordinate Geometry
5. Plane Geometry
6. Trigonometry

Remember these strategies when approaching math questions:

STRATEGIES AND TECHNIQUES

Pictures Are Worth...at Least a Couple of Points

It really helps sometimes to visualize the problem. This strategy should not take a lot of time and can prevent careless errors. Your sketches can be quick and even a little messy. Sometimes they give you a picture, sometimes you have to just make your own.

Think Before Computing

Most of the calculations are fairly simple and actually will not require the use of a calculator. In fact, the ACT test writers are just as likely to be attempting to test your logical reasoning ability or your ability to follow directions as they are to test your ability to punch information into your calculator. If you do use your calculator, be sure that you have a good idea of what your answer should look like ahead of time. If the answer you get from your calculator is not at least in the ballpark that you expected, try again.

Answer the Question That They Ask You

If the problem requires three steps to reach a solution and you only completed two of the steps, it is likely that the answer you arrived at will be one of the choices. However, it will not be the correct choice! Don't quit early — reason your way through the problem so that it makes sense. Keep in mind, though, that these questions have been designed to take an average of 1 minute each to complete. They do not involve intensive calculations.

Check the Choices

Take a quick peek at the choices as you read the problem for the first time. They can provide valuable clues about how to proceed. For example, you may be able to substitute answer choices for variables in a given equation.

Quit When You Are Finished

Don't overcompute. Most of the math questions involve simple calculations. Keep checking the answer choices to see when you have something that might work as an answer.

Test the Answers

Sometimes the quickest way to answer an ACT math question is to try the answer choices that they give you. The questions on the ACT Mathematics Test have five answer choices each, and the numerical choices are always arranged in ascending or descending order. This means that if you are "trying out" answer choices, it makes sense to try the middle value (Choice C or Choice H) first. If the middle value is too small, you can eliminate the other two smaller choices. And, if it is too large, you can eliminate the other two larger choices.

Stand-ins Can Be Stars

You can sometimes simplify your work on a given problem by using actual numbers as "stand-ins" for variables. This strategy works when you have variables in the question and some of the same variables in the answer choices. You can simplify the answer choices by substituting actual numbers for the variables. If you use this strategy, remember that numbers on the ACT can be positive or negative and are sometimes whole numbers and sometimes fractions. You should also be careful not to use 1 or 0 as your stand-ins because they can create "identities," which can lead to more than one seemingly correct answer choice.

Quitters Prosper

The ACT Mathematics Test has sixty questions. There are bound to be a few that you are going to get wrong on any given testing day. The questions are each weighted the same as one another. In other words, you don't get any extra points for answering the harder questions. So, you would be foolish to waste time on a question when you aren't making any progress. Go find some questions that are easier for you and come back to the tougher ones only if you have time.

The Whole Is Equal to Exactly the Sum of Its Parts

When you are looking at ratio problems, note whether the question is giving a part-to-part ratio or a part-to-whole ratio. For example, the ratio of girls to boys in a class is a part-to-part ratio. The ratio of girls to students in a class is a part-to-whole ratio.

Weird Doesn't Equal Hard

Some of the questions on the Mathematics section will involve new operations that you have never seen. They may appear very unfair at first. However, if you take a moment to read the whole question, you'll find that the new "operation" is defined for you. This means that these questions are pretty straightforward substitution questions. Just apply the definition that is given in the question and the actual mathematics part is usually easy.

■■■■ MATH CONCEPT REVIEW

Pre-Algebra

The fourteen Pre-Algebra (seventh- or eighth-grade level) questions make up about 23% of the total number of questions on the ACT Mathematics Test. The questions test basic algebraic concepts such as:

1. Operations Using Whole Numbers, Fractions, and Decimals
2. Square Roots
3. Exponents
4. Scientific Notation
5. Ratios, Proportions, and Percent
6. Linear Equations with One Variable
7. Absolute Value
8. Simple Probability

Operations Using Whole Numbers, Decimals, and Fractions

The ACT Mathematics Test will require you to add, subtract, multiply, and divide whole numbers, fractions, and decimals. When performing these operations, be sure to keep track of negative signs and line up decimal points in order to eliminate careless mistakes.

The following are some simple rules to keep in mind regarding whole numbers, fractions, and decimals:

1. Ordering is the process of arranging numbers from smallest to greatest or from greatest to smallest. The symbol $>$ is used to represent "greater than," and the symbol $<$ is used to represent "less than." To represent "greater than and equal to," use the symbol $\geq$; to represent "less than and equal to," use the symbol $\leq$.
2. The Commutative Property of Multiplication is expressed as $a \times b = b \times a$, or $ab = ba$.
3. The Distributive Property of Multiplication is expressed as $a(b + c) = ab + ac$.
4. The order of operations for whole numbers can be remembered by using the acronym **PEMDAS**:

   A. First, do the operations within the **parentheses**, if any.
   B. Next, do the **exponents**.
   C. Next, do the **multiplication** and **division**, in order from left to right.
   D. Finally, do the **addition** and **subtraction**, in order from left to right.

5. When a number is expressed as the product of two or more numbers, it is in factored form. *Factors* are all of the numbers that will divide evenly into one number.

6. A number is called a *multiple* of another number if it can be expressed as the product of that number and a second number. For example, the multiples of 4 are 4, 8, 12, 16, etc., because $4 \times 1 = 4$, $4 \times 2 = 8$, $4 \times 3 = 12$, $4 \times 4 = 16$, etc.

7. The Greatest Common Factor (GCF) is the largest number that will divide evenly into any two or more numbers. The Least Common Multiple (LCM) is the smallest number into which any two or more numbers will divide evenly. For example, the Greatest Common Factor of 24 and 36 is 12, because 12 is the largest number that will divide evenly into both 24 and 36. The Least Common Multiple of 24 and 36 is 72, because 72 is the smallest number into which both 24 and 36 will divide evenly.

8. Multiplying and dividing both the numerator and the denominator of a fraction by the same nonzero number will result in an equivalent fraction.

9. When multiplying fractions, multiply the numerators to get the numerator of the product, and multiply the denominators to get the denominator of the product. For example, $\frac{3}{5} \times \frac{7}{8} = \frac{21}{40}$.

10. To divide fractions, multiply the first fraction by the reciprocal of the second fraction. For example, $\frac{1}{3} \div \frac{1}{4} = \frac{1}{3} \times \frac{4}{1}$, which equals $\frac{4}{3}$.

11. When adding and subtracting like fractions, add or subtract the numerators and write the sum or difference over the denominator. So, $\frac{1}{8} + \frac{2}{8} = \frac{3}{8}$, and $\frac{4}{7} - \frac{2}{7} = \frac{2}{7}$.

12. When adding or subtracting unlike fractions, first find the Lowest Common Denominator. The Lowest Common Denominator is the smallest number into which all of the denominators will divide evenly. For example, to add $\frac{3}{4}$ and $\frac{5}{6}$, find the smallest number into which both 4 and 6 will divide evenly. That number is 12, so the Lowest Common Denominator is 12. Multiply $\frac{3}{4}$ by $\frac{3}{3}$ to get $\frac{9}{12}$, and multiply $\frac{5}{6}$ by $\frac{2}{2}$ to get $\frac{10}{12}$. Now add the fractions: $\frac{9}{12} + \frac{10}{12} = \frac{19}{12}$, which can be simplified to $1\frac{7}{12}$.

13. *Place value* refers to the value of a digit in a number relative to its position. Starting from the left of the decimal point, the values of the digits are 1's, 10's, 100's, etc. Starting to the right of the decimal point, the values of the digits are 10ths, 100ths, 1000ths, etc.

14. When converting a fraction to a decimal, divide the numerator by the denominator.

Square Roots

A square root is written as $\sqrt{n}$, and is the nonnegative value a that fulfills the expression $a^2 = n$. For example, the square root of 25 would be written as $\sqrt{25}$, which is equivalent to 5^2, or 5×5. A number is considered a perfect square when the square root of that number is a whole number. So, 25 is a perfect square because the square root of 25 is 5.

Exponents

When a whole number is multiplied by itself, the number of times it is multiplied is referred to as the *exponent*. As shown above with square roots, the exponent of 5^2 is 2 and it signifies 5×5. Any number can be raised to any exponential value. For example, $7^6 = 7 \times 7 \times 7 \times 7 \times 7 \times 7 = 117,649$.

Scientific Notation

When numbers are very large or very small, scientific notation is used to shorten them. Scientific notation is expressed by setting a positive number, N, equal to a number less than 10, times 10 raised to an integer. To form the scientific notation of a number, the decimal point is moved until it is placed after the first nonzero digit from the left in the number. For example, 568,000,000 written in scientific notation would be 5.68×10^8, because the decimal point was moved 8 places to the left. Likewise, 0.0000000354 written in scientific notation would be 3.54×10^{-8}, because the decimal point was moved 8 places to the right.

Ratio, Proportion, and Percent

A *ratio* is the relation between two quantities expressed as one divided by the other. For example, if there are 3 blue cars and 5 red cars, the ratio of blue cars to red cars is 3/5, or 3:5. A *proportion* indicates that one ratio is equal to another ratio. For example, if the ratio of blue cars to red cars is 3/5, and there are 8 total cars, you could set up a proportion to calculate the percent of blue cars, as follows:

(1) 3 cars is to 8 cars as x percent is to 100 percent
(2) $3/8 = x/100$; solve for x
(3) $8x = 300$
(4) $x = 37.5\%$

A percent is a fraction whose denominator is 100. The fraction $\dfrac{55}{100}$ is equal to 55%.

Linear Equations with One Variable

In a linear equation with one variable, the variable cannot have an exponent or be in the denominator of a fraction. An example of a linear equation is $2x + 13 = 43$. The ACT Mathematics Test will most likely require you to solve for x in that equation. Do this by isolating x on the left side of the equation, as follows:

(1) $2x + 13 = 43$
(2) $2x = 43 - 13$
(3) $2x = 30$
(4) $x = \dfrac{30}{2}$, or 15.

One common ACT example of a linear equation with one variable is in questions involving speed of travel. The basic formula to remember is Rate $\times$ Time = Distance. The question will give you two of these values and you will have to solve for the remaining value.

Absolute Value

The absolute value of a number is indicated by placing that number inside two vertical lines. For example, the absolute value of 10 is written as follows: |10|. Absolute value can be defined as the numerical value of a real number without regard to its sign. This means that the absolute value of 10, |10|, is the same as the absolute value of -10, $|-10|$, in that they both equal 10. Think of it as the distance from -10 to 0 on the number line, and the distance from 0 to 10 on the number line: Both distances equal 10 units.

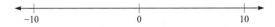

Simple Probability

Probability is used to measure how likely an event is to occur. It is always between 0 and 1; an event that will definitely not occur has a probability of 0, whereas an event that will certainly occur has a probability of 1. To determine probability, divide the number of outcomes that fit the conditions of an event by the total number of outcomes. For example, the chance of getting heads when flipping a coin is 1 out of 2, or $\frac{1}{2}$. There are two possible outcomes (heads or tails) but only one outcome (heads) that fits the conditions of the event. Therefore, the probability of the coin toss resulting in heads is 0.5.

When two events are independent, meaning the outcome of one event does not affect the other, you can calculate the probability of both occurring by multiplying the probabilities of each of the events together. For example, the probability of flipping three heads in a row would be $\frac{1}{2} \times \frac{1}{2} \times \frac{1}{2}$, or $\frac{1}{8}$. The ACT Mathematics Test will assess your ability to calculate simple probabilities in every-day situations.

Elementary Algebra

The ten Elementary Algebra (eighth- or ninth-grade level) questions make up about 17% of the total number of questions on the ACT Mathematics Test. The questions test elementary algebraic concepts such as:

1. Functions
2. Polynomial Operations and Factoring Simple Quadratic Expressions
3. Linear Inequalities with One Variable
4. Properties of Integer Exponents and Square Roots

Functions

A function is a set of ordered pairs where no two of the ordered pairs has the same x-value. In a function, each input (x-value) has exactly one output (y-value). An example of this relationship would be $y = x^2$. Here, y is a function of x, because for any value of x there is exactly one value of y. However, x is not a function of y, because for certain values of y there is more than one value of x. The *domain* of a function refers to the x-values, while the *range* of a function refers to the y-values. If the values in the domain corresponded to more than one value in the range, the relation is not a function. The following is an example of a function question that may appear on the ACT Mathematics Test:

For the function $f(x) = x^2 - 3x$, what is the value of $f(5)$?

Solve this problem by substituting 5 for x wherever x appears in the function:

(1) $f(x) = x^2 - 3x$
(2) $f(5) = (5)^2 - (3)(5)$
(3) $f(5) = 25 - 15$
(4) $f(5) = 10$

Polynomial Operations and Factoring Simple Quadratic Expressions

A polynomial is the sum or difference of expressions like $2x^2$ and $14x$. The most common polynomial takes the form of a simple quadratic expression, such as $2x^2 + 14x + 8$, with the terms in decreasing order. The standard form of a simple quadratic expression is $ax^2 + bx + c$, where a, b, and c are whole numbers. When the terms include both a number and a variable, such as x, the number is called the *coefficient*. For example, in the expression $2x$, 2 is the coefficient of x.

The ACT Mathematics Test will often require you to evaluate, or solve a polynomial, by substituting a given value for the variable, as follows:

For $x = -2$, $2x^2 + 14x + 8 = ?$

(1) $2(-2)^2 + 14(-2) + 8 =$
(2) $2(4) + (-28) + 8 =$
(3) $8 - 28 + 8 = -12$

You will also be required to add, subtract, multiply, and divide polynomials. To add or subtract polynomials, simply combine like terms, as in the following examples:

(1) $(2x^2 + 14x + 8) + (3x^2 + 5x + 32) =$
(2) $5x^2 + 19x + 40$

and

(3) $(8x^2 + 11x + 23) - (7x^2 + 3x + 13) =$
(4) $x^2 + 8x + 10$

To multiply polynomials, use the distributive property to multiply each term of one polynomial by each term of the other polynomial. Following are some examples:

(1) $(3x)(x^2 + 4x - 2) =$
(2) $(3x^3 + 12x^2 - 6x)$

and

(3) $(2x^2 + 5x)(x - 3)$

Remember the **FOIL** Method whenever you see this type of multiplication: multiply the **F**irst terms, then the **O**utside terms, then the **I**nside terms, then the **L**ast terms.

(4) $(2x^2 + 5x)(x - 3) =$
(5) **F**irst terms: $(2x^2)(x) = 2x^3$
(6) **O**utside terms: $(2x^2)(-3) = -6x^2$
(7) **I**nside terms: $(5x)(x) = 5x^2$
(8) **L**ast terms: $(5x)(-3) = -15x$

Now put the terms in decreasing order:

(9) $2x^3 + (-6x^2) + 5x^2 + (-15x) =$
(10) $2x^3 - 1x^2 - 15x$

You may also be asked to find the factors or solution sets of certain simple quadratic expressions. A factor or solution set takes the form $(x \pm \text{some number})$. Simple quadratic expressions will usually have two of these factors or solution sets. Remember that the standard form of a simple quadratic expression is $ax^2 + bx + c$. To factor the equation, find two numbers that when multiplied together will give you c, and when added together will give you b.

The ACT Mathematics Test includes questions similar to the following:
What are the solutions sets for $x^2 + 9x + 20$?

(1) $x^2 + 9x + 20 =$
(2) $(x + \underline{\quad})(x + \underline{\quad})$
(3) 5 and 4 are two numbers that when multiplied together give you 20, and when added together give you 9.
(4) $(x + 5)(x + 4)$ are the two solution sets for $x^2 + 9x + 20$

Linear Inequalities with One Variable

Linear inequalities with one variable are solved in almost the same manner as linear equations with one variable: By isolating the variable on one side of the inequality. Remember, though, that when multiplying one side of an inequality by a negative number, the direction of the sign must be reversed. The ACT Mathematics Test will include questions similar to those that follow:
For which values of x is $3x + 4 > 2x + 1$?

(1) $3x + 4 > 2x + 1$
(2) $3x - 2x > 1 - 4$
(3) $x > -3$

and

For which values of x is $10x - 32 < 6x + 12$?

(4) $6x - 32 < 10x + 12$
(5) $6x - 10x < 32 + 12$
(6) $-4x < 20$

Now, since you have to divide both sides by -4, remember to reverse the inequality sign.

(7) $x > -5$

Properties of Integer Exponents

The ACT Mathematics Test will assess your ability to multiply and divide numbers with exponents. The following are the rules for operations involving exponents:

(1) $x^m \cdot x^n = x^{(m+n)}$
(2) $(x^m)^n = x^{mn}$
(3) $(xy)^m = x^m \cdot y^m$
(4) $\left[\dfrac{x}{y}\right]^m = \dfrac{x^m}{y^m}$
(5) $x^0 = 1$, when $x \neq 0$
(6) $x^{-m} = \dfrac{1}{x^m}$, when $x \neq 0$
(7) $\dfrac{a}{x^{-m}} = ax^m$, when $x \neq 0$

Intermediate Algebra

The nine Intermediate Algebra (ninth- or tenth-grade level) questions make up about 15% of the total number of questions on the ACT Mathematics Test. The questions test intermediate algebraic concepts such as:

1. Quadratic Formula
2. Radical and Rational Expressions

3. Inequalities and Absolute Value Equations
4. Sequences
5. Systems of Equations
6. Logarithms
7. Roots of Polynomials
8. Complex Numbers

Quadratic Formula

The quadratic formula is expressed as $x = \dfrac{-b \pm \sqrt{(b^2 - 4ac)}}{2a}$. This formula finds solutions to quadratic equations of the form $ax^2 + bx + c = 0$. It is the method that can be used in place of factoring for more complex polynomial expressions. The part of the formula $b^2 - 4ac$ is called the *discriminant* and can be used to determine quickly at what kind of answer you should arrive. If the discriminant is 0, then you will have only one solution. If the discriminant is positive, then you will have two real solutions. If the discriminant is negative, then you will have two complex solutions.

Radical and Rational Expressions

A radical is the root of a given quantity, indicated by the radical sign, $\sqrt{\ }$. For example, $\sqrt{9}$ is considered a radical, and 9 is the *radicand*. The following rules apply to radicals:

(1) $\sqrt{a}$ means the "square root of a," $\sqrt[3]{a}$ means the "cube root of a," etc.
(2) $\sqrt{a} \cdot \sqrt{b} = \sqrt{(ab)}$
(3) $\sqrt[n]{a^n} = a$
(4) $\sqrt[n]{\sqrt[m]{a}} = \sqrt[nm]{a}$

A *rational number* is a number that can be expressed as a ratio of two integers. Fractions are rational numbers that represent a part of a whole number. To find the square root of a fraction, simply divide the square root of the numerator by the square root of the denominator. If the denominator is not a perfect square, rationalize the denominator by multiplying both the numerator and the denominator by a number that would make the denominator a perfect square. For example:

(1) $\sqrt{\left[\dfrac{1}{3}\right]} =$

(2) $\dfrac{\sqrt{1 \cdot 12}}{\sqrt{3 \cdot 12}} =$

(3) $\dfrac{\sqrt{12}}{\sqrt{36}} = \dfrac{\sqrt{(4)(3)}}{6} =$

(4) $\dfrac{2\sqrt{3}}{6} = \dfrac{\sqrt{3}}{3}$

Inequalities and Absolute Value Equations

An inequality with an absolute value will be in the form of $|ax + b| > c$, or $|ax + b| < c$. To solve $|ax + b| > c$, first drop the absolute value and create two separate inequalities with the word OR between them. To solve $|ax + b| < c$, first drop the absolute value and create two separate inequalities with the word AND between them. To remember this, think of the inequality sign that is being used in the equation. If it is a "greatOR" than sign, use OR. If it is a "less 'thAND'" sign, use AND. The first inequality will look just like the original inequality without the absolute value. For the second inequality, you must switch the inequality sign and change the sign of c.

To solve $|x+3| > 5$, first drop the absolute value sign and create two separate inequalities with the word OR between them:

(1) $x+3 > 5$ OR $x+3 < -5$. Then solve for x:
(2) $x > 2$ OR $x < -8$.

To solve $|x+3| < 5$, first drop the absolute value sign and create two separate inequalities with the word AND between them:

(3) $x+3 < 5$ AND $x+3 > -5$. Then solve for x:
(4) $x < 2$ AND $x > -8$.

Sequences

An arithmetic sequence is one in which the difference between consecutive terms is the same. For example, 2, 4, 6, 8..., is an arithmetic sequence where 2 is the constant difference. In an arithmetic sequence, the nth term can be found using the formula $a_n = a_1 + (n-1)d$, where d is the common difference. A geometric sequence is one in which the ratio between two terms is constant. For example, $\frac{1}{2}$, 1, 2, 4, 8..., is a geometric sequence where 2 is the constant ratio. With geometric sequences, you can find the nth term using the formula $a_n = a_1(r)^{n-1}$, where r is the constant ratio.

Systems of Equations

The most common type of system of equations tested on the ACT Mathematics Test is two equations and two unknowns. To solve a system of equations, follow the steps below:

$$4x + 5y = 21$$
$$5x + 10y = 30$$

If you multiply the top equation by -2, you will get:

(1) $-8x - 10y = -42$

Now, you can add the two equations together.

(2) $(-8x + 5x) = -3x$
(3) $(-10y + 10y) = 0$
(4) $-42 + 30 = -12$
(5) $-3x = -12$

Notice that the two y-terms cancel each other out. Solving for x, you get $x = 4$. Now, choose one of the original two equations, plug 4 in for x, and solve for y:

(6) $4(4) + 5y = 21$
(7) $16 + 5y = 21$
(8) $5y = 5$
(9) $y = 1$

Logarithms

Logarithms are used to indicate exponents of certain numbers called bases, where $\log_a b = c$, if $a^c = b$. For example, $\log_2 16 = 4$, which means the log to the base 2 of 16 is 4, because $2^4 = 16$.

The following is the kind of logarithm problem you are likely to see on the ACT Mathematics Test:

Which of the following is the value of x that satisfies $\log_x 9 = 2$?

(1) $\log_x 9 = 2$ means the log to the base x of $9 = 2$.
(2) So, x^2 must equal 9, and x must equal 3.

Roots of Polynomials

When given a quadratic equation, $ax^2 + bx + c = 0$, you may be asked to find the roots of the equation. This means you need to find what value(s) of x make the equation true. You may either choose to factor the quadratic equation or you may choose to use the quadratic formula. For example, find the roots of $x^2 + 6x + 8 = 0$.

(1) $x^2 + 6x + 8 = 0$
(2) $(x + 4)(x + 2) = 0$; solve for x
(3) $x + 4 = 0$ and $x + 2 = 0$, so $x = -4$ and $x = -2$.

The roots of $x^2 + 6x + 8 = 0$ are $x = -4$ and $x = -2$. Using the quadratic formula will yield the same solution.

Complex Numbers

Complex numbers are written in the form of $a + bi$, where i is an imaginary number equal to the square root of -1. Thus, $i = \sqrt{(-1)}$. It also follows that $i^2 = (i)(i) = (\sqrt{(-1)})(\sqrt{(-1)}) = -1$, $i^3 = (i^2)(i) = (-1)i = -i$, and $i^4 = (i^2)(i^2) = (-1)(-1) = 1$.

Complex numbers can be added, subtracted, multiplied, and divided as shown below:

Add: $(5 + 3i) + (7 + 2i) = 12 + 5i$ Simply combine like terms.
Subtract: $(3 + 6i) - (4 + 3i) = -1 + 3i$ Simply combine like terms.
Multiply: $(2 + 3i)(4 - 2i) =$ Use the **FOIL** Method.

(1) $8 - 4i + 12i - 6i^2 =$
(2) $8 + 12i + 6 = 14 + 12i$ Combine like terms, remembering that $i^2 = -1$.

When dividing, complex numbers, you must first get rid of all imaginary numbers from the denominator. You do this by multiplying the complex number in the denominator by its *conjugate*. The conjugate of $(a + bi)$ is simply $(a - bi)$. So:

Divide: $\dfrac{(5 + 3i)}{(3 + 2i)}$

First, multiply the numerator and denominator by $(3 - 2i)$; this will eliminate the imaginary number from the denominator.

(1) $\dfrac{(5 + 3i)(3 - 2i)}{(3 + 2i)(3 - 2i)}$

(2) $\dfrac{15 - 10i + 9i - 6i^2}{9 - 6i + 6i - 4i^2} =$

(3) $\dfrac{15 - i - 6(-1)}{9 - 4(-1)} = \dfrac{21 - i}{13}$

Coordinate Geometry

The nine Coordinate Geometry (Cartesian Coordinate Plane) questions make up about 15% of the total number of questions on the ACT Mathematics Test. The questions test coordinate geometry concepts such as:

1. Number Line Graphs
2. Graphs of Points, Lines, Polynomials, and Other Curves
3. Equation of a Line
4. Slope
5. Parallel and Perpendicular Lines
6. Distance and Midpoint Formulas

Number Line Graphs

The most basic type of graphing is graphing on a number line. For the most part, you will be asked to graph inequalities. Below are four of the most common types of problems you will be asked to graph on the ACT Mathematics Test:

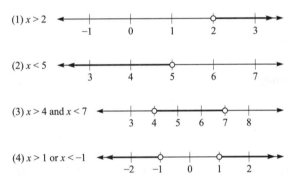

For any of the above graphs, if the inequality sign had been "greater than or equal to," or "less than or equal to," you would use a closed circle instead of an open circle.

Equation of a Line

There are three forms used to write an equation of a line. The standard form of an equation of a line is in the form $Ax + By = C$. This can be transformed into the slope-intercept form of $y = mx + b$, where m is the slope of the line and b is the y-intercept (that is, the point at which the graph of the line crosses the y-axis). The third form is point-slope form, which is $(y - y_1) = m(x - x_1)$, where m is the slope and (x_1, y_1) is a given point on the line. The ACT Mathematics Test will often require you to put the equation of a line into the slope-intercept form to determine either the slope or the y-intercept of a line as follows:

What is the slope of the line given by the equation $3x + 7y - 16 = 0$?

(1) $3x + 7y - 16 = 0$; isolate y on the left side of the equation.
(2) $7y = -3x + 16$
(3) $y = \dfrac{-3}{7}x + \dfrac{16}{7}$

The slope of the line is $-\dfrac{3}{7}$.

Slope

The slope of a line is the grade at which the line increases or decreases. Commonly defined as "rise over run," the slope is a value that is calculated by taking the change in y-coordinates divided by the change in x-coordinates from two given points on a line. The formula for slope is $m = \frac{(y_2 - y_1)}{(x_2 - x_1)}$ where (x_1, y_1) and (x_2, y_2) are the two given points. For example, if you are given (3,2) and (5,6) as two points on a line, the slope would be $m = \frac{6-2}{5-3} = \frac{4}{2} = 2$. A positive slope will mean the graph of the line will go up and to the right. A negative slope will mean the graph of the line will go down and to the right. A horizontal line has slope 0, while a vertical line has an undefined slope.

Parallel and Perpendicular Lines

Two lines are parallel if and only if they have the same slope. Two lines are perpendicular if and only if the slope of one of the lines is the negative reciprocal of the slope of the other line. If the slope of line a is 5, then the slope of line b must be $-\frac{1}{5}$ for the lines to be perpendicular.

Distance and Midpoint Formulas

To find the distance between two points on a coordinate graph, use the formula $\sqrt{([x_2 - x_1]^2 + [y_2 - y_1]^2)}$, where (x_1, y_1) and (x_2, y_2) are the two given points. For instance, the distance between (3,2) and (7,6) is $\sqrt{([7-3]^2 + [6-2]^2)} = \sqrt{(16+16)} = \sqrt{(32)} = \sqrt{(4)(8)} = 2\sqrt{8}$.

Note: This formula is based on the Pythagorean Theorem and if you can't remember it on test day, just draw a right triangle in on your test booklet and proceed from there.

To find the midpoint of a line given two points on the line, use the formula $\left(\frac{x_1 + x_2}{2}, \frac{y_1 + y_2}{2}\right)$. For example, the midpoint between (5,4) and (9,2) is $\left(\frac{5+9}{2}, \frac{4+2}{2}\right) = (7,3)$

Plane Geometry

Plane Geometry questions make up about 23% of the total number of questions on the ACT Mathematics Test. The questions test plane geometry concepts such as:

1. Properties and Relations of Plane Figures

   a. Triangles
   b. Circles
   c. Rectangles
   d. Parallelograms
   e. Trapezoids

2. Angles, Parallel Lines, and Perpendicular Lines
3. Translations, Rotations, and Reflections
4. Simple Three-Dimensional Geometry
5. Perimeter, Area, and Volume

Properties and Relations of Plane Figures

Triangles

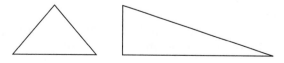

A triangle is a polygon with three sides and three angles. If the measure of all three angles in the triangle are the same and all three sides of the triangle are the same length, then the triangle is an *equilateral* triangle. If the measure of two of the angles and two of the sides of the triangle are the same, then the triangle is an *isosceles* triangle.

The sum of the interior angles in a triangle is always 180°. If the measure of one of the angles in the triangle is 90° (a right angle), then the triangle is a right triangle, as shown below.

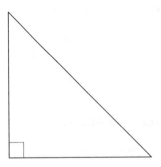

Some right triangles have unique relationships between the angles and the lengths of the sides. These are called *Special Right Triangles*. It may be helpful to remember the following information:

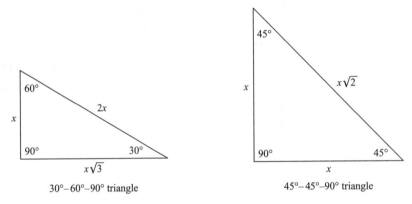

30°–60°–90° triangle   45°–45°–90° triangle

The perimeter of a triangle is the sum of the lengths of the sides. The area of a triangle is $A = \frac{1}{2}$(base)(height). For any right triangle, the Pythagorean Theorem states that $a^2 + b^2 = c^2$, where a and b are legs (sides) and c is the hypotenuse.

Circles

The equation of a circle centered at the point (h, k) is $(x - h)^2 + (y - k)^2 = r^2$, where r is the radius of the circle. The radius of a circle is the distance from the center of the circle to any point on the circle. The diameter of a circle is twice the radius. The formula for the circumference of a circle is $C = 2\pi r$, while the formula for the area of a circle is $A = \pi r^2$.

Rectangles

A rectangle is a polygon with four sides (two sets of congruent, or equal sides) and four right angles. The sum of the angles in a rectangle is always 360°.

The perimeter of a rectangle is $P = 2l + 2w$, where l is the length and w is the width. The area of a rectangle is $A = lw$. The lengths of the diagonals of a rectangle are congruent, or equal. A square is a special rectangle where all four sides are of equal length, as shown here:

Parallelograms

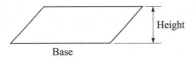

A parallelogram is a polygon with four sides and four angles that are **NOT** right angles. A parallelogram has two sets of congruent sides and two sets of congruent angles.

Again, the sum of the angles of a parallelogram is 360°. The perimeter of a parallelogram is $P = 2l + 2w$. The area of a parallelogram is $A = \text{(base)(height)}$. The height is the distance from top to bottom. A rhombus is a special parallelogram with four congruent sides.

Trapezoids

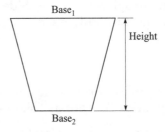

A trapezoid is a polygon with four sides and four angles. The bases of the trapezoids (top and bottom) are never the same length. The sides of the trapezoid can be the same length (isosceles trapezoid), or they may not be. The perimeter of the trapezoid is the sum of the lengths of the sides. The area of a trapezoid is $A = \frac{1}{2}(\text{Base}_1 + \text{Base}_2)(\text{Height})$. Height is the distance between the bases. The diagonals of a trapezoid have a unique feature. When the diagonals of a trapezoid intersect, the ratio of the top of the diagonals to the bottom of the diagonals is the same as the ratio of the top base to the bottom base.

Angles, Parallel Lines, and Perpendicular Lines

Angles can be classified as acute, obtuse, or right. An acute angle is any angle less than 90°. An obtuse angle is any angle that is greater than 90° and less than 180°. A right angle is an angle that is 90°.

When two parallel lines are cut by a perpendicular line, right angles are created, as follows:

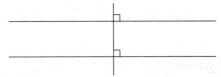

When two parallel lines are cut by a transversal, the angles created have special properties. Each of the parallel lines cut by the transversal has four angles surrounding the intersection that are matched in measure and position with a counterpart at the other parallel line. The vertical (opposite) angles are congruent, and the adjacent angles are supplementary; that is, the sum of the two supplementary angles is 180°.

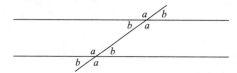

Note: Almost every ACT ever administered has a diagram similar to the one above as part of at least one math question.

Perimeter, Area, and Volume

Perimeter

The formulas for calculating the perimeter of shapes that appear on the ACT Mathematics Test are as follows:

(1) Triangle: Sum of the Sides
(2) Rectangle and Parallelogram: $2l + 2w$
(3) Square: $4s$ (s is Length of Side)
(4) Trapezoid: Sum of the Sides
(5) Circle (Circumference): $2\pi r$

Area

The formulas for calculating the area of shapes that appear on the ACT Mathematics Test are as follows:

(1) Triangle: $\frac{1}{2}$(Base)(Height)
(2) Rectangle and Square: (Length)(Width)
(3) Parallelogram: (Base)(Height)
(4) Trapezoid: $\frac{1}{2}$(Base 1 + Base 2)(Height)
(5) Circle: πr^2

Volume

The formulas for calculating the volume of basic three-dimensional shapes that appear on the ACT Mathematics Test are as follows:

(1) Rectangular Box and Cube: (Length)(Width)(Height)
(2) Sphere: $\frac{4}{3}\pi r^3$
(3) Right Circular Cylinder: $\pi r^2 h$ (h is the height)
(4) Right Circular Cone: $\frac{1}{3}\pi r^2 h$ (h is the height)
(5) Prism: (Area of the Base)(Height)

Trigonometry

The four trigonometry questions make up about 7% of the total number of questions on the ACT Mathematics Test. If you have never had trigonometry, you may still be able to learn enough here to get by on at least a couple of the four questions. (Even if you NEVER learn trigonometry don't worry, four questions is not likely to seriously affect your score.) The questions test basic trigonometric concepts (which only apply to right triangles, as shown below) such as:

SOHCAHTOA

SINE = **O**pposite/**H**ypotenuse (SOH)
COSINE = **A**djacent/**H**ypotenuse (CAH)
TANGENT = **O**pposite/**A**djacent (TOA)

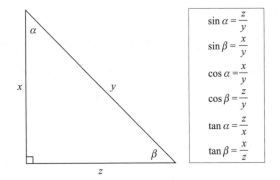

$$\sin \alpha = \frac{z}{y}$$

$$\sin \beta = \frac{x}{y}$$

$$\cos \alpha = \frac{x}{y}$$

$$\cos \beta = \frac{z}{y}$$

$$\tan \alpha = \frac{z}{x}$$

$$\tan \beta = \frac{x}{z}$$

Basic Trigonometric Concepts

The hypotenuse is the side that is opposite the right angle. Sometimes the graph or diagram shown in the question will have the triangle rotated, so make sure that you know where the right angle is and, of course, the hypotenuse, which is directly opposite the right angle.

Note: The following information will be extremely confusing and intimidating for anyone who has never heard of it before. This information is included only as a review for those readers who have had a trigonometry class. The rest of you, just guess on the two or three questions that might include these concepts.

The secant, cosecant, and cotangent can be found as follows:

$$\text{SEC(secant)} = \frac{1}{\text{COS}} \quad \text{CSC(cosecant)} = \frac{1}{\text{SIN}} \quad \text{COT(cotangent)} = \frac{1}{\text{TAN}}$$

Remember the following Pythagorean Identities:

$$\sin^2 \theta + \cos^2 \theta = 1 \quad 1 + \tan^2 \theta = \sec^2 \theta \quad 1 + \cot^2 \theta = \csc^2 \theta$$

Remember the following Trigonometric Identities:

$$\sin(-\theta) = -\sin \theta \quad \cos(-\theta) = \cos \theta \quad \tan(-\theta) = -\tan \theta$$
$$\csc(-\theta) = -\csc \theta \quad \sec(-\theta) = \sec(\theta) \quad \cot(-\theta) = -\cot \theta$$

$$\left.\begin{array}{l} \sin(\alpha + \beta) = \sin \alpha \cos \beta + \sin \beta \cos \alpha \\ \sin(\alpha - \beta) = \sin \alpha \cos \beta - \sin \beta \cos \alpha \\ \cos(\alpha + \beta) = \cos \alpha \cos \beta - \sin \alpha \sin \beta \\ \cos(\alpha - \beta) = \cos \alpha \cos \beta + \sin \alpha \sin \beta \end{array}\right\} \text{Addition and Subtraction Formulas}$$

$$\sin 2\theta = 2\sin\theta\cos\theta$$

$$\cos 2\theta = \cos^2\theta - \sin^2\theta = 1 - 2\sin^2\theta = 2\cos^2\theta - 1 \Big\} \text{Double-angle Formulas}$$

$$\sin^2\theta = \frac{(1 - \cos^2\theta)}{2} \qquad \cos^2\theta = \frac{(1 + \cos^2\theta)}{2} \qquad \text{Half-angle Formulas}$$

To change from degrees to radians, take the number of degrees, divide by 180, and add π to the numerator. For example, $120° = \dfrac{120\pi}{180} = \dfrac{2\pi}{3}$ radians. Conversely, to change from radians to degrees, take the number of radians, multiply by 180, and drop the π.

PRACTICE QUESTIONS

DIRECTIONS: The following are problems that are representative of the kinds of questions you will see on the ACT Mathematics Test. Solve each problem and circle the letter of the correct answer. Do not linger over problems that take too much time; come back to them later. You are permitted to use a calculator, but remember to use it wisely. The figures are NOT necessarily drawn to scale, all geometric figures lie in a plane, and the word *line* indicates a straight line. An Answer Key and Detailed Explanations are included at the end of this section.

1. On a real number line, point X has a coordinate of -2 and point Y has a coordinate of 6. What is the length of line $\overline{XY}$?
   A. -4
   B. 0
   C. 4
   D. 6
   E. 8

DO YOUR FIGURING HERE.

2. Given the right triangle below, how many units long is side AC?

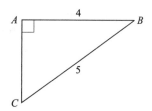

   F. 1
   G. $\sqrt{5}$
   H. 3
   J. $\sqrt{41}$
   K. 9

3. The area of a cylinder can be approximated by multiplying 3.14 by the radius squared. Which of the following expresses this approximation?
   A. $A \approx (3.14)2r$
   B. $A \approx \dfrac{3.14}{r^2}$
   C. $A \approx \sqrt{3.14r}$
   D. $A \approx 3.14r^2$
   E. $A \approx (3.14r)^2$

GO ON TO THE NEXT PAGE.

DO YOUR FIGURING HERE.

4. José has 7 blue shirts and 5 white shirts in one drawer in his dresser. Because he is late for school, he reaches into the drawer and randomly grabs a shirt. What is the probability that José grabs a white shirt?
   F. 1:12
   G. 1:5
   H. 5:12
   J. 5:7
   K. 7:5

5. Ryan bought a pair of shorts on clearance for $15.75. If the shorts were 30% off, what was the original price of the shorts?
   A. $4.73
   B. $6.75
   C. $20.48
   D. $22.50
   E. $52.50

6. Stephanie was s years old 5 years ago. How old will she be 4 years from now?
   F. $s+4$
   G. $5(s+4)$
   H. $(s+5)+4$
   J. $(s+4)-5$
   K. $(s-4)+5$

7. What is the sum of the polynomials $4x^2y + 2x^2y^3$ and $-2xy + x^2y^3$?
   A. $4x^2y + 3x^2y^3 - 2xy$
   B. $4x^2y + 2x^2y^3 - 2x^2y^3$
   C. $2x^2y + 2x^2y^3 + xy$
   D. $2x^2 - 4x^2y^3 - 2xy^3$
   E. $-2x^2y - 2x^2y^3 + x^2y^3$

8. If $t = -7$, what is the value of $|t - 2|$?
   F. -9
   G. -5
   H. 5
   J. 9
   K. 14

9. For all a, $4 - 2(x + 1) = ?$
   A. $2 - 2x$
   B. $4 + x$
   C. $3 - 2x$
   D. $2x - 4$
   E. $4 - x$

10. $(x^4)^{15}$ is equivalent to:
    F. x^{11}
    G. x^{19}
    H. x^{60}
    J. $15x^4$
    K. $60x$

11. What is the sum of the 2 solutions to the equation $x^2 - 2x - 15 = 0$?
    A. -8
    B. -2
    C. 2
    D. 8
    E. 15

GO ON TO THE NEXT PAGE.

12. What is the 209th digit after the decimal point in the repeating decimal $0.\overline{76234}$?
    F. 5
    G. 4
    H. 3
    J. 2
    K. 0

13. How many minutes would it take a car to travel 18 miles at a constant speed of 45 miles per hour?
    A. 20
    B. 24
    C. 28
    D. 34
    E. 40

14. The area of a trapezoid is found by using the equation $\frac{1}{2}h(b_1 + b_2)$, where h is the height and b_1 and b_2 are the lengths of the bases. What is the area of the trapezoid shown below?

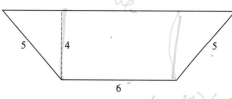

    F. 18
    G. 20
    H. 24
    J. 30
    K. 36

15. For the area of a square to triple, the new side lengths must be the old side lengths multiplied by what number?
    A. $\sqrt{3}$
    B. 2
    C. $2\sqrt{3}$
    D. 3
    E. 9

16. In the triangles below, $\overline{PQ}$ is 4 centimeters, $\overline{QC}$ is 3 centimeters, $\overline{AB}$ is 8 centimeters, and $\overline{BP}$ is 5. How long in centimeters is $\overline{AQ}$?

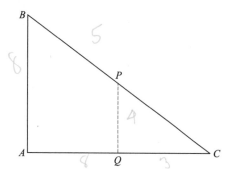

    F. 2
    G. 3
    H. 4
    J. 5
    K. 6

GO ON TO THE NEXT PAGE.

DO YOUR FIGURING HERE.

17. A rectangular classroom is 4 feet wider than it is long and has an area of 480 square feet. What is the length of the classroom in feet?
    A. 12
    B. 16
    C. 20
    D. 24
    E. 28

18. In the standard (x, y) coordinate plant, a line has a slope of $\frac{2}{3}$ and passes through $(-1, 1)$. Which of the following points does this line also pass through?
    F. $(2, 3)$
    G. $(2, 1)$
    H. $(2, 2)$
    J. $(3, 2)$
    K. $(3, 3)$

19. If $\log_x 256 = 4$, then $x = ?$
    A. 4
    B. 16
    C. 64
    D. $\dfrac{64}{\log_x}$
    E. 256^4

20. What is the slope of the line with equation $2x - 3y = 6$?
    F. -3
    G. -2
    H. $\dfrac{2}{3}$
    J. 1
    K. $\dfrac{3}{2}$

21. $\dfrac{3}{5} \cdot \dfrac{4}{6} \cdot \dfrac{5}{7} \cdot \dfrac{6}{8} \cdot \dfrac{7}{9} = ?$
    A. $\dfrac{1}{2}$
    B. $\dfrac{1}{3}$
    C. $\dfrac{1}{6}$
    D. $\dfrac{3}{8}$
    E. $\dfrac{4}{9}$

22. The points, P $(1, 2)$, Q $(5, 2)$, and R $(1, -2)$ in the standard (x, y) coordinate plane are 3 vertices of square $PQRS$. Which of the following points is the fourth vertex, S?
    F. $(5, -2)$
    G. $(1, 5)$
    H. $(5, -1)$
    J. $(2, -5)$
    K. $(5, 2)$

23. The equation $x^2 - 12x + b = 0$ has only 1 solution for x. What is the value of b?
    A. 0
    B. 3
    C. 4
    D. 24
    E. 36

GO ON TO THE NEXT PAGE.

24. If $0° \leq x° \leq 90°$ and $\tan x - 1 = 0$, then $x° = ?$
    F. 0
    G. 15
    H. 30
    J. 45
    K. 60

25. The operation $\otimes$ is defined by the following:
$$a \otimes b = 2 - a + b + a \times b$$

For example, $2 \otimes 3 = 2 - 2 + 3 + 2 \times 3 = 9$.
If $a = -7$ and $b = 2$, then $a \otimes b = ?$
    A. -3
    B. 0
    C. 8
    D. 28
    E. 72

ANSWERS AND EXPLANATIONS

1. **The correct answer is E.** You are given that point X is -2 on the number line and point Y is 6 on the number line. Draw a number line and measure the distance between those 2 points:

The distance between point X and point Y on the number line is 8 units, answer choice E.

2. **The correct answer is H.** To find the length of the sides of a right triangle, use the Pythagorean Theorem: $a^2 + b^2 = c^2$, where c is the hypotenuse, and a and b are the remaining two sides. The hypotenuse is the side opposite the right angle. According to the information given, the hypotenuse is side $\overline{BC}$, which has a length of 5 units. Side $\overline{AB}$ has a length of 4 units, so you must find the length of side $\overline{AC}$. Simply plug the given lengths into the Pythagorean Theorem and solve the equation.

(1) $4^2 + b^2 = 5^2$

(2) $b^2 = 5^2 - 4^2$

(3) $b^2 = 25 - 16$

(4) $b^2 = 9$, so b equals $\sqrt{9}$, or 3, answer choice H.

3. **The correct answer is D.** The first step in answering this question is to square the radius. The radius squared is equivalent to r^2. Eliminate answer choices A and C, which do not square the radius. Since you are told that you must multiply 3.14 by the radius squared, eliminate answer choice B, which divides 3.14 by the radius squared. You can also eliminate answer choice E, which squares the quantity $(3.14r)$; you are only required to square the radius, r. This leaves $3.14r^2$, answer choice D.

4. **The correct answer is H.** *Probability* refers to how likely it is that something will happen. In this case, how likely is it that José will grab a white shirt from the drawer? José has 5 white shirts and 7 blue shirts in the drawer; therefore he has a total of 12 shirts in the drawer. He has 5 chances to grab a white shirt out of the 12 total shirts, because he has 5 white shirts. So, the likelihood of José grabbing a white shirt is 5 out of 12, which can also be expressed as 5:12, answer choice H.

5. **The correct answer is D.** This question asks you to solve for an unknown price. Set the unknown price (the original price) to P. Since the shorts were on sale for 30% off, Ryan paid $100\% - 30\%$, or 70% of the original price, P. Multiply P by 0.70, the decimal equivalent of 70%:

(1) $P \times 0.70 = \$15.75$.

Set up a proportion to solve for P:

(2) $\$15.75$ is to P as 70% is to 100%

(3) $\dfrac{15.75}{P} = \dfrac{70}{100}$; cross-multiply and solve for P.

(4) $70P = 1,575$

(5) $P = \$22.50$, answer choice D.

6. **The correct answer is H.** If Stephanie was s years old 5 years ago, she must $s + 5$ years old today. In 4 years from now, she will be $(s + 5) + 4$ years old, answer choice H.

7. **The correct answer is A.** To find the sum of the polynomials, you must add the like terms together. Like terms have the same variables raised to the same powers. The only like terms given in the problem are $2x^2y^3$ and x^2y^3; add them together to get $3x^2y^3$. Therefore, the correct answer is $4x^2y + 3x^2y^3 - 2xy$, answer choice A.

8. **The correct answer is J.** The absolute value of any number is always a positive value. The first step in solving this problem is to perform the math function inside the absolute value signs. Plug in -7 for t in the equation $t - 2$: $-7 - 2 = -9$. Now take the absolute value: The absolute value of -9 is 9, answer choice J.

9. **The correct answer is A.** This is an order of operations question, so the first step is to multiply the quantity in the parenthesis by 2:

(1) $2(x + 1) = 2x + 2$.

Next, subtract this quantity from 4, combining like terms and keeping track of the negative sign:

(2) $4 - (2x + 2) = (4 - 2) - 2x$

(3) $2 - 2x$, answer choice A.

10. **The correct answer is H.** When exponents are raised to an exponential power, the rules state that you must multiply the exponents by the power to which they are raised. So, $(x^4)^{15} = x^{(4 \times 15)} = x^{60}$, answer choice H.

11. **The correct answer is C.** The first step in solving this problem is to factor the equation $x^2 - 2x - 15 = 0$.

(1) $(x - \underline{\quad})(x + \underline{\quad}) = 0$.

Find 2 numbers that when multiplied together give you -15, and when added together give you -2. The only numbers that satisfy both operations are -5 and 3.

(2) $(x - 5)(x + 3) = 0$.

(3) $x - 5 = 0$; $x = 5$

(4) $x + 3 = 0$; $x = -3$

Since the problem asks for the sum of the 2 solutions, add 5 and -3 to get 2, answer choice C.

12. **The correct answer is H.** Notice that there are 5 digits in the repeating decimal (only count the digits after the decimal point). The fifth digit is the number 4, so every place that is a multiple of 5 will be the number 4. Since 210 is a multiple of 5, the 210th digit will be 4. In the repeating decimal, the number 4 always follows the number 3, so the 209th digit will be 3, answer choice H.

13. **The correct answer is B.** There are 60 minutes in 1 hour. This means that the car is traveling at a constant speed of 45 miles per 60 minutes. Set up a proportion to calculate the number of minutes it would take the car to travel 18 miles:

(1) 18 miles is to 45 miles as x minutes is to 60 minutes.

(2) $\dfrac{18}{45} = \dfrac{x}{60}$; cross-multiply and solve for x.

(3) $45x = 1,080$

(4) $x = 24$ minutes, answer choice B.

14. **The correct answer is K.** You are given the height (4) and the length of b_2 (6). The first step in solving this problem is to calculate the length of b_1. A trapezoid is formed by adding 2 right triangles to the ends of a rectangle. Since you are given that the length of 1 leg of the triangles is 4 and the length of the hypotenuse is 5, you know that the length of the other leg must be 3. Draw a diagram to help visualize the dimensions:

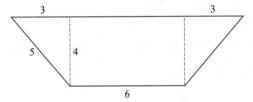

So $b_1 = 6 + 3 + 3$, or 12. Plug the values for h, b_1 and b_2 into the equation and calculate the area:

(1) $1/2(b_1 + b_2)h =$

(2) $1/2(12 + 6)(4) =$

(3) $1/2(18)(4) =$

(4) $(9)(4) = 36$, answer choice K.

15. **The correct answer is A.** The area of a square is equal to side times side, or side^2. Set the length of a side in the original square equal to 1. The area of the original square is 1^2, or 1. The area of the new square will be 3 times 1, or 3. If 3 is equal to side^2, then the length of a side must be equal to $\sqrt{3}$, answer choice A.

16. **The correct answer is G.** The best way to solve this problem is to show the given values on the triangle:

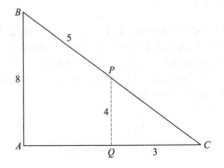

According to information in the problem, both of the triangles are right triangles. Therefore, you can use the Pythagorean Theorem to determine the missing lengths. The first step is to calculate the length of $\overline{PC}$. The Pythagorean Theorem states that $a^2 + b^2 = c^2$, where c is the hypotenuse. Substitute the known values and solve for c:

(1) $\overline{PQ}^2 + \overline{QC}^2 = \overline{PC}^2$

(2) $4^2 + 3^2 = c^2$

(3) $25 = c^2$, so $c = 5$.

Therefore the length of $\overline{PC}$ is 5, and the length of $\overline{BC}$ is $5 + 5$, or 10. Now use the Pythagorean Theorem again to calculate the length of $\overline{AC}$:

(1) $\overline{AB}^2 + \overline{AC}^2 = \overline{BC}^2$

(2) $8^2 + \overline{AC}^2 = 10^2$

(3) $64 + \overline{AC}^2 = 100$

(4) $\overline{AC}^2 = 36$, so $\overline{AC} = 6$

Finally, you can calculate the length of $\overline{AQ}$.

(1) $\overline{AC} = \overline{AQ} + \overline{AC}$

(2) $6 = \overline{AQ} + 3$

(3) $\overline{AQ} = 3$, answer choice G.

17. **The correct answer is C.** The area of a Rectangle = length × width. Since the classroom is 4 feet wider than it is long, set the length to x feet, and the width to $x + 4$ feet. You are given that the area is equal to 480 square feet. Plug these values into the equation and solve for x:

(1) $x(x + 4) = 480$

(2) $x^2 + 4x = 480$

(3) $x^2 + 4x - 480 = 0$

(4) $(x + 24)(x - 20) = 0$

(5) $x + 24 = 0$; $x = -24$

(6) $x - 20 = 0$; $x = 20$

Since the length cannot be a negative number, the length of the classroom must be 20 feet, answer choice C.

18. **The correct answer is F.** The slope of a line is defined as the change in the y-values over the change in the x-values in the standard (x, y) coordinate plane. Slope can be calculated by using the following formula:

$$\frac{(y_1 - y_2)}{(x_1 - x_2)}.$$

Since the slope is $\frac{2}{3}$, for every positive change in 2 on the y-axis, there must be a positive change in 3 on the x-axis. In other words, as you go up 2 in the value of y, you also must go 3 to the right in the value of x. Therefore, the line will pass through the x-coordinate with value $-1 + 3$ or 2, and will pass through the y-coordinate with value $1 + 2$, or 3. That point is $(2, 3)$, answer choice F.

19. **The correct answer is A.** Logarithms are used to indicate exponents of certain numbers called bases. This problem tells you that log to the base x of 4 equals 256. By definition, $\log_a b = c$, if $a^c = b$. So, the question is, when x is raised to the power of 4, you get 256; what is x? By definition, $\log_x 256 = 4$ when $x^4 = 256$. The fourth root of 256 is 4, answer choice A.

20. **The correct answer is H.** The standard form of the equation of a line is $y = mx + b$, where m is the slope. Put the equation in the standard form:

(1) $2x - 3y = 6$

(2) $-3y = -2x + 6$

(3) $y = \frac{2}{3} + 6$

The slope of the line is $\frac{2}{3}$, answer choice H.

21. **The correct answer is C.** The first step in solving this problem is to reduce some of the fractions.

(1) $\frac{4}{6} = \frac{2}{3}$ and $\frac{6}{8} = \frac{3}{4}$

When you multiply fractions, simply multiply all of the numerators, then multiply all of the denominators:

(2) $3 \times 2 \times 5 \times 3 \times 7 = 630$ in the numerator

(3) $5 \times 3 \times 7 \times 4 \times 9 = 3,780$ in the denominator

Now reduce the fraction by dividing both the numerator and the denominator by 630:

(4) $\frac{630}{3,780} \div \frac{630}{630} = \frac{1}{6}$, answer choice C.

22. **The correct answer is F.** Draw a diagram to help visualize this problem:

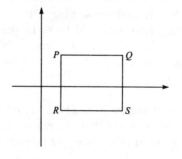

Based on the diagram, point S must have a negative y-coordinate. Eliminate answer choices G and K because they have positive y-coordinates. Since point P is at $(1, 2)$ and point Q is at $(5, 2)$, you know that the distance between the points along the x-axis is 4. A square has 4 sides of equal length, so the distance from point Q to point S must also be 4. Since the y-coordinate of point Q is 2, the y-coordinate of point S must be -2. The only remaining answer choice with a y-coordinate of -2 is answer choice F.

23. **The correct answer is E.** Since the equation $x^2 - 12x + b = 0$ has only 1 solution for x, the equation is a perfect square. This means that $x^2 - 12x + b$ is equivalent to $(x - 6)^2$. Use the *FOIL* method as follows to solve for b:

    (1) $(x - 6)(x - 6) = 0$

    (2) First terms: $(x)(x) = x^2$

    (3) Outside terms: $(-6)(x) = -6x$

    (4) Inside terms: $(-6)(x) = -6x$

    (5) Last terms: $(-6)(-6) = 36$

So, $(x - 6)(x - 6) = x^2 - 12x + 36$; b is 36, answer choice E.

24. **The correct answer is J.** You are given that $\tan x - 1 = 0$, so $\tan x = 1$. By definition, $\tan 45° = 1$, so x must equal 45, answer choice J.

25. **The correct answer is A.** Don't be alarmed by this "new operation." This is strictly a substitution problem. Since the new operation is defined, you can simply plug the values given for a and b into the operation and solve (keep track of the negative signs and remember the order of the operations!):

    (1) The operation is defined as: $a \otimes b = 2 - a + b + a \times b$

    (2) You are given that $a = -7$ and $b = 2$

    (3) So, $a \otimes b = 2 - (-7) + (2) + (-7) \times 2$. Do the multiplication first.

    (4) $a \otimes b = 2 - (-7) + 2 + (-14)$

    (5) $a \otimes b = 2 + 7 + 2 - 14$

    (6) $a \otimes b = 11 - 14$, or -3

CHAPTER 5

ACT READING TEST: STRATEGIES AND CONCEPT REVIEW

The ACT Reading Test has four passages of about 700–900 words each, that are each followed by ten questions, for a total of forty questions. The questions can be answered based on information found in the passage. There is virtually no prior knowledge tested on the Reading Test. You will have thirty-five minutes to complete your work on this section.

The test authors choose subject matter that they think will be representative of the type of material that you will have to read in college. All of the passages on the actual ACT come from material that has been previously published. Therefore, you can rely on the fact that the passages are well edited and will be correct in terms of their grammar, punctuation, and overall structure.

The four passages will be of four different types, as follows:

1. **Prose Fiction** (excerpts from novels and short stories)
2. **Humanities** (passages with topics from arts and literature, often biographies of famous authors, artists, musicians, etc.)
3. **Social Sciences** (History, Sociology, Psychology, and other areas of Social Studies)
4. **Natural Sciences** (Biology, Chemistry, Physics, etc.)

Your ACT score report will include an overall scaled score, which comes from your total number of correct answers out of forty, and, a subscore for Social Studies/Sciences which combines your performance on the Social Science and Natural Science passages. There is also a subscore given for Arts/Literature, which is derived from the twenty questions on Prose Fiction and Humanities.

It turns out that you can't just add up your two subscores to get your Reading score. There is a little statistical mumbo-jumbo behind the scenes at ACT. So, the subscores might not add up just exactly to your Reading score, but they will be very close.

TIMING

If you choose to answer all of the questions on the Reading Test, you will have about eight minutes to work on each of the four passages and still have enough time to mark the answers on your answer sheet. For many students, it makes sense to slow down a bit and focus on two or three of the passages, and simply guess on the remaining questions. Whether you choose to work on all four of the passages or not will depend on where you are on the scoring scale. The truth of the scoring patterns on the ACT exam is that, if you get thirty out of the forty questions correct, you end up with a scaled Reading Score of about a 29. (There is minor variation in scaled scores from one exam to the next.) A 29 on the Reading Test means that your reading score would be well within the top 10% of reading scores nationwide.

In fact, the national average ACT Reading Test score is around a 20 or 21 on the scale. This means that the average ACT taker gets just about exactly one half of the questions correct on the Reading Test. Of course, we recommend that you strive to do your best and we hope that all readers of this book will be well into the above-average range on the ACT. However, it pays to be realistic about what is possible for you on test day. If, after a reasonable amount of practice and study, you are still only able to tackle three of the four passages comfortably within the thirty-five minutes you are given, you are not in very bad shape. If you can get most of those thirty questions correct, and pick up a few correct answers by guessing on the remaining ten, you could still realistically hope to end up with a top 10% score on the Reading Test.

If you are closer to the average ACT Reading test taker, and find that you are only able to really understand two passages and their accompanying questions in the time allowed, you are still likely to get credit for a few more correct responses by guessing on the remaining twenty questions. In fact, since there are four answer choices for each question, you should predict that you would get about 25% correct when guessing at random. This means that guessing on twenty questions should yield about five correct answers. If you manage to get only fifteen correct of the twenty questions that go with the two passages that you work on carefully, you would still have a scaled score of approximately 20 or 21, which is an above-average score.

Therefore, most students should not attempt all four of the passages on the Reading Test. Most students should choose a passage or two that will be "sacrificed" in the interest of time management. There are a few factors to consider when deciding which passage(s) you will sacrifice. For example, you should certainly look at the subject matter. Most students have distinct preferences for one or two of the passage types mentioned previously. Conversely, there is probably at least one type of passage that always seems to account for the bulk of the questions that you miss on practice Reading Tests. Let your practice testing help you to decide whether to attack all four passages or not. If you decide to focus on two or three passages on test day, let your practice help guide you when deciding which passages to sacrifice.

Remember to always fill in every answer "bubble" on your answer sheet since there is no extra penalty for guessing incorrectly as there is on some other tests, like the SAT.

While vocabulary is not tested directly on the ACT, there is certainly an advantage to knowing what the words mean as you try to decipher a passage. We have included a vocabulary list (Appendix 2), which includes words that have appeared on past ACTs and may appear again. Even if none of the words on the list shows up on your exam, you should at least get an idea of the type of word that is likely to be seen and the level of difficulty that you can expect to find on your test.

QUESTION TYPES

1. **Main Idea/Point of View.** These questions may ask about the main idea of the passage or a specific paragraph. They also ask about the author's point of view or perspective, and the intended audience. Questions 1 and 2 in the Practice Section are examples of Main Idea/Point of View questions.

2. **Specific Detail.** These questions can be as basic as asking you about a fact that is readily found by referring to a part of the passage. Often, they are a bit more difficult because they ask you to interpret the information that is referred to. Questions 7, 12, 13, 14, 16, 19, and 20 in the Practice Section are examples of Specific Detail questions.

3. **Conclusion/Inference.** These questions require the test taker to put together information in the passage and use it as evidence for a conclusion. You will have to find language in the passage that will lead you to arrive at the inference that the question demands. (To "infer" is to draw a conclusion based on information in the passage.) Questions 4, 5, 9, 10, and 17 in the Practice Section are examples of Conclusion/Inference questions.

4. **Extrapolation.** These questions ask you to go beyond the passage itself and find answers that are *probably* true based on what you know from the passage. They can be based on the author's tone, or on detailed information in the passage. Questions 3 and 18 in the Practice Section are examples of Extrapolation questions.

5. **Vocabulary.** The ACT does not have a separate vocabulary test. However, there are occasional questions that ask what a specific word means from the passage. The context of the passage should lead you to an educated guess even if you don't know the specific word being asked about. Questions 6, 8, 11, and 15 in the Practice Section are examples of Vocabulary in context questions.

STRATEGIES AND TECHNIQUES

Don't "Study" the Passage

Probably the biggest mistake that you could make is to read these passages as though you are studying for an exam in high school or college. The truth is that the ACT Reading Test (and the Science Reasoning Test also) is in an open-book format. The open-book aspect of the Reading Test means that you should read in a way that helps your brain to work through the information efficiently. You should not read slowly and carefully as though you will have to remember the information for a long period of time. You should read loosely and only dwell on information that you are sure is important because you need it to answer a question.

The test writers are not interested in whether you can store information for a long period of time and then recall it on an exam day or weeks later. The admissions folks at the colleges you are applying to will rely on your Grade Point Average to tell them how well you do that kind of thinking and reading. This test is meant to measure a slightly different skill set. This type of reading should be very goal-oriented. If the information you are looking at does not help to answer a question that the test writers find important, then you should not be lingering over it.

When you read for a high school test, you are probably reading carefully so that you don't miss some detail or subtle nuance that is likely to help you to answer an exam question later. You are probably rereading any part of your material that doesn't make sense immediately. You are probably also making connections to your prior knowledge, visualizing as much as you can and subvocalizing (reading "aloud" silently). If you find a new word, you probably slow down or stop reading and try to figure out what the word means by using context cues. You may also underline, or highlight, important-looking facts, or make margin notes to help you understand and recall information when you review later.

All of these skills are very useful for the type of reading that you must do when preparing for an exam that comes days, or even hours, after your study session. However, they are not very useful in the context of the ACT Reading Test. In fact, if you read these passages in the same way that you read when you are studying for a closed-book exam, you are falling into some of the traps that are set by the psychometricians mentioned earlier in this book.

The test writers know a lot about how the human brain works. They know about something called *negative transference of learning* that occurs when we have skills that are "adaptive" or useful in our environment. But, when the environment changes, and we keep using our old skills, they can be "maladaptive" or harmful. There are many examples of negative transference of learning that range from the comical to the downright tragic. For instance, there have been airplane crashes that resulted from pilots applying habits that they developed in one type of plane to piloting a new type of plane that had the controls arranged a bit differently. We have all experienced something similar (though perhaps not as dangerous) when trying to drive someone else's car and finding that the controls for the turn signals and windshield wipers were in different places.

So, what we are really discussing are your reading habits. You should take stock of your current reading habits and compare them to the strategies explained below, and make changes where you must in order to get a higher ACT score. Don't feel that you have to give up all of the reading skills that you have acquired thus far in your educational career. However, it is a good idea to add to your "tool box" so that you can adapt your approach to the requirements of the reading "environment" in which you find yourself.

The best scores on this section are usually earned by students who have two key skills: paraphrasing and skimming, which will be discussed later.

Read the Question Stems First

Once you have decided to attack a specific passage, you should have a plan for *how* to do it. The single most powerful strategy for Reading is to read the question stems first. The *question* stems are the prompts, or stimuli, that appear before the four answer choices. Don't read the answer choices before you read the passage. Most of the answer choices are wrong and, in fact, are referred to by testing professionals as *distractors*. If you read them before you read the passage, you will be much more likely to get confused. The questions themselves, though, may contain useful information. You may find that the questions repeatedly refer to specific names or terms. You will find other questions that contain references to the line numbers that are printed down the left side of the passage. These can be very useful in focusing your attention and energy on the parts of the passage that are likely to lead to correct answers to questions.

You can do a little experiment with a couple of friends. Tell one friend to pay attention to one aspect of your environment for a specified period of time. For instance, you might tell him or her that the "game" will consist of counting the number of blue cars on the road. Don't tell the other friend exactly what to look for but tell him or her to pay close attention to everything in the surrounding area. Then, after a reasonable time, ask your two friends to tell you how many blue cars were on the road. The odds are overwhelming that only the one who knew what to look for will be correct. The truth is that focus matters and we humans can only focus on a limited number of things at a time.

Read for Main Idea First

The main idea has three components: "What?", "What About It?" and, "Why did the author write this?" If you can answer these three questions, then you understand the main idea.

Too often, students confuse topic with main idea. The topic of a passage only answers the questions of "What is the passage about?" If that is all that you notice, you are missing some very important information.

For example, consider a passage that has a topic that we are all at least somewhat familiar with: rain forests. Let's say that you are faced with one passage that is about the ongoing destruction of the rain forests and includes a call for the reader to get involved and help to stop the destruction in some way. The "What?" = rain forests. The "What About It?" = destruction, and the "Why?" = to get the reader to do something.

Now, say that we keep the same topic, rain forests, but change the other two dimensions so that the "What About It?" = biodiversity (species variation) and the "Why?" = to educate the reader. Then we are reading a very different passage. You need all three dimensions of main idea to really understand all that you need to in order to answer the questions correctly.

So, read a little more slowly at the beginning until you get a grip on the three questions and then you can shift to the next-higher gear and skim the rest of the passage.

Skim

Don't highlight/underline. Don't use context clues. When you come to a word or phrase that is unfamiliar, just blow past it. There is always time to come back, if you need to. But, there is strong chance that you won't need to bother figuring out exactly what that one word or phrase means in order to answer the bulk of the ten questions that follow the passage. If you waste some of your precious time, you'll never get it back. This habit can be hard to break. But, with perseverance and practice, you will start to get comfortable with a less-than-perfect understanding of the passage.

The goal at this stage is to get a general understanding of the structure of the passage so that you can find what you are looking for when you refer back to the passage. You should pay attention to paragraph breaks and try to quickly determine the subtopic for each one. The first sentence is not always the topic sentence. So, don't believe those who say that you can read the first and last sentence of each paragraph and skip the rest of the sentences completely. You are better off skimming over all of the words even if you end up forgetting most of what you read almost immediately.

Remember that you can write in your test booklet. So, when you see a topic word, circle it. If you can sum up a paragraph in a word or two, jot it down in the margin. Remember that the idea at this stage is to not waste time. Keep moving through the material.

Read and Answer the Questions

Start at the beginning of each group of questions. Read the question and make sure that you understand it. Paraphrase it, if you need to. This means to put the question into your own words. If you paraphrase, keep your language simple. Pretend you are "translating" the question to an average eighth grader. If you can make sure that the eighth grader you are imagining can understand the question, then you are ready to answer it.

Refer Back to the Passage

Go back to the part of the passage that will probably contain the answer to your question. It is true that some of the questions on the ACT ask you draw conclusions based on the information that you read. However, even these questions should be answered based on the information in the passage. There will always be some strong hints, or evidence, that will lead you to an answer.

Some of the questions contain references to specific lines of the passage. The trick in those cases is to read a little before and a little after the specific line that is mentioned. At least read the entire sentence that contains the line that is referenced.

Some of the questions don't really tell you where to look for the answer, or they are about the passage as a whole. In those cases, think about what you learned about the passage while you were skimming it. Note the subtopics for the paragraphs, and let them guide you to the part of the passage that contains the information for which you are looking.

One of the important skills rewarded by the ACT is the ability to sift through text and find the word or concept for which you are looking. This skill improves with practice.

Predict an answer

Once you have found the information in the passage that will provide the answer for which you are looking, try to answer the question in your mind. Do this before you look at the answer choices. Remember: three out of every four answer choices are incorrect. Not only are they incorrect, but they were written by experts to confuse you. They are less likely to confuse you if you have a clear idea of an answer before you read the answer choices. If you can predict an answer for the question, then skim the choices presented and look for your answer. You may have to be a little flexible to recognize it. Your answer may be there dressed up in different words. If you can recognize a paraphrase of your predicted answer, mark it. The odds that you will manage to predict one of the "distractor" (incorrect) answer choices are slim. Mark the question if you are unsure. You can always come back to the question later if there is time.

Process of Elimination

Someone once asked Michelangelo how he could sculpt a figure as lifelike as his David. The great artist reportedly responded (certainly with a glint of humor in his eye), "I simply chipped away all of the stone that did not look like David." This is just like the process that most test takers use for all of the questions that they answer. It is reliable but slow. It is useful to you as a back-up strategy for the questions where you either cannot predict an answer or you find that your prediction is not listed as a choice.

The process of elimination is a good tool. It just shouldn't be the only tool in your box. It can be hard to break the habit of almost always applying the process of elimination. You have developed this habit because of the fact that you have been given too much time on most exams that you have taken.

Teachers tend to allow long periods of time for exams for a number of different reasons. The first is that teachers have to allow enough time for even the slower students to have a fair chance to answer questions. Another is that testing time for students is often break time for the instructor. He or she might be able to catch up on paperwork or read a newspaper during the time that students are testing. These factors tend to lead to students who get used to a leisurely pace on exams.

That habit can be a problem in the ACT testing environment, which, as mentioned previously, has time limits that aren't even realistic for most students. The way to overcome this little problem is to form some new habits by practicing with ACT reading passages under realistic conditions.

Don't be afraid to refer back to the passage repeatedly, and don't be reluctant to skip around within the ten-question group that accompanies each of the four passages. In fact, many students report success with a strategy of actually skipping back and forth among passages. This plan won't work for everyone. It probably would just create confusion for most test takers. But, if you feel comfortable with it after trying it on practice tests, then we can't think of any reason not to do it on test day.

STRATEGIES FOR SPECIFIC QUESTION TYPES

Main Idea

Answer according to your understanding of the three components of the main idea that are mentioned previously (What? What About It? and Why?). It is also worth noting that the incorrect choices are usually either too broad or too narrow. You should eliminate the choices that focus on a specific part of the passage and also eliminate the choices that are too general and could describe other passages besides the one that you are working on.

Specific Detail

Refer back to the passage to find the answer to the question. Use line or paragraph references in the questions, if they are given. Recognize that sometimes the answer choices are paraphrased, and don't just choose the answers that contain words that appeared in the passage. Make sure that the choice you select is responsive to the question.

Conclusion/Inference

Although you have to do a bit of thinking for these questions, you should be able to find very strong evidence for your answer. If you find yourself creating a long chain of reasoning and including information from outside the passage when "selling" the answer to yourself, stop and reconsider. The ACT rewards short, strong connections between the evidence in the passage and the answer that is credited.

Extrapolation

This question type asks you about what is probably true based on information in the passage. You need to be sensitive to any clues about the author's tone or attitude and any clues about how the characters in the passage feel. Eliminate any choices that are outside the scope of the passage. As with Inference questions above, the ACT rewards short, strong connections between the passage and the correct answers.

Vocabulary

The ACT only asks a few vocabulary questions and always in the context of a passage. The best way to answer these questions is the simplest way, just read the answer choices back into the sentence mentioned in the question stem and choose the one that changes the meaning of the sentence the least.

PRACTICE QUESTIONS

DIRECTIONS: This practice section includes two passages, each followed by ten questions. Read the passage and choose the best answer to each question. Circle the answer you choose. You should refer to the passages as often as necessary when answering the questions.

Passage I
PROSE FICTION: *Fear of Success*

"You appear to have a fear of success," her doctor said.

"You mean a fear of failure, don't you?"

"No. A fear of *success*."

5 "You don't know what you're talking about!" she exclaimed as she stormed out of the doctor's office. As she passed the receptionist's desk, she wryly declared, "You can cancel all the rest of my appointments with Dr. Mornington. I'm cured."

10 "Are you sure you want to do that? The doctor has a nine-month waiting list. If you change your mind, you'll have to go to the end of the list."

"Don't worry. I won't be changing my mind. Like I said, 'I'm cured.'" She knew the receptionist

15 hadn't missed the sarcasm in her voice.

This exchange had occurred three months ago. She was now beginning to ruefully realize the accuracy of the saying, "the truth hurts."

At first, she had continued to scoff the doctor's

20 interpretation of her life's events as a fear of success. The incidents the doctor focused on had been mere errors in judgment — or corrections of past errors. But then, as she tried to justify her own point of view, she began to see the doctor's perspective.

25 In the third grade, she had been caught copying from Bobby Jacobs' paper. Most kids made the mistake of cheating at some point in their life. But she had copied from Bobby — a boy who struggled to earn C's. Why?

30 In high school, as her academic and athletic success was propelling her toward an Ivy League school, she conspicuously shoplifted some candy in front of the shopkeeper. When confronted, she blatantly lied, even as the evidence was pulled from

35 her pocket and a videotape of the events played and replayed for her. As her best friend paid for the candy and begged for mercy, the store owner shook his head, but let her go.

Her college career was marked with small lapses

40 in judgment, such as the vandalism of a campus bus,

but as her Yale graduation approached, she ardently prepared for an interview with a prominent investment banking firm. "The hours are brutal!" she announced to her roommate, "but if I can survive the

45 first two years, I'll be making well over six figures before I'm twenty-five!" She got the job and moved to the company's Atlanta office. She was well paid for the long hours, but she seldom had the opportunity to meet new friends with whom to spend her

50 hard-earned money, and so, twenty-one months into the job, she quit.

For years, she had been applauding herself for making this wise personal decision. She didn't want to be one of those money-grubbers with no

55 personal life! But what quality of life had she subsequently obtained? She flitted from one career to another, staying in each job just long enough to get out of debt. Each time, she quit to pursue her "true calling."

60 Her parents continued to let her live in the downstairs apartment of the working-class neighborhood home in which she had grown up. When she was working, she paid them rent; when she was unemployed, she didn't. What did they care? The old

65 house was paid for and they weren't likely to spend the money on themselves. They would probably just save it for her modest inheritance. It was her money either way. Besides, her parents had never really understood her. They had recognized her intelligence

70 only when her grade-school teachers had pointed it out. Her dad, a bricklayer by day and a coach by night, had been integral in her athletic success, but intellectually, she had passed him by the time she hit high school. Her mom, a school nurse, was ever

75 the concerned mom but couldn't understand her daughter's caprice.

So, was the doctor right? Was she afraid of success? Was she afraid of being a misfit in the world outside her working-class neighborhood? Or was she

80 afraid of falling in love, marrying, and having a child

GO ON TO THE NEXT PAGE.

like herself? With a heavy sigh, she reached for the phone.

"Hi. I'd like to make an appointment with Dr. Mornington."

85   "Are you a current patient?"

"No."

"The first available appointment is in ten months..."

1. The passage is written from the point of view of:
   A. an unidentifiable narrator.
   B. the doctor of a very disturbed woman.
   C. a mother confused by her daughter's strange decisions.
   D. a working-class man.

2. Which of the following best describes the author's approach to presenting the story of the main character's discovery about herself?
   F. Starting immediately with a statement of the discovery in the character's voice and continuing with scenes that reveal how the discovery came about.
   G. Revealing the character's self-awareness through a blend of reflection and scenes from the character's youth and adulthood.
   H. Describing the physical details of scenes and summarizing their significance in a concluding statement in the character's voice.
   J. Using dialogue in the midst of scenes from the character's youth and adulthood.

3. Each of the events from the main character's youth and early adulthood reveal:
   A. the increasing antagonism between the main character and her doctor.
   B. the judgmental attitude of the main character's parents.
   C. the main character's failure to make wise decisions.
   D. the main character's inability to keep a job.

4. The main character's adamant denial of shoplifting is most likely indicative of:
   F. her conviction of her own innocence.
   G. the demonstration of similar crimes by other members of her family.
   H. her brilliance.
   J. a subconscious wish to be caught.

5. As she is revealed in the shoplifting incident, the main character's best friend can best be characterized as:
   A. jealous.
   B. genuinely concerned.
   C. apathetic and uncaring.
   D. naïve.

6. As it is used in line 41, the word, *ardently* most nearly means:
   F. half-heartedly.
   G. hotly.
   H. enthusiastically.
   J. loyally.

7. The main character's childhood home was:
   A. a working-class neighborhood of an unnamed city.
   B. a wealthy suburb in Connecticut.
   C. Atlanta.
   D. not mentioned in the passage.

8. The use of the phrase "true calling" in line 59 indicates that the main character:
   F. heard voices from God.
   G. worked in the tele-communications industry.
   H. was struggling to find her purpose in life.
   J. hated investment banking, but loved her next job.

9. The passage states that the main character's mother "couldn't understand her daughter's caprice." This most nearly means that the main character's mother:
   A. didn't understand the collegiate words that her daughter used.
   B. was concerned about her daughter's need to see a psychologist.
   C. thought her daughter spent too much of her time playing sports.
   D. did not know what caused her daughter's impulsive behavior.

10. Based on the telephone conversation at the end of the passage, it can most reasonably be inferred that:
   F. the main character is ready to trust her doctor and make positive changes in her life.
   G. Dr. Mornington's receptionist is lying about the long wait to meet with the doctor.
   H. the main character will not see Dr. Mornington.
   J. the main character is unwilling to recognize the need for change in her life.

GO ON TO THE NEXT PAGE.

Passage II
NATURAL SCIENCE: *An Enemy Within*

The human body's defense mechanisms are truly remarkable. When injured, the human body immediately begins to repair itself; when attacked by germs, it increases production of white blood cells to
5 defend itself and fight back against the germs. And, throughout life, the brain and heart never take a break. With an ever-expanding understanding of how the body keeps itself healthy, modern medicine attempts to work with this predictable machine,
10 supplementing the natural defenses where possible. Unfortunately, the machine occasionally malfunctions, and the very cells designed to protect the body instead attack its allies. For example, leukocytes (white blood cells) occasionally increase for no
15 apparent reason, fighting not against germs, but healthy blood cells; this is commonly referred to as *leukemia*. Although certainly not a desired disease, doctors have made tremendous progress in successfully curing leukemia. Such is not the case for
20 Huntington's Disease (HD).

HD is a devastating, degenerative brain disorder for which there is no effective treatment or cure. The disease results from genetically programmed degeneration of brain cells, called *neurons*, in certain areas
25 of the brain. This degeneration causes uncontrolled movements, loss of intellectual faculties, and emotional disturbance. Early symptoms of Huntington's Disease may affect cognitive ability or mobility and include depression, mood swings, forgetfulness, irri-
30 tability, clumsiness, involuntary twitching, and lack of coordination. As the disease progresses, concentration and short-term memory diminish and involuntary movements of the head, trunk, and limbs increase. Walking, speaking, and swallowing abilities
35 deteriorate. Eventually, HD sufferers become unable to care for themselves and are totally dependent upon others. Death follows from complications such as choking, infection, or heart failure.

HD typically begins in midlife, between the ages
40 of thirty and forty-five, though onset may occur as early as the age of two. Children who develop the juvenile form of the disease rarely live to adulthood. HD affects males and females equally and crosses all ethnic and racial boundaries.

45 HD is a familial disease, passed from parent to child through a mutation in the normal gene. Each child of an HD parent has a 50–50 chance of inheriting the HD gene. If a child does not inherit the HD gene, he or she will not develop the disease
50 and cannot pass it to subsequent generations. A person who inherits the HD gene will sooner or later develop the disease. Whether one child inherits the gene has no bearing on whether others will or will not inherit the gene. The rate of disease progression
55 and the age of onset vary from person to person. A genetic test, coupled with a complete medical history and neurological and laboratory tests, help physicians diagnose HD. Presymptomatic testing is available for individuals who are at risk for carry-
60 ing the HD gene. The test cannot predict when symptoms will begin, and, in the absence of a cure, some individuals "at risk" elect not to take the test. Strangely, in 1 to 3 percent of individuals with HD, no family history of HD can be found.

65 Named for Dr. George Huntington, who first described this hereditary disorder in 1872, HD is now recognized as one of the more common genetic disorders. More than a quarter of a million Americans have HD or are "at risk" of inheriting
70 the disease from an affected parent. Since there is no known way to stop or reverse the course of HD, researchers are continuing to study the HD gene with an eye toward understanding how it causes disease in the human body. In the meantime, physicians
75 prescribe a number of medications to help control emotional and movement problems associated with HD.

Until a cure is found, Huntington's Disease affects entire families: physically, emotionally,
80 socially, and economically. For those afflicted, the gradual loss of capacities is humiliating; the realization that they may have passed the disease along to their offspring is horrifying. For the families, the physical and financial strain of caring for the afflicted
85 is coupled with the realization that they may someday suffer the same fate. Given the current lack of treatment, HD is nothing less than an insidious villain, which lurks within its victims who, in turn, are helpless against the malice.

11. As it is used the in the first paragraph, the word *machine* most nearly means:
   A. the aggregate of human functions.
   B. a coin-operated device.
   C. a highly organized political group.
   D. a newly discovered medical tool.

12. According to the passage, medical researchers have made tremendous progress in their ability to cure:
   F. leukemia.
   G. Huntington's Disease.
   H. most types of cancer.
   J. white blood cells.

13. According to the passage, all of the following are examples of symptoms of Huntington's Disease EXCEPT:
   A. difficulty swallowing.
   B. forgetfulness.
   C. frequent rashes.
   D. involuntary twitching.

14. The symptoms of Huntington's Disease begin when:
   F. white blood cells multiply too quickly.
   G. leukocytes attack other cells.
   H. brain cells are cured.
   J. neurons degenerate.

15. As it is used in the passage, the word *juvenile* (line 42) most nearly means:
   A. naive.
   B. emotionally immature.
   C. misbehaving.
   D. occurring in childhood.

GO ON TO THE NEXT PAGE.

16. According to the passage, Huntington's Disease occurs in:
    F. caucasians of European descent only.
    G. people who carry the HD gene only.
    H. adults between the ages of thirty and forty-five only.
    J. all people with leukemia.

17. According to the passage, if someone carries the Huntington's Disease gene:
    A. he or she may never develop symptoms of HD.
    B. he or she will eventually lose his or her cognitive ability and coordination.
    C. he or she is likely to have unusual physical traits recognizable before the onset of symptoms.
    D. there is no way of knowing it until symptoms begin.

18. According to the passage, George Huntington:
    F. was the first person diagnosed with HD.
    G. was the doctor who developed a cure for HD.
    H. was the first doctor to describe the symptoms and hereditary nature of the disease.
    J. suffered from drastic mood swings.

19. The author of the passage, compares HD to:
    A. a fly in the ointment.
    B. an insidious villain with malicious intent.
    C. a monkey wrench in the machine.
    D. a black-widow spider.

20. According to the passage, HD directly affects:
    I. those who carry the HD gene.
    II. the families of people with HD.
    III. the patients of those who carry the HD gene.
    F. I only
    G. I and II only
    H. II and III only
    J. I, II, and III

▬ ANSWERS AND EXPLANATIONS

PASSAGE I

1. **The best answer is A.** Although the doctor, mother, and working-class man are all mentioned in the passage, the narrator is an unnamed observer of the main character, who is also unnamed.

2. **The best answer is G.** The main character discovers her character flaws by reflecting on scenes from her life. The passage does not begin with a statement of discovery. Although dialogue is used at the beginning and end of the passage, it is not used throughout, nor does the main character offer a concluding statement of summary at the end.

3. **The best answer is C.** It is clear based on the details in the passage that the main character seems to lack common sense and does not make wise decisions. The antagonism between the main character and her doctor is evident in the opening paragraphs, but there is no mention of the doctor in other scenes of the main character's life. Although the main character's parents may have judged their daughter's actions, it is not central to the story. Finally, although the main character jumped from one career to another, it is also not a factor in all of the scenes.

4. **The best answer is J.** Given the other hints that the main character was self-destructive due to a fear of success, we can infer that she subconsciously wished to be caught in her crime. The passage says that the main character shoplifted the candy; therefore, she was not convinced of her innocence. We have no reason to believe that shoplifting had ever been committed by other members of her family. Although the main character was academically intelligent, shoplifting was not an example of this.

5. **The best answer is B.** The passage states that "her best friend paid for the candy and begged for mercy." These are not the actions of anyone who is jealous, apathetic, or naïve, but it is indicative of someone genuinely concerned for her friend.

6. **The best answer is H.** Although *ardent* can mean "hotly," it can also mean "enthusiastic" or "whole-hearted." The main character "enthusiastically" prepared for her interview, because, at that time, she really wanted the job.

7. **The best answer is A.** The main character's first job was in Atlanta and she attended college in Connecticut, but the main character grew up on a working-class neighborhood. The name of the city is not mentioned.

8. **The best answer is H.** Given that the main character repeatedly went from one job to another, each time thinking she was answering her "true calling," you can infer that she was struggling to find her purpose in life. The passage

does not tell us what each of those jobs was nor does it infer that she heard voices.

9. **The best answer is D**. *Caprice* is defined as "sudden, impulsive and seemingly unmotivated notions or actions." This definition is supported by the passage. Although the main character was well educated, the passage does not imply that the mother's vocabulary was not equal to that of her daughter's. The passage does not imply that the mother was aware that her daughter saw a psychologist. Nor does it imply that the mother thought her daughter spent too much time playing sports.

10. **The best answer is F**. Based on the reflections leading up to the telephone conversation at the end, and the "heavy sigh" (which implies a new resolve), you can infer that the main character is willing to trust the doctor and begin trying to make positive changes in her life. The other answer choices are not supported by the passage.

PASSAGE II

11. **The best answer is A**. Although humans are not routinely referred to as "machines," the routine, predictable functions of the human body can be likened to a machine. The other options are all legitimate definitions of the word, "machine," but are inappropriate in this context.

12. **The best answer is F**. The first paragraph clearly states that doctors "have made tremendous progress in successfully curing leukemia. Such is not the case for Huntington's Disease (HD)." The other answer choices are not supported by details in the passage.

13. **The best answer is C**. Difficulty swallowing, forgetfulness, and involuntary twitching are all listed as symptoms of Huntington's Disease. Frequent rashes are not mentioned.

14. **The best answer is J**. HD is the result of the degeneration of neurons (a type of brain cell).

White blood cells (leukocytes) are mentioned in the opening paragraph in relation to leukemia. *Degenerate* means "to break down."

15. **The best answer is D**. The word *juvenile* can be used to mean "naïve" or "emotionally immature," but in this context, it means "occurring in childhood." Juvenile delinquents frequently "misbehave," but his notion is not discussed in the passage.

16. **The best answer is G**. The passage states that if someone "does not inherit the HD gene, he or she will not develop the disease" Therefore, you can infer that HD occurs only in those people who carry the gene. It is not more prevalent in one racial or ethnic group than another. Although symptoms of HD usually appear between the ages of thirty and forty-five, symptoms can begin at any age. HD has nothing to do with leukemia.

17. **The best answer is B**. Anyone with the HD gene will eventually develop HD (and lose cognitive ability and coordination). Prior to developing symptoms, people with the HD gene do not look any different than people without it. A blood test can determine if someone carries the HD gene, whether or not he or she has symptoms of the disease.

18. **The best answer is H**. As stated in the fifth paragraph, Dr. George Huntington first described the hereditary disorder. He did not have the disease, nor did he develop a cure.

19. **The best answer is B**. In the last sentence, HD is described as "an insidious villain which lurks within its victims who, in turn, are helpless against the malice." The other answer choices are not supported by the passage.

20. **The best answer is G**. The passage only mentions the effects of HD on those afflicted with the disease and their families. Roman numeral III is not supported by the passage.

CHAPTER 6

ACT SCIENCE REASONING TEST: STRATEGIES AND CONCEPT REVIEW

The ACT Science Reasoning Test measures the interpretation, analysis, evaluation, reasoning, and problem-solving skills that apply to the study of the natural sciences. The questions require you to recognize and understand the basic concepts related to the information contained within the passages, critically examine the hypotheses developed, and generalize from given information to draw conclusions, or make predictions. The ACT Science Reasoning Test includes seven passages, each followed by four to seven multiple-choice questions, for a total of forty questions. The content areas found in the passages are Biology, Chemistry, Physics, and Earth Sciences. You do not need to have advanced knowledge of these content areas; you only need to be able to interpret the data as it is presented and understand the scientific method and experimental design. All of the information you need to answer the questions is in the passages. Usually, if you've completed two years of science coursework in high school, you will have all of the background knowledge necessary to understand the passages and answer the questions correctly.

You may have to do some math on the ACT Science Reasoning Test. You are not, however, allowed to use a calculator. Only basic arithmetic computation will be necessary to answer these questions. You can do math scratch work right on your test booklet.

The ACT Science Reasoning Test has passages in three basic formats:

1. **Data Representation** These passages are mostly charts and graphs. The questions ask you to read information from them or spot trends within the data presented.
2. **Research Summaries** These passages explain the set-up of an experiment or a series of experiments and the results that were obtained.
3. **Conflicting Viewpoints** These passages are a lot like the Reading passages. There will usually be two scientists or two students who disagree on a specific scientific point and each will present an argument defending his or her position and/or attacking the other, conflicting position.

STRATEGIES AND TECHNIQUES

Prioritize

Remember that you may end up working through only four or five of the seven passages. Choose the format at which you are best. If you are having a hard time making sense of the passage that you start with, move on to some less confusing material. The best way to know which passages to do first on test day is to practice ahead of time so that you can recognize the passages that are likely to give you the most points for the time that you put in.

Think First

Once you have chosen a passage to attack, take a moment or two to understand the main idea or ideas presented before you dig into the questions. Unlike the Reading Test, these questions are not likely to add anything to your understanding of the passages. Reading them first will be likely to confuse you. Common sense will help to keep you from being fooled by some of the distractors that are "way out." For instance, if the passage is describing an experiment done with living animals in a laboratory, and the question asks about temperatures that are likely to result in a certain behavior, you could certainly rule out an answer choice that says, "400° Fahrenheit."

Be "Trendy"

Many of the Science Reasoning questions reward test takers who can spot trends in the data presented. When charts or graphs are given, take a moment to figure out which variables are being charted and note any apparent relationships between them. A *direct relationship* is when one variable increases as the other increases. An *inverse relationship* is when one variable decreases as another increases. Sometimes the data reveals a lack of relationship. As you have learned in your science classes, this is often the result of experimentation and observation.

Don't Let Them Scare You with Complex Vocabulary

There will certainly be language on the Science Reasoning Test that is new to you. Don't get worried when you see words that you have never seen before. The ACT usually defines terms that are absolutely essential to your understanding. You can answer questions about some terms without even knowing exactly what they mean as long as you focus on the overall idea of the passage.

Don't "Listen" to Science

Don't ever spend time trying to figure out how to pronounce any of the unfamiliar terms that you run across. That is simply a waste of time and energy.

The rest of this chapter will provide an overview of the Scientific Method, a brief review of basic scientific concepts, an introduction to the types of questions you will see on the ACT Science Test and sample questions with explanations.

THE SCIENTIFIC METHOD

The Scientific Method is the process by which scientists attempt to construct an accurate representation of the world. This process is fundamental to scientific investigation and acquisition of new knowledge, based upon actual physical evidence and careful observation. The Scientific Method is a means of building a supportable, documented understanding of our world.

The Scientific Method includes four essential elements:

1. Observation
2. Hypothesis
3. Prediction
4. Experiment

During the **observation** phase, the experimenter will directly observe and measure the phenomenon that is being studied. Careful notes should be taken and all pertinent data should be recorded so that the phenomenon (the thing observed) can be accurately described.

The experimenter will then generate a **hypothesis** to explain the phenomenon. He or she will speculate as to the reason for the phenomenon, based on the observations made and recorded.

Next, the experimenter will make **predictions** to test the hypothesis. These predictions are tested with scientific experiments, designed to either prove or disprove the hypothesis. The Scientific Method requires that any hypothesis either be ruled out or modified if the predictions are clearly and consistently incompatible with experimental results.

If the **experiments** bear out the hypothesis, it may come to be regarded as a *theory* or *law of nature*. However, it is possible that new information and discoveries could contradict any hypothesis, at any stage of experimentation.

The passages included on the ACT Science Reasoning Test have been written with the Scientific Method in mind. You can often use common sense along with a basic understanding of the this process to answer many of the questions.

Experimental Design

When scientists design experiments to test their hypotheses, they have to be careful to avoid "confounding of variables." This means that they have to isolate, as much as possible, one variable at a time so that they can reveal the relationships between the variables, if any. An **independent variable** (manipulated by the experimenter) is under the control of the scientist. As the scientist changes the independent variable, it is hoped that the **dependent variable** (observed by the experimenter) will change as a result, and that a relationship can be established. A **control** is an element of the experiment that is not subjected to the same changes in the independent variable as the **experimental** elements are. For instance, if we want to find out how the consumption of sugar impacts the fatigue level of ACT takers, we would have to be sure to have at least a few ACT takers who do not consume any sugar so that we can measure the "baseline" or "natural" fatigue level of ACT takers for comparison to the group who consumes sugar. If there were no control group, we wouldn't be able to say for sure that sugar has any impact on the fatigue level of ACT takers. If all of the test takers consumed sugar, and if all of them were sleepy, we would face a confounding of variables situation because the sleepiness could be caused by any other factor that the group had in common, like the ACT itself! (By the way, sugar does cause increased fatigue levels after the initial "sugar buzz" wears off. It is best to avoid it before your ACT exam.)

Some of the ACT Science Reasoning Passages refer to "studies" rather than experiments. An experiment is an artificial situation that is created by the researcher. A study is simply a careful, documented observation. Studies can include some of the elements of experiments, such as control groups.

PRACTICE QUESTIONS

DIRECTIONS: There are three passages in this Practice section. Each passage is followed by several questions. After reading a passage, choose the best answer to each question. Circle the letter of the answer you choose.

Data Representation

Data Representation passages present scientific information in tables, charts, graphs, and figures similar to those you might find in a scientific journal or other scientific publication. The questions associated with Data Representation passages will ask you to interpret and analyze the data shown in the tables, charts, graphs, and figures. The following is a Data Representation passage and several questions. The answers and explanations are at the end of this chapter.

Passage I

Soybeans have been bred to exhibit a hereditary association of several characteristics: flower color, leaf shape, the color of the hypocotyls (the part of the seedling that is below the seed leaf), plant height, and pod length. Some of these characteristics, or traits, are considered *qualitative*, because the trait is influenced by only a few genes. Other traits are considered *quantitative*, because they show continuous variation, and are influenced by a number of genes. Alternative versions of a gene are called *alleles*. The dominant and recessive alleles for each soybean characteristic are displayed in Table 1. Dominant alleles are visible traits that mask all other traits, and they are more likely to be passed along from one generation to the next. Recessive alleles are hidden characteristics that are masked by dominant ones. A soybean plant may carry a recessive gene, whose traits will show up only in later generations.

	Table 1	
	Dominant alleles	Recessive alleles
Qualitative traits		
Flower color	purple	white
Leaf shape	round	narrow
Color of hypocotyls	purple	green
Quantitative traits		
Plant height	short	tall
Pod length	long	short

Figure 1 is an illustration of how some of the genetic traits may be passed from 1 generation of soybean plants to the next. Each parent passes only 1 trait on to successive generations. The plants are numbered consecutively within each generation.

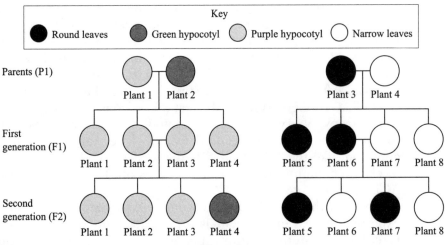

Figure 1

1. Based on Figure 1, what is the relationship between Plant 1 and Plant 2 in row F2?
   A. Plant 1 is dominant over Plant 2.
   B. Plant 1 is recessive to Plant 2.
   C. Plant 1 and Plant 2 are members of the same generation.
   D. Plant 1 and Plant 2 both have green hypocotyls.

2. In row F2, green hypocotyls appear in the offspring for the first time. Which of the following is the most reasonable explanation for this?
   F. None of the other offspring of generation F2 inherited the gene.
   G. The members of generations P1 and F1 do not carry the gene.
   H. The gene for green hypocotyls is recessive.
   J. The gene for purple hypocotyls is recessive.

3. Based on Table 1, a soybean with purple flowers and round leaves will most likely:
   A. pass those traits on to later generations.
   B. not be able to pass on qualitative traits.
   C. yield offspring with white flowers and narrow leaves only.
   D. only be able to pass on quantitative traits.

4. According to the passage, plant height is most likely considered a quantitative trait because:
   F. plant height is a recessive characteristic in soybean plants.
   G. all soybean plants are short.
   H. quantitative traits are dominant over qualitative traits.
   J. plant height varies over the lifespan of the soybean plant.

Research Summaries

Research Summary passages provide descriptions of one or more related experiments or studies. The passages usually include a discussion of the design, methods, and results of the experiments or studies. The corresponding questions will ask you to comprehend, evaluate, and interpret the procedures and results. The following is a Research Summary passage and several questions. The answers and explanations are at the end of this chapter.

Passage II

Water pressure influences the rate at which water flows. As water pressure increases, so does the rate of flow. Water pressure can be defined as the amount of force that the water exerts on the container it's in. The more water that is in the container, the greater the water pressure will be. Students conducted the following experiment.

Experiment

Students used push pins to punch holes in an empty, plastic 2-liter bottle. The students created 4 holes, each 1-inch apart, from top to bottom. The pins were left in each hole as it was created. The bottle was filled to the top with water and placed on a table. An 8-inch by 9-inch pan with a piece of blotting paper was placed lengthwise in front of the bottle. A ruler was placed in the pan to measure the spot at which the water stream touched the paper. The students removed the pin nearest the top of the bottle and marked the spot where the water stream touched the paper. The pin was then replaced, the bottle was filled to the top, and the next pin was removed. The spot where the water stream touched the paper was measured. Rate of flow was indicated by the length of the water stream. This was repeated a total of 4 times, once for each pin. The results are recorded in Table 1.

Table 1		
Pin	Position of pin in the bottle	Length of water stream (inches)
A	First (top)	1.5
B	Second	2.0
C	Third	3.0
D	Fourth (bottom)	3.5

5. Based on Table 1, water pressure is greatest:
   A. at the top of the full container.
   B. at the bottom of the full container.
   C. when the water stream is 1.5 inches long.
   D. when the water stream is 3.0 inches long.

6. Which of the following is an assumption that the students made prior to beginning the experiment?
   F. Water pressure has no effect on the length of the water stream produced.
   G. The rate of flow cannot be accurately determined using push pins and plastic bottles.
   H. The rate of flow corresponds directly to the length of the water stream produced.
   J. Water pressure and rate of flow are the two most important characteristics of water.

7. Which of the following graphs best represents the relationship between water presssure and rate of flow, according to the passage?

A.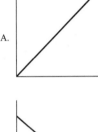

B.

C.

D.

8. Based on the results of the experiment, removal of Pin C:
   F. created a 3.5-inch water stream.
   G. caused the bottle to empty more quickly than did removal of Pin D.
   H. increased the total water pressure in the bottle.
   J. created a 3-inch water stream.

9. Suppose that the students removed the pins in order, replaced each pin after measuring the water stream, but did not refill the bottle after removing and replacing each pin. According to the passage, the water-stream lengths would most likely:
   A. be identical to the first experiment.
   B. increase for each pin removed.
   C. decrease after removal of the first pin.
   D. be equal for each pin removed.

Conflicting Viewpoints

Conflicting Viewpoints passages provide information on more than one alternative hypothesis or theory related to an observable event or phenomenon. The viewpoints presented are usually inconsistent with one another. Questions associated with Conflicting Viewpoint passages ask you to comprehend, evaluate, and compare differing hypothesis and theories. The following is a Conflicting Viewpoints passage and several questions. The answers and explanations are at the end of this chapter.

Passage III

The theory that complex life exists on other planets or worlds outside of our solar system has been debated for decades. Two scientists present their viewpoints regarding the possibility of life on planets other than Earth.

Scientist 1

Earth is the only model of planetary life about which we know. Therefore, a determination about what is common about the natural world and the formation of life is almost impossible to make. It is highly unlikely that planets with characteristics that enable them to support complex life are also located in zones of solar mass stars that are habitable for complex life. Even if such a planet existed, it is doubtful that a planet outside of our solar system could remain within secure orbits for any real length of time. Even then, if a planet were to be located in a place that could spawn or sustain complex life, that planet might not have the characteristics of Earth that make complex life possible. The factors that enable complex life to exist on Earth include planet mass, abundance of water and carbon, and oxygen. These factors are essential for the existence of complex life as we know it. In addition, if one takes into account planetary disasters, the possibility of complex life decreases. Therefore, I believe that there is little or no chance for complex life existing or having existed on other planets or worlds.

Scientist 2

Earth has select properties that allow it to sustain complex life. However, it is not impossible that there is another set of characteristics and properties that together are also able to support complex life. Although free oxygen is essential to complex life on Earth and has not been found elsewhere, complex life-forms outside of our solar system may use another gas for respiration. In addition, complex or intelligent life may not appear simultaneously. One complex life-form might never discover or know about a life-form that existed before or after the extinction of the first life-form. Studies suggest that 95% of known stars in space appear to have systems very similar to ours. This is very encouraging to those who believe that other complex life currently exists or has existed on planets other than Earth.

10. If the arguments of Scientist 1 are correct, which of the following statements about complex life is most accurate, according to the information in the passage?
    F. The possibility of development or existence of complex life is affected by many different factors.
    G. Complex life is dependent on the balance of oxygen, carbon dioxide, and neon gas.
    H. Complex life will most certainly exist if a planet is located in the correct place and has the proper assortment of elements and traits.
    J. It is unlikely that complex life-forms will ever exist on a planet other than Earth, because 95% of star systems are similar to our solar system.

11. Which of the following issues is raised by Scientist 1, but NOT by Scientist 2?
    A. The presence of oxygen is required for complex life to exist on Earth.
    B. Most of the known stars appear to have planetary systems similar to that of Earth.
    C. Planetary disasters could account for the lack of complex life on other planets.
    D. Complex life may not appear simultaneously on planets in different solar systems.

12. Studies have shown that a planet existed that was almost identical to Earth and was located in a place that was conducive to complex life. However, there are no signs that complex life existed. What explanation might Scientist 1 give, based on the information presented in the passage?
    F. Ninety-five percent of the stars near this planet had planetary systems that contained complex life.
    G. Planetary disasters might have eliminated or prevented complex life.
    H. The planet had an overabundance of carbon, oxygen, and water.
    J. The complex life-forms that would have inhabited this planet used another gas for respiration.

13. According to the passage, Scientist 2 would agree with which of the following statements, if true?
    A. Planetary disasters are the primary reason for the existence of complex life on other planets.
    B. Five percent of stars in the universe have systems identical to our own.
    C. Free oxygen is not essential to the existence of complex life on other planets.
    D. All complex life-forms will eventually discover one another.

14. Both Scientist 1 and Scientist 2 would agree with which of the following statements, if true?
    F. Oxygen is necessary for the existence of complex life on Earth.
    G. Planets outside of our solar system are not likely to maintain orbits secure enough for complex life.
    H. Complex life-forms are likely to exist or have existed on other planets.
    J. Complex life-forms are able to easily withstand planetary disasters.

15. Humans on Earth have yet to find another form of complex life on another planet. Scientist 2 would probably account for this by maintaining that:
    A. complex life-forms probably do not exist because other planets do not have the same characteristics and properties as Earth.
    B. complex life may have existed on other planets before the existence of humans on Earth.
    C. complex life has not been found because we have yet to find stars with a system similar to ours.
    D. complex life will only emerge when humans on Earth can survive without water and oxygen.

ANSWERS AND EXPLANATIONS

1. **The correct answer is C.** Based on Figure 1, Plant 1 and Plant 2 in row F2 both have purple hypocotyls, so you cannot conclude that one is dominant over the other. Eliminate answer choices A, B, and D. Since row F2 signifies the second generation of plants, both Plant 1 and Plant 2 are members of the same generation, answer choice C.

2. **The correct answer is H.** The passage states that a "soybean plant may carry a recessive gene, whose traits will show up only in later generations." The passage also indicates that green hypocotyls are a recessive allele. Both of these statements support answer choice H.

3. **The correct answer is A.** According to Table 1, both purple flowers and round leaves are dominant alleles. Therefore, it is most likely that these traits will be passed on to later generations. The other answer choices are not supported by the passage.

4. **The correct answer is J.** According to the passage, a quantitative trait shows "continuous variation." Therefore, it makes the most sense that plant height is considered a quantitative trait because plant height varies over the lifespan of the soybean plant. The other answer choices are not supported by the passage.

5. **The correct answer is B.** The passage states that as "water pressure increases, so does the rate of flow." The passage also indicates that rate of flow corresponds to the length of the water stream. Since the rate of flow was greatest when Pin D was removed, you can conclude that the water pressure was greatest at the bottom of the full container.

6. **The correct answer is H.** In designing the experiment, the students must have assumed that they could accurately correspond the rate of flow to the length of the water stream. The other answer choices are not supported by information presented in the experiment.

7. **The correct answer is A.** Based on information in the passage, there is a direct relationship between water pressure and rate of flow — as water pressure increases, so does the rate of flow. This relationship is indicated by the graph in answer choice A.

8. **The correct answer is J.** Table 1 indicates that the length of the water stream produced when Pin C was removed is 3.0 inches. The other answer choices are not supported by the passage.

9. **The correct answer is C.** According to the passage, the "more water that is in the container, the greater the water pressure will be." This suggests that, if the amount of water in the container is reduced, the water pressure will also be reduced. So, if the students do not replace the water in the container, it is likely that the lengths of the water streams will decrease after the first pin is removed.

10. **The correct answer is F.** Scientist 1 argues that the location, security of the planet's orbit, planetary disasters, and characteristics of planets determine the probability of complex life. This argument best supports answer choice F.

11. **The correct answer is C.** Scientist 1 argues that "if one takes into account planetary disasters, the possibility of complex life decreases." The other answer choices are either discussed by both scientists or by Scientist 2 only.

12. **The correct answer is G.** Scientist 1 argues that it takes many precise factors together to allow complex life to form. In addition Scientist 1 says, "if one takes into account planetary disasters, the possibility of complex life decreases." The other answer choices are not supported by the passage.

13. **The correct answer is C.** Scientist 2 says that "it is not impossible that there is another set of characteristics and properties that together are also able to support complex life." Scientist 2 goes on to say that "... complex life-forms outside of our solar system may use another gas for respiration." These statements best support answer choice C.

14. **The correct answer is F.** According to the passage, both scientists agree that oxygen is necessary for the existence of complex life on earth. The other answer choices are supported by either one or the other scientist, but not both, or they are not supported at all by the passage.

15. **The correct answer is B.** Scientist 2 states that "complex or intelligent life may not appear simultaneously. ... One complex life-form might never discover or know about a life-form that existed before or after the extinction of the first life-form." This statement best supports answer choice B.

CHAPTER 7

ACT WRITING TEST: STRATEGIES AND REVIEW

The ACT Writing Test is optional, meaning that students can choose to take it or not. The decision depends on to which colleges and universities you plan to apply. If you take the Writing Test, it will come after the ACT exam. You will have a short break between the ACT multiple-choice sections and the Writing Test.

The Writing Test consists of a "prompt" or "stimulus," which is a brief discussion of a topic to which you must respond, and some blank, lined space in which to write your answer. You will have thirty minutes to complete the test. Time is rarely a problem for most students, and space is almost never a problem. (If you start to run out of space on this test, you are simply writing too much! There is more detailed discussion of controlling the length of your response later in this chapter.) The graders are not looking for long answers; they are looking for quality answers.

The Writing Test is scored on a 2-point through 12-point scale. Two professional, trained readers will evaluate your answer, and each of them will assign a point value of 1 (worst) through 6 (best) (see "Simplified Essay Scoring Rubric"); the two scores are then totaled. If the two readers assign scores that differ by more than 1 point, then a third reader will be called in to read your essay and make the final decision regarding your score.

The scores are *holistic* scores, which means that your essay is judged as a whole without assigning point values to the specific characteristics for which the graders are looking.

The most important thing to know about this essay is that THERE IS NO CORRECT ANSWER! The readers are looking at the essay as an example of your ability to write a clear, concise, persuasive piece. DO NOT WASTE TIME by trying to figure out which position the test writers want you to choose.

This part of the ACT is designed to measure your writing skills. The test writers specifically choose topics that are probably relevant to high school students, and they even give a couple of different points of view from which to choose. They are looking for essays that pick a position and support it. The graders will reward you with more points if you stay on your main idea throughout your essay and back up your position by giving specific examples and information. You will certainly do well if you have a clear, logical structure and if your language is correct and free of errors in grammar or vocabulary. Don't take any vocabulary risks when writing this essay. If you are not sure what a word means, don't use it. It should go without saying, but remember that you should not fill your essay with vernacular, slang, jargon, or profanity.

There is a big overlap between the English section of the ACT and the Writing Test. If you can recognize proper English and point out common errors on the multiple-choice portion of the ACT, you should be able to avoid making those same errors on the Writing Test.

The folks at ACT will give you a couple of different positions on the issue that they present in the stimulus. While you are not strictly limited to either point of view, it is probably easier to pick one of them and use it as your position on the subject.

You will have some "scratch paper" on this part of the ACT. Later in the chapter, we'll discuss some specific ideas for the best way to use it. Be certain that you do use it. This is not the time to just jump in and start writing a stream-of-consciousness, shoot-from-the-hip answer off the top of your head. You might not have time to do a full first and second draft of this essay, but you should make use of the time that is given to you. Be sure that you plan out what you are going to say before you actually start writing out your final answer.

At this point in your ACT testing day, you are likely to be somewhat tired. Try to focus on the fact that you are almost finished, and do what you can to keep your focus for the last thirty minutes. In some cases, this essay will be important to people who make admissions decisions at the institutions to which you are applying.

SCORING

The ACT graders use something called a *rubric* when they assign scores to essays. Basically, a rubric is a checklist of characteristics that the grader is supposed to look for when reading your essay. If your essay is more like the one described in the rubric as being a 5 than a 4, the grader will assign your essay a 5. The rubrics are posted on the ACT Web site and listed in ACT publications.

Since everyone knows what is expected, and there is virtually no chance that the grader will know the person who wrote a given essay, the system is reasonably fair. Here is the simplified version of the rubric that describes an essay that rates a score of 6, which is the highest possible score.

> **6:** The essay takes a clear position and discusses other perspectives, including perspectives that may differ from the author's. The essay is logical and complete. There are good transitions and very little, or no, irrelevant information. The introduction and conclusion are solid and consistent with each other and with the argument presented. While there may be a few errors, they are minor and infrequent. Grammar, spelling, and punctuation are nearly perfect. Vocabulary is effective and appropriate.

Note that the graders are allowed to give a 6 to an essay that is somewhat less than perfect. The graders know that you have limited time to write, that you are doing this after you have just taken what may be the toughest exam of your life up to now, and that your fatigue and stress levels are likely to be elevated as a result.

Note that neatness is not specifically mentioned. However, the colleges to which you are applying will have access to your essay — and so will your high school. This means that the people who are deciding on your applications may take your neatness into account. It also may have an impact on the graders as they assign a score to your essay. Since the scale runs from 1 through 6, there are some fine distinctions between say, a 4 and a 5. That difference could be important to the admissions personnel whom you are trying to impress. But, the rubric descriptions of these two scores are very similar to each other. The difference between a 4 and a 5 could hinge on how the grader interprets words like *competent* (5) and *adequate* (4) or, what exactly makes an error "distracting."

So, make it easy on your grader to interpret those differences in your favor. Keep your essay neat and your handwriting legible. Nothing in the rules prevents you from printing rather than writing in cursive. So, if your printing will be easier for graders and admissions officials to read than your cursive, then by all means, print.

We've decided not to include a detailed description of the entire rubric and how each point level is described. Suffice it to say that a 1 or a 2 usually indicates to graders and colleges that the person who wrote the essay either did not put forth a reasonable effort or is probably incapable of handling even basic college writing tasks. A 3 or 4 score means that the grader sees some fairly solid basic skills, but that there is plenty of room for improvement, and a 5 or 6 means that the author appears to be ready for challenging college-level work.

Keep in mind that the scores that are assigned by the graders are based on the essay only. The graders do not get to see your ACT multiple-choice scores. They just assign a point value to the essay and move on to the next one. They are not making comments on your worth as a human being, or even your intelligence or ability. They are just giving feedback regarding how the essay stacks up to the rubric.

In addition to the numerical score, there will be between one and four different sets of written comments on your essay. These will be similar to the kind of feedback that most high school writing teachers give to their students, and they may include suggestions for improvement as well as specific comments on the good and not-so-good parts of your essay.

ACT will also report a Combined English/Writing score that will be on the same 1-through-36 scale as the multiple-choice portions of the ACT. The combined score, while it does depend, in part, on the scaled score of your English multiple-choice section, does not change the score that you earn on the English Test.

Colleges are likely to make use of the scoring information in different ways. You should do thorough research of the colleges to which you are applying and find out how they interpret ACT results in general, and Combined English/Writing scores specifically.

THE PROMPT

The prompt will be a few sentences long and will mention an issue that can cause some disagreement. It will probably be an issue that is relevant to high school students. Some past subjects have included school dress codes, requirements that student do community service before graduating from high school, separation of males from females during classroom instruction, and the linking of school performance to driving privileges.

It will also include at least two different positions on the issue and then instructions to take a position on the issue in your essay. The page following the prompt will be blank on both sides, except for a note that says that anything that you put on those two pages will not be scored. The idea is that the ACT folks are giving you some "scratch" paper so that you can jot down whatever notes you want to, or do some outlining to help keep yourself on track as you write in your answer document.

Four pages of lined answer space follow the blank pages. You are to confine your response to those four pages. It may not sound like a lot of space, but we have found that the students who write the most and complain about not having enough room to finish are usually spending too much time on irrelevant discussion or have needless repetition in their answers. You may use pencil only. No ink is allowed. You should probably write with a medium pressure since, if you don't press hard enough, your words might not scan. If you press too hard, you will have a hard time keeping your essay neat if you need to erase.

The prompt essentially describes a debate on an issue about which you are likely to have some strong feelings. If you do have strong feelings, you should just stick with your first response to the issue and work from there. If you don't, the fact that ACT will give you at least two different responses to the issue that other people have had, means that you can just choose one of them as your starting point. If you have a different response from the two that are mentioned in the stimulus, then you may write about it. However, this choice is significantly more difficult for most students and should be considered a very advanced technique.

TECHNIQUES

Here are the steps that are likely to result in the best essay that you can write. The steps are laid out so that you can perform them one at a time. This is not the time for "multitasking." If you were to simply read the stimulus and then try to write your answer out from the beginning to the end on the lined pages, you would certainly be doing several tasks at once. You would be creating the logical structure of your essay, you would also be searching your memory banks for vocabulary words, and anticipating counterarguments, at the same time that you would be trying to correctly apply the rules of grammar, punctuation, and spelling, as well as remembering some good, relevant examples to plug into your essay structure. In short, those students who try to write without planning are setting themselves up for a score that is less than their potential, because they are trying to do too many things at one time.

1. Read the Stimulus

It's okay to read the stimulus over more than once to be certain that you understand what you are reading. The test booklet is a resource for you to consume, so don't be afraid to underline, circle, and so on. The stimulus is short, so reading carefully will not take up much of your time. However, it may save you from making a mistake in responding to the prompt.

For example, many students write essays that argue vehemently against school *uniforms* when responding to a prompt that mentions school *dress codes* but never actually mentions uniforms at all. While it is possible to write an essay that takes the idea of dress codes one step further and actually advocates for the dress codes, it reveals a clear misunderstanding of the stimulus to write an essay that argues against something that is never even mentioned. This type of mistake is tragic when an otherwise extremely well written essay can probably not get higher than a 3 on the point scale.

You must know what the task is before you begin. Rushing through this step can cost valuable points and make some of your hard work worthless.

One or two minutes will probably be sufficient time to read the prompt carefully.

2. Think

If the topic is something that you have thought about, or discussed in the past, then you may already have an opinion. If not, then take a short time to formulate your opinion. That is what these essays are really all about: opinion. That is why there is really no correct or incorrect position to take. The truth is that either side can be supported. The test writers are careful to choose topics that have at least two sides that can be argued successfully. Remember that one of the characteristics of the rubric is taking a position on the issue. This is not the time to be overly diplomatic. Take a side and defend your choice.

This thinking process should not take very long, a few minutes at most.

3. Plan Your Essay

Your essay should start out with a clear statement of your position on the issue. There should be no doubt in the reader's mind about which side you are on from the beginning of your essay. You should use the scratch paper that is provided to outline the structure of your essay.

There is an old saying about effective essays. It is said that you should "tell them what you are going to tell them. Then tell them. Then, tell them what you told them." In other words, you should have a clear introduction, a body, and a conclusion that echoes the introduction. You may choose to do a traditional five-paragraph essay. But it is possible to do a very effective essay with more paragraphs, or fewer.

Your outline does not have to include complete sentences. It does have to include the ideas that you will put into your final draft. You need to be sure that you have a clear picture of where you are going and how you will get there before you start to write on the answer document.

You will hear some of the other test takers around you scratching furiously with their pencils from the beginning of the thirty-minute period. Sometimes that sound can make you feel like you are falling behind. You are not. Thirty minutes is a long time to write two to four pages on a one-paragraph stimulus. The planning stage is the most important stage. Even if you spend over fifteen minutes on this stage, you will probably still be able to finish on time. Your essay will certainly be better than if you had simply started writing your thoughts with no planning.

4. Write Your Essay Out on the Answer Pages

You should also remember that there are really four categories of information when you are writing a persuasive essay and the opposition's position is clearly understood:

1. Positive for your position
2. Negative for your position
3. Positive for the other side
4. Negative for the other side

An effective essay uses facts from all four categories. You can think of your side as "correct" and the other side as "incorrect." When you write a paragraph that is focused on the "correct" side of the issue, you should mention at least one aspect of your choice that may be seen as a negative by some people. Your essay will be much more persuasive if you do not ignore potential problems with your side of the debate. Of course, you should be sure to mention plenty of positive information in order to overcome the potential down side to which you are admitting.

The same technique can be applied to the part of your essay where you discuss the opposition's position. You should admit that the other side of the debate has at least one strong point. Then, follow up with enough discussion of the pitfalls associated with the other side of the argument that your side ends up looking like the clear winner.

This is known as dealing with counterarguments, and it is the most effective way of presenting a persuasive written argument. To do this properly requires certain transition words. There are four basic categories of transition words that you will probably have to use:

> **Contrast:** *But, However, On the other hand, Conversely, Although, Even though,* etc.
> **Similarity:** *Likewise, Similarly,* etc.
> **Evidence:** *Since, Because, In light of, First, Second, Third,* etc.
> **Conclusion:** *Therefore, Thus, As a result, So, It follows that, In conclusion,* etc.

An example of a sentence structure that will allow you to deal with these positive and negative categories of facts follows:

The opposition makes a valid point regarding the initial cost of my solution; the truth is that my solution would only cost a few dollars more per user than their option would, and, furthermore, would result in significant maintenance savings over the long run that would more than make up for the slightly higher start-up costs.

This sentence effectively deals with the potential objection that the other side might raise in two ways. First, it reduces the impact of the higher cost of the author's proposal by pointing out that the difference really isn't very large when considered as a cost per user. Then, it points out that the costs will be recaptured in the future through increased savings. In addition, the sentence makes proper use of a semicolon. A semicolon is used correctly when it you could erase it and replace it with a period and a capital letter. In other words, the semicolon links two independent clauses, which could stand alone as sentences in their own right. You should use the semicolon when the two sentences are very closely related and are continuing the same thought.

COMMON MISTAKES

There are many common errors that students make on the ACT Writing Test essay. If you know what to avoid, you'll not only be a better writer, but, you'll have a much easier time on the English multiple-choice test.

1. Too General

The scoring rubric awards points for specific examples. Think of the best teachers you have had. They tend to tell you the general concept that they are teaching and then give one or more specific, memorable examples. This strategy works because of the memorable examples.

If you are told that there is no progress without determination and hard work, you might accept the statement as true and you may even remember it. However, you will have a much better chance of fully grasping the idea and remembering it later, if you are given a specific example like Thomas Edison, who tried thousands and thousands of different filament materials in his lightbulbs before finally settling on one that gave acceptable light and lasted a reasonable period of time.

Too often, students make broad, general statements in their essays without giving any specific support. Make sure that you provide clear, simple examples of the general statements that you make.

2. Too Emotional and Opinionated

While it is true that the stimulus will be asking you for an opinion, you should not make the entire essay about your feelings. You should state what your opinion is and then back up your opinion with well-reasoned logical support. Tell the reader *why* you feel the way you do rather than just telling *how* you feel.

Also, exclamation points are rarely appropriate for a Writing Test essay. Smiley faces or other "emoticons" are never appropriate.

3. Too Complicated

Many coaches and teachers have suggested that students apply the K.I.S.S. principle. While there is a slightly less polite formulation, we'll explain the K.I.S.S. principle as an acronym for "Keep It Short and Sweet." Do not use three words when one will do.

For example, if you want to say, "I do not think that the proposal will work," do not write, "I believe that my feelings on this matter are correct when I state plainly and clearly that the previously proposed solution to this complicated problem will be somewhat less than completely effective as compared to other potential solutions, which have been brought forth concurrently."

The graders are not going to be blown away by your amazing ability to use a dozen words to state a plain idea. They are going to be blown away if you are able to make your point cleanly and clearly.

4. Risky Vocabulary

If you are not sure what a word means, or whether it would be appropriate to your essay, don't use it. Many an otherwise wonderful essay has been sunk by a word or two used incorrectly, which made the grader start to question the author's abilities.

For instance, if you were grading an essay that said, "High school students are often *condemned* for their kindness," you might know that the author meant to say, "High school students are often *commended* for their kindness." But, you would still have to note the error and take it into account in scoring the essay.

5. Poor Penmanship

As mentioned previously in the chapter, the grader has to assign a score to your essay that depends on the grader's interpretation of the terms in the rubric. In order to help the grader interpret those terms in your favor when he or she is making judgment calls, you should write, or print, as neatly as you can. Make it easy for the graders to find the good things about your essay that will allow them to give you all of the points that your hard work deserves.

6. Shaky Logic

The essay that you must write for the Writing Test is an argument. It is an essay written with the purpose of defending a position. That position is your conclusion, and the support you are offering is evidence for that conclusion. There should be a cause-and-effect relationship between your evidence and your conclusion. In other words, the body of your essay should lead the reader to see the wisdom of your position.

If you are taking the position in your essay that students should be subject to an 11:00 p.m. curfew, do not spend time discussing how you felt about your bedtime when you were seven years old.

Choose relevant examples that are connected to your position in a direct way. One way to do this is to use examples that point out the benefits of your position. For example, "I believe that anyone under the age of 18 should have an 11:00 p.m. curfew on school nights. This is because school starts at 8:00 a.m., which means that most students have to get up at 7:00 a.m., or even earlier. Since students, like everyone, need adequate sleep in order to learn well, an 11:00 p.m. curfew would help students to succeed in school."

While you may disagree with the conclusion of the above argument, you have to admit that there is a cause-and-effect connection between the evidence presented and the position that the author takes.

7. Unsafe Assumptions

There are two components to an argument: evidence and conclusion. Consider the following statement:

Evidence leads to conclusions. You need at least two pieces of evidence to support one conclusion. So, if you only give one piece of evidence, you must be making an assumption. Logic professors refer to assumptions as "suppressed premises," which is just a fancy way to say, "unstated evidence." If you leave too much of your evidence unstated, your argument starts to get weak.

For example, if an essay says, "Curfews are dangerous because what if I have to be somewhere after 11:00?" The reader immediately starts to wonder, "Where could you have to be? What will you be doing?" There are simply too many unanswered questions. If you happen to agree with the position that the writer is taking, you tend to "help" with the assumptions and provide your own examples and answers to the unanswered questions. You might read the statement above and fill in an example from your own life or one that you would consider plausible. The graders at ACT will not do that extra thinking work for you as they read your essay. You have to be aware of the completeness of your essay and try to minimize the unanswered questions.

8. Too Conversational

This essay is supposed to be an example of your command of Standard Written English. The fact is that we often let each other "get away with" language in conversation that is simply not correct for Standard Written English. For example, if a friend uses *ain't* or *ya'll* in conversation, we would rarely correct him or her. Similarly we all tend to use the term *you* when we really are speaking of people in general or people in a certain position, and not referring specifically to the reader or listener.

For example: "*You* could feel the tension in the room when Jeff had a pizza delivered to American History class." The person making that statement should have said, "*I* could feel the tension..." or "*We could all* feel the tension."

In general, you should try to leave *you* and *me* out of your essays. It is acceptable to use a personal example and refer to yourself once or twice. However, some students get carried away and make the whole essay about them. The topics are meant to be relevant to high school students in general and usually refer to a policy matter. The stimulus is not an invitation to write a brief autobiography.

In conversation we often try to be inclusive and gender neutral. The goal of including everyone is an ideal that this author shares. However, English forces us to use a gender-specific pronoun such as *he* or *she* or *him* or *her*. In conversation, we often ignore the incongruity when someone says, "Whoever forgot *their* umbrella is going to be sorry." The statement should be, "Whoever forgot *his or her* umbrella is going to be sorry."

One way to be inclusive is to alternate between male and female pronouns throughout your piece. This method can create some confusion for your reader. Another method is to use a plural phrasing rather than a singular phrasing: "*Those* who forgot *their umbrellas* are going to be sorry."

The overall thing to keep in mind is that your essay needs to be a formal document. It is not appropriate to write in the same idiom that you use with friends in informal conversation.

HOW TO PREPARE

As was noted earlier in this book, humans acquire skills through practice. Since the Writing Test is a test of your writing skills, you should practice writing in order to score better. Specifically, you should practice the type of writing that is rewarded by the scoring rubric. The best way to make sure that you are on track is to have someone with experience in this area, someone you trust, give you specific feedback on the good and not-so-good parts of your practice essays. You can gain something by reading your own essays and comparing them to a rubric. But, writers tend to develop blind spots when it comes to areas that need improvement in their own essays. It is always a good idea to get a fresh set of eyes to review your work. Anyone who has worked with high school teachers for any length of time can tell you that most of them would be delighted if a student came to them for help on a practice essay. It does not take long for an experienced grader to give feedback that can be immensely valuable to a student.

SIMPLIFIED ESSAY SCORING RUBRIC

6: The essay takes a clear position and discusses other perspectives, including perspectives that may differ from the author's. The essay is logical and complete. There are good transitions and very little, or no, irrelevant information. The introduction and conclusion are solid and consistent with each other and with the argument presented. The essay predicts, and deals with counter arguments. While there may be a few errors, they are minor and infrequent. Grammar, spelling, and punctuation are nearly perfect. Vocabulary is effective and appropriate.

5: The essay takes a clear position on the topic and might give an overall context. The essay deals with some of the complex issues surrounding the topic and at least raises some counterarguments. There are specific examples given. Organization is clear and concise even if it is not creative. Transition signals are used. The author uses language competently and there is some variation in word choice. Any errors present are relatively minor and not distracting.

4: The essay demonstrates an understanding of the issue and the purpose of the essay is clear. The author states a position on the main issue and at least raises some potential counterarguments. There is adequate development of ideas and some specific reasons and/or examples are given. There is some logical sequence. Most transitions are simple. There is some variety in sentence length and word choice. There are some distracting errors but the essay is still understandable.

3: The essay reveals that the author has some understanding of the task. There is a clear position but no real overall context is provided. There may be some mention of counterarguments but they are cursory or not clearly stated. The essay may be repetitious or redundant. The essay stays within the general subject but may stray from the specific issue. The organization is simple and predictable. Transitions, if any, are simple and predictable. Introduction and conclusion are present but not well developed. Word choice is generally appropriate but sentences lack variety in length or structure. There are distracting errors that impact understandability.

2: The essay shows that the author misunderstood the assignment. There is no position taken on the main issue or there are no reasons given. There may be a general example or two but no specific examples offered. There are problems with the relevance of some of the statements made. Transition words may be incorrect or misleading. There are several distracting errors that affect the understandability of the essay.

1: The author demonstrates almost no grasp of the assignment. The essay fails to take a position or fails to support a position taken. It may be excessively redundant. There is little or no structure or coherence. There are several errors that nearly prevent understanding the author's point, if any.

0: The answer document was blank. Or, the essay was on a topic of the author's own choosing. Or, the essay was either completely or nearly illegible.

SAMPLE STUDENT RESPONSES

The following is a Sample Writing Prompt and examples of essays representing each level of the Scoring Rubric:

Prompt

Some high schools in the United States have wired their classrooms with Internet connections. Some educators think that students must be given the most up-to-date learning tools. Other teachers think that Internet connections can create distractions during class and even promote cheating among students. In your opinion, should high school classrooms provide Internet connections for students?

In your essay, take a position on this question. You may write about one of the points of view mentioned above, or you may give another point of view on this issue. Use specific examples and reasons for your position.

1: Of course we should have computers in classrooms. Computers are everywhere now. Kid might play games sometimes or whatever but so what? Kids will always find a way to waste time. Sometimes, I read magazines, in class, anyway, but I still learned. Everyone knows that computers are everywhere now and you can't really get a job without knowing how to work one. I don't think that we should go without computers just because they pay teachers too much or waste money on other things like cheerleading outfits and that kinds of stuff. Other schools have computers and its not fair if everyone don't have them just because they are rich!!

This essay scores a 1 because it demonstrates very little understanding of the task. The author assumes that Internet connections and computers are the same thing. He fails to consider that classrooms can have computers without having Internet connections. There are several distracting grammatical errors and the discussion is focused on irrelevant personal details. The author also fails to consider the other side of the argument, even though it is mentioned in the prompt. There are some interesting points raised, such as equality of opportunity and budget priorities, but they are not developed at all. Overall, this essay is poor.

2: Computers is important and the Internets helps computers work right but I can see the problem with putting it all around in school. Maybe theres other ways. I could do it anways I guess so it probly don't matter or either it does but if you can't help it, why worry?

If there was enough computers to go around then it would be more better and no one would have to go without one and we could all communicate and share stuff for class and not just chat with our friends who have computers also.

I can't say for sure that there should be Internet all around because of hackers and security. I know that some things on the Internet arent really good for our mind. So, in the end, I will conclude that therefore we should get computers if the Internet is the best thing for us to learn on.

This essay scores a 2 mainly because it fails to take a clear position on the issue. While this essay does stay focused on the relevant issue, it does not answer the question posed by the prompt and it contains several very distracting errors. Some of the ideas are potentially interesting but are left almost completely undeveloped. The grammar and punctuation errors are sufficient to guarantee that this essay will receive a well-below-average score. This essay does consider counterarguments. However, it allows the counterarguments to obscure the author's position.

3: I think that an Internet connection would help to get us to use computers more for research and to send e-mails to teachers. It is everywhere now and everything is on the Internet. I used a web sight to write my paper and I got an A. Other students might use the Internet for cheating but the teachers can catch us right away if they use the internet too. If I am going to use computers and the Internet all the time in college anyway, we may as well get started now so that we now how to do it right and get good grades in college so we can get good jobs later in life. Isn't that the point of school anyway? So we can get ready for our jobs? I think so and so do my parents and I'm sure that they agree that we should have internet computers in class. If we don't, then what are we going to do? Just work out of books like my grandma did? And do work on the board? I don't think that is the best way to learn about how to survive in the modern world. And, that is what the schools should do for us all!

This essay scores a 3 because it shows some skill in responding to the prompt. There is a clear point of view and it is supported by examples. This essay does consider counterarguments. However, there is irrelevant information and some grammar and punctuation issues. The essay does a fairly good job of responding to counterarguments and has some structure. However, the essay leaves most of its potential undeveloped, and the conclusion does not effectively respond to the prompt or tie in to the author's main point. The author also uses us *as synonymous with* students. *This is an example of a low average essay.*

4: I believe that wiring our classrooms for the Internet would be in the best interests of the students and the teachers also. Teachers would find ways to use the Internet help students in many ways.

First, teachers can use the Web to show students web sites to help teach important subjects that are not in our books yet. A lot of information that is newer can only be found on the web. For example, there are web sites that show pictures of Mars from NASA that are so new that they aren't in any of our books. They are interesting and can get students excited to learn more. If our class didn't have Internet access, we might not get to see the pictures at all.

Second, the Internet can save steps in doing research for papers and assignments. Instead of trying to find books in the library, students can search the Web and find great resources to support our thesis statements. For example, students could use encyclopedia sites to search for information much more quickly than walking up and down the rows of shelves in the library and trying to find books that aren't even there sometimes anyway.

Finally, e-mail can be a great way to ask questions even after class. Teachers can answer e-mail questions whenever they get a chance and maybe even take a little extra time to look up some answers for their students. For example, if a student asks to learn about Mars in an e-mail, a teacher can find details and maybe some links and put them in the answer to the student.

Therefore, as shown, it is clear that schools should have the Internet in the classrooms so that teachers can teach students better.

This essay scores a 4. This essay has a simple, straightforward structure and uses examples to support its points. There are few technical errors and the vocabulary is varied and used appropriately. The introduction and conclusion echo each other and there is little or no irrelevant information in the passage. The author is not excessively self-referential as some of the previous authors were. Overall, a good, solid, well-constructed essay in the high average range.

5: As schools consider the question of wiring classrooms for the Internet, it seems that the best choice would be in favor of the Internet. After considering both sides of the issue, it should be clear that the Internet is more of a positive than a negative. It is important for students to have the most up-to-date tools as they pursue their education.

Everyone should agree that computer use is only likely to increase in the future. Students will need to have computer skills in order to compete in college and in the job market later. While it may be true that there are some issues to consider, there are several good reasons to provide Internet access to classrooms.

For instance, educators can access a wide variety of useful and current information at their fingertips, such as fresh images from outer space to help explain planets and galaxies to students. Students are sure to respond better to beautiful photos from the orbiting Hubble telescope than to the tired, old models that are found in most school science classrooms.

Even though students may find ways to abuse Internet connections, it seems that teachers and staff should be able to control things like cheating and chatting or surfing during class time. It is true that there are sites that sell term papers to students, the teachers can access the same sites and should not be fooled unless they are not on the ball. As for chatting and surfing, the computers can be turned off when they aren't being used just like cell phones are now.

E-mail can be important also. Students and teachers can exchange e-mail messages on weekends or during holidays. Teachers can send e-mails out to an entire class reminding them of quizzes or exams, or giving links to important web sites that can help students to understand subjects.

Finally, I think that it comes down to a simple matter of staying up with the times. In earlier generations, students used chalkboards and shared books that were only updated every few years. As society progressed, we began to add chemistry labs and biology dissections along with slide and movie projectors and televisions with educational videotapes. It seems to me that the next obvious step is to get up with the times and get computers in the classrooms where they belong.

This essay scores a 5. While not perfect, it is nearly error-free and well structured. The author's points are clearly stated and then backed up with relevant examples. The paragraphs are each built around a subtopic that adds support to the author's response to the prompt. The essay reveals a depth of thought and creativity in raising potential arguments and dealing with them effectively. The vocabulary choices are appropriate and varied. This is a well-above-average essay.

6: There are those who are concerned with the negative potential of the Internet. They cite the possibility of cheating or time wasting by students. Their concerns stem from the fact that the Internet and, more specifically, the World Wide Web, is a source of both good and bad information. It is true that there are sites that actually offer term papers for sale. Even students who do not go to that extreme may be tempted to plagiarize from legitimate web sites. Students may also find that e-mail is an efficient tool for sharing gossip and other information that does not contribute to their education. And, of course, the computers and the Internet are often used for playing games that usually have little to no educational value.

However, all educational technology, from the pencil, to videotape, has the potential to be abused. Just because students have always used pencil and paper to write notes to, and about, each other, does not mean that classrooms would be better off without them. In fact, as technology improves it always finds its way into the learning environment. Take videotape, for example. At first videotape was for professionals only, and then Hollywood found a way to exploit the profit potential. Finally, the educational potential of the technology was unleashed when schools invested in VCR's and students were able to view educational programming on a flexible schedule. No one can deny that VCR's are a useful tool for educators.

Now is the time for schools to move forward and adopt the latest technology again. Computers are a fact of life and they are only becoming more prevalent.

Schools did not turn their backs on videotape simply because some teachers could potentially have shirked their responsibilities by showing "movies" almost every day rather than actually teaching their classes. Nor, should schools turn their backs on the amazing potential of computers and the Internet simply because there are possibilities of abuse.

The advantages of computers are many. Instructors can use web sites as support for lectures, and student can use them as sources for information. E-mail can be a means of flexible communication that can keep students in touch with each other and their teachers. Electronic communication can save precious resources such as paper and ink and there is research that shows that students tend to stay on a task longer on the computer than on paper.

Also, we should consider the fact that some students come from homes with computers and some do not. If there are no Internet connections in the schools, then only some students will have Internet access; some students will be left behind simply because their families can't afford computers.

In conclusion, even though there are arguments against wiring schools for the Internet, it should be clear that it is the right thing to do for a number of reasons. The benefits outweigh the risks. The schools that do not have Internet connections should move forward and get online.

This essay scores a 6. It is superior in its logical structure and its vocabulary use. The author combines creativity with a clear logical development of ideas and makes almost no technical errors. The essay also raises less obvious aspects of the issue under discussion and weaves them into a persuasive essay. Note that this essay is longer than the others. It is not always necessary to write a long essay to get a good score. However, it is difficult to get a 5 or a 6 with an extremely short essay because there won't be sufficient room to fully develop the ideas in the essay.

PART IV

FOUR PRACTICE TESTS

ACT PRACTICE TESTS

These tests should help you to evaluate your progress in preparing for the ACT. Take the tests under realistic conditions (preferably early in the morning in a quiet location), and allow approximately 3.5 hours for each entire test. Each of the test sections should be taken in the time indicated at the beginning of the sections, and in the order in which they appear. Fill in the bubbles on your answer sheet once you have made your selections.

When you have finished each test, check your answers against the Answer Key. Follow the directions on how to score your test. Then, read the Explanations, paying close attention to the explanations for the questions that you missed.

■ ANSWER SHEET

ACT PRACTICE TEST 1
Answer Sheet

ENGLISH

1 Ⓐ Ⓑ Ⓒ Ⓓ	21 Ⓐ Ⓑ Ⓒ Ⓓ	41 Ⓐ Ⓑ Ⓒ Ⓓ	61 Ⓐ Ⓑ Ⓒ Ⓓ
2 Ⓕ Ⓖ Ⓗ Ⓙ	22 Ⓕ Ⓖ Ⓗ Ⓙ	42 Ⓕ Ⓖ Ⓗ Ⓙ	62 Ⓕ Ⓖ Ⓗ Ⓙ
3 Ⓐ Ⓑ Ⓒ Ⓓ	23 Ⓐ Ⓑ Ⓒ Ⓓ	43 Ⓐ Ⓑ Ⓒ Ⓓ	63 Ⓐ Ⓑ Ⓒ Ⓓ
4 Ⓕ Ⓖ Ⓗ Ⓙ	24 Ⓕ Ⓖ Ⓗ Ⓙ	44 Ⓕ Ⓖ Ⓗ Ⓙ	64 Ⓕ Ⓖ Ⓗ Ⓙ
5 Ⓐ Ⓑ Ⓒ Ⓓ	25 Ⓐ Ⓑ Ⓒ Ⓓ	45 Ⓐ Ⓑ Ⓒ Ⓓ	65 Ⓐ Ⓑ Ⓒ Ⓓ
6 Ⓕ Ⓖ Ⓗ Ⓙ	26 Ⓕ Ⓖ Ⓗ Ⓙ	46 Ⓕ Ⓖ Ⓗ Ⓙ	66 Ⓕ Ⓖ Ⓗ Ⓙ
7 Ⓐ Ⓑ Ⓒ Ⓓ	27 Ⓐ Ⓑ Ⓒ Ⓓ	47 Ⓐ Ⓑ Ⓒ Ⓓ	67 Ⓐ Ⓑ Ⓒ Ⓓ
8 Ⓕ Ⓖ Ⓗ Ⓙ	28 Ⓕ Ⓖ Ⓗ Ⓙ	48 Ⓕ Ⓖ Ⓗ Ⓙ	68 Ⓕ Ⓖ Ⓗ Ⓙ
9 Ⓐ Ⓑ Ⓒ Ⓓ	29 Ⓐ Ⓑ Ⓒ Ⓓ	49 Ⓐ Ⓑ Ⓒ Ⓓ	69 Ⓐ Ⓑ Ⓒ Ⓓ
10 Ⓕ Ⓖ Ⓗ Ⓙ	30 Ⓕ Ⓖ Ⓗ Ⓙ	50 Ⓕ Ⓖ Ⓗ Ⓙ	70 Ⓕ Ⓖ Ⓗ Ⓙ
11 Ⓐ Ⓑ Ⓒ Ⓓ	31 Ⓐ Ⓑ Ⓒ Ⓓ	51 Ⓐ Ⓑ Ⓒ Ⓓ	71 Ⓐ Ⓑ Ⓒ Ⓓ
12 Ⓕ Ⓖ Ⓗ Ⓙ	32 Ⓕ Ⓖ Ⓗ Ⓙ	52 Ⓕ Ⓖ Ⓗ Ⓙ	72 Ⓕ Ⓖ Ⓗ Ⓙ
13 Ⓐ Ⓑ Ⓒ Ⓓ	33 Ⓐ Ⓑ Ⓒ Ⓓ	53 Ⓐ Ⓑ Ⓒ Ⓓ	73 Ⓐ Ⓑ Ⓒ Ⓓ
14 Ⓕ Ⓖ Ⓗ Ⓙ	34 Ⓕ Ⓖ Ⓗ Ⓙ	54 Ⓕ Ⓖ Ⓗ Ⓙ	74 Ⓕ Ⓖ Ⓗ Ⓙ
15 Ⓐ Ⓑ Ⓒ Ⓓ	35 Ⓐ Ⓑ Ⓒ Ⓓ	55 Ⓐ Ⓑ Ⓒ Ⓓ	75 Ⓐ Ⓑ Ⓒ Ⓓ
16 Ⓕ Ⓖ Ⓗ Ⓙ	36 Ⓕ Ⓖ Ⓗ Ⓙ	56 Ⓕ Ⓖ Ⓗ Ⓙ	
17 Ⓐ Ⓑ Ⓒ Ⓓ	37 Ⓐ Ⓑ Ⓒ Ⓓ	57 Ⓐ Ⓑ Ⓒ Ⓓ	
18 Ⓕ Ⓖ Ⓗ Ⓙ	38 Ⓕ Ⓖ Ⓗ Ⓙ	58 Ⓕ Ⓖ Ⓗ Ⓙ	
19 Ⓐ Ⓑ Ⓒ Ⓓ	39 Ⓐ Ⓑ Ⓒ Ⓓ	59 Ⓐ Ⓑ Ⓒ Ⓓ	
20 Ⓕ Ⓖ Ⓗ Ⓙ	40 Ⓕ Ⓖ Ⓗ Ⓙ	60 Ⓕ Ⓖ Ⓗ Ⓙ	

MATH

1 Ⓐ Ⓑ Ⓒ Ⓓ Ⓔ	16 Ⓕ Ⓖ Ⓗ Ⓙ Ⓚ	31 Ⓐ Ⓑ Ⓒ Ⓓ Ⓔ	46 Ⓕ Ⓖ Ⓗ Ⓙ Ⓚ
2 Ⓕ Ⓖ Ⓗ Ⓙ Ⓚ	17 Ⓐ Ⓑ Ⓒ Ⓓ Ⓔ	32 Ⓕ Ⓖ Ⓗ Ⓙ Ⓚ	47 Ⓐ Ⓑ Ⓒ Ⓓ Ⓔ
3 Ⓐ Ⓑ Ⓒ Ⓓ Ⓔ	18 Ⓕ Ⓖ Ⓗ Ⓙ Ⓚ	33 Ⓐ Ⓑ Ⓒ Ⓓ Ⓔ	48 Ⓕ Ⓖ Ⓗ Ⓙ Ⓚ
4 Ⓕ Ⓖ Ⓗ Ⓙ Ⓚ	19 Ⓐ Ⓑ Ⓒ Ⓓ Ⓔ	34 Ⓕ Ⓖ Ⓗ Ⓙ Ⓚ	49 Ⓐ Ⓑ Ⓒ Ⓓ Ⓔ
5 Ⓐ Ⓑ Ⓒ Ⓓ Ⓔ	20 Ⓕ Ⓖ Ⓗ Ⓙ Ⓚ	35 Ⓐ Ⓑ Ⓒ Ⓓ Ⓔ	50 Ⓕ Ⓖ Ⓗ Ⓙ Ⓚ
6 Ⓕ Ⓖ Ⓗ Ⓙ Ⓚ	21 Ⓐ Ⓑ Ⓒ Ⓓ Ⓔ	36 Ⓕ Ⓖ Ⓗ Ⓙ Ⓚ	51 Ⓐ Ⓑ Ⓒ Ⓓ Ⓔ
7 Ⓐ Ⓑ Ⓒ Ⓓ Ⓔ	22 Ⓕ Ⓖ Ⓗ Ⓙ Ⓚ	37 Ⓐ Ⓑ Ⓒ Ⓓ Ⓔ	52 Ⓕ Ⓖ Ⓗ Ⓙ Ⓚ
8 Ⓕ Ⓖ Ⓗ Ⓙ Ⓚ	23 Ⓐ Ⓑ Ⓒ Ⓓ Ⓔ	38 Ⓕ Ⓖ Ⓗ Ⓙ Ⓚ	53 Ⓐ Ⓑ Ⓒ Ⓓ Ⓔ
9 Ⓐ Ⓑ Ⓒ Ⓓ Ⓔ	24 Ⓕ Ⓖ Ⓗ Ⓙ Ⓚ	39 Ⓐ Ⓑ Ⓒ Ⓓ Ⓔ	54 Ⓕ Ⓖ Ⓗ Ⓙ Ⓚ
10 Ⓕ Ⓖ Ⓗ Ⓙ Ⓚ	25 Ⓐ Ⓑ Ⓒ Ⓓ Ⓔ	40 Ⓕ Ⓖ Ⓗ Ⓙ Ⓚ	55 Ⓐ Ⓑ Ⓒ Ⓓ Ⓔ
11 Ⓐ Ⓑ Ⓒ Ⓓ Ⓔ	26 Ⓕ Ⓖ Ⓗ Ⓙ Ⓚ	41 Ⓐ Ⓑ Ⓒ Ⓓ Ⓔ	56 Ⓕ Ⓖ Ⓗ Ⓙ Ⓚ
12 Ⓕ Ⓖ Ⓗ Ⓙ Ⓚ	27 Ⓐ Ⓑ Ⓒ Ⓓ Ⓔ	42 Ⓕ Ⓖ Ⓗ Ⓙ Ⓚ	57 Ⓐ Ⓑ Ⓒ Ⓓ Ⓔ
13 Ⓐ Ⓑ Ⓒ Ⓓ Ⓔ	28 Ⓕ Ⓖ Ⓗ Ⓙ Ⓚ	43 Ⓐ Ⓑ Ⓒ Ⓓ Ⓔ	58 Ⓕ Ⓖ Ⓗ Ⓙ Ⓚ
14 Ⓕ Ⓖ Ⓗ Ⓙ Ⓚ	29 Ⓐ Ⓑ Ⓒ Ⓓ Ⓔ	44 Ⓕ Ⓖ Ⓗ Ⓙ Ⓚ	59 Ⓐ Ⓑ Ⓒ Ⓓ Ⓔ
15 Ⓐ Ⓑ Ⓒ Ⓓ Ⓔ	30 Ⓕ Ⓖ Ⓗ Ⓙ Ⓚ	45 Ⓐ Ⓑ Ⓒ Ⓓ Ⓔ	60 Ⓕ Ⓖ Ⓗ Ⓙ Ⓚ

READING

1 (A) (B) (C) (D)	11 (A) (B) (C) (D)	21 (A) (B) (C) (D)	31 (A) (B) (C) (D)
2 (F) (G) (H) (J)	12 (F) (G) (H) (J)	22 (F) (G) (H) (J)	32 (F) (G) (H) (J)
3 (A) (B) (C) (D)	13 (A) (B) (C) (D)	23 (A) (B) (C) (D)	33 (A) (B) (C) (D)
4 (F) (G) (H) (J)	14 (F) (G) (H) (J)	24 (F) (G) (H) (J)	34 (F) (G) (H) (J)
5 (A) (B) (C) (D)	15 (A) (B) (C) (D)	25 (A) (B) (C) (D)	35 (A) (B) (C) (D)
6 (F) (G) (H) (J)	16 (F) (G) (H) (J)	26 (F) (G) (H) (J)	36 (F) (G) (H) (J)
7 (A) (B) (C) (D)	17 (A) (B) (C) (D)	27 (A) (B) (C) (D)	37 (A) (B) (C) (D)
8 (F) (G) (H) (J)	18 (F) (G) (H) (J)	28 (F) (G) (H) (J)	38 (F) (G) (H) (J)
9 (A) (B) (C) (D)	19 (A) (B) (C) (D)	29 (A) (B) (C) (D)	39 (A) (B) (C) (D)
10 (F) (G) (H) (J)	20 (F) (G) (H) (J)	30 (F) (G) (H) (J)	40 (F) (G) (H) (J)

SCIENCE

1 (A) (B) (C) (D)	11 (A) (B) (C) (D)	21 (A) (B) (C) (D)	31 (A) (B) (C) (D)
2 (F) (G) (H) (J)	12 (F) (G) (H) (J)	22 (F) (G) (H) (J)	32 (F) (G) (H) (J)
3 (A) (B) (C) (D)	13 (A) (B) (C) (D)	23 (A) (B) (C) (D)	33 (A) (B) (C) (D)
4 (F) (G) (H) (J)	14 (F) (G) (H) (J)	24 (F) (G) (H) (J)	34 (F) (G) (H) (J)
5 (A) (B) (C) (D)	15 (A) (B) (C) (D)	25 (A) (B) (C) (D)	35 (A) (B) (C) (D)
6 (F) (G) (H) (J)	16 (F) (G) (H) (J)	26 (F) (G) (H) (J)	36 (F) (G) (H) (J)
7 (A) (B) (C) (D)	17 (A) (B) (C) (D)	27 (A) (B) (C) (D)	37 (A) (B) (C) (D)
8 (F) (G) (H) (J)	18 (F) (G) (H) (J)	28 (F) (G) (H) (J)	38 (F) (G) (H) (J)
9 (A) (B) (C) (D)	19 (A) (B) (C) (D)	29 (A) (B) (C) (D)	39 (A) (B) (C) (D)
10 (F) (G) (H) (J)	20 (F) (G) (H) (J)	30 (F) (G) (H) (J)	40 (F) (G) (H) (J)

RAW SCORES	**SCALE SCORES**	DATE TAKEN:
ENGLISH _____	ENGLISH _____	
MATH _____	MATH _____	ENGLISH/WRITING _____
READING _____	READING _____	
SCIENCE _____	SCIENCE _____	**COMPOSITE SCORE**

1 ■ ■ ■ ■ ■ ■ ■ ■ 1

ENGLISH TEST

45 Minutes – 75 Questions

DIRECTIONS: In the passages that follow, some words and phrases are underlined and numbered. In the answer column, you will find alternatives for the words and phrases that are underlined. Choose the alternative that you think is best and fill in the corresponding bubble on your answer sheet. If you think that the original version is best, choose "NO CHANGE," which will always be either answer choice A or F. You will also find questions about a particular section of the passage, or about the entire passage. These questions will be identified by either an underlined portion or by a number in a box. Look for the answer that clearly expresses the idea, is consistent with the style and tone of the passage, and makes the correct use of standard written English. Read the passage through once before answering the questions. For some questions, you should read beyond the indicated portion before you answer.

PASSAGE I

A Focused Intelligence

Aviator Charles A. Lindbergh was undeniably a man of genius. In 1927, he was the first person to fly from New York to Paris. Such success is not the result of academic excellence, but the result of ingenuity and determination.
<u>excellence, but the result of ingenuity</u>
₁

1. **A.** NO CHANGE
   B. excellence, but the result, of ingenuity,
   C. excellence but the result of, ingenuity
   D. excellence

Throughout his childhood and early <u>adulthood</u> being
₂
Charles Lindbergh was not interested in erudition. In 1918, with the U.S. in the throes of World <u>War I, as a result of which</u>
₃
Lindbergh eagerly agreed to return to the farm to grow food for the war effort in exchange for his high school diploma. Though the small Minnesota <u>farm, under his</u>
₄
<u>care, thrived,</u> his passion was not for agriculture, but
₄
for things mechanical. When he expressed these interests to his parents (a congressman and a <u>teacher),</u> encouraged
₅
him to obtain a more formal education.

2. **F.** NO CHANGE
   G. adulthood, he,
   H. adulthood, which was
   J. adulthood,

3. **A.** NO CHANGE
   B. War I;
   C. War I,
   D. War I, the result was that

4. **F.** NO CHANGE
   G. farm thrived, under his care
   H. farm thrived under his care,
   J. under his care, the farm thrived,

5. **A.** NO CHANGE
   B. teacher). They
   C. teacher), they
   D. teacher; they

Lindbergh attended the University of Wisconsin to study engineering. However, Lindbergh's penchant for "hands-on" learning, combined with a lack of scholarly discipline and study skills, <u>because of</u> academic probation
₆
after barely two years. Realizing that the only practical

6. **F.** NO CHANGE
   G. resulted in
   H. as a result of
   J. primarily resulting from

GO ON TO THE NEXT PAGE.

1 ■ ■ ■ ■ ■ ■ ■ ■ 1

knowledge he had gained in college was through his participation in the Reserve Officers' Training Corps (R.O.T.C.), Lindbergh dropped out of college, never to <u>return in pursuit of a degree.</u>
₇

7. **A.** NO CHANGE
   B. return.
   C. return without a bodyguard.
   D. return without kicking and screaming.

In 1922, after brief aviation training at the Nebraska Aircraft Corporation, Lindbergh spent two summers traveling from state to state <u>performing: as a</u>
₈
<u>barnstormer,</u> wingwalker, parachutist, and sky diver.
₈

8. **F.** NO CHANGE
   G. performing, as a barnstormer
   H. performing; as a barnstormer,
   J. performing as a barnstormer,

Having now <u>found</u> his true passion as a pilot, Lindbergh
₉
enlisted in the Army along with 103 other would-be flying cadets. Despite his aversion to classroom learning, he <u>focused</u> his efforts and learned to truly study
₁₀
during ground school. Failing any one test would have resulted in being "washed out," but Lindbergh passed his tests with "flying" colors. <u>In 1925, at graduation,</u>
₁₁
only eighteen cadets remained — with Lindbergh achieving the highest ranking among all of the members of his class.

9. **A.** NO CHANGE
   B. able to find
   C. discovers
   D. finding

10. **F.** NO CHANGE
    G. has focused
    H. was focusing
    J. focuses

11. **A.** NO CHANGE
    B. At graduation, which was in 1925,
    C. When he graduated in 1925,
    D. At graduation, in 1925, he and

<u>Despite his</u> disinterest in formal education, Lindbergh
₁₂
displayed an enjoyment for learning throughout his life,

12. **F.** NO CHANGE
    G. Despite, his
    H. Due to his
    J. Irregardless of his

<u>seeking and accepted</u> new challenges. He charted
₁₃
transcontinental and transoceanic air routes that are still used today. His sister-in-law's fatal heart condition

13. **A.** NO CHANGE
    B. sought and accepting
    C. seeking and accepting
    D. seeks and accepts

<u>led to his work in the development (with surgeon Alexis</u>
₁₄
<u>Carrel) of a perfusion pump</u> which enabled a
₁₄
damaged heart to continue pumping while doctors

14. **F.** NO CHANGE
    G. led to his work with surgeon Alexis Carrel on the development of a perfusion pump
    H. led to the development of a perfusion pump with surgeon Alexis Carrel
    J. led to the surgeon Alexis Carrel and his work with him to develop a perfusion pump

GO ON TO THE NEXT PAGE.

worked to repair it. ⬚15

15. Which of the following choices should the writer use here to provide an appropriate conclusion to the essay?
  A. Charles Lindbergh dedicated his efforts toward preserving wildlife and the environment for the rest of his life.
  B. Charles Lindbergh realized that his initial admiration of Hitler's leadership had been wrong and he helped the U.S. defeat the Axis powers during World War II.
  C. Charles Lindbergh developed cancer and spent his last days in Hawaii, surrounded by family.
  D. Charles Lindbergh could look back with the wisdom of life's experiences, knowing that he had focused his intelligence in untraditional ways and changed the world.

Crude Sophistication

The Vikings of Scandinavia (what is now Norway, Sweden, and Denmark) led what would today be considered a crude existence. In many ways, <u>hence,</u>
16
they were far more advanced than their contemporaries.

16. The writer wants to emphasize that the Vikings, though crude in many ways, were sophisticated in many others. Which choice does that best?
  F. NO CHANGE
  G. similarly,
  H. however,
  J. to that end,

⬚17 This argument, however, is moot, given that the Native Americans beat them both by thousands of years.

The Vikings were among the first international

17. Which of the following sentences, if inserted here, would best illustrate the accomplishments of the Vikings?
  A. Vikings were very loyal to family members, even if they did something wrong.
  B. Vikings gained much of their wealth by robbing and plundering, finding easy victims in Christian monasteries.
  C. Vikings traveled far and wide.
  D. Although Christopher Columbus is credited with "discovering" America in 1492, Viking explorers appear to have reached North America much earlier.

<u>seafaring, traders with</u> purpose-built,
18

18. F. NO CHANGE
  G. seafaring traders: with
  H. seafaring traders, with,
  J. seafaring traders with

<u>wooden trading ships.</u> Vikings sailed from Norway
19
through the Straits of Gibraltar to the eastern Mediterranean. Vikings also crossed the Atlantic Ocean,

19. A. NO CHANGE
  B. trading ships constructed of wooden products.
  C. wooden ships for trading.
  D. ships, constructed of wood, for trading.

GO ON TO THE NEXT PAGE.

1 ■ ■ ■ ■ ■ ■ ■ ■ **1**

settling in Iceland and Greenland. From there, the Vikings of Scandinavian countries crossed a much [20] shorter distance over to the North American continent where archaeological evidence of their landing has been found in what is now northern Newfoundland, Canada. Whether they arrived "first" or not; their distant travel [21] during the ninth to twelfth centuries is, nevertheless, remarkable.

The Vikings were skillful boat-builders and sailors. Their varied boats were built for many purposes, and included small river boats, ocean-going cargo ships, and even warships used to raid their Christian neighbors. [22] Viking traders sailed around the Baltic sea, obtaining furs

and amber. In Russia, they will meet up and traded goods [23] with Arab traders carrying silks and spices.

Vikings possessed many complicated skills. For example, their steel sword and ax blades were heavy and [24] powerful. Similar craftsmanship was used by leather [24] workers on shoes, harnesses, and saddlery. The women

also possessed diverse skills. Making butter, cheese, [25] and ale, and often weaving intricate geometric designs

into their multi-colored fabrics (woven fabrics are still [26] used inclothes throughout the world today). [26]
One way in which the Vikings were behind their contemporaries was in reading and writing. Few Vikings could read or write, so those who could were considered [27] valuable. Records of brave deeds were etched on large

standing stones. These runes; were made up of sixteen [28] different symbols. Because so few Vikings could read, they

20. F. NO CHANGE
G. they
H. the Vikings of Scandinavia
J. Scandinavian Vikings

21. A. NO CHANGE
B. not, their
C. not: their
D. not; they're

22. F. NO CHANGE
G. evenly to
H. up evenly to
J. even for

23. A. NO CHANGE
B. met
C. would meet
D. would be meeting

24. Given that all of them are true, which choice supports the paragraph by giving the most specific details?
F. NO CHANGE
G. well made.
H. often inlaid with intricate designs in silver.
J. made of steel.

25. A. NO CHANGE
B. skills? Making
C. skills! Making
D. skills, making

26. F. NO CHANGE
G. fabrics; fabrics like those used in today's clothes.
H. fabrics — clothes are made from fabrics.
J. fabrics.

27. A. NO CHANGE
B. was considering
C. that were considerate
D. considered

28. F. NO CHANGE
G. These rune's
H. These runes
J. They're runes

GO ON TO THE NEXT PAGE.

believed that runes <u>were</u> magical and could be used to cast
29
spells. Because they wrote down very little of their history
or beliefs, most of what is known of the Vikings today is
the result of archaeologists' discoveries and 30 .

29. A. NO CHANGE
  B. had been
  C. were being
  D. was being

30. The writer wants the final statement to reflect
  information previously provided in the essay. Given
  that all of the following concluding phrases are true,
  which one, if inserted here, would do that best?
  F. written records of people who met them, such as
    their Christian neighbors (and victims) and the
    Arabs with whom they traded.
  G. other research.
  H. some recovered runes, which were often used by
    the archaeologists to cast spells and make
    predictions.
  J. the testimonies of Scandinavian immigrants to
    America.

PASSAGE III

> The following paragraphs may or may not be in the
> most logical order. You may be asked questions about
> the logical order of the paragraphs, as well as where to
> place sentences logically within any given paragraph.

Everybody Loves Kari

[1]

Kari has always been one of my favorite cousins. She
and <u>me were</u> allies against the older, bigger cousins in
31
games of hide-and-seek.

But <u>Kari's appeal</u> to me isn't unique
32

31. A. NO CHANGE
  B. I was
  C. I were
  D. me was

32. F. NO CHANGE
  G. the appeal of Kari
  H. the appealingness of Kari
  J. Kari's level of appeal

— it's universal! <u>She has a</u> pretty face and long legs make
33
her irresistible to boys. Her genuine concern for others
combined with her occasional forgetfulness makes her

nonthreatening among <u>girls; and her</u> gregarious
34
nature juxtaposed with a genuine sweetness appeals

33. A. NO CHANGE
  B. She's
  C. It's her
  D. Her

34. F. NO CHANGE
  G. girls: her
  H. girls her
  J. girls, and her

GO ON TO THE NEXT PAGE.

1 ▪ ▪ ▪ ▪ ▪ ▪ ▪ ▪ 1

to adults. Despite her overwhelming popularity,

her congeniality occasionally gets her into trouble. ☐35

[2]

Girls State provides promising High School Juniors the

opportunity of participating on hands-on citizenship
                              ———————————
                                   36
training. They learn about government by electing each

other as public officials on the local, county, and state

levels and then by carrying out the respective duties of

their offices. From each Girls State, two Senators are

chosen to continue on to Girls Nation. Kari

was of course chosen to be one of her state's senators.
———————————
        37

[3]

At Girls Nation, the schedule was packed from
                        —————————
                            38
morning until night — with one exception: The girls were

allowed one afternoon to sight-see according to their own

agenda. Kari had been sightseeing for about five minutes

when she was meeting a nice young military
            ——————————
                39

cadet, who gallantly offered, to show her around the
————————————————————
            40
nation's capital. After a fun (and surprisingly educational)

day together, Kari vowed to write often. Unlike most

people who promises to write, Kari actually does.
       ————————————————————————————
                    41

[4]

[1] Kari and the cadet were pen pals for several months

until one fateful day when Kari wrote to a girlfriend from

35. Which of the following sentences, if added here, would most effectively signal the essay's shift in focus occurring at this point?
   A. *Congeniality* is defined as "pleasant," "sociable," or "genial."
   B. Take, for example, the time she was chosen to represent her home town at the American Legion Auxiliary Girls State convention.
   C. Kari doesn't get into trouble with the law — just embarrassing situations like you see on television comedies.
   D. I could give you many examples.

36. F. NO CHANGE
   G. of participating in
   H. in participation of
   J. to participate in

37. A. NO CHANGE
   B. was of course chosen:
   C. was of, course chosen,
   D. was, of course, chosen

38. F. NO CHANGE
   G. schedule
   H. schedules was
   J. schedules where

39. A. NO CHANGE
   B. met
   C. had meeted
   D. had a meeting with

40. F. NO CHANGE
   G. cadet, who, gallantly offered
   H. cadet who gallantly offered:
   J. cadet, who gallantly offered

41. A. NO CHANGE
   B. who promise to write, Kari actually does.
   C. Kari actually does write when she promises she'll write.
   D. to whom they promise to write to, Kari does it.

GO ON TO THE NEXT PAGE.

1 ■ ■ ■ ■ ■ ■ ■ **1**

camp. [2] Her letter to her girlfriend was newsy and filled with many confidences. [3] Kari had attended three proms (with three different boys) that spring, and she had enjoyed herself at each. [4] Her favorite, however, had been with a very cute boy from a town 100 miles away. [5] (How Kari met him is another long story, the details of which she did *not* omit in her letter to her girlfriend.) [42] [6] The same day, Kari wrote a letter to the cadet. [7] However, out of consideration for the hard-working young man, she omitted information about the many social events she had recently attended. [8] A week later, she received a brief note from the cadet with her letter returned. [9] It said, "I believe you intended

the enclosed letter for another friend." [43]

Kari and the cadet stopped corresponding.
44

42. The writer had considered deleting the italics on the word *not* in the preceding sentence and revising *did not* to read as the contraction *didn't*. If the writer had done this, the sentence would have lost its:

   I. emphasis on the difference between Kari's letter to her girlfriend and her letter to the cadet.

   II. implication that this information was insignificant in the letter.

   III. suggestion that this information would be critical later in the essay.

F. I only
G. III only
H. I and II only
J. I and III only

43. The writer is considering the division of Paragraph 4 into two separate paragraphs. In terms of the logic and coherence of the essay, the best course of action to take would be to:

A. begin a new paragraph with Sentence 3.
B. begin a new paragraph with Sentence 4.
C. begin a new paragraph with Sentence 6.
D. begin a new paragraph with Sentence 7.

44. The writer wishes to add a light note at this point, supporting the essay's sense of completion by tying the ending back to the essay's beginning. Given that all are true, which choice would best accomplish this?

F. NO CHANGE
G. Okay, so *almost* everybody loves Kari.
H. When Kari grew up, she became a minister.
J. The cadet eventually left the military.

The following question asks about the essay as a whole.

45. Suppose the writer had been assigned to write an essay describing the many opportunities that Girls State offered to high school juniors. Would this essay successfully fulfill the assignment?

A. Yes, because the essay indicates that Girls State offers many opportunities to high school juniors.
B. Yes, because Kari was selected to be one of her state's senators.
C. No, because the essay proves that Girls State did not provide high school juniors with any opportunities.
D. No, because the essay is a personal recollection of a favorite cousin.

GO ON TO THE NEXT PAGE.

1 ■ ■ ■ ■ ■ ■ ■ ■ 1

PASSAGE IV

The following paragraphs may or may not be in the most logical order. You may be asked questions about the logical order of the paragraphs, as well as where to place sentences logically within any given paragraph.

Field of Error

[1]

"Hey, Clint!" I shouted. "Did you know that each stalk of corn only has one ear of corn on it?"

"No way! That seven-foot tall stalk only produces one ear of corn?"

"Really! Isn't that amazing? Get it? A-maize-ing!"

[2]

Have you ever asserted yourself as an expert, only to have your "expertise" challenged and proven wrong? The experience can <u>be, humbling,</u> embarrassing, and
46
seemingly never-ending.

[3]

<u>Growing up on a farm in Iowa where I spent my</u>
47
<u>evenings, weekends, and summers performing</u>
47
<u>menial labor.</u> In the course of doing my chores, I picked
47
up a few bits of trivia — like the one-ear-of-corn-per-stalk information. After high school, I went away to

<u>college, and</u> took great pains to ensure that I always
48
had summer jobs lined up that did *not* involve farm labor.

[4]

After college, I moved to the city, where my friends enjoyed hearing occasional anecdotes and bits of trivia about life on the farm. <u>Therefore,</u> the truth as I knew it
49
had changed.

46. **F.** NO CHANGE
     G. be humbling,
     H. be, humbling
     J. be humbling

47. **A.** NO CHANGE
     B. On a farm in Iowa, I grew up where I spent my evenings, weekends, and summers doing menial labor.
     C. Performing menial labor in the evenings, on weekends and in summers, I grew up on a farm in Iowa where I did those things.
     D. I grew up on a farm in Iowa where I spent my evenings, weekends, and summers performing menial labor.

48. **F.** NO CHANGE
     G. college and
     H. college,
     J. college

49. **A.** NO CHANGE
     B. Unfortunately,
     C. In other words,
     D. Hence,

GO ON TO THE NEXT PAGE.

1 ■ ■ ■ ■ ■ ■ ■ ■ 1

[5]

Apparently, while I was away at college and beginning
50
my career, genetic engineering had been employed in the
field of agriculture and corn stalks now regularly sported
two ears of corn instead of one. I learned this the
51
hard way.
51

One day, as my friend Clint and his friends were
52

about to tee off from hole number five, Clint spied a
53
cornfield.

[6]

54 "Hey guys! I'll bet you ten bucks that not one stalk of
corn out there has more than one ear on it." "You're
crazy!" they replied. "We'll take that bet!" And so
Clint lost ten dollars and some measure of pride.

I on the other hand lost all credibility.
55

It's now much later, ten years later, in fact, and
56

I cannot see Clint without reminding me of his
57

lost bet. 58

---

50. F. NO CHANGE
G. In addition,
H. Regardless,
J. Similarly,

51. A. NO CHANGE
B. This, I learned, the hard way.
C. I learned something like this the hard way.
D. The hard way is how I learned this.

52. F. NO CHANGE
G. Once in a while
H. One day long ago
J. One day, a while back,

53. A. NO CHANGE
B. from the hole at the far end of the golf course from the club house,
C. from the fifth hole,
D. OMIT the underlined portion.

54. At this point, the writer would like the reader to imagine the emotion and motivation behind Clint's next words. Which of the following sentences, if added here, would most effectively accomplish this?
F. "Here's a bet I'm sure to win!" he thought to himself.
G. "Golfing is a dumb game," he mused.
H. "I know something about corn," he said.
J. "There's a cornfield," Clint thought to himself.

55. A. NO CHANGE
B. I, on the other hand lost
C. I on the other hand, lost,
D. I, on the other hand, lost

56. F. NO CHANGE
G. Now, after ten long years,
H. It's been ten years,
J. Ten long years have gone by

57. A. NO CHANGE
B. without his reminding me
C. without being reminded by him
D. without receiving a reminder from him

58. The writer would like to add an introductory sentence to Paragraph 6 that shows why Clint challenged his friends. Which of the choices does that best?
F. My friend Clint likes to make small bets with his golfing buddies.
G. My friend Clint has been to Las Vegas many times.
H. My friend Clint loves to golf.
J. My friend Clint attended the University of Michigan.

GO ON TO THE NEXT PAGE.

1 ■ ■ ■ ■ ■ ■ ■ ■ 1

Questions 59 and 60 ask about the essay as a whole.

59. The writer is considering adding the following sentence to the essay, in order to emphasize that she did not intentionally mislead her friends.

With the exception of occasionally exaggerating some of the "characters" in my stories, I told my friends the truth.

If added, this new sentence would best support and be placed after the first sentence in Paragraph:

A. 2
B. 3
C. 4
D. 5

60. Suppose the writer had been assigned to write an article for a farming magazine that described the impact of genetic engineering on agriculture. Would this essay successfully fulfill the assignment?
F. No, because the essay describes the writer's experience with the repercussions of authoritatively sharing outdated information.
G. No, because the essay focuses on the golf habits of her friend and does not describe genetic engineering in agriculture in detail.
H. Yes, because the essay focuses on how genetic engineering has increased corn yields.
J. Yes, because the essay states that corn stalks now contain two ears of corn where there previously was only one.

PASSAGE V

The Perfect Part-Time Job

Like most college students, I usually needed extra cash. However, I was a bit too discriminating in how I earned that money. Since my parents were paying my tuition, I couldn't very well get a job that interfered with my classes, <u>where</u> did I want to give up any of my
61
extracurricular activities. Babysitting often fit within these parameters, but it usually didn't pay very well. I scoured the campus papers, but the good jobs were always taken by the time <u>one could call.</u> And then,
62
one day, I found it — the perfect part-time job.

As I left my sociology class one day, I saw the flyer <u>posting nearly outside</u> the door. "Help wanted for
63
Psychology Dissertation Research — Acting Experience

61. A. NO CHANGE
B. and
C. nor
D. but

62. F. NO CHANGE
G. I called.
H. you could call.
J. you can call.

63. A. NO CHANGE
B. just flying outside
C. posted just outside
D. it was posted just outside

GO ON TO THE NEXT PAGE.

1 ■ ■ ■ ■ ■ ■ ■ ■ 1

Requested." Now, normally, I avoided any opportunities

that involved psychology research because <u>it</u> generally
₆₄

involved some form of pain or deprivation for a very

small <u>stipend, which can range from twenty to</u>
₆₅

<u>fifty dollars.</u> Nevertheless, I was intrigued by the
₆₅

request for "acting experience," <u>and</u> since most of my
₆₆

extracurricular time was spent on stage, I decided this

one warranted a phone call.

    As it turned out, I was to be the <u>experimenter; not</u> the
₆₇

subject. And I did not have to inflict any pain. Essentially,

I read the same series of questions to the <u>subjects of</u> the
₆₈

experiment and <u>providing varied levels of feedback</u> to
₆₉

each subjects' answers. In some cases, I would say nothing

and simply read the questions. In other cases, I would say

things like, "Uh huh," or "Yeah, that happened to me

<u>once!"</u> In some cases, I kept my face devoid of emotion
₇₀

and made very little eye contact. In other cases, I nodded,

smiled, leaned forward, showed concern, and so on, in

response to the subject's answers. By combining these

<u>verbal, and nonverbal,</u> responses, I played four different
₇₁

roles.

    [1] Although the pay was minimal, I found the work

<u>exhausting.</u> [2] I would have loved for the experiments
₇₂

to continue, but the research grant money was running

low and the experiments had already yielded definitive

results. [3] All too soon, the experiments were completed.

64. **F.** NO CHANGE
    G. they
    H. it's
    J. its

65. **A.** NO CHANGE
    B. stipend.
    C. twenty to fifty-dollar stipend.
    D. stipend. These are usually in the twenty to fifty-dollar range.

66. **F.** NO CHANGE
    G. request for "acting experience" and
    H. requesting "acting experience," and
    J. request for "acting, experience," and

67. **A.** NO CHANGE
    B. experimenter — not
    C. experimenter: not
    D. experimenter — not,

68. **F.** NO CHANGE
    G. subjects in
    H. subject to
    J. subjective of

69. **A.** NO CHANGE
    B. various levels of feedback were provided
    C. providing varying levels of feedback
    D. provided varying levels of feedback

70. **F.** NO CHANGE
    G. once!" and in
    H. once!" so in
    J. once!", because in

71. **A.** NO CHANGE
    B. verbal, and nonverbal
    C. verbal and nonverbal
    D. verbal, and, nonverbal

72. The writer wishes to conclude this sentence with a phrase that would explain why she would have liked the job to continue. Which choice would best accomplish this?
    F. NO CHANGE
    G. fascinating and fun.
    H. about the same as babysitting.
    J. better than nothing.

GO ON TO THE NEXT PAGE.

1 ■ ■ ■ ■ ■ ■ ■ ■ 1

[4] To avoid inadvertently skewing the results, I was not allowed to know the researcher's hypothesis ahead of time. [5] When the experiments were complete, my suspicions were confirmed: Body language (nonverbal feedback) affects what (and how much) people tell you far more than anything you say. 73

73. For the sake of unity and coherence, Sentence 3 of the last paragraph should be placed:
A. where it is now.
B. immediately before Sentence 1.
C. immediately before Sentence 2.
D. immediately before Sentence 5.

Questions 74 and 75 ask about the essay as a whole.

74. The writer is considering the addition of the following sentence to the essay:

William James Hall is the building where classes for both the Sociology Department and the Psychology Department are held.

Given that this statement is true, should it be added to the essay, and if so, where?

F. Yes, at the very beginning, because the sentence effectively introduces the subject of this essay.
G. Yes, at the beginning of the second paragraph, because the sentence explains why the writer would have seen a psychology flyer outside a sociology classroom.
H. No, because the information does not add value to this essay about a part-time job.
J. No, because it is unlikely that any of the students know who William James is.

75. Suppose that the editor of a magazine had assigned the writer to depict a firsthand account of an undergraduate majoring in Sociology. Does the essay successfully fulfill this assignment?
A. Yes, because the essay describes what happens when the writer is leaving a sociology class.
B. Yes, because sociology and psychology are closely linked.
C. No, because the essay describes a part-time job working on a psychology dissertation research project.
D. No, because the essay's tone is too formal and too personal for such an assignment.

END OF THE ENGLISH TEST
STOP! IF YOU HAVE TIME LEFT OVER, CHECK YOUR WORK ON THIS SECTION ONLY.

2      **2**

MATHEMATICS TEST

60 Minutes – 60 Questions

DIRECTIONS: Solve each of the problems in the time allowed, then fill in the corresponding bubble on your answer sheet. Do not spend too much time on any one problem; skip the more difficult problems and go back to them later. You may use a calculator on this test. For this test you should assume that figures are NOT necessarily drawn to scale, that all geometric figures lie in a plane, and that the word *line* is used to indicate a straight line.

---

1. If $2x + 5 = 17$, then $x = ?$
   A. 3
   B. 6
   C. 10
   D. 11
   E. 24

2. Consider the 3 statements below to be true.

   All horses that run fast are brown.

   Horse A is not brown.

   Horse B runs fast.

   Which of the following statements is true?

   F. Horse B is not brown.
   G. Horse B is brown.
   H. All brown horses run fast.
   J. Horse A runs fast.
   K. Both horse A and horse B are brown.

3. If the probability that John will oversleep is 0.2, what is the probability that he will NOT oversleep?
   A. 0.0
   B. 0.2
   C. 0.4
   D. 0.8
   E. 1.2

4. Sam bought 2 stuffed animals for $3.59 each and 2 others for $6.49 each. What was the average price per stuffed animal that she paid for these 4 stuffed animals?

   F. $\dfrac{\$3.59}{2} + \dfrac{\$6.49}{2}$

   G. $\dfrac{2(\$3.59) + 2(\$6.49)}{4}$

   H. $\dfrac{\$3.59 + \$6.49}{4}$

   J. $\dfrac{\$3.59 + \$6.49}{3}$

   K. $\dfrac{2(\$3.59) + 2(\$6.49)}{2}$

DO YOUR FIGURING HERE.

GO ON TO THE NEXT PAGE.

2   **2**

DO YOUR FIGURING HERE.

5. On Saturday, Mike received his pay and spent $\frac{1}{3}$ of it. On Sunday he spent $\frac{1}{3}$ of the remaining money, and on Monday he spent $\frac{1}{2}$ of what remained from Sunday. If \$10 then remained, how much pay did he receive originally?
   A. \$27
   B. \$36
   C. \$45
   D. \$60
   E. \$180

6. If $a^2 = 64$ and $b^2 = 81$, which of the following CANNOT be the value of $a + b$?
   F. -17
   G. -1
   H. 1
   J. 17
   K. 145

7. In the figure below, B is the midpoint of $\overline{AC}$, $\overline{AC}$ is parallel to $\overline{DG}$, and $\overline{BE}$ is congruent to $\overline{BF}$. What is the measure of angle BFG?

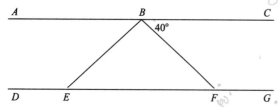

   A. $40°$
   B. $80°$
   C. $90°$
   D. $140°$
   E. $180°$

8. If $x = -3$, then $x^2 - 6x - 18 = ?$
   F. 9
   G. 0
   H. -9
   J. -27
   K. -45

9. The average of 5 numbers is 4.2. If each of the numbers is increased by 2.5, what is the average of the 5 new numbers?
   A. 1.7
   B. 2.5
   C. 4.2
   D. 6.7
   E. 9.2

10. The expression $8x - 8y$ is equivalent to which of the following?
    F. $8(x - y)$
    G. $8(x + y)$
    H. $8xy$
    J. $-8(x + y)$
    K. $-8xy$

GO ON TO THE NEXT PAGE.

2 △ △ △ △ △ △ △ △ **2**

DO YOUR FIGURING HERE.

11. For each day that you stuff envelopes, you receive $17.00 plus a fixed amount for each envelope that you stuff. Currently you are earning $52.00 per day for stuffing 350 envelopes. Today you are assigned to stuff an additional 250 envelopes. What will be your new daily earnings?
   A. $17.00
   B. $27.00
   C. $52.00
   D. $52.25
   E. $77.00

12. If $\dfrac{2}{x} \geq \dfrac{1}{7}$, what is the largest possible value for x?
   F. $\dfrac{1}{2}$
   G. 7
   H. 14
   J. 15
   K. 28

13. A circle with a circumference of 46π is divided evenly into 12 sectors. What is the total measure, in degrees, of 5 sectors?
   A. $46°$
   B. $60°$
   C. $115°$
   D. $150°$
   E. $230°$

14. In the standard (x,y) coordinate plane below, $PQRS$ is a parallelogram. Which of the following could be the coordinates of point Q?

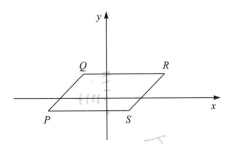

   F. $(6,4)$
   G. $(4,-1)$
   H. $(-6,-1)$
   J. $(-4,1)$
   K. $(0,-1)$

15. Which of the following equations has both $x=-3$ and $x=6$ as solutions?
   A. $(x-6)(x+3)=0$
   B. $(x+6)(x+3)=0$
   C. $(x+6)(x-3)=0$
   D. $(x-6)(x-3)=0$
   E. $x-6=x+3$

GO ON TO THE NEXT PAGE.

2   **2**

DO YOUR FIGURING HERE.

16. A classroom has $(r - 3s)$ rows of seats and $4t$ seats in each row. Which of the following is an expression for the number of seats in the entire classroom?

   F. $r(-3s)4t$
   G. $(4r \cdot 12s) + (4r \cdot 4t)$
   H. $4t + (r(-3s))$
   J. $r - 3s + 4t$
   K. $(4t \cdot r) - (4t \cdot 3s)$

17. If 60% of x equals 90, then $x = ?$

   A. 5.4
   B. 15
   C. 54
   D. 150
   E. 1,500

18. The price of 1 box of popcorn and 1 drink together is $5.10. The price of 2 boxes of popcorn and 1 drink together is $8.35. What is the cost of 1 drink?

   F. $0.75
   G. $1.85
   H. $2.15
   J. $2.55
   K. $3.25

19. You are standing in line at the cash register to pay for 2 lamps priced at $8.99 each. A sales tax of 7% of the cost of the lamps will be added (rounded to the nearest cent) to the price of the 2 lamps. You have 20 one-dollar bills. How much will you need in coins if you want to have exact change ready?

   A. $0.24
   B. $0.38
   C. $0.62
   D. $0.76
   E. $0.87

20. For which nonnegative value of x is the expression $\dfrac{1}{(300 - 3x^2)}$ undefined?

   F. 0
   G. 5
   H. 10
   J. 30
   K. 300

21. What is the correct order of π, $\dfrac{7}{3}$, and $\dfrac{9}{2}$ from least to greatest?

   A. $\dfrac{9}{2} < \pi < \dfrac{7}{3}$
   B. $\dfrac{7}{3} < \pi < \dfrac{9}{2}$
   C. $\pi < \dfrac{9}{2} < \dfrac{7}{3}$
   D. $\pi < \dfrac{7}{3} < \dfrac{9}{2}$
   E. $\dfrac{9}{2} < \dfrac{7}{3} < \pi$

GO ON TO THE NEXT PAGE.

2   **2**

DO YOUR FIGURING HERE.

22. What number can you add to the numerator and denominator of $\frac{9}{13}$ to get $\frac{3}{4}$?

   F. -3
   G. $-1\frac{1}{4}$
   H. $1\frac{1}{2}$
   J. 3
   K. 6

23. The ratio of the radii of 2 circles is 4:9. What is the ratio of their areas?
   A. 4:81
   B. 16:81
   C. 4:9
   D. 16:9
   E. 81:16

24. Which of the following gives all the solutions of $x^2 - 4x = 12$?
   F. -6 and 2
   G. -2 and 6
   H. -4 and 3
   J. -6 only
   K. 12 only

25. If $(t+v)^2 = 289$ and $tv = 30$, then $t^2 - v^2 = ?$
   A. -11
   B. 1
   C. 11
   D. 61
   E. 229

26. If, for all x, $(x^{3a+5})^4 = x^{44}$, then $a = ?$
   F. 1
   G. 2
   H. $\frac{16}{3}$
   J. $\frac{53}{12}$
   K. 5

27. Which of the following is a value of x that satisfies $\log_x 16 = 2$?
   A. 2
   B. 4
   C. 8
   D. 16
   E. 32

28. One endpoint of a line segment in the (x,y) coordinate plane has coordinates $(-2,9)$. The midpoint of the segment has coordinates $(4,4)$. What are the coordinates of the other endpoint of the segment?
   F. $(-8,13)$
   G. $(-6,5)$
   H. $(2,13)$
   J. $(10,-1)$
   K. $(-8,36)$

GO ON TO THE NEXT PAGE.

2   **2**

29. In the (x,y) coordinate plane, what is the radius of the circle $(x-4)^2 + (y-1)^2 = 14$?
   A. 7
   B. 14
   C. $\sqrt{7}$
   D. $\sqrt{14}$
   E. 296

DO YOUR FIGURING HERE.

30. In the right triangle shown below, $\cos \angle A = ?$

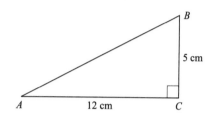

   F. $\dfrac{5}{12}$

   G. $\dfrac{5}{13}$

   H. $\dfrac{12}{13}$

   J. $\dfrac{13}{12}$

   K. $\dfrac{12}{5}$

31. For all nonzero a and b, $\dfrac{(13a^2b^4)(-8a^3b^5)}{(4a^2b^6)} = ?$
   A. $26a^3b^{14}$
   B. $-26a^3b^3$
   C. $\dfrac{a^3b^3}{-26}$
   D. $-26a^4b^9$
   E. $\dfrac{-26}{ab}$

32. Which of the following sets of 3 numbers could be the side lengths, in feet, of an isosceles triangle?
   F. 1, 2, 3
   G. 2, 2, 2
   H. 2, $2\sqrt{3}$, 4
   J. 1, 2, $2\sqrt{2}$
   K. 2, 2, $2\sqrt{2}$

GO ON TO THE NEXT PAGE.

2   **2**

33. The figure below shows square *ABCD* and also shows the circle centered at *D* with radii $\overline{DC}$ and $\overline{DA}$. If the area of the square is 64 units, what is the circumference of the circle, in units?

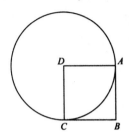

   A. 4π
   B. 8π
   C. 16π
   D. 32π
   E. 64π

34. Which of the following logical statements identifies the same set as the graph shown below?

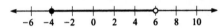

   F. $x \geq -4$ and $x < 6$
   G. $x > -4$ and $x < 6$
   H. $x \geq -4$ or $x < 6$
   J. $x \leq -4$ and $x > 6$
   K. $x \leq -4$ or $x > 6$

35. Jeff leans a 12-foot ladder against the side of his garage. The side of the garage is perpendicular to the ground so that the base of the ladder is 7 feet away from the base of the garage. To the nearest foot, how far up the garage does the ladder reach?
   A. 5 feet
   B. 7 feet
   C. 10 feet
   D. 12 feet
   E. 19 feet

36. If x and y are real and $\sqrt{3}\left(\dfrac{x^2}{2y}\right) = 4$, then what must be true of the values of x and y?
   F. x and y must both be negative
   G. x and y must both be positive
   H. x and y must both be positive or both be negative
   J. x and y must have opposite signs
   K. x and y may have any value

37. For all pairs of real numbers A and S where $A = 2S + 9$, $S = ?$

   A. $\dfrac{A}{9} + 2$

   B. $\dfrac{A}{9} - 2$

   C. $9A - 2$

   D. $\dfrac{A - 9}{2}$

   E. $\dfrac{A + 9}{2}$

DO YOUR FIGURING HERE.

GO ON TO THE NEXT PAGE.

2   **2**

DO YOUR FIGURING HERE.

38. What is the slope of any line perpendicular to the *y*-axis in the (*x,y*) coordinate plane?
    F. −1
    G. 0
    H. 1
    J. Undefined
    K. Cannot be determined from the given information

39. Which of the following lines has the smallest slope?
    A. $y = 3x - 5$
    B. $y = x + 4$
    C. $4y = 24x - 8$
    D. $3y = 9x + 6$
    E. $y = -7x + 8$

40. A right triangle has side lengths as shown below. What is (tan α)(cos β)?

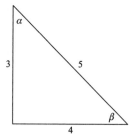

    F. $\dfrac{5}{12}$

    G. $\dfrac{4}{9}$

    H. $\dfrac{15}{20}$

    J. $\dfrac{2}{15}$

    K. $\dfrac{16}{15}$

41. Amy can run 3 miles in *s* minutes. At that pace, how many miles can she run in 50 minutes?

    A. $\dfrac{3s}{50}$

    B. $\dfrac{50s}{3}$

    C. $50\dfrac{(s)}{3}$

    D. $3(50s)$

    E. $\dfrac{150}{s}$

42. An oil tank contains 4,800 gallons of oil. Each gallon of oil weighs approximately 6 pounds. About how many pounds does the oil in the tank weigh?
    F. 800
    G. 4,806
    H. 6,000
    J. 28,800
    K. 46,800

GO ON TO THE NEXT PAGE.

2   **2**

43. In triangle ABC, the measure of $\angle A$ is 30° and the measure of $\angle B$ is 60°. If $\overline{AB}$ is 16 units long, what is the area, in square units, of triangle ABC?

   A. 16
   B. $16\sqrt{3}$
   C. $32\sqrt{3}$
   D. 256
   E. $256\sqrt{3}$

44. Trapezoid $FGHJ$ below is isosceles, with side lengths as marked. Its diagonals intersect at K. What is the ratio of the length of $\overline{HK}$ to the length of $\overline{GK}$?

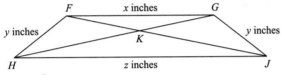

   F. $\dfrac{z}{x}$
   G. $\dfrac{x}{z}$
   H. $\dfrac{y}{z}$
   J. 1
   K. $\dfrac{z}{y}$

45. A certain rectangle is 2 times as long as it is wide. Suppose the length is tripled and the width is doubled. The area of the second rectangle is how many times as large as the area of the first?

   A. 2
   B. 3
   C. 6
   D. 9
   E. 12

46. For what value of z would the following system of equations have an infinite number of solutions?

$$24x - 15y = 108$$
$$72x - 45y = 9z$$

   F. 3
   G. 9
   H. 12
   J. 36
   K. 108

47. How many prime numbers are there between 36 and 53?

   A. 4
   B. 5
   C. 6
   D. 7
   E. 8

GO ON TO THE NEXT PAGE.

2

48. If $\tan A = \dfrac{x}{y}$, $x > 0$, $y > 0$, and $0 < A < 90°$, what is $\sin A$?

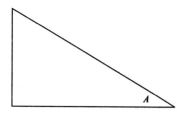

F. $\dfrac{x}{y}$

G. $\dfrac{y}{x}$

H. $\dfrac{x}{\sqrt{x^2 + y^2}}$

J. $\dfrac{y}{\sqrt{x^2 + y^2}}$

K. $\dfrac{\sqrt{x^2 + y^2}}{x}$

49. In the parallelogram below, lengths are given in centimeters. What is the area of the parallelogram, in square centimeters?

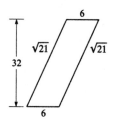

A. $\sqrt{21}$
B. $2\sqrt{21}$
C. $\sqrt{105}$
D. 96
E. 192

50. Points A, B, and C lie on the same line. If the length of $\overline{AB}$ is 9 meters and the length of $\overline{BC}$ is 11 meters, then what are all the possible lengths, in meters, for $\overline{AC}$?
   F. 20 only
   G. 2 only
   H. 2 and 20 only
   J. Any number less than 2 or greater than 20
   K. Any number greater than 20 or less than 2

GO ON TO THE NEXT PAGE.

2 △ △ △ △ △ △ △ △ **2**

51. Given the vertices of parallelogram *FGHJ* in the standard *(x,y)* coordinate plane below,

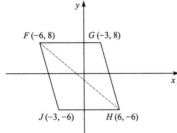

what is the area of triangle *FGH*, in square units?

A. 9.0
B. 21.0
C. 31.5
D. 63.0
E. 126.0

DO YOUR FIGURING HERE.

52. If $6a^5b^7 < 0$, then which of the following must be true?
  F. $a > 0$ and $b > 0$ or $a < 0$ and $b < 0$
  G. $a > 0$ and $b < 0$ or $a < 0$ and $b > 0$
  H. $a = b$
  J. $a < 0$ and $b < 0$
  K. $a > b$

53. Mandy visited 7 patients on her first day as a nurse. Her goal was to visit 3 more patients on each successive day than she had visited the day before. If Mandy met, but did not exceed her goal, how many patients did she visit in all during her first 5 days as a nurse?
  A. 19
  B. 35
  C. 65
  D. 105
  E. 325

54. What is the smallest possible value for the product of 2 real numbers that differ by 8?
  F. −16
  G. −4
  H. −2
  J. 6
  K. 8

55. If $0° \leq x \leq 90°$ and $\cos x = \frac{4}{5}$, then $\sin x = ?$

  A. $\frac{3}{5}$

  B. $\frac{3}{4}$

  C. $\frac{4}{5}$

  D. $\frac{5}{4}$

  E. $\frac{4}{3}$

GO ON TO THE NEXT PAGE.

DO YOUR FIGURING HERE.

56. For every dollar decrease in price of a set of books, the bookstore sells 1,200 more sets of books per month. The bookstore normally sells 1,750 sets of books per month at \$9.50 per set of books. Which of the following expressions represents the number of sets of books sold per month if the cost is reduced by x dollars per set of books?

  F. $1,750 + 1,200x$
  G. $1,750 - 1,200x$
  H. $(2.50 - x)(1,750 + 1,200x)$
  J. $2.50 + 1,200x$
  K. $1,750 + 2.50x$

57. In a game, 45 marbles numbered 00 through 44 are placed in a box. A player draws 1 marble at random from the box. Without replacing the first marble, the player draws a second marble at random. If the numbers on both marbles drawn have a sum greater than 45 (that is, the sum of Marble 1 and Marble 2 exceeds 45), the player is a winner. If the first marble Martin draws is numbered 17, what is the probability that Martin will be a winner on the next draw?

  A. 4/11
  B. 16/45
  C. 17/44
  D. 17/45
  E. 16/43

58. In the figure below, all of the line segments are either horizontal or vertical, as shown, and the dimensions are given in centimeters. What is the perimeter, in centimeters, of the figure?

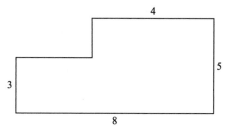

  F. 26
  G. 29
  H. 31
  J. 32
  K. 81

59. In the standard (x,y) coordinate plane, the vertices of a square have coordinates (0,4), (4,4), (4,0), and (0,0). Which of the following is an equation of a circle that is inscribed in the square?

  A $(x+2)^2 + (y+2)^2 = 2$
  B. $(x-2)^2 + (y-2)^2 = 2$
  C. $(x-2)^2 + (y-2)^2 = 4$
  D. $(x+2)^2 + (y-2)^2 = 4$
  E. $(x+2)^2 + (y+2)^2 = 8$

GO ON TO THE NEXT PAGE.

2 △ △ △ △ △ △ △ △ **2**

60. On Monday, a skirt was priced at $60.00. On Wednesday, the price was reduced by 15%. Two weeks later, the price was further reduced by 20%. What percent of the original price is this last price?
   F. 35%
   G. 40%
   H. 51%
   J. 65%
   K. 68%

DO YOUR FIGURING HERE.

END OF THE MATH TEST
STOP! IF YOU HAVE TIME LEFT OVER, CHECK YOUR WORK ON THIS SECTION ONLY.

3 ████████████████████████████████████ **3**

READING TEST

35 Minutes – 40 Questions

DIRECTIONS: This test includes four passages, each followed by ten questions. Read the passage and choose the best answer to each question. After you have selected your answer, fill in the corresponding bubble on your answer sheet. You should refer to the passages as often as necessary when answering the questions.

Passage I

PROSE FICTION: *This passage is adapted from "The Awakening," by Kate Chopin, originally published in 1899.*

Mrs. Pontellier's eyes were quick and bright; they were a yellowish brown, about the color of her hair. She had a way of turning them swiftly upon an object and holding them there as if lost in some inward
5 maze of contemplation or thought. Her eyebrows were a shade darker than her hair. They were thick and almost horizontal, emphasizing the depth of her eyes. She was rather more handsome than beautiful. Her face was captivating by reason of a certain
10 frankness of expression and a contradictory subtle play of features. Her manner was engaging.

Robert LeBruns had a cigar in his pocket which Mr. Pontellier had presented him with, and he was saving it for his after-dinner smoke. This seemed
15 quite proper and natural on his part. In coloring he was not unlike his companion. A clean-shaved face made the resemblance more pronounced than it would otherwise have been. There rested no shadow of care upon his open countenance. His eyes gathered
20 in and reflected the light and languor of the summer day.

Mrs. Pontellier reached over for a palm-leaf fan that lay on the porch and began to fan herself, while she and Robert chatted incessantly; about the things
25 around them; their amusing adventure out in the water — it had again assumed its entertaining aspect; about the wind, the trees, the people who had gone to the Cheniere; about the children playing croquet under the oaks, and the Farival twins, who were now
30 performing the overture to "The Poet and the Peasant."

Robert talked a good deal about himself. He was very young, and did not know any better. Mrs. Pontellier talked a little about herself for the same
35 reason. Each was interested in what the other said. Robert spoke of his intention to go to Mexico in the autumn, where fortune awaited him. He was always intending to go to Mexico, but some way never got there. Meanwhile, he held on to his modest position in
40 the mercantile house in New Orleans, where an equal familiarity with English, French, and Spanish gave him no small value as a clerk and correspondent.

He was spending his summer vacation, as he always did, with his mother at Grand Isle. In former
45 times, before Robert could remember, "the house" had been a summer luxury of the LeBruns. Now, flanked by its dozen or more cottages, which were always filled with exclusive tenants from the "Quartier Francais," it enabled Madame LeBruns to
50 maintain the easy and comfortable existence which appeared to be her birthright.

Mrs. Pontellier talked about her father's Mississippi plantation and her girlhood home in the old Kentucky bluegrass country. She was an
55 American woman, with a small infusion of French which seemed to have been lost in dilution. She read a letter from her sister, who was away in the East, and who had engaged herself to be married. Robert was interested, and wanted to know what manner of
60 girls the sisters were, what the father was like, and how long the mother had been dead.

When Mrs. Pontellier folded the letter it was time for her to dress for the early dinner. "I see Leonce isn't coming back," she said, with a glance in the
65 direction whence her husband had disappeared. Robert supposed he was not, as there were a good many New Orleans club men over at Klein's. When Mrs. Pontellier left him to enter her room, the young man descended the steps and strolled over toward the
70 croquet players, where, during the half-hour before dinner, he amused himself with the little Pontellier children, who were very fond of him.

1. When Mrs. Pontellier says "I see Leonce isn't coming back," she is expressing her belief that:
   A. she will be having dinner without her husband.
   B. Robert knew her husband wasn't returning.
   C. her husband has left her.
   D. she must go to Klein's for dinner.

2. It can reasonably be inferred from their conversation that Mrs. Pontellier and Robert are:
   F. related to each other.
   G. each married to someone else.
   H. about the same age.
   J. long-time friends.

GO ON TO THE NEXT PAGE.

3 ██ **3**

3. The idea that Robert aspires to gain more wealth and social stature than he currently has is best exemplified by which of the following quotations from the passage?
   A. "... where fortune awaited him."
   B. "... the young man descended the steps and strolled over toward the croquet players ..."
   C. "... gave him no small value as a clerk and correspondent."
   D. "Robert talked a good deal about himself."

4. As it is used in paragraph 3, "She and Robert chatted incessantly" most nearly means that:
   F. they each talked about themselves.
   G. they had a long and lively conversation.
   H. they weren't listening to each other.
   J. they both spoke in loud voices.

5. The passage makes it clear that Mrs. Pontellier and her husband:
   A. never spend time together.
   B. do not get along.
   C. enjoy Robert's company.
   D. have children.

6. In the second paragraph, Robert's physical appearance is compared to:
   F. Mrs. Pontellier's.
   G. Leonce's.
   H. a clean-shaved face.
   J. Mr. Pontellier's.

7. We may reasonably infer from details in the passage that all of the characters in the story are:
   A. poor.
   B. sociable.
   C. kind.
   D. generous.

8. Paragraph 4 indicates that Robert's feelings about himself are best described as:
   F. unfulfilled.
   G. disinterested.
   H. mournful.
   J. confident.

9. It can be reasonably inferred from information in the passage that:
   A. Robert's mother was better off financially in an earlier time.
   B. Robert is visiting his mother to help her out.
   C. Robert will never go to Mexico.
   D. Robert pretends to be more well-off than he is.

10. Details in the passage suggest that Mrs. Pontellier:
   F. longs to go back to her family home.
   G. feels like a stranger at Grand Isle.
   H. does not enjoy being a wife and mother.
   J. is accustomed to being without her husband.

GO ON TO THE NEXT PAGE.

3 ██ **3**

Passage II
SOCIAL SCIENCE: *Whales in Inuit Life*

As a result of the overhunting of whales by commercial whaling ships, many whales became endangered — some to the point of near extinction. In response, the motto, "Save the Whales" became
5 a common phrase. The thought of killing this large mammal for human consumption was appalling to many westerners. And so, in 1977, the International Whaling Committee (IWC) imposed a moratorium on all whaling. Almost immediately, a great cry
10 sounded from the Inuit — the indigenous people of the Arctic Circle who rely on the whale for their very survival.

Since about 800 A.D., Inuit whalers have hunted bowhead whales. Whaling songs date back nearly as
15 far. The whale has many uses, and no part of the animal is wasted. The *baleen* (whalebone) is used to house equipment and insulate boots; the huge vertebrae are used for seats. The stomach and bladder are used for drums. The remainder, inclu-
20 ding even the tongue, skin, and other organs, are used for food.

This food is surprisingly nutritious. A serving of whale meat is 95 percent protein. The meat is also rich in iron, niacin, vitamin E, and phosphorus. A
25 favorite snack, *maktaaq* (whale skin) is rich in calcium, selenium, and Omega-3 fatty acids. A study of Inuit eating habits found that those who consumed primarily traditional Inuit food (60 to 70 percent whale meat) were less likely to be obese
30 than Inuit who consumed a more Western diet.

Although the whale itself is prized for the sum of its parts, the process of whaling contributes to the Inuit sense of community. The communal nature of the hunt and the sharing of the whale give the
35 animal a central place in their cultural and spiritual life. The whole village helps haul in the whale, butcher it, cook it, and distribute it. Sharing the whale throughout the community, and with neighboring communities, is an old, respected practice. At
40 the butchering site, the parts of the whale are divided among the whaling crews, with some shares reserved for elders and widows; other parts are saved for festivals, along with meat from seals and fish.

The whaling captain's family and crew feed the
45 whole community after the first successful hunt. At this time of thanksgiving and sharing, the successful crew shares a portion of the catch with the community. In mid-June, at the end of the whaling season, *Naluqatak*, is celebrated. This feast extends
50 throughout the day, and features a blanket toss, dancing, and many whale delicacies such as *mikigaq* (fermented whale meat) and other traditional Inuit foods such as fish or caribou soup. This simple celebration is actually indicative of the structure of
55 Inuit relationships.

Family is at the center of Inuit culture, with extended family playing an important role in the lives of each family member. The relationship of whaling captain to crew often mimics this familial
60 model. Similarly, the traditional blanket toss at *Naluqatak* is symbolic of the whaling experience.

The process requires the coordinated action of many people pulling on a large piece of *ugruk* (seal) skin to toss an individual into the air, thereby creating
65 a communal version of a trampoline. Finally, at *Naluqatak* and at Thanksgiving and Christmas as well, the food of the whale is given to everyone who comes to take part. In this way, tons of whale meat find their way throughout the region all
70 year long.

Because Inuit culture cannot be separated from the environment, the Inuit respect their surroundings. They believe the Arctic animals, land, sea, and weather are all part of their culture. The
75 Inuit believe that animals are on Earth to provide food and clothing for their survival; to show their respect, they hunt only as many animals as they need. Similarly, even though the hunting season for bowhead whales extends from about
80 mid-April to mid-June as the animals migrate down the coast to their summer feeding grounds, many Inuit never hunt beyond the end of May, to avoid the time when calving females are passing through.

85 The whale provides life, meaning, and identity to the Inuit whalers and their communities. Undoubtedly, prohibiting whaling would endanger Inuit culture far more than the Inuit would ever endanger the whales.

11. According to the passage, the traditional Inuit diet includes all of the following EXCEPT:
    A. *mikigaq*.
    B. baleen.
    C. *maktaaq*.
    D. caribou.

12. According to the passage, the Inuit traditionally hunt which type of whale?
    F. *Naluqatak*
    G. Bowhead
    H. Humpback
    J. *Maktaaq*

13. According to the information presented in the passage, which of the following best describes the relationship between the Inuit and whales?
    A. The Inuit have hunted whales to the point of near extinction.
    B. The Inuit feel that whale hunting is a crime perpetrated by Westerners.
    C. The Inuit worship whales.
    D. The Inuit consider the whales a gift over which they are very protective.

14. According to the passage, whale meat is nutritionally high in all of the following EXCEPT:
    F. phosphorus.
    G. niacin.
    H. riboflavin.
    J. vitamin E.

GO ON TO THE NEXT PAGE.

3 ▬▬▬▬▬▬▬▬▬▬▬▬▬▬▬▬▬▬▬▬▬▬▬▬▬▬▬▬ **3**

15. As it is used in the passage (line 8), the word *moratorium* most nearly means:
    A. a funeral home.
    B. a common phrase.
    C. a suspension of activity.
    D. the relative incidence of disease.

18. It can be inferred from the passage that the Inuit perspective toward the elderly is one of:
    F. respect.
    G. pity.
    H. apathy.
    J. condescension.

16. As it is depicted in the passage, *Naluqatak* can best be described as:
    F. a harvest feast.
    G. a pagan celebration.
    H. a whale delicacy.
    J. a solemn ceremony.

19. According to the passage, some whalers stop hunting at the end of May because:
    A. that is when the calving females are passing through.
    B. that is when the hunting season officially ends.
    C. they don't want to miss *Naluqatak*.
    D. they have caught their quota by then.

17. It can be inferred that the word *coordinated*, as it is used in line 62, primarily refers to:
    A. matching in design, color, and/or texture.
    B. a set of numbers used in specifying a location.
    C. moving together in a smooth, organized way.
    D. athletic and graceful.

20. It can be inferred from the passage that, in addition to whales, the Inuit also hunt:
    F. penguins.
    G. fox.
    H. moose.
    J. seals.

GO ON TO THE NEXT PAGE.

3 ████████████████████████████████████ **3**

Passage III
HUMANITIES: *"Bobby" Jones*

Tiger Woods is often referred to as "the child prodigy of golf." However, eighty years before Woods, another youth made headlines in the world of golf. Robert "Bobby" Tyre Jones, Jr. (1902–1971), is described in the *Oxford Companion to World Sports and Games* as "probably the greatest player the game has known."

At age fourteen, Bobby became the youngest player ever to enter the U.S. amateur championship. At this young age, the precocious Jones was known as a temperamental perfectionist, frequently throwing tantrums (as well as balls and clubs). Atlanta sportswriter O. B. "Pop" Keeler became Bobby's friend and publicist. This mentor helped focus Bobby's passion, and he became known as not only a gracious winner and loser but also a remarkably honorable gentleman.

After two years on the Amateur circuit, Jones entered Georgia Tech to earn his degree in mechanical engineering. While there, he continued to play amateur golf and played on his college team. Immediately after graduation, Jones enrolled at Harvard where, since his collegiate eligibility had been exhausted, he earned a varsity letter as the assistant manager of Harvard's golf team. It is difficult to imagine one of today's professional athletes volunteering to be the assistant manager of a college team!

Perhaps the best story of Jones's sense of fair play comes to us from the 1925 U.S. Open. As he addressed his ball on the long grass on a steep bank near one of the greens, the ball moved. Against official objections, he insisted on adding a penalty stroke to his score. When people remarked on this noble gesture, he replied, "You might as well praise me for not breaking into banks. There is only one way to play this game."

Between 1922 and 1930, Jones placed first or second in eleven U.S. and British Open championship games. In 1924, he earned his Bachelor of Arts degree from Harvard, with a concentration in English. He then obtained a law degree from Emory University, passing the Georgia bar exam in 1928.

At age twenty-eight, Jones won golf's "Grand Slam" of all four major championships in one year and became the only individual ever to receive two New York City tickertape parades. And then, content with his achievements, he retired from competitive golf. Ironically, when Tiger Woods won today's version of the Grand Slam, the fourth win was at the Masters — the golf course (and competition) designed by Bobby Jones. When Tiger Woods entitled his book *How I Play Golf*, it was the same title Bobby Jones had used in his first instructional film series. When Tiger Woods was asked to name his "dream foursome," Woods included Bobby Jones.

Sadly, Jones played his last full round of golf in 1948. He suffered from *syringeomyelia*, a rare spinal disease that degenerates the motor and sensory nerves, which confined Jones to a wheelchair. Although the disease filled his later years with pain, Jones stoically managed to continue to enjoy life. When asked how he coped with the painful spinal condition, his reply belied his suffering: "Remember, we play the ball as it lies."

Bobby Jones never had a formal golf lesson in his life and was known to store his golf clubs most winters. Despite this appearance of nonchalance, Jones was a serious athlete whose skill and grace many still try to emulate.

21. The passage suggests that Tiger Woods, when compared to Bobby Jones, is:
   A. a poor imitation.
   B. similar in many ways.
   C. a more talented athlete.
   D. eighty years older.

22. It can reasonably be inferred from the second paragraph that "Pop" Keeler could be called:
   F. the first sports psychologist.
   G. a controlling and manipulative man.
   H. a swindler and a crook.
   J. a positive force in Jones's life.

23. The passage primarily emphasizes the idea that Jones's golfing success was:
   A. the only thing that mattered in his life.
   B. the result of extensive lessons.
   C. but one highlight of a life well lived.
   D. due to constant practice.

24. As it is used throughout the passage, the word *amateur* means:
   F. one who loves a given activity.
   G. one who plays golf in order to earn fame and fortune.
   H. one lacking in competence.
   J. one who does not receive money for participating in an activity.

25. It can be inferred from the passage that Jones's perspective on higher education was that it:
   A. was important to a well-rounded life.
   B. was really difficult.
   C. was just a way to play more sports.
   D. was entirely unnecessary.

26. In the context of the passage, "You might as well praise me for not breaking into banks" suggests that Jones:
   F. had committed a felony in his temperamental youth.
   G. felt the rules of golf were as unbendable as laws against crime.
   H. hated to receive praise.
   J. thought his admirers were foolish.

GO ON TO THE NEXT PAGE.

3 ████████████████████████████████████ **3**

27. According to the passage, Jones accomplished all of the following in his life, EXCEPT:
    A. designing a world-famous golf course.
    B. passing the bar exam.
    C. graduating from Harvard.
    D. writing a book called *How I Play Golf*.

28. According to the passage, *syringeomyelia*:
    F. occurs most often among golfers.
    G. forced Jones to retire.
    H. gradually left Jones incapacitated.
    J. involves many needles and injections.

29. When Jones commented about playing "the ball where it lies," he was referring to:
    A. his penalty stroke at the 1925 U.S. Open.
    B. his debilitating disease.
    C. a fundamental rule of golf.
    D. being honest.

30. Based on the overall tone of the passage, it can be inferred that the author's opinion of Jones is one of:
    F. admiration and respect.
    G. aloof observation.
    H. utter disdain.
    J. silent suffering.

GO ON TO THE NEXT PAGE.

3 ████████████████████████████████████ **3**

Passage IV
NATURAL SCIENCE: *Wily Coyote*

For decades, aficionados of Saturday morning cartoons have enjoyed the cunning capers of fictional character, Wile E. Coyote. Humorous tales of the coyote did not originate on the Looney
5 Tunes drawing board, however. For hundreds of years, Native American storytellers have shared colorful fables of the beast. These humorous, and occasionally bawdy, "Trickster Tales" are packed with hidden practical advice, moral lessons, and
10 spiritual overtones. Why did Looney Tunes and multiple tribes of Native Americans all cast the coyote as a leading character which is, at any given time, protagonist and antagonist? The answer is in the very nature of the beast itself.

15 Coyotes do, in fact, exhibit some naturally crafty traits. They are smart and learn quickly. They are also remarkably opportunistic and adaptable. Furthermore, they exhibit some remarkable physical feats. In size and shape, coyotes look somewhat like
20 a medium-sized collie, although the coyote's bone structure is lighter and its tail is round and bushy. Despite the physical resemblance (as well as the genetic similarity) to the domestic dog, the coyote is a significantly wilder, more cunning member of the
25 *Canis* family.

For an example of the coyote's opportunistic adaptability, examine the coyote's feeding habits. Coyotes will eat almost anything they can chew, including frogs, snakes, rabbits, mice, and various
30 other small creatures. They eat birds, carrion, and most wild animals. They sometimes kill sheep, poultry and young livestock. In urban areas, coyotes are attracted to garbage, garden vegetables, and pet foods; if opportunities exist, they will prey
35 on unattended small dogs and cats. Insects, fruits, berries, plants, and seeds round out their diet. In essence, they will kill and eat whatever is easiest to come by.

If food is not readily available, the normally
40 solitary (but ever adaptable) coyotes will join forces to hunt larger animals such as deer and antelope. To accomplish this, they will take turns pursuing the animal until it tires or will work as a group to drive the prey toward a hidden member of the pack.
45 Occasionally, coyotes will even form "hunting partnerships" with a badger. The two move together, the coyote using its keen sense of smell to locate burrowing rodents and the badger digging them up with its powerful claws. Both predators
50 then share the proceeds.

The coyotes' clever hunting skills are further aided by their physical abilities. Known to run up to forty miles per hour, they can easily leap an eight-foot fence and have even been known to leap up to
55 fourteen feet. Although generally not known to have exceptional climbing skills, they have nevertheless been spotted climbing over a fourteen-foot cyclone fence. Strong swimmers, coyotes do not hesitate to enter the water after their prey.

60 Another example of the coyotes' adaptability is in their wide range of habitats. They prefer habitats that do not contain wolves, but beyond that, they are not particular, living in clear cuts and farms as readily as in forests or woodlots. Coyotes have a
65 high tolerance for human activity and are rapidly increasing in the suburbs of large cities. Although the coyote usually digs its own den (a wide-mouthed tunnel), it will sometimes enlarge an old badger hole or fix up a natural hole in a rocky ledge.

70 Even the coyotes' reproduction displays their adaptability. Where predators are prevalent and the coyote population is threatened, the typical litter of six pups will often double — and even triple — with up to nineteen pups resulting.

75 In combination with these versatile traits, the final part of the coyote's mystique may stem from the quavering howl and short, high-pitched yips it makes at night. Although these are merely the animal's way of communicating, the human who
80 overhears may experience a tingling fear of primitive danger.

Coyotes originated in the western United States. Despite years of being trapped, shot, and poisoned, coyotes have maintained their numbers there and
85 continue to increase in the East. Today, coyotes are the dominant terrestrial carnivore on most of North America and are found from Central America to the Arctic. Their adaptability, combined with the elimination of most of their predators, including
90 wolves, mountain lions, and bears, has resulted in the coyotes' tremendous expansion.

31. From the author's reference to the coyote as both "protagonist and antagonist," it can be inferred that the coyote exhibits behavior that is both:
A. wise and clever.
B. admirable and despicable.
C. evil and unkind.
D. conniving and deceitful.

32. According to information in the passage, the coyote exhibits all of the following abilities EXCEPT the ability to:
F. run forty miles per hour.
G. locate prey with a keen sense of smell.
H. dig efficiently.
J. overtake its prey in the water.

33. The passage indicates that, unlike domestic collies, coyotes:
A. do not have pointed ears.
B. are generally larger.
C. have a lighter bone structure.
D. carry their tails high in the air.

GO ON TO THE NEXT PAGE.

3 ██████████████████████████████████████ **3**

34. According to the passage, coyotes team up with badgers in order to take advantage of the badger's:
    F. digging abilities.
    G. exceptional climbing skills.
    H. keen sense of smell.
    J. ability to chase deer toward the coyote.

35. It may be reasonably inferred from the passage that if evidence of a coyote is discovered, residents of the community should:
    A. carefully watch their small pets when the pets are outside.
    B. feed their pets outside.
    C. take the garbage out the night before scheduled pick-up.
    D. install a fourteen-foot fence around their property.

36. The passage indicates that the number of pups in a coyote litter is affected by:
    F. the moon.
    G. the availability of food.
    H. bone structure.
    J. the prevalence of predators.

37. According to the passage, coyotes are NOT known for being good:
    A. hunters.
    B. swimmers.
    C. eaters.
    D. climbers.

38. The passage indicates that coyote populations:
    F. are threatened to the point of extinction, due to the use of poisons.
    G. have spread from their original native habitats.
    H. are decreasing in the East.
    J. are increasing in the West.

39. According to the passage, all of the following are predators of the coyote EXCEPT:
    A. bears.
    B. mountain lions.
    C. badgers.
    D. wolves.

40. The author of the passage suggests that the coyote's mystique stems, in part, from its:
    F. strange howl.
    G. partnerships with other animals.
    H. portrayal in cartoons.
    J. affinity for eating cats.

END OF THE READING TEST
STOP! IF YOU HAVE TIME LEFT OVER, CHECK YOUR WORK ON THIS SECTION ONLY.

4

SCIENCE REASONING TEST

35 Minutes – 40 Questions

DIRECTIONS: This test includes seven passages, each followed by several questions. Read the passage and choose the best answer to each question. After you have selected your answer, fill in the corresponding bubble on your answer sheet. You should refer to the passages as often as necessary when answering the questions.

You may NOT use a calculator on this test.

Passage I

Several scientists considered the different environmental factors and their influence on the growth of certain bacteria. The following experiments used *E. coli* bacteria and a controlled temperature to measure the effect of pH levels, nutrients, and growth factors in biosynthesis on the number of bacteria produced within a given time period.

Experiment 1
An *E. coli* bacterium was placed in each of 3 petri dishes with the same nutrient concentration. The pH level of each nutrient concentration was varied according to Table 1. The lids of the petri dishes were replaced and the dishes were left alone. After 6 hours, the percent growth of *E. coli* bacteria was recorded (Table 1).

Table 1		
Dish	pH level	Percent growth
1	6	34
2	7	84
3	8	26

Experiment 2
An *E. coli* bacterium was placed in each of 3 petri dishes with different nutrient concentrations in the form of organic compounds. The lids of the petri dishes were replaced and the dishes were left alone. After 6 hours, the percent growth of *E. coli* bacteria was recorded (Table 2).

Table 2			
Dish	Organic compound	Percent of dry weight	Percent growth
1	Carbon	50	26
	Oxygen	20	
	Nitrogen	14	
2	Carbon	25	14
	Oxygen	10	
	Nitrogen	7	
3	Carbon	12.5	9
	Oxygen	5	
	Nitrogen	3.5	

Experiment 3
An *E. coli* bacterium was placed in each of 3 petri dishes with one of 3 growth factors. Most bacteria, unlike *E. coli*, have 2 requirements for reproduction: growth factors to synthesize nucleic acids and proteins, and small amounts of different vitamins. Experiment 3 was run to ensure that the 3 growth factors have minimal to no effect on growth. The lids of the petri dishes were replaced and the dishes were left alone. After 6 hours, the percent growth of *E. coli* bacteria was recorded (Table 3).

Table 3		
Dish	Growth factors	Percent growth
1	Purines	81
2	Amino acids	79
3	Vitamins	83

GO ON TO THE NEXT PAGE.

4 ◯ ◯ ◯ ◯ ◯ ◯ ◯ ◯ **4**

1. According to Table 1, what might best contribute to the growth of *E. coli* bacteria?
   A. A pH level above 8
   B. A pH level below 6
   C. A pH level near 7
   D. A pH level above 7

2. According to the results of the 3 experiments, *E. coli* bacteria is different from most bacteria in that:
   F. it does not require growth factors to reproduce.
   G. it does not reproduce if a light source is present.
   H. it does not reproduce if amino acids are not available.
   J. it requires a specific nutrient concentration to reproduce.

3. Which of the following conclusions is strengthened by the results of Experiment 1?
   A. *E. coli* bacteria reproduce most efficiently at a pH level of 7.
   B. *E. coli* bacteria cannot reproduce at a pH level below 8.
   C. *E. coli* bacteria cannot reproduce at a pH level above 6.
   D. *E. coli* bacteria can only reproduce if the pH level is near 7.

4. Bacteria will often reproduce until all of the nutrients available have been depleted. How could the experiment be altered to maximize the length of time that bacteria will reproduce?
   F. Change the observation time from 6 hours to 12 hours.
   G. Regularly resupply each group of bacteria with unlimited nutrients.
   H. Increase the rate of growth by decreasing the pH levels.
   J. Do not test the effect of different nutrient combinations on growth.

5. The nutritional requirements of a bacterium are determined by the makeup of the elements within its cells. According to the experiments, which of the following elements are present in the cells of an *E. coli* bacterium?
   A. Oxygen and Hydrogen
   B. Purines and Vitamins
   C. Nitrogen and Amino acids
   D. Carbon and Nitrogen

6. The experiments recorded the percent growth that occurred after a 6-hour period. Bacteria often reproduce at a rate that drastically varies from one stage to the next. The best way to study the different stages of growth would be to record the percent growth:
   F. after 2 hours only.
   G. after 4 hours, then again after 6 hours.
   H. after 8 hours only.
   J. every 15 minutes for 3 hours.

GO ON TO THE NEXT PAGE.

4 ◯ ◯ ◯ ◯ ◯ ◯ ◯ ◯ ◯ **4**

Passage II

The San Francisco Bay Area in California has several fault lines that extend throughout the entire region. The Loma Prieta, the Bay Area's last major earthquake, occurred in 1989 along the San Andreas Fault. The Loma Prieta was centered in a mountainous region that was not heavily populated, unlike San Francisco, which lies only 50 miles south. Experts believe that accurate predictions will allow people in populated areas to take the necessary precautions to minimize earthquake damage. Two scientists discuss the probability of the next major earthquake powerful enough to cause widespread damage in the Bay Area.

Scientist 1

The probability of an earthquake occurring in a heavily populated area is extremely difficult to predict. After the massive earthquake of 1906, the rate of powerful, damaging earthquakes in the Bay Area dropped considerably, even though the area is covered with major fault lines. The probability of an earthquake is determined by considering two activities: tectonic plate motions of the Earth's outer shell and the pressure that is released during an earthquake. Global Positioning Systems (GPS) allow scientists to determine the amount of plate motion and the strain it loads onto faults, the first element of predicting quakes, easily and with much certainty. The amount of strain, or pressure, released, however, is much more difficult to estimate. Scientists currently inspect trenches, analyze data from seismograms, and use historical data to estimate the amount of strain that is released during an earthquake. The main problem is that historical accounts only date back to the 1900s, hardly long enough to illustrate a clear picture of quake activities. Therefore, predictions of the location and the magnitude of an earthquake cannot be made accurately.

Scientist 2

There is a high probability that a major quake will take place within the next 25 years in the Bay Area. Experts can forecast the location and magnitude of an earthquake with a compelling amount of certainty. The probability of an earthquake increases if the strain from plate motion outweighs the amount of pressure released during an actual earthquake. This analysis is complemented with findings from fault line research. The length of fault line ruptures and trenches speak volumes on the magnitude and fault slip of future earthquakes. The 1906 earthquake released over 25 feet of slip — enough to lessen strain in the entire area, thus reducing the frequency and intensity of earthquakes. Because of plate motion, however, strain has been slowly building up. At some point, the equation must balance out again. The only time fault strain is released is during an earthquake, and many populated areas in the Bay Area

are near, or even sandwiched between, numerous major fault lines. A damaging earthquake in the near future is inevitable.

7. Which of the following best illustrates the major difference between the 2 scientists' opinions?
   A. The magnitude of the next earthquake
   B. The location of the next earthquake
   C. The fault line that will erupt
   D. The ability to predict the next earthquake

8. According to Scientist 1, when the probability of an earthquake is calculated, determination of the amount of strain released, as compared to determination of strain loaded onto faults from plate motion, is an element that is:
   F. just as difficult to do.
   G. more difficult to do.
   H. slightly less difficult to do.
   J. simple to do.

9. The opinion of Scientist 2 suggests that the strain on a fault increases when:
   A. more pressure is released.
   B. fault slip decreases.
   C. plates shift over time.
   D. the magnitude increases.

10. According to Scientist 1, which of the following statements best illustrates why an earthquake cannot be accurately predicted?
    F. The amount of tectonic plate motion has no influence on the amount of strain put on fault lines.
    G. The amount of strain released during earthquakes has not been recorded for a long enough period of time.
    H. No system is capable of tracking plate motion to an acceptable degree for predicting earthquakes.
    J. No system is capable of measuring the magnitude of an earthquake.

11. A handful of small earthquakes has been recorded in various mountainous regions during the past year. According to Scientist 2, the probability of a large earthquake occurring in those regions would:
    A. decrease because some of the strain was released.
    B. decrease because plate motion ceased.
    C. increase because fault slip would outweigh the strain.
    D. increase because strain has not built up.

GO ON TO THE NEXT PAGE.

12. With which of the following statements would both scientists most likely agree? The San Francisco Bay Area:

   F. is not in danger of the possibility of an earthquake.
   G. is not populated enough to worry about predicting the next earthquake.
   H. has a higher chance of experiencing an earthquake than any other area.
   J. has fault lines extending throughout the entire region.

13. The argument made by Scientist 2 would be *strengthened* by which of the following statements about earthquakes, if true?

   A. A team of scientists in Ecuador predicts the occurrence of an earthquake near the coast that occurs within days of the date they estimated.
   B. A scientist in Alaska announces that the last century's earthquake records are inaccurate and not applicable for current research.
   C. An earthquake occurs in the eastern Mediterranean Sea at a depth of 4.1 kilometers and a magnitude of 5.8.
   D. The latest statistics show that the population of Oakland, Calfornia, has been slowly declining for the past 12 years.

GO ON TO THE NEXT PAGE.

4 ◯ ◯ ◯ ◯ ◯ ◯ ◯ ◯ **4**

Passage III

A series of experiments performed by the Italian scientist Alessandro Volta disproved an earlier theory by Luigi Galvani that an electric current was dependent on the presence of animal tissue. Volta also discovered the means of converting chemical energy into electric energy, which is the basis for the modern battery.

Volta's research built from the earlier work of Luigi Galvani, who discovered *galvanism*. *Galvanism* is a direct electric current produced by chemical reactions. Galvani discovered this phenomenon when he stuck a copper hook through a dead frog and touched the frog's leg with a piece of iron. The dead frog's leg jerked as if it were alive. Galvani believed that an electric fluid present in animal tissue created this movement. Volta used the following experiments to disprove Galvani's theory that an electric fluid was creating the electric current.

Experiment 1
Volta experimented by putting 2 different metals on his tongue. He experienced pain and concluded that this pain meant that electricity was flowing.

Experiment 2
Volta submerged copper and zinc near each other in an inorganic acidic solution and noted an electrical interaction.

Experiment 3
Volta made a battery cell by placing paper soaked in electrolytes between 2 different metals and produced a consistent flow of electricity.

Experiment 4
Volta built piles using 30, 40, or 60 layers of metal and separated them with a piece of material dampened by an acid solution. Volta discovered that the intensity of the electric shock was greater when the piles contained 60 layers of metal rather than 30 or 40 layers.

14. Given the results of Experiment 1, which of the following statements best explains why this experiment did not disprove Galvani's earlier theory involving electric fluid?
    F. Galvani used more than 2 metals in his frog experiment to create an electric current.
    G. Volta's tongue is animal tissue and could have contained electric fluid.
    H. Galvani's frog was dead, so it could not feel pain to verify the presence of an electric current.
    J. The surface of Volta's tongue was moist and the dead frog leg was not.

15. Which of the following was probably thought to be true in designing Experiment 1?
    A. Animal tissue was not needed to produce an electric current.
    B. Two metals were sufficient to produce an electric current.
    C. Pain was the most accurate way to measure the power of an electric current.
    D. A moist surface was not necessary to produce an electric current.

16. The data from this passage best supports the conclusion that:
    F. animal tissues do not contain any fluid that can be used to conduct an electric current.
    G. only copper and zinc will produce an electric current in inorganic solutions.
    H. Galvani did not discover that an electric current is produced by chemical reactions.
    J. more than 2 pieces or layers of metal can be used to produce an electric current.

17. Which of the following hypotheses is best supported by the results in Experiment 4?
    A. The larger the number of metal layers piled and separated by material dampened in an acidic solution, the greater the intensity of the electric shock.
    B. In order to produce an electric shock, an acidic solution is needed to create the electric current.
    C. The intensity of the electric shock is likely to be dependent on the weight of the individual elements used as well as the density of the elements.
    D. Certain elements create a greater electric shock when combined than others.

18. To test the hypothesis that an acidic solution is always needed to create an electric current, the researcher should determine:
    F. whether the type of acidic solution used in Volta's experiments is present in dead frogs' legs.
    G. whether the tongue and electrolytes contain an acidic solution.
    H. whether all acidic solutions are inorganic in origin.
    J. whether copper or zinc respond to different acidic solutions.

19. Which of the 4 experiments disproved Galvani's theory that a direct electric current is produced by chemical reactions?
    A. Experiments 2, 3, and 4, because they did not involve animal tissue.
    B. Experiment 1, because it involved living human tissue.
    C. None of the experiments necessarily disprove Galvani's theory that a direct electric current is produced by chemical reactions.
    D. Experiment 3, because Volta created a consistent flow of energy.

GO ON TO THE NEXT PAGE.

4   **4**

Passage IV

A study was conducted to compare the accuracy of 2 commercially available swimming pool water testing kits (Kit A and Kit B) in determining the levels of chlorine, bromine, pH, and alkalinity in 2 different water samples. The water samples were kept at a constant temperature of 72°F throughout the entire study. The results include the ideal level or concentration of each chemical and the readings of each kit for 2 different 100 milliliters (ml) samples of water (Table 1).

Table 1		
Chemical	Sample 1	Sample 2
Chlorine (in ppm)		
Ideal	1.0–3.0	1.0–3.0
Kit A	2.40	3.4
Kit B	2.10	3.6
Bromine (in ppm)		
Ideal	2.0–4.0	2.0–4.0
Kit A	4.00	3.5
Kit B	3.75	3.35
pH		
Ideal	7.4–7.6	7.4–7.6
Kit A	7.40	6.2
Kit B	7.90	6.7
Alkalinity (in ppm)		
Ideal	85–105	85–105
Kit A	85	84
Kit B	85	84

The pH scale measures how acidic or basic a substance is on a scale of 0 to 14. Lower numbers indicate increasing acidity, and higher numbers indicate increasing basicity. The ideal pH level of a swimming pool is near 7.5. The minimum and maximum pH levels for a standard swimming pool are 7.2 and 7.8, respectively. Most residential swimming pools, however, have a tendency to drift toward a pH level of 8.

The pH level of a sample of water has a tremendous impact on the effectiveness of chlorine. Chlorine is used to destroy contaminants and, at higher levels, is capable of having a bleaching effect on colors and a corrosive effect on surfaces. pH levels are tested using *phenol red*, a dark red powder that is added to a sample and will change the color of the water, depending on the pH level. The presence of too much chlorine may bleach the dye in phenol red. The effectiveness of chlorine at different pH levels is shown in Figure 1, as a percentage of chlorine's effectiveness at destroying harmful contaminants.

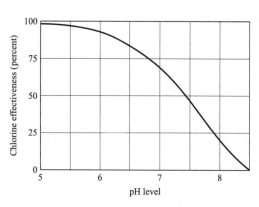

Figure 1

20. Which of the following statements best describes the effectiveness of the chlorine in Sample 2?
    F. The concentration of chlorine in Sample 2 is at an ideal level.
    G. The concentration of chlorine in Sample 2 may be corrosive to surfaces.
    H. The concentration of chlorine in Sample 2 is too weak to destroy contaminants.
    J. The Sample 2 reading of chlorine from Kit A was higher than the reading from Kit B.

21. An ideal alkalinity level prevents pH levels from becoming too basic. Which statement is best supported by this fact? When testing pool water:
    A. an alkalinity test is not necessary for residential swimming pools.
    B. an alkalinity level above 105 is ideal for residential swimming pools.
    C. check alkalinity levels before attempting to adjust pH levels.
    D. a high pH level is most common in swimming pools with a low water temperature.

22. The readings from Kit A of Sample 1 indicate that:
    F. the water from Sample 1 is probably balanced and safe.
    G. the water from Sample 1 is probably harmful to swimmers.
    H. bromine levels are difficult to accurately measure.
    J. Kit B is inferior to Kit A in measuring pH levels.

23. Another water sample was tested using Kit B. The results indicate that the effectiveness of the chlorine in the sample was just above 80%. What is the estimated pH level of the water sample?
    A. 5.0
    B. 6.5
    C. 7.5
    D. 8.0.

24. A pool owner uses phenol red to test the pH level in his overchlorinated pool. The most likely explanation for the resulting colorless water is that:
    F. phenol red cannot be used to test pH levels.
    G. pH levels cannot be measured.
    H. chlorine bleached the color out.
    J. chlorine levels are not affected by pH levels.

GO ON TO THE NEXT PAGE.

Passage V

The human body is a system of many complex processes. The body has a specific process for meeting the demands of working muscles during exercise.

When the muscles are working, the body turns adenosine diphosphates (ADP) and adenosine monophosphates (AMP) into adenosine triphosphate (ATP). ATP is then converted into energy, which is a biochemical requirement of any contraction of the muscle and keeps the muscles working. Figure 1 shows the 3 biochemical systems that act as a source of ATP for the body.

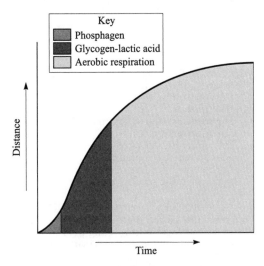

Figure 1

After only 2 minutes of exercise, the body responds by breaking down glucose into carbon dioxide and water to supply the muscles with oxygen. This process is called *aerobic respiration*. Table 1 shows the sources of glucose that are used during aerobic respiration.

Table 1	
Source	Process
Liver	Breaks down in liver, transported in blood
Muscles	Remaining glycogen supplies are used
Intestine	Absorbed from food, transported in blood
Reserves	Carbohydrates taken first, then fatty acids from fat reserves, and in extreme cases like starvation, proteins are taken last

An individual's fitness level can be determined by measuring the maximum amount of oxygen that can be used in 1 minute of activity per kilogram of body weight, or VO2 max. Figure 2 shows the milliliters (ml) of oxygen that can be consumed in 1 minute per kilogram of body weight for both females and males at a "Poor" and at an "Excellent" fitness level.

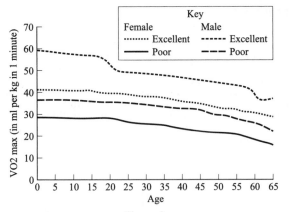

Figure 2

25. According to Figure 1, which system is most likely to continue to produce ATP to fuel the muscles of a long-distance runner (as opposed to a sprinter)?
    A. Phosphagen
    B. Glycogen-lactic acid
    C. Aerobic respiration
    D. Anaerobic respiration

26. How many minutes of exercise does it take for the body to begin certain processes to supply the muscles with oxygen?
    F. 2 minutes
    G. 30 minutes
    H. 1 hour
    J. 3 hours

27. A healthy body absorbs glucose from carbohydrates first, and then from fatty acid from fat reserves during regular exercise. In what case might the body turn to proteins as a source of glucose?
    A. Dehydration
    B. Starvation
    C. Lack of fluids
    D. High humidity

28. As compared to a 50-year-old male in excellent physical condition, a woman of the same age and fitness level consumes approximately how much less oxygen (in milliliters per minute per kilogram, ml/min/kg, body weight)?
    F. 0
    G. 12
    H. 33
    J. 45

29. A 27-year-old female in poor physical condition would consume between:
    A. 25 to 30 milliliters of oxygen per minute.
    B. 33 to 35 milliliters of oxygen per minute.
    C. 37 to 41 milliliters of oxygen per minute.
    D. 47 to 52 milliliters of oxygen per minute.

GO ON TO THE NEXT PAGE.

4 ◯ ◯ ◯ ◯ ◯ ◯ ◯ ◯ 4

Passage VI

Cholesterol is a soft, waxy compound that is found in many foods and throughout the entire human body. The body's liver produces all of the cholesterol that it needs to form and maintain cell membranes, some hormones, and vitamin D. The liver is also responsible for eliminating cholesterol from the body. Excessive levels of cholesterol in the blood, however, can lead to health problems, including heart disease.

The dietary consumption of specific types of fats is a major factor influencing the levels of low-density lipo-protein cholesterol (LDL), or "bad" cholesterol, and high-density lipoprotein (HDL), or "good" cholesterol. Cholesterol is carried by LDL and HDL in the blood. The circulation of too much LDL cholesterol in the blood can lead to buildup in the arteries and subsequently, the development of heart disease. The presence of higher levels of HDL cholesterol helps to protect against the development of heart disease.

Table 1 shows specific types of fats and their effect on cholesterol levels.

Table 1		
	Effect on cholesterol	
Type of fat	LDL	HDL
Monounsaturated	Decrease	Increase
Polyunsaturated	Decrease	Increase
Saturated	Increase	Increase
Trans	Increase	Decrease

30. Approximately 75% of the cholesterol in the blood is produced in the body. According to the passage, the remaining 25% of cholesterol that can be found in the blood comes from:
  F. diet.
  G. LDL.
  H. genetics.
  J. HDL.

31. If HDL protects against the development of heart disease, which of the following statements is most likely to be true?
  A. HDL carries cholesterol to the liver where it can be eliminated.
  B. HDL dissolves in the bloodstream and increases total cholesterol levels.
  C. HDL becomes "bad" cholesterol after it enters the bloodstream.
  D. HDL cholesterol cannot be affected by diet or any other risk factor.

32. Which type of fat has the greatest negative net effect on cholesterol levels?
  F. Monounsaturated fats
  G. Polyunsaturated fats
  H. Trans fats
  J. Saturated fats

33. According to the following table, which type of cooking oil would most likely be suggested for a person with high cholesterol?

Oil	Saturated	Monounsaturated	Polyunsaturated	Trans
Canola	8	57	26	0
Palm	50	37	10	0
Coconut	87	6	2	0

  A. Coconut oil, because it has the least amount of polyunsaturated fats.
  B. Palm oil, because it has a good amount of both mono- and polyunsaturated fats.
  C. Canola oil, because it has the least amount of saturated fats and a low amount of polyunsaturated fats.
  D. Canola oil, because it has the least amount of saturated fats and the most unsaturated fats.

34. Omega-3 fatty acid (found in fish such as mackerel, salmon, sardines, or swordfish) is known for its potential to lower the risk of heart disease. Which of the following best explains why this statement may be true? Omega-3 fatty acid:
  F. is a form of saturated fat that increases the levels of both HDL and LDL in the bloodstream.
  G. is a form of monounsaturated fat that lowers the level of HDL and increases the level of LDL.
  H. is a form of polyunsaturated fat that lowers the level of HDL and increases the level of LDL.
  J. is a form of polyunsaturated fat that lowers the level of LDL and increases the level of HDL.

GO ON TO THE NEXT PAGE.

4 ○ ○ ○ ○ ○ ○ ○ ○ **4**

Passage VII

Friction is the resistive force to motion. If an object is moving in 1 direction, friction is pulling in the opposite direction and allows an object to stop moving or stay in place. Friction depends mostly on the smoothness of the surfaces that come into contact with an object, and the magnitude of force (or weight) of one object on the other. A rough surface, for example, increases friction, making it more difficult for one object to slide over the other.

Some students conducted 3 experiments to test their hypotheses about the influence of surface material and speed on the force of friction. The students created a ramp and runway from different-sized blocks and 2 pieces of plywood (Figure 1). They used a toy car to test the effect of friction on the speed and distance that the car was able to travel, once it reaches the flat surface. The same car was used in all of the experiments.

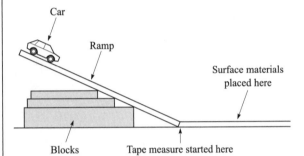

Figure 1

Experiment 1

The ramp in this experiment was placed on a 45° angle. The students changed the angle (or height) of the ramp in order to change the speed that the car could travel. The car was placed at the top of the ramp and released. A tape measure was used to determine the distance that the car traveled once it left the ramp until it stopped on different materials that covered the flat surface at the bottom of the ramp. For each material, the experiment was repeated three times and the results are shown in Table 1.

Table 1				
	Distance (in inches)			
Surface	T1	T2	T3	Avg
Waxpaper	42.0	40.5	43.5	42.0
Plywood	11.0	12.5	11.75	11.75
Carpet	4.25	5.00	5.25	4.83
Asphalt	22.0	23.5	21.75	22.42

Experiment 2

The experiment was repeated with the ramp placed on a 30° angle. The results are shown in Table 2.

Table 2				
	Distance (in inches)			
Surface	T1	T2	T3	Avg
Waxpaper	32.0	30.0	32.5	31.5
Plywood	7.00	7.50	7.25	7.25
Carpet	3.00	3.25	3.5	3.25
Asphalt	16.0	16.5	17.25	16.58

Experiment 3

The experiment was repeated with the ramp placed on a 15° angle. The results are shown in Table 3.

Table 3				
	Distance (in inches)			
Surface	T1	T2	T3	Avg
Waxpaper	18.0	20.75	19.75	19.5
Plywood	4.00	3.75	4.00	3.92
Carpet	1.75	2.25	2.00	2.00
Asphalt	10.25	12.75	11.5	11.5

35. In each experiment, the material used affected the force of friction and, as a result, the distance that the car traveled before it came to a stop. Based on the experiments, it is most likely that the stronger the friction the:
    A. heavier the object is compared to the material.
    B. lighter the object is compared to the material.
    C. longer the distance the car could travel.
    D. shorter the distance the car could travel.

36. Using a smoother surface would most likely:
    F. both decrease friction and increase the distance traveled before the car came to a stop.
    G. both decrease friction and decrease the distance traveled before the car came to a stop.
    H. both increase friction and increase the distance traveled before the car came to a stop.
    J. both increase friction and decrease the distance traveled before the car came to a stop.

GO ON TO THE NEXT PAGE.

4 ◯ ◯ ◯ ◯ ◯ ◯ ◯ ◯ ◯ **4**

37. If each of the following materials was used, as in the experiments, to cover the flat surface at the bottom of the ramp, the friction exerted will likely be the least with which material?
    A. Brick
    B. Lace
    C. Aluminum foil
    D. Window screens

38. Which of the following statements best explains why lubricant or oil is used to decrease the friction between 2 objects?
    F. It increases the magnitude of force on each object, making it harder to slide 1 object past the other.
    G. It smoothes the surfaces of both objects, making it easier for 1 object to slide past the other.
    H. It increases the gravitational pull on the objects, making it harder to slide 1 object past the other.
    J. It decreases the weight of each object, making it easier to slide 1 object past the other.

39. Which variable was kept constant throughout the experiments?
    A. The mass of the car
    B. The speed of the car
    C. The height at which the car was released
    D. The angle of the ramp

40. According to the results of the experiments, increasing the ramp's height increased the distance the car could travel, regardless of the material used. Increasing the height of the ramp:
    F. both decreased the speed of the car and increased friction.
    G. both decreased the speed of the car and decreased friction.
    H. both increased the speed of the car and increased the distance traveled before friction could stop it.
    J. both increased the speed of the car and decreased the distance traveled before friction could stop it.

**END OF THE SCIENCE REASONING TEST
STOP! IF YOU HAVE TIME LEFT OVER, CHECK YOUR WORK ON THIS SECTION ONLY.**

5   5

WRITING TEST

DIRECTIONS: This test is designed to assess your writing skills. You have thirty (30) minutes to plan and write an essay based on the stimulus provided. Be sure to take a position on the issue and support your position using logical reasoning and relevant examples. Organize your ideas in a focused and logical way, and use the English language to clearly and effectively express your position.

When you have finished writing, refer to the Scoring Rubrics discussed in Chapter 7 to estimate your score.

Note: On the actual ACT you will receive approximately 2.5 pages of scratch paper on which to develop your essay, and approximately 4 pages of notebook paper on which to write your essay. We recommend that you limit yourself to this number of pages when you write your practice essays.

Essay Prompt

In some high schools, athletes are required to submit to random chemical testing for illegal drug use. Some coaches and administrators feel that the testing is necessary to help get control of a problem that faces many student athletes. Other coaches and administrators think that random drug testing treats all athletes as though they are guilty of wrongdoing rather than allowing them the presumption of innocence. In your opinion, should high school athletes be subject to random drug testing?

In your essay, take a position on this question. You may write about one of the points of view mentioned above, or you may give another point of view on this issue. Use specific examples and reasons for your position.

ANSWER KEY

English Test

1. A	21. B	41. B	61. C
2. J	22. F	42. J	62. G
3. C	23. B	43. C	63. C
4. H	24. H	44. G	64. G
5. C	25. D	45. D	65. B
6. G	26. J	46. G	66. F
7. B	27. A	47. D	67. B
8. J	28. H	48. G	68. F
9. A	29. A	49. B	69. D
10. F	30. F	50. F	70. F
11. C	31. C	51. A	71. C
12. F	32. F	52. F	72. G
13. C	33. D	53. D	73. C
14. G	34. J	54. F	74. H
15. D	35. B	55. D	75. C
16. H	36. J	56. H	
17. D	37. D	57. B	
18. J	38. F	58. F	
19. A	39. B	59. C	
20. G	40. J	60. F	

Mathematics Test

1. B	21. B	41. E
2. G	22. J	42. J
3. D	23. B	43. C
4. G	24. G	44. F
5. C	25. E	45. C
6. K	26. G	46. J
7. D	27. B	47. A
8. F	28. J	48. H
9. D	29. D	49. E
10. F	30. H	50. H
11. E	31. B	51. D
12. H	32. K	52. G
13. D	33. C	53. C
14. J	34. F	54. F
15. A	35. C	55. A
16. K	36. H	56. F
17. D	37. D	57. A
18. G	38. G	58. F
19. A	39. E	59. C
20. H	40. K	60. K

Reading Test

1. A	21. B
2. H	22. J
3. A	23. C
4. G	24. J
5. D	25. A
6. F	26. G
7. B	27. D
8. J	28. H
9. A	29. B
10. J	30. F
11. B	31. B
12. G	32. H
13. D	33. C
14. H	34. F
15. C	35. A
16. F	36. J
17. C	37. D
18. F	38. G
19. A	39. C
20. J	40. F

Science Reasoning Test

1. C	21. C
2. F	22. F
3. A	23. B
4. G	24. H
5. D	25. C
6. J	26. F
7. D	27. B
8. G	28. G
9. C	29. A
10. G	30. F
11. A	31. A
12. J	32. H
13. A	33. D
14. G	34. J
15. B	35. D
16. J	36. F
17. A	37. C
18. G	38. G
19. C	39. A
20. G	40. H

■ SCORING GUIDE

Your final reported score is your COMPOSITE SCORE. Your COMPOSITE SCORE is the average of all of your SCALED SCORES.

Your SCALED SCORES for the four multiple-choice sections are derived from the Scoring Table on the next page. Use your RAW SCORE, or the number of questions that you answered correctly for each section, to determine your SCALED SCORE. If you got a RAW SCORE of 60 on the English test, for example, you correctly answered 60 out of 75 questions.

Step 1   Determine your RAW SCORE for each of the four multiple-choice sections:

English   _____

Mathematics   _____

Reading   _____

Science Reasoning   _____

The following Raw Score Table shows the total possible points for each section.

RAW SCORE TABLE	
KNOWLEDGE AND SKILL AREAS	**RAW SCORES**
ENGLISH	75
MATHEMATICS	60
READING	40
SCIENCE REASONING	40
WRITING	12

Multiple-Choice Scoring Worksheet

Step 2   Determine your SCALED SCORE for each of the four multiple-choice sections using the following Scoring Worksheet. Each SCALED SCORE should be rounded to the nearest number according to normal rules. For example, $31.2 \approx 31$ and $31.5 \approx 32$. If you answered 61 questions correctly on the English section, for example, your SCALED SCORE would be 28.

English

$$\underline{\hspace{3cm}} \times 36 = \underline{\hspace{3cm}} \div 75 = \underline{\hspace{3cm}}$$
RAW SCORE

$$\underline{-\ 2} \quad \text{(*correction factor)}$$

SCALED SCORE

Mathematics

$$\underline{\hspace{3cm}} \times 36 = \underline{\hspace{3cm}} \div 60 = \underline{\hspace{3cm}}$$
RAW SCORE

$$\underline{+\ 1} \quad \text{(*correction factor)}$$

SCALED SCORE

Reading

$$\underline{\hspace{3cm}} \times 36 = \underline{\hspace{3cm}} \div 40 = \underline{\hspace{3cm}}$$
RAW SCORE

$$\underline{+\ 2} \quad \text{(*correction factor)}$$

SCALED SCORE

Science Reasoning

$$\underline{\hspace{3cm}} \times 36 = \underline{\hspace{3cm}} \div 40 = \underline{\hspace{3cm}}$$
RAW SCORE

$$\underline{+\ 1.5} \quad \text{(*correction factor)}$$

SCALED SCORE

   *The correction factor is an approximation based on the average from several recent ACT tests. It is most valid for scores in the middle 50% (approximately 16–24 scaled composite score) of the scoring range.
   The scores are all approximate. Actual ACT scoring scales vary from one administration to the next based upon several factors.

   If you take the optional Writing Test, you will need to combine your English and Writing scores to obtain your final COMPOSITE SCORE. Refer to Chapter 7 for guidelines on scoring your Writing Test Essay. Once you have determined a score for your essay out of 12 possible points, you will need to determine your ENGLISH/WRITING SCALED SCORE, using both your ENGLISH SCALED SCORE and your WRITING TEST SCORE. The combination of the two scores will give you an ENGLISH/WRITING SCALED SCORE, from 1 to 36, that will be used to determine your COMPOSITE SCORE mentioned earlier.

   Using the English/Writing Scoring Table, find your ENGLISH SCALED SCORE on the left or right hand side of the table and your WRITING TEST SCORE on the top of the table. Follow your ENGLISH SCALED SCORE over and your WRITING TEST SCORE down until the two columns meet at a number. This number is your ENGLISH/WRITING SCALED SCORE and will be used to determine your COMPOSITE SCORE.

Step 3   Determine your ENGLISH/WRITING SCALED SCORE using the English/Writing Scoring Table on the following page:

   English   _____
   Writing   _____
   English/Writing _____

ENGLISH/WRITING SCORING TABLE

ENGLISH SCALED SCORE	WRITING TEST SCORE											ENGLISH SCALED SCORE
	2	3	4	5	6	7	8	9	10	11	12	
36	26	27	28	29	30	31	32	33	34	32	36	36
35	26	27	28	29	30	31	31	32	33	34	35	35
34	25	26	27	28	29	30	31	32	33	34	35	34
33	24	25	26	27	28	29	30	31	32	33	34	33
32	24	25	25	26	27	28	29	30	31	32	33	32
31	23	24	25	26	27	28	29	30	30	31	32	31
30	22	23	24	25	26	27	28	29	30	31	32	30
29	21	22	23	24	25	26	27	28	29	30	31	29
28	21	22	23	24	24	25	26	27	28	29	30	28
27	20	21	22	23	24	25	26	27	28	28	29	27
26	19	20	21	22	23	24	25	26	27	28	29	26
25	18	19	20	21	22	23	24	25	26	27	28	25
24	18	19	20	21	22	23	23	24	25	26	27	24
23	17	18	19	20	21	22	23	24	25	26	27	23
22	16	17	18	19	20	21	22	23	24	25	26	22
21	16	17	17	18	19	20	21	22	23	24	25	21
20	15	16	17	18	19	20	21	21	22	23	24	20
19	14	15	16	17	18	19	20	21	22	23	24	19
18	13	14	15	16	17	18	19	20	21	22	23	18
17	13	14	15	16	16	17	18	19	20	21	22	17
16	12	13	14	15	16	17	18	19	20	20	21	16
15	11	12	13	14	15	16	17	18	19	20	21	15
14	10	11	12	13	14	15	16	17	18	19	20	14
13	10	11	12	13	14	14	15	16	17	18	19	13
12	9	10	11	12	13	14	15	16	17	18	19	12
11	8	9	10	11	12	13	14	15	16	17	18	11
10	8	9	9	10	11	12	13	14	15	16	17	10
9	7	8	9	10	11	12	13	13	14	15	16	9
8	6	7	8	9	10	11	12	13	14	15	16	8
7	5	6	7	8	9	10	11	12	13	14	15	7
6	5	6	7	7	8	9	10	11	12	13	14	6
5	4	5	6	7	8	9	10	11	12	12	13	5
4	3	4	5	6	7	8	9	10	11	12	13	4
3	2	3	4	5	6	7	8	9	10	11	12	3
2	2	3	4	5	6	6	7	8	9	10	11	2
1	1	2	3	4	5	6	7	8	9	10	11	1

Step 4 Determine your COMPOSITE SCORE by finding the sum of all your SCALED SCORES for each of the four sections: English only (if you do not choose to take the optional Writing Test) *or* English/Writing (if you choose to take the optional Writing Test), Mathematics, Reading, and Science Reasoning, and divide by 4 to find the average. Round your COMPOSITE SCORE according to normal rules. For example, $31.2 \approx 31$ and $31.5 \approx 32$.

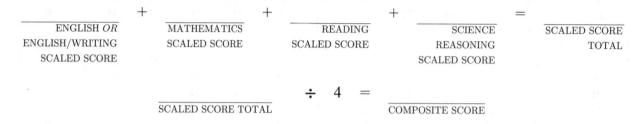

ANSWERS AND EXPLANATIONS

English Test Explanations

PASSAGE I

1. **The best answer is A.** As it is written, the sentence is complete. The other answer choices do not create complete sentences.

2. **The best answer is J.** As it is written, the sentence lacks a main verb. Removing the participle *being* allows *was* to take that position. A comma needs to follow *adulthood* in order to separate the descriptive clause from the main sentence.

3. **The best answer is C.** The clause *with the U.S. in the throes …* implies a causal relationship with what comes next. That makes *as a result* redundant and unnecessary. Finally, the introductory clauses are not complete sentences. Therefore, they should be separated from the main clause with a comma, not a semicolon.

4. **The best answer is H.** The subject and verb of the clause should be kept together (as should the adjective *Minnesota* and noun *farm*). The phrase *under his care* belongs to the first clause, not the second (*his passion was not for agriculture*), and therefore should be followed by a comma, not preceded by one.

5. **The best answer is C.** The verb *encouraged* needs a subject, so the pronoun *they* should be added. The *when* clause is not a complete sentence, and therefore should be separated only by a comma, not a period or semicolon.

6. **The correct answer is G.** The sentence as it is written implies that Lindbergh's academic probation caused his poor study skills. In fact, it was the other way around. Answer choice G, "resulted in" gets the cause right and is also the most concise choice.

7. **The correct answer is B.** The final clause, *in pursuit of a degree*, is implied in the phrase "never to return". It is unnecessary, and should be deleted. The other answer choices are not supported by information in the passage and should be eliminated.

8. **The correct answer is J.** While colons can be used to introduce examples or lists (as in this case), the clause before the colon should be an independent clause. Since here it is not, no punctuation is necessary to separate the clause from the list of activities.

9. **The correct answer is A.** To maintain parallel construction within this paragraph, you need to use the past tense of the verb *find*, which is *found*. Notice that other sentences in the paragraph use the past tense for their main verbs. The verb forms should agree, that is, have the same tense.

10. **The correct answer is F.** To maintain parallel construction within this sentence, the verb *focused* should agree in tense with the verb *learned*. As this is the case, no change is necessary.

11. **The correct answer is C.** This question requires you to select the choice that best expresses the idea. Answer choice D contains an unnecessary comma after the word *graduation*, so it can be eliminated. The other answer choices, while correct, do not express the main idea of the sentence as clearly as does answer choice C.

12. **The correct answer is F.** The correct form is *despite*. Because *despite* is a necessary part of its clause, it should not be separated from it by a comma.

13. **The correct answer is C.** To maintain parallel construction within the sentence, the verbal forms of *seek* and *accept* should be the same. The correct form is the progressive participle (*-ing*) to indicate that the actions continued over time.

14. **The correct answer is G.** This question requires you to keep the ideas consistent in this sentence while arranging them in a more logical order. The clause should start with *led to his work* because the essay is about Lindbergh, and any other order would take the emphasis away from him. Next should be the name of his collaborator, in order to group together the people doing the "work." Last should be what was worked on: the development of a perfusion pump. This order creates a logical flow telling you who did something (in order of importance), followed by what was done.

15. **The correct answer is D.** The focus of the passage is on Lindbergh's intellectual growth and the untraditional ways in which he trained and used his intelligence. Only choice D sums up this message and provides an appropriate conclusion to the essay.

PASSAGE II

16. **The correct answer is H.** The second sentence contains a contrast to what comes before. That is, the first sentence says Vikings were crude; the second appears to contradict that by saying they were advanced. The word *however* is the only choice to signal this contrast.

17. **The correct answer is D.** Because the new sentence would follow an assertion that the Vikings were advanced, the logical choice would contain an example of some sort of accomplishment. Answer choice D describes an accomplishment: the Vikings' "discovery" of North America hundreds of years before Columbus.

18. **The correct answer is J.** The phrase *seafaring traders* is a collective noun that is used to describe the Vikings. You should not use a comma to separate the elements of this phrase. It is also not appropriate to use a colon or a comma after the word *with*.

19. **The correct answer is A.** The sentence as it is written is the most concise statement of the information. Therefore, no change is necessary.

20. **The correct answer is G.** The paragraph has a clear subject: Vikings. This sentence is giving more detailed information about the Vikings. Since there has been no change in subject, and it has already been stated that the Vikings are from Scandinavia, a pronoun (*they*) is clear and concise.

21. **The correct answer is B.** The first step in answering this question is to recognize that you must use the possessive pronoun *their*, not the conjunction of *they are*. Eliminate answer choice D. The clause *whether they arrived* is not an independent clause. Therefore, it cannot be separated from the rest by a semicolon. A colon would be used if what followed were an example or list. Since it's not, a comma is the only punctuation necessary.

22. **The correct answer is F.** None of the other items listed in the sentence are preceded by a preposition. Therefore, none is needed here. Answer choice F, *no change*, is the best answer since it is the only one that does not add a preposition.

23. **The correct answer is B.** In order to maintain parallel construction, the tense of *meet* has to match the tense of its paired verb, *trade*. Here,

the author tells you that, in the past, Vikings traded often with Arabs. Since *met* is the past tense of *meet*, answer choice B is correct.

24. **The correct answer is H.** While "heavy and powerful" might be a good description of swords and ax blades, the correct answer should mirror the description of the leather goods in the next sentence. You know they have to match because the next sentence starts with the comparative, *similar*. The answer choice that contains the most specific description is answer choice H.

25. **The correct answer is D.** The phrase beginning *Making butter . . .* is not a complete sentence; it lacks a finite verb. Therefore, you should not use any form of end punctuation before that phrase. It is most appropriate to use a comma.

26. **The correct answer is J.** The information included in answer choices F, G, and H is irrelevant. There is no need to further discuss fabrics — it will not add any useful information to the passage.

27. **The correct answer is A.** The subject here is the Vikings who could read. However, they are not the ones doing the action — other people consider them to be valuable. Since the sentence uses a passive verb, answer choice A is the only selection that is correct.

28. **The correct answer is H.** Like periods, semicolons are used to separate complete sentences. *These runes* is not an independent clause. Therefore, the semicolon should be removed. The sentence is correct without any additional punctuation. Also, answer choice G indicates the possessive form of *rune*, which is not appropriate here.

29. **The correct answer is A.** In order to maintain parallel construction within the paragraph, this verb needs to be in the past tense. It also needs to be plural because the subject, *runes*, is plural. The plural past tense of *to be* is *were*. Note that the other main verbs are also in the past tense: *was, were, believed, wrote*, and so on.

30. **The correct answer is F.** The information given in answer choice F directly reflects the information provided in the third paragraph. Answer choice G is too vague. Answer choice H contradicts information in the last paragraph (the Vikings wrote down little of their history). Answer choice J simply is not mentioned in the passage.

PASSAGE III

31. The correct answer is C. When you have a compound subject, all nouns must be in the subject case. Here, the pronoun *I* is needed because *I* denotes a subject (*I get the ball*), while *me* denotes an object (*He gave the ball to me*). Further, the main verb must be plural. In other words, while *she* and *I* are each singular, when they are combined they become a plural subject and require a plural verb (e.g., *She and I were allies*).

32. The correct answer is F. The sentence as it is written is concise and grammatically correct. No change is needed.

33. The correct answer is D. The sentence already has a main verb, *make*. Therefore, additional finite verbs, like *has* or *is* (implied in *She's* and *It's*, respectively), are unnecessary.

34. The correct answer is J. If two related main clauses are linked by a coordinating conjunction (e.g., *and*), a separating comma is generally used before the conjunction. This is especially true if the clauses are long, as they are here.

35. The correct answer is B. To answer this question correctly, look forward to the next paragraph to see what direction the essay is going to take. In this case, the author shifts from a description of Kari to a description of the Girls State convention. Answer choice B not only provides an introduction to Girls State, it links Kari to it through her participation in the convention. That makes it an effective transitional sentence.

36. The correct answer is J. The present-tense verb *provides* tells the reader that the opportunities occur now and can be assumed to continue into the future. The phrase *to participate in* suggests that the opportunities are ongoing. Also you would most likely say "participate in," rather than "participate on," so eliminate answer choice F.

37. The correct answer is D. *Of course* is a nonrestrictive clause, and must be set off by commas. This means it is extra information and can be removed without changing the meaning of the sentence. Answer choice D is the only choice that has a comma at the beginning and at the end of the nonrestrictive clause.

38. The correct answer is F. As it is written, the sentence is in agreement between the plural subject (i.e., *schedule*) and the singular verb (i.e., *was*). Either a plural or a singular subject could be correct, but it must agree with the verb. Only answer choice F meets this requirement.

39. The correct answer is B. The author is describing a one-time event: the introduction of Kari to a military cadet. Answer choice B captures this meaning and places it in the appropriate past tense. Answer choice D implies that the meeting was prearranged. Nothing in the passage indicates this was the case. Answer choice A's "was meeting" implies that there were multiple meetings. Answer choice C uses both the wrong tense and a nonstandard past tense of *meet*.

40. The correct answer is J. The underlined phrase describes the cadet's offer to Kari. You are asked to find the best punctuation for this phrase. The cadet offered to show her around the capital. The verb *offered* should not be separated from its object, that is, the following clause. Moreover, the relative pronoun *who* introduces a nonrestrictive relative clause. The pronoun should be preceded by a comma, but it shouldn't be separated from the rest of the clause.

41. The correct answer is B. As it is written, the singular verb of the relative clause (*promises*) does not agree with its plural subject (*most people*). Answer choice B corrects this problem. The other two choices are awkward, wordy, and repetitious.

42. The correct answer is J. Roman numeral II is easy to eliminate; words are italicized to emphasize their significance, not insignificance. Therefore, eliminate answer choice H. Roman numeral I is more subtle, but Sentence 5 makes a distinction between what Kari told her friend and what she told the cadet in the other letter. Roman numeral I makes sense, so eliminate answer choice G. The italics indicate that something significant has been communicated. It's logical to assume (and it turns out to be the case) that this information *is* significant to what comes next, so roman numeral III also makes sense.

43. The correct answer is C. The first half of the paragraph focuses on Kari's letter to her girlfriend. At Sentence 6, however, the author begins to talk about Kari's letter to the cadet and his response to what he actually received. This shift in focus marks the most appropriate place to begin a new paragraph.

44. The correct answer is G. The main idea of this essay is a description of an extremely popular girl who, every now and again, gets in trouble despite herself. Answer choice G reminds the reader that Kari is very popular, while still acknowledging that not everyone feels positively about her. It also says this in a humorous way. The other answer choices don't sum up the essay and are much more serious in tone.

45. **The correct answer is D.** The essay reflects the author's personal reminiscence of a cousin, Kari, and includes details about certain events in Kari's life. While the essay mentions that Kari took advantage of one of the opportunities provided by Girls State, that is not the main focus of the essay.

PASSAGE IV

46. **The correct answer is G.** Commas are used to separate adjectives in a list like this one. However, it is unnecessary to add a comma before the list begins. Only answer choice G is correct.

47. **The correct answer is D.** The sentence as it is written lacks a main verb, and thus is incomplete. Answer choice D puts the main idea of the sentence first ("I grew up on a farm in Iowa"). The descriptive clause follows, giving additional information. This order is the most concise and logical of any of the answer choices.

48. **The correct answer is G.** The clause after the comma (*and took great pains . . .*) is not independent, meaning it could not stand on its own as a complete sentence. Therefore, a comma should not be used to separate it from the preceding clause.

49. **The correct answer is B.** Answer choices A and D (*Therefore* and *Hence*) indicate that the following sentence is a result of what's come before. In this case, the sentences are not connected causally, so neither answer choice is correct. Also, the last sentence of the paragraph is not a restatement of the previous sentences. Therefore, answer choice C is incorrect. Answer choice B, however, implies that a change has occurred and that this will be significant later in the essay. This implication best matches the sense of the essay.

50. **The correct answer is F.** Paragraph 5 begins the explanation for the changed truth mentioned at the end of Paragraph 4. The current sentence captures this meaning and therefore F is the best answer. The other answer choices are not supported by the context of the passage.

51. **The correct answer is A.** Answer choice A is written in the active voice, which means that the subject is the one performing the action of the verb. The active voice is almost always better than the passive voice. Answer choice B is also

in the active voice, but it has an unnecessary comma separating the verb from its object.

52. **The correct answer is F.** The sentence as it is written is clear and concise. The other answer choices are wordy and redundant.

53. **The correct answer is D.** Any mention of where Clint and his friends are on the golf course is irrelevant to the main idea of the paragraph. The best option is to omit the underlined portion, answer choice D.

54. **The correct answer is F.** Clint's next words refer to gambling — he bets his friends ten dollars based on information given to him by the author. While the information itself is about corn, the implication is that he wouldn't bet ten dollars on that information if he was not sure he would win. Only answer choice F contains this implication.

55. **The correct answer is D.** *On the other hand* is a logical connective that implies contrast. That means it links what comes before to what comes after but emphasizes the difference between the two. It is logically helpful, but not necessary for the sense of the sentence. Therefore, it is a nonrestrictive clause and needs to be enclosed by commas. Only answer choice D has both commas.

56. **The correct answer is H.** The directions require you to select the answer choice that expresses the idea most clearly and simply. Answer choices F, G, and J are wordy and awkward and should be eliminated.

57. **The correct answer is B.** Since the "reminding" belongs to Clint, it is correct to use the possessive pronoun *his*. The other answer choices are awkward and do not convey the clear meaning of the sentence.

58. **The correct answer is F.** Paragraph 6 discusses the bet that Clint made with his friends about the ear of corn. Therefore it makes sense that Clint challenged his friends because he enjoys making small bets with them. The other answer choices are not supported by the passage.

59. **The correct answer is C.** The first sentence in Paragraph 4 includes mention of the author "sharing occasional anecdotes and bits of trivia." It seems most appropriate to insert a sentence here that gives more information about the stories that the author tells. The sentence does not make sense placed elsewhere in the passage.

60. The correct answer is F. This question asks you to identify the main idea of the essay. The main idea is suggested as early as Paragraph 2: "only to have your 'expertise' challenged and proven wrong." Agriculture and golf habits are only mentioned to illustrate this main point. Therefore, the essay would not be appropriate for the farming magazine because "the essay describes the writer's experience with the repercussions of authoritatively sharing outdated information."

PASSAGE V

61. The correct answer is C. The inversion of the verb and subject (*did I* instead of the usual *I did*) is used after a negative term, like *never*, *nowhere*, and *nor*. The author did not want to give up any of her extracurricular activities, so *nor* is the best selection.

62. The correct answer is G. In order to maintain parallel construction, pronoun use should be consistent. The rest of the paragraph is in the first-person singular; that is, the story is told from the point of view of the narrator, using the pronoun *I*.

63. The correct answer is C. By the time the author has seen the flyer, the action of posting it has been completed. Therefore, the past tense, *posted*, must be used. Answer choice D is incorrect because it would create an independent clause, which would require a semicolon or a period after *flyer*.

64. The correct answer is G. The underlined pronoun in this sentence refers back to the noun *opportunities*. Because *opportunities* is plural, its pronoun must be plural, too. Therefore, the pronoun *they* is the correct. Answer choice H can be eliminated because it is the contraction of *it is*.

65. The correct answer is B. The focus of the paragraph is how the author found her job. The actual amount of the stipend is irrelevant and should be deleted.

66. The correct answer is F. It is necessary to use a comma after *acting experience* because it separates the two main clauses of the sentence. The comma should be placed inside the quotation marks. It is not appropriate to use *requesting* in this sentence, so eliminate answer choice H.

67. The correct answer is B. In this example, the semicolon is incorrect because the final clause is not an independent clause. A colon would introduce an example or list. Neither of these

occurs, so eliminate answer choices A and C. A dash, however, is appropriate because it can be used in place of a comma to separate a clause from the main sentence. No comma is needed after the word *not* because it would interrupt the meaning of the clause, so eliminate answer choice D.

68. The correct answer is F. The sentence as it is written is correct because *subjects of the experiment* is a genitive (or possessive) phrase. To test this reading, change the wording to *the experiment's subjects* (also a possessive phrase). Since the alternate wording makes sense, answer choice F is correct.

69. The correct answer is D. In order to maintain parallel construction, the verb forms must stay consistent. In this sentence, the author "read" (a past tense) to the subjects, therefore she must have "provided" (also past tense) varying levels of feedback. Answer choice B is also in the past tense, but it is in the passive voice, which is not consistent with the rest of the sentence.

70. The correct answer is F. In this paragraph, the author presents examples in an alternating rhetorical pattern of *In some cases, ...* and *In other cases, ...* Each example is a complete sentence. Therefore, in order to maintain parallel construction, the underlined portion should include end punctuation and capitalization to indicate two complete sentences.

71. The correct answer is C. In this example, *verbal* and *nonverbal* are adjectives modifying the noun, *responses*. Because there are only two of them, there is no need to separate them by using commas.

72. The correct answer is G. The question asks you to find a phrase that would explain why the author would like to continue her work. This implies something positive, like answer choice G ("fascinating and fun"). Answer choices F and J are clearly negative, and the author has already stated that answer choice H, babysitting, is underpaid; eliminate these answer choices.

73. The correct answer is C. Sentence 3 describes the end of the experiments. The subject, *experiments*, is obviously plural — this gives us a clue for its proper placement. You should have noticed that Sentence 2 appears to have the wrong third person pronoun — it uses *them* instead of the *it* required by the singular noun *work* in the previous sentence. If we place Sentence 3, with its plural subject, immediately before Sentence 2, the plural pronoun *them* becomes correct. The paragraph still makes logical sense with Sentence 3 in this new position. Therefore, answer choice C is correct.

74. **The correct answer is H.** This question asks that you identify the main idea of the essay. The main idea is stated at the end of the first paragraph: a description of "the perfect part-time job." Since this is the case, the additional sentence does not belong anywhere in the passage because it does not contribute meaningful information to the essay. Therefore, answer choice H is the best selection.

75. **The correct answer is C.** This question also relies on identifying the main idea of the essay. The main idea is stated at the end of the first paragraph: a description of "the perfect part-time job." The author's perfect job is in psychology, not sociology. In fact, there is no indication that the author is even a sociology major. Therefore, the essay would not be appropriate for the magazine article because its content is off-topic.

Mathematics Test Explanations

1. **The correct answer is B.** This is a basic Algebra problem that requires you to solve for x. Isolate the variable, x, on one side of the equation, as follows:

   (1) $2x + 5 = 17$

   (2) $2x = 12$

   (3) $x = \dfrac{12}{2} = 6$, answer choice B.

2. **The correct answer is G.** The best way to answer this question is to look at the answer choices given and decide whether each choice is true, based on the 3 statements, or false because it contradicts 1 or more of the 3 statements.

   (1) Answer choice F states that Horse B is not brown. Since the problem states that Horse B runs fast and that all horses that run fast are brown, Horse B must be brown. Eliminate answer choice F.

   (2) Answer choice G states that Horse B is brown. Since you know that Horse B also runs fast, and that all horses that run fast are brown, answer choice G must be true, and, therefore is the correct answer.

3. **The correct answer is D.** *Probability* refers to how likely it is that something will happen. You can look at probability in this problem as a percentage. Convert the 0.2 probability that John will oversleep into a 20% chance that John will oversleep. The question asks you for the probability that John will NOT oversleep, which is 100%−20%, or 80%. Convert 80% into decimal form, 0.8, to arrive at answer choice D.

4. **The correct answer is G.** To find the average price that Sam paid per stuffed animal, you must divide the total dollar amount that Sam paid for the stuffed animals by the number of stuffed animals that Sam bought. The total dollar amount that Sam paid for the stuffed animals can be set up like this:

   (1) 2 stuffed animals for \$3.59 each + 2 stuffed animals for \$6.49 each

   (2) $2(\$3.59) + 2(\$6.49)$

   You know from information in the problem that Sam purchased a total of 4 videos. Divide the total dollar amount that he paid, $2(\$3.59) + 2(\$6.49)$ by 4:

   (3) $\dfrac{2(\$3.59) + 2(\$6.49)}{4}$, answer choice G.

5. **The correct answer is C.** The easiest way to solve this problem is to work backwards. Since \$10

was $\frac{1}{2}$ of what remained from Sunday, then there must have been $\$10 \cdot 2$, or \$20 remaining from Sunday. Since Mike spent $\frac{1}{3}$ of the money on Sunday and still had \$20 remaining, \$20 must be $\frac{2}{3}$ of the money that he started out with on Sunday. Calculate the amount of money that he started out with on Sunday (x):

   (1) $20 = \dfrac{2}{3}x$

   (2) $\dfrac{20}{x} = \dfrac{2}{3}$; cross multiply and solve for x.

   (3) $2x = 60$

   (4) $x = 30$

So, after spending $\frac{1}{3}$ of his pay on Saturday, Mike had \$30 left. Since he spent $\frac{1}{3}$ of his pay on Saturday and still had \$30 left, \$30 must be $\frac{2}{3}$ of the money that he started out with on Saturday. Calculate the amount of money that he started out with on Saturday (x):

   (1) $30 = \dfrac{2}{3}x$

   (2) $\dfrac{30}{x} = \dfrac{2}{3}$; cross-multiply and solve for x.

   (3) $2x = 90$

   (4) $x = 45$

Mike received \$45 originally, answer choice C.

6. **The correct answer is K.** To find the value of a and b, first find the square root of 64 and 81. Since a negative number squared results in a positive number, consider both the negative and positive values:

   (1) $\sqrt{64} = 8$ or -8 and $\sqrt{81} = 9$ or -9

   Find all of the possibilities for $a + b$: $-8 + -9 = -17$, $8 + -9 = -1$, $-8 + 9 = 1$, and $8 + 9 = 17$. This means that 145 is NOT a value of $a + b$, so answer choice K is correct.

7. **The correct answer is D.** Triangle *BEF* is an isosceles triangle with 2 congruent sides, $\overline{BE}$ and $\overline{BF}$, and 2 angles with equal measure, *BFE* and *BEF*. $\overline{BF}$ is also the transversal between 2 parallel lines, $\overline{AC}$ and $\overline{DG}$, making angles *CBF* and *BFE* alternate interior angles, which are congruent. By definition, if angle *CBF* is 40°, angle *BFE* is also 40°. Since there are 180° in a line, angle *BFG* must equal 180° − 40°, or 140°, answer choice D.

8. **The correct answer is F.** Simply plug −3 in for x wherever x appears in the equation and solve the equation. Don't forget to keep track of the negative signs!

(1) $(-3)^2 - 6(-3) - 18 =$

(2) $(9) - (-18) - 18 =$

(3) $9 + 18 - 18 =$

(4) $9 + 0 = 9$, answer choice F.

9. **The correct answer is D.** If the average of 5 numbers is 4.2, then the total of the 5 numbers is 5×4.2, or 21. If each of the 5 numbers is increased by 2.5, then the total of the 5 new numbers is $21 + 5(2.5)$, or $21 + 12.5$, which is 33.5. To find the average, divide 33.5 by 5, to get 6.7, answer choice D.

10. **The correct answer is F.** This question tests your ability to recognize and apply the distributive property. According to the distributive property, for any numbers a, b, and c, $c(a + b) = ca + cb$. In this problem, c is 8 so you can simplify the expression $8x - 8y$ into $8(x - y)$, answer choice F.

11. **The correct answer is E.** The first step in solving this problem is to calculate the amount of money that you earn each day for stuffing envelopes:

(1) $52.00 (total amount earned per day) – $17.00 (fixed amount earned per day) = $35.00 (amount earned for envelopes stuffed).

Next, calculate the amount that you earn per envelope:

(2) $35.00 (amount earned for stuffed envelopes) $\div$ 350 (number of envelopes stuffed) = $0.10 (amount earned per envelope stuffed).

Now determine the amount that you will earn today for stuffing the extra envelopes:

(3) 250 (additional number of stuffed envelopes) $\times$ $0.10 (amount earned per envelope stuffed) = $25.00 (additional income for the day).

Finally, add this amount to your fixed daily earnings:

(4) $52.00 + $25.00 = $77.00, answer choice E.

12. **The correct answer is H.** The easiest way to solve this problem is to plug the answer choices into the inequality and solve. Because the question asks you for the largest possible value of x, start with the largest answer choice (note that the answer choices are in ascending order):

(1) $\frac{2}{28} \geq \frac{1}{7}$; $\frac{2}{28} = \frac{1}{14}$, which is less than $\frac{1}{7}$, so eliminate answer choice K.

Try the next largest number:

(2) $\frac{2}{15} \geq \frac{1}{7}$; $\frac{2}{15} = \frac{1}{7.5}$, which is less than $\frac{1}{7}$, so eliminate answer choice J.

Try the next largest number:

(3) $\frac{2}{14} \geq \frac{1}{7}$; $\frac{2}{14} = \frac{1}{7}$

This satisfies the inequality and is the largest remaining answer choice, so answer choice H must be correct.

13. **The correct answer is D.** There are $360°$ in a circle. To calculate the number of degrees in 5 of the 12 sectors, perform the following operations:

(1) $360° \div 12 = 30°$. Each sector is equivalent to $30°$.

(2) $30° \times 5$ (the number of sectors) $= 150°$, answer choice D.

14. **The correct answer is J.** The first step in choosing the correct answer is to locate point Q in the coordinate plane. You will see that it is located in the upper left quadrant, which means that x-coordinate must be negative and y-coordinate must be positive. Eliminate answer choices F and G because they both include positive x-coordinates. You can also eliminate answer choices H and K, because they both include negative y-coordinates. That leaves answer choice J as the only possible correct answer.

15. **The correct answer is A.** To solve this problem, set each element of the equations in the answer choices equal to 0 and solve for x:

(1) $(x - 6) = 0$; $x = 6$

(2) $(x + 3) = 0$; $x = -3$

Since this equation has solutions of 6 and –3, answer choice A is correct.

16. **The correct answer is K.** To find the total number of seats in the entire classroom, you must multiply the number of rows, $(r - 3s)$, by the number of seats in each row, $4t$, using the Distributive Property:

(1) $(r - 3s) \times 4t = (4t \times r) - (4t \times 3s)$, answer choice K.

17. **The correct answer is D.** The first step in selecting the correct answer to this problem is to recognize that x cannot be less than 90. This means that answer choices A, B, and C can be eliminated. Set up a proportion to calculate the correct answer:

(1) 90 is to x as 60% is to 100%.

(2) $\frac{90}{x} = \frac{60}{100}$; cross-multiply and solve for x.

(3) $60x = 9,000$

(4) $x = 150$, answer choice D.

18. **The correct answer is G.** To solve this problem, calculate the price of 1 box of popcorn and subtract it from the price of 1 box of popcorn and 1 drink.

    (1) $8.35 (2 boxes and 1 drink) − $5.10 (1 box and 1 drink) = $3.25 (1 box of popcorn)

    (2) $5.10 (1 box and 1 drink) − $3.25 (1 box of popcorn) = $1.85

    The price of 1 drink is $1.85, answer choice G.

19. **The correct answer is A.** In order to solve this problem you must first calculate the total cost of the lamps, including tax. Since the sales tax is 7%, multiply the price of the 2 lamps ($8.99 × 2) by 0.07, the decimal equivalent of 7%:

    (1) $8.99 × 2 = $17.98

    (2) $17.98 × 0.07 = 1.2586

    (3) $1.2586 rounded to the nearest cent is $1.26.

    Now, add the sales tax to the price of the lamps:

    (4) $17.98 + $1.26 = $19.24.

    Based on these calculations, you will need $0.24 in exact change, answer choice A.

20. **The correct answer is H.** An expression is undefined when the denominator equals 0. Set the denominator equal to 0 and solve for x:

    (1) $300 − 3x^2 = 0$

    (2) $300 = 3x^2$

    (3) $100 = x^2$

    (4) $x = 10$, answer choice H.

21. **The correct answer is B.** In order to solve this problem you must know that π is approximately equal to 3.14. The next step is to find the value of the fractions $\frac{7}{3}$ and $\frac{9}{2}$. To do this, divide the numerators by the denominators: $7 \div 3 = 2.33$, and $9 \div 2 = 4.5$. Now, put the values in order from least to greatest: $2.33 < 3.14 < 4.5$, or $\frac{7}{3} < \pi < \frac{9}{2}$, answer choice B.

22. **The correct answer is J.** The question can be solved using the following equation: $\frac{9 + x}{13 + x} = \frac{3}{4}$. Cross-multiply to get $4(9 + x) = 3(13 + x)$. Solve for x:

    (1) $4(9 + x) = 3(13 + x)$

    (2) $36 + 4x = 39 + 3x$

(3) $4x − 3x = 39 − 36$

(4) $x = 3$, answer choice J.

23. **The correct answer is B.** If the ratio of the radii of 2 circles is 4:9, then you can assume that circle a has a radius, r, of 4 and circle b has a radius, r, of 9. Knowing this, you can find the area of each circle using the formula πr^2: the area of circle a is 16π and the area of circle b is 81π. Thus, the ratio of the areas of the circles is 16:81, answer choice B.

24. **The correct answer is G.** To find the solutions of the expression $x^2 − 4x = 12$, first put it in the correct quadratic equation form by subtracting 12 from both sides: $x^2 − 4x − 12 = 0$. Now you can factor the polynomial $x^2 − 4x − 12$:

    (1) $(x + \underline{\quad})(x − \underline{\quad}) = 0$.

    Find two factors of −12 that, when added together give you −4, and plug them into the solution sets:

    (2) $(x + 2)(x − 6) = 0$.

    (3) Now, solve for x: $(x + 2) = 0$, so $x = −2$; and $(x − 6) = 0$, so $x = 6$

    The solutions of $x^2 − 4x = 12$ are −2 and 6, answer choice G.

25. **The correct answer is E.** The key to solving this problem is to recognize that, if $(2t + v)^2 = 289$, then $2t + v$ must equal 17, because 17^2 equals 289. Now, since you are given that $tv = 30$, you need to find 2 numbers that, when added together give you 17, and when multiplied together give you 30. The only 2 numbers that will satisfy both operations are 15 and 2. Substitute 15 for t and 2 for v in the final equation:

    (1) $15^2 + 2^2$

    (2) $225 + 4 = 229$, answer choice E.

26. **The correct answer is G.** When exponents are raised to an exponential power, the rules state that you must multiply the exponents by the power to which they are raised. In this problem, x is raised to the $(3a + 5)$ power. This exponent is then raised to the fourth power, so you should multiply $3a + 5$ by 4: $4(3a + 5) = 12a + 20$. You now have the equation $x^{12a + 20} = x^{44}$. Since the coefficients are equal (x), the exponents must also be equal, so $12a + 20 = 44$. Solve for a:

    (1) $12a + 20 = 44$

    (2) $12a = 24$

(3) $a = \dfrac{24}{12} = 2$, answer choice G.

27. **The correct answer is B.** Logarithms are used to indicate exponents of certain numbers called bases. This problem tells you that log to the base x of 2 equals 16. By definition, $\log_a b = c$, if $a^c = b$. So, the question is, when x is raised to the power of 2, you get 16; what is x? By definition, $\log_x 16 = 2$ when $x^2 = 16$. Since the square root of 16 is 4, answer choice B is correct.

28. **The correct answer is J.** To solve this problem you should use the Midpoint Formula. The midpoint of a line, M, is equal to the average of the x-coordinates and the average of the y-coordinates. The formula looks like this:

$$M = \left(\frac{x_1 + x_2}{2}, \frac{y_1 + y_2}{2}\right)$$

You are given 1 point on the line, $(-2, 9)$ and the midpoint of the line $(4,4)$. Since the midpoint is $(4,4)$ the average of the x-coordinates is 4, and the average of the y-coordinates is 4. Set up equations to solve for the other endpoint:

(1) $4 = \dfrac{-2 + x_2}{2}$

(2) $8 = -2 + x_2$

(3) $10 = x_2$

The x-coordinate of the other endpoint is 10. Since only answer choice J includes an x-coordinate of 10, it must be the correct answer. If you solve for the y-coordinate in the same way that you solved for the x-coordinate, you will get -1.

29. **The correct answer is D.** A circle centered at (a,b) with a radius r, has the equation $(x - a)^2 + (y - b)^2 = r^2$. Based on this definition, a circle with the equation $(x - 4)^2 + (y + 1)^2 = 14$ would have a radius of $\sqrt{14}$. If $r^2 = 14$, then $r = \sqrt{14}$, answer choice D.

30. **The correct answer is H.** The cosine of any angle is calculated by dividing the length of the side adjacent to the acute angle by the hypotenuse ($\cos = \dfrac{\text{adj}}{\text{hyp}}$), so the $\cos \angle A = \dfrac{12}{x}$. To find the length of the hypotenuse, use the Pythagorean Theorem, $a^2 + b^2 = c^2$:

(1) $12^2 + 5^2 = c^2$

(2) $144 + 25 = 169 = c^2$

(3) $\sqrt{169} = \sqrt{c^2}$, so $c = 13$

The $\cos$ of $\angle A = \dfrac{12}{13}$, answer choice H.

31. **The correct answer is B.** You should think of this problem as a basic fraction, where $(13a^2b^4)(-8a^3b^5)$ is the numerator and $(4a^2b^6)$ is the denominator. The first step is to multiply together the 2 elements in the numerator, as follows:

(1) When multiplying exponents, the rules state that you should add exponents with like coefficients, so $(13a^2b^4)(-8a^3b^5) = -104a^5b^9$.

To solve a fraction, you simply divide the numerator by the denominator.

(2) When dividing exponents, the rules state that you should subtract exponents of the same coefficients in the denominator from the exponents of the same coefficients in the numerator, so $-104a^5b^9 \div (4a^2b^6) = -26a^3b^3$, answer choice B.

32. **The correct answer is K.** By definition, a right isosceles triangle has 2 sides of equal length, and the hypotenuse is equal to $\sqrt{2}$ times the length of either of the sides (only for a right isosceles triangle). Therefore, a right isosceles triangle could have side lengths equal to 2, 2, and $2\sqrt{2}$, answer choice K.

33. **The correct answer is C.** A square is a parallelogram with 4 right angles and 4 sides of the same length. The area of a square is the length of 1 side squared. Since the area is given as 64, the length of each side of the square must be $\sqrt{64}$, or 8. This means that radii $\overline{DA}$ and $\overline{DC}$ are both equal to 8. The circumference of a circle is calculated using the formula $C = 2\pi r$. Plug 8 in for r and solve:

(1) $C = 2\pi r$, or $2(8)\pi$

(2) $C = 16\pi$, answer choice C.

34. **The correct answer is F.** According to the graph shown, the number -4 is included, but the number 6 is not included. This means that x must be greater than or equal to -4 ($x \geq -4$) and/or x must be less than 6 ($x < 6$). You can eliminate answer choices J and K, which both say that x is less than or equal to -4 ($x \leq -4$). You can also eliminate answer choice G, which says that x is greater than, but not equal to, -4 ($x > -4$). Now you must decide whether to use *and* or to use *or*. Since the sets overlap on the graph, the correct answer is $x \geq -4$ and $x < 6$, answer choice F.

35. **The correct answer is C.** To determine how far the ladder reaches up the garage, draw a diagram

to help you visualize the problem:

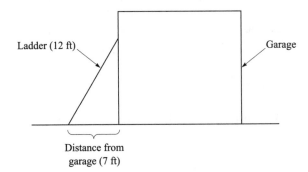

Ladder (12 ft)

Garage

Distance from
garage (7 ft)

The ladder leaning against the garage forms a right triangle. The hypotenuse of the triangle is 12 feet, and the base is 7 feet. The final side is the distance that the ladder reaches up the garage and can be calculated by using the Pythagorean Theorem, $a^2 + b^2 = c^2$:

(1) $7^2 + b^2 = 12^2$

(2) $49 + b^2 = 144$

(3) $b^2 = 95$

(4) $b = 9.746$

The ladder reaches up the building 9.746 feet which, when rounded to the nearest foot, is 10 feet, answer choice C.

36. **The correct answer is H.** Because a negative number cannot have a square root, the value under a square root sign *must* be positive. In this problem, the value under the square root sign is $3\left(\dfrac{x^3}{2y}\right)$, or $\dfrac{3x^3}{2y}$. Choose values for the answer choices and eliminate those choices that could give you a negative value under the square root sign:

(1) If x is negative, then x^3 will be negative. If y is also negative, then $2y$ will also be negative, so the value under the square root sign will be positive. Answer choice F will work.

(2) If x is positive, then x^3 will be positive. If y is also positive, then $2y$ will also be positive, so the value under the square root sign will be positive. Answer choice G will also work.

(3) Answer choices J and K are not true, because you have just determined that both x and y must both be either positive or negative.

Since answer choices F and G cannot both be correct, you are left with answer choice H.

37. **The correct answer is D.** The question asks you to solve for S, so perform the following operations:

(1) $A = 2S + 9$

(2) $A - 9 = 2S$

(3) $\dfrac{A - 9}{2} = S$, answer choice D.

38. **The correct answer is G.** The slope of a line measures the steepness of a line, and can be calculated by using the following formula: $\dfrac{(y_1 - y_2)}{(x_1 - x_2)}$. Any line perpendicular to the y-axis is a horizontal line. Because there is no change in y, the numerator $(y_1 - y_2)$, is 0. This means that the slope of a horizontal line is 0, answer choice G.

39. **The correct answer is E.** The standard form of a line is $y = mx + b$, where m is the slope. In order to determine which line has the smallest slope, you must first put all of the answer choices into the standard form. Answer choices A, B, and E are already in the standard form. The slopes of those lines are 3, 1, and −7, respectively. Calculate the slope of answer choices C and D:

(1) $4y = 4x - 8$

(2) $y = \dfrac{4}{4x} - \dfrac{8}{4}; y = x - 2$

Answer choice C has a slope of 1.

(1) $3y = 9x + 6$

(2) $y = \dfrac{9}{3x} + \dfrac{6}{3}; y = 3x + 2$

Answer choice D has a slope of 3. Therefore, the line with the smallest slope is answer choice E, with a slope of −7.

40. **The correct answer is K.** To solve this problem, you must calculate the $\tan \alpha$ and the $\cos \beta$. The tangent of any acute angle is calculated by dividing the length of the side opposite the acute angle by the length of the side adjacent to the acute angle ($\tan = \dfrac{\text{opp}}{\text{adj}}$). The cosine of any acute angle is calculated by dividing the length of the side adjacent to the acute angle by the hypotenuse ($\cos = \dfrac{\text{adj}}{\text{hyp}}$). The tan of angle α is $\dfrac{4}{3}$, and the cos of angle β is $\dfrac{4}{5}$. Now you can plug these values into the equation given in the problem and solve:

(1) $(\tan \alpha)(\cos \beta) = \left(\dfrac{4}{3}\right)\left(\dfrac{4}{5}\right) = \dfrac{16}{15}$, answer choice K.

41. **The correct answer is E.** According to information in the problem, Amy can run 3 miles in s minutes, or $\dfrac{3}{s}$. The question asks you to calculate the distance she can run in 50 minutes. In other

words, Amy can run x miles per 50 minutes, or $\frac{x}{50}$. Set up a proportion and solve for x:

(1) $\frac{3}{s} = \frac{x}{50}$

(2) $sx = 150$

(3) $x = \frac{150}{s}$, answer choice E.

42. **The correct answer is J.** The problem states that each gallon of oil weighs 6 pounds. Multiply the number of pounds per gallon (6) by the number of gallons that the tank contains (4,800):

(1) $6 \times 4,800 = 28,800$, answer choice J.

43. **The correct answer is C.** The area of a triangle is calculated using the formula $A = \frac{1}{2}(bh)$, where b is the length of the base, and h is the height. Based on the measures of the angles given, you can draw triangle ABC as shown below:

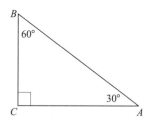

You are given that $\overline{AB}$, the hypotenuse, is 16 units long. Because this is a $30° - 60° - 90°$ triangle, you can calculate the lengths of the height $(\overline{BC})$ and the base $(\overline{AC})$. The relationship between the sides of a $30° - 60° - 90°$ triangle is as follows: The side opposite the $30°$ is equal to $\frac{1}{2}$ of the length of the hypotenuse, and the side opposite the $60°$ is equal to $\frac{1}{2}$ of the length of the hypotenuse times $\sqrt{3}$. Calculate the lengths of the sides:

(1) Side $\overline{AC}$ (the base) $= \frac{1}{2}(16\sqrt{3}) = 8\sqrt{3}$

(2) Side $\overline{BC}$ (the height) $= \frac{1}{2}(16) = 8$

Now you can plug these values into the formula for the area of a triangle:

(3) $A = \frac{1}{2}(8)(8\sqrt{3}) = 4(8\sqrt{3}) = 32\sqrt{3}$, answer choice C.

44. **The correct answer is F.** For isosceles trapezoids, the ratio of the bottom part of the diagonal to the top part of the diagonal is equal to the ratio of the bottom side of the trapezoid to the top side of the trapezoid. Therefore, the ratio of $\overline{HK}$

(the bottom part of the diagonal) to $\overline{GK}$ (the top part of the diagonal) is equal to the ratio of $\overline{HJ}$ (the bottom of the trapezoid) to $\overline{FG}$ (the top of the trapezoid). This statement is expressed as $\frac{HK}{GK} = \frac{HJ}{FG}$. Since HJ is z inches, and FG is x inches, $\frac{HK}{GK}$ is equal to $\frac{z}{x}$, answer choice F.

45. **The correct answer is C.** The area of a rectangle is calculated by multiplying the width by the length ($A = w \times l$). Calculate the area of the first rectangle as follows:

(1) Set the width equal to x, and the length equal to $2x$.

(2) $A = x(2x) \times = 2x^2$.

Now calculate the area of the second triangle:

(1) The length is tripled and the width is doubled, so the length $= 3(2x)$ and the width $= 2x$.

(2) $A = 3(2x)(2x) = 6x \times 2x = 12x^2$.

The area of the second triangle is $12x^2$, which is 6 times greater than the area of the first triangle ($2x^2$), answer choice C.

46. **The correct answer is J.** Systems of equations will have an infinite number of solutions when the equations are equal to each other. The first step in solving this problem is to recognize that the second equation is exactly 3 times the value of the first equation: $72x = 3(24x)$, $45y = 3(15y)$, so $9z$ must equal $3(108)$. Solve for z:

(1) $9z = 3(108)$

(2) $9z = 324$

(3) $z = 36$, answer choice J.

47. **The correct answer is A.** A prime number is a number that is only divisible by 1 and itself. If you list all of the numbers between 36 and 53, not including 36 and 53, you will find the prime numbers 37, 41, 43, and 47. There are 4 prime number between 36 and 53, answer choice A.

48. **The correct answer is H.** The tangent of any acute angle is calculated by dividing the length of the side opposite the acute angle by the length of the side adjacent to the acute angle ($\tan = \frac{\text{opp}}{\text{adj}}$). If $\tan A = \frac{x}{y}$, then $\sin A = \frac{x}{\text{hypotenuse}}$. The sin of any acute angle is calculated by dividing the length of the side opposite to the acute angle by the hypotenuse ($\sin = \frac{\text{adj}}{\text{hyp}}$). To determine the

length of the hypotenuse, use the Pythagorean Theorem, $a^2 + b^2 = c^2$. According to this equation, $a^2 + b^2 = x^2 + y^2$, so $c^2 = x^2 + y^2$, and $c = \sqrt{x^2 + y^2}$. Now that you know the value of the hypotenuse, you can solve for sin A. Sin A is $\dfrac{x}{\sqrt{x^2 + y^2}}$, answer choice H.

49. **The correct answer is E.** The area of a parallelogram is calculated by using the formula $A = (b \times h)$, where b is the base, and h is the height. The length of the side, $\sqrt{21}$, is not relevant. Plug the given values into the formula:

    (1) $A = (6 \times 32)$

    (2) $A = 192$, answer choice E.

50. **The correct answer is H.** The easiest way to solve this problem is to draw a line and place the given points on the line, as follows:

    (1)

    Based on the line above, 1 possible length of BC is 20. Eliminate answer choices G, J, and K. Since you are left with answer choices F and H, you need to determine if AC could also be 2 meters long. Draw another line, and change the order of the points:

    (2)

    Based on this line, another possible length of AC is 2, so answer choice H must be correct.

51. **The correct answer is D.** The area of a parallelogram is calculated by using the formula $A = (b \times h)$, where b is the base, and h is the height. The area of a triangle is $\frac{1}{2}(b \times h)$. You can determine the base by measuring the distance along the x-axis, and you can determine the height by measuring the distance along the y-axis:

    (1) The distance between -6 and 3 on the x-axis is 9 units. Likewise, the distance between -3 and 6 is 9 units. The length of the base is 9.

    (2) The distance between 8 and -6 on the y-axis is 14. The height is 14.

    Now plug these values into the formula for the area of a triangle:

    (1) $A = \frac{1}{2}(b \times h)$

    (2) $A = \frac{1}{2}(9 \times 14)$

    (3) $A = \frac{1}{2}(126) = 63.0$, answer choice D.

52. **The correct answer is G.** In this problem, the quantity $6a^5b^7$ is less than 0, which means it must be negative. 6 is positive and a^5 and b^7 can be positive or negative. Since a negative number times a negative number yields a positive number, either a^5 or b^7 must be negative, but not both. Eliminate answer choice F. By definition, if you raise a negative number to an odd numbered power, the result will be negative. Since the problem asks which must be true, answer choice G is the best because it makes either a or b negative, but not both.

53. **The correct answer is C.** The easiest way to solve this problem is to determine the number of patients Mandy visited each day and calculate the total number of visits on all 5 days.

    (1) Day 1: 7 visits
        Day 2: $7 + 3 = 10$ visits
        Day 3: $10 + 3 = 13$ visits
        Day 4: $13 + 3 = 16$ visits
        Day 5: $16 + 3 = 19$ visits

    (2) $7 + 10 + 13 + 16 + 19 = 65$ visits, answer choice C.

54. **The correct answer is F.** If 2 numbers, x and y, differ by 8, that means that $x - y = 8$. Multiplying the 2 numbers, $(x)(y)$, will yield the product. Solve the first equation for x, and then substitute the result for x in the second equation, as follows:

    (1) $x - y = 8$

    (2) $x = y + 8$

    (3) $(y + 8)y =$

    Since one of the answer choices must be the solution to that equation, plug in the answer choices, starting with the smallest value (note that the answer choices are in ascending order):

    (1) $(y + 8)y = -16$

    (2) $y^2 + 8y = -16$

    (3) $y^2 + 8y + 16 = 0$

    (4) $(y + 4)^2 = 0$

    (5) $y = -4$

Now, substitute -4 for y in the first equation and solve for x:

(1) $x-(-4)=8$

(2) $x=4$

Since $(4)(-4)=-16$, and -16 is the smallest answer, answer choice F is correct.

55. **The correct answer is A.** Because angle x is less than $90°$, it is an acute angle. The cosine of any acute angle is calculated by dividing the length of the side adjacent to the acute angle by the hypotenuse $(\cos=\dfrac{\text{adj}}{\text{hyp}})$. This means that the length of the side adjacent to angle x is 4, and the length of the hypotenuse is 5. The sine of any acute angle is calculated by dividing the length of the side opposite to the acute angle by the hypotenuse $(\sin=\dfrac{\text{opp}}{\text{hyp}})$. Since you know the measure of the side adjacent to angle x and the length of the hypotenuse, you can use the Pythagorean Theorem to calculate the length of the side opposite angle x.

Pythagorean Theorem: $a^2+b^2=c^2$, where c is the hypotenuse.

(1) $4^2+b^2=7^2$

(2) $16+b^2=25$

(3) $b^2=9$

(4) $b=3$

The side opposite angle x is 3, so the sin of angle x is $\dfrac{3}{5}$, answer choice A.

56. **The correct answer is F.** The problem asks for an expression that represents the *number* of sets of books sold, not the *price* of the sets of books sold. The easiest way to understand the problem is to make a table and notice the pattern:

Change is $ per set of books	Number of books sold
Original price of $9.50	1,750 books sold (given in problem)
Decrease by $1.00 = $8.50	1,750 + 1,200(1) books sold
Decrease by $2.00 = $7.50	1,750 + 1,200(2) = 1,750 + 2,400 books sold
Decrease by $3.00 = $6.50	1,750 + 1,200(3) = 1,750 + 3,600 books sold
Decrease by $x = (9.50 − x)	1,750 + 1,200x books sold

Answer H would be correct if the question asked for the price of the set of books. Since the problem asks for the number of books sold, answer choice F is correct.

57. **The correct answer is A.** The rules of the game state that a player is a winner if 2 marbles drawn have a sum greater than 45. Martin has already drawn the marble numbered 17. In order to win, Martin must draw another marble with a number greater than 28 $(17+28=45)$. The possible winning marbles are 29, 30, 31 ... 44. Therefore, Martin has 16 chances to draw a winning marble. Since he has already drawn one of the 45 marbles and did not put it back, he has 16 chances out of 44 to draw a winning marble. $\dfrac{16}{44}$ can be reduced to $\dfrac{4}{11}$, answer choice A.

58. **The correct answer is F.** The perimeter is the distance around an object. Calculate the perimeter by adding the lengths of the sides. First, find the missing lengths:

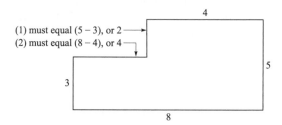

The lengths of the sides are $3+4+5+8+2+4$, which is 26. Therefore, the perimeter is 26, answer choice F.

59. **The correct answer is C.** A circle that is inscribed in the square will be contained completely inside the square, and will touch all 4 sides of the square. Draw a picture to help you visualize the problem:

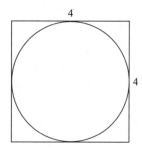

If the vertices, or corners of the square, are at the coordinates given, the length of each of the sides of the square must be 4. This means that the diameter of the circle is 4, and the radius is 2. The equation of a circle centered at (a,b) with a radius r, is $(x-a)^2+(y+b)^2=r^2$. Substitute 2 for r and get a value of 4 for r^2. You can eliminate answer choice A, B, and E, which indicate that r^2 is equal to either 2 or 8. Answer choice C matches the standard form of the equation of a circle, so it is the correct choice.

60. The correct answer is K. To solve this problem, you must first calculate the last price of the skirt. On Wednesday, the price ($60) was reduced by 15%. This means that the new price is 100% −15%, or 85% of $60. Multiply $60 by 0.85, the decimal equivalent of 85%, to get $51. Two weeks later, the new price ($51) is further reduced by 20%. Calculate this reduced price:

(1) 100%−20%=80%

(2) ($51) 0.80=$40.80

Set up a proportion to calculate the percent this price is of the original price:

(1) $40.80 is to $60 as x% is to 100%

(2) $\dfrac{40.80}{60.00}=\dfrac{x}{100}$; cross-multiply and solve for x.

(3) $60x=4,080$

(4) $x=68$, answer choice K.

Reading Test Explanations

PASSAGE I

1. **The best answer is A.** The first sentence of the last paragraph indicates that it was time for Mrs. Pontellier to dress for dinner. She then makes the comment about her husband not returning, so it is most likely that she is expressing her belief that she will be having dinner without her husband, answer choice A.

2. **The best answer is H.** Paragraph 4 indicates that Robert talked a good deal about himself because "he was very young, and did not know any better." The passage goes on to say that "Mrs. Pontellier talked a little about herself for the same reason." You can infer that the two are about the same age, answer choice H.

3. **The best answer is A.** According to the passage, Robert intended to "go to Mexico in the autumn, where fortune awaited him." This suggests that he wanted to seek his fortune in Mexico in order to gain more wealth and social stature than he currently has.

4. **The best answer is G.** The word *incessantly* means "long and uninterrupted." This definition best supports answer choice G. Based on the context of the passage, you could have eliminated answer choices H and J. While it is true that they each talked about themselves, the use of the word *incessantly* suggests that the conversation was long.

5. **The best answer is D.** The only selection that is made clear in the passage about both Mrs. Pontellier and her husband is that they have children, answer choice D. There is no discussion about the way that Mr. Pontellier feels about Robert, or about how Mr. and Mrs. Pontellier get along. While the passage suggests that Mrs. Pontellier will not be having dinner with her husband, the passage does not make it clear that they never spend time together.

6. **The best answer is F.** The second paragraph states that Robert, "in coloring ... was not unlike his companion." His physical appearance is, therefore, compared to Mrs. Pontellier, answer choice F.

7. **The best answer is B.** All of the characters in the story seem to enjoy the company of others, so it makes sense that they are all sociable, answer choice B. The other answer choices are not supported by details in the passage.

8. **The best answer is J.** In paragraph 4, Robert talks a good deal about himself, mentioning that he speaks three languages, which "gave him no small value as a clerk and correspondent." He appears to be quite confident, answer choice J. The other answer choices have negative connotations, which are not supported by the passage.

9. **The best answer is A.** According to the passage, "In former times ... 'the house' had been a summer luxury of the LeBruns." Now, the cottages surrounding the house were rented by visitors, which "enabled Madame LeBruns to maintain the easy and comfortable existence which appeared to be her birthright." This suggest that Robert's mother, Madame LeBruns, was better off financially earlier in her life, answer choice A.

10. **The best answer is J.** Mrs. Pontellier did not seem to be concerned that she would be dining without her husband, which suggests that she is accustomed to being without him. Her friendly and easy conversation with Robert also supports answer choice J. The other answer choices are not supported by the passage.

PASSAGE II

11. **The best answer is B.** The passage states that *baleen* is whalebone, which was used for things like storage and insulation, but not for food. All of the other answer choices are mentioned specifically as being part of the Inuit diet.

12. **The best answer is G.** The passage states that, "Since about 800 A.D., Inuit whalers have hunted bowhead whales." *Maktaaq* is whale skin, and *Naluqatak* is a feast. The humpback whale is not mentioned in the passage.

13. **The best answer is D.** The Inuit culture is tied to the environment, and the Inuit "believe the Arctic animals ... are all part of their culture." They have a great respect for the whales, and hunt only as many animals as they need to survive. This information best supports answer choice D.

14. **The best answer is H.** The passage explicitly states that whale meat is rich in phosphorous, niacin, and vitamin E. Riboflavin is not mentioned.

15. **The best answer is C.** In Paragraph 1, the word *moratorium* is used in reference to the International Whaling Committee's response to the over-hunting of whales. Therefore, it makes sense that a moratorium would be a suspension of activity. The other answer choices are not supported by the passage.

16. The best answer is F. According to the passage, *Naluqatak* is a feast that is celebrated at the end of the whaling season. It is a "time of thanksgiving and sharing." Therefore, it can best be described as a harvest feast, answer choice F.

17. The best answer is C. Paragraph 6 indicates that the traditional blanket toss "requires the coordinated action of many people … creating a communal version of a trampoline." The use of the word *coordinated* refers to the organized movement of the people, answer choice C.

18. The best answer is F. A main theme of the passage is the importance of family and community to the Inuit people. It would make sense, then, that the Inuit would respect their elders, answer choice F. The passage also states that the shares of the whale meat are "reserved for elders and widows." The other answer choices are somewhat negative, and do not fit within the context of the passage.

19. The best answer is A. The passage states that "many Inuit never hunt beyond the end of May, to avoid the time when calving females are passing through."

20. The best answer is J. Since, according to the passage, "meat from seals and fish" is saved for festivals. You can conclude that the Inuit also hunt seals, answer choice J.

PASSAGE III

21. The best answer is B. The passage indicates that, like Tiger Woods, Bobby Jones was also a very talented golfer at a young age. Tiger Woods entitled his book, *How I Play Golf*, which was the same title that Bobby Jones used for his instructional film series. There, and other details form the passage, suggest that both of the men were similar in many ways, answer choice B.

22. The best answer is J. Paragraph 2 states that "Pop" Keeler was a mentor for Bobby, and helped Bobby to become a gracious winner and loser, as well as "a remarkably honorable gentlemen." This indicates that "Pop" Keeler was a positive force in Bobby's life, answer choice J.

23. The best answer is C. The passage discusses many accomplishments that Jones made throughout his life, including furthering his education. The passage also mentions that Jones did not take lessons or practice constantly. Answer choices A, B, and D can be eliminated, because they are not supported by details in the passage.

24. The best answer is J. As it is used in the passage, the word *amateur* refers to Bobby Jones's status as a golfer who is not paid to golf. Therefore, answer choice J is best.

25. The best answer is A. Since Jones took time away from golfing to earn his college degrees, it is clear that his perspective on higher education was that it was important. The other answer choices are not supported by the passage.

26. The best answer is G. The statement appears in the fourth paragraph, where Jones insisted on following the rules of the game, "adding a penalty stroke to his score." This suggests that he placed as great an emphasis on the rules of golf, as he did on the laws against crime.

27. The best answer is D. The passage states that Tiger Woods, not Bobby Jones, wrote a book called *How I Play Golf*.

28. The best answer is H. According to the passage, *syringeomyelia* is a rare spinal disease, which eventually confined Jones to a wheelchair. This suggests that the disease gradually left him incapacitated, answer choice H. He had retired from golf years earlier, so answer choice G can be eliminated. The other answer choices are not supported by the passage.

29. The best answer is B. Jones' comment in the seventh paragraph was in response to a question about his debilitating disease.

30. The best answer is F. The overall tone of the passage is very positive, and indicates that the author admired and respected Bobby Jones. The other answer choices are not supported by the passage.

PASSAGE IV

31. The best answer is B. Since "protagonistic" behavior is opposite of "antagonistic" behavior, find the answer choice that contains a word pair that have opposite meanings. *Admirable* is opposite of *despicable*, so answer choice B is best. The other answer choices contain pairs of words that have similar meanings.

32. The best answer is H. The passage states that a coyote can run "up to forty miles per hour," use its "keen sense of smell to locate burrowing rodents," and swim strongly after its prey. There is no mention in the passage of the coyote's ability to dig efficiently. In fact, according to the passage, coyotes sometimes join forces with badgers, relying on the other animals "powerful claws" to dig up prey.

33. **The best answer is C.** According to the passage, coyotes are "somewhat like a medium-sized collie, although the coyote's bone structure is lighter." The other answer choices are not supported by details in the passage.

34. **The best answer is F.** Paragraph 4 indicates that the coyote will join forces with a badger to take advantage of its "powerful claws." This supports answer choice F.

35. **The best answer is A.** Since the passage indicates that coyotes will "prey on unattended small dogs and cats." it makes sense that, if evidence of a coyote is discovered, residents of the community should carefully watch their small pets when the pets are outside. The other answer choices are not supported by the passage.

36. **The best answer is J.** The seventh paragraph states that if "predators are prevalent and the coyote population is threatened, the typical litter of six pups will often double — and even triple." This supports answer choice J.

37. **The best answer is D.** The passage states that coyotes are "generally not known to have

exceptional climbing skills," answer choice D. The other answer choices are not supported by details in the passage.

38. **The best answer is G.** According to the passage, despite being hunted and killed, "coyotes have maintained their numbers ... and continue to increase in the East." Eliminate answer choice H, which says that they are decreasing in the East. Since coyotes originated in the West and are expanding into the East, you can conclude that coyote population have spread from their native habitats, answer choice G.

39. **The best answer is C.** According to the passage, the coyote sometimes forms a "hunting partnership" with a badger. It is unlikely, then, that badgers are predators of coyotes. The other answer choices are mentioned explicitly in the passage.

40. **The best answer is F.** Paragraph 8 states that "the final part of the coyotes' mystique may stem from the quavering howl," which supports answer choice F. The other answer choices are mentioned in the passage, but not in connection with the coyotes' mystique.

Science Reasoning Test Explanations

PASSAGE I

1. The correct answer is C. Table 1 shows that petri dish 2 had a pH level of 7 and experienced the highest percent growth of *E. coli* bacteria, as compared to petri dishes 1 and 2. Therefore, answer choice C, a pH level near 7, is correct.

2. The correct answer is F. The description of Experiment 3 indicates that *most* bacteria, unlike *E. coli*, need certain growth factors and vitamins to reproduce. In addition, the experiment was run to "ensure that the 3 growth factors have minimal to no effect on growth."

3. The correct answer is A. Table 1 shows that *E. coli* bacteria reproduce most efficiently at a pH level of 7, so answer choice A is correct. Answer choice D is not correct because Table 1 shows that *E. coli* can still reproduce at different pH levels, just not as efficiently.

4. The correct answer is G. The question states that bacteria often reproduce until all available nutrients have been depleted. By supplying each group of bacteria with unlimited nutrients, the bacteria will reproduce for a longer time.

5. The correct answer is D. To answer this question, you must look at Table 2, which shows the nutrients required for *E. coli* to reproduce. If the compounds are listed as requirements, then you must assume that the compounds are present in the cells of *E. coli* bacteria. The only nutrients listed are carbon, oxygen, and nitrogen. Based on this information, the only correct answer is D.

6. The correct answer is J. Since the reproduction rate varies drastically from one stage to the next, the best way to study the different growth stages would be to record the growth changes more frequently.

PASSAGE II

7. The correct answer is D. The major difference between the scientists' opinions is whether or not earthquakes can be accurately predicted. Scientist 1 believes that predictions cannot be made with accuracy. Scientist 2 believes that accurate predictions can be made about the location and magnitude of the next earthquake.

8. The correct answer is G. Scientist 1 claims that Global Positioning Systems can determine the amount of strain that is loaded onto faults from plate motion "easily and with much certainty." On the other hand, Scientist 1 claims that the amount of strain *released* is "much more difficult to estimate."

9. The correct answer is C. According to Scientist 2, the movement of the tectonic plates is causing strain to build up. This claim best supports answer choice C.

10. The correct answer is G. Scientist 1 states that the main problem in predicting earthquakes is that historical data do not date back far enough to illustrate quake activities clearly. The other answer choices are not supported by the passage.

11. The correct answer is A. Scientist 2 claims that an earthquake is caused by the buildup of pressure on a fault line and the only way to release that pressure is through an earthquake. Therefore, if a handful of small earthquakes released some of the pressure along a fault line, there would be a decrease in the probability of another earthquake, answer choice A.

12. The correct answer is J. Based on their opinions, the only statement that both scientists would agree with is that the San Francisco Bay Area has fault lines extending through the entire region. Scientist 1 says that the Bay Area is covered with major fault lines and Scientist 2 says that many populated areas in the Bay Area are "near, or even sandwiched between," major fault lines.

13. The correct answer is A. Scientist 2 claims that earthquakes can be predicted with much certainty. The only statement that strengthens his claim is answer choice A, which says that the predictions of a group of scientists were accurate.

PASSAGE III

14. The correct answer is G. Galvani claimed an electric fluid was present in animal tissue that created an electric current. Volta was trying to prove that you did not need animal tissue or electric fluid to create an electric current. By using his tongue, which is animal tissue, Volta did not disprove Galvani's theory that animal tissue contains electric fluid.

15. The correct answer is B. Galvani used 2 metals in his experiment with the leg of the dead frog. Volta also believed that 2 metals were sufficient to produce an electric current, or he likely would have used a third metal in this experiment. The other answer choices are not supported by the passage.

16. **The correct answer is J.** Volta used several layers of the elements/metals piled on each other, separated by the moist material. We know that he used as many as 60 layers of metal to produce an electric current, which supports answer choice J.

17. **The correct answer is A.** According to Experiment 4, 60 layers of metal produced a greater intensity than 30 or 40 layers. It could be reasonably assumed that the greater the number of layers, the greater the intensity of the electric current.

18. **The correct answer is G.** In Experiment 2, Volta noted an electrical interaction between copper and zinc in an acidic solution. In Experiment 4, he separated layers of metal with material dampened by an acidic solution. If researchers were able to determine that substances used in the other 2 experiments (the human tongue and paper soaked in electrolytes) also contained an acidic solution, the hypothesis that an acidic solution is needed to create an electric current would be supported.

19. **The correct answer is C.** None of the experiments directly disprove the theory that a direct electric current is produced by chemical reactions. Volta only proved that animal tissue was not needed to produce electric currents. In fact, the first paragraph states that "Volta also discovered the means of converting chemical energy into electric energy which is the basis for the modern battery."

PASSAGE IV

20. **The correct answer is G.** The passage states that high levels of chlorine are capable of having a corrosive effect on surfaces. The chlorine levels in Sample 2 are too high to fall into the ideal range, so it can be inferred that the water from Sample 2 may be corrosive.

21. **The correct answer is C.** Since alkalinity is related to pH levels, then the most logical thing to do is check the alkalinity levels in the pool before adjusting pH levels. The other answer choices are not supported by the passage.

22. **The correct answer is F.** According to Table 1, the results from the tests on Sample 1 all fall within the ideal range, which most likely means that the water is balanced and safe for swimmers, answer choice F.

23. **The correct answer is B.** To answer this question, look at Figure 1. Find the point just above 80% on the y-axis and move to the right until you reach the line. Once you reach the line, move down until you arrive at the x-axis. The point on the x-axis that corresponds to this point on the line is a pH of 6.5, answer choice B.

24. **The correct answer is H.** The passage states that the presence of too much chlorine may bleach the dye in phenol red. If the pool is overchlorinated, then there is a possibility that the chlorine will bleach the dye in the phenol red and result in a clear water sample.

PASSAGE V

25. **The correct answer is C.** According to Figure 1, as Time and Distance increase, the body goes through 3 different phases to produce ATP for the muscles. The phosphagen phase and the glycogen-lactic acid phase are first and, as it appears in Figure 1, occur within a short period of time and within short distances. The final phase, aerobic respiration, continues on into longer periods of time and longer distances. Therefore, a long-distance runner will most likely continue to produce ATP through aerobic respiration, answer choice C.

26. **The correct answer is F.** The passages states that aerobic respiration begins after only 2 minutes of exercise, answer choice F.

27. **The correct answer is B.** According to Table 1, reserves are a source of glucose used during aerobic respiration. The body uses carbohydrates first, then fatty acids, and, in extreme cases, like starvation, the body turns to proteins. Therefore, answer choice B, starvation, is correct.

28. **The correct answer is G.** The question is asking you to look at Figure 2 and determine the VO2 max of a 50-year-old male in "Excellent" physical condition and compare it to a female of the same age and fitness level.

   (1) Find 50 on the x-axis (Age) and follow it up to the line that corresponds to a male in excellent condition from the Key. Once you reach the line, move to the left until you reach the y-axis (VO2 max). This point is at a VO2 max of approximately 45.

   (2) Find 50 on the x-axis (Age) again and follow it up to the line that corresponds to a female in excellent condition from the Key. Once you reach the line, move to the left until you reach the y-axis (VO2 max). This point is at a VO2 max of approximately 33.

(3) 45 (male) − 33 (female) = 12

The female consumes 12 milliliters less oxygen (per minute per kilogram of body weight), answer choice G.

29. **The correct answer is A.** Look at Figure 2 and find 27 on the *x*-axis (Age). Follow it up to the line that corresponds to a female in poor physical condition from the Key. Once you reach the line, move to the left until you reach the *y*-axis (VO2 max). This point is at a VO2 max of between 25 and 30, answer choice A.

PASSAGE VI

30. **The correct answer is F.** According to the passage, the body produces all of the cholesterol that it needs. Therefore, cholesterol is found in the body or in particular foods only. It can be inferred that any other cholesterol in the body that was not created there must come from what you eat, answer choice F.

31. **The correct answer is A.** HDL protects against the development of heart disease and is considered "good" cholesterol. Answer choice B says that HDL increases cholesterol levels and answer choice C claims that HDL is "bad" cholesterol, so you can eliminate both of these choices. You know from the passage that answer choice D is also false, so answer choice A must be correct. The passage also states that the liver is responsible for cholesterol from the body.

32. **The correct answer is H.** According to Table 1, trans fats are the only type of fats that increase "bad" LDL cholesterol and decrease "good" HDL cholesterol. Therefore, this type of fat would have the greatest net negative effect on cholesterol levels.

33. **The correct answer is D.** According to Table 1, monounsaturated and polyunsaturated fats are the best for overall cholesterol levels. Saturated and trans fats are the worst for overall cholesterol levels. Based on this information and the data in the question, you can eliminate answer choices A and B. Both palm and coconut oil have high amounts of saturated fats, which increase "bad" cholesterol levels. Canola oil is the best choice, but not because it is low in polyunsaturated fats, which increase "good" cholesterol levels, so answer choice C can also be eliminated. Canola oil is the best choice because it is high in monounsaturated and polyunsaturated fats and low in saturated fats, answer choice D.

34. **The correct answer is J.** According to the question, omega-3 fatty acid is known to lower the risk of heart disease. You know from the passage that high cholesterol levels can cause heart disease, so you can assume that omega-3 fatty acid lowers cholesterol levels. You can also assume that omega-3 fatty acids have lower amounts of "bad" LDL cholesterol and higher amounts of "good" HDL cholesterol. Therefore, lowering the level of "bad" LDL cholesterol and increasing the levels of "good" HDL cholesterol would probably lower the risk of heart disease.

PASSAGE VII

35. **The correct answer is D.** The passage states that friction depends mostly on the smoothness of the surfaces that come into contact with an object. Rough surfaces, like the carpet or driftwood used in the experiments, increase friction because it is harder for the car to travel on these surfaces than on a smoother surface. Therefore, the stronger the friction, the shorter the distance the car can travel, answer choice D.

36. **The correct answer is F.** The passage states that friction depends mostly on the smoothness of the surfaces that come into contact with an object. The smoother the surface, the less friction there will be to stop the car from traveling farther. If the surface is smoother, the friction will be decreased, and the car will be able to travel a longer distance, answer choice F.

37. **The correct answer is C.** According to the passage, friction depends mostly on the smoothness of the surfaces that come into contact with an object. Friction will be the least powerful on a smooth surface, like aluminum foil, answer choice C.

38. **The correct answer is G.** According to the passage, friction depends mostly on the smoothness of the surfaces that come into contact with an object. The smoother the surfaces of the 2 objects attempting to slide past one another, the less friction there will be to stop or slow the movement. Lubricants or oils cause the surface of an object to become slippery, or smoother, which is why the materials are used to decrease friction, answer choice G. The other answer choices are not supported by the passage.

39. **The correct answer is A.** The passage states that the same car was used in all of the experiments. Therefore, it can be inferred that the mass of the

car was kept constant in each experiment, answer choice A.

40. **The correct answer is H.** The passage states that raising the height of the ramp increased the speed that the car could travel, so you can eliminate answer choices F and G. Based on information given in the passage and the results of the experiments, you know that the faster the car traveled, the longer the distance it traveled before friction stopped it. Therefore, increasing the height of the ramp both increased the speed and increased the distance traveled, answer choice H.

ACT PRACTICE TEST 2
Answer Sheet

ENGLISH

1 Ⓐ Ⓑ Ⓒ Ⓓ	21 Ⓐ Ⓑ Ⓒ Ⓓ	41 Ⓐ Ⓑ Ⓒ Ⓓ	61 Ⓐ Ⓑ Ⓒ Ⓓ
2 Ⓕ Ⓖ Ⓗ Ⓙ	22 Ⓕ Ⓖ Ⓗ Ⓙ	42 Ⓕ Ⓖ Ⓗ Ⓙ	62 Ⓕ Ⓖ Ⓗ Ⓙ
3 Ⓐ Ⓑ Ⓒ Ⓓ	23 Ⓐ Ⓑ Ⓒ Ⓓ	43 Ⓐ Ⓑ Ⓒ Ⓓ	63 Ⓐ Ⓑ Ⓒ Ⓓ
4 Ⓕ Ⓖ Ⓗ Ⓙ	24 Ⓕ Ⓖ Ⓗ Ⓙ	44 Ⓕ Ⓖ Ⓗ Ⓙ	64 Ⓕ Ⓖ Ⓗ Ⓙ
5 Ⓐ Ⓑ Ⓒ Ⓓ	25 Ⓐ Ⓑ Ⓒ Ⓓ	45 Ⓐ Ⓑ Ⓒ Ⓓ	65 Ⓐ Ⓑ Ⓒ Ⓓ
6 Ⓕ Ⓖ Ⓗ Ⓙ	26 Ⓕ Ⓖ Ⓗ Ⓙ	46 Ⓕ Ⓖ Ⓗ Ⓙ	66 Ⓕ Ⓖ Ⓗ Ⓙ
7 Ⓐ Ⓑ Ⓒ Ⓓ	27 Ⓐ Ⓑ Ⓒ Ⓓ	47 Ⓐ Ⓑ Ⓒ Ⓓ	67 Ⓐ Ⓑ Ⓒ Ⓓ
8 Ⓕ Ⓖ Ⓗ Ⓙ	28 Ⓕ Ⓖ Ⓗ Ⓙ	48 Ⓕ Ⓖ Ⓗ Ⓙ	68 Ⓕ Ⓖ Ⓗ Ⓙ
9 Ⓐ Ⓑ Ⓒ Ⓓ	29 Ⓐ Ⓑ Ⓒ Ⓓ	49 Ⓐ Ⓑ Ⓒ Ⓓ	69 Ⓐ Ⓑ Ⓒ Ⓓ
10 Ⓕ Ⓖ Ⓗ Ⓙ	30 Ⓕ Ⓖ Ⓗ Ⓙ	50 Ⓕ Ⓖ Ⓗ Ⓙ	70 Ⓕ Ⓖ Ⓗ Ⓙ
11 Ⓐ Ⓑ Ⓒ Ⓓ	31 Ⓐ Ⓑ Ⓒ Ⓓ	51 Ⓐ Ⓑ Ⓒ Ⓓ	71 Ⓐ Ⓑ Ⓒ Ⓓ
12 Ⓕ Ⓖ Ⓗ Ⓙ	32 Ⓕ Ⓖ Ⓗ Ⓙ	52 Ⓕ Ⓖ Ⓗ Ⓙ	72 Ⓕ Ⓖ Ⓗ Ⓙ
13 Ⓐ Ⓑ Ⓒ Ⓓ	33 Ⓐ Ⓑ Ⓒ Ⓓ	53 Ⓐ Ⓑ Ⓒ Ⓓ	73 Ⓐ Ⓑ Ⓒ Ⓓ
14 Ⓕ Ⓖ Ⓗ Ⓙ	34 Ⓕ Ⓖ Ⓗ Ⓙ	54 Ⓕ Ⓖ Ⓗ Ⓙ	74 Ⓕ Ⓖ Ⓗ Ⓙ
15 Ⓐ Ⓑ Ⓒ Ⓓ	35 Ⓐ Ⓑ Ⓒ Ⓓ	55 Ⓐ Ⓑ Ⓒ Ⓓ	75 Ⓐ Ⓑ Ⓒ Ⓓ
16 Ⓕ Ⓖ Ⓗ Ⓙ	36 Ⓕ Ⓖ Ⓗ Ⓙ	56 Ⓕ Ⓖ Ⓗ Ⓙ	
17 Ⓐ Ⓑ Ⓒ Ⓓ	37 Ⓐ Ⓑ Ⓒ Ⓓ	57 Ⓐ Ⓑ Ⓒ Ⓓ	
18 Ⓕ Ⓖ Ⓗ Ⓙ	38 Ⓕ Ⓖ Ⓗ Ⓙ	58 Ⓕ Ⓖ Ⓗ Ⓙ	
19 Ⓐ Ⓑ Ⓒ Ⓓ	39 Ⓐ Ⓑ Ⓒ Ⓓ	59 Ⓐ Ⓑ Ⓒ Ⓓ	
20 Ⓕ Ⓖ Ⓗ Ⓙ	40 Ⓕ Ⓖ Ⓗ Ⓙ	60 Ⓕ Ⓖ Ⓗ Ⓙ	

MATH

1 Ⓐ Ⓑ Ⓒ Ⓓ Ⓔ	16 Ⓕ Ⓖ Ⓗ Ⓙ Ⓚ	31 Ⓐ Ⓑ Ⓒ Ⓓ Ⓔ	46 Ⓕ Ⓖ Ⓗ Ⓙ Ⓚ
2 Ⓕ Ⓖ Ⓗ Ⓙ Ⓚ	17 Ⓐ Ⓑ Ⓒ Ⓓ Ⓔ	32 Ⓕ Ⓖ Ⓗ Ⓙ Ⓚ	47 Ⓐ Ⓑ Ⓒ Ⓓ Ⓔ
3 Ⓐ Ⓑ Ⓒ Ⓓ Ⓔ	18 Ⓕ Ⓖ Ⓗ Ⓙ Ⓚ	33 Ⓐ Ⓑ Ⓒ Ⓓ Ⓔ	48 Ⓕ Ⓖ Ⓗ Ⓙ Ⓚ
4 Ⓕ Ⓖ Ⓗ Ⓙ Ⓚ	19 Ⓐ Ⓑ Ⓒ Ⓓ Ⓔ	34 Ⓕ Ⓖ Ⓗ Ⓙ Ⓚ	49 Ⓐ Ⓑ Ⓒ Ⓓ Ⓔ
5 Ⓐ Ⓑ Ⓒ Ⓓ Ⓔ	20 Ⓕ Ⓖ Ⓗ Ⓙ Ⓚ	35 Ⓐ Ⓑ Ⓒ Ⓓ Ⓔ	50 Ⓕ Ⓖ Ⓗ Ⓙ Ⓚ
6 Ⓕ Ⓖ Ⓗ Ⓙ Ⓚ	21 Ⓐ Ⓑ Ⓒ Ⓓ Ⓔ	36 Ⓕ Ⓖ Ⓗ Ⓙ Ⓚ	51 Ⓐ Ⓑ Ⓒ Ⓓ Ⓔ
7 Ⓐ Ⓑ Ⓒ Ⓓ Ⓔ	22 Ⓕ Ⓖ Ⓗ Ⓙ Ⓚ	37 Ⓐ Ⓑ Ⓒ Ⓓ Ⓔ	52 Ⓕ Ⓖ Ⓗ Ⓙ Ⓚ
8 Ⓕ Ⓖ Ⓗ Ⓙ Ⓚ	23 Ⓐ Ⓑ Ⓒ Ⓓ Ⓔ	38 Ⓕ Ⓖ Ⓗ Ⓙ Ⓚ	53 Ⓐ Ⓑ Ⓒ Ⓓ Ⓔ
9 Ⓐ Ⓑ Ⓒ Ⓓ Ⓔ	24 Ⓕ Ⓖ Ⓗ Ⓙ Ⓚ	39 Ⓐ Ⓑ Ⓒ Ⓓ Ⓔ	54 Ⓕ Ⓖ Ⓗ Ⓙ Ⓚ
10 Ⓕ Ⓖ Ⓗ Ⓙ Ⓚ	25 Ⓐ Ⓑ Ⓒ Ⓓ Ⓔ	40 Ⓕ Ⓖ Ⓗ Ⓙ Ⓚ	55 Ⓐ Ⓑ Ⓒ Ⓓ Ⓔ
11 Ⓐ Ⓑ Ⓒ Ⓓ Ⓔ	26 Ⓕ Ⓖ Ⓗ Ⓙ Ⓚ	41 Ⓐ Ⓑ Ⓒ Ⓓ Ⓔ	56 Ⓕ Ⓖ Ⓗ Ⓙ Ⓚ
12 Ⓕ Ⓖ Ⓗ Ⓙ Ⓚ	27 Ⓐ Ⓑ Ⓒ Ⓓ Ⓔ	42 Ⓕ Ⓖ Ⓗ Ⓙ Ⓚ	57 Ⓐ Ⓑ Ⓒ Ⓓ Ⓔ
13 Ⓐ Ⓑ Ⓒ Ⓓ Ⓔ	28 Ⓕ Ⓖ Ⓗ Ⓙ Ⓚ	43 Ⓐ Ⓑ Ⓒ Ⓓ Ⓔ	58 Ⓕ Ⓖ Ⓗ Ⓙ Ⓚ
14 Ⓕ Ⓖ Ⓗ Ⓙ Ⓚ	29 Ⓐ Ⓑ Ⓒ Ⓓ Ⓔ	44 Ⓕ Ⓖ Ⓗ Ⓙ Ⓚ	59 Ⓐ Ⓑ Ⓒ Ⓓ Ⓔ
15 Ⓐ Ⓑ Ⓒ Ⓓ Ⓔ	30 Ⓕ Ⓖ Ⓗ Ⓙ Ⓚ	45 Ⓐ Ⓑ Ⓒ Ⓓ Ⓔ	60 Ⓕ Ⓖ Ⓗ Ⓙ Ⓚ

READING

1 Ⓐ Ⓑ Ⓒ Ⓓ	11 Ⓐ Ⓑ Ⓒ Ⓓ	21 Ⓐ Ⓑ Ⓒ Ⓓ	31 Ⓐ Ⓑ Ⓒ Ⓓ
2 Ⓕ Ⓖ Ⓗ Ⓙ	12 Ⓕ Ⓖ Ⓗ Ⓙ	22 Ⓕ Ⓖ Ⓗ Ⓙ	32 Ⓕ Ⓖ Ⓗ Ⓙ
3 Ⓐ Ⓑ Ⓒ Ⓓ	13 Ⓐ Ⓑ Ⓒ Ⓓ	23 Ⓐ Ⓑ Ⓒ Ⓓ	33 Ⓐ Ⓑ Ⓒ Ⓓ
4 Ⓕ Ⓖ Ⓗ Ⓙ	14 Ⓕ Ⓖ Ⓗ Ⓙ	24 Ⓕ Ⓖ Ⓗ Ⓙ	34 Ⓕ Ⓖ Ⓗ Ⓙ
5 Ⓐ Ⓑ Ⓒ Ⓓ	15 Ⓐ Ⓑ Ⓒ Ⓓ	25 Ⓐ Ⓑ Ⓒ Ⓓ	35 Ⓐ Ⓑ Ⓒ Ⓓ
6 Ⓕ Ⓖ Ⓗ Ⓙ	16 Ⓕ Ⓖ Ⓗ Ⓙ	26 Ⓕ Ⓖ Ⓗ Ⓙ	36 Ⓕ Ⓖ Ⓗ Ⓙ
7 Ⓐ Ⓑ Ⓒ Ⓓ	17 Ⓐ Ⓑ Ⓒ Ⓓ	27 Ⓐ Ⓑ Ⓒ Ⓓ	37 Ⓐ Ⓑ Ⓒ Ⓓ
8 Ⓕ Ⓖ Ⓗ Ⓙ	18 Ⓕ Ⓖ Ⓗ Ⓙ	28 Ⓕ Ⓖ Ⓗ Ⓙ	38 Ⓕ Ⓖ Ⓗ Ⓙ
9 Ⓐ Ⓑ Ⓒ Ⓓ	19 Ⓐ Ⓑ Ⓒ Ⓓ	29 Ⓐ Ⓑ Ⓒ Ⓓ	39 Ⓐ Ⓑ Ⓒ Ⓓ
10 Ⓕ Ⓖ Ⓗ Ⓙ	20 Ⓕ Ⓖ Ⓗ Ⓙ	30 Ⓕ Ⓖ Ⓗ Ⓙ	40 Ⓕ Ⓖ Ⓗ Ⓙ

SCIENCE

1 Ⓐ Ⓑ Ⓒ Ⓓ	11 Ⓐ Ⓑ Ⓒ Ⓓ	21 Ⓐ Ⓑ Ⓒ Ⓓ	31 Ⓐ Ⓑ Ⓒ Ⓓ
2 Ⓕ Ⓖ Ⓗ Ⓙ	12 Ⓕ Ⓖ Ⓗ Ⓙ	22 Ⓕ Ⓖ Ⓗ Ⓙ	32 Ⓕ Ⓖ Ⓗ Ⓙ
3 Ⓐ Ⓑ Ⓒ Ⓓ	13 Ⓐ Ⓑ Ⓒ Ⓓ	23 Ⓐ Ⓑ Ⓒ Ⓓ	33 Ⓐ Ⓑ Ⓒ Ⓓ
4 Ⓕ Ⓖ Ⓗ Ⓙ	14 Ⓕ Ⓖ Ⓗ Ⓙ	24 Ⓕ Ⓖ Ⓗ Ⓙ	34 Ⓕ Ⓖ Ⓗ Ⓙ
5 Ⓐ Ⓑ Ⓒ Ⓓ	15 Ⓐ Ⓑ Ⓒ Ⓓ	25 Ⓐ Ⓑ Ⓒ Ⓓ	35 Ⓐ Ⓑ Ⓒ Ⓓ
6 Ⓕ Ⓖ Ⓗ Ⓙ	16 Ⓕ Ⓖ Ⓗ Ⓙ	26 Ⓕ Ⓖ Ⓗ Ⓙ	36 Ⓕ Ⓖ Ⓗ Ⓙ
7 Ⓐ Ⓑ Ⓒ Ⓓ	17 Ⓐ Ⓑ Ⓒ Ⓓ	27 Ⓐ Ⓑ Ⓒ Ⓓ	37 Ⓐ Ⓑ Ⓒ Ⓓ
8 Ⓕ Ⓖ Ⓗ Ⓙ	18 Ⓕ Ⓖ Ⓗ Ⓙ	28 Ⓕ Ⓖ Ⓗ Ⓙ	38 Ⓕ Ⓖ Ⓗ Ⓙ
9 Ⓐ Ⓑ Ⓒ Ⓓ	19 Ⓐ Ⓑ Ⓒ Ⓓ	29 Ⓐ Ⓑ Ⓒ Ⓓ	39 Ⓐ Ⓑ Ⓒ Ⓓ
10 Ⓕ Ⓖ Ⓗ Ⓙ	20 Ⓕ Ⓖ Ⓗ Ⓙ	30 Ⓕ Ⓖ Ⓗ Ⓙ	40 Ⓕ Ⓖ Ⓗ Ⓙ

RAW SCORES	**SCALE SCORES**	DATE TAKEN:
ENGLISH _____	ENGLISH _____	
MATH _____	MATH _____	ENGLISH/WRITING _____
READING _____	READING _____	
SCIENCE _____	SCIENCE _____	**COMPOSITE SCORE**

ENGLISH TEST

45 Minutes – 75 Questions

DIRECTIONS: In the passages that follow, some words and phrases are underlined and numbered. In the answer column, you will find alternatives for the words and phrases that are underlined. Choose the alternative that you think is best and fill in the corresponding bubble on your answer sheet. If you think that the original version is best, choose "NO CHANGE," which will always be either answer choice A or F. You will also find questions about a particular section of the passage, or about the entire passage. These questions will be identified by either an underlined portion or by a number in a box. Look for the answer that clearly expresses the idea, is consistent with the style and tone of the passage, and makes the correct use of standard written English. Read the passage through once before answering the questions. For some questions, you should read beyond the indicated portion before you answer.

PASSAGE I

> The following paragraphs may or may not be in the most logical order. You may be asked questions about the logical order of the paragraphs, as well as where to place sentences logically within any given paragraph.

Noh Theatre

[1]

A highly ritualized form of drama, called "Noh," <u>originates</u> in Medieval Japan as a type of play performed in front of nobility. Noh theatre reached its apex in the fourteenth and fifteenth centuries with a <u>playwright named Kannami and his son Zeami,</u> and it

<u>has been largely unchanged.</u>

[2]

There are certain traits that make Noh unique in the Japanese theatrical world. The stage is always sparse, and always <u>only decorated solely</u> with a painted pine tree as a backdrop. Props are minimal, and often symbolic.

<u>A fan for example is a staple of Noh theater, and it</u> usually symbolizes another object. The costumes are

1. **A.** NO CHANGE
   B. original
   C. originating
   D. originated

2. **F.** NO CHANGE
   G. playwright, named Kannami, and his son, Zeami,
   H. playwright named Kannami and his son Zeami;
   J. playwright named Kannami; and his son Zeami,

3. **A.** NO CHANGE
   B. has remained largely unchanged.
   C. will be largely unchanged.
   D. will largely be unchanged.

4. **F.** NO CHANGE
   G. decorated solely
   H. just decorated solely
   J. decorated only solely

5. **A.** NO CHANGE
   B. A fan, for example, is a staple of Noh theater,
   C. A fan for example, is a staple of Noh theater,
   D. A fan, for example is a staple, of Noh theater,

GO ON TO THE NEXT PAGE.

1 ■ ■ ■ ■ ■ ■ ■ ■ 1

lavish and colorful, and the colors of the costumes are also symbolic. There is a chorus that often narrates, and musicians who add to the ambience with the unique and otherworldly music it plays.
                                    6

[3]

7 If the audience is familiar with Noh, it can

recognize the characters in the stylized masks that the
                          8
actors wear. Certain masks represent certain types of characters and are intended to show specific traits possessed by these characters. The masks are intentionally painted in such a way that the different angles actually look like different facial expressions. 9

[4]

Noh theater combines poetry, dance, and music;
                                  10
and often deals with supernatural themes. It is a very
        10
sophisticated and subtle form of drama, and, according

to legend, was considered to possess something called
           11
"*yugen*." An approximate English translation of this abstract concept refers to mystery, and to what lies beneath the surface.

6. **F.** NO CHANGE
   G. they play for.
   H. they play.
   J. it will play.

7. Which of the following sentences (assuming all are true), if added here, would best introduce the new subject of Paragraph 3?
   A. In the early days, Noh theater was sponsored by the elite rulers of Japan.
   B. Japanese theater has been popular for centuries.
   C. Masks play an important role in Noh theater.
   D. There are archetypal characters who show up repeatedly in the repertoire of plays.

8. **F.** NO CHANGE
   G. with
   H. by
   J. for

9. At this point, the writer would like to highlight a very unique talent that Noh actors must develop in order to be convincing. Which of the following sentences, (assuming all are true) if added here, would most successfully achieve this effect?
   A. The actors wearing them must be skilled at tilting their heads in order to express nuances in emotion.
   B. The masks the actors wear are colorful and detailed and truly works of art.
   C. The actors must learn to express themselves in ways that are often unfamiliar to viewers of Western theater.
   D. Noh actors begin training at a very young age, so by the time they are much older, they have become very accomplished in their trade.

10. **F.** NO CHANGE
    G. Noh theater combines poetry dance and, music, and often deals with supernatural themes.
    H. Noh theater combines poetry, dance and music — and often deals with supernatural themes.
    J. Noh theater combines poetry, dance, and music and often deals with supernatural themes.

11. **A.** NO CHANGE
    B. is thought to possess
    C. has possessed
    D. possesses

GO ON TO THE NEXT PAGE.

[5]

[1] Most of the plays being performed today are the originals written by Kannami and Zeami, although a few new ones <u>had been written</u> since then. [2] Noh is not the
₁₂

most popular form of theater in Japan today, <u>but it's</u>
₁₃
performers are extremely dedicated, and people still buy tickets to enjoy this classic art form. [3] The fact that it has remained essentially in its original form for over 600 years <u>speak</u> to its incredible beauty, mystique, and lasting
₁₄
elegance.

PASSAGE II

Calligraphy

[1]

Art takes many forms, from watercolor painting, to pencil sketching, <u>to photography or sculpture</u>. One
₁₆
lesser known and perhaps less appreciated art form is calligraphy, the elegant script of letters and figures. Many modern-day computer fonts are attempts to replicate this ancient art. [17]

12. F. NO CHANGE
    G. will have been written
    H. have been wrote
    J. have been written

13. A. NO CHANGE
    B. also its
    C. but its
    D. because it's

14. F. NO CHANGE
    G. will speak
    H. speaks
    J. speaked

Question 15 asks about the passage as a whole.

15. In reviewing notes, the writer discovers that the following information has been left out of the essay:

    Zeami also wrote a treatise on the methodology of Noh, which is still studied by Noh actors.

    If added to the essay, the sentence would most logically be placed after Sentence:
    A. 2 in Paragraph 2.
    B. 1 in Paragraph 5.
    C. 2 in Paragraph 3.
    D. 3 in Paragraph 5.

16. F. NO CHANGE
    G. to photography, sculpture
    H. to photography and to sculpture
    J. to photography, to sculpture

17. The writer is considering adding the following true statement after the preceding sentence:

    Computer fonts, however, cannot fully exemplify the artistry and talent of an accomplished calligrapher.

    Would this be a relevant addition to the paragraph?
    A. Yes, because the writer goes on to discuss how calligraphy is an art form.
    B. Yes, because the passage continues to make references to modern technology.
    C. No, because the writer is focusing on calligraphy itself, not on specific calligraphers.
    D. No, because computer fonts have nothing to do with the art of calligraphy.

GO ON TO THE NEXT PAGE.

1 ■ ■ ■ ■ ■ ■ ■ ■ 1

The word *calligraphy* is <u>derived from</u> the Greek words
₁₈
kalli, which means "beautiful," and *graphia*, which means
"writing." It is difficult to say from which civilization
calligraphy emerged directly, as many ancient peoples
<u>were interested in</u> the written word and had some form
₁₉
of written records. Since the printing press wasn't
invented until the mid-fifteenth century, legible
handwriting was an important and useful skill <u>throughout</u>
₂₀
the known world.

Chinese calligraphy <u>date back to</u> nearly 5,000 years.
₂₁
Around 200 B.C., a 3,000-character index was established

<u>for use of</u> Chinese scholars. These scribes
₂₂

<u>have quickly developed their own</u> styles
₂₃

<u>when replicating the characters</u> by varying the
₂₄
thickness of the lines, the amount of ink, and the

types of paper. <u>However,</u> true "artists of script"
₂₅

emerged and the <u>Japanese adapted</u> Chinese calligraphy
₂₆

around the seventh <u>century; developing</u> their own style,
₂₇

18. **F.** NO CHANGE
    G. derived with
    H. derived by
    J. derived to

19. **A.** NO CHANGE
    B. relied upon
    C. were accomplished readers of
    D. preferred

20. **F.** NO CHANGE
    G. all, around
    H. throughout which
    J. around which

21. **A.** NO CHANGE
    B. dated back to
    C. dates back
    D. dated back

22. **F.** NO CHANGE
    G. for the use by
    H. for the use with
    J. for use by

23. **A.** NO CHANGE
    B. has quickly developed their own
    C. quickly developed their own
    D. who have quickly developed their own

24. **F.** NO CHANGE
    G. when replicating the various characters
    H. when replicating
    J. OMIT the underlined portion

25. **A.** NO CHANGE
    B. Soon,
    C. Yet,
    D. Otherwise,

26. **F.** NO CHANGE
    G. Japanese, adapted
    H. Japanese adapted,
    J. Japanese having adapted

27. **A.** NO CHANGE
    B. century developing
    C. century. Developing
    D. century, developing

GO ON TO THE NEXT PAGE.

1 ■ ■ ■ ■ ■ ■ ■ ■ 1

which included an appreciation for imperfection as well as technical ability.

In Europe, calligraphy was greatly influenced by the development of the Church during the Middle Ages.

<u>28</u>

Manual recording and duplication of religious texts demanded an abundance of beautiful calligraphy. Most of this work was done by European monks. A variety of styles soon emerged, including Gothic calligraphy. In the Gothic style, the letters are more spaced closely

<u>29</u>

together and the lines are much narrower than with other styles. Because the print takes up less space, less paper is required than with other styles.

Today, calligraphy continues to fascinate both scribes and art aficionados. Modern calligraphy equipment, such as specialized pens, inks, and paper, make the art easier

<u>30</u>

to learn than it was in the past.

28. **F.** NO CHANGE
    G. the development of calligraphy greatly influenced the Church
    H. the Church greatly influenced the development of calligraphy
    J. calligraphy greatly influenced the development of the Church

29. **A.** NO CHANGE
    B. closely
    C. more closely spaced
    D. spaced closely

30. **F.** NO CHANGE
    G. pens, inks and, paper
    H. pens, inks, and paper
    J. pens inks, and paper

PASSAGE III

Fur Trappers

The myth of the early American mountain men paints

<u>31</u>

a picture of romance, adventure, and intrigue. In reality,

most mountain men were fur traders choosing to compete

<u>32</u>

in a tough business that sent them for months at a time to the vast rivers and mountains of the American West. For the most part, beaver pelts were the primary target of these unconventional businessmen, as beaver hats and

31. **A.** NO CHANGE
    B. paint
    C. will paint
    D. painting

32. **F.** NO CHANGE
    G. competing
    H. chosen to compete
    J. OMIT the underlined portion

GO ON TO THE NEXT PAGE.

1 ■ ■ ■ ■ ■ ■ ■ ■ 1

coats were all the rage in early American towns and cities. ⬛33

While some fur trappers and traders traveled alone, many worked together in groups for a particular trading company. The Hudson Bay Company,

<u>first operated in Britain,</u> initially dominated the fur trade
34

scene. The <u>buyers for this company</u> would rendezvous at
35
designated sites where the trappers presented their furs in

exchange for money or essential goods. ⬛36 While the

mountain man <u>appear to</u> personify "rugged individu-
37
alism," he was completely dependent upon his ability to

trap wild animals and, therefore, relied upon consumer

<u>demanding</u> for those pelts.
38

33. At this point, the writer is considering adding the following sentence:

> While not inexpensive, harvesting beaver pelts directly from North America was far cheaper than importing them from across the ocean.

Would this be a relevant addition to make here?
A. Yes, because the writer needs to establish that beaver pelts were very expensive.
B. Yes, because the sentence emphasizes the importance of the American mountain man's contribution.
C. No, because the paragraph focuses on the American mountain man, not on beaver pelts.
D. No, because beaver pelts from other countries cost more than those obtained in America.

34. The writer wants to emphasize the characterization that the Hudson Bay Company was originally run by the British. Given this purpose, which choice would work best?
F. NO CHANGE
G. though not American-owned,
H. operated outside of North America,
J. OMIT the underlined portion.

35. A. NO CHANGE
B. buyers that worked for this company
C. buyers of this company
D. company's buyers

36. Given that all of the following sentences are true, which one should be placed here to offer a logical explanation for why trappers traded their furs for money or goods?
F. While mountain men were skilled hunters and could capture their own food, they still needed many supplies in order to survive.
G. Many Indian tribes were willing to trade goods and supplies with the mountain men.
H. Some mountain men had families back in the cities and towns, so furs and pelts were important.
J. Trappers enjoyed trading goods and supplies among themselves, as long as the Hudson Bay Company approved.

37. A. NO CHANGE
B. appeared to
C. appear
D. appears to

38. F. NO CHANGE
G. their demand
H. they're demand
J. demand

GO ON TO THE NEXT PAGE.

While some of the trappers were <u>in control of</u> a
                                    39
particular fur company, others chose a more independent

relationship. Men <u>hired directly, by a fur company</u> were
                            40
called "engagers," and all furs they obtained were

company property <u>that belonged to the fur company.</u>
                              41

The "free-trapper" was the most autonomous of <u>all; he</u>
                                                    42
trapped wherever and with whomever he chose. He also

traded or sold his furs at his own discretion. While the

free-trappers were considered by their peers to be tough

and hardy <u>because of</u> their abilities to endure the hard-
              43
ships of mountain living, many of them either succumbed

to those hardships or found safe haven

<u>by living in the mountains.</u>
              44

39. **A.** NO CHANGE
    B. under the control with
    C. controlled by
    D. OMIT the underlined portion.

40. **F.** NO CHANGE
    G. hired directly, by a fur company
    H. hired directly by a fur company
    J. hired, directly by a fur company

41. **A.** NO CHANGE
    B. that were given directly to the company.
    C. and did not belong to them.
    D. OMIT the underlined portion and end the sentence with a period.

42. **F.** NO CHANGE
    G. all:
    H. all, he
    J. all he

43. **A.** NO CHANGE
    B. in regards with
    C. regards to
    D. irregardless

44. **F.** NO CHANGE
    G. by striking out on their own.
    H. with groups of Native Americans
    J. OMIT the underlined portion and end the sentence with a period.

Question 45 asks about the passage as a whole.

45. Suppose the writer had intended to write an essay that explored the myth of the American mountain man. Would this essay successfully fulfill the writer's goal?
    A. No, because the essay focuses on American myths in general, not just the myth of the American mountain man.
    B. No, because there really were American mountain men, which means that they were not a myth.
    C. Yes, because the writer explains how the American mountain man story is really a myth.
    D. Yes, because the writer discusses the contrast between the romantic, mythical side of a mountain man's life and the reality of the job of a mountain man.

GO ON TO THE NEXT PAGE.

1 ■ ■ ■ ■ ■ ■ ■ ■ **1**

PASSAGE IV

The Green Bay Packers

[1]

In 1919, Curly Lambeau returned home to Green Bay, Wisconsin, to playing football at Notre Dame from a severe case of tonsillitis· In a conversation with his friend George Calhoun, he expressed regret at not being able to play football since returning home. Calhoun decides to recommend that he start a team in his home town. Excited by the idea, Lambeau convinced his boss at the Indian Packing Company to donate uniforms and the use of an athletic field.

Calhoun ran ads in the local newspaper, inviting other athletes to join the new team. Only 20 football players joined the team the first year. Although Lambeau named the team the Big Bay Blues, fans and players fittingly called the team the Packers.

The conditions under which the Packers played during that first year were a far cry from those enjoyed by modern present-day football teams. They played their games in an empty field behind Hagemeister Brewery. There were no locker rooms, so players normally changed into their uniforms at home before the game. There were no gates or bleachers; so there was no way to charge admission or get an accurate count of attendance.

46. **F.** NO CHANGE
   G. from playing football at Notre Dame, due to a severe case of tonsillitis.
   H. from a case of severe tonsillitis, which was due to playing football at Notre Dame.
   J. from playing football at Notre Dame, which was due to a severe case of tonsillitis.

47. **A.** NO CHANGE
   B. recommended to him a decision
   C. recommended
   D. gives his recommendation

48. **F.** NO CHANGE
   G. fans and players called the team the Packers, fittingly.
   H. the team was called the Packers by fitting fans and players.
   J. the Packers fittingly called the fans and players the team.

49. **A.** NO CHANGE
   B. contemporary
   C. up-to-date
   D. OMIT the underlined portion

50. **F.** NO CHANGE
   G. before the game into their uniforms at home.
   H. uniforms at their home before the game.
   J. into their uniforms, which were at home before the game.

51. **A.** NO CHANGE
   B. gates or bleachers, so there was no way to charge admission
   C. gates, or bleachers, so there was no way to charge admission
   D. gates or bleachers. So there was no way to charge admission

GO ON TO THE NEXT PAGE.

1 ■ ■ ■ ■ ■ ■ ■ ■ 1

Without fences and stands, the only way by raising money
                                        ————————
                                             52

was to actually pass a hat around to spectators, for
    ———————————————————————————————————
                        53

donations. 54

In 1920, bleachers were built on one side of

Hagemeister Park, located behind the brewery. The

largest recorded attendance at that location was 6,000

fans, for the game against the Minneapolis Marines on

October 23, 1921.

That was the Packers' first official game that was played
                                          ——————————————
                                               55

as part of the new American Professional Football

Association, which is now known as the National

Football League. 56

From their humble beginnings, the Packers have gone

on to win more NFL championships than any other team,

including three Super Bowls. The Packers now play in a

newly renovated stadium, which was being named
                        ————————————————————
                                 57

Lambeau Field after the entrepreneurship
                 ————————————————————————
                            58
and legendary status of the team's founder. The stadium
————————————————————————————————————
             58
now seats 72,515 — and over 60,000 people are on the

waiting list for season tickets! The team has come a long

52. **F.** NO CHANGE
    G. it raised
    H. to raise
    J. fundraising

53. **A.** NO CHANGE
    B. to actually, pass a hat around to spectators,
    C. to actually pass a hat around, to spectators
    D. to actually pass a hat around to spectators

54. The writer is considering changing the first sentence of this paragraph (assuming that if there is an error, it has been fixed). Which sentence would be the best choice?
    F. The writer should not replace the sentence.
    G. The Packers endured brutal conditions in the first year, and all for the love of the game.
    H. When the Packers played their first season, professional football was not very popular nationwide.
    J. Equipped with a popular new name, the Packers were ready to begin their first season.

55. **A.** NO CHANGE
    B. they played
    C. for playing
    D. OMIT the underlined portion

56. The writer would like to link the information already presented about the Green Bay Packers to the information in this paragraph. Assuming all are true, which of the following sentences best achieves this effect?
    F. Vince Lombardi coached the Packers with great success in the 1960s.
    G. The Packers are the only publicly owned team in the NFL.
    H. In the 1950s, Curly Lambeau was fired by the Packers as part of an internal power struggle.
    J. This historic game marked the beginning of the Green Bay Packers, one of the oldest franchises in professional football.

57. **A.** NO CHANGE
    B. named after Curly Lambeau,
    C. named
    D. naming

58. **F.** NO CHANGE
    G. after the team's entrepreneurial and legendary founder.
    H. after the entrepreneurial legend of the team's founder.
    J. after the team founder's legendary entrepreneurship.

GO ON TO THE NEXT PAGE.

1 ■ ■ ■ ■ ■ ■ ■ ■ 1

way from wearing donated uniforms and passing
                                                    59
a hat around a nearly empty field.
                                                    59

59. A. NO CHANGE
B. way, from wearing donated uniforms, and passing a hat around an empty field.
C. way from wearing donated uniforms; and passing a hat around an empty field.
D. way from wearing donated uniforms and passing a hat around, an empty field.

Question 60 asks about the passage as a whole.

---

60. Suppose the writer had been assigned to write a brief essay illustrating the economic influence of the Packers on the city of Green Bay. Would this essay fulfill that assignment?
F. Yes, because the essay indicates that the team relied on a corporate sponsorship to get started.
G. Yes, because the essay indicates that the team has been very successful.
H. No, because the essay primarily focuses on how the team was started.
J. No, because the essay notes that the team relied on donations rather than charging admission.

PASSAGE V

The Starfish Inn

[1]

"Are we really planning on staying here?" Sophie asked me incredulously. "I feel like we have no choice!" I responded. The place in question was the Starfish Inn, a motel of dubious character on the beach in Jacksonville, Florida. We ended up here largely of our own
                                              61

irresponsibility. It was our freshman year of college, yet yearning to escape the cold and dreary weather for
62
spring break, we decided to head south. It was a last-minute decision; we did not make reservations anywhere.

When we arrived in Florida, we tried to book a room in a decent, but affordable hotel. After going to six hotels and finding no vacancy, we stopped at an information
                                                    63
booth. A kind and helpful woman delivered the discouraging news that, if we didn't have reservations

61. A. NO CHANGE
B. instead of
C. because of
D. in part of

62. F. NO CHANGE
G. and,
H. but
J. where

63. A. NO CHANGE
B. were stopped by
C. had to stop in
D. will stop at

GO ON TO THE NEXT PAGE.

1 ■ ■ ■ ■ ■ ■ ■ ■ 1

anywhere, it would be very difficult for us to possess
64

lodging. She recommended that we check a couple of

places, but they all seemed far beyond our

budget, which was small. Then she said that the Starfish
65

Inn was reasonably priced, but that she would not want

her daughters to stay there!

So there's how we got into our predicament. After
66

paying the proprietor of the motel, we dragged our

luggage to the room, where we opened the door with great
67

trepidation. The room was a starfish-themed nightmare!

Everything was in shades of blue, green, and turquoise,

with real and depicted starfish on nearly every

surface; so the place looked like it hadn't been
68

redecorated since 1975!
68

[1] With grim determining, we shuffled across the
69

somewhat gritty floor to further check out the place.

[2] The couch was threadbare and lumpy, and not exactly

inviting. [3] The television was equipped with a rusty
70

old antenna, which reminded me of the television that my
70

grandpa kept in his basement workshop. [4] On the down
71

side, the small kitchen table was so rickety that I was

afraid to actually use it. [5] On the plus side, the room did

have a kitchenette, so we could save money by cooking

some meals inside. 72

Confronted with all of these problems, Sophie and I

decided we had one option — to make the best of it and

enjoy ourselves! We thought that it was about time to

64. Which choice provides the most appropriate image?
   F. NO CHANGE
   G. secure
   H. capture
   J. grab

65. A. NO CHANGE
   B. budget.
   C. budget. Our budget was pretty typical for college
      students.
   D. budget. I wanted to have enough money left to
      buy souvenirs.

66. F. NO CHANGE
   G. this is
   H. that's
   J. there is

67. A. NO CHANGE
   B. so
   C. we
   D. OMIT the underlined portion

68. F. NO CHANGE
   G. surface, the place looked like it hadn't been
      redecorated since 1975!
   H. surface. (the place looked like it hadn't been
      redecorated since 1975!)
   J. surface; the place looked like it hadn't been
      redecorated since 1975!

69. A. NO CHANGE
   B. determined
   C. determination
   D. determine

70. F. NO CHANGE
   G. with a rusty, old antenna,
   H. with a rusty old, antenna
   J. with a rusty old antenna

71. A. NO CHANGE
   B. will keep
   C. does keep
   D. keep

72. For the sake of unity and coherence, Sentence 5 of
   this paragraph should be placed:
   F. where it is now.
   G. immediately before Sentence 2.
   H. immediately before Sentence 3.
   J. immediately before Sentence 4.

GO ON TO THE NEXT PAGE.

escape the pseudo-undersea atmosphere of the room and

enjoy some real ocean views 73 .

73. The writer would like to conclude the final paragraph with a sentence that shows the shift in attitude she and her friend Sophie experienced. Which choice would best accomplish this?

A. I begrudgingly accepted the fact that our motel room was terrible as we headed to the beach.

B. As the old saying goes: "When life gives you lemons, make lemonade."

C. We headed to the beach moaning about our crazy motel room.

D. I decided that my next spring break trip will definitely not be in Florida!

Questions 74 and 75 ask about the passage as a whole.

---

74. The writer is considering the addition of the following sentence to the essay:

> I couldn't help but be reminded of one of the most fascinating facts about starfish; that if you chop one up, a new starfish will grow from each remaining stump.

Given that this statement is true, should it be added to the essay, and if so, where?

F. Yes, at the end of the second paragraph because the lady at the information booth mentioned the Starfish Inn. Adding the sentence would be an effective way for the writer to foreshadow the troubles she and her friend would soon have at the motel.

G. Yes, at the end of the third paragraph, because the writer had just finished describing the starfish theme of the room.

H. No, because it is evident that the writer is not interested in scientific facts.

J. No, because a scientific statement would be out of context in an essay describing the personal experiences of the writer and her friend.

75. Suppose a travel agent hired the writer to write an article warning of the possible hazards of being unprepared for a vacation. Does this essay successfully fulfill the assignment?

A. Yes, because the first paragraph clearly states that the writer and her friend did not make reservations.

B. Yes, because the essay gives an example of what can happen when you don't make reservations before going on vacation.

C. No, because the essay is primarily intended to be a humorous story about being forced to stay at a dilapidated motel.

D. No, because the essay concerns college students, and does not consider that others may also be unprepared for a vacation.

END OF THE ENGLISH TEST
STOP! IF YOU HAVE TIME LEFT OVER, CHECK YOUR WORK ON THIS SECTION ONLY.

2   **2**

MATHEMATICS TEST

60 Minutes – 60 Questions

DIRECTIONS: Solve each of the problems in the time allowed, then fill in the corresponding bubble on your answer sheet. Do not spend too much time on any one problem; skip the more difficult problems and go back to them later. You may use a calculator on this test. For this test you should assume that figures are NOT necessarily drawn to scale, that all geometric figures lie in a plane, and that the word *line* is used to indicate a straight line.

---

1. If $5x - 6 = 12$, then $x = ?$
   A. $\dfrac{6}{5}$
   B. $\dfrac{18}{5}$
   C. 11
   D. 13
   E. 23

DO YOUR FIGURING HERE.

2. The expression $a(b - 2c)$ is equivalent to:
   F. $ab - 2a - 2c$
   G. $ab - 2ac$
   H. $ab - 2bc$
   J. $ab - b - 2c$
   K. $ab - 2b - c$

3. Which 3 numbers should be placed in the blanks below so that the difference between consecutive numbers is the same?

   $$\_\_ , 3, 10, \_\_ , 24 \_\_$$

   A. $-4, 17, 31$
   B. $0, 17, 30$
   C. $1, 13, 31$
   D. $2, 17, 25$
   E. $5, 15, 31$

4. Diane bought 1 DVD for $20.00 and 5 others that were on sale for $8.49 each. What was the average price per DVD that she paid for these 6 DVDs?
   F. $\$20.00 + \dfrac{\$8.49}{5}$
   G. $\dfrac{\$20.00 + 5(\$8.49)}{6}$
   H. $\dfrac{\$20.00 + \$8.49}{6}$
   J. $\dfrac{\$20.00 + \$8.49}{2}$
   K. $\dfrac{(\$20.00) + 5(\$8.49)}{2}$

GO ON TO THE NEXT PAGE.

2   **2**

5. On Saturday, Stephanie received her pay and spent $\frac{1}{3}$ of it. On Sunday she spent $\frac{1}{2}$ of the remaining money, and on Monday she spent $\frac{1}{2}$ of what remained from Sunday. If $15.00 then remained, how much pay did she receive originally?
   A. $15.00
   B. $30.00
   C. $60.00
   D. $90.00
   E. $120.00

6. $2x^3 \cdot 3x^2y^2 \cdot 3x^2y = ?$
   F. $9x^6y^3$
   G. $9x^7y^2$
   H. $18x^7y^3$
   J. $18x^{12}y^3$
   K. $18x^{12}y^2$

7. A rectangular garden measures 60 feet by 25 feet. A fence completely encloses the garden. What is the length, in feet, of the fence?
   A. 85
   B. 170
   C. 256
   D. 625
   E. 1,500

8. If $x = -6$, then $-x^2 - 2x + 21 = ?$
   F. -27
   G. -3
   H. 21
   J. 45
   K. 69

9. The formula for the volume of a sphere is $V = \frac{4}{3}\pi r^3$. If the radius, r, of a spherical ball is 2 inches, what is its volume, to the nearest cubic inch?
   A. 8
   B. 19
   C. 25
   D. 34
   E. 96

10. The expression $4c - 2d$ is equivalent to which of the following?
    F. $4(c - 2d)$
    G. $2cd$
    H. $2(c - d)$
    J. $4(c - d)$
    K. $2(2c - d)$

11. For each day on the job, you receive $20.00 plus a fixed amount for each lawn that you mow. Currently you are earning $95.00 per day for mowing 5 lawns. Today you are assigned to mow an additional 2 lawns. What will be your new daily earnings?
    A. $50.00
    B. $75.00
    C. $100.00
    D. $125.00
    E. $150.00

DO YOUR FIGURING HERE.

GO ON TO THE NEXT PAGE.

2   **2**

DO YOUR FIGURING HERE.

12. Which of the following is a simplified form of $4x + 2x + y - x$?
   F. $3x + y$
   G. $5x + y$
   H. $2(x + 2)(x + y)$
   J. $6x - y$
   K. $x(6 + y)$

13. When graphed in the standard (x,y) coordinate plane, which of the following equations does NOT represent a line?
   A. $x = 3$
   B. $2y = 7$
   C. $-y = 2x + 1$
   D. $y = \frac{3}{4}x$
   E. $x^2 = y - 7$

14. What is the number of degrees that the minute hand of a clock moves in 30 minutes?
   F. $30°$
   G. $60°$
   H. $100°$
   J. $180°$
   K. $360°$

15. Which of the following solution sets has both $x = 5$ and $x = 6$ as solutions?
   A. $(x - 6)(x + 5) = 0$
   B. $(x + 6)(x + 5) = 0$
   C. $(x + 6)(x - 5) = 0$
   D. $(x - 5)(x - 6) = 0$
   E. $x - 6 = x - 5$

16. If 75% of x equals 180, then $x = ?$
   F. 24
   G. 45
   H. 240
   J. 450
   K. 2,400

17. A conference room has $(2r + s)$ rows of seats and $(4t)$ seats in each row. Which of the following is an expression for the number of seats in the entire conference room?
   A. $4rs + 2rt$
   B. $4(rs + 2t)$
   C. $8tr + 4ts$
   D. $8r + 4rts$
   E. $24rts$

18. Tony is participating in a charity event and must collect pledges for every mile that he runs in the next 30 days. His friend pledges 9 cents per mile for the first 25 miles that he runs, and 7 cents per mile for each additional mile. Tony's goal is to run 63 miles in the next 30 days. Assuming he meets but does not exceed his goal, what is the total amount Tony should collect from his friend?
   F. $2.25
   G. $4.91
   H. $6.66
   J. $8.33
   K. $10.08

GO ON TO THE NEXT PAGE.

2   **2**

19. If the inequality $|x| > |y|$ is true, then which of the following must be true?

A. $x > 0$
B. $x < y$
C. $x = y$
D. $x \neq y$
E. $x > y$

20. For which nonnegative value of x is the expression $\dfrac{1}{(100 - 4x^2)}$ undefined?

F. 0
G. 5
H. 10
J. 100
K. 400

21. What is the correct order of π, 3, and $\dfrac{5}{2}$ from least to greatest?

A. $\dfrac{5}{2} < \pi < 3$

B. $3 < \pi < \dfrac{5}{2}$

C. $\pi < \dfrac{5}{2} < 3$

D. $\pi < 3 < \dfrac{5}{2}$

E. $\dfrac{5}{2} < 3 < \pi$

22. The 2 squares below have the same dimensions. The vertex of 1 square is at the center of the other square. What is the area of the shaded region, in square centimeters?

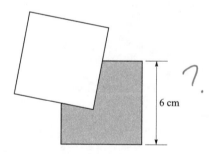

6 cm

F. 9
G. 12
H. 27
J. 36
K. 72

23. The lengths of the sides of a triangle are 3, 4, and 5 inches. What is the length, in inches, of the shortest side of a similar triangle that has a perimeter of 36 inches?

A. 6
B. 9
C. 12
D. 15
E. 18

GO ON TO THE NEXT PAGE.

2   **2**

24. Which of the following gives all the solutions of $x^2 - 6x = 16$?
    F. −2 and 8
    G. 2 and 8
    H. −4 and 4
    J. −6 only
    K. 16 only

25. A CD that normally sells for $14.95 is on sale for 30% off. What is the cost of the CD during the sale, to the nearest cent?
    A. $4.49
    B. $10.46
    C. $11.21
    D. $11.96
    E. $44.85

26. If, for all x, $(x^{7a-2})^3 = x^{57}$, then $a = ?$
    F. 2
    G. 3
    H. $\dfrac{31}{5}$
    J. $\dfrac{51}{21}$
    K. 57

27. If $(3r - s)^2 = 36$ and $rs = 45$, then $r^2 + s^2 = ?$
    A. 18
    B. 99
    C. 106
    D. 189
    E. 675

28. One endpoint of a line segment in the (x,y) coordinate plane has coordinates $(-5,3)$. The midpoint of the segment has coordinates $(9,-1)$. What are the coordinates of the other endpoint of the segment?
    F. $(-45,-3)$
    G. $(-14,4)$
    H. $(2,1)$
    J. $(23,-5)$
    K. $(4,2)$

29. In the standard (x,y) coordinate plane, what is the radius of the circle $(x-3)^2 + (y-4)^2 = 25$?
    A. 3
    B. 4
    C. 5
    D. 16
    E. 25

DO YOUR FIGURING HERE.

GO ON TO THE NEXT PAGE.

30. In the right triangle pictured below, r, s, and t are the lengths of its sides. What is the value of $\tan \alpha$?

DO YOUR FIGURING HERE.

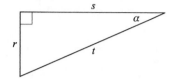

F. $\dfrac{r}{t}$

G. $\dfrac{s}{t}$

H. $\dfrac{t}{r}$

J. $\dfrac{r}{s}$

K. $\dfrac{t}{s}$

31. For all $x > 0$, $\dfrac{1}{x} - \dfrac{3}{4} =$

A. $\dfrac{3}{4x}$

B. $3 - 4x$

C. $\dfrac{4}{x} - 3$

D. $\dfrac{3}{x} - \dfrac{4}{x}$

E. $\dfrac{4 - 3x}{4x}$

32. In the figure below, lines m and n are parallel, lines o and p are parallel, and the measure of angle α is 40°. What is the measure of angle β?

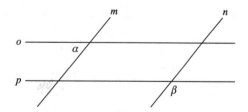

F. 40°
G. 50°
H. 110°
J. 140°
K. 180°

GO ON TO THE NEXT PAGE.

2   **2**

33. The figure below shows square *LMNO* and also shows the circle centered at M with radii MN and ML. If the perimeter of the square is 64 units, what is the area of the circle, in square units?

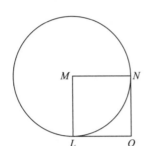

DO YOUR FIGURING HERE.

    A. 4π
    B. 8π
    C. 16π
    D. 64π
    E. 256π

34. Among the points graphed on the number line below, which is the closest to $1\frac{3}{4}$?

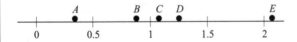

    F. *A*
    G. *B*
    H. *C*
    J. *D*
    K. *E*

35. The sides of a triangle measure $3\sqrt{2}$ meters, 3 meters, and 3 meters. What are the measures of the angles of the triangle, in degrees?
    A. 30°–60°–90°
    B. 90°–30°–30°
    C. 40°–50°–90°
    D. 90°–45°–45°
    E. 45°–60°–90°

GO ON TO THE NEXT PAGE.

2   **2**

36. Which of the following figures is NOT a quadrilateral?

DO YOUR FIGURING HERE.

F.

G.

H.

J.

K.

37. If p is a positive integer that divides both 45 and 60, but divides neither 9 nor 10, what should you get when you add the digits in p?
   A. 3
   B. 2
   C. 5
   D. 6
   E. 9

38. What is the slope of any line perpendicular to the x-axis in the (x,y) coordinate plane?
   F. −1
   G. 0
   H. 1
   J. Undefined
   K. Cannot be determined from the given information

39. Which of the following lines has the largest slope?
   A. $y = 3x - 5$
   B. $y = x + 4$
   C. $y = 7x + 8$
   D. $3y = 9x + 6$
   E. $2y = 8x - 8$

GO ON TO THE NEXT PAGE.

2   △ △ **2**

40. If $\tan \beta = \frac{3}{4}$, then $\sin \beta = ?$

   F. $\frac{3}{5}$

   G. $\frac{3}{4}$

   H. $\frac{4}{5}$

   J. $\frac{4}{3}$

   K. $\frac{5}{4}$

DO YOUR FIGURING HERE.

SOhcahtoa

41. Jenny can walk 4 miles in $(m + 3)$ minutes. At that pace, how many miles can she walk in 15 minutes?

   A. $\frac{(m+3)}{60}$

   B. $\frac{m}{180}$

   C. $60(m+3)$

   D. $\frac{60}{(m+3)}$

   E. $\frac{15}{4(m+3)}$

42. Which of the following calculations will yield an even integer for any integer n?

   F. $4n^2$
   G. $3n^2 + 1$
   H. $5n^2 - 1$
   J. $3n$
   K. $n^2 - 2n$

43. In triangle CAB, the measure of $\angle A$ is $45°$ and the measure of $\angle B$ is $45°$. If $\overline{AC}$ is 12 units long, what is the perimeter, in units, of triangle CAB?

   A. 36
   B. $36\sqrt{2}$
   C. 72
   D. $24 + 12\sqrt{2}$
   E. $24 + 12\sqrt{3}$

44. A certain circle has a circumference of 42π. What is the area of the circle?

   F. 21π
   G. 42π
   H. 168π
   J. 441π
   K. $1,764\pi$

45. A certain rectangle is 3 times as long as it is wide. Suppose the length stays the same but the width is tripled. The area of the second rectangle is how many times as large as the area of the first?

   A. 1.5
   B. 3
   C. 6
   D. 4.5
   E. 9

GO ON TO THE NEXT PAGE.

2 △ △ △ △ △ △ △ △ **2**

46. For what value of a would the following system of equations have an infinite number of solutions?

$$12x - 19y = 20$$

$$36x - 57y = 30a$$

- **F.** 2
- **G.** 3
- **H.** 10
- **J.** 15
- **K.** 50

47. If $\log_x 169 = 2$, then $x = ?$
- **A.** 2
- **B.** 13
- **C.** 84.5
- **D.** 169
- **E.** 338

48. If $A = \begin{pmatrix} 2 & -2 \\ 3 & 2 \end{pmatrix}$ and $B = \begin{pmatrix} 1 & 3 \\ -2 & 4 \end{pmatrix}$, then $A + B = ?$

- **F.** $\begin{pmatrix} 3 & 5 \\ 5 & 6 \end{pmatrix}$
- **G.** $\begin{pmatrix} 3 & 1 \\ 1 & 6 \end{pmatrix}$
- **H.** $\begin{pmatrix} 2 & -6 \\ -6 & 8 \end{pmatrix}$
- **J.** $\begin{pmatrix} 5 & -4 \\ -1 & 7 \end{pmatrix}$
- **K.** $\begin{pmatrix} 0 & 5 \\ 4 & 2 \end{pmatrix}$

49. In the parallelogram below, lengths are given in centimeters. What is the area of the parallelogram, in square centimeters?

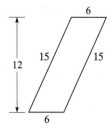

- **A.** 36
- **B.** 45
- **C.** 72
- **D.** 90
- **E.** 18

GO ON TO THE NEXT PAGE.

2   **2**

50. In the standard (x,y) coordinate plane, if the x-coordinate of each point on a line is 3 more than twice the corresponding y-coordinate, the slope of the line is:

F. $-\dfrac{1}{2}$

G. $\dfrac{1}{2}$

H. 2

J. 3

K. 6

51. Given the vertices of parallelogram $JFGH$ in the standard (x,y) coordinate plane below,

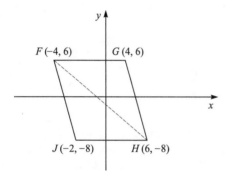

what is the area of triangle FGH, in square units?

A. 14

B. 28

C. 42

D. 56

E. 112

52. If X, Y, and Z are real numbers, and $XYZ = 1$, then which of the following conditions must be true?

F. $XY = \dfrac{1}{z}$

G. X, Y, and $Z > 0$

H. Either $X = 1$, $Y = 1$, or $Z = 1$

J. Either $X = 0$, $Y = 0$, or $Z = 0$

K. Either $X < 1$, $Y < 1$, or $Z < 1$

53. In the standard (x,y) coordinate plane, the y-intercept of the line $5x + y = 9$ is?

A. -9

B. -5

C. $\dfrac{5}{9}$

D. 9

E. 45

54. The average of a set of 7 integers is 24. When an 8th number is included in the set, the average of the set increases to 31. What is the 8th number?

F. 31

G. 55

H. 80

J. 168

K. 217

DO YOUR FIGURING HERE.

GO ON TO THE NEXT PAGE.

2 △ △ △ △ △ △ △ △ **2**

55. The area of a rectangular kitchen is 180 square feet. If the length of the floor is 2 feet less than twice the width, what is the width of the floor in feet?
  A. 5
  B. 10
  C. 12
  D. 16
  E. 24

DO YOUR FIGURING HERE.

56. For every cent increase in price of a pound of apples, the grocery store sells 35 fewer pounds per day. The grocery store normally sells 625 pounds of apples per day at $1.19 per pound. Which of the following expressions represents the number of pounds of apples sold per day if the cost is increased by $6x$ cents per pound of apples?
  F. $(1.19 - 6x)(625 - 210x)$
  G. $625 - 35x$
  H. $625 - 210(1.19)x$
  J. $625 + 35x$
  K. $625 - 210x$

57. Jordan has been hired to build a circular wading pool in his neighbor's backyard. The rectangular backyard measures 40 feet wide by 70 feet long. Jordan's neighbors want the pool to be as large as possible, with the edge of the pool at least 4 feet from the edge of the backyard all around. How long should the radius of the pool be, in feet?
  A. 16
  B. 32
  C. 36
  D. 40
  E. 62

58. Three distinct lines contained within a plane, separate the plane into distinct regions. How many possible distinct regions of the plane may be separated by any 3 such lines?
  F. 4, 7, 8
  G. 4, 6, 7
  H. 3, 6, 7
  J. 3, 5, 8
  K. 3, 4, 6

GO ON TO THE NEXT PAGE.

59. In a game, 97 marbles numbered 00 through 96 are placed in a box. A player draws 1 marble at random from the box. Without replacing the first marble, the player draws a second marble at random. If both marbles drawn have the same 10s digit (that is, both marbles are numbered between 00 and 09, or 10 and 19, or 20 and 29, etc.), the player is a winner. If the first marble Dave draws is numbered 17, what is the probability that Dave will be a winner on the next draw?

A. $\dfrac{3}{32}$

B. $\dfrac{1}{10}$

C. $\dfrac{17}{97}$

D. $\dfrac{17}{32}$

E. $\dfrac{96}{97}$

DO YOUR FIGURING HERE.

60. What is the smallest possible value for the product of 2 real numbers that differ by 4?

F. -4

G. -3

H. 0

J. 5

K. 8

END OF THE MATH TEST
STOP! IF YOU HAVE TIME LEFT OVER, CHECK YOUR WORK ON THIS SECTION ONLY.

3 ▌ **3**

READING TEST

35 Minutes – 40 Questions

DIRECTIONS: This test includes four passages, each followed by ten questions. Read the passage and choose the best answer to each question. After you have selected your answer, fill in the corresponding bubble on your answer sheet. You should refer to the passages as often as necessary when answering the questions.

Passage I
PROSE FICTION: *Born in Paradise*

Martin spent most of his childhood in a tropical paradise, on the island of Barbados. Despite the pleasant climate, Martin's early life was difficult. His father left when Martin was a baby, and his
5 mother, Sheila, worked long hours as a housekeeper at a nearby hotel. Martin was left to be cared for by his teen-age brothers. In the best of times, the selfish boys let Martin fend for himself; in the worst of times, they made Martin the target of their pranks.
10 Eventually, Martin's mother recognized his plight and enlisted the help of Martin's grandmother.

Granny loved Martin dearly, but the elderly woman did not have the energy to keep up with a feisty toddler. As often as possible, she took Martin
15 to the rundown neighborhood playground so that he could burn off some of his excess energy. On the endless rainy days of summer, she was often heard to exclaim, "Oh, Martin! What am I gonna do with you?"

20 To help fill the long, muggy days, Granny began taking Martin to the island's library. There they sat for hours as she slowly read him story after story. When her voice grew tired, young Martin would beg her to teach him to read. "Oh, Martin. You're too
25 young to read, dear," she would reply. But Martin was determined, and his inquisitiveness prevailed. Soon, the symbols on the page took on meaning; as the rainy season ended, Martin begged to continue their library excursions.

30 "Sheila, Martin is special."

Sheila absently looked up.

"What's that, Mom?"

"I said, 'Martin is special!'"

"Oh. Yeah. And, listen, I really appreciate you
35 taking care of him like you have. In a couple years he can go to school and then it will all be so much easier!"

"I'm not sure it will. When I said he was special I didn't just say it because I'm his grandmother. He's
40 special." She paused and then continued, "You know, he can read."

"It is wonderful the way he likes books and all."

"Have you ever let him read to you?"

"Of course! He comes into my room almost every
45 morning and recites his favorite book. He even turns the pages. It's very cute!"

"Sheila! Pay attention! I know you're tired from working long hours, but Martin isn't reciting — he's reading! In all my years I have never seen a four-year-
50 old like him. By next month he'll be reading books that are beyond me!"

Sheila's mother continued: "Honey, the schools here will be too easy for Martin, and you can't afford to send him to one of those fancy international
55 schools. You have got to get to America where they'll have schools for a child like Martin."

"Mom, think what you're saying! I can't just pick up and move to another country! The older boys aren't even finished with school yet, and there's no
60 way they'd leave their friends! Besides, I can't possibly afford to move to America. Do you have any idea how much it costs to live there?"

"Slow down! I'm not telling you to leave today. I'm telling you to start planning and saving. Your
65 older boys will be done with school in a few years. Then they can fend for themselves. Oh, don't give me that look — I'll look after 'em! But you gotta start makin' plans for Martin. Honey, he doesn't like to be bored, and that's gonna be a problem pretty soon.
70 He's a good boy, and he'll behave in these schools while he's still young. But I can't promise that he'll be able to control himself when he realizes he knows more than the teachers! I don't want to see that precious baby wasting his life and getting into trouble!
75 Sweetie, he's got a gift, and you gotta do something with that gift."

Sheila paused for a long moment as she struggled to comprehend all that her mother was telling her. Finally, she sighed. "Okay."

80 "What's that?"

GO ON TO THE NEXT PAGE.

"I said, 'okay.' I trust you. I'll start finding out what I need to do to get Martin and me to America. But I don't know what we're gonna do when we get there!"

85 "Just work on getting there. You can figure out the rest later."

1. When Granny says, "I'm not sure it will," she is expressing her concern that:
   A. schools in Barbados are dangerous.
   B. Martin is hyperactive and will likely behave poorly in school.
   C. school will not provide the academic challenge that Martin requires.
   D. life never gets any easier.

2. It can be reasonably inferred from their conversation that Granny believes Sheila is:
   F. not as well-educated as Martin is.
   G. too overworked to recognize Martin's gift.
   H. an incompetent parent.
   J. overly solicitous with her sons.

3. The idea that Martin's mother is unaware of his abilities is best exemplified by which of the following quotations from the passage?
   A. "He even turns the pages. It's very cute!"
   B. "Do you have any idea how much it costs to live there?"
   C. "Mom, think what you're saying!"
   D. "I really appreciate you taking care of him like you have."

4. As it is used in line 10, the word *plight* most nearly means:
   F. happiness.
   G. engagement.
   H. predicament.
   J. flexibility.

5. It can be inferred from the passage that Granny is:
   A. Martin's paternal grandmother.
   B. Sheila's mother-in-law.
   C. Martin's maternal grandmother.
   D. an unknown wealthy benefactor.

6. The passage makes it clear that Martin and his mother:
   F. plan to move to America.
   G. will remain distant.
   H. will be alienated from Martin's brothers.
   J. may never see Granny again.

7. You may reasonably infer from the details in the passage that Sheila is:
   A. self-confident.
   B. in her early 20s.
   C. negligent in her care of her older sons.
   D. willing to do whatever it takes to help Martin succeed.

8. You may reasonably infer from the passage that Martin's brothers:
   F. attended a school for juvenile delinquents.
   G. mistreated Martin because they were jealous of his intelligence.
   H. were not well-liked in school.
   J. cared more for themselves than for Martin.

9. The word *gift*, as it is used in the passage, most nearly means:
   A. endowment.
   B. interest.
   C. talent.
   D. present.

10. The title, "Born in Paradise," combined with details presented in the passage imply that:
    F. everyone loves a tropical island.
    G. Caribbean islands tend to have subpar educational systems.
    H. children in single-parent homes need someone like Granny.
    J. paradise is a relative term.

GO ON TO THE NEXT PAGE.

3 ████████████████████████████████ **3**

Passage II

SOCIAL SCIENCE: *This passage is adapted from "History of the Donner Party," by C. F. McGlashan, originally published in 1880.*

The pioneers of a new country are deserving of a niche in the country's history. The pioneers who became martyrs to the cause of the development of an almost unknown land deserve to have a place in
5　the hearts of its inhabitants. The members of the far-famed Donner Party are, in a peculiar sense, pioneer martyrs of California. Before the discovery of gold, before the highway across the continent was fairly marked out, while untold dangers lurked by the way-
10　side, and unnumbered foes awaited the emigrants, the Donner Party started for California. None but the brave and venturesome, none but the energetic and courageous, could undertake such a journey. In 1846, comparatively few had dared attempt to cross the
15　almost unexplored plains, which lay between the Mississippi and the fair, young land called California. Hence it is that a certain grandeur, a certain heroism seems to cling about the men and women composing this party, even from the day they began their
20　perilous journey across the plains. California, with her golden harvests, her beautiful homes, her dazzling wealth, and her marvelous commercial facilities, may well enshrine the memory of these noble-hearted pioneers, pathfinders, martyrs.
25　The states along the Mississippi were but sparsely settled in 1846, yet the fame of the fruitfulness, the healthfulness, and the almost tropical beauty of the land bordering the Pacific tempted the members of the Donner Party to leave their homes. These homes
30　were situated in Illinois, Iowa, Tennessee, Missouri, and Ohio. Families from each of these states joined the train and participated in its terrible fate; yet the party proper was organized in Sangamon County, Illinois, by George and Jacob Donner and James
35　F. Reed. Early in April of 1846, the party set out from Springfield, Illinois, and by the first week in May reached Independence, Missouri. Here, the party was increased by additional members, and the train comprised about one hundred persons.
40　Independence was on the frontier in those days, and every care was taken to have ample provisions laid in and all necessary preparations made for the long journey. It was a long journey for many in the party! Great was the enthusiasm and eagerness with
45　which these noble-hearted pioneers caught up the cry of the times, "Ho! for California!" It is doubtful if presentiments of the fate to be encountered were not occasionally entertained. The road was difficult, and in places almost unbroken; warlike Indians guarded
50　the way, and death, in a thousand forms, hovered about their march through the great wilderness.
In the party were aged fathers with their trusting families about them, mothers whose very lives were wrapped up in their children, men in the prime and
55　vigor of manhood, maidens in all the sweetness and freshness of budding womanhood, children full of glee and mirthfulness, and babes nestling on maternal breasts. Lovers there were, to whom the journey was tinged with rainbow hues of joy and happiness, and
60　strong, manly hearts whose constant support and

encouragement was the memory of dear ones left behind in homeland. The cloud of doom, which finally settled down in a death-pall over their heads, was not yet perceptible; though, as we shall soon see,
65　its mists began to collect almost at the outset, in the delays that marked the journey.
The wonderment that all experience in viewing the scenery along the line of the old emigrant road was peculiarly vivid to these people. Few descrip-
70　tions had been given of the route, and all was novel and unexpected. In later years the road was broadly and deeply marked, and good camping grounds were distinctly indicated. The bleaching bones of cattle that had perished, or the broken fragments of
75　wagons or cast-away articles, were thickly strewn on either side of the highway. But in 1846 the way was through almost trackless valleys waving with grass, along rivers where few paths were visible, save those made by the feet of buffaloes and antelope, and over
80　mountains and plains where little more than the westward course of the sun guided the travelers. Trading posts were stationed at only a few widely distant points, and rarely did the party meet with any human beings, save wandering bands of Indians.
85　Yet these first days are written about by survivors as being crowned with peaceful enjoyment and pleasant anticipations. There were beautiful flowers by the roadside, an abundance of game in the meadows and mountains, and at night there were singing, dancing,
90　and innocent plays. Several musical instruments, and many excellent voices, were in the party, and the kindliest feeling and good fellowship prevailed among the members.

11. It can be reasonably inferred that the conclusions made about the courage of the Donner Party are based on:
  A. journal entries discovered decades later.
  B. historical fact that references the country's development in the 1840s.
  C. firsthand accounts by ancestors of the Donner Party.
  D. anecdotal evidence of the group's trip to California.

12. The focus of the passage can best be summarized as a study of both the:
  F. Donner Party and the characteristics of the United States in 1846.
  G. history of the California Gold Rush and the Donner Party.
  H. Donner Party and the discovery of gold.
  J. wealth and innocence of the Donner Party.

GO ON TO THE NEXT PAGE.

3 ▬▬▬▬▬▬▬▬▬▬▬▬▬▬▬▬▬▬▬▬▬▬▬▬▬ **3**

13. According to information presented in the passage, which of the following best describes the relationship between the Donner Party and other American pioneers?
   A. Other American pioneers also traveled west in search of opportunity.
   B. The Donner Party was one of the first pioneer groups to cross the country to California.
   C. The Donner Party ignored the advice of earlier pioneers.
   D. The Donner Party successfully reached their destination while other pioneers did not.

14. According to the passage, the motivation for the Donner Party's journey was to:
   F. gain independence.
   G. explore the Mississippi.
   H. flee religious tyranny.
   J. reach California.

15. As it is used in the third paragraph, the word *unbroken* most nearly means:
   A. intact.
   B. easy to follow.
   C. not constructed.
   D. well-built.

16. As it is depicted in the passage, the initial mood of the Donner Party can best be described as:
   F. eagerly determined.
   G. hopelessly discouraged.
   H. predominantly cautious.
   J. wildly happy.

17. It can be inferred that the word *train* as it is used in line 39 refers to:
   A. the land bordering the Pacific.
   B. an early steam engine.
   C. America's first passenger train.
   D. a line of wagons.

18. According to the passage, which of the following were dangers faced by the Donner Party?
   F. Lack of food and water
   G. Savage attacks
   H. Wagons breaking down
   J. Boredom and bad weather

19. As it relates to the passage, all of the following were members of the Donner Party EXCEPT:
   A. aged fathers.
   B. Californians.
   C. young children.
   D. musicians.

20. According to the passage, in the early part of their journey, the Donner Party enjoyed all of the following EXCEPT the:
   F. beautiful scenery.
   G. road conditions.
   H. camaraderie.
   J. night-time stops.

GO ON TO THE NEXT PAGE.

3 ▬▬▬▬▬▬▬▬▬▬▬▬▬▬▬▬▬▬▬▬ **3**

Passage III
HUMANITIES: *The Passion of Perugino*

I remember feeling slightly disconcerted as I looked up at the unsmiling saints, the Virgin Mary, and even Jesus as I wandered through the hushed halls of the museum. The unworldly
5　experience continues to haunt my memory as I recall the unflinching gazes of Pietro Perugino's subjects staring blankly at me as I admired the power and beauty of the great Italian Renaissance master's most famous works of art. For years, I had
10　studied great artists of the past and present, but not even the breathtaking landscapes of Monet could prepare me for the moment that I was confronted with the genius of one of the least well known artists of the Italian Renaissance. In that moment, my
15　admiration for artists like Renoir and Manet of the French Impressionist Movement, was eclipsed by the austere exquisiteness of these fifteenth century paintings.

Since that day in the museum, I have gained
20　more knowledge and expertise about the Italian Renaissance movement, and I recognize that Pietro Perugino's work is not beyond critique. His paintings have been described as monotonous and unimaginative because the people portrayed often
25　look alike without any distinguishing features. His paintings lack the ingenuity and fluidity of Sandro Botticelli. Perugino's own pupil, Raphael, could surpass his teacher in creating emotion on the canvas. The genius Michelangelo could evoke
30　dreaminess in his work that creates a feast for the imagination, while keeping minuscule details in perfect perspective. And yet, Pietro Perugino's paintings are still the ones that I see in my mind when I hear the words *Italian Renaissance*.

35　I remember staring awestruck as I viewed his fresco *The Delivery of the Keys* (1482) and noticing the elegant simplicity of the painting, which portrayed St. Peter accepting the keys to heaven. The painting should have paled next to the other
40　more dramatic work in the Sistine Chapel, but *The Delivery of the Keys* held its own with its voluminous clouds and elegant gothic buildings in the background. In this piece, Pietro Perugino showed how far art had come since the medieval
45　times. Instead of flat and cardboard-like characters, the subjects in *The Delivery of the Keys* display awe, disbelief, and amazement while engrossed in conversation with each other. Perugino also experimented with depth, and he rivaled Leonardo da
50　Vinci in his ability to create a definite background and foreground. *The Delivery of the Keys* boasts a gorgeous mountain landscape that truly appears to be miles away from St. Peter as he accepts the key to eternity.

55　During our tour of the Sistine Chapel, the guide had shared with us the story of Perugino's life. Perugino would almost starve to death because he forgot to eat or sleep while painting. Rest was never an option for this driven artist. His dedication
60　shined through in his meticulous, yet passionate work. The love that Perugino had for painting shows in the careful detail of works like *The Delivery of the*

Keys. In my mind, Perugino's passion for art gives his pieces their distinction and this passion more
65　than makes up for any deficiencies that his critics might find.

I have seen the works of several painters during the Italian Renaissance that are considered far greater than anything created by Perugino. Paintings
70　by Michelangelo, Leonardo da Vinci, and Botticelli are certainly more in demand and enjoy mainstream popularity and acceptance. All of these three artists seemed capable of creating more dramatic and majestic pieces than did Perugino. The work
75　of da Vinci and Michelangelo is seen on postcards and reprinted on cheap posters everywhere because of its universal appeal. Although the brilliance of all of the Italian Renaissance masters is undeniable, the awe-inspiring beauty of Michelangelo's work or
80　the subtle detail of da Vinci's *Mona Lisa* cannot match the simple passion evident in Perugino's paintings. In spite of being more simple and less appealing to the masses, Perugino's paintings reveal raw talent and skill that I have never seen
85　equaled by another artist anywhere in the world.

21. Which of the following descriptions most accurately and completely represents this passage?
　A. A reminiscent and passionate recollection of the narrator's introduction to Perugino's art
　B. An independent critical analysis of Monet, Renoir, and Manet in relation to Perugino
　C. An impartial evaluation of the paintings of Perugino
　D. An all-inclusive biographical outline of Perugino's life

22. All of the following were unmistakably identified as painters in this passage EXCEPT:
　F. Leonardo da Vinci
　G. Michelangelo
　H. Botticelli
　J. Donatello

23. Which of the following quotations best expresses the main point of the passage?
　A. "Since that day in the museum, I have gained more knowledge and experience with the Italian Renaissance movement and I recognize that Pietro Perugino's work is not beyond critique."
　B. "I have seen the works of several painters during the Italian Renaissance that are considered far greater than any thing created by Perugino."
　C. "In this piece, Pietro Perugino showed how far art had come since the medieval times."
　D. "In my mind, Perugino's passion for art gives his pieces their distinction and this passion more than makes up for any deficiencies that the critics might find."

GO ON TO THE NEXT PAGE.

3 ▬▬▬▬▬▬▬▬▬▬▬▬▬▬▬▬▬▬▬▬▬▬▬ **3**

24. As it is used in the passage (line 26), the word *ingenuity* most nearly means:
   F. resourcefulness.
   G. inventiveness.
   H. quality.
   J. versatility.

25. It can be inferred from the passage that the narrator most highly values which of the following in an artist?
   A. Fluidity and volatility
   B. Unique appearance of subjects
   C. Devotion and passion for art
   D. Classical training from the masters

26. It can be most reasonably concluded from the writer's quote, "In that moment, my admiration for artists like Renoir and Manet of the French Impressionist Movement, was eclipsed by the austere exquisiteness of these fifteenth century paintings," that:
   F. few of the painters of the French Impressionist Movement were as impressive as the artists of the Italian Renaissance.
   G. the masters of the Italian Renaissance are more universally accepted than Renoir and Manet.
   H. the narrator believes that the technical skill and creativity of Perugino surpasses that of Renoir and Manet.
   J. the narrator's admiration of Perugino is so great, he or she believes that Perugino's work outshines that of more well-known painters.

27. According to the passage, what are characteristics of Perugino's work?
   I. austerity
   II. showing the passion of the artist
   III. ability to display depth
   IV. abstraction
   A. I, II, III only
   B. I, II only
   C. I, IV only
   D. I, II, IV only

28. Which of the following best describes the narrator's instant reaction upon seeing Perugino's paintings for the first time?
   F. Disbelief in the quality of the work
   G. Unsettled by some of the features of the paintings
   H. Envious of Perugino's genius and artistic ability
   J. Intent on comparing Perugino's work to French Impressionist artists

29. All of the following are a criticism of Perugino's paintings mentioned in the passage EXCEPT:
   A. Perugino's paintings show a lack of imagination.
   B. Perugino's technique in creating depth was not as advanced as Leonardo Da Vinci's.
   C. the subjects or people of Perugino's paintings often look alike.
   D. Raphael could create more emotion in his paintings than Perugino.

30. The narrator states his or her opinion about famous artists and their work throughout the passage. All of the following opinions are clearly stated in the passage EXCEPT:
   F. Manet's work is reprinted on postcards and cheap posters because of its popularity.
   G. Leonardo da Vinci and Perugino could both display depth well.
   H. Botticelli's work shows fluidity and ingenuity.
   J. the painting *Mona Lisa* by Leonardo da Vinci shows subtle detail.

GO ON TO THE NEXT PAGE.

3 ⬛⬛⬛⬛⬛⬛⬛⬛⬛⬛⬛⬛⬛⬛⬛⬛⬛ **3**

Passage IV
NATURAL SCIENCE: *The Prickly Porcupine*

As we timidly watched the lumbering escape efforts of this oversized rodent, we were struck by its own apparent lack of fear and panic. Then it dawned on us that, unlike most other animals in the
5 wild, the porcupine's mere outward appearance provides more than adequate reason for it rarely to become alarmed or excited. Even knowing that the "shooting-quills" forest legend really is just that, stumbling upon this threatening creature is sure to
10 cause fear and panic only from the human's point of view and not vice versa.

The *Erethizon dorsatum* (Latin for "irritable back") comes equipped with more than 30,000 quills on its back, sides, and tail. Each of these
15 quills contains several barbs, or hook-like structures, that can imbed themselves into the flesh of a predator. Rather than throwing their quills, however, porcupines are able to implant them into their would-be attacker when the animal or human
20 gets too close. Porcupines also swing their tails back and forth, rather like hammering nails into their adversaries. Since these quills are hollow, they fill up with the host's blood once imbedded, making them even more difficult to remove. Many a dog has
25 found itself with a noseful or mouthful of porcupine quills, which need to be tended to right away. Often, clipping an inch or so off the end of the quills before removing them can aid in their extraction and relieve the excruciating pain.

30 The porcupine ranks second in size to the beaver among the rodent family. A full-grown porcupine can range anywhere from two to three and a half feet in length and generally weighs between eight and fourteen pounds. However, a porcupine with
35 a plentiful food supply can weigh considerably more. Female porcupines generally give birth once a year to a single offspring. The long, seven-month gestation period ensures a well-developed infant that is nearly ready at birth to take care of itself. Born
40 with soft quills, it takes only a few hours after birth for these quills to harden and be ready for an attack. There are some animals, however, that are able to break down the porcupine's powerful defense system by carefully turning the porcupine
45 over onto its back, exposing its soft and vulnerable underbelly. Bobcats, cougars, and coyotes are especially adept at this technique and pose a major threat to the porcupine.

Porcupines are mostly found in northern
50 and cold climates. They are particularly fond of forested areas, as mature trees provide both food and shelter. During the winter months, porcupines chew almost exclusively on tree bark. As nocturnal animals, porcupines generally sleep high up in a tree
55 during the day, though they also use underground burrows, particularly in the spring while tending their newborns.

According to the Yukon Department of Environment, the porcupine has been useful to and
60 appreciated by many. Quills are often used in jewelry- and basket-making, as well as in decorating clothing and shoes. Porcupine meat is even considered to be a tasty meal and fairly easy to obtain. In British Columbia, however, the porcupine
65 has developed a negative reputation due to its appetite for wood, damaging trees and even wooden buildings.

While porcupines can be a source of worry to some people, they are fascinating animals to
70 observe. Because of their incredible defense systems, they take their time to escape a potential enemy, which allows for a great opportunity to view these animals fairly closely. Just don't get too close!

31. The author likens porcupines' tails to "hammering nails" in Paragraph 2 because:
A. porcupines can pound their quills into an enemy with their tails.
B. a porcupine's quills are as hard as nails.
C. the swinging tail of a porcupine makes a hammering sound.
D. the porcupine's tail is shaped like a hammer.

32. The author calls the porcupine a "threatening creature" in the first paragraph because:
F. it throws its quills at its enemies.
G. no one can survive being attacked by a porcupine.
H. it becomes alarmed and excited.
J. it has a frightening appearance.

33. The passage indicates that, unlike some other wild animals, the porcupine:
A. has a descriptive scientific name.
B. does not have a defense mechanism.
C. is not easily frightened.
D. generally finds plenty of food.

34. According to the author, the porcupine moves slowly because:
F. its quills add extra weight.
G. it has no reason to move quickly.
H. it has no predators.
J. it has short legs.

35. Based on information in the passage, the author feels dogs are especially threatened by porcupines because:
A. quills can cause great discomfort.
B. dogs are likely to touch porcupines with their noses and mouths.
C. porcupines routinely attack dogs.
D. porcupines often wander into peoples' backyards.

GO ON TO THE NEXT PAGE.

3 ████████████████████████████████ **3**

36. The passage indicates that the Yukon government considers porcupines to be both:
   F. scarce and endangered.
   G. interesting and useful.
   H. dangerous and unthreatening.
   J. appreciated and disliked.

39. The passage indicates that, if imbedded, a porcupine's quills:
   A. can cause death.
   B. can be very painful.
   C. should be left alone.
   D. will eventually fall out on their own.

37. What does the passage state is one of the porcupine's biggest enemies?
   A. Cougars
   B. Humans
   C. Dogs
   D. Rodents

38. The passage indicates that, in British Columbia, porcupines are damaging:
   F. dogs.
   G. forests.
   H. lakes.
   J. baskets.

40. According to the passage, the scientific name for the porcupine means:
   F. "prickly animal."
   G. "shooting quills."
   H. "threatening creature."
   J. "irritable back."

END OF THE READING TEST
STOP! IF YOU HAVE TIME LEFT OVER, CHECK YOUR WORK ON THIS SECTION ONLY.

4 ◯ ◯ ◯ ◯ ◯ ◯ ◯ ◯ ◯ **4**

SCIENCE REASONING TEST

35 Minutes – 40 Questions

DIRECTIONS: There are seven passages in this test. Each passage is followed by several questions. You should refer to the passages as often as necessary in order to choose the best answer to each question. Once you have selected your answer, fill in the corresponding bubble on your answer sheet.

You may NOT use a calculator on this test.

Passage I

A hurricane is a large, rotating storm centered around an area of very low pressure with strong winds blowing at an average speed in excess of 74 miles per hour. Hurricanes are dangerous natural hazards to people and the environment. However, they are essential features of the Earth's atmosphere. Hurricanes transfer heat and energy between the equator and the cooler regions toward the poles.

Two meteorologists present their views on hurricane formation.

Meteorologist 1

The most influential factors that turn a storm into a hurricane are a source of very warm, moist air coming from tropical oceans having surface temperatures greater than 26°C, and sufficient spin from the Earth's rotation. The warm ocean heats the air above it, causing a current of very warm, moist air to rise quickly. This creates a center of low pressure at the surface. Trade winds rush in toward the area of low pressure, which forces the inward-spiraling winds to whirl upward, releasing heat and moisture. The rotation of the Earth causes the rising column to twist. The rising air cools and produces towering cumulus and cumulonimbus clouds. When the warm water evaporates from the tropical ocean, energy is stored in the water vapor. As the air rises, the majority of the stored energy is released by condensation, resulting in cumulus clouds

and rain. The hurricane becomes a self-sustaining heat engine because the release of heat energy warms the air locally and causes a further decrease in pressure. Air rises faster to fill the low-pressure area and more warm, moist air is drawn off the sea. This gives the system even more energy. A hurricane causes major destruction when its path takes it over land, but this also leads to the destruction of the hurricane itself.

Meteorologist 2

Hurricanes start out as a group of storms that begin to rotate when they encounter converging winds. They are not necessarily formed where the surface temperature of the ocean is warm, nor does the Earth's rotation have any bearing on whether or not storms turn into hurricanes. The converging winds spin the group of storms until they organize into a more powerful spiraling storm. The storm takes the form of a cylinder whirling around an "eye" of relatively still air. The spinning storm heats the surface of the ocean until the warm water turns into water vapor. The water vapor rises very quickly, rotating with the storms, and helps to increase the wind speed. The cycle repeats itself and eventually the water vapor is released as condensation, resulting in a tremendous amount of rain. For the hurricane to die, land must be in its path. The hurricane causes major destruction when it hits land, but it destroys itself at the same time. Over the past 3 decades, studies have shown that higher-than-average tropical ocean temperatures did not result in more hurricanes.

GO ON TO THE NEXT PAGE.

4   **4**

1. Assuming that increased levels of atmospheric carbon dioxide (CO_2) cause an increase in air temperatures, which of the following figures best represents the relationship between CO_2 levels and the number of hurricanes, according to Meteorologist 1?

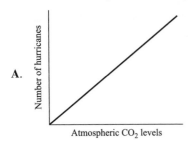

A.

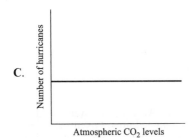

B.

C.

D.

2. Which of the following would Meteorologist 1 suggest leads to an increase in the number of hurricanes, assuming that increased levels of atmospheric CO_2 cause an increase in air temperature?
   F. Decreased levels of atmospheric CO_2
   G. Increased marine life in the oceans
   H. Decreased production and release of particles that increase water temperatures in tropical oceans
   J. Reduced number of forests and trees that help remove CO_2 from the atmosphere during photosynthesis

3. It has been found that nontropical oceans and seas contain higher numbers of marine animals. This results in increased water temperatures at the surface due to the energy that is transferred from the movement of the marine life. However, hurricanes do not occur in these waters. This information would best support the view of:
   A. Meteorologist 1, because hurricanes are mostly self-sustaining.
   B. Meteorologist 1, because increased water temperatures cause hurricanes.
   C. Meteorologist 2, because increased water temperatures do not cause hurricanes.
   D. Meteorologist 2, because there are no converging winds in these waters.

4. According to the hypothesis of Meteorologist 1, which of the following results is expected if global temperatures increase and water temperatures rise?
   F. There will be an increase in the number of hurricanes.
   G. There will be a decrease in the number of hurricanes.
   H. There will no change in the number of hurricanes.
   J. Hurricanes will be easier to predict.

5. The views of both meteorologists are similar because they imply that:
   A. increased water temperatures alone help create hurricanes.
   B. converging winds are not a necessary component in hurricane formation and duration.
   C. hurricanes become stronger and more destructive with the presence of warm water and water vapor.
   D. there is a correlation between average water temperatures and the number of hurricanes.

6. Meteorologist 2 states that higher:
   F. surface water temperatures cause hurricanes.
   G. surface water temperatures do not cause hurricanes.
   H. wind speeds do not cause hurricanes.
   J. levels of CO_2 cause hurricanes.

7. The hypothesis of Meteorologist 2 could best be tested by:
   A. recording the surface temperature of nontropical oceans and seas over the next 10 years.
   B. recording the surface temperature of tropical oceans and seas over the next 10 years and comparing the data with the number of hurricanes recorded during the same time period.
   C. combining waters with cooler surface temperatures and high converging winds, and recording the data for at least 10 years.
   D. combining waters with warmer surface temperatures and high converging winds, and recording the data for at least 10 years.

GO ON TO THE NEXT PAGE.

4 ◯ ◯ ◯ ◯ ◯ ◯ ◯ ◯ **4**

Passage II

Gas diffusion occurs when a gas moves from a syringe into a sealed vacuumed area where it can spread widely and thinly throughout the entire vacuumed area. A 50 ml gas sample in a syringe is forced into a sealed vacuumed area. The molecular mass in a.m.u. (atomic mass units), for 6 noble gases, as well as the time required for the gases to completely diffuse throughout the entire 10-cubic-foot (c^3) vacuumed area, are recorded in Table 1. The densities (mass/volume), boiling point (Kelvin, or K), and melting point (Kelvin, or K) are also given.

Table 1					
Gas	Diffusion time (sec)	Molecular mass (a.m.u.)	Density (g/cm^3)	Boiling point (K)	Melting point (K)
He	13	4	0.25	5	1
Ne	18	20	1.00	27	25
Ar	28	40	2.00	87	84
Kr	43	84	4.00	120	116
Xe	58	131	6.00	165	161
Rn	73	222	10.0	211	202

Note: Figures are all rounded to the nearest number.

Figure 1 shows a graph of the diffusion time versus the molecular mass of the noble gases.

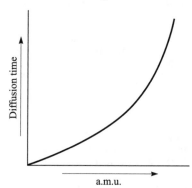

Figure 1

8. Given the information in Table 1, the difference in diffusion times is greatest between which of the following pairs of noble gases?
   F. He and Kr
   G. Ne and Ar
   H. Kr and Rn
   J. Ne and Xe

9. Based on the passage, what is the relationship between molecular mass and diffusion time?
   A. Molecular mass increases as diffusion time increases.
   B. Molecular mass decreases as diffusion time increases.
   C. Molecular mass stays constant as diffusion time decreases.
   D. Molecular mass stays constant as diffusion time increases.

10. Six vacuumed areas of identical shape and size are placed side by side. Six syringes, each containing 50 milliliters (ml) of one of the noble gases is forced into each vacuumed area. According to the data in Table 1, if these areas are kept under the same conditions, which gas should completely diffuse first?
    F. He
    G. Ne
    H. Ar
    J. Kr

11. A 50-ml sample of Ar gas is allowed to diffuse in a 10-cubic-foot vacuumed area. Given the information in Table 1, what percentage of the vacuumed area will NOT have Ar gas molecules after 14 seconds?
    A. 12.25%
    B. 25%
    C. 50%
    D. 75%

12. According to Table 1, if a vacuumed area of unknown volume is filled with Ne gas, and it takes 54 seconds for this Ne gas to completely diffuse, which of the measurements is closest to the volume of the vacuumed area?
    F. 2.5 cubic feet
    G. 5 cubic feet
    H. 20 cubic feet
    J. 30 cubic feet

GO ON TO THE NEXT PAGE.

4 ○ ○ ○ ○ ○ ○ ○ ○ ○ **4**

Passage III

A study was conducted to determine whether 2 processes (Process A and Process B) provided reliable data on the content of forest soil samples of varying acidity (acid concentration). The concentrations of several compounds commonly tested for in forest soil samples were measured. The results are presented in the Table 1. The results for the processes were compared to estimates obtained using Standard Methods, which provide extremely accurate estimates.

13. From the results of the study, one would conclude that at a pH level of 2, Process A is most accurate in measuring the concentration of which of the following compounds, relative to the Standard Method?
A. Dissolved O_2
B. Dissolved CO_2
C. Calcium chloride
D. Dissolved $CaCO_3$

14. The data from which of the measurement procedures supports the conclusion that the concentration of calcium chloride increases as the level of acidity increases?
F. Standard Method only
G. Process A only
H. Standard Method and Process A only
J. Standard Method, Process A, and Process B

	Table 1				
Concentration	Acidity of sample (pH level)				
(mg/L) of :	2	3	4	5	6
Dissolved O_2					
Standard	5.6	5.2	4.6	4.4	3.9
Process A	5.6	5.1	4.4	4.1	3.7
Process B	5.7	5.3	4.7	4.4	4.0
Dissolved CO_2					
Standard	36.5	22.4	10.1	2.2	44.7
Process A	32.4	20.8	11.3	3.4	42.1
Process B	35.6	19.9	9.5	4.4	41.2
Calcium chloride					
Standard	23.5	1920	5350	9507	11346
Process A	22.9	1875	5167	8909	12544
Process B	23.7	2002	5454	9589	11543
Dissolved $CaCO_2$					
Standard	78.5	78.8	79.7	81.2	104.4
Process A	73.3	78.2	80.4	85.0	101.2
Process B	66.8	67.8	78.9	89.8	153.2
Dissolved NH_3					
Standard	0.41	0.43	0.88	0.91	0.69
Process A	0.48	0.52	0.68	0.81	0.76
Process B	0.42	0.45	0.86	0.92	0.67

15. Is the conclusion that Process A is more accurate than Process B for estimation of NH_3 concentration supported by the results in the table?
A. Yes, because the estimates using Process A are consistently lower than are the estimates using Process B.
B. Yes, because the estimates using Process A are more similar to the estimates using the Standard Method than are the estimates using Process B.
C. No, because the estimates using Process B are more similar to the estimates using the Standard Method than are the estimates using Process A.
D. No, because the estimates using Process B are consistently higher than the estimates using Process A.

GO ON TO THE NEXT PAGE.

16. Which of the following graphs best represents the relationship between the level of acidity and the concentration of dissolved CO_2 as estimated by Process A?

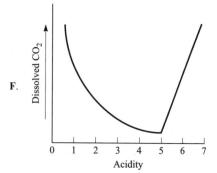

F.

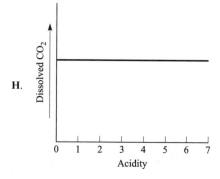

G.

H.

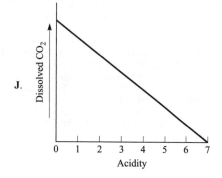

J.

17. A forest soil sample of unknown acidity was tested using Process A. The concentrations, in milligrams per liter (mg/l), of selected compounds in this sample were: dissolved $O_2 = 5.5$, $CaCO_3 = 72.1$, and $NH_3 = 0.49$. According to the data in the table, one would predict that the most likely level of acidity was:
  A. 6
  B. 5
  C. 4
  D. 2

GO ON TO THE NEXT PAGE.

4 ◯ ◯ ◯ ◯ ◯ ◯ ◯ ◯ ◯ **4**

Passage IV

Pesticides are often used to kill and repel fleas and ticks on dogs. Two experiments were designed to measure the effectiveness of different pesticides on fleas and ticks. The pesticides work by making contact with the fleas and ticks during the application, and by coating the dogs' skin.

Experiment 1

A biologist tested 2 types of flea and tick pesticides on flea- and tick-infested dogs. Ten dogs were washed with a shampoo containing 8 oz. of Pesticide A, and 10 other dogs were washed with a shampoo containing 8 oz. of Pesticide B. All dogs weighed between 15 and 20 pounds (lbs) and were noted to have at least 10 visible ticks each. The shampoo volumes were identical. The dogs were then inspected for live fleas and ticks. The total number of remaining fleas and ticks were counted, averaged, and recorded 24 hours after treatment and 48 hours after treatment. The results are shown in Table 1.

Table 1				
	Average count at 24 hr		Average count at 48 hr	
	Fleas	Ticks	Fleas	Ticks
Pesticide A	27	5	4	4
Pesticide B	10	11	3	9
Note: The average number of fleas per dog before treatment = 57 The average number of ticks per dog before treatment = 13				

Experiment 2

A biologist tested 3 types of flea and tick shampoos: one containing only Pesticide A and one containing only Pesticide B, and a combination of the shampoos (Pesticide A + B), which contained 50% of Pesticide A and 50% of Pesticide B, on dogs with long and short coats. The experiment was conducted in the same manner as Experiment 1, except fleas and ticks were only counted and averaged after 24 hours. The results are shown in Table 2.

Table 2				
	Average count at 24 hrs		Average count at 24 hrs	
	Long coat		Short coat	
	Fleas	Ticks	Fleas	Ticks
Pesticide A	34	7	26	4
Pesticide B	15	12	9	10
Pesticide A + B	20	10	13	8
Note: The average number of fleas per dog before treatment = 57 The average number of ticks per dog before treatment = 13				

Information on average coat length of the dogs in both experiments is given in Table 3.

Table 3	
Coat type	Length (in.)
Long	1.5 > 3.5
Short	0 > 1.5

18. The results of Experiments 1 and 2 indicate that which type of pesticide was most effective in removing fleas?
    F. Pesticide A
    G. Pesticide B
    H. Pesticide A + B
    J. Neither pesticide removed fleas

19. Which scenario would most reduce the number of ticks on a dog?
    A. Applying Pesticide B to a dog with a long coat
    B. Applying Pesticide A + B to a dog with a short coat
    C. Applying Pesticide B to a dog with a short coat
    D. Applying Pesticide A to a dog with a short coat

20. Based on the results of Experiment 2, shorter coat length leads to:
    F. reduced effectiveness of all pesticides.
    G. increased effectiveness of Pesticide A only.
    H. increased effectiveness of all pesticides.
    J. reduced effectives of Pesticide B only.

21. Which of the following best explains why Pesticide A + B did not drastically reduce the number of both fleas and ticks?
    A. The 2 pesticides interfered with each other's effectiveness.
    B. The outcome depended on whether the dog had a long or short coat.
    C. The pesticides did not remain in sufficient contact with the fleas and ticks.
    D. The combined volume of Pesticide A + B was less than that of the other pesticides.

22. Assuming a coat length of 2 inches, what is the average number of ticks per dog 24 hours after application of Pesticide A?
    F. 4
    G. 7
    H. 10
    J. 12

GO ON TO THE NEXT PAGE.

4 ○ ○ ○ ○ ○ ○ ○ ○ ○ **4**

Passage V

Radioactive decay is a natural process by which an atom of a radioactive isotope spontaneously decays into another element. The unstable nucleus disintegrates by emitting alpha or beta particles or gamma rays. This process changes the composition of the nucleus and continues to take place until a stable nucleus is reached. Half-life is the amount of time it takes for half of the atoms in a sample to decay.

Figure 1 shows the decay from Fluorine 22 to Neon 22.

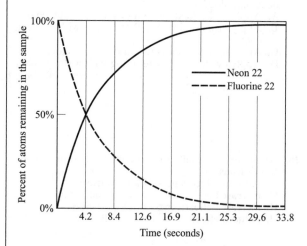

Figure 1

Figure 2 shows the decay from Oxygen 22 to Fluorine 22 to Neon 22.

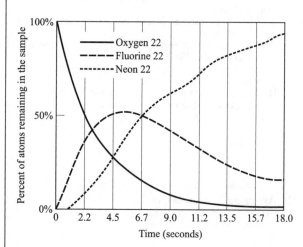

Figure 2

Table 1 shows the decay products and associated energy in Mev, million electron volts, and velocity, measured as a fraction of the speed of light.

Table 1			
Isotope	Decay product	Energy (Mev)	Particle velocity
Phosphorus 42	Sulfur 42	17.300	0.9995
Nitrogen 22	Oxygen 22	22.800	0.9997
Oxygen 22	Fluorine 22	6.490	0.9973
Fluorine 22	Neon 22	10.818	0.9989

23. According to Figure 1, what is the approximate half-life of Fluorine 22?
    A. 16.9 seconds
    B. 8.4 seconds
    C. 4.2 seconds
    D. 29.6 seconds

24. Based on the passage, radioactive decay:
    F. is unstable.
    G. does not occur in nature.
    H. is a natural process.
    J. only occurs in half of the atoms.

25. Based on Table 1, what is the relationship between decay energy and decay particle velocity?
    A. Lower decay energy leads to lower particle velocity.
    B. Lower particle velocity leads to higher decay energy.
    C. Decay energy does not impact particle velocity.
    D. Higher decay energy leads to lower particle velocity.

26. When Cerium 53 decays into Lanthanum 127, the decay energy is 6.100 Mev. According to the data in Table 1, the decay particle velocity is most likely:
    F. greater than the particle velocity of Oxygen 22.
    G. equal to the particle velocity of Flourine 22.
    H. greater than the particle velocity of Nitrogen 22.
    J. equal to the particle velocity of Oxygen 22.

27. Based on Figure 2, at which time do Oxygen 22 and Neon 22 have the same percent of atoms remaining?
    A. 2.2 seconds
    B. 4.5 seconds
    C. 6.7 seconds
    D. 15.7 seconds

28. What statement best explains the meaning of the shape of the Fluorine 22 curve in Figure 1 and the Oxygen 22 curve in Figure 2?
    F. Decay happens at a steady rate regardless of the number of atoms.
    G. Decay starts off slowly and then speeds up.
    H. Decay occurs very quickly at first and slows as the number of atoms is reduced.
    J. The rate of decay is erratic.

GO ON TO THE NEXT PAGE.

4 ○ ○ ○ ○ ○ ○ ○ ○ ○ **4**

Passage VI

A study was conducted on the effects of pesticide exposure on domestic chicken breeds. Some zoologists believe that exposure to pesticides can lead to lower birth rates and increased susceptibility to illness. Table 1 shows the average number of eggs laid, average number of eggs that hatch, and resistance to illness before being exposed to a pesticide for several different domestic chicken breeds.

Table 1			
Chicken Breed	Resistance to Illness	Average Number of Eggs Laid	Average Number of Eggs Hatched
A	High	10	9
B	High	8	7
C	Medium	11	8
D	Medium	7	5
E	Low	15	9

Figure 1 shows how pesticide exposure affects the chicken's susceptibility to illness.

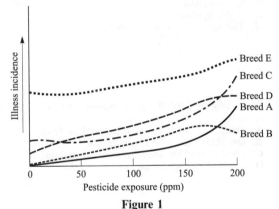

Figure 1

Figure 2 shows the average number of eggs laid and subsequent number of eggs that hatched after exposure to pesticide.

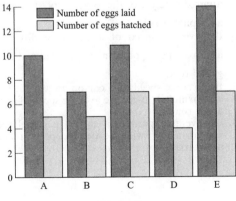

Figure 2

29. Based on the results of the study, if chicken Breed F has a low resistance to illness, approximately how many eggs would you expect to hatch from an average of 20 eggs laid, before pesticide exposure?
    A. 5
    B. 12
    C. 17
    D. 20

30. Based on the information in Figure 1, which breed has the fewest illness incidences at the highest pesticide exposure [200 parts per million (ppm)]?
    F. Breed E
    G. Breed C
    H. Breed B
    J. Breed A

31. Based on the data in Figures 1 and 2, which breed is likely to have a higher number of eggs hatch per number of eggs laid, and have a low incidence of illness when exposed to pesticide?
    A. Breed B
    B. Breed A
    C. Breed E
    D. Breed C

32. According to Table 1, what is the relationship between resistance to illness and average number of eggs laid?
    F. The average number of eggs laid remains constant.
    G. There is no direct relationship.
    H. As resistance increases, the average number of eggs laid increases.
    J. As resistance increases, the average number of eggs laid decreases.

33. According to Figure 1, which breed is the most affected by pesticide exposure?
    A. Breed A
    B. Breed B
    C. Breed D
    D. Breed E

34. Based on the passage, which of the following statements is true?
    F. The average number of eggs hatched for all chicken breeds is not affected by pesticide exposure.
    G. Chicken breed C has the lowest resistance to illness.
    H. Chicken breed A had the lowest number of eggs hatch before exposure to pesticide.
    J. The average number of eggs laid by all breeds is not affected by pesticide exposure.

35. According to Table 1, which chicken breed laid the most eggs before pesticide exposure?
    A. E
    B. C
    C. B
    D. A

GO ON TO THE NEXT PAGE.

4 ◯ ◯ ◯ ◯ ◯ ◯ ◯ ◯ ◯ **4**

Passage VII

Some students performed 3 studies to measure the average speed of a remote-controlled car on different surfaces. Each study was conducted on a fair day with no wind. A 100-foot-long flat surface was measured, and the car's travel time was measured from start to finish with a stopwatch. The car was not modified in any way and the car's batteries were fully charged before each trial.

Study 1

The students placed the car on a smooth asphalt road. One student started the car as the other student started the stopwatch. The student stopped the stopwatch as the car crossed the 100-foot mark. The students calculated the results of 3 separate trials and averaged the results (see Table 1).

Table 1		
Trial	Time (s)	Speed (ft/s)
1	12	8.33
2	11.3	8.85
3	11.7	8.55
Average:	11.7	8.58

Study 2

The students repeated the procedure used in Study 1, except they placed the car on a rough gravel road. The results are shown in Table 2.

Table 2		
Trial	Time (s)	Speed (ft/s)
1	22.1	4.52
2	21.8	4.59
3	22.4	4.46
Average:	22.4	4.52

Study 3

The students repeated the procedure used in Study 1, except they placed the car on a powdery, dry, dirt road. The results are shown in Table 3.

Table 3		
Trial	Time (s)	Speed (ft/s)
1	15.8	6.33
2	16.2	6.17
3	15.7	6.37
Average:	15.9	6.29

36. The highest average speeds resulted from using which surface?
  F. Dirt road
  G. Gravel road
  H. Asphalt road
  J. The speeds remained constant.

37. According to Table 1, the average speed for all three trials is:
  A. greater than the speed measured in Trial 2.
  B. less than the speed measured in Trial 3.
  C. greater than the speed measured in Trial 1.
  D. equal to the speed measured in Trial 2.

38. According to Tables 1, 2, and 3:
  F. the average speed of a car on a gravel road is approximately $\frac{1}{2}$ of the average speed of a car on an asphalt road.
  G. the average speed of a car on a dirt road is approximately $\frac{1}{2}$ of the average speed of a car on a gravel road.
  H. the average speed of a car on an asphalt road is approximately twice the average speed of a car on a dirt road.
  J. the average speed of a car on a gravel road is approximately twice the average speed of a car on a dirt road.

GO ON TO THE NEXT PAGE.

4 ◯ ◯ ◯ ◯ ◯ ◯ ◯ ◯ ◯ **4**

39. Based on the passage, the lower average speeds were probably a result of:
   A. error.
   B. greater friction.
   C. wind resistance.
   D. cloud cover.

40. During which of the following was the travel time of the car the slowest?
   F. Study 1, Trial 2
   G. Study 2, Trial 2
   H. Study 2, Trial 3
   J. Study 3, Trial 2

END OF THE SCIENCE REASONING TEST
STOP! IF YOU HAVE TIME LEFT OVER, CHECK YOUR WORK ON THIS SECTION ONLY.

5 ☆ ☆ ☆ ☆ ☆ ☆ ☆ ☆ 5

WRITING TEST

DIRECTIONS: This test is designed to assess your writing skills. You have thirty (30) minutes to plan and write an essay based on the stimulus provided. Be sure to take a position on the issue and support your position using logical reasoning and relevant examples. Organize your ideas in a focused and logical way, and use the English language to clearly and effectively express your position.

When you have finished writing, refer to the Scoring Rubrics discussed in Chapter 7 to estimate your score.

Note: On the actual ACT you will receive approximately 2.5 pages of scratch paper on which to develop your essay, and approximately 4 pages of notebook paper on which to write your essay. We recommend that you limit yourself to this number of pages when you write your practice essays.

Essay Prompt

Some states have laws that require all drivers to reach age eighteen before they are allowed to drive a car with more than one passenger. Some people think that the law is a common-sense safety measure since so many high school students die each year in accidents involving a single car with several teenagers as passengers and a teen driver. Other people think that such laws punish all teen drivers for the mistakes of a few irresponsible, unsafe drivers. In your opinion, should the law prohibit younger drivers from taking more than one passenger?

In your essay, take a position on this question. You may write about one of the points of view mentioned above, or you may give another point of view on this issue. Use specific examples and reasons for your position.

ANSWER KEY

English Test

1. D	21. C	41. D	61. C
2. F	22. J	42. F	62. G
3. B	23. C	43. A	63. A
4. G	24. J	44. H	64. G
5. B	25. B	45. D	65. B
6. H	26. F	46. G	66. H
7. C	27. D	47. C	67. A
8. H	28. H	48. F	68. J
9. A	29. D	49. D	69. C
10. J	30. F	50. F	70. G
11. D	31. A	51. B	71. A
12. J	32. G	52. H	72. J
13. C	33. C	53. D	73. B
14. H	34. J	54. F	74. J
15. B	35. D	55. D	75. C
16. J	36. F	56. J	
17. A	37. B	57. C	
18. F	38. J	58. G	
19. B	39. C	59. A	
20. F	40. H	60. H	

Mathematics Test

1. B	21. E	41. D
2. G	22. H	42. F
3. A	23. B	43. D
4. G	24. F	44. J
5. D	25. B	45. B
6. H	26. G	46. F
7. B	27. C	47. B
8. G	28. J	48. G
9. D	29. C	49. C
10. K	30. J	50. G
11. D	31. E	51. D
12. G	32. J	52. F
13. E	33. E	53. D
14. J	34. K	54. H
15. D	35. D	55. B
16. H	36. H	56. K
17. C	37. D	57. A
18. G	38. J	58. G
19. D	39. C	59. A
20. G	40. F	60. F

Reading Test

1. C	21. A
2. G	22. J
3. A	23. D
4. H	24. G
5. C	25. C
6. F	26. J
7. D	27. A
8. J	28. G
9. C	29. B
10. J	30. F
11. A	31. A
12. F	32. J
13. B	33. C
14. J	34. G
15. C	35. B
16. F	36. G
17. D	37. A
18. H	38. G
19. B	39. B
20. G	40. J

Science Reasoning Test

1. A	21. A
2. J	22. G
3. C	23. C
4. F	24. H
5. C	25. A
6. G	26. G
7. B	27. B
8. J	28. H
9. A	29. B
10. F	30. H
11. C	31. A
12. J	32. G
13. A	33. D
14. J	34. J
15. C	35. A
16. F	36. H
17. D	37. C
18. G	38. F
19. D	39. B
20. H	40. H

SCORING GUIDE

Your final reported score is your COMPOSITE SCORE. Your COMPOSITE SCORE is the average of all of your SCALED SCORES.

Your SCALED SCORES for the four multiple-choice sections are derived from the Scoring Table on the next page. Use your RAW SCORE, or the number of questions that you answered correctly for each section, to determine your SCALED SCORE. If you got a RAW SCORE of 60 on the English test, for example, you correctly answered 60 out of 75 questions.

Step 1   Determine your RAW SCORE for each of the four multiple-choice sections:

English   _____

Mathematics   _____

Reading   _____

Science Reasoning   _____

The following Raw Score Table shows the total possible points for each section.

RAW SCORE TABLE	
KNOWLEDGE AND SKILL AREAS	**RAW SCORES**
ENGLISH	75
MATHEMATICS	60
READING	40
SCIENCE REASONING	40
WRITING	12

Multiple-Choice Scoring Worksheet

Step 2   Determine your SCALED SCORE for each of the four multiple-choice sections using the following Scoring Worksheet. Each SCALED SCORE should be rounded to the nearest number according to normal rules. For example, $31.2 \approx 31$ and $31.5 \approx 32$. If you answered 61 questions correctly on the English section, for example, your SCALED SCORE would be 28.

English

_____ × 36 = _____ ÷ 75 = _____
RAW SCORE

              − 2   (*correction factor)

              SCALED SCORE

Mathematics

_____ × 36 = _____ ÷ 60 = _____
RAW SCORE

              + 1   (*correction factor)

              SCALED SCORE

Reading

_____ × 36 = _____ ÷ 40 = _____
RAW SCORE

              + 2   (*correction factor)

              SCALED SCORE

Science Reasoning

_____ × 36 = _____ ÷ 40 = _____
RAW SCORE

              + 1.5   (*correction factor)

              SCALED SCORE

   *The correction factor is an approximation based on the average from several recent ACT tests. It is most valid for scores in the middle 50% (approximately 16–24 scaled composite score) of the scoring range.

   The scores are all approximate. Actual ACT scoring scales vary from one administration to the next based upon several factors.

   If you take the optional Writing Test, you will need to combine your English and Writing scores to obtain your final COMPOSITE SCORE. Refer to Chapter 7 for guidelines on scoring your Writing Test Essay. Once you have determined a score for your essay out of 12 possible points, you will need to determine your ENGLISH/WRITING SCALED SCORE, using both your ENGLISH SCALED SCORE and your WRITING TEST SCORE. The combination of the two scores will give you an ENGLISH/WRITING SCALED SCORE, from 1 to 36, that will be used to determine your COMPOSITE SCORE mentioned earlier.

   Using the English/Writing Scoring Table, find your ENGLISH SCALED SCORE on the left or right hand side of the table and your WRITING TEST SCORE on the top of the table. Follow your ENGLISH SCALED SCORE over and your WRITING TEST SCORE down until the two columns meet at a number. This number is your ENGLISH/WRITING SCALED SCORE and will be used to determine your COMPOSITE SCORE.

Step 3   Determine your ENGLISH/WRITING SCALED SCORE using the English/Writing Scoring Table on the following page:

      English   _____

      Writing   _____

      English/Writing   _____

ENGLISH/WRITING SCORING TABLE

ENGLISH SCALED SCORE	WRITING TEST SCORE											ENGLISH SCALED SCORE
	2	3	4	5	6	7	8	9	10	11	12	
36	26	27	28	29	30	31	32	33	34	32	36	36
35	26	27	28	29	30	31	31	32	33	34	35	35
34	25	26	27	28	29	30	31	32	33	34	35	34
33	24	25	26	27	28	29	30	31	32	33	34	33
32	24	25	25	26	27	28	29	30	31	32	33	32
31	23	24	25	26	27	28	29	30	30	31	32	31
30	22	23	24	25	26	27	28	29	30	31	32	30
29	21	22	23	24	25	26	27	28	29	30	31	29
28	21	22	23	24	24	25	26	27	28	29	30	28
27	20	21	22	23	24	25	26	27	28	28	29	27
26	19	20	21	22	23	24	25	26	27	28	29	26
25	18	19	20	21	22	23	24	25	26	27	28	25
24	18	19	20	21	22	23	23	24	25	26	27	24
23	17	18	19	20	21	22	23	24	25	26	27	23
22	16	17	18	19	20	21	22	23	24	25	26	22
21	16	17	17	18	19	20	21	22	23	24	25	21
20	15	16	17	18	19	20	21	21	22	23	24	20
19	14	15	16	17	18	19	20	21	22	23	24	19
18	13	14	15	16	17	18	19	20	21	22	23	18
17	13	14	15	16	16	17	18	19	20	21	22	17
16	12	13	14	15	16	17	18	19	20	20	21	16
15	11	12	13	14	15	16	17	18	19	20	21	15
14	10	11	12	13	14	15	16	17	18	19	20	14
13	10	11	12	13	14	14	15	16	17	18	19	13
12	9	10	11	12	13	14	15	16	17	18	19	12
11	8	9	10	11	12	13	14	15	16	17	18	11
10	8	9	9	10	11	12	13	14	15	16	17	10
9	7	8	9	10	11	12	13	13	14	15	16	9
8	6	7	8	9	10	11	12	13	14	15	16	8
7	5	6	7	8	9	10	11	12	13	14	15	7
6	5	6	7	7	8	9	10	11	12	13	14	6
5	4	5	6	7	8	9	10	11	12	12	13	5
4	3	4	5	6	7	8	9	10	11	12	13	4
3	2	3	4	5	6	7	8	9	10	11	12	3
2	2	3	4	5	6	6	7	8	9	10	11	2
1	1	2	3	4	5	6	7	8	9	10	11	1

Step 4 Determine your COMPOSITE SCORE by finding the sum of all your SCALED SCORES for each of the four sections: English only (if you do not choose to take the optional Writing Test) *or* English/Writing (if you choose to take the optional Writing Test), Mathematics, Reading, and Science Reasoning, and divide by 4 to find the average. Round your COMPOSITE SCORE according to normal rules. For example, $31.2 \approx 31$ and $31.5 \approx 32$.

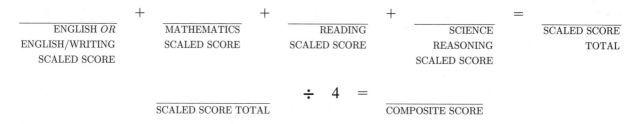

| ENGLISH *OR* ENGLISH/WRITING SCALED SCORE | + | MATHEMATICS SCALED SCORE | + | READING SCALED SCORE | + | SCIENCE REASONING SCALED SCORE | = | SCALED SCORE TOTAL |

$$\underline{\hspace{4cm}} \div \ 4 \ = \ \underline{\hspace{3cm}}$$

SCALED SCORE TOTAL   COMPOSITE SCORE

ANSWERS AND EXPLANATIONS

English Test Explanations
PASSAGE I

1. **The best answer is D.** According to the context of the first paragraph, Noh theater originated sometime around the fourteenth century, which is in the past. Therefore, the verb in the first sentence should be past tense. Eliminate answer choice A, because it uses the present tense: *originates.* *Original* is not a verb, so eliminate answer choice B. If you use *originating* you will create an incomplete sentence, so eliminate answer choice C.

2. **The best answer is F.** This question requires you to select the correct punctuation for the underlined portion. Answer choice G has unnecessary commas. Both H and J improperly use semicolons.

3. **The best answer is B.** The phrase *has remained largely unchanged* suggests that Noh theater is very much the same as it was in the fourteenth and fifteenth centuries. This fits the context of the paragraph.

4. **The best answer is G.** The words *only*, *just*, and *solely* all have the same meaning. To avoid redundancy, you should use only one of them in the sentence. Eliminate answer choices F, H, and J.

5. **The best answer is B.** The conjunctive phrase *for example* should always be set off by commas when it appears within a sentence. The only answer choice that places a comma before and after *for example* is answer choice B.

6. **The best answer is H.** The noun being replaced by the pronoun in this sentence is *musicians*, which is plural. Therefore, you must use the plural pronoun *they*. Eliminate answer choices F and J. You should not end a sentence with a preposition, so eliminate answer choice G.

7. **The best answer is C.** Paragraph 3 discusses the "stylized masks" worn by the actors to reflect certain characters. The sentence that best introduces this topic is answer choice C.

8. **The best answer is H.** The actors, not the characters that they portray, wear the masks, so you can eliminate answer choice F. The word *with* suggests that the audience is wearing the masks; eliminate answer choice G. The audience is most likely to recognize the characters "by the stylized masks that the actors" wear, answer choice H.

9. **The best answer is A.** This question requires you to select an answer choice that discusses a "unique talent." Answer choice A explains that "tilting their heads" is a specific skill that must be learned, so it is the best selection. The other answer choices are either too general, or they include information about the masks, not the actors.

10. **The best answer is J.** A semicolon must be followed by an independent clause, or a phrase that starts with a conjunction such as *therefore*. Eliminate answer choice F because the semicolon is not followed by an independent clause. The items in a list must be separated by commas if there are three or more items in the list. The only remaining choice that includes correct comma placement is answer choice J.

11. **The best answer is D.** To maintain parallelism in the sentence, the verb forms must match. It "is" a sophisticated form of drama that "possesses" something called *yugen.* Both answer choices A and C include past-tense verb forms and should be eliminated. While answer choice B contains a present-tense verb form, it is too wordy, so answer choice D is the best selection.

12. **The best answer is J.** In order to maintain consistency in this sentence, you must use the participle *have been.* Eliminate answer choices F and G because they include the wrong form of the verb *to be.* H is incorrect because it includes the wrong form of the verb *to write.*

13. **The best answer is C.** First, decide whether you should use *its* or *it's.* In this sentence, the noun *theater* is being replaced by the pronoun *it.* The "performers" belong to the theater, so you should use the possessive form of *it*, which is *its.* Eliminate answer choices A and D. There is a contrast suggested in the second half of the sentence, so the correct conjunction is *but*, making answer choice C correct.

14. **The best answer is H.** To maintain parallelism in the sentence, the subject must match the verb. Since the subject of this sentence, *fact* is a singular noun, the correct form of the verb is *speaks,* answer choice H. It is the "fact" that "speaks," not the "years" that "speak."

15. **The best answer is B.** The sentence contains information on Zeami, one of the original playwrights. Zeami is not discussed in either Paragraph 2 or Paragraph 3, so eliminate answer choices A and C. Since you are left with Paragraph 5, decide whether the sentence should be placed after Sentence 1 or Sentence 3. Since Sentence 1 mentions Zeami, it would make sense to place the new sentence after Sentence 1.

PASSAGE II

16. **The best answer is J.** The items in a list must be separated by commas. While answer choice G contains the correct number of commas, it deletes the word *to*, which is essential to the sentence.

17. **The best answer is A.** The preceding sentence mentions computer fonts. It is appropriate to provide a transition into the rest of the passage that is concerned with calligraphy as an art form.

18. **The best answer is F.** The phrase *derived from* is an idiomatic, or commonly used, phrase to indicate the origin of something. The word *calligraphy* comes *from* two different Greek words. The phrase *derived by* can also be used idiomatically, but it is usually followed by a verb ending in *–ing*.

19. **The best answer is B.** This question requires you to select an answer choice that will emphasize the importance of written records. The phrase *relied upon* suggests that the written word was important to many ancient peoples. Answer choices A, C, and D do not place enough emphasis on the importance of the written word.

20. **The best answer is F.** This question requires you to best express the idea that legible handwriting was important and useful in many places. Answer choices H and J create incomplete sentences and should be eliminated. Answer choice G contains an unnecessary comma, so it should be eliminated as well. The sentence is best written as it is.

21. **The best answer is C.** To maintain parallelism in this sentence, the subject must match the verb. Since the subject, *Chinese calligraphy* is singular, the correct verb form is *dates back*, answer choice C. Also, because the action is currently taking place, it is appropriate to use the present-tense form of the verb. Eliminate answer choices B and D because they include the past-tense form of the verb.

22. **The best answer is J.** The Chinese scholars used the index. Therefore, the index was established "for use by" the Chinese scholars. The other answer choices are awkward.

23. **The best answer is C.** According to the passage, the scribes started using the index around 200 B.C., which is clearly in the past. Therefore, you should use the simple past-tense form of the verb *develop*. Since there is more than one scribe, you can eliminate answer choice B, which contains the singular auxiliary verb *has*. The use of an auxiliary verb like *have* indicates past, present, or future perfect tense, which is not appropriate here.

24. **The best answer is J.** This question requires you to express the idea clearly and concisely. It is implied in the paragraph that the scribes replicate the characters when the scribes use the index. Therefore, it is not necessary to include any phrase about "replicating" the characters. If you omit, or remove, the underlined portion, the sentence does not lose any meaning.

25. **The best answer is B.** This question requires you to choose the best conjunctive adverb. A conjunctive adverb can be used to join two independent but related ideas, and is often used at the beginning of a sentence, if that sentence is related to the one directly preceding it. The conjunctive adverbs *however*, *yet*, and *otherwise* suggest a contrast that doesn't exist in this paragraph. It makes sense that "soon" after the scribes developed their own, individual styles, the scribes would emerge as artists.

26. **The best answer is F.** The subject of the sentence *the Japanese* is followed directly by the verb *adapted*. You should not separate the subject from the verb with a comma. It is not necessary to use any punctuation at all in the underlined portion.

27. **The best answer is D.** A semicolon should be followed by an independent clause, which is not the case in the sentence as it is written. Likewise, eliminate answer choice C because it creates an incomplete sentence. You should use a comma to separate the two main clauses of the sentence, which is why answer choice D is better than answer choice B.

28. **The best answer is H.** This question requires you to express the idea clearly and concisely. First, determine whether it is the "Church" or the "calligraphy" that is being influenced. Based on the context of the passage, it makes sense that the "calligraphy" is being influenced.

Eliminate answer choices G and J, which suggest that "calligraphy" influenced the "Church." It is better to use the active voice, as in answer choice H, which clearly indicates that the "Church" influenced "calligraphy."

29. **The best answer is D.** This question requires you to express the idea clearly and concisely. Answer choices A and C are wordy and awkward, and should be eliminated. Answer choice B eliminates the verb, which is a necessary component of any sentence. Answer choice D clearly indicates the positioning of the letters in Gothic calligraphy.

30. **The best answer is F.** Items in a list must be separated with commas. Therefore, there should be a comma after *pens*, and a comma after *inks*. Eliminate answer choices G and J. The phrase *such as specialized pens, inks, and paper* is a dependent clause, and should be set off with commas. In other words, you need a comma before and after the phrase, making answer choice F correct.

PASSAGE III

31. **The best answer is A.** To maintain parallelism, the subject must match the verb. The subject of this sentence, *the myth*, is singular and, therefore, requires a singular verb. The sentence is correct as it is written. The helping verb *will* suggests that the action hasn't happened yet, which is inconsistent with the context of the paragraph.

32. **The best answer is G.** This question requires you to express the idea clearly and concisely. Nothing in the passage suggests that the mountain men were "chosen," so eliminate answer choice H. If you omit, or remove, the underlined portion, you will remove the verb, so eliminate answer choice J. While *choosing to compete* is grammatically correct, it is not the simplest way to express the idea, so eliminate answer choice F.

33. **The best answer is C.** The primary focus of the first paragraph is the mountain man, not the beaver pelts that he harvested. Therefore, the sentence would not be a relevant addition to the paragraph. Answer choice D is not correct because the statement is off-topic.

34. **The best answer is J.** The fact that the Hudson Bay company was a British company adds nothing to the passage's main idea about American mountain men. The meaning of the sentence is not changed and the sentence is still complete without the underlined portion. So, the best choice is to OMIT, or delete, the underlined portion.

35. **The best answer is D.** This question requires you to express the idea clearly and simply. The phrase *buyers for this company* has the same meaning as *company's buyers*, but *company's buyers* is more concise. Eliminate answer choice C because it suggests that the company is being sold, which is not supported by information in the passage.

36. **The best answer is F.** The only answer choice that is relevant to the passage is answer choice F. It makes sense that the mountain men would need supplies other than the food they captured. The other answer choices contain information that is outside the scope of the passage.

37. **The best answer is B.** It is important to maintain parallelism within the sentence. So, the subject and verb must have the same form. Since the subject, *mountain man*, is singular, the verb must also be singular. Eliminate answer choices A and C. The other verb forms in the sentence, *was* and *relied*, are past tense, so eliminate answer choice D, which includes the present-tense verb *appears*.

38. **The best answer is J.** This question requires you to express the idea clearly and concisely. The phrase that makes the most sense is that the mountain man *relied upon the demands of consumers*, answer choice J. You can eliminate answer choice H because *they're* is a contraction of *they are*. The sentence would not make sense if you said "relied upon they are demand."

39. **The best answer is C.** The context of the passage does not support the idea that the trappers were "in control of" a fur company, so eliminate answer choice A. The phrase *under the control with* is not idiomatic, so eliminate answer choice B. If you omit, or remove the underlined portion, the sentence does not make sense and is grammatically incorrect. Therefore, answer choice D is incorrect.

40. **The best answer is H.** This question requires you to determine the correct use of commas. A good rule-of-thumb when it comes to commas is to use them where you would naturally pause when reading the sentence. The phrase *hired directly by a fur company* is a descriptive phrase. Since you would not naturally pause anywhere while reading that phrase, it does not require any commas.

41. **The best answer is D.** The sentence already says that the furs were "company property," so it is not necessary to include any more information about to whom the furs belonged. Answer

choices A, B, and C are all redundant and should be eliminated.

42. **The best answer is F.** A semicolon should be followed by a main clause that provides more information about the first part of the sentence. The sentence as it is written is correct. You should not use a comma to separate two main clauses — this is known as a comma splice. Eliminate answer choice H. It is necessary to include some form of punctuation, so eliminate answer choice J. By removing the word *he* in answer choice G, an incomplete sentence is created.

43. **The best answer is A.** The sentence structure suggests a cause-and-effect relationship. The phrase *because of* provides the proper connection between the cause and the effect. The phrase *in regards with* is not idiomatic and, therefore, is not acceptable for standard written English. Eliminate answer choice B. Answer choice C, while idiomatic in some circumstances, does not effectively complete this sentence, so it should be eliminated. *Irregardless* is not a word and should never be used, so eliminate answer choice D.

44. **The best answer is H.** It makes sense that the mountain men would find "safe haven" somewhere, so omitting, or removing, the underlined portion is not best here. Eliminate answer choice J. The sentence indicates that living in the mountains was hard, so it is not likely that the mountains themselves would provide a "safe haven." Eliminate answer choice F. Striking out on their own does not necessarily guarantee "save haven," so eliminate answer choice G. Answer choice H clearly indicates where the "safe haven" may be found.

45. **The best answer is D.** This question requires you to determine the main idea of the essay. The essay introduces the concept of the myth of the mountain man, and then goes on to describe the reality of living as a mountain man, which is quite different. Answer choice D best supports the ideas presented in the essay.

PASSAGE IV

46. **The best answer is G.** This question requires you to express the idea clearly and concisely. Since Curly Lambeau returned home "to Green Bay" he must have returned "from somewhere." Eliminate answer choice F. He did not return "from a severe case of tonsillitis," so eliminate answer choice H. It is not necessary to include

the word *which* after the comma, so eliminate answer choice J.

47. **The best answer is C.** It is important to maintain parallelism. This means that the verb forms should match. The verbs *returned*, *expressed*, and *convinced* are all past tense. Therefore, a past-tense verb should be used in the underlined portion. Eliminate answer choices A and D. The simplest way to express the idea conveyed in the sentence is to use *recommended*, answer choice C.

48. **The best answer is F.** This question requires you to express the idea clearly and concisely. First, decide who was performing the action of "calling." Since the Packers did not call the fans and players the team, eliminate answer choice G. Answer choice H should be eliminated because it is the passive voice. Active voice is generally preferred. Since the word *fittingly* is an adverb that describes the verb *called*, it should directly precede the verb. Therefore, eliminate answer choice G.

49. **The best answer is D.** The phrases *present-day*, *contemporary*, and *up-to-date* all have the same meaning, so none of them can be the correct answer. Since the sentence already includes the word *modern*, it would be redundant to include any of the answer choices. It would be best to omit the underlined portion, answer choice D.

50. **The best answer is F.** This question requires you to express the idea clearly and concisely. Answer choice H suggests that they were already wearing uniforms and had to change into different uniforms at home. This is not supported by information in the paragraph, so eliminate answer choice H. Answer choices G and J are awkward and should be eliminated.

51. **The best answer is B.** The phrase beginning with *so* is an adverbial phrase and should be preceded by a comma when found in the middle of a sentence. Semicolons should be followed by an independent clause, so eliminate answer choice A. Answer choice D creates an incomplete sentence and should be eliminated. Answer choice C contains an extra comma after *gates*.

52. **The best answer is H.** This question requires you to express the idea clearly and concisely. Answer choice G contains an ambiguous pronoun; it is unclear which noun is being replaced by the word *it*. The best way to express the idea is to say "…the only way to raise money…," answer choice H.

53. The best answer is D. This question requires you to determine the correct use of commas. A good rule of thumb when it comes to commas is to use them where you would naturally pause when reading the sentence. There are no natural pauses in this sentence, so no commas are needed.

54. The best answer is F. The first sentence as it is written adequately introduces the main idea of the paragraph and does not need to be replaced. While the conditions under which the Packers played football during the first year were difficult, the paragraph does not support the idea that the conditions were "brutal," so eliminate answer choice G. The other answer choices are not supported by the context of the paragraph.

55. The best answer is D. The pronoun *that* is used to indicate the game that was played on October 23, 1921. Therefore, it is not necessary to use any form of the verb *play* in the sentence. If you omit, or remove, the underlined portion, the sentence retains its meaning and is no longer redundant.

56. The best answer is J. This question asks you to find a way to "link" information already given in the passage with the information that is to follow. Since the paragraph introduces the "historic game" played at Hagemeister Park and indicates that it was the first game that the Packers played as professionals, answer choice J makes the most sense. The other answer choices refer specifically to individuals or contain irrelevant information.

57. The best answer is C. This question requires you to express the idea clearly and concisely. The stadium is "named" Lambeau Field, so answer choice C is best. The other answer choices are awkward or contain redundant information.

58. The best answer is G. This question requires you to express the idea clearly and concisely. The words *legendary* and *entrepreneurial* refer to the team's founder, Curly Lambeau. Eliminate answer choice F because it is awkward and wordy. Answer choice H suggests that the "legend," not Curly Lambeau, was entrepreneurial, so it should be eliminated. The stadium was named after Curly Lambeau, not his "legendary entrepreneurship." Eliminate answer choice J.

59. The best answer is A. This question requires you to determine the correct use of commas. A good rule-of-thumb when it comes to commas is to use them where you would naturally pause when reading the sentence. There are no natural pauses in this sentence, so no commas are needed.

60. The best answer is H. This question requires you to determine the main idea of the essay. The essay focuses primarily on the beginnings of the Green Bay Packers, and doesn't really have anything to do with any economic influence the team may have had on the city of Green Bay.

PASSAGE V

61. The best answer is C. The sentence following the sentence containing the underlined portion explains how the author and her friend ended up at the Starfish Inn. The conjunction *because of* implies that the reason they ended up at the Starfish Inn was their own irresponsibility. Answer choice C makes the most sense.

62. The best answer is G. The coordinate conjunction *and* suggests that, in addition to it being their freshman year of college, the friends wanted to get away for spring break. *Yet* and *but* suggest a contrast that doesn't exist, so eliminate answer choices F and H. The word *where* suggests a specific location; freshman year of college is not a location, so eliminate answer choice J.

63. The best answer is A. The sentence as it is makes the most sense. Since the action took place in the past, you can eliminate answer choice D, which suggests a future action. It does not make sense that the information booth stopped the girls, so eliminate answer choice B. Nothing in the paragraph suggests that the girls "had to stop in" the information booth.

64. The best answer is G. It is idiomatic to say "secure lodging," so answer choice G is best. The other answer choices are not commonly used and do not convey an appropriate image based on the context of the passage.

65. The best answer is B. The sentence implies that the girls had a small budget, since they could not afford the hotel rates. Eliminate answer choice A. Answer choices C and D contain irrelevant information that does not add anything significant to the passage, so they should be eliminated as well.

66. The best answer is H. The phrase *that is* indicates that the preceding paragraph explains how the girls came to stay at the Starfish Inn. *That's* is the contraction of *that is* and is the best selection. *This is* suggests that the explanation will follow the sentence containing the underlined portion, so eliminate answer choice G. *There's* is the conjunction of *there is*, so both answer choice F and answer choice J should be eliminated.

67. **The best answer is A.** The word *where* indicates a location. The girls dragged their luggage to the room (the location) and then opened the door. The remaining answer choices create incomplete sentences and should be eliminated.

68. **The best answer is J.** This question requires you to select the correct punctuation to use, while maintaining the meaning of the sentence. A semicolon should be followed by an independent clause, which is the case in answer choice J. Since the phrase. *The place looked like it hadn't been redecorated since 1975!* is an independent clause, you cannot use a comma. This creates what is called a comma splice, so eliminate answer choice G. By the same token, you should capitalize the word *the* inside the parentheses, so answer choice H is incorrect.

69. **The best answer is C.** The correct word to use in this sentence will be a noun. *Determining*, *determine*, and *determined* are always used as either verbs or adjectives, so these answer choices should be eliminated. *Determination* is a noun, so answer choice C is correct.

70. **The best answer is G.** The relative pronoun *which* should be preceded by a comma in this case because it refers to a specific television set. Eliminate answer choices H and J. If two adjectives modify a noun in the same way, they are called coordinate adjectives. Coordinate adjectives can be joined with *and*. *Rusty* and *old* are coordinate adjectives, so there should be a comma separating them.

71. **The best answer is A.** In order to maintain parallelism in the sentence, the verb forms should match. The verbs *equipped* and *reminded*

are past tense, so the past tense verb *kept* is correct. *Keep* is a plural verb, and *grandpa* is a singular noun, so you should eliminate answer choice D.

72. **The best answer is J.** It makes the most sense to place Sentence 5 immediately before Sentence 4, because Sentence 5 introduces the "kitchenette" and Sentence 4 provides some additional information about the "kitchenette." The sentence would be inappropriate placed anywhere else in the paragraph.

73. **The best answer is B.** The writer and her friend are originally very disappointed with the condition of the motel room. However, they decide to "make the best of it and enjoy" themselves. This suggests that they took a bad situation and turned it into a good one. The selection that best acknowledges this shift is answer choice B.

74. **The best answer is J.** This question requires you to identify the main idea of the essay. The essay is primarily about the difficulties that the friends encountered on their trip and how they ended up staying at a subpar motel. Even though the motel was called the Starfish Inn, any information included in the passage about actual starfish would be irrelevant.

75. **The best answer is C.** Although the essay does provide an example of what could go wrong if you don't make reservations before going on vacation, it does not fully discuss possible hazards of being unprepared for a vacation. The essay is a humorous account of being forced to stay at a dilapidated motel, answer choice C.

Mathematics Test Explanations

1. **The correct answer is B.** This is a basic algebra problem that requires you to solve for x. Isolate the variable, x, on one side of the equation, as follows:

   (1) $5x - 6 = 12$

   (2) $5x = 18$

   (3) $x = \dfrac{18}{5}$, answer choice B.

2. **The correct answer is G.** This question tests your ability to recognize and apply the distributive property. According to the distributive property, for any numbers a, b, and c, $c(a + b) = ca + cb$. If you distribute the a value, you get $ab - a2c$, or $ab - 2ac$, answer choice G.

3. **The correct answer is A.** The first step in solving this problem is to determine what the difference is between the consecutive numbers. You are given 2 consecutive numbers, 3 and 10, which differ by 7. Think of the numbers as being on a number line. Since the first number must be 7 units from the number 3, and the numbers are in ascending order, the first number must be 7 units to the left of 3 on the number line. Count backwards 7 units from 3 and you will arrive at -4. Since only answer choice A includes -4 in the first blank, answer choice A must be correct.

4. **The correct answer is G.** To find the average price that Diane paid per DVD, you must divide the total dollar amount that Diane paid for the DVDs by the number of DVDs that Diane bought. The total dollar amount that Diane paid for the DVDs can be set up like this:

   (1) 1 DVD for $20.00 + 5 DVDs for $8.49 each

   (2) $20.00 + 5($8.49)

   You know from information in the problem that Diane purchased a total of 6 DVDs. Divide the total dollar amount that she paid, $20.00 + 5($8.49), by 6:

   (3) $\dfrac{\$20.00 + 5(\$8.49)}{6}$, answer choice G.

5. **The correct answer is D.** The easiest way to solve this problem is to work backwards. Since $15.00 was $\dfrac{1}{2}$ of what remained from Sunday, then there must have been $15.00 \cdot 2$, or $30.00 remaining from Sunday. Since Stephanie spent $\dfrac{1}{2}$ of the money on Sunday and still had $30.00 remaining, $30.00 must be $\dfrac{1}{2}$ of the money that she started out with on Sunday. This means that she must have

started out with $60.00 on Sunday. Since she spent $\dfrac{1}{3}$ of her pay on Saturday and still had $60.00 left, $60.00 must be $\dfrac{2}{3}$ of the money that she started out with on Saturday. Calculate the amount of money that she started out with on Saturday (x):

   (1) $60 = \dfrac{2}{3}x$

   (2) $\dfrac{60}{x} = \dfrac{2}{3}$; cross-multiply and solve for x.

   (3) $2x = 180$

   (4) $x = 90$

   Stephanie received $90.00 originally, answer choice D.

6. **The correct answer is H.** The first step in this problem is to multiply the coefficients of the like terms. In other words, multiply the coefficients of the x's ($2 \cdot 3 \cdot 3 = 18$), then multiply the coefficients of the y's ($1 \cdot 1 = 1$). The solution must contain $18x$, so eliminate answer choices F and G. Now look at the exponents. The rule of exponents states that when you multiply numbers with exponents, you should add the values of the exponents. Therefore, $x^3 \cdot x^2 \cdot x^2 = x^7$, and $y^2 \cdot y = y^3$, since y has an exponent of 1. This means that the solution must be $18x^7y^3$, answer choice H.

7. **The correct answer is B.** According to the problem, the fence completely encloses the garden. This means that it goes all the way around the garden. Therefore, the length of the fence must be equal to the perimeter of the garden. One formula for calculating the perimeter of a rectangle is $2l(\text{length}) + 2w(\text{width})$. Plug the numbers from the problem into this formula:

   (1) $2(60) + 2(25) =$

   (2) $120 + 50 = 170$, answer choice B.

8. **The correct answer is G.** Simply plug -6 in for x wherever x appears in the equation and solve the equation. Don't forget to keep track of the negative signs!

   (1) $-(-6^2) - 2(-6) + 21 =$

   (2) $-(36) - (-12) + 21 =$

   (3) $-36 + 12 + 21 = -3$, answer choice G.

9. **The correct answer is D.** Substitute the value for the radius given in the problem, 2, into the equation and solve:

   (1) $V = \dfrac{4}{3}\pi r^3$

(2) $V = \frac{4}{3}\pi(2)^3$

(3) $V = \frac{4}{3}\pi 8$

(4) $V = (8)\left(\frac{4}{3}\right)\pi$

(5) $V = \frac{32}{3}\pi$

(6) $V = 10.67\pi$

You also need to know that π is approximately equal to 3.14. Multiply 10.67 by 3.14 and round: $10.67 \cdot 3.14 = 33.5$, which means that the volume, to the nearest cubic inch, is 34, answer choice D.

10. **The correct answer is K.** This problem tests your ability to recognize and apply the distributive property; however, you must work backwards. According to the distributive property, for any numbers a, b, and c, $c(a+b)=ca+cb$. In this problem, since 2 is the common factor for both 4 and 2, you can "factor out" 2. Eliminate answer choices F and J, which have incorrectly factored out 4. Once you factor out 2, the expression will look like this: $2(2c-d)$, answer choice K.

11. **The correct answer is D.** The first step in solving this problem is to calculate the amount of money that you earn each day for mowing lawns:

(1) $95.00 (total amount earned per day)
      − $20.00 (fixed amount earned per day) =
      $75.00 (amount earned for lawns mowed).

Next, calculate the amount that you earn per lawn that you mow:

(2) $75.00 (amount earned for lawns mowed) ÷ 5 (number of lawns mowed) = $15.00 (amount earned per lawn mowed).

Now determine the amount that you will earn today for mowing the extra lawns:

(3) 2 (additional number of lawns mowed) · $15.00 (amount earned per lawn mowed) = $30.00 (additional income for the day).

Finally, add this amount to your fixed daily earnings:

(4) $95.00 + $30.00 = $125.00, answer choice D.

12. **The correct answer is G.** In the expression $4x + 2x + y - x$, $4x$ and $2x$ and $-x$ are like terms and can be added together:

(1) $4x + 2x + (-x) = 5x$

The term with x and the term with y cannot be added because they contain different variables, so the simplified form of $4x + 2x + y - x$ is $5x + y$, answer choice G.

13. **The correct answer is E.** The slope-intercept form of the equation of a line is $y = mx + b$. If y equals 0, and the slope of the line is 1, then $x = 3$ could be the equation of a line, so eliminate answer choice A. Answer choice E is actually the equation for a parabola, which is NOT a line, so answer choice E is correct.

14. **The correct answer is J.** In order to solve this problem you must know that there are 360° in a circle. The minute hand of a clock moves halfway around the face of the clock in 30 minutes; therefore, the minute hand moves 360° ÷ 2, or 180°, answer choice J.

15. **The correct answer is D.** To solve this equation, set each element of the equations in the answer choices equal to 0 and solve for x. When you get the solutions 5 and 6, that will be the correct answer.

(1) $(x-6)=0$; $x=6$ and $(x+5)=0$; $x=-5$; eliminate answer choice A.

(2) $(x+6)=0$; $x=-6$ and $(x+5)=0$; $x=-5$; eliminate answer choice B.

(3) $(x+6)=0$; $x=-6$ and $(x-5)=0$; $x=5$; eliminate answer choice C.

(4) $(x-5)=0$; $x=5$ and $(x-6)=0$; $x=6$; answer choice D is correct.

16. **The correct answer is H.** The first step in selecting the correct answer to this problem is to recognize that x cannot be less than 180. This means that answer choices F and G can be eliminated. To solve this problem mathematically, set up a proportion:

(1) 180 is to x as 75% is to 100%.

(2) $\frac{180}{x} = \frac{75}{100}$; cross-multiply and solve for x.

(3) $75x = 18,000$

(4) $x = 240$, answer choice H.

17. **The correct answer is C.** To find the total number of seats in the entire conference room, you must multiply the number of rows, $(2r+s)$, by the number of seats in each row, $(4t)$, using the rules of the distributive property. According to the distributive property, for any numbers a, b, and c, $c(a+b)=ca+cb$.

(1) $(4t)(2r+s)=(8tr)+(4ts)$, answer choice C.

18. **The correct answer is G.** The first step in solving this problem is to calculate the amount of money Tony's friend will donate for the first 25 miles that Tony runs:

(1) 25 miles · $0.09 = $2.25.

Next, calculate the amount of money Tony's friend will donate for the remaining miles:

(2) 63 miles (Tony's goal) − 25 miles = 38 miles

(3) 38 miles · $0.07 = $2.66.

Now, add the 2 amounts together to get the total:

(4) $2.25 + $2.66 = $4.91, answer choice G.

19. **The correct answer is D.** The absolute value of any number is always positive. Therefore, even if x is a negative number, the absolute value of x will be a positive value. Eliminate answer choice A, because x does not have to be greater than zero. By the same token, x can be greater than or less than y, because the absolute value of x will always be a positive number. So even if $x = -3$ and $y = 2$, the inequality given in the problem will be true. Eliminate answer choices B and E. The only instance in which the absolute value of x could possibly be greater than the absolute value of y is when x is not equal to y, answer choice D.

20. **The correct answer is G.** An expression is undefined when the denominator equals 0. Set the denominator equal to 0 and solve for x:

(1) $100 - 4x^2 = 0$

(2) $100 = 4x^2$

(3) $25 = x^2$

(4) $5 = x$, answer choice G.

21. **The correct answer is E.** In order to solve this problem you must know that π is approximately equal to 3.14. The next step is to find the value of the fraction $\frac{5}{2}$. To do this, divide the numerator (5) by the denominator (2): $5 \div 2 = 2.5$. Now, put the values in order from least to greatest: $2.5 \left(\frac{5}{2}\right) < 3 < 3.14$, answer choice E.

22. **The correct answer is H.** The best approach to this problem is to extend the sides of the shaded square into the nonshaded square, as shown below:

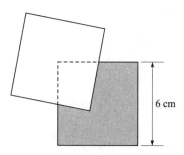

6 cm

By doing this you will see that the shaded region is $\frac{3}{4}$ of one of the squares. Since the squares have the same dimensions, calculate the area of the shaded square: Area of a square = side². Each side is equal to 6 centimeters, so the area is 6^2, or 36 square centimeters. Multiply the total area of the square, 36, by $\frac{3}{4}$ to get the area of the shaded region: $36 \cdot \frac{3}{4} = \frac{108}{4}$, which is 27, answer choice H. Once you determined that the shaded region was $\frac{3}{4}$ of the total area, 36, you could have eliminated answer choices F and G as being too small, and answer choices J and K as being too big, leaving you with answer choice H.

23. **The correct answer is B.** Similar triangles have the same shape and the same proportions. The perimeter of the first triangle is $3 + 4 + 5$, or 12 inches. You are given that a similar triangle has a perimeter of 36, which is 3 times the perimeter of the first triangle. Therefore, each side in the second triangle must be 3 times the length of the corresponding side in the first triangle. Since the shortest side of the first triangle is 3 inches, the shortest side of the second triangle must be $3 \cdot 3$, or 9 inches, answer choice B.

24. **The correct answer is F.** To find all of the solutions of the expression $x^2 - 6x = 16$, first put it in the correct quadratic form by subtracting 16 from both sides: $x^2 - 6x - 16 = 0$. Now you can factor the polynomial $x^2 - 6x - 16$:

(1) $(x + \_)(x - \_) = 0$.

Find two factors of −16 that, when added together give you −6, and plug them into the solution sets:

(2) $(x + 2)(x - 8) = 0$.

Now, solve for x:

(3) $(x + 2) = 0$, so $x = -2$

(4) $(x - 8) = 0$, so $x = 8$.

The solutions of $x^2 + 2x = 8$ are −2 and 8, answer choice F.

25. **The correct answer is B.** The first step in solving this problem is to calculate 30% of $14.95. Convert 30% to 0.30, its decimal equivalent, then multiply $14.95 by 0.30:

(1) $14.95(0.30) = $4.485, rounded to the nearest cent is $4.49.

Next, subtract the amount off ($4.49) from the regular price of the CD ($14.95):

(2) $\$14.95 - \$4.49 = \$10.46$, answer choice B.

26. The correct answer is G. When exponents are raised to an exponential power, the rules state that you must multiply the exponents by the power to which they are raised. In this problem, x is raised to the $(7a - 2)$ power. This exponent is then cubed, so you should multiply $7a - 2$ by 3: $3(7a - 2) = 21a - 6$. You now have the equation $x^{21a - 6} = x^{57}$. Since the coefficients are equal (x), the exponents must also be equal, so $21a - 6 = 57$. Solve for a:

(1) $21a - 6 = 57$

(2) $21a = 63$

(3) $a = 3$, answer choice G.

27. The correct answer is C. The key to solving this problem is to recognize that, if $(3r - s)^2 = 36$, then $3r - s$ must equal 6, because 6^2 equals 36. And, if $3r - s = 6$, then $-s = -3r + 6$ and $s = 3r - 6$. Since you are given that $rs = 45$, you can substitute $3r - 6$ for s and get $r(3r - 6) = 45$.

Use the Distributive Property:

(1) $r(3r - 6) = 45$

(2) $3r^2 - 6r = 45$

When you put it in standard quadratic equation form, you get $3r^2 - 6r - 45 = 0$. Factoring this gives you $(3r + 9)(r - 5) = 0$. Solve for r:

(3) $(3r + 9)(r - 5) = 0$

(4) $r = -3$ and 5

If you plug 5 in for r, you get $5s = 45$, or $s = 9$. Now plug 5 in for r and 9 in for s to see if it fits the other equation. $3(5) - 9 = 6$; it does fit. If you plug -3 in for r, you get $-3s = 45$, or $s = -15$. Now plug -3 in for r and -15 in for s and see if it fits the other equation. $3(-3) - (-15) = 6$. Now plug -3 in for r and -15 in for s and see if it fits the other equation. $3(-3) - (-15) = 5$. It also fits. Substitute 5 for r and 9 for s in the final equation:

(5) $r^2 + s^2 = 9^2 + 5^2 = 81 + 25 = 106$, answer choice C.

Substitute -3 for r and -15 for s in the final equation.

(6) $r^2 + s^2 = (-3)^2 + (-15)^2 = 3 + 225 = 234$.

Since this is not an answer choice, the correct answer must be C.

28. The correct answer is J. To solve this problem you should use the Midpoint Formula. The midpoint of a line, M, is equal to the average of the x-coordinates and the average of the y-coordinates. The formula looks like this:

$$M = \left(\frac{x_1 + x_2}{2}, \frac{y_1 + y_2}{2}\right)$$

You are given 1 point on the line, $(-5, 3)$ and the midpoint of the line $(9, -1)$. Since the midpoint is $(9, -1)$ the average of the x-coordinates is 9, and the average of the y-coordinates is -1. Set up equations to solve for the other endpoint:

(1) $9 = \dfrac{-5 + x_2}{2}$

(2) $18 = -5 + x_2$

(3) $23 = x_2$

The x-coordinate of the other endpoint is 23. Since only answer choice J includes an x-coordinate of 23, it must be the correct answer. If you solve for the y-coordinate in the same way that you solved for the x-coordinate, you will get -5.

29. The correct answer is C. A circle centered at (a, b) with a radius r, has the equation $(x - a)^2 + (y - b)^2 = r^2$. Based on this definition, a circle with the equation $(x - 3)^2 + (y - 4)^2 = 25$ would have a radius of $\sqrt{25}$. If $r^2 = 25$, then $r = \sqrt{25}$, or 5, answer choice C.

30. The correct answer is J. The tangent of any acute angle is calculated by dividing the length of the side opposite the acute angle by the length of the side adjacent to the acute angle $\left(\tan = \dfrac{\text{opp}}{\text{adj}}\right)$. In this problem, the length of the side opposite angle α is r, and the length of the side adjacent to angle α is s. Therefore, the tan of angle α is $\dfrac{r}{s}$, answer choice J.

31. The correct answer is E. When you subtract fractions you must first find the common denominator. Multiply the denominators to get $4x$ as the common denominator, then solve for x:

(1) $\dfrac{1}{x} - \dfrac{3}{4} =$

(2) $\dfrac{(4)(1)}{(4)(x)} - \dfrac{(3)(x)}{(4)(x)} =$

(3) $\dfrac{4}{4x} - \dfrac{3x}{4x} = \dfrac{4 - 3x}{4x}$, answer choice E.

32. The correct answer is J. The figure in the problem represents 2 parallel lines cut by 2 parallel transversals. The angles created as a result have special properties. Where each of the parallel lines is cut by a transversal, there are 2 pairs of vertical, or opposite angles. Each angle in the pair is congruent to, or equal to, the other angle in the pair. Therefore, where m cuts o and also where it cuts p, two 40° angles are formed, which means that angle $\alpha = 40°$; in addition, two 140° are formed that are adjacent to the 40° angles, since a straight line has 180°. So, since the same angles are created where n cuts o and p, and angle β is opposite of the 140° angle that is adjacent to angle α, angle β must be equal to 140°, answer choice J.

33. **The correct answer is E.** A square is a parallelogram with 4 right angles and 4 sides of the same length. The perimeter of a square is the distance around the square, or the sum of all 4 sides. Since the perimeter is given as 64, the length of each side of the square must be $64 \div 4$, or 16. This means that radii DA and DC are both equal to 16. The area of a circle is calculated using the formula $A = \pi r^2$. Plug 16 in for r and solve:

(1) $A = \pi r^2 = \pi (16)^2$

(2) $A = \pi 256$, or 256π, answer choice E.

34. **The correct answer is K.** In order to solve this problem you must recognize that $1\frac{3}{4}$ is exactly halfway between 1.5 (which equals $1\frac{1}{2}$) and 2 on the number line. This means that the point closest to $1\frac{3}{4}$ on the number line is point E, answer choice K.

35. **The correct answer is D.** By definition, the legs of a 45°–45°–90° have the same length, and the hypotenuse is $\sqrt{2}$ times as long as either leg. Since you are given that the length of 2 legs is 3 meters, and the length of the third leg, the hypotenuse, is $3\sqrt{2}$ meters, this must be a 45°–45°–90° triangle, answer choice D. Also, since the measure of the angles in a triangle must equal 180°, you can eliminate answer choices B and E.

36. **The correct answer is H.** A quadrilateral is a closed 2-dimensional figure with 4 sides that are line segments. A curved line is not a line segment, therefore the figure shown in answer choice H is NOT a quadrilateral.

37. **The correct answer is D.** To solve this problem, first list all of the distinct factors of 45: 1, 3, 5, 9, 15, 45. All of these numbers divide evenly into 45. Next, list all of the distinct factors of 60: 1, 2, 3, 4, 5, 6, 10, 12, 15, 30, 60. All of these numbers divide evenly into 60. The only factors that both 45 and 60 have in common are 1, 3,

5, and 15. Since you are told that p is NOT a factor of either 9 or 10, you can eliminate 1, 3, and 5, which factor evenly into either 9 or 10. This leaves you with a value for p of 15. When you add the digits $(1 + 5)$ you get 6, answer choice D.

38. **The correct answer is J.** The slope of a line is defined as the change in the y-values over the change in the x-values in the standard (x, y) coordinate plane. Slope can be calculated by using the following formula: $\frac{(y_1 - y_2)}{(x_1 - x_2)}$. Any line perpendicular to the x-axis is a vertical line: The x values do not change (see diagram).

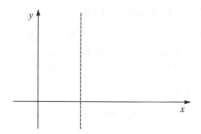

The slope of a vertical line is undefined, answer choice J, because there is no change in x, which means that the denominator $(x_1 - x_2)$ is 0.

39. **The correct answer is C.** The slope-intercept form of a line is $y = mx + b$, where m is the slope. In order to determine which line has the largest slope, you must first put all of the answer choices into the slope-intercept form. Answer choices A, B, and C are already in the slope-intercept form. The slopes of those lines are 3, 1, and 7, respectively. Calculate the slope of answer choices D and E:

(1) $3y = 9x + 6$
(2) $y = \frac{9}{3}x + \frac{6}{3}$; $y = 3x + 2$

Answer choice D has a slope of 3.

(1) $2y = 8x - 8$
(2) $y = \frac{8}{2}x - \frac{8}{2}$; $y = 4x - 4$

Answer choice E has a slope of 4. Therefore, the line with the largest slope is answer choice C, with a slope of 7.

40. **The correct answer is F.** The tangent of any acute angle is calculated by dividing the length of the side opposite the acute angle by the length of the side adjacent to the acute angle ($\tan = \frac{\text{opp}}{\text{adj}}$). The sine of any acute angle is calculated by dividing the length of the side opposite the acute angle by the hypotenuse ($\sin = \frac{\text{opp}}{\text{hyp}}$). In this problem, the tangent of angle β is $\frac{3}{4}$. This means that the

length of the side opposite angle β is 3 units, and the length of the side adjacent to angle β is 4 units. Therefore, by definition, the sine must be 3 units (the length of the side opposite angle β) over some number greater than 4, since the hypotenuse is always the longest side. The only answer choice that will work is $\frac{3}{5}$, answer choice F.

41. **The correct answer is D.** This problem requires you to set up a simple proportion and solve for a variable. According to information in the problem, Jenny can walk 4 miles in $m+3$ minutes. This means that she can walk 4 miles per $m+3$ minutes, or $\frac{4}{m+3}$. The question asks you to calculate the number of miles that she can walk in 15 minutes. In other words, Jenny can walk x miles per 15 minutes, or $\frac{x}{15}$; what is the value of x? Set up a proportion and solve for x:

(1) $\dfrac{4}{m+3} = \dfrac{x}{15}$

(2) $15\dfrac{(4)}{m+3} = x$

(3) $\dfrac{60}{m+3} = x$, answer choice D.

42. **The correct answer is F.** The best approach to this problem is to pick some numbers for n, plug them into the answer choices, and eliminate the answer choices that do not always yield an even number.

   (1) If $n=1$, then $4n^2 = 4(1)^2 = 4$, which is even. If $n=2$, then $4n^2 = 4(2)^2 = 16$, another even number. Because you are multiplying n^2 by 4, an even number, the result will always be even. Answer choice F is correct. Check the other answer choices:

   (2) If $n=2$, then $3n^2 + 1 = 3(2)^2 + 1 = 12 + 1 = 13$, which is odd. Eliminate answer choice G.

   (3) If $n=1$, then $5n^2 = 5(1)^2 = 5$, which is odd. Eliminate answer choice H.

   (4) If $n=1$, then $3n = 3(1) = 3$, which is odd. Eliminate answer choice J.

   (5) If $n=3$, then $n^2 - 2n = (3)^2 - 2(3) = 3$, which is odd. Eliminate answer choice K.

   Answer choice F is the only choice that will always give you an even number for any value of n.

43. **The correct answer is D.** The perimeter of a triangle is calculated by adding together the lengths of all 3 sides. Based on the measures of the angles given, you can draw triangle CAB as shown below:

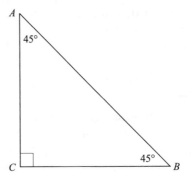

You are given that $\overline{AC}$, one of the legs, is 12 units long. Because this is a 45°–45°–90° triangle, the length of the other leg, $\overline{CB}$ is also 12 units long. In a 45°–45°–90° triangle, the hypotenuse is $\sqrt{2}$ times longer than either leg. Therefore, the length of the hypotenuse is $12\sqrt{2}$. Add together the lengths of all 3 sides to find the perimeter:

(1) $12 + 12 + 12\sqrt{2} = 24 + 12\sqrt{2}$, answer choice D.

44. **The correct answer is J.** The circumference of a circle is calculated using the formula $C = 2\pi r$. You are given that the circumference, C, is equal to 42π. This means that 42 must be equal to $2r$, so r must be 21. The area of a circle is calculated using the formula $A = \pi r^2$. When you substitute 21 for r, you find that the area, A, $= \pi 21^2$, which equals $\pi 441$, or $\pi 441$, answer choice J.

45. **The correct answer is B.** The area of a rectangle is calculated by multiplying the length by the width ($A = w \times l$). Calculate the area of the first rectangle as follows:

   (1) Set the width equal to x, and the length equal to $3x$.

   (2) Area of rectangle$_1 = x(3x) = 3x^2$.

   Now calculate the area of the second triangle:

   (1) The length stays the same, so the length $= 3x$, but the width is tripled, so the width $= 3x$ as well.

   (2) Area of rectangle$_2 = (3x)(3x) = 9x^2$.

   The area of the second triangle is $9x^2$, which is 3 times greater than the area of the first triangle ($3x^2$), answer choice B.

46. The correct answer is F. Systems of equations will have an infinite number of solutions when the equations are equal to each other. The first step in solving this problem is to recognize that the second equation is exactly 3 times the value of the first equation: $36x = 3(12x)$, $57y = 3(19y)$, so $30a$ must equal $3(20)$. Solve for a:

(1) $30a = 3(20)$

(2) $30a = 60$

(3) $a = 2$, answer choice F.

47. The correct answer is B. Logarithms are used to indicate exponents of certain numbers called bases. This problem tells you that log to the base x of 2 equals 169. By definition, $\log_a b = c$ if $a^c = b$. So, the question is, when x is raised to the power of 2, you get 169; what is x? By definition, $\log_x 169 = 2$ when $x^2 = 169$. Since the square root of 169 is 13, answer choice B is correct.

48. The correct answer is G. To find the sum of the 2 sets of numbers, add the entries in A to the corresponding entries in B. The sum of the entries in the first row is $2 + 1$ or 3, and $-2 + 3$, or 1. The first row of A + B will include 3 and 1. Only answer choice G contains these values, so it must be correct. When you add the entries in the second row ($3 + -2 = 1$; $2 + 4 = 6$) you will find that the sums correspond to the second row of $A + B$ in answer choice G.

49. The correct answer is C. The area of a parallelogram is calculated by using the formula $A = (b \times h)$, where b is the base, and h is the height. The length of the sides 15, is not relevant in calculating the area. Plug the given values into the formula:

(1) $A = (6 \cdot 12)$

(2) $A = 72$, answer choice C.

50. The correct answer is G. You can express the phrase *the x-coordinate is 3 more than twice the corresponding y-coordinate* as follows: $x = 2y + 3$. The slope–intercept form for the equation of a line is $y = mx + b$, where m is the slope. Put the equation in the slope-intercept form:

(1) $x = 2y + 3$

(2) $-2y = -x + 3$

(3) $y = \frac{1}{2}x - \frac{3}{2}$; the slope is $\frac{1}{2}$, answer choice G.

51. The correct answer is D. The area of a triangle is $\frac{1}{2}(bh)$, where b is the base, and h is the height. You can determine the base by measuring the distance along the x-axis, and you can determine the height by measuring the distance along the y-axis:

(1) The distance between -4 and 4 on the x-axis is 8 units; likewise, the distance between -2 and 6 on the x-axis is 8 units. The length of the base is 8.

(2) The distance between 6 and -8 on the y-axis is 14. The height is 14.

Now plug these values into the formula for the area of a triangle:

(1) $A = \frac{1}{2}(bh)$

(2) $A = \frac{1}{2}(8 \cdot 14)$

(3) $A = \frac{1}{2}(112) = 56$, answer choice D.

52. The correct answer is F. If $XYZ = 1$, then Z cannot equal 0. If Z (or X or Y, for that matter) were 0, then XYZ would equal 0. Both sides of the equation can be divided by Z, which gives you $XY = \frac{1}{Z}$, answer choice F. Answer choice G is incorrect because 2 of the values *could* be -1. Answer choice H is incorrect because 2 of the values *could* be fractions and the third value *could* be a whole number, that, when multiplied by the fractions give you 1. Answer choices J and K are incorrect because you have already determined that none of the values can be equal to 0.

53. The correct answer is D. The slope-intercept form of a line is $y = mx + b$, where m is the slope and b is the y-intercept. Put the equation given in the problem in the slope-intercept form:

(1) $5x + y = 9$

(2) $y = -5x + 9$; the y-intercept is 9, answer choice D.

54. The correct answer is H. If the average of 7 integers is 24, then the total must be $7 \cdot 24$, or 168. If the average of 8 integers is 31, then the total must be $8 \cdot 31$, or 248. Since you are adding an 8th integer to the set, the value of the 8th integer will be the difference between 248 and 168: $248 - 168 = 80$, answer choice H.

55. **The correct answer is B.** The area of a rectangle is calculated by multiplying the width by the length ($w \times l$). You are given that the length is 2 feet less than twice the width. Set the width equal to x; the length is then $2x - 2$. Plug these values into the equation for the area of a rectangle:

(1) $(x)(2x - 2) = 180$

(2) $2x^2 - 2x = 180$

Put this equation into the quadratic form and factor to find the solutions for x:

(3) $2x^2 - 2x - 180 = 0$

(4) $(2x + \underline{\hspace{0.5cm}})(x - \underline{\hspace{0.5cm}}) = 0$

(5) $(2x + 18)(x - 10) = 0$

(6) $(2x + 18) = 0$; $2x = -18$; $x = -9$

(7) $(x - 10) = 0$; $x = 10$

Since the width of a room cannot have a negative value, the width must be 10, answer choice B.

56. **The correct answer is K.** The problem asks for an expression that represents the *number* of pounds of apples sold, not the *cost* of the pounds of apples sold. The easiest way to understand the problem is to make a table and notice the pattern.

Change is $ per Pound of Apples	Number of Pounds of Apples
Original price of $1.19	625 pounds of apples sold (given in the problem)
Decrease by $0.01 = $1.18	$625 - 35(1) = 625 - 35$ pounds of apples sold
Decrease by $0.02 = $1.17	$625 - 35(2) = 625 - 70$ pounds of apples sold
Decrease by $0.03 = $1.16	$625 - 35(3) = 625 - 105$ pounds of apples sold
Decrease by $x = $1.19 - x$	$625 - 35x$ pounds of apples sold
Decrease by $6(x) = $1.19 - 6(x)$	$625 - 35(6x) = 625 - 210x$ pounds of apples sold

Answer F would be correct if the question asked for the price of the apples. Since the problem asks for the number of apples, the correct answer is K.

57. **The correct answer is A.** First, draw the picture of the wading pool according to the information given in the problem, where the distance from the edge of the pool to the edge of the long side

of the rectangular region is 4 feet. The distance from the edge of the pool to the edge of the short side of the rectangular region can be anything greater than 4, but it is not necessary to know this distance to solve the problem:

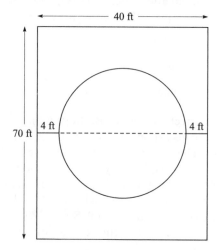

Now you can determine the diameter of the circular pool. The diameter is the maximum distance from 1 point on a circle to another (the dashed line). Since the short side of the rectangular region is 40 feet, and the distance from the edge of the circular pool to each edge of the long sides of the rectangular region is set at 4 feet, the diameter of the circle must be 40 feet $- 2(4$ feet$)$, or 40 feet $- 8$ feet, or 32 feet. The question asks for the radius of the pool, which is $\frac{1}{2}$ of the diameter. $32 \div 2 = 16$, answer choice A.

58. **The correct answer is G.** To solve this problem, start by drawing 3 parallel lines.

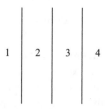

This creates 4 distinct regions, so the minimum number of distinct regions must be 4. Eliminate answer choices H, J, and K, which give the minimum number of distinct regions as 3. Now, try drawing 3 lines in other configurations, and you will see that there will always be either 6 or 7 regions:

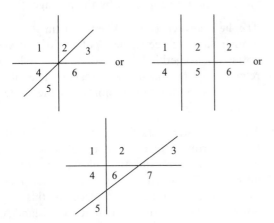

Therefore, the correct answer is 4, 6, or 7 distinct regions, answer choice G.

59. **The correct answer is A.** The rules of the game state that a player is a winner if 2 marbles drawn have the same 10s digit. The player has already drawn the marble numbered 17, which has a 1 in the 10s digit. In order to win, the player must draw another marble with a 1 in the 10s digit. The possible winning marbles are 10, 11, 12, 13, 14, 15, 16, 18, and 19. Therefore, the player has 9 chances to draw a winning marble. Since he has already drawn 1 of the 97 marbles and did not put it back, he has 9 chances out of 96 to draw a winning marble. $\frac{9}{96}$ can be reduced to $\frac{3}{32}$, answer choice A.

60. **The correct answer is F.** If 2 numbers, x and y, differ by 4, that means that $x - y = 4$. Multiplying the 2 numbers, $(x)(y)$, will yield the product. Solve the first equation for x.

(1) $x - y = 4$

(2) $x = y + 4$

Substitute the result for x in the second equation.

(3) $(y + 4)y =$

Since one of the answer choices must be the solution to that equation, plug in the answer choices, starting with the smallest value (note that the answer choices are in ascending order):

(4) $(y + 4)y = -4$

(5) $y^2 + 4y + 4 = 0$

(6) $(y + 2)^2 = 0$

(7) $y = -2$

Now, substitute -2 for y in the first equation and solve for x:

(9) $x - (-2) = 4$

(10) $x = 2$

Since $(2)(-2) = -4$ and -4 is the smallest answer available, answer choice F is correct.

Reading Test Explanations

PASSAGE I

1. **The best answer is C.** Granny makes this statement in response to Sheila's comment that, once Martin goes to school, "it will all be so much easier." This suggests that Granny was not convinced that school would challenge Martin effectively. The other answer choices are not supported by the passage.

2. **The best answer is G.** During the conversation Granny says, "I know you're tired from working long hours, but Martin isn't reciting — he's reading!" You can infer that Granny believes Sheila is too overworked to recognize Martin's gift, answer choice G.

3. **The best answer is A.** When Martin's mother says, "He even turns the pages. It's very cute!," she indicates that she doesn't actually think that he can read. This is the best example of the idea that she is unaware of his abilities. The other answer choices do not reflect Sheila's ignorance of her son's reading ability.

4. **The best answer is H.** The word *plight* is used in the first paragraph to indicate Martin's situation. Based on the context of the paragraph, his situation is not easy. Therefore, *plight* most nearly means "predicament," which refers to a difficult situation. The other answer choices are not supported by the context of the passage.

5. **The best answer is C.** Throughout the passage, Granny is clearly referred to as Martin's grandmother, so answer choice D should be eliminated. It is also made clear that Granny is Sheila's mother. Therefore, since Sheila is Martin's mother, Granny must be Martin's maternal grandmother, answer choice C.

6. **The best answer is F.** At the end of the passage, Martin's mother agrees that she will start finding out how to get to America with Martin. This best supports answer choice F.

7. **The best answer is D.** Sheila states in the passage, "I'll start finding out what I need to do to get Martin and me to America." This suggests that she understands the importance of going to America and will probably do whatever she can to help Martin succeed. The other answer choices are not supported by details in the passage.

8. **The best answer is J.** The first paragraph states that Martin's brothers are selfish boys, who "let Martin fend for himself" and "made him the target of their pranks." This suggests that Martin's brothers cared more for themselves than they did for Martin. The other answer choices are not supported by the passage.

9. **The best answer is C.** When Martin's grandmother says, "Sweetie, he's got a gift and you gotta do something with that gift," she is referring to his talent as a reader. The other answer choices are not supported by the context of the passage.

10. **The best answer is J.** The first paragraph states that "Martin spent most of his childhood in a tropical paradise" but that his "early life was difficult." The word *paradise* most often refers to a delightful or beautiful place. In this case, however, despite the fact that the island of Barbados contains the natural beauty associated with a paradise, the living conditions were not so delightful. This best supports answer choice J.

PASSAGE II

11. **The best answer is A.** The passage makes it clear that the Donner Party began its journey in 1846. According to information about the source of the passage, it was written nearly forty years later. Also, the last paragraph states that the "first days are written about by the survivors" which suggests that journal entries were discovered on which to base the conclusions made about the coverage of the Donner Party.

12. **The best answer is F.** The passage discusses the type of people who were members of the Donner Party and their experiences of the journey. Also discussed in the passage are some of the characteristics of the United States in 1846: "the almost unexplored plains, which lay between the Mississippi and the fair young land called California," "the States along the Mississippi were but sparsely settled," "the way was through almost trackless valleys waving with grass." This best supports answer choice F.

13. **The best answer is B.** According to the passage, at the time that the Donner Party began its journey, "comparatively few had dared attempt to cross the almost unexplored plains, which lay between the Mississippi and the fair young land called California." This suggests that the Donner Party was among the first to cross the country to California, answer choice B. The other answer choices are not supported by details in the passage, or they are too general to explain the relationship between the Donner Party and other pioneers.

14. The best answer is J. The passage clearly indicates that the Donner Party was attempting to reach California. The other answer choices are not supported by details in the passage.

15. The best answer is C. The third paragraph states that the "road was difficult, and in places almost unbroken." This statement does not support the idea that *unbroken* means "intact," "easy to follow," or "well-built," so you can eliminate answer choices A, B, and D. Answer choice C fits the context of the sentence, so it is correct.

16. The best answer is F. In the third paragraph, the statement is made that the "noble-hearted pioneers" of the Donner Party were enthusiastic and eager to begin their journey. Even though the journey would prove to be difficult and tragic, early on the members of the party were determined to succeed and even enjoy the experience. This best supports answer choice F.

17. The best answer is D. It is reasonable to infer that the word *train*, as it used in the passage — "the train comprised about one hundred persons" — refers to a line of wagons, answer choice D. The other answer choices are not supported by the passage.

18. The best answer is H. The fifth paragraph mentions that "in later years ... the broken fragments of wagons ... were thickly strewn on either side of the highway." Also, the discussion of the poor condition of the roads would suggest that one danger that the Donner Party faced was wagons breaking down, answer choice H. The other answer choices are not supported by details in the passage.

19. The best answer is B. The passage indicates that the Donner Party was on its way to California, but nowhere does it mention that Californians were members of the party. All of the other answer choices are listed explicitly in the passage.

20. The best answer is G. It is clearly indicated in the passage that the road conditions were poor, so it is unlikely that the Donner Party would enjoy the road conditions at any point in their journey. The last paragraph states that they did enjoy the scenery, the stops at night that included singing, and the "good-fellowship" that existed among the members.

PASSAGE III

21. The best answer is A. The narrator states in the introduction that "the unworldly experience continues to haunt my memory as I recall the unflinching gazes of Pietro Perugino's subjects staring blankly at me as I admired the power and beauty of the great Italian Renaissance master's most famous works of art." Although the narrator briefly speaks about the work of other painters in relation to Perugino, this is not the focus of the paragraph. The narrator is also not impartial about the work of Perugino. In fact, the narrator admits that Perugino is one of his favorite painters. The passage also tells very little about Perugino's life outside of his contributions to art. Eliminate answer choice B, C, and D.

22. The best answer is J. The passage does not mention Donatello as a painter. However, all of the other answer choices are explicitly identified as painters in the passage.

23. The best answer is D. Throughout the passage the narrator discussed his or her strong feelings about Perugino's art. The answer choice that best supports this main idea is answer choice D.

24. The best answer is G. *Ingenuity* is another word for *creativity*. The narrator is acknowledging that despite his or her admiration for Perugino's work, it lacked the originality of Botticelli.

25. The best answer is C. The narrator states "although the brilliance of all of the Italian Renaissance masters is undeniable, the awe-inspiring beauty of Michelangelo's work or the subtle detail of da Vinci's *Mona Lisa* cannot match the simple passion evident in Perugino's paintings." Even though Perugino's work may not show some of the technical skill of other Renaissance painters, the narrator believes Perugino's work outshines the more complicated pieces because of his devotion to and passion for his craft.

26. The best answer is J. The use of the word *eclipsed* suggests that the work of Renoir and Manet was overshadowed by Perugino's work.

27. The best answer is A. All of the following quotes appear in the passage: "In that moment, my admiration for artists like Renoir and Manet of the French Impressionist Movement, was eclipsed by the austere exquisiteness of these fifteenth-century paintings," "cannot match the simple passion evident in Perugino's paintings," "Perugino also experimented with depth and he rivaled Leonardo da Vinci in his ability to create a definite background and foreground." These statements best support answer choice A. Abstraction is not mentioned in the passage.

28. The best answer is G. The narrator writes, "I remember feeling slightly disconcerted as I looked up at the unsmiling saints, the Virgin Mary, and even Jesus as I wandered through the hushed halls of the museum." *Disconcerted* is a synonym for *unsettled*.

29. The best answer is B. The passage states that "Perugino also experimented with depth, and he rivaled Leonardo da Vinci in his ability to create a definite background and foreground." This suggests that he was as talented as Leonardo da Vinci at creating depth, which would not be a criticism.

30. The best answer is F. The passage states that "The work of da Vinci and Michelangelo is seen on postcards and reprinted on cheap posters everywhere because of its universal appeal." These are the only artists mentioned in the passage who have their work reprinted on postcards and cheap posters.

PASSAGE IV

31. The best answer is A. The passage states, in paragraph 2, that "Porcupines also swing their tails back and forth, rather like hammering nails into their adversaries." This best supports answer choice A.

32. The best answer is J. The first paragraph states that "the porcupine's mere outward appearance provides more than adequate reason for it rarely to become alarmed or excited." The passage goes on to describe the porcupine as a "threatening creature," which suggests that its appearance is what makes it threatening. The other answer choices are not supported by the passage.

33. The best answer is C. According to the passage, the porcupine, "unlike most other animals in the wild," has a threatening appearance that allows it to remain unexcited in the face of danger. The other answer choices are not supported by details in the passage.

34. The best answer is G. The author's statement that "the porcupine's mere outward appearance provides more than adequate reason for it rarely to become alarmed or excited" suggests that the porcupine moves slowly because it has no reason to move quickly, answer choice G.

35. The best answer is B. Information in the passage indicates that "a noseful or mouthful of porcupine quills" can cause "excruciating pain." This best supports answer choice B.

36. The best answer is G. According to the passage, the Yukon Department of Environment considers the porcupine useful, and believes that it has been and can be "appreciated by many." The passage goes on to give examples of the utility of the porcupine quill. This best supports answer choice G.

37. The best answer is A. While the passage mentions humans, dogs, and rodents, it specifically states that "cougars ... pose a major threat to the porcupine," answer choice A.

38. The best answer is G. The passage states that, in British Columbia, "the porcupine has developed a negative reputation due to its appetite for wood, damaging trees and even wooden buildings." This suggests that porcupines are damaging forests. The other answer choices are not supported by the passage.

39. The best answer is B. According to the passage, if a dog gets a noseful or mouthful of quills, it should be "tended to right away," so eliminate answer choice C. The passage goes on to say that extraction of the quills can "relieve the excruciating pain," so it makes sense that imbedded porcupine quills can be very painful, answer choice B.

40. The best answer is J. The scientific name for the porcupine is *Erethizon dorsatum*, which is Latin for "irritable back." The other answer choices are mentioned in the passage, but not in reference to the scientific name of the porcupine.

Science Reasoning Test Explanations

PASSAGE I

1. **The correct answer is A.** Meteorologist 1 believes that the presence of very warm air is one of the things that most influences hurricane formation. Since higher levels of CO_2 increase air temperatures, it is likely that Meteorologist 1 would suggest a direct relationship between CO_2 levels and the number of hurricanes. The graph in answer choice A shows a direct relationship — as CO_2 levels increase, so does the number of hurricanes.

2. **The correct answer is J.** Meteorologist 1 believes that higher air temperatures contribute to hurricane formations. It is given that increased levels of atmospheric CO_2 cause an increase in air temperature. Therefore, reducing the number of forests and trees, which remove CO_2 from the atmosphere, would lead to higher levels of CO_2 in the atmosphere, higher air temperatures, and an increased number of hurricanes.

3. **The correct answer is C.** According to Meteorologist 2, higher water temperatures do not necessarily lead to hurricane formation. Therefore, any evidence suggesting that hurricanes do not occur in areas of the ocean with higher water temperatures would support Meteorologist 2's viewpoint. This best supports answer choice C.

4. **The correct answer is F.** Meteorologist 1 believes that higher air and water temperatures contribute to hurricane formation. Therefore, it is likely that Meteorologist 1 would predict an increase in the number of hurricanes if both air and water temperatures increased. The other answer choices are not supported by Meteorologist 1's viewpoint.

5. **The correct answer is C.** Based on the passage, both meteorologists believe that hurricanes become stronger and more destructive with the presence of warm water and water vapor. While Meteorologist 2 does not believe that higher water temperatures cause hurricanes, the passage indicates that Meteorologist 2 does believe that higher water temperatures increase water vapor levels, which leads to an increase in wind speed.

6. **The correct answer is G.** Meteorologist 2 states that hurricanes "are not necessarily formed where the surface temperature of the ocean is warm," which best supports answer choice G.

7. **The correct answer is B.** Meteorologist 2 suggests that higher water temperatures are not a factor in hurricane formation. A good way to test this theory would be to record surface temperatures of tropical oceans and seas over time, and compare that data with the number of hurricanes recorded during the same time period, answer choice B.

PASSAGE II

8. **The correct answer is J.** To answer this question, calculate the difference in diffusion time between each pair of gases in each answer choice:

   (F) He and Kr: 13 and 43; the difference is 30 seconds
   (G) Ne and Ar: 18 and 28; the difference is 10 seconds
   (H) Kr and Rm: 43 and 73; the difference is 30 seconds
   (J) Ne and Xe: 18 and 58; the difference is 40 seconds

   The greatest difference in diffusion time occurs between Ne and Xe, answer choice J.

9. **The correct answer is A.** According to Figure 1 and Table 1, as molecular mass (a.m.u.) increases, diffusion time also increases. The other answer choices are not supported by the data.

10. **The correct answer is F.** Since, according to Table 1, He has the shortest diffusion time, it should completely diffuse first.

11. **The correct answer is C.** According to Table 1, the diffusion time of Ar is 28 seconds. Since 14 is half, or 50%, of 28, it is safe to assume that after 14 seconds, 50% of the vacuumed area will NOT have any Ar gas molecules left, answer choice C.

12. **The correct answer is J.** According to Table 1, in a 10-cubic-foot vacuumed area it takes Ne 18 seconds to diffuse. 18×3 is 54, so the volume of the vacuumed area described in the question is most likely 10×3, or 30 cubic feet, answer choice J.

PASSAGE III

13. **The correct answer is A.** Process A will be most accurate as compared to the Standard Method when the measurements obtained using Process A are similar to the measurements obtained using the Standard Method. If you look at Table 1 you see that, at a pH level of 2, the concentration of dissolved O_2 is identical using both Process A and the Standard Method. Therefore, answer choice A is correct.

14. **The correct answer is J.** The first step in answering this question is to find calcium chloride, $CaCO_3$, on Table 1. Then, see what happens to the concentration levels as you move across the table from left to right. In the Standard Method, Process A, and Process B, the concentration levels all increase significantly, which means that answer choice J is correct.

15. **The correct answer is C.** Process A will be more accurate than Process B if the measurements obtained using Process A are similar to the measurements obtained using the Standard Method. Find NH_3 on Table 1, and compare the results obtained from each method. You will see that, at each acidity level, the results obtained using Process B are closer to the results obtained using the Standard Method. Therefore, you can eliminate answer choices A and B, which both say that Process A is more accurate. Answer choice C is most consistent with the data in Table 1, so it is correct.

16. **The correct answer is F.** First, find CO_2 on Table 1, and look at the concentration levels obtained by using Process A. You will see that, from acidity levels 2 through 5, there is a gradual reduction in CO_2 concentration, but at an acidity level of 6, the CO_2 concentration jumps up dramatically. This is best represented by the graph in answer choice F.

17. **The correct answer is D.** To solve this problem, look at Table 1 and determine the acidity level that corresponds the closest to the concentration values given in the problem for Process A. The data best supports answer choice D.

PASSAGE IV

18. **The correct answer is G.** To answer this question, look at Table 1 and Table 2, and determine which pesticide application resulted in the lowest number of fleas remaining. Note that the average number of fleas per dog before treatment in both experiments was 57. In both experiments, application of Pesticide B resulted in fewer fleas than did application of Pesticide A, or Pesticide A+B. Therefore, answer choice G is correct.

19. **The correct answer is D.** According to Table 2, dogs with short coats had fewer ticks after all pesticide applications than did dogs with long coats. You can eliminate answer choices A and B. Now, look at Table 2 to determine whether Pesticide A or Pesticide B most reduced the number of ticks on a dog. Since all of the dogs started out with an average of 13 ticks before

treatment, and the Pesticide A application resulted in only 4 ticks per dog, while the Pesticide B application resulted in 10 ticks per dog, answer choice D must be correct.

20. **The correct answer is H.** It is clear based on the data in Table 2 that shorter coat length leads to increased effectiveness of all pesticides, answer choice H.

21. **The correct answer is A.** The passage indicates that Pesticide A+B shampoo contained only 50% of each pesticide, while the other shampoos contained 100% of either Pesticide A or Pesticide B. Therefore, the most likely reason for the relative ineffectiveness of Pesticide A+B is that the two pesticides reduced each other's effectiveness, answer choice A. The other answer choices are not supported by the passage.

22. **The correct answer is G.** Based on Table 3, an average coat length of 2 inches would be considered long. On Table 2, find the average number of ticks per dog 24 hours after application of Pesticide A. That number is 7, answer choice G.

PASSAGE V

23. **The correct answer is C.** The passage defines half-life as the "amount of time it takes for half of the atoms in a sample to decay." Locate the line on the graph in Figure 1 that corresponds to Fluorine 22, and find the time at which half, or 50%, of the atoms are remaining in the sample. The half-life of Fluorine 22 is 4.2 seconds, answer choice C.

24. **The correct answer is H.** The passage indicates that radioactive decay is "a natural process by which an atom of a radioactive isotope spontaneously decays into another element." The other answer choices are not supported by details in the passage.

25. **The correct answer is A.** Table 1 indicates that lower decay energy values result in lower particle velocity, answer choice A.

26. **The correct answer is G.** The decay energy of Cerium 53 into Lanthanum 127 (6.100) is closest to the decay energy of Oxygen 22 into Fluorine 22 (6.490). Therefore, it is likely that the particle velocity will be similar to Fluorine 22 as well. This best supports answer choice G.

27. **The correct answer is B.** Oxygen 22 and Neon 22 will have the same percent of atoms remaining at the point where the lines representing each

product cross on the graph. When you locate the appropriate lines, you see that they cross at 4.5 seconds, answer choice B.

28. **The correct answer is H.** Both of the curves mentioned in the question show a rather rapid initial decay rate that appears to slow and stabilize as the percentage of atoms remaining is reduced:

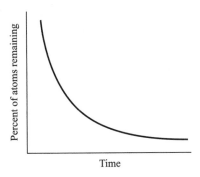

This best supports answer choice H.

PASSAGE VI

29. **The correct answer is B.** Table 1 shows the average number of eggs laid and the average number of eggs hatched before pesticide exposure. Since Breed F has a low resistance to illness, it would probably have a similar eggs laid to eggs hatched ratio as that of Breed E. Since 9 out of 15, or 3 out of 5 of Breed E's eggs hatched, you can assume that the same fraction of Breed F's eggs would hatch: $\frac{3}{5} = \frac{x}{20}$; $x = 12$, answer choice B.

30. **The correct answer is H.** To answer this question, look at Figure 1 and find the breed that, at the far right end of the figure, has an illness incidence closest to zero. This will be Breed B, answer choice H.

31. **The correct answer is A.** According to Figure 1, both Breed E and Breed C have a high incidence of illness, so you can eliminate answer choices C and D. Although, according to Figure 2, Breed B lays fewer eggs than does Breed A, more of them hatch. Therefore, Breed B is likely to have a higher number of eggs hatch and have a low incidence of illness.

32. **The correct answer is G.** According to Table 1, the average number of eggs laid does not seem to be affected by the resistance to illness. Therefore, there is no direct relationship, answer choice G.

33. **The correct answer is D.** The breed that is most affected by pesticide exposure will likely be the breed that has the highest illness incidence after exposure. According to Figure 1, breed E has the highest illness incidence.

34. **The correct answer is J.** The only statement that is supported by the passage is that the average number of eggs laid by all breeds is not affected by pesticide exposure. The data in both Table 1 and Figure 2 supports this conclusion.

35. **The correct answer is A.** According to Table 1, Breed E laid an average of 15 eggs before exposure to pesticide, more than any other breed.

PASSAGE VII

36. **The correct answer is H.** Based on the data in all 3 tables, the highest average speed was recorded in Table 1. Table 1 shows the results of Study 1, which placed the car on a smooth asphalt road. Therefore, the highest average speeds resulted from using a asphalt road, answer choice H.

37. **The correct answer is C.** The average speed recorded in Table 1 is 8.58 feet per second. This speed is not greater than the speed recorded in Trial 2 (8.85 ft/s); likewise, it is not less than the speed recorded in Trial 3 (8.55 ft/s); eliminate answer choices A and B. The average speed recorded in Table 1 (8.58 ft/s) is greater than the speed recorded in Trial 1 (8.33 ft/s), so answer choice C must be correct.

38. **The correct answer is F.** To answer this question, you must remember that Table 1 is associated with a blacktop road, Table 2 is associated with a gravel road, and Table 3 is associated with a dirt road. When you compare the average recorded speed, you will see that the average speed of a car on a gravel road (4.52 ft/s) is approximately half of the average speed of a car on a blacktop road (8.58 ft/s) answer choice F.

39. **The correct answer is B.** Since the passage indicates that all 3 of the studies were "conducted on a fair day with no wind," you can eliminate answer choices C and D. The studies were also conducted over different ground cover, so the most likely reason for the lower average speeds is greater friction, answer choice B.

40. The correct answer is H. Look at each of the answer choices and compare the travel times:

(F) Study 1, Trial 2 = 8.85 ft/s

(G) Study 2, Trial 2 = 4.59 ft/s

(H) Study 2, Trial 3 = 4.46 ft/s

(J) Study 3, Trial 3 = 6.17 ft/s

The slowest travel time was recorded in Study 2, Trial 3, answer choice H.

ACT PRACTICE TEST 3
Answer Sheet

ENGLISH

1 Ⓐ Ⓑ Ⓒ Ⓓ	21 Ⓐ Ⓑ Ⓒ Ⓓ	41 Ⓐ Ⓑ Ⓒ Ⓓ	61 Ⓐ Ⓑ Ⓒ Ⓓ
2 Ⓕ Ⓖ Ⓗ Ⓙ	22 Ⓕ Ⓖ Ⓗ Ⓙ	42 Ⓕ Ⓖ Ⓗ Ⓙ	62 Ⓕ Ⓖ Ⓗ Ⓙ
3 Ⓐ Ⓑ Ⓒ Ⓓ	23 Ⓐ Ⓑ Ⓒ Ⓓ	43 Ⓐ Ⓑ Ⓒ Ⓓ	63 Ⓐ Ⓑ Ⓒ Ⓓ
4 Ⓕ Ⓖ Ⓗ Ⓙ	24 Ⓕ Ⓖ Ⓗ Ⓙ	44 Ⓕ Ⓖ Ⓗ Ⓙ	64 Ⓕ Ⓖ Ⓗ Ⓙ
5 Ⓐ Ⓑ Ⓒ Ⓓ	25 Ⓐ Ⓑ Ⓒ Ⓓ	45 Ⓐ Ⓑ Ⓒ Ⓓ	65 Ⓐ Ⓑ Ⓒ Ⓓ
6 Ⓕ Ⓖ Ⓗ Ⓙ	26 Ⓕ Ⓖ Ⓗ Ⓙ	46 Ⓕ Ⓖ Ⓗ Ⓙ	66 Ⓕ Ⓖ Ⓗ Ⓙ
7 Ⓐ Ⓑ Ⓒ Ⓓ	27 Ⓐ Ⓑ Ⓒ Ⓓ	47 Ⓐ Ⓑ Ⓒ Ⓓ	67 Ⓐ Ⓑ Ⓒ Ⓓ
8 Ⓕ Ⓖ Ⓗ Ⓙ	28 Ⓕ Ⓖ Ⓗ Ⓙ	48 Ⓕ Ⓖ Ⓗ Ⓙ	68 Ⓕ Ⓖ Ⓗ Ⓙ
9 Ⓐ Ⓑ Ⓒ Ⓓ	29 Ⓐ Ⓑ Ⓒ Ⓓ	49 Ⓐ Ⓑ Ⓒ Ⓓ	69 Ⓐ Ⓑ Ⓒ Ⓓ
10 Ⓕ Ⓖ Ⓗ Ⓙ	30 Ⓕ Ⓖ Ⓗ Ⓙ	50 Ⓕ Ⓖ Ⓗ Ⓙ	70 Ⓕ Ⓖ Ⓗ Ⓙ
11 Ⓐ Ⓑ Ⓒ Ⓓ	31 Ⓐ Ⓑ Ⓒ Ⓓ	51 Ⓐ Ⓑ Ⓒ Ⓓ	71 Ⓐ Ⓑ Ⓒ Ⓓ
12 Ⓕ Ⓖ Ⓗ Ⓙ	32 Ⓕ Ⓖ Ⓗ Ⓙ	52 Ⓕ Ⓖ Ⓗ Ⓙ	72 Ⓕ Ⓖ Ⓗ Ⓙ
13 Ⓐ Ⓑ Ⓒ Ⓓ	33 Ⓐ Ⓑ Ⓒ Ⓓ	53 Ⓐ Ⓑ Ⓒ Ⓓ	73 Ⓐ Ⓑ Ⓒ Ⓓ
14 Ⓕ Ⓖ Ⓗ Ⓙ	34 Ⓕ Ⓖ Ⓗ Ⓙ	54 Ⓕ Ⓖ Ⓗ Ⓙ	74 Ⓕ Ⓖ Ⓗ Ⓙ
15 Ⓐ Ⓑ Ⓒ Ⓓ	35 Ⓐ Ⓑ Ⓒ Ⓓ	55 Ⓐ Ⓑ Ⓒ Ⓓ	75 Ⓐ Ⓑ Ⓒ Ⓓ
16 Ⓕ Ⓖ Ⓗ Ⓙ	36 Ⓕ Ⓖ Ⓗ Ⓙ	56 Ⓕ Ⓖ Ⓗ Ⓙ	
17 Ⓐ Ⓑ Ⓒ Ⓓ	37 Ⓐ Ⓑ Ⓒ Ⓓ	57 Ⓐ Ⓑ Ⓒ Ⓓ	
18 Ⓕ Ⓖ Ⓗ Ⓙ	38 Ⓕ Ⓖ Ⓗ Ⓙ	58 Ⓕ Ⓖ Ⓗ Ⓙ	
19 Ⓐ Ⓑ Ⓒ Ⓓ	39 Ⓐ Ⓑ Ⓒ Ⓓ	59 Ⓐ Ⓑ Ⓒ Ⓓ	
20 Ⓕ Ⓖ Ⓗ Ⓙ	40 Ⓕ Ⓖ Ⓗ Ⓙ	60 Ⓕ Ⓖ Ⓗ Ⓙ	

MATH

1 Ⓐ Ⓑ Ⓒ Ⓓ Ⓔ	16 Ⓕ Ⓖ Ⓗ Ⓙ Ⓚ	31 Ⓐ Ⓑ Ⓒ Ⓓ Ⓔ	46 Ⓕ Ⓖ Ⓗ Ⓙ Ⓚ
2 Ⓕ Ⓖ Ⓗ Ⓙ Ⓚ	17 Ⓐ Ⓑ Ⓒ Ⓓ Ⓔ	32 Ⓕ Ⓖ Ⓗ Ⓙ Ⓚ	47 Ⓐ Ⓑ Ⓒ Ⓓ Ⓔ
3 Ⓐ Ⓑ Ⓒ Ⓓ Ⓔ	18 Ⓕ Ⓖ Ⓗ Ⓙ Ⓚ	33 Ⓐ Ⓑ Ⓒ Ⓓ Ⓔ	48 Ⓕ Ⓖ Ⓗ Ⓙ Ⓚ
4 Ⓕ Ⓖ Ⓗ Ⓙ Ⓚ	19 Ⓐ Ⓑ Ⓒ Ⓓ Ⓔ	34 Ⓕ Ⓖ Ⓗ Ⓙ Ⓚ	49 Ⓐ Ⓑ Ⓒ Ⓓ Ⓔ
5 Ⓐ Ⓑ Ⓒ Ⓓ Ⓔ	20 Ⓕ Ⓖ Ⓗ Ⓙ Ⓚ	35 Ⓐ Ⓑ Ⓒ Ⓓ Ⓔ	50 Ⓕ Ⓖ Ⓗ Ⓙ Ⓚ
6 Ⓕ Ⓖ Ⓗ Ⓙ Ⓚ	21 Ⓐ Ⓑ Ⓒ Ⓓ Ⓔ	36 Ⓕ Ⓖ Ⓗ Ⓙ Ⓚ	51 Ⓐ Ⓑ Ⓒ Ⓓ Ⓔ
7 Ⓐ Ⓑ Ⓒ Ⓓ Ⓔ	22 Ⓕ Ⓖ Ⓗ Ⓙ Ⓚ	37 Ⓐ Ⓑ Ⓒ Ⓓ Ⓔ	52 Ⓕ Ⓖ Ⓗ Ⓙ Ⓚ
8 Ⓕ Ⓖ Ⓗ Ⓙ Ⓚ	23 Ⓐ Ⓑ Ⓒ Ⓓ Ⓔ	38 Ⓕ Ⓖ Ⓗ Ⓙ Ⓚ	53 Ⓐ Ⓑ Ⓒ Ⓓ Ⓔ
9 Ⓐ Ⓑ Ⓒ Ⓓ Ⓔ	24 Ⓕ Ⓖ Ⓗ Ⓙ Ⓚ	39 Ⓐ Ⓑ Ⓒ Ⓓ Ⓔ	54 Ⓕ Ⓖ Ⓗ Ⓙ Ⓚ
10 Ⓕ Ⓖ Ⓗ Ⓙ Ⓚ	25 Ⓐ Ⓑ Ⓒ Ⓓ Ⓔ	40 Ⓕ Ⓖ Ⓗ Ⓙ Ⓚ	55 Ⓐ Ⓑ Ⓒ Ⓓ Ⓔ
11 Ⓐ Ⓑ Ⓒ Ⓓ Ⓔ	26 Ⓕ Ⓖ Ⓗ Ⓙ Ⓚ	41 Ⓐ Ⓑ Ⓒ Ⓓ Ⓔ	56 Ⓕ Ⓖ Ⓗ Ⓙ Ⓚ
12 Ⓕ Ⓖ Ⓗ Ⓙ Ⓚ	27 Ⓐ Ⓑ Ⓒ Ⓓ Ⓔ	42 Ⓕ Ⓖ Ⓗ Ⓙ Ⓚ	57 Ⓐ Ⓑ Ⓒ Ⓓ Ⓔ
13 Ⓐ Ⓑ Ⓒ Ⓓ Ⓔ	28 Ⓕ Ⓖ Ⓗ Ⓙ Ⓚ	43 Ⓐ Ⓑ Ⓒ Ⓓ Ⓔ	58 Ⓕ Ⓖ Ⓗ Ⓙ Ⓚ
14 Ⓕ Ⓖ Ⓗ Ⓙ Ⓚ	29 Ⓐ Ⓑ Ⓒ Ⓓ Ⓔ	44 Ⓕ Ⓖ Ⓗ Ⓙ Ⓚ	59 Ⓐ Ⓑ Ⓒ Ⓓ Ⓔ
15 Ⓐ Ⓑ Ⓒ Ⓓ Ⓔ	30 Ⓕ Ⓖ Ⓗ Ⓙ Ⓚ	45 Ⓐ Ⓑ Ⓒ Ⓓ Ⓔ	60 Ⓕ Ⓖ Ⓗ Ⓙ Ⓚ

READING

1 Ⓐ Ⓑ Ⓒ Ⓓ	11 Ⓐ Ⓑ Ⓒ Ⓓ	21 Ⓐ Ⓑ Ⓒ Ⓓ	31 Ⓐ Ⓑ Ⓒ Ⓓ
2 Ⓕ Ⓖ Ⓗ Ⓙ	12 Ⓕ Ⓖ Ⓗ Ⓙ	22 Ⓕ Ⓖ Ⓗ Ⓙ	32 Ⓕ Ⓖ Ⓗ Ⓙ
3 Ⓐ Ⓑ Ⓒ Ⓓ	13 Ⓐ Ⓑ Ⓒ Ⓓ	23 Ⓐ Ⓑ Ⓒ Ⓓ	33 Ⓐ Ⓑ Ⓒ Ⓓ
4 Ⓕ Ⓖ Ⓗ Ⓙ	14 Ⓕ Ⓖ Ⓗ Ⓙ	24 Ⓕ Ⓖ Ⓗ Ⓙ	34 Ⓕ Ⓖ Ⓗ Ⓙ
5 Ⓐ Ⓑ Ⓒ Ⓓ	15 Ⓐ Ⓑ Ⓒ Ⓓ	25 Ⓐ Ⓑ Ⓒ Ⓓ	35 Ⓐ Ⓑ Ⓒ Ⓓ
6 Ⓕ Ⓖ Ⓗ Ⓙ	16 Ⓕ Ⓖ Ⓗ Ⓙ	26 Ⓕ Ⓖ Ⓗ Ⓙ	36 Ⓕ Ⓖ Ⓗ Ⓙ
7 Ⓐ Ⓑ Ⓒ Ⓓ	17 Ⓐ Ⓑ Ⓒ Ⓓ	27 Ⓐ Ⓑ Ⓒ Ⓓ	37 Ⓐ Ⓑ Ⓒ Ⓓ
8 Ⓕ Ⓖ Ⓗ Ⓙ	18 Ⓕ Ⓖ Ⓗ Ⓙ	28 Ⓕ Ⓖ Ⓗ Ⓙ	38 Ⓕ Ⓖ Ⓗ Ⓙ
9 Ⓐ Ⓑ Ⓒ Ⓓ	19 Ⓐ Ⓑ Ⓒ Ⓓ	29 Ⓐ Ⓑ Ⓒ Ⓓ	39 Ⓐ Ⓑ Ⓒ Ⓓ
10 Ⓕ Ⓖ Ⓗ Ⓙ	20 Ⓕ Ⓖ Ⓗ Ⓙ	30 Ⓕ Ⓖ Ⓗ Ⓙ	40 Ⓕ Ⓖ Ⓗ Ⓙ

SCIENCE

1 Ⓐ Ⓑ Ⓒ Ⓓ	11 Ⓐ Ⓑ Ⓒ Ⓓ	21 Ⓐ Ⓑ Ⓒ Ⓓ	31 Ⓐ Ⓑ Ⓒ Ⓓ
2 Ⓕ Ⓖ Ⓗ Ⓙ	12 Ⓕ Ⓖ Ⓗ Ⓙ	22 Ⓕ Ⓖ Ⓗ Ⓙ	32 Ⓕ Ⓖ Ⓗ Ⓙ
3 Ⓐ Ⓑ Ⓒ Ⓓ	13 Ⓐ Ⓑ Ⓒ Ⓓ	23 Ⓐ Ⓑ Ⓒ Ⓓ	33 Ⓐ Ⓑ Ⓒ Ⓓ
4 Ⓕ Ⓖ Ⓗ Ⓙ	14 Ⓕ Ⓖ Ⓗ Ⓙ	24 Ⓕ Ⓖ Ⓗ Ⓙ	34 Ⓕ Ⓖ Ⓗ Ⓙ
5 Ⓐ Ⓑ Ⓒ Ⓓ	15 Ⓐ Ⓑ Ⓒ Ⓓ	25 Ⓐ Ⓑ Ⓒ Ⓓ	35 Ⓐ Ⓑ Ⓒ Ⓓ
6 Ⓕ Ⓖ Ⓗ Ⓙ	16 Ⓕ Ⓖ Ⓗ Ⓙ	26 Ⓕ Ⓖ Ⓗ Ⓙ	36 Ⓕ Ⓖ Ⓗ Ⓙ
7 Ⓐ Ⓑ Ⓒ Ⓓ	17 Ⓐ Ⓑ Ⓒ Ⓓ	27 Ⓐ Ⓑ Ⓒ Ⓓ	37 Ⓐ Ⓑ Ⓒ Ⓓ
8 Ⓕ Ⓖ Ⓗ Ⓙ	18 Ⓕ Ⓖ Ⓗ Ⓙ	28 Ⓕ Ⓖ Ⓗ Ⓙ	38 Ⓕ Ⓖ Ⓗ Ⓙ
9 Ⓐ Ⓑ Ⓒ Ⓓ	19 Ⓐ Ⓑ Ⓒ Ⓓ	29 Ⓐ Ⓑ Ⓒ Ⓓ	39 Ⓐ Ⓑ Ⓒ Ⓓ
10 Ⓕ Ⓖ Ⓗ Ⓙ	20 Ⓕ Ⓖ Ⓗ Ⓙ	30 Ⓕ Ⓖ Ⓗ Ⓙ	40 Ⓕ Ⓖ Ⓗ Ⓙ

RAW SCORES

ENGLISH _____

MATH _____

READING _____

SCIENCE _____

SCALE SCORES

ENGLISH _____

MATH _____

READING _____

SCIENCE _____

DATE TAKEN:

ENGLISH/WRITING _____

COMPOSITE SCORE

1 ■ ■ ■ ■ ■ ■ ■ ■ 1

ENGLISH TEST

45 Minutes – 75 Questions

DIRECTIONS: In the passages that follow, some words and phrases are underlined and numbered. In the answer column, you will find alternatives for the words and phrases that are underlined. Choose the alternative that you think is best and fill in the corresponding bubble on your answer sheet. If you think that the original version is best, choose "NO CHANGE," which will always be either answer choice A or F. You will also find questions about a particular section of the passage, or about the entire passage. These questions will be identified by either an underlined portion or by a number in a box. Look for the answer that clearly expresses the idea, is consistent with the style and tone of the passage, and makes the correct use of standard written English. Read the passage through once before answering the questions. For some questions, you should read beyond the indicated portion before you answer.

PASSAGE I

Born to Hunt

I watch his black leather nose as it sporadically quivers,

sensing new smells in the air,

desperately trying to identify them. His head remains
<u>   </u>
                    1

1. The writer is describing the attributes of a particular dog. Based on the information in this first paragraph, which choice is most relevant?
   A. NO CHANGE
   B. thinking about identifying them.
   C. attempting to flee.
   D. shaking his head in disgust.

perfectly erect, his body perfectly still. His longish white
<u>   </u>
          2

2. **F.** NO CHANGE
   G. perfectly erect his body
   H. perfectly, erect his body
   J. perfectly erect his body,

tail curls into the letter "C." He appear to be perfectly
                                  <u>   </u>
                                      3
balanced, a beautiful specimen, poised at the starting

3. **A.** NO CHANGE
   B. appeared
   C. appears
   D. has appeared

point of the two-track road. How did my son know, about
                                              <u>   </u>
                                                  4
this adorable canine was a mere twelve weeks old, that his

name should be Hunter?

4. **F.** NO CHANGE
   G. when
   H. what
   J. how

We had already revisited the local animal shelter three
   <u>   </u>
           5
times in the previous six months, searching for the perfect

boy/dog chemistry. Disappointed after trial playtimes

with several older animals, we suddenly realized we had

yet to visit the nursery, which was full of puppies.

5. **A.** NO CHANGE
   B. had visited
   C. already visited again
   D. have revisited already

GO ON TO THE NEXT PAGE.

1 ■ ■ ■ ■ ■ ■ ■ ■ 1

There he <u>was,</u> a short-haired, pink-skinned, white and
     ₆
black spotted angel of a puppy.

The bond was instant.

    Hunter <u>is his name, and, a hunter</u> is what he aspires to
                     ₇

be. His black, velvet ears <u>are raising</u> and held firmly back
                     ₈
as he attempts to capture even the slightest of sounds.

I know, as I watch him, that at any moment he may

choose to ignore the meager training <u>I give</u> him and
                         ₉
bound off

mindlessly <u>into the woods,</u> 100 acres of which are "his."
          ₁₀
I could lose him; I know this. Even the neon orange,

bell-adorned collar around his neck is no assurance.

    As I stand there watching, <u>marvel</u> at the instincts
                         ₁₁
coursing through his entire being,

<u>I know that he, too, is torn.</u> "Should I pursue the dark
    ₁₂
but enticing unknowns of the forest before me, or stay

back with the comfort and warmth of those who care for

me?" He turns his head toward me as I beckon to him,

then <u>races back</u> to the yard, grabbing his plastic flying
      ₁₃
disc in his mouth,

bounding into the air as he runs, <u>happy to be alive.</u>
                            ₁₄

6. **F.** NO CHANGE
   G. were
   H. is
   J. are

7. **A.** NO CHANGE
   B. is his name; and a hunter
   C. is his name, and a hunter
   D. is his name. And a hunter

8. **F.** NO CHANGE
   G. have risen
   H. are raised
   J. raised up

9. **A.** NO CHANGE
   B. I did give
   C. I once gave
   D. I had given

10. Which of the following would NOT be acceptable
    alternatives to the underlined portion?
   F. toward the woods
   G. to the woods
   H. over toward the direction of the woods
   J. in the direction of the woods

11. **A.** NO CHANGE
   B. marveling
   C. and marvels
   D. I marveled

12. The underlined portion would best be placed:
   F. where it is now.
   G. after the word *watching*.
   H. after the word *there*.
   J. before the word *as*.

13. Which choice best describes the way the dog returns
    to the writer of the story?
   A. NO CHANGE
   B. lopes back
   C. returns at a slow trot
   D. sadly comes home

14. If the last part of this sentence was deleted, the
    paragraph would lose:
   F. the disappointment of the dog's owner.
   G. an understanding of the dog's hunting instincts.
   H. a description of the dog's attitude.
   J. the depth of dog ownership.

GO ON TO THE NEXT PAGE.

1 ■ ■ ■ ■ ■ ■ ■ ■ 1

Question 15 asks about the passage as a whole.

15. Suppose the writer's goal for this passage was to convince the reader to train dogs to hunt. Would this essay fulfill the writer's goal?
    A. Yes, because the writer is very accepting of the dog's natural instincts to hunt.
    B. Yes, because the writer knows that, with better training, the dog would be a good hunting dog.
    C. No, because the passage specifically encourages readers not to train dogs to hunt.
    D. No, because the passage restricts its focus to a discussion of a family pet.

PASSAGE II

Don't Fence Me In

One of the first tasks of a new homeowner is often centered around the issue, of "the fence." Most people
16
are naturally territorial, at least to some extent, and are inclined to mark off their boundaries as a statement to their neighbors, it's a way to say, "Here's my line, don't
17
cross it." However, a civilized society dictates that this

fencing to be done in a genial manner. Excuses are
18
offered to the neighbor such as, "We need to keep our dog confined," or "This fence is only necessary for our children." In reality, fences are most often erected not to keep loved ones in, but to keep outsiders out.

People also respect their privacy, and a solid wood
19
fence or concrete wall will certainly accomplish that goal. Sometimes, however, the neighbor is on the second or third level of his home, in this case all the goings-on
20

in a private backyard are clearly visible. Rather then
21
constructing a solid screen such as a fence or wall, some people prefer to take a more subtle route, such

16. **F.** NO CHANGE
    G. the, issue of
    H. the issue of
    J. the, issue of,

17. **A.** NO CHANGE
    B. their neighbors; it's a way
    C. their neighbors: its a way
    D. their neighbors. Its a way

18. **F.** NO CHANGE
    G. be done
    H. needs be done
    J. will be done

19. **A.** NO CHANGE
    B. reject
    C. value
    D. undermine

20. **F.** NO CHANGE
    G. home; in case
    H. home. In this case,
    J. home, in case

21. **A.** NO CHANGE
    B. Rather, than
    C. Rather than
    D. Rather, then,

GO ON TO THE NEXT PAGE.

1 ■ ■ ■ ■ ■ ■ ■ ■ 1

as planting <u>trees, shrubs, vines and the like</u>. This option
                ₂₂
works well as long as the fence is easy to maintain
year-round. Keep in mind, though, that these plants
require some time to grow. Climbing ivies or deciduous
trees that <u>lose their foliage</u> prove to be ineffective
           ₂₃

barriers <u>of</u> prying eyes and perked ears. Evergreen trees
       ₂₄
and shrubs are excellent choices for fences,

<u>and are better than deciduous trees</u> as they keep their
             ₂₅
leaves and needles throughout the year. One must take
care, however, to select species that are suited to their
intended purpose and environment. Planting tall, thin
Cryptomeria trees <u>too far apart for example</u> is not a
                  ₂₆
good idea. You should plant two or three rows of the trees
rather than a single row of trees along a property line.

    When considering how to mark a property line and
create <u>privacy and security,</u> it is important to
       ₂₇

<u>be cautious, and</u> carefully plan out the type of fence you
    ₂₈
want to construct, as well as the statement you want to

make to your neighbors. <u>Privacy</u> fences can take time
                   ₂₉
to come to full maturity, and more permanent

fencing can be <u>costly</u>.
       ₃₀

22. **F.** NO CHANGE
    G. trees, shrubs vines, and the like
    H. trees shrubs vines, and the like
    J. trees, shrubs, vines, and the like

23. **A.** NO CHANGE
    B. lose they're foliage
    C. lose its foliage
    D. lose it's foliage

24. **F.** NO CHANGE
    G. at
    H. with
    J. to

25. **A.** NO CHANGE
    B. in place of deciduous trees
    C. as opposed to deciduous trees
    D. OMIT the underlined portion

26. **F.** NO CHANGE
    G. too far apart for, example
    H. too far apart, for example,
    J. too far apart for example,

27. Which of the following creates the most appropriate
    image?
    A. NO CHANGE
    B. fun and enjoyment,
    C. relaxation and vacation time,
    D. safety and recreation,

28. **F.** NO CHANGE
    G. cautiously and
    H. take care to
    J. OMIT the underlined portion

29. **A.** NO CHANGE
    B. Natural
    C. Tall
    D. OMIT the underlined portion

30. **F.** NO CHANGE
    G. costfull.
    H. a lot of money.
    J. expensive to build.

GO ON TO THE NEXT PAGE.

1 ■ ■ ■ ■ ■ ■ ■ ■ 1

PASSAGE III

Maya Angelou

A woman of incredible inner beauty an ingenious
                                   31

gift with words, and a golden heart: that is Maya
                                       32
Angelou. Born in 1928 in St. Louis, Missouri, Maya

Angelou experienced a difficult and transient childhood.

Much of what her young life was is related and reflected
          33
in her first book, *I Know Why the Caged Bird Sings*.

As suggested by its title, this autobiography describes the

tumultuous and often frightening aspects of her

teen years, causing the reader to both sympathize with
       34
and marvel at Maya's ability to cope with, even rise

above, many adverse circumstances. Following one

particularly traumatic incident, Maya spent the next five
          35
years in total and utter silence, refusing to speak and

causing her mother to send Maya to live in Stamps,

Arkansas, with Maya's grandmother.

     As a young woman, Angelou performed a variety

of jobs, including dancing, singing, and acting.

☐36 Angelou went on to become active in the

civil rights movement and, pursued her dream of
          37
becoming a writer as well. She has published many

volumes of poetry and over a dozen books. Since 1981,

Angelou has resided at Wake Forest University where she

is the first Reynolds Professor of American Studies, a

31. **A.** NO CHANGE
      B. beauty; an ingenious
      C. beauty an ingenious,
      D. beauty, with an ingenious

32. **F.** NO CHANGE
      G. who is
      H. whom is
      J. that was

33. **A.** NO CHANGE
      B. her young life
      C. her current life
      D. that her young life

34. Which of the following alternatives to the underlined
      portion would NOT be acceptable?
      F. teen years, which causes the reader to
      G. teen years. This causes the reader to
      H. teen years; the reader can
      J. teen years. Causing the reader to

35. If the writer of this essay deleted the phrase
      particularly traumatic incident, the essay would
      primarily lose:
      A. an explanation for Angelou's subsequent
          behavior.
      B. the essence of the entire passage.
      C. an argument for the writer's point of view.
      D. an unnecessary detail about Angelou's life.

36. Which of the following words from the preceding
      sentence could be deleted without negatively impac-
      ting the grammar and clarity of the sentence?
      F. variety of jobs
      G. performed
      H. singing
      J. a young woman

37. **A.** NO CHANGE
      B. civil rights movement and
      C. civil rights, movement, and
      D. civil, rights, movement

GO ON TO THE NEXT PAGE.

1 ■ ■ ■ ■ ■ ■ ■ ■ 1

prestigious position. 38 She is one of only two people ever to have read her own poetry at the inauguration of a

United States President Bill Clinton.
                                            39

    Listening or watching to an interview with Maya
                                            40
Angelou is truly a treat. With her deep, throaty voice and

her ability to make words sound like either

blossomed flowers or deafening cannons, Maya
        41

Angelou can sense and instill of wonder and joy in even
                    42
the most hardened listener. Angelou has the ability

and eliciting emotion in such a way that
        43

any listener would become heavy with gratitude for life,
    44
and hope for humanity.

38. At this point, the writer is considering adding the following true statement:

> The appointment as Professor of American Studies is a lifetime appointment.

Should the writer make this addition here?

F. Yes, because it indicates that Angelou will keep this position for the rest of her life.
G. Yes, because it shows how important the Reynolds professorship appointment is for Angelou's career.
H. No, because it detracts from the points regarding Angelou's difficult childhood.
J. No, because it does not substantially add to the essence of the essay.

39. A. NO CHANGE
    B. president, Bill Clinton.
    C. president.
    D. president; Bill Clinton.

40. F. NO CHANGE
    G. Listening to or watching
    H. Listening to or watching with
    J. Listening, or watching

41. A. NO CHANGE
    B. blossoming flowers
    C. blossoms of flowers
    D. blossoms and flowers

42. F. NO CHANGE
    G. a sense of wonder and joy can instill
    H. a sense she can instill of wonder and joy
    J. can instill a sense of wonder and joy

43. A. NO CHANGE
    B. for eliciting
    C. to elicit
    D. with eliciting

44. F. NO CHANGE
    G. a listener has
    H. all who listen will have
    J. OMIT the underlined portion.

Question 45 asks about the essay as a whole.
---

45. Suppose the writer had intended to write an essay focusing on southern poverty. Would this essay successfully fulfill the writer's goal?
    A. Yes, because the writer clearly states that Angelou grew up in Arkansas under difficult circumstances.
    B. Yes, because the essay discusses Angelou's first book about poverty, *I Know Why the Caged Bird Sings*.
    C. No, because the writer's goal is to describe how people can rise above bad situations.
    D. No, because the essay's main focus is on the life of Maya Angelou, both the good and bad times.

GO ON TO THE NEXT PAGE.

1 ■ ■ ■ ■ ■ ■ ■ ■ 1

PASSAGE IV

Summer Visits

[1] Visiting my grandparents every summer was a definite highlight of my youth. [2] Grandma and I would
₄₆

46. **F.** NO CHANGE
    G. my younger days as a teenager.
    H. my summer visits.
    J. my young childhood.

take the city bus just to go up the road one mile, to the
₄₇

47. **A.** NO CHANGE
    B. one mile to the
    C. one mile; to the
    D. one mile: to the

nearest shopping center. [3] That one mile seems as if a
₄₈

48. **F.** NO CHANGE
    G. seemed a
    H. seeming like a
    J. seems as a

happy eternity to me. [4] There, at the "five-and-dime," Grandma would purchase yards and yards of fabric to take home to my mother. [5]Grandma would let me help choose the material, knowing that much of it would become my new fall school clothes. ⁴⁹

49. The writer is considering adding the following sentence to further describe her mother's talent for sewing.

    My mother had become an excellent seamstress under the tutelage of my grandmother.

    The new sentence would best amplify and be placed after Sentence:

    A. 2
    B. 3
    C. 4
    D. 5

Before Grandma Ritz and I spent much of our time
₅₀

50. **F.** NO CHANGE
    G. Except
    H. Because
    J. As for

together, I must admit the brief moments with Grandpa

Ritz are truly my most memorable. Grandpa always
₅₁

51. Which of the following choices would NOT be an acceptable alternative for the underlined portion?
    A. are most memorable.
    B. truly are my most memorable.
    C. are the ones I remember most.
    D. my most memorable.

seemed to be in-and-out, but mostly out. ⁵² I do remember his over-sized, green chair and matching mammoth ottoman. The chair and ottoman

52. If the writer deleted the phrase *but mostly out* from the preceding sentence, the sentence would primarily lose:
    F. the implication that the writer's grandfather was gone much of the time.
    G. details about the writer's relationship with her grandmother.
    H. a sense of the grandparents' relationship with each other.
    J. an explanation of where the grandfather spent most of his time.

GO ON TO THE NEXT PAGE.

1 ■ ■ ■ ■ ■ ■ ■ ■ 1

<u>was forbidden</u> to all of the grandchildren,
₅₃

<u>even when</u> Grandpa was off on one of his many
₅₄

excursions. Right next to Grandpa's chair was his

cherished bookstand, complete with reading lamp and

reading glasses. I can still picture Grandpa sitting in that

chair in front of his radio (and later a black-and-white

television set), happily reading his favorite Hemingway

novel. <u>Even as a child, Grandpa to me seemed</u>
₅₅

<u>like a small man</u>, and, indeed, he only stood about five
₅₅

and a half feet tall. Still, Grandpa was a <u>royal king</u> in that
₅₆

chair.

My fondest memories are of Grandpa and his fishing

lures. An avid fly-fisherman, Grandpa probably fished

every river within driving distance of his home.

<u>When he was</u> out in his waders somewhere, he could often
₅₇

be found bent over his garage workbench, a single

lightbulb hanging over his head, putting together bobbers,

colorful feathers, and shiny metal fish bodies.

Occasionally, Grandpa would invite me to accompany

him to the garage, <u>where he would show me how</u> to tie
₅₈

all of the parts together with a piece of thin fishing wire.

He always assured me that my humble creation would be

an asset on his next fishing expedition. Maybe it would

even nab the big one!

When I became a teenager, my lone summer visits to

my grandparents ended. By then, <u>they had</u> moved out of
₅₉

the city and into the country, where they purchased acres

---

53. **A.** NO CHANGE
   B. were forbidden
   C. are being forbidden
   D. will be forbidden

54. **F.** NO CHANGE
   G. despite the fact that
   H. including any time when
   J. instead of when

55. **A.** NO CHANGE
   B. Grandpa, even when I was a child, to me seemed like a small man
   C. Grandpa seemed like a small man to me, even when I was a child
   D. Grandpa seemed to me, even as a child, like a small man

56. **F.** NO CHANGE
   G. royalty
   H. king
   J. king of royalty

57. **A.** NO CHANGE
   B. When he wasn't
   C. Whenever he was
   D. Whenever he is

58. **F.** NO CHANGE
   G. he showed me how
   H. so he would show me how
   J. because he could show me how

59. **A.** NO CHANGE
   B. they
   C. my grandparents had
   D. it had

GO ON TO THE NEXT PAGE.

1 ■ ■ ■ ■ ■ ■ ■ ■ 1

and acres of hilly woods. While I never grew to love their new home as I did the old one, this property became my Grandpa's sanctuary. He spent every day of every month cleaning out the deadwood, carving walking paths along the creek, and building wooden birdhouses.

Question 60 asks about the essay as a whole.

60. Suppose the writer had intended to write an essay describing the relationship between her grandparents. Would this essay accomplish the writer's goal?
   F. Yes, because the writer clearly describes how important her grandparents were during her childhood.
   G. Yes, because the writer recalls fond memories of both her grandparents.
   H. No, because the essay does not mention the writer's grandparents' relationship with one another.
   J. No, because the writer clearly spent more time with her grandmother than with her grandfather.

PASSAGE V

The Electric Motor Team

   In 1834, Thomas Davenport, a poor blacksmith with no formal education, and his wife Emily, jointly worked
                                                                              61
together to make one of the most
   61

misused inventions in the history of the world—the
  62
electric motor. Thomas was working in Vermont when he

heard of an innovative technique used to more efficiently
                                                       63
separate iron ore with an electromagnet.
   63

He was so convinced, that he intrigued his brother to
                                                  64
raise money, and the two of them purchased an

electromagnet.

61. A. NO CHANGE
    B. jointly worked with each other
    C. worked with each other together on a project
    D. worked together

62. Which of the choices would be most appropriate here?
    F. NO CHANGE
    G. justified
    H. important
    J. authoritative

63. A. NO CHANGE
    B. more efficiently separating
    C. separates more efficiently
    D. separate more efficiently

64. F. NO CHANGE
    G. His brother was so intrigued that he convinced him to
    H. He was so intrigued that he convinced his brother to
    J. He was so convinced and intrigued that his brother to

GO ON TO THE NEXT PAGE.

1 ■ ■ ■ ■ ■ ■ ■ ■ 1

Thomas brought it home and began to experiment
with it, first by disassembling it. His wife, Emily, took a
keen interest in the project. Thomas's brother, who
witnessed much of their work, said that Emily "had a
fine education and was as enthusiastic as he was, . . . [She]
wrote

down exactly the way the wire was winded on, and all
about it, from beginning to end." Thomas began work on
his own electromagnet by constructing a core of wound
iron wires, but he realized he needed an insulator for the
wires. Emily sacrificed her silk, wedding dress, and
tore it into strips. Thomas and Emily then used these

strips of silk torn from her dress to insulate the wires.

[1] Thomas was convinced that the improved
electromagnet they built could be accustomed to spin
a wheel with attached magnets. [2] Thomas grew very
frustrated, until Emily suggested that mercury might be
used as a conductor. [3] For several months, Thomas
could not get it to work. [4] The wheel would start as the
underlying magnets attracted those on the wheel, but as
soon as the underlying magnets were opposite the
magnets on the wheel, the wheel would stop. [5] There was
no way to quickly reverse the current in the electromagnet
before the wheel stopped. [6] They were trying it, and the

wheel turned continuously, as expected. 72

65. **A.** NO CHANGE
B. brother, who witnessed much of their work, said
that Emily;
C. brother who witnessed much of their work, said
that Emily
D. brother, who witnessed much of their work said
that Emily

66. **F.** NO CHANGE
G. was wound
H. have been wound
J. was wounded

67. **A.** NO CHANGE
B. silk wedding dress; and tore it into strips.
C. silk wedding dress and tore it, into strips.
D. silk wedding dress and tore it into strips.

68. **F.** NO CHANGE
G. strips of silk
H. torn strips of wedding silk
J. strips of silk wedding dress fabric

69. **A.** NO CHANGE
B. utilized
C. used to
D. weary of

70. **F.** NO CHANGE
G. The wheels would start
H. The wheel commenced to start
J. The wheel, would, start

71. **A.** NO CHANGE
B. would of tried
C. had been trying
D. tried

72. For the sake of the unity and coherence of this
paragraph, Sentence 2 should be placed:
F. where it is now.
G. after Sentence 4.
H. after Sentence 5.
J. after Sentence 6.

GO ON TO THE NEXT PAGE.

[73] After building several more sophisticated models, he finally received the patent for the first electric motor in 1837. Although there was great initial excitement in the scientific community and the media the electric motor did not gain widespread popularity until after Thomas Davenport's death. However, within forty years of his death, electric motors were being commonly used in trains and trolleys, and now they are used in thousands of efficient and time-saving machines all over the world.

73. Which of the following sentences offers the best introduction to this paragraph?
A. Emily Davenport's contribution to the electric motor was invaluable.
B. Building a working electric motor was very difficult and expensive.
C. Thomas's first application for a patent was rejected, at a time when there were no other electrical patents at all.
D. The U.S. Patent Office was first proposed by Thomas Jefferson.

74. F. NO CHANGE
G. the scientific community and the media, the electric motor
H. the scientific community and the media and the electric motor
J. the scientific community, the media, and the electric motor

75. What function does the underlined portion serve in the essay?
A. The author is showing that electric motors save time.
B. The author is showing that modern electric motors are more efficient than the model the Davenports invented.
C. The author is showing that modern machines have replaced trains and trolleys.
D. The author is showing that the Davenports' invention directly impacts the modern world.

**END OF THE ENGLISH TEST
STOP! IF YOU HAVE TIME LEFT OVER, CHECK YOUR WORK ON THIS SECTION ONLY.**

2   **2**

MATHEMATICS TEST

60 Minutes – 60 Questions

DIRECTIONS: Solve each of the problems in the time allowed, then fill in the corresponding bubble on your answer sheet. Do not spend too much time on any one problem; skip the more difficult problems and go back to them later. You may use a calculator on this test. For this test you should assume that figures are NOT necessarily drawn to scale, that all geometric figures lie in a plane, and that the word *line* is used to indicate a straight line.

DO YOUR FIGURING HERE.

1. At the "Parkway" Bridge, a vehicle must be, at most, 1,500 pounds to cross the bridge. If w represents the car's weight, in pounds, this requirement can be indicated by which of the following inequalities?
   A. $w > 1,500$
   B. $w < 1,500$
   C. $w \geq 1,500$
   D. $w \leq 1,500$
   E. $w \neq 1,500$

2. What is the smallest positive integer that is a multiple of 2, of 6, and of 9?
   F. 12
   G. 17
   H. 18
   J. 56
   K. 112

3. If $\dfrac{z(x+y)^v}{u} = 1$, which of the numbers u, v, x, y or z CANNOT be 0?
   A. u
   B. v
   C. x
   D. y
   E. z

4. In a town called Hortonville, exactly 648 of the 2,160 residents have a white house. What percentage of the Hortonville residents do NOT have a white house?
   F. 30%
   G. 50%
   H. 70%
   J. 80%
   K. 90%

5. If $q = -1$ and $s = 3$, what is the value of the expression $\dfrac{(q-s)}{3q}$?
   A. -1
   B. $-\dfrac{2}{3}$
   C. $\dfrac{2}{3}$
   D. $\dfrac{4}{3}$
   E. 4

GO ON TO THE NEXT PAGE.

2 2

6. What is the slope-intercept form of the equation $\frac{1}{4}y - 3x = 5$?

    (Note: Slope-intercept form is $y = mx + b$, for constants m and b.)

  F. $y = -\frac{4}{3}x + 5$

  G. $\frac{3}{4}y = -\frac{4}{3}x + 5$

  H. $\frac{1}{4} = 3x + y$

  J. $20 = 12y + x$

  K. $y = 12x + 20$

7. Given: p and q are parallel lines
          s is a transversal crossing lines p and q
          o, m, and n are angles
          $m + n = 230°$
What is the measure of angle o below?

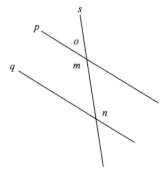

  A. 25°
  B. 65°
  C. 115°
  D. 130°
  E. 140°

8. The volume of a cylinder is $\pi r^2 h$, where r is the radius of the base of the cylinder and h is the height of the cylinder. What is the volume, in cubic inches, of a cylinder of height 5 inches that has a base of radius 4 inches?

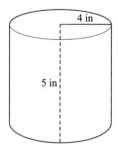

  F. 9π
  G. 20π
  H. 40π
  J. 80π
  K. 100π

GO ON TO THE NEXT PAGE.

2   △ △ △ △ **2**

9. What is the value of $|4 - x|$ if $x = 7$?
   A. -11
   B. -3
   C. 3
   D. 11
   E. 47

DO YOUR FIGURING HERE.

10. In the figure below, where the triangle is created by 3 lines that intersect at the angles indicated, the measure of angle $q = ?$

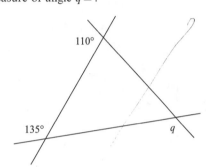

110°

135° q

   F. 45°
   G. 65°
   H. 70°
   J. 110°
   K. 115°

11. $(\sqrt{2} - 6)(\sqrt{2} - 4) = ?$
   A. $10\sqrt{2} - 22$
   B. $12\sqrt{2} + 24$
   C. $24 - \sqrt{2}$
   D. $26 - 10\sqrt{2}$
   E. $10 - 11\sqrt{2}$

$\sqrt{2}(-6\sqrt{2}) + 24 (-4\sqrt{2})$

$\sqrt{2} - 10\sqrt{2} + 24$

$26 - 10\sqrt{2}$

12. For all real numbers x and y, $(x - 3y)^2 = ?$
   F. $2x - 6y$
   G. $x^2 - 6xy + 9y^2$
   H. $x^2 - 9y^2$
   J. $x^2 - 9x^2y^2 - 9y^2$
   K. $x^2 + 9xy + 9y^2$

$(x - 3y)(x - 3y)$

$x^2 - 3yx + 9y - 3yx$

$x^2 - 6yx + 9y^2$

13. For all real numbers x and y, $x - 4y + 3(x + 3y) = ?$
   A. $3x - 12y$
   B. $3x - y$
   C. $4x + 5y$
   D. $4x - y$
   E. $4x + 7y$

$3 \cdot 3xy$

$3(x + 3y) = 3x + 9y$

$x - 4y + 3x + 9y$

$4x + 5y$

14. Which of the following has the same graph as $x + 8y = 3$?
   F. $3x + 11y = 6$
   G. $2x + 10y = 5$
   H. $3x + y = 8$
   J. $3x + 24y = 9$
   K. $x - 8y = -3$

GO ON TO THE NEXT PAGE.

2 △ △ △ △ △ △ △ △ **2**

15. Anne is 3 times as old as Kyle. If their combined age is 24, how old is Anne?
- **A.** 24
- **B.** 18
- **C.** 12
- **D.** 9
- **E.** 6

DO YOUR FIGURING HERE.

16. In the figure below, the 2 intersecting lines QS and PT form triangles PRQ and SRT. Lines PQ and ST are parallel. If angle P is 65° and angle S is 85°, what is the measure of angle T?

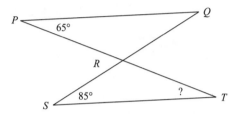

- **F.** 45°
- **G.** 55°
- **H.** 65°
- **J.** 75°
- **K.** 85°

17. A cafeteria serves a choice of 4 meats, 3 vegetables, and 5 desserts. How many different meal options does a student have for a meal consisting of 1 serving of meat, 1 serving of vegetables, and 1 dessert?
- **A.** 5
- **B.** 12
- **C.** 15
- **D.** 30
- **E.** 60

18. If $0.2a + 1.8 = a - 2.2$, then $a = ?$
- **F.** 4
- **G.** 5
- **H.** 8
- **J.** 12
- **K.** 20

19. What is the smallest integer, x, satisfying the condition that $-\sqrt{8} + x$ is negative?
- **A.** 2
- **B.** 3
- **C.** 4
- **D.** 5
- **E.** 6

20. At a dealership 265 of the vehicles are cars, while the remaining 435 vehicles are trucks. Approximately what percentage of the vehicles at the dealership are NOT cars?
- **F.** 17%
- **G.** 38%
- **H.** 62%
- **J.** 76%
- **K.** 83%

GO ON TO THE NEXT PAGE.

2   **2**

21. A circle has an area of 49π. What is the diameter of the circle?
- **A.** 7
- **B.** 14
- **C.** 24.5
- **D.** 49
- **E.** 153

DO YOUR FIGURING HERE.

22. What is the area, in square centimeters, of the figure shown below?

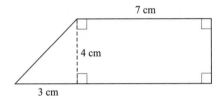

- **F.** 21
- **G.** 24
- **H.** 34
- **J.** 40
- **K.** 84

23. For all positive a, b, and c, $\dfrac{3a^2b^{-4}c^2}{2^{-2}ac^{-2}} = ?$
- **A.** $\dfrac{3a^3b^4}{4}$
- **B.** $\dfrac{12a^3}{b^4}$
- **C.** $\dfrac{3ac^4}{4b^4}$
- **D.** $\dfrac{12ac^4}{b^4}$
- **E.** $\dfrac{12a^4c}{b^2}$

24. If the monthly car payment, P dollars, on a car that costs C dollars, is given by the formula, $P = \dfrac{C}{240} - 0.007P + 35$, what is the cost, to the nearest dollar, of a car that has a monthly payment of \$233.00?
- **F.** \$23,611
- **G.** \$23,956
- **H.** \$46,812
- **J.** \$47,911
- **K.** \$63,929

25. Which of the following gives the complete solution for the quadratic equation $3x^2 = 4x$?
- **A.** $x = 3$ or $x = \dfrac{3}{4}$
- **B.** $x = -3$ or $x = -4$
- **C.** $x = 0$ or $x = \dfrac{3}{4}$
- **D.** $x = 0$ or $x = \dfrac{4}{3}$
- **E.** $x = \dfrac{3}{4}$ or $x = -\dfrac{3}{4}$

GO ON TO THE NEXT PAGE.

2   **2**

DO YOUR FIGURING HERE.

26. In the standard (x,y) coordinate plane, what is the slope of a line containing the points $(3,-8)$ and $(4,7)$?

F. $-\dfrac{1}{15}$

G. -1

H. $\dfrac{3}{7}$

J. 7

K. 15

27. In the standard (x, y) coordinate plane, which of the following is an equation of the circle with a center located at $(2, -7)$ and a radius of 5?

A. $(x+2)^2+(y-7)^2=25$

B. $(x-2)^2+(y+7)^2=25$

C. $(x-2)+(y+7)=5$

D. $(x-7)^2+(y+2)^2=25$

E. $x^2+y^2=25$

28. If $8x^2-8x-6=(ax-3)(4x+a)$, what is the value of a?

F. -2

G. 1

H. 2

J. 3

K. 4

29. Which of the following is the slope-intercept form of a line that is perpendicular to $y=-\dfrac{1}{4}x+1$ in the standard (x, y) coordinate plane and that also contains the point $(0, -5)$?

A. $y=4x-5$

B. $y=-\dfrac{1}{4}x$

C. $y=4x+5$

D. $y=-\dfrac{1}{4}x-5$

E. $y=-5x+4$

30. When baking cookies, the quantity of flour needed is a constant proportion of the number of cookies being made. If 24 cookies require 2 cups of flour, how many cups of flour will 60 cookies require?

F. 2

G. $2\dfrac{1}{4}$

H. 3

J. $4\dfrac{1}{2}$

K. 5

31. What value of p will satisfy the equation $0.1(p-1,800)=p$?

A. $2,000$

B. $1,620$

C. 800

D. 200

E. 180

GO ON TO THE NEXT PAGE.

2   **2**

32. Which of the following is an equation of the circle shown below?

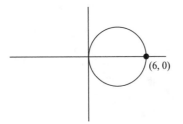

(6, 0)

   F. $(x-3)^2 + y^2 = 9$
   G. $(x-6)^2 + (y-3)^2 = 9$
   H. $x^2 - (y-6)^2 = 3$
   J. $x^2 + (y+3)^2 = 9$
   K. $(x-3)^2 + (y-3)^2 = 9$

33. Which of the following is the solution statement for the inequality $x + 2(5 - x) \leq 2x + 3$?

   A. $x \leq -7$
   B. $x \geq \dfrac{7}{3}$
   C. $x \geq 3$
   D. $x \leq \dfrac{7}{3}$
   E. $x \geq 0$

34. Given the figure below, with the lengths of the sides of the triangle shown in centimeters, how many centimeters long is side YZ?

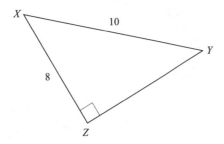

   F. $2\sqrt{41}$
   G. 6
   H. $2\sqrt{3}$
   J. 9
   K. 18

GO ON TO THE NEXT PAGE.

35. Given the parallelogram below, what is the area of the shaded region?

- **A.** 24
- **B.** 26
- **C.** 32
- **D.** 38
- **E.** 40

36. What is the only possible solution for x in the equation $\frac{3}{4}x - \frac{3}{8} = \frac{1}{4} + \frac{5}{8}x$?

- **F.** $\frac{1}{8}$
- **G.** $\frac{5}{8}$
- **H.** 3
- **J.** $\frac{8}{5}$
- **K.** 5

37. Two similar isosceles right triangles are shown below. The hypotenuse of the smaller triangle is $2\sqrt{2}$ cm. If the perimeter of the larger triangle is twice that of the smaller triangle, what is the length, in centimeters, of each of the 2 congruent legs of the larger triangle?

 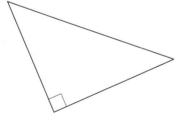

- **A.** 2
- **B.** $2\sqrt{2}$
- **C.** $4\sqrt{2}$
- **D.** 4
- **E.** $\sqrt{2}$

GO ON TO THE NEXT PAGE.

2 △ △ △ △ △ △ △ △ **2**

38. In the figure below, $MNOQ$ is a parallelogram and OPQ is a right triangle. The side lengths shown are in centimeters. What is the area, in square centimeters, of figure $MNOP$?

DO YOUR FIGURING HERE.

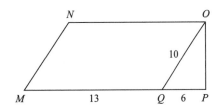

F. 104
G. 128
H. 136
J. 190
K. 208

39. In the triangle below, $\sin a =$?

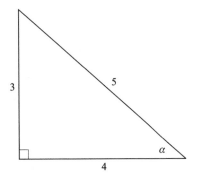

A. $\dfrac{3}{4}$

B. $\dfrac{4}{5}$

C. $\dfrac{3}{5}$

D. $\dfrac{4}{3}$

E. $\dfrac{5}{4}$

40. If $x = -3$ and $x = 5$ are solutions to the equation $(x+m)(x+n) = 0$, then $m + n =$?
F. -15
G. -8
H. -2
J. 2
K. 8

GO ON TO THE NEXT PAGE.

2   **2**

41. What is the x coordinate if $(x,5)$ is on a line that passes through $(-2,-1)$ and $(2,2)$ in the standard (x, y) coordinate plane?

A. 3
B. 4
C. 5
D. 6
E. 7

DO YOUR FIGURING HERE.

42. If $\cos B = \dfrac{10}{17}$ and the $\sin B = \dfrac{7}{17}$, then $\tan B = ?$

F. $\dfrac{7}{10}$

G. $\dfrac{24}{17}$

H. $\dfrac{10}{7}$

J. $\dfrac{17}{10}$

K. $\dfrac{24}{10}$

43. Which of the following expressions is illustrated in the (x, y) coordinate plane below?

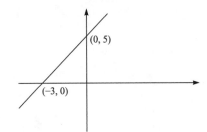

A. $y = \dfrac{5}{3}x + 5$

B. $y = -\dfrac{5}{3}x + 5$

C. $y = \dfrac{3}{5}x - 5$

D. $y = -\dfrac{5}{3}x - 5$

E. $5y - 3x = 0$

44. In the square $SPQR$ shown below, the diagonal of the square is QS, which is 8 centimeters long. What is the area of square $SPQR$?

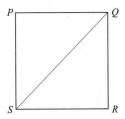

F. 64
G. 32
H. $8\sqrt{2}$
J. 8
K. $\sqrt{2}$

GO ON TO THE NEXT PAGE.

2   **2**

45. The circumference of a circle is 7π. What is the radius of the circle?

   A. $\dfrac{7}{4}$

   B. $\dfrac{7}{2}$

   C. 7
   D. 14
   E. 49

46. Each side of a certain cube has a length of 5 centimeters. What is the volume of the cube, in cubic centimeters?
   F. 3^5
   G. 4^3
   H. 5^3
   J. 5^4
   K. 6^3

47. For what values of x is $3x^2 + 4x - 15$ positive?

   A. $x < -\dfrac{5}{3}$ or $x > 3$

   B. $x < -5$ or $x > 3$
   C. $x < -3$ or $x > 3$
   D. $x < 5$ or $x > -3$

   E. $x < -3$ or $x > \dfrac{5}{3}$

48. Which of the following is a perfect square trinomial?
   F. $4x^2 + 12x + 9$
   G. $9x^2 - 6x + 10$
   H. $2x^2 + 4x + 16$
   J. $9x^2 - 10$
   K. $4x^2 + 16x + 4$

49. Assuming both p and q are negative integers, if $p = 2q$, which of the following must be a rational number?

   I. $p + q$

   II. $\dfrac{p}{q}$

   III. $\dfrac{q}{p}$

   A. I only
   B. II only
   C. III only
   D. II and III only
   E. I, II, and III

50. Marcia rode her bike to Alan's house to visit. The trip to Alan's house took x minutes. Returning home, Marcia was able to travel at an average speed 2 times faster than the speed at which she biked to Alan's house. Which of the following is an expression for the total number of minutes Marcia biked on the entire trip?
   F. $2x$

   G. $\dfrac{x}{2}$

   H. $x + 2$

   J. $\dfrac{3x}{2}$

   K. $3x$

DO YOUR FIGURING HERE.

GO ON TO THE NEXT PAGE.

2   **2**

51. In the figure below, line AB is parallel to the base of the triangle and creates a smaller triangle inside of the original triangle. If the lengths of the sides are as shown and the smaller triangle has an area of 10 centimeters square (cm^2), what is the area, in square centimeters, of the original triangle?

DO YOUR FIGURING HERE.

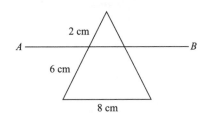

- **A.** 20
- **B.** 40
- **C.** 80
- **D.** 160
- **E.** 200

52. The figure below is a regular octagon. What is the measure of 1 of the interior angles of the octagon?

- **F.** 45°
- **G.** 60°
- **H.** 90°
- **J.** 120°
- **K.** 135°

53. It is estimated that, from the beginning of 1995 to the end of 1999, the average number of CDs bought by teenagers increased from 5 per year to 9 per year. During the same time period, the average number of videogames purchased by teenagers increased from 2 per year to 10 per year. Assuming that in each case the consumption rates are the same, in what year did teenagers buy the same average number of CDs and videogames?
- **A.** 1995
- **B.** 1996
- **C.** 1997
- **D.** 1998
- **E.** 1999

54. If $x^2 - 15b^2 = 2xb$, what are the 2 solutions for x in terms of b?
- **F.** 15b and 2b
- **G.** −5b and 3b
- **H.** 2b and 3b
- **J.** 15b and −5b
- **K.** −3b and 5b

GO ON TO THE NEXT PAGE.

2 △ △ △ △ △ △ △ △ **2**

55. Which of the following is (are) equivalent to the mathematical operation $a(b+c)$ for all real numbers a, b, and c?

    I. $ca+ba$
    II. $ab+ac$
    III. $(b+c)a$

A. I only
B. II only
C. III only
D. I and II only
E. I, II, and III

56. For values of x where $\sin x$, $\cos x$, and $\tan x$ are all defined, $\dfrac{(\tan x)}{(\sin x \cos x)} = ?$

F. $\dfrac{1}{\cos^2 x}$
G. $\cot x$
H. 1
J. $\sin^2 x$
K. $\sec x$

57. What is the solution set for the equation $|x^3| = -x^3$?
A. All real numbers
B. All $x \geq 0$
C. All $x \leq 0$
D. All odd numbers
E. Only $x = 1$

58. For which of the following values of c will there be 2 distinct solutions to the equation $3x^2 + 2x + c = 0$?
F. -1
G. 1
H. 2
J. 3
K. 4

59. In the figure below, angle QPR and angle PRS are right angles. If the length of line $\overline{PS}$ is 20 units and the length of line $\overline{PR}$ is 12 units, what is the length of line $\overline{RS}$?

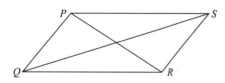

A. $\sqrt{12}$
B. 16
C. $\sqrt{20}$
D. $4\sqrt{2}$
E. 20

DO YOUR FIGURING HERE.

GO ON TO THE NEXT PAGE.

2 △ △ △ △ △ △ △ △ **2**

60. The figure below shows a loading ramp at a hardware store that is s feet high and has a slope of t, where $t > 0$. Which of the following expressions gives the length of the ramp, in feet?

DO YOUR FIGURING HERE.

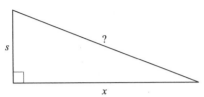

F. $\dfrac{t}{s}$

G. $t^2 + s^2$

H. $\left(\dfrac{t}{s}\right)^2$

J. $\dfrac{s}{t}$

K. $\sqrt{\left(\dfrac{s}{t}\right)^2 + s^2}$

END OF THE MATH TEST
STOP! IF YOU HAVE TIME LEFT OVER, CHECK YOUR WORK ON THIS SECTION ONLY.

3 ███████████████████████████████ **3**

READING TEST

35 Minutes – 40 Questions

DIRECTIONS: This test includes four passages, each followed by ten questions. Read the passage and choose the best answer to each question. After you have selected your answer, fill in the corresponding bubble on your answer sheet. You should refer to the passages as often as necessary when answering the questions.

Passage I

PROSE FICTION: *This passage is adapted from "The Magic Shop," by H. G. Wells, originally published in 1903.*

I had seen the Magic Shop from afar several times; I had passed it once or twice, a shop window of alluring little objects, magic balls, magic hens, wonderful cones, ventriloquist dolls, the basket trick,
5 packs of cards that LOOKED all right, and all that sort of thing, but never had I thought of going in, until one day, almost without warning, Gip hauled me by my finger right up to the window and so conducted himself that there was nothing for it but
10 to take him in. I had not even been sure that the place was there, to tell the truth. It was a modest-sized frontage in Regent Street, between the picture shop and the place where the chicks run about just out of patent incubators, but there it was sure enough.
15 I had fancied it was down nearer the Circus, or round the corner in Oxford Street, or even in Holborn; always over the way and a little inaccessible it had been, with something of the mirage in its position; but here it was now quite indisputably,
20 and the fat end of Gip's pointing finger made a noise upon the glass. "If I was rich," said Gip, dabbing a finger at the Disappearing Egg, "I'd buy myself that. And that"—which was The Crying Baby, Very Human—"and that", which was a mystery,
25 and called, so a neat card asserted, "Buy One and Astonish Your Friends." "Anything," said Gip, "will disappear under one of those cones. I have read about it in a book. And there, dadda, is the Vanishing Halfpenny—, only they've put it this way
30 up so's we can't see how it's done." Gip, dear boy, inherits his mother's breeding, and he did not propose to enter the shop or worry in any way; only, you know, quite unconsciously he lugged my finger doorward, and he made his interest clear.
35 "That," he said, and pointed to the Magic Bottle. "If you had that?" I said; at which promising inquiry he looked up with a sudden radiance. "I could show it to Jessie," he said, thoughtful as ever of others.

"It's less than a hundred days to your birthday,
40 Gibbles," I said, and laid my hand on the door-handle. Gip made no answer, but his grip tightened

on my finger, and so we came into the shop. It was no common shop this; it was a magic shop, and all the prancing precedence Gip would have taken in
45 the matter of mere toys was wanting. He left the burden of the conversation to me. It was a little, narrow shop, not very well lit, and the door-bell pinged again with a plaintive note as we closed it behind us. For a moment or so, we were alone
50 and could glance about us. There was a tiger in papier-mâché on the glass case that covered the low counter—a grave, kind-eyed tiger that waggled his head in a methodical manner; there were several crystal spheres, a china hand holding magic cards,
55 a stock of magic fish-bowls in various sizes, and an immodest magic hat that shamelessly displayed its springs. On the floor were magic mirrors; one to draw you out long and thin, one to swell your head and vanish your legs, and one to make you short
60 and fat; and while we were laughing at these, the shopman came in.

At any rate, there he was behind the counter—a curious, sallow, dark man, with one ear larger than the other and a chin like the toe-cap of a boot. "What
65 can we have the pleasure?" he said, spreading his long, magic fingers on the glass case; and so with a start we were aware of him. "I want," I said, "to buy my little boy a few simple tricks." "Legerdemain?" he asked. "Mechanical? Domestic?" "Anything
70 amusing?" said I. "Um!" said the shopman, and scratched his head for a moment as if thinking. Then, quite distinctly, he drew from his head a glass ball. "Something in this way?" he said, and held it out. The action was unexpected. I had seen the trick done
75 at entertainments endless times before—it's part of the common stock of conjurers—but I had not expected it here. "That's good," I said, with a laugh. "Isn't it?" said the shopman. Gip stretched out his disengaged hand to take this object and found merely
80 a blank palm. "It's in your pocket," said the shopman, and there it was! "How much will that be?" I asked. "We make no charge for glass balls," said the shopman politely. "We get them"—he picked one out of his elbow as he spoke—"free."
85 He produced another from the back of his neck, and he laid it beside its predecessor on the counter.

GO ON TO THE NEXT PAGE.

3 ██████████████████████████████████████ **3**

Gip regarded his glass ball sagely, then directed a look of inquiry at the two on the counter, and finally brought his round-eyed scrutiny to the shopman,
90 who smiled. "You may have those too," said the shopman, "and, if you DON'T mind, one from my mouth, SO!" Gip counseled me mutely for a moment, and then in a profound silence he put away the four balls, resumed my reassuring finger, and nerved
95 himself for the next event.

1. As it is used in the passage (line 15), the word *fancied* most nearly means:
   A. forgotten.
   B. imagined.
   C. stated
   D. pretended.

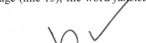

2. The narrator states that he was confused about:
   F. which store Gip wanted to enter.
   G. whether or not to go into the store.
   H. the location of the Magic Shop.
   J. Gip's feelings about the Magic Shop's clerk.

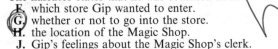

3. The passage suggests that the narrator first learned about the Magic Shop:
   A. when he had passed it before.
   B. when Gip led him there.
   C. when he was a little boy.
   D. when he moved into the town.

4. The narrator states that Gip "did not propose to enter the shop or worry in any way" in the second paragraph. This description suggests that Gip:
   F. was worried about his mother.
   G. began to have a temper tantrum because he wanted to go into the store.
   H. was not capable of speaking.
   J. was a polite child.

5. The narrator considers the clerk's behavior, as it is described in Paragraph 4, as:
   A. surprising.
   B. frightening.
   C. confusing.
   D. predictable.

6. Gip's reaction to the shopman's first trick can best be described as:
   F. quietly astonished; he takes the glass balls and then goes back to holding his father's hand.
   G. uncomfortably disturbed; he signals to his father that he wishes to leave the shop.
   H. obviously frustrated; he wants to know how the tricks are done.
   J. unamused; he feels the shopman is playing tricks on him.

7. The narrator's desire to purchase a magic trick, as mentioned in Paragraph 4, depends primarily on:
   A. Gip's birthday wishes.
   B. its appropriateness to Gip's age.
   C. which tricks the shopkeeper can show him.
   D. how much fun the trick will be.

8. It can be reasonably inferred that Gip's feeling about entering the Magic Shop is:
   F. frustration.
   G. anxiety.
   H. uncertainty.
   J. excitement.

9. The description in Paragraph 4 suggests that the shopman's sudden presence causes the narrator and his son to:
   A. stop laughing together.
   B. begin asking endless questions.
   C. leave the shop.
   D. laugh at him.

10. According to the last sentence in the passage, Gip was ready to:
    F. start crying.
    G. make his purchases.
    H. run out of the store.
    J. see the next trick.

GO ON TO THE NEXT PAGE.

3 ██ **3**

Passage II
SOCIAL SCIENCE: *Alaska the Beautiful?*

I was a ten-year-old girl, in the middle of fifth grade, on the day that Alaska garnered the forty-ninth star on the American flag. I remember clearly all the hoopla and celebration, knowing that Hawaii
5 was close to becoming star number 50. Nearly fifty years later, however, Alaska remains an enigma to me. Having never visited this remote area, I still think of Alaska as little but cold, dark and desolate, in stark contrast to my image of Hawaii's golden
10 sunshine and warm breezes. At one point in our married life, my husband and I discussed the possibility of pulling up stakes and moving the family to Alaska to teach. A friend of ours had done so several years before and was now earning six digits as a high
15 school principal there. As tempting as it sounded, however, I couldn't get past the idea of living in the vicinity of Siberia, so we never went, not even for a visit with our friend.

So how did this vast and relatively untouched
20 land become a state in a country like ours, a state that is so geographically, and seemingly in all other ways, so far removed? The evolution of this nearly 600,000 square miles of land from U.S. territory to statehood took almost 100 years from beginning
25 to end. In March of 1867, an agreement then known as "Seward's Folly" was made between Russia and then Secretary of State William H. Seward, to obtain this territory for a mere $7.2 million. As the name of this pact suggests, many people back home
30 marveled at the apparent stupidity of such a plan. What, after all, did this place called Alaska have to offer the rest of the country?

The Klondike Gold Rush in 1897 was probably the first concrete evidence that Alaska did have
35 something to offer. For over a decade, more than 30,000 miners, fishermen, and trappers entered regions of Alaska, developing a colonial economy in which Alaska's land and water resources were taken out and sold elsewhere. In effect, Alaska's
40 own natural wealth was being stripped for the benefit of a handful of outside entrepreneurs. At this time, Alaska was functioning under the First Organic Act of 1884 which provided the territory with judges, clerks, and marshals. These officials,
45 however, numbered only 13 in a population of 32,000 people; all but 430 of these 32,000 people were white settlers. As Alaska's resources were being exploited and public unrest brewing, the Second Organic Act was passed by Congress in 1912. This
50 act gave official territory status to Alaska and also appropriated a legislature of eight elected Senators and sixteen elected Members of the House. However, the territory's governor was to be appointed by Congress rather than freely elected,
55 and all acts passed by the local bodies of government were subject to the approval of Congress. The federal government also maintained power over Alaska's vast resources, power that probably ultimately led to Alaska's statehood. These acts of
60 Congress did, however, seal the concept of Alaska being a part of the United States.

Alaska's first bill requesting statehood was introduced to Congress in 1916. Without a push from Alaska's 58,000 residents, however, the bill was
65 unsuccessful. Ironically, the bombing of Pearl Harbor in the Hawaiian Islands, though thousands of miles away, also brought Alaska into the forefront of national attention. It was two years earlier, in 1940, when Congress had appropriated
70 funds for military bases in Alaska, convinced that Alaska and the nearby Aleutian Island chain were threatened by their proximity to Japan. The bombing of Pearl Harbor and Japanese occupation of two of the islands in the Aleutian chain propelled
75 Congress to provide Alaska with billions of dollars in defense spending, as well as for the construction of the Alaska Highway. By 1943, a solid three quarters of Alaska's 233,000 residents were part of the military, changing Alaska forever. After many
80 more years of political wrangling, Alaska finally gained its statehood on January 3, 1959, due primarily to growing and organized public and political pressure.

At some point in my life I have gained at least
85 some familiarity with every state in the continental United States. And, while never having been to Hawaii, I plan to go there someday soon and dread only the thought of the twelve-hour plane trip. In my head, I'm already enjoying the multitude of fragrant,
90 colorful blossoms, the red-orange sunsets, and the lapping of soft waves on the beach. Alaska, on the other hand, despite glowing reports received from my friend, will probably never mean more to me than the forty-ninth star on the American flag.

11. As it is depicted in the passage, Alaska can most reasonably be characterized as:
    A. an undeveloped territory with few resources.
    B. a region of land that shouldn't be a part of the United States.
    C. a vast, unpopulated region that is difficult to visit.
    D. a distant state that encountered difficulty in achieving statehood.

12. As it is used in line 6, the word *enigma* most nearly means:
    F. image.
    G. mystery.
    H. picture.
    J. enemy.

13. Based on information in the passage, you can conclude that the author:
    A. is almost sixty years old.
    B. is a young girl.
    C. was born in 1959.
    D. is a resident of Alaska.

GO ON TO THE NEXT PAGE.

3 3

14. The passage states that:
    F. both Hawaii and Alaska became states in 1959.
    G. the Alaska Highway was never completed.
    H. the Aleutian Islands are somewhat close to Japan.
    J. Alaska was bombed during World War II.

15. It can most reasonably be inferred that the author asks the question "So how did this vast and relatively untouched land become a state in a country like ours …?" in Paragraph 2 in order to:
    A. explain why Alaskans were determined to make their territory an official state.
    B. introduce the rest of the information in the paragraph about Alaska's struggle for statehood.
    C. introduce arguments against Alaska's chances at becoming a state.
    D. elaborate on "Seward's Folly."

16. Which of the following statements best describes the author's method of addressing her audience?
    F. She makes an emotional appeal to the reader by describing her childhood.
    G. She describes her personal experiences about her visits to Alaska.
    H. She presents historical background information regarding the topic.
    J. She presents a series of arguments similar to those presented when Alaskans were working toward statehood.

17. It is most reasonable to infer that when the author claims that "Alaska's own natural wealth was being stripped for the benefit of a handful of outside entrepreneurs" in the third paragraph, she means that:
    A. Alaska's benefits to the rest of the country were short-lived.
    B. Alaskans were greedy and did not want outsiders to settle there.
    C. Alaskans were not reaping the benefits of their own land's resources.
    D. Alaskans did not believe in capitalism.

18. As it is used in line 74, the word *propelled* most nearly means:
    F. motivated.
    G. supported.
    H. prospered.
    J. silenced.

19. It can most reasonably be inferred that the author contrasts Alaska and Hawaii throughout the passage in order to:
    A. show how much alike they really are.
    B. encourage the reader to visit Hawaii.
    C. provide a history of Alaska's statehood.
    D. emphasize her personal impressions of each state.

20. According to the author, Alaska's eventual success at gaining statehood can mostly be attributed to:
    F. the public's growing desire to make it happen.
    G. the bombing of Pearl Harbor.
    H. the realization that Alaska had plenty of natural resources.
    J. politicians who forced the issue against the people's wishes.

GO ON TO THE NEXT PAGE.

3 ████████████████████████████████████ **3**

Passage III

HUMANITIES: *This passage is adapted from "Alma Gluck," by Alma Gluck; published in The Etude Magazine, February 1921)*

Many seem surprised when I tell them that my vocal training did not begin until I was twenty years of age. It seems to me that it is a very great mistake for any girl to begin the serious study
5 of singing before that age, as the feminine voice, in most instances, is hardly settled until then. Vocal study before that time is likely to be injurious, though some survive it in the hands of very careful and understanding teachers.

10 The first kind of repertoire that a student should acquire is a repertoire of *solfeggios* (technical exercises). I am a great believer in the *solfeggio*. Using that for a basis, one is assured of acquiring facility and musical accuracy. The experienced
15 listener can tell at once the voice that has had such training. Always remember that musicianship carries one much further than a good natural voice. The voice, even more than the hands, needs a kind of exhaustive technical drill. This is because in
20 this training you are really building the instrument itself. In the piano, one has the instrument complete before he begins; but in the case of the voice, the instrument has to be developed and sometimes made by study. When the pupil is practicing, tones
25 grow in volume, richness, and fluency.

There are exercises by Bordogni, Concone, Vaccai, Marchesi, Panofka, Panserson, and many others, which are marvelously beneficial when intelligently studied. These I sang on the syllable
30 "Ah," and not with the customary syllable names. It has been said that the syllables Do, Re, Mi, Fa, etc., aid one in reading. To my mind, they are often confusing.

After a thorough drilling in *solfeggios*, I would
35 have the student work on the operatic arias of Bellini, Rossini, Donizetti, Verdi, and others. These men knew how to write for the human voice! Their arias are so vocal that the voice develops under them and the student gains vocal assurance.
40 They were written before modern philosophy entered into music—when music was intended for the ear rather than for the mind. I cannot lay too much stress on the importance of using these arias. They are a tonic for the voice and bring back the
45 elasticity which the more subdued singing of songs taxes.

Then when the student has her voice under complete control, it is safe to take up the lyric repertoire of Mendelssohn, Old English songs,
50 etc. How simple and charming they are! The works of the lighter French composers, Hahn, Massenet, Chaminade, Gounod, and others. Then Handel, Haydn, Mozart, Loew, Schubert, Schumann, and Brahms. Later the student will continue
55 with Strauss, Wolf, Reger, Rimsky-Korsakoff, Mousorgsky, Borodin, and Rachmaninoff. Then the modern French composers, Ravel, Debussy, Geroges, Kocklin, Hue, Chausson, and others. I leave French for the last because it is, in many ways,

60 more difficult for an English-speaking person to sing. It is so full of complex and trying vowels that it requires the utmost subtlety to overcome these difficulties and still retain clarity in diction. For that reason the student should have the advice of a
65 native French coach. When one has traveled this long road, then she is qualified to sing English songs and ballads.

In this country we are rich in the quantity of songs rather than in the quality. The singer has to go
70 through hundreds of compositions before she finds one that really says something. Commercialism overwhelms our composers. They approach their work with the question, "Will this go?" The spirit in which a work is conceived is that in which it will be
75 executed. Inspired by the purse rather than the soul, the mercenary side fairly screams in many of the works put out by everyday American publishers. This does not mean that a song should be strange or ugly to be novel or immortal. It means that the
80 sincerity of the art worker must permeate it as naturally as the green leaves break through the dead branches in springtime. Of the vast number of new American composers, there are hardly more than a dozen who seem to approach their work in the
85 proper spirit of artistic reverence.

Nothing annoys me quite so much as the hysterical hypocrites who are forever prating about "art for art's sake." What nonsense! The student who deceives himself into thinking that she is giving
90 her life like an ascetic in the spirit of sacrifice for art is the victim of a deplorable species of egotism. Art for art's sake is just as iniquitous an attitude, in its way, as art for money's sake. The real artist has no idea that she is sacrificing herself for art. She does
95 what she does for one reason and one reason only— she can't help doing it. Just as the bird sings or the butterfly soars, because it is her natural characteristic, so the artist works.

21. The passage suggests that the author has strong opinions about:
    A. modern philosophy.
    B. voice training.
    C. earning a living by singing.
    D. playing the piano.

22. The passage suggests that the reason the narrator was twenty years old when she began her voice training was because:
    F. she believed it was better for her voice to wait until age twenty.
    G. she was too poor to afford voice lessons until she was twenty.
    H. her parents were against voice training until the age of twenty.
    J. she did not have a natural voice until the age of twenty.

GO ON TO THE NEXT PAGE.

23. The passage states that the first part of vocal training should revolve around:
  A. listening to classical music.
  B. playing the piano.
  C. learning music theory.
  D. vocal exercises.

24. The narrator's claim that "These men knew how to write for the human voice!," suggests that:
  F. she understands different types of music.
  G. no other type of music should be sung by voice students.
  H. the human voice is difficult to develop.
  J. instrumental music cannot be sung.

25. Information in the fifth paragraph supports the narrator's claim that:
  A. all songs should be sung with lyrics.
  B. most lyrics ruin the melody of Old English songs.
  C. lyrics should only be sung when the voice is developed and ready.
  D. only lyrical music should be learned by a serious singer.

26. It is most reasonable to infer that when Gluck claims that "the student should have the advice of a native French coach" in the fifth paragraph, she is referring to her opinion that:
  F. French songs should be translated into English before being sung by English-speaking singers.
  G. French songs are difficult to learn because of the nature of the French language.
  H. only French teachers are able to teach French songs.
  J. to be a great vocalist, one must study music in France.

27. Which of the following best describes Gluck's method of and purpose for addressing her audience?
  A. She relates her own experiences of learning to sing to convince the reader to learn the same way.
  B. She cites the advice of music composers regarding vocal instruction to show support for the composers.
  C. She presents information about voice physiology and its development in humans to indicate the value of voice training.
  D. She presents her personal opinions about the appropriate steps in learning to sing to provide the reader with useful information.

28. It is most reasonable to infer that when Gluck claims that in America "we are rich in the quantity of songs rather than in the quality," she most nearly means:
  F. there are too many American composers.
  G. there is a great deal of European influence in American composing.
  H. there are many songs, some of which are poorly composed.
  J. Americans enjoy singing.

29. As it is used in line 92, the word *iniquitous* most nearly means:
  A. agreeable.
  B. unjust.
  C. truthful.
  D. spiritual.

30. It can most reasonably be inferred that Gluck compares the "real artist" to a bird singing in the last paragraph because:
  F. both have been taught to sing.
  G. they are both examples of "practice makes perfect."
  H. they are both naturally driven to sing.
  J. all good singers sound like birds.

GO ON TO THE NEXT PAGE.

3

Passage IV
NATURAL SCIENCE: *Dangerous Visitor*

The huge billboard at the side of the highway is no joke; transporting firewood in certain areas of Michigan and Ohio is a federal crime, punishable by a whopping four thousand dollar fine. The reason?
5 Emerald Ash Borer disease, or EAB disease, a new addition to the long list of dangerous foreign pest infestations on American soil. It was in 2002 when this bug, the Emerald Ash Borer beetle, was first discovered in southeastern lower Michigan. Not
10 long after, it was found in Toledo, Ohio. Originally an Asian insect, this metallic green beetle (*Agrilus planipennis*) probably found its way to North America via a wooden crate or pallet made of ash wood, and immediately settled into the bark of a
15 local ash tree. In little time, the species managed to fully establish itself, decimating millions of ash trees as well as a thirty million dollar annual market for this once sought-after landscape choice. To date, over 5,000 square miles of Michigan and Canadian
20 land, as well as several outlying areas in Ohio and Indiana, are officially considered infested, and work is underway to eradicate the disease before ash trees end up in the same category as the elm and chestnut trees which are all but extinct in many areas.

25 Ash Borer infestations are particularly troublesome because they are difficult to identify until the ash tree is heavily infested. The larvae of these bugs hide deep within the tree's bark while the adults settle high within the tree's canopy. In addition,
30 other ash trees in the area surrounding the source are probably also being invaded. This can occur within up to a half mile radius from the source tree. This makes control and eradication a monumental task, not to mention an extremely costly one.

35 Researchers are working on a variety of issues related to the control and ultimate elimination of this harmful beetle. For example, it has been discovered that Asian ash trees are not devastated by this native borer as are the ash trees in North
40 America. The presumption is that, over time, Asian ash trees have developed genes resistant to the insect; therein perhaps lies the secret to controlling this pest in North American ash trees as well. Insecticide treatment is also being explored on
45 several fronts. Research is underway to determine which insecticides are proving to be the most successful, as well as their proper application— directly treating the tree, as opposed to injecting the soil, for example. Proper timing of the insecticide is
50 also an important consideration. And, as always, the benefits of insecticide treatments must be carefully weighed against their potential harm to other plant life and living beings.

These, however, are all long-range solutions
55 requiring a great deal of study and research. In the meantime, careful steps must be taken to prevent the spread of ash tree disease. Methodical identification of infested trees is taking place in all susceptible areas. As questions are raised and research is
60 conducted to answer those questions, the invasive ash borer continues to lay its eggs and prey on the nutrients of its host tree. This means that identified

trees are being cut down and destroyed, along with the beetle colonies, or "galleries." Ultimately, this
65 puts a huge drain on town and city budgets, as mature tree removal can be extremely expensive. Along with tree removal expenses comes the additional outlay of funds for replacement trees, often an unexpected and unplanned emergency
70 budget item.

Even though it will be expensive to deal with this problem in the short term, the costs of doing nothing could be far higher since we could conceivably lose an entire species of tree.

31. Information in the passage suggests that the author of the passage:
A. is a scientist.
B. is cautiously optimistic about the success of EAB disease eradication.
C. is personally involved with the study of EAB disease in Michigan and Ohio.
D. disagrees with the outrageous fines for transporting firewood.

32. The passage indicates that the Emerald Ash Borer beetle:
F. is resistant to insecticides.
G. is clearly visible on the ash tree.
H. is native to North America.
J. occurs naturally in Asia.

33. The four thousand dollars referred to in Paragraph 1 relates to:
A. a fine for having an infested tree on your property.
B. the cost of removing an infected ash tree.
C. a fine for moving firewood.
D. the cost of uninfected ash firewood.

34. The main worry expressed in the first paragraph is:
F. the cost of EAB infestation to the tree industry.
G. the transporting of EAB to American soil.
H. the time period during which the bugs were discovered.
J. the decimation of ash trees in North America.

35. The author's attitude toward the study of EAB disease is best characterized as one of:
A. interested concern.
B. emotional panic.
C. scholarly interest.
D. scientific knowledge.

GO ON TO THE NEXT PAGE.

3 ████████████████████████████████ **3**

36. The passage identifies *Agrilus planipennis* as:
    F. North American ash wood.
    G. pest infestations.
    H. beetle eggs.
    J. Emerald Ash Borer beetle.

37. According to the passage, "galleries" are:
    A. beetle colonies.
    B. places from which to observe the beetles.
    C. insecticide application processes.
    D. infected trees.

38. The passage indicates that EAB beetles might also be correctly identified as:
    F. a North American insect.
    G. a Canadian beetle.
    H. an Asian beetle.
    J. Dutch elm beetles.

39. The passage states that EAB adults live:
    A. under the tree bark of various local trees.
    B. in the soil of the ash tree.
    C. deep within the tree trunk.
    D. in the upper branches of the ash tree.

40. The passage claims that one of the methods currently being used to control EAB disease is:
    F. building monuments.
    G. tree removal.
    H. insecticide spray.
    J. gene replacement.

END OF THE READING TEST
STOP! IF YOU HAVE TIME LEFT OVER, CHECK YOUR WORK ON THIS SECTION ONLY.

SCIENCE REASONING TEST

35 Minutes – 40 Questions

DIRECTIONS: There are seven passages in this test. Each passage is followed by several questions. You should refer to the passages as often as necessary in order to choose the best answer to each question. Once you have selected your answer, fill in the corresponding bubble on your answer sheet. You may NOT use a calculator on this test.

Passage I

Traditionally, oral drugs in pill or capsule form have been designed to release the dose of medicine in the upper gastrointestinal tract, where drugs are more readily dissolved and absorbed. New research has targeted the colon as an ideal environment for drug absorption to treat certain illnesses. To reach the colon, the drug must first pass through the stomach and small intestine. Table 1 details several drug-delivery systems, and the following experiments test two of the drug-delivery systems.

Table 1		
Drug-delivery system	Mechanics	Drawback
pH	* Dissolves at a higher pH in the small intestine.	Releases early or not at all.
Pressure	* Higher pressure in the colon ruptures capsule. * Capsule size and wall thickness are varied to withstand lower pressures and rupture at higher pressures in the colon.	Food taken with the capsule may alter the pressure enough to disintegrate the capsule in the stomach.
Bacteria	* Synthetic polymer or natural (guar gum) coatings are resistant to bacteria in the stomach and small intestine but are dissolved by the higher content of bacteria in the colon.	Safety and toxicity guidelines for synthetic polymers have not been established.
Time	* Outer coating dissolves upon entering the small intestine. * Inner barrier delays release by selling, eroding, or dissolving.	Transit (movement) is slower in the evening than in the morning. Cannot adapt to an individual's transit time.

GO ON TO THE NEXT PAGE.

4 ◯ ◯ ◯ ◯ ◯ ◯ ◯ ◯ ◯ 4

Experiment 1

Bacteria-dependent delivery. This experiment measured the average time it took a coated tablet to travel from the stomach (gastric emptying) through the small intestine (small intestine transit) to arrive in the colon. Twelve healthy men aged 23 to 25 years old and weighing between 55 and 70 kilograms (kg) who had fasted overnight were divided into 3 groups. They each swallowed 1 tablet, which contained a tracer (A or B) and 1 of 2 natural coatings (1 or 2). The location of the tracer was measured every half-hour for 12 hours. The average times are recorded in Table 2.

Experiment 2

Time-dependent delivery. The methods were the same as those used in Experiment 1, except that the tablets all contained the same tracer and 1 of 2 outer coatings (A or B) and one of two inner barriers (1 or 2). The average times are recorded in Table 3.

Table 2						
Group	Gastric emptying (h)	Small intestine transit (h)	Colonic arrival (h)	Tracer	Coating	Target
I	0.63	2.75	3.35	A	1	Colon
II	0.62	2.13	2.78	A	2	Colon
III	0.61	3.25	2.63	B	1	Stomach

Table 3						
Group	Gastric emptying (h)	Small intestine transit (h)	Colonic arrival (h)	Outer coating	Inner coating	Target
I	0.63	2.65	3.15	A	1	Colon
II	0.62	3.15	3.25	A	2	Colon
III	0.61	2.25	2.78	B	1	Colon

1. Based on Table 1, which drug-delivery system can be affected by food intake?
   A. pH-dependent delivery
   B. Time-dependent delivery
   C. Pressure-dependent delivery
   D. Bacteria-dependent delivery

2. According to Experiment 2, which combination of outer and inner coatings caused the tablet to reach its intended target most quickly?
   F. A and 1
   G. A and 2
   H. B and 1
   J. B and 2

3. The results of Experiment 1 suggest that:
   A. the tracer affects the drug's target destination more than the coating does.
   B. the coating affects colonic arrival time.
   C. the coating affects the drug's target destination more than the tracer does.
   D. the tracer affects gastric emptying time.

4. Which average time is standard for both experiments?
   F. Small intestine transit time.
   G. Colonic arrival time.
   H. Small intestine transit time and colonic arrival time.
   J. Gastric emptying time.

5. Which of the following is true about time-dependent delivery?
   A. Synthetic polymers may be unsafe and may disintegrate in the stomach.
   B. Taking food may disintegrate the capsule before it reaches the colon.
   C. Delivery depends on the bacteria in the colon for delivery.
   D. An inner barrier delays release of the medicine.

GO ON TO THE NEXT PAGE.

4 ◯ ◯ ◯ ◯ ◯ ◯ ◯ ◯ ◯ **4**

Passage II

The process of altering solid rocks by changes in temperature, pressure, and chemistry is called *metamorphism. Foliation* refers to the alternating layers of different mineral compositions. Table 1 lists foliated and nonfoliated rocks. Table 2 shows a source rock and its result after undergoing metamorphism.

Table 1	
Foliated	Nonfoliated
Slate	Quartzite
Phyllite	Marble
Schist	Amphibolite
Gneiss	Metaconglomerate
	Hornfels

Table 2	
Source Rock	Result
Shale	Slate
Slate	Schist
Schist	Gneiss
Rhyolite	Schist
Basalt	Schist
Basalt	Amphibolite
Limestone	Marble
Sandstone	Quartzite

Figure 1 shows the metamorphic intensity of four types of rock.

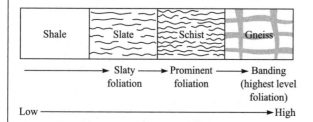

Figure 1

6. Which source rock's metamorphic result can be either foliated or nonfoliated?
   F. Shale
   G. Granite
   H. Schist
   J. Basalt

7. According to the passage, the source rock for marble is:
   A. shale.
   B. sandstone.
   C. limestone.
   D. granite.

8. According to Figure 1, foliation:
   F. increases as metamorphic intensity increases.
   G. decreases as metamorphic intensity increases.
   H. increases as metamorphic intensity decreases.
   J. is not dependant on metamorphic intensity.

9. Based on the passage, which of the following statements is true?
   A. Slate and gneiss form at approximately the same intensity.
   B. Slate forms at a lower intensity than schist.
   C. Basalt metamorphism results in only foliated rock.
   D. Schist forms rhyolite at high metamorphic intensity.

10. According to Figure 1 and Table 2, it would be expected that:
    F. foliation will increase during metamorphism from rhyolite to schist to gneiss.
    G. foliation will decrease during metamorphism from shale to schist to gneiss.
    H. metamorphic intensity will decrease from prominent foliation to banding.
    J. metamorphic intensity will increase from prominent foliation to slate foliation.

11. According to the passage, schist can result from which of the following source rocks?
    A. Slate only
    B. Slate, Shale, and Basalt
    C. Slate, Rhyolite, and Basalt
    D. Slate and Basalt only

GO ON TO THE NEXT PAGE.

4 ◯ ◯ ◯ ◯ ◯ ◯ ◯ ◯ ◯ **4**

Passage III

Researchers interested in studying the interactions between solvents' physical characteristics and the rapidity of dissolution in various solutes conducted 2 experiments. The results are shown below.

A tablet containing 1,285 milligrams (mg) sodium bicarbonate and 1,000 mg citric acid was placed in each of six, 50 milliliter (mL) beakers. The tablets were either whole, crushed into a coarse powder, or crushed into a fine powder. Either 15 mL of water at a constant temperature of 25°C, or 15 mL of hydrochloric acid (HCl) was added to each beaker. The time it took the tablet to dissolve was recorded.

Experiment 1

Each 50 mL beaker contained a tablet (1,285 mg sodium bicarbonate and 1,000 mg citric acid), which was either whole or crushed. Fifteen milliliters of water (25°C) or hydrochloric acid (HCl) was added to each beaker, and the time it took in seconds (s) for the tablet to dissolve was recorded in Table 1.

Table 1			
Beaker	Tablet form	Time (s)	Solvent
1	Whole	35	Water
2	Coarse powder	22	Water
3	Fine powder	17	Water
4	Whole	31	HCl
5	Coarse powder	17	HCl
6	Fine powder	10	HCl

Experiment 2

To each of the 6 beakers, 1 whole tablet (containing 1,285 mg sodium bicarbonate and 1,000 mg citric acid) was added. Fifteen milliliters of water of varying temperatures was added to the beakers, and the time it took in seconds (s) for the tablet to dissolve was recorded in Table 2.

Table 2		
Beaker	Temperature (°C)	Time (s)
1	10	46
2	20	38
3	40	30
4	60	21
5	80	12
6	100	4

12. In Experiment 1, which of the following scenarios caused the tablet to dissolve the fastest?
   F. Fine powder in water
   G. Coarse powder in HCl
   H. Fine powder in HCl
   J. Coarse powder in water

13. In what ways are the methods of Experiments 1 and 2 different?
   A. The solvent was varied in Experiment 1 but held constant in Experiment 2.
   B. The temperature was varied in Experiment 1 but held constant in Experiment 2.
   C. The tablet type was varied in Experiment 2 but held constant in Experiment 1.
   D. The solvent was varied in Experiment 2 but held constant in Experiment 1.

14. What observation can be made from the data in Table 1?
   F. Crushing the tablet does not affect dissolution time.
   G. Solvents do not affect dissolution time.
   H. Crushing the tablet results in slower dissolution time.
   J. Crushing the tablet results in faster dissolution time.

15. What would the result most likely be if 15 mL of 80°C water was added to a beaker containing a finely crushed tablet?
   A. The dissolution rate would be slower than 17 seconds.
   B. The dissolution rate would be faster than 12 seconds.
   C. The dissolution rate would be slower than 12 seconds.
   D. Crushing the tablet would have no effect on dissolution rate.

16. Based on the experiments, what can be done to slow the dissolution rate?
   F. Increase the water temperature
   G. Crush the tablet
   H. Use HCl to dissolve the tablet
   J. Decrease the water temperature

17. Based on the experiments, which method resulted in the slowest dissolution rate?
   A. Whole tablet dissolved in 10°C water
   B. Finely crushed tablet dissolved in 25°C water
   C. Finely crushed tablet dissolved in HCl
   D. Whole tablet in 80°C water

GO ON TO THE NEXT PAGE.

4 ◯ ◯ ◯ ◯ ◯ ◯ ◯ ◯ ◯ **4**

Passage IV

A biologist wanted to test the effects of nutrition on the growth of young rats. Two experiments were conducted using different feeds and vitamin supplements. For both experiments, 4 groups of 20 rats each were given a different type of feed over a 6-week period. The rats were measured and weighed weekly. The rats in each group had an average starting weight of 30 grams (g) and an average starting length of 10 centimeters (cm).

Experiment 1
- Group 1 was fed a high-protein feed (Feed W).
- Group 2 was fed a grain-based feed with vitamin supplements (Feed X).
- Group 3 (control group) was fed a grain-based feed without supplements (Feed Y).
- Group 4 was fed a grain-based feed without supplements plus fruits and vegetables (Feed Z).

The results and average measurements are recorded in Table 1.

Table 1		
Group	Average weight after 6 weeks (g)	Average length after 6 weeks (cm)
1	50	16.25
2	47	18.00
3	43	14.50
4	43	17.00

Experiment 2
- Group 5 was fed a high-protein feed plus fruits and vegetables (Feed M).
- Group 6 was fed a grain-based feed with vitamin supplements plus fruits and vegetables (Feed N).
- Group 7 (control group) was fed a grain-based feed without supplements (Feed O).
- Group 8 was fed a grain-based feed without supplements plus fruits and vegetables (Feed P).

The results and average measurements are recorded in Table 2 below.

Table 2		
Group	Average weight after 6 weeks (g)	Average length after 6 weeks (cm)
5	52	17.00
6	49	18.25
7	42	14.25
8	44	15.75

18. Based on the results of both experiments, the rats in which group increased the most in average length?
    F. Group 6
    G. Group 2
    H. Group 7
    J. Group 4

19. Based on the results of Experiment 2, which feed resulted in the greatest weight gain?
    A. Feed M
    B. Feed N
    C. Feed O
    D. Feed P

20. Based on the results of both experiments, the rats in which of the following groups gained the least amount of weight?
    F. Group 1
    G. Group 3
    H. Group 5
    J. Group 7

21. If the biologist added vitamin supplements to Feed M for a new group (Group 9), what might the result be after 6 weeks?
    A. Group 9 would weigh less than Group 5.
    B. Group 9 would weigh less than Group 6.
    C. Group 9 would have a greater length than Group 5.
    D. Group 9 would have a shorter average length than Group 5.

22. Which of the following statements is true, according to Table 2?
    F. Feed N produces rats that are almost twice as long as those in the control group.
    G. Feed M produces rats that weigh 3 times as much as those in the control group.
    H. Feed P produces rats with the greatest average length.
    J. Feed O produces rats similar to those produced by Feed P.

GO ON TO THE NEXT PAGE.

4 ◯ ◯ ◯ ◯ ◯ ◯ ◯ ◯ ◯ **4**

Passage V

Igneous rocks are formed by the cooling and solidification of molten magma either above ground, when magma, or lava, reaches the Earth's surface and cools, or deep below the surface of the Earth, when magma gets trapped in small pockets and cools. Table 1 lists rock textures and cooling characteristics of igneous rocks. Figure 1 shows the cooling rate and associated grain size of igneous rock textures. Table 2 lists igneous rocks and their respective textures.

Table 1		
Rock texture	Description	Cooling characteristics
Glassy	No distinct visible grains.	Cools rapidly and above the temperature for crystals to form.
Aphanitic	Minerals are too small to be seen without a microscope.	Cools quickly but more slowly than glassy-textured rocks.
Phaneritic	Interlocking grains form a mosaic pattern; can be seen without a microscope.	Cools very slowly at a uniform rate.
Porphyritic	Has two grain sizes.	Undergoes two stages of cooling: usually cools slowly first then rapidly.

Table 2	
Rock	Texture
Rhyolite	Aphanitic
Andesite	Aphanitic
Basalt	Aphanitic
Granite	Phaneritic
Diorite	Phaneritic
Gabbro	Phaneritic

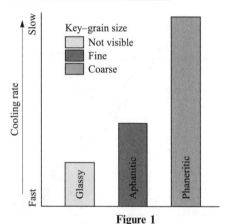

Figure 1

23. Which of the following is true about granite?
    A. It is fine grained and cools slowly.
    B. It is fine grained and cools quickly.
    C. It is coarse grained and cools quickly.
    D. It is coarse grained and cools slowly.

24. Rhyolite and andesite have which of the following in common?
    F. They cool very slowly at a uniform rate.
    G. They are phaneritic.
    H. They cool quickly but more slowly than glassy rocks.
    J. They are coarse grained.

25. Using the data in Table 1 and Figure 1, what conclusion can be made about (crystal) grain size?
    A. The slower a rock cools, the larger the crystals will be.
    B. The faster a rock cools, the larger the crystals will be.
    C. Glassy rocks have large crystals.
    D. The slower a rock cools, the smaller the crystals will be.

26. Which rock texture is formed by rapid cooling from a high temperature?
    F. Porphyritic
    G. Glassy
    H. Phaneretic
    J. Aphanitic

27. Based on information in the passage, which rocks cooled quickly?
    A. Rhyolite, granite, and diorite
    B. Granite, gabbro, and peridotite
    C. Rhyolite, andesite, and basalt
    D. Andesite, basalt, and granite

28. Peridotite is an igneous rock with interlocking grains that can be seen without a microscope. What are the likely cooling characteristics of peridotite?
    F. It cools quickly.
    G. It cools at a very slow and uniform rate.
    H. It cools slowly at first, and then speeds up.
    J. It cools at a rapid, constant rate.

GO ON TO THE NEXT PAGE.

4 ◯ ◯ ◯ ◯ ◯ ◯ ◯ ◯ 4

Passage VI

Stars can be classified according to color, surface temperature, mass, radius, and luminosity. Table 1 shows the spectral classification of star types. Figure 1 is a cluster diagram plotting stars near the sun by temperature and luminosity (total brightness). Main sequence stars are young stars shown in Figure 1 as the central band.

Table 1					
Star type	Color	Surface temperature (K)	Mass (solar mass)	Radius (solar radius)	Luminosity (solar units)
O	Blue	28,000–60,000	60	15	1,400,000
B	Blue	10,000–28,000	18	7	20,000
A	Blue	7,500–10,000	3.2	2.5	80
F	Blue to white	6,000–7,500	1.7	1.3	6
G	White to yellow	5,000–6,000	1.1	1.1	1.2
K	Orange to red	3,500–5,000	0.8	0.9	0.4
M	Red	<3,500	0.3	0.4	0.04 (very faint)

Notes: Mass, radius, and luminosity are averages. The sun has the following spectral classifications: mass = 1; radius = 1; luminosity = 1.

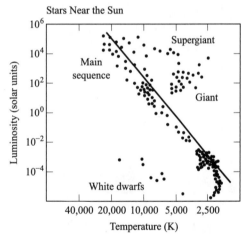

Figure 1

29. According to Table 1, which type of star has a mass 18 times that of the sun?
A. O
B. B
C. F
D. K

30. What color are stars with an approximate surface temperature of 2,500 K?
F. Blue
G. White
H. Yellow
J. Red

31. What is the color range of the giant stars shown on Figure 1?
A. Orange to red
B. Blue to white
C. White to yellow
D. Blue to orange

32. The main sequence stars on Figure 1 represent all the star types EXCEPT:
F. M
G. A
H. O
J. K

33. A new star with a temperature of 15,000 K and luminosity of 10^{-4} solar units is plotted on Figure 1. Based on the passage, what category of star is it?
A. Main sequence
B. White dwarf
C. Supergiant
D. Giant

GO ON TO THE NEXT PAGE.

4 ⃝ ⃝ ⃝ ⃝ ⃝ ⃝ ⃝ ⃝ ⃝ 4

Passage VII

A student wanted to test the absorbency of several brands of cat litter to determine which absorbed the most water the fastest. The student conducted 2 experiments to test the litters.

Experiment 1

The student filled nine 12-inch × 9-inch glass pans 2 inches deep with 1 of 3 types of cat litter (A, B, or C). The student placed each type of litter in 3 areas with different relative humidity levels. The student then poured 100 milliliters (mL) of water into each pan. The student recorded the time it took for each pan of litter to absorb the water. Results are shown in Table 1.

Table 1

Relative humidity (%)	Time for A (hr)	Time for B (hr)	Time for C (hr)
40	4	2	1
60	7	5	3
80	16	9	5

Experiment 2

The student repeated the previous experiment but used only 3 pans (one of each litter) and added 4 ounces of baking soda (sodium bicarbonate) to each pan. The student mixed the litter and baking soda thoroughly before adding 100 mL of water to each pan. The room had a constant relative humidity of 40% during the experiment. Results are shown in Table 2.

Table 2

Litter	Time (hr)
A	3.5
B	2.0
C	1.5

34. Based on the experiments, which type of litter absorbs water fastest at 40% relative humidity?
   F. Litter A + baking soda
   G. Litter C
   H. Litter B
   J. Litter C + baking soda

35. If the relative humidity was increased to 90%, how long might Litter B take to absorb all of the water?
   A. 5 hours
   B. 7 hours
   C. 9 hours
   D. >9 hours

36. Based on the results of Experiment 1, which of the following is true of Litter A?
   F. It took almost twice as long as Litter B and more than 3 times as long as Litter C to absorb the water at 80% relative humidity.
   G. It absorbed the water almost twice as fast as Litter B and almost 3 times as fast as Litter C at 80% humidity.
   H. It absorbed the water faster than both Litter B and Litter C.
   J. It absorbed the water faster than Litter B at 60% relative humidity.

37. How does Experiment 1 differ from Experiment 2?
   A. Baking soda was added to the litter in Experiment 1.
   B. The amount of water varied in Experiment 2.
   C. Relative humidity is constant in Experiment 2 but varies in Experiment 1.
   D. Relative humidity is constant in Experiment 1 but varies in Experiment 2.

38. How did adding baking soda effect the water absorption times of the litter?
   F. It decreased the absorption time for Litter A only.
   G. It increased the absorption time for Litter A and Litter B.
   H. It decreased the absorption time for Litter B only.
   J. It increased the absorption time for Litter B and Litter C.

39. If the student were to repeat Experiment 2, but reduced the quantity of water added by 50%, how would the absorption time most likely be affected?
   A. It would stay the same for all litter types.
   B. It would decrease for Litter A only.
   C. It would increase for all litter types.
   D. It would decrease for all litter types.

40. According to the results of the experiments, which of the following conclusions can be reached?
   F. Relative humidity levels have no effect on absorption rates.
   G. Absorption rates will decrease at higher relative humidity levels for all litter types.
   H. The type of litter has the greatest effect on absorption rates at all relative humidity levels.
   J. Adding baking soda to cat litter increases the absorption rate for all litter types.

END OF THE SCIENCE REASONING TEST
STOP! IF YOU HAVE TIME LEFT OVER, CHECK YOUR WORK ON THIS SECTION ONLY.

5  **5**

WRITING TEST

DIRECTIONS: This test is designed to assess your writing skills. You have thirty (30) minutes to plan and write an essay based on the stimulus provided. Be sure to take a position on the issue and support your position using logical reasoning and relevant examples. Organize your ideas in a focused and logical way, and use the English language to clearly and effectively express your position.

When you have finished writing, refer to the Scoring Rubrics discussed in Chapter 7 to estimate your score.

Note: On the actual ACT you will receive approximately 2.5 pages of scratch paper on which to develop your essay, and approximately 4 pages of notebook paper on which to write your essay. We recommend that you limit yourself to this number of pages when you write your practice essays.

Essay Prompt

Some high schools require students to pass two years of a foreign language in order to graduate. Some teachers and parents think that the requirement is needed since the world is becoming more interconnected all the time. Other people think that the rule is not necessary since many of the people in the world speak English as a second language and their numbers are increasing. In your opinion, should high school students be required to pass two years of a foreign language in order to graduate?

In your essay, take a position on this question. You may write about one of the points of view mentioned above, or you may give another point of view on this issue. Use specific examples and reasons for your position.

■ ANSWER KEY

English Test

1. A	21. C	41. B	61. D
2. F	22. J	42. J	62. H
3. C	23. A	43. C	63. A
4. G	24. J	44. F	64. H
5. B	25. D	45. D	65. A
6. F	26. H	46. F	66. G
7. C	27. A	47. B	67. D
8. H	28. J	48. G	68. G
9. D	29. B	49. C	69. C
10. H	30. F	50. H	70. F
11. B	31. D	51. D	71. D
12. F	32. F	52. F	72. H
13. A	33. B	53. B	73. C
14. H	34. J	54. F	74. G
15. D	35. A	55. C	75. D
16. H	36. H	56. H	
17. B	37. B	57. B	
18. G	38. J	58. F	
19. C	39. C	59. C	
20. H	40. G	60. H	

Mathematics Test

1. D	21. B	41. D
2. H	22. H	42. F
3. A	23. D	43. A
4. H	24. J	44. G
5. D	25. D	45. B
6. K	26. K	46. H
7. B	27. B	47. E
8. J	28. H	48. F
9. C	29. A	49. E
10. K	30. K	50. J
11. D	31. D	51. D
12. G	32. F	52. K
13. C	33. B	53. D
14. J	34. G	54. K
15. B	35. B	55. E
16. H	36. K	56. F
17. E	37. D	57. C
18. G	38. G	58. F
19. A	39. C	59. B
20. H	40. H	60. K

Reading Test

1. B	21. B
2. H	22. F
3. A	23. D
4. J	24. F
5. A	25. C
6. F	26. G
7. D	27. D
8. J	28. H
9. A	29. B
10. J	30. H
11. D	31. B
12. G	32. J
13. A	33. C
14. H	34. J
15. B	35. A
16. H	36. J
17. C	37. A
18. F	38. H
19. D	39. D
20. F	40. G

Science Reasoning Test

1. C	21. C
2. H	22. J
3. B	23. D
4. J	24. H
5. D	25. A
6. J	26. G
7. C	27. C
8. F	28. G
9. B	29. B
10. F	30. J
11. C	31. A
12. H	32. H
13. A	33. B
14. J	34. G
15. B	35. D
16. J	36. F
17. A	37. C
18. F	38. F
19. A	39. D
20. J	40. H

▇▇▇ SCORING GUIDE

Your final reported score is your COMPOSITE SCORE. Your COMPOSITE SCORE is the average of all of your SCALED SCORES.

Your SCALED SCORES for the four multiple-choice sections are derived from the Scoring Table on the next page. Use your RAW SCORE, or the number of questions that you answered correctly for each section, to determine your SCALED SCORE. If you got a RAW SCORE of 60 on the English test, for example, you correctly answered 60 out of 75 questions.

Step 1   Determine your RAW SCORE for each of the four multiple-choice sections:

English   _____

Mathematics   _____

Reading   _____

Science Reasoning   _____

The following Raw Score Table shows the total possible points for each section.

RAW SCORE TABLE	
KNOWLEDGE AND SKILL AREAS	**RAW SCORES**
ENGLISH	75
MATHEMATICS	60
READING	40
SCIENCE REASONING	40
WRITING	12

Multiple-Choice Scoring Worksheet

Step 2   Determine your SCALED SCORE for each of the four multiple-choice sections using the following Scoring Worksheet. Each SCALED SCORE should be rounded to the nearest number according to normal rules. For example, $31.2 \approx 31$ and $31.5 \approx 32$. If you answered 61 questions correctly on the English section, for example, your SCALED SCORE would be 28.

English

$\underline{\hspace{3cm}}_{\text{RAW SCORE}} \times 36 = \underline{\hspace{3cm}} \div 75 = \underline{\hspace{3cm}}$

$\underline{-\ 2}$ (*correction factor)

$\underline{\hspace{3cm}}$
SCALED SCORE

Mathematics

$\underline{\hspace{3cm}}_{\text{RAW SCORE}} \times 36 = \underline{\hspace{3cm}} \div 60 = \underline{\hspace{3cm}}$

$\underline{+\ 1}$ (*correction factor)

$\underline{\hspace{3cm}}$
SCALED SCORE

Reading

$\underline{\hspace{3cm}}_{\text{RAW SCORE}} \times 36 = \underline{\hspace{3cm}} \div 40 = \underline{\hspace{3cm}}$

$\underline{+\ 2}$ (*correction factor)

$\underline{\hspace{3cm}}$
SCALED SCORE

Science Reasoning

$\underline{\hspace{3cm}}_{\text{RAW SCORE}} \times 36 = \underline{\hspace{3cm}} \div 40 = \underline{\hspace{3cm}}$

$\underline{+\ 1.5}$ (*correction factor)

$\underline{\hspace{3cm}}$
SCALED SCORE

---

*The correction factor is an approximation based on the average from several recent ACT tests. It is most valid for scores in the middle 50% (approximately 16–24 scaled composite score) of the scoring range.

The scores are all approximate. Actual ACT scoring scales vary from one administration to the next based upon several factors.

If you take the optional Writing Test, you will need to combine your English and Writing scores to obtain your final COMPOSITE SCORE. Refer to Chapter 7 for guidelines on scoring your Writing Test Essay. Once you have determined a score for your essay out of 12 possible points, you will need to determine your ENGLISH/WRITING SCALED SCORE, using both your ENGLISH SCALED SCORE and your WRITING TEST SCORE. The combination of the two scores will give you an ENGLISH/WRITING SCALED SCORE, from 1 to 36, that will be used to determine your COMPOSITE SCORE mentioned earlier.

Using the English/Writing Scoring Table on the next page, find your ENGLISH SCALED SCORE on the left or right hand side of the table and your WRITING TEST SCORE on the top of the table. Follow your ENGLISH SCALED SCORE over and your WRITING TEST SCORE down until the two columns meet at a number. This number is your ENGLISH/WRITING SCALED SCORE and will be used to determine your COMPOSITE SCORE.

Step 3   Determine your ENGLISH/WRITING SCALED SCORE using the English/Writing Scoring Table on the following page:

English   _____

Writing   _____

English/Writing   _____

ENGLISH/WRITING SCORING TABLE

ENGLISH SCALED SCORE	WRITING TEST SCORE											ENGLISH SCALED SCORE
	2	3	4	5	6	7	8	9	10	11	12	
36	26	27	28	29	30	31	32	33	34	32	36	36
35	26	27	28	29	30	31	31	32	33	34	35	35
34	25	26	27	28	29	30	31	32	33	34	35	34
33	24	25	26	27	28	29	30	31	32	33	34	33
32	24	25	25	26	27	28	29	30	31	32	33	32
31	23	24	25	26	27	28	29	30	30	31	32	31
30	22	23	24	25	26	27	28	29	30	31	32	30
29	21	22	23	24	25	26	27	28	29	30	31	29
28	21	22	23	24	24	25	26	27	28	29	30	28
27	20	21	22	23	24	25	26	27	28	28	29	27
26	19	20	21	22	23	24	25	26	27	28	29	26
25	18	19	20	21	22	23	24	25	26	27	28	25
24	18	19	20	21	22	23	23	24	25	26	27	24
23	17	18	19	20	21	22	23	24	25	26	27	23
22	16	17	18	19	20	21	22	23	24	25	26	22
21	16	17	17	18	19	20	21	22	23	24	25	21
20	15	16	17	18	19	20	21	21	22	23	24	20
19	14	15	16	17	18	19	20	21	22	23	24	19
18	13	14	15	16	17	18	19	20	21	22	23	18
17	13	14	15	16	16	17	18	19	20	21	22	17
16	12	13	14	15	16	17	18	19	20	20	21	16
15	11	12	13	14	15	16	17	18	19	20	21	15
14	10	11	12	13	14	15	16	17	18	19	20	14
13	10	11	12	13	14	14	15	16	17	18	19	13
12	9	10	11	12	13	14	15	16	17	18	19	12
11	8	9	10	11	12	13	14	15	16	17	18	11
10	8	9	9	10	11	12	13	14	15	16	17	10
9	7	8	9	10	11	12	13	13	14	15	16	9
8	6	7	8	9	10	11	12	13	14	15	16	8
7	5	6	7	8	9	10	11	12	13	14	15	7
6	5	6	7	7	8	9	10	11	12	13	14	6
5	4	5	6	7	8	9	10	11	12	12	13	5
4	3	4	5	6	7	8	9	10	11	12	13	4
3	2	3	4	5	6	7	8	9	10	11	12	3
2	2	3	4	5	6	6	7	8	9	10	11	2
1	1	2	3	4	5	6	7	8	9	10	11	1

Step 4 Determine your COMPOSITE SCORE by finding the sum of all your SCALED SCORES for each of the four sections: English only (if you do not choose to take the optional Writing Test) *or* English/Writing (if you choose to take the optional Writing Test), Mathematics, Reading, and Science Reasoning, and divide by 4 to find the average. Round your COMPOSITE SCORE according to normal rules. For example, $31.2 \approx 31$ and $31.5 \approx 32$.

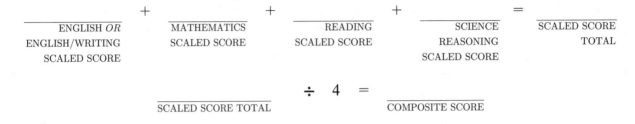

	+		+		+		=	
ENGLISH *OR* ENGLISH/WRITING SCALED SCORE		MATHEMATICS SCALED SCORE		READING SCALED SCORE		SCIENCE REASONING SCALED SCORE		SCALED SCORE TOTAL

$$\underline{\hspace{4cm}} \div \; 4 \; = \; \underline{\hspace{4cm}}$$

SCALED SCORE TOTAL   COMPOSITE SCORE

ANSWERS AND EXPLANATIONS

English Test Explanations

PASSAGE I

1. **The best answer is A.** The sentence indicates that the dog is "sensing new smells in the air." You can imply that the dog is doing this in order to identify the new smells. The context of the passage best supports answer choice A. There is nothing at this point in the passage to suggest that the dog wants to run away, so eliminate answer choice C.

2. **The best answer is F.** This question asks you to correctly punctuate the underlined portion. Because *perfectly* directly modifies *erect*, you should not separate the words with a comma. Eliminate answer choice H. You should, however, use a comma to separate the two clauses in the sentence.

3. **The best answer is C.** In order to maintain parallel construction in the paragraph, the verb forms should match. The verbs *watch, remains,* and *curls* are all in the present tense. Therefore, you should use the present-tense singular verb *appears,* answer choice C.

4. **The best answer is G.** The relative pronoun *when* denotes time. The idea being expressed here is that, at the time the puppy was twelve-weeks old, the writer's son named it Hunter.

5. **The best answer is B.** This question tests your ability to recognize redundancy in a sentence. The words *already* and *again* suggest that the writer had visited the animal shelter on at least one previous occasion. Likewise, the word *revisited* indicates the same thing. It is not necessary to express this concept more than once in the sentence, so eliminate answer choices A, C and D.

6. **The best answer is F.** The singular verb *was* follows the singular pronoun *he*; this sentence is correct as it is written. It is clear that the writer is referring to only one of the puppies in the nursery, so eliminate answer choices G and J, which include plural verb forms. Because this action took place in the past, you can also eliminate answer choice H.

7. **The best answer is C.** This question requires you to determine the correct punctuation. Eliminate answer choice D because it creates an incomplete sentence. A semicolon should be followed by an independent clause, so eliminate answer choice B. A good rule of thumb when it comes to commas is to use them where you would naturally pause when reading the sentence. There is a natural pause in the middle of the sentence, so it makes sense to place a comma after *name.* Also, it is necessary to use a comma before a coordinate conjunction like *and* to separate main clauses in a sentence.

8. **The best answer is H.** The verb forms in a sentence should be parallel, which means that they should match. Because the dog's ears are "held" back they should be "raised," answer choice H. If you substitute the other answer choices into the sentence, it will not make sense.

9. **The best answer is D.** The context of the passage implies that the writer has already trained the dog, so you should use a past-tense verb. Eliminate answer choices A and B. Answer choice D is best because it includes the past perfect tense of the verb *give,* which suggests that the training took place some time before the writer brought her dog to the edge of the woods.

10. **The best answer is H.** The best way to answer this question is to try the answer choices in the sentence. The only one that does not make sense and is, therefore, NOT a good alternative, is answer choice H. It is too wordy and awkward.

11. **The best answer is B.** It is important to maintain consistent verb forms within a sentence. Since the writer is "watching," she should also be "marveling," answer choice B.

12. **The best answer is F.** The underlined portion makes the most sense where it is. Placing it anywhere else in the sentence would create confusion as to who is doing the "watching" and "marveling."

13. **The best answer is A.** The context of the paragraph indicates that the dog is excited and happy to be returning to its owner. The phrase that best conveys that idea is *races back,* which is the original version. The other answer choices are not supported by the context of the paragraph.

14. **The best answer is H.** The underlined portion, "happy to be alive," indicates the dog's perceived attitude toward returning to its owner. If this part of the sentence were deleted, the sentence would lose its description of the dog's attitude, answer choice H.

15. **The best answer is D.** This question requires you to determine the main idea of the passage. The passage is primarily about the writer's experience with her dog, not about training her dog to hunt. You can eliminate answer choices A and B. There is nothing in the passage that encourages readers not to train dogs to hunt, so eliminate answer choice C.

PASSAGE II

16. **The best answer is H.** This question requires you to determine the correct use of commas. A good rule of thumb when it comes to commas is to use them where you would naturally pause when reading the sentence. It is not necessary to use any commas within the underlined portion.

17. **The best answer is B.** This question requires you to determine the correct punctuation, as well as to decide whether *its* or *it's* is correct. In this case, you should use the conjunction of *it is*, which is *it's*. Eliminate answer choices C and D because they contain the possessive pronoun *its*. You should not use a comma to separate two main clauses of a sentence; this is known as a comma splice. Eliminate answer choice A.

18. **The best answer is G.** The word *fencing* is implied by the previous sentence, so you don't need to include it again; eliminate answer choice F. If you select answer choices H or J, the pronoun *this* becomes ambiguous; it is unclear what noun the pronoun is supposed to replace.

19. **The best answer is C.** In this sentence, the underlined portion refers to the people who are building the fence. While they may "respect" someone else's privacy, it makes more sense that they are building a fence because they "value" their own privacy. Answer choices B and D do not make sense in the context of the passage.

20. **The best answer is H.** This question requires you to determine the correct punctuation. You should not use a comma to separate two main clauses of a sentence; this is known as a comma splice. Eliminate answer choice F. It is necessary to include the word *this* in order to maintain the meaning of the sentence. The best thing to do is to begin a new sentence, answer choice H.

21. **The best answer is C.** The first step in answering this question is to decide whether to use *then* or *than*. The word *then* indicates the passage of time, which is not appropriate here. Eliminate answer choices A and D. Now look at the punctuation. It is not necessary to include a comma after the word *rather*, so eliminate answer choice B.

22. **The best answer is J.** This question requires you to determine the correct use of commas. It is necessary to set off each item in a list with a comma. Therefore, you should place a comma after *trees, shrubs, vines,* answer choice J.

23. **The best answer is A.** Because the noun *deciduous trees* is plural, you should use the plural pronoun *their*. *They're* is the contraction of *they are*, so eliminate answer choice B. *Its* is a singular pronoun, so eliminate answer choice C. *It's* is the contraction of *it is*, so eliminate answer choice D.

24. **The best answer is J.** The sentence implies that the ivy and deciduous trees would be "ineffective barriers to prying eyes." It does not make sense to say "barriers of, barriers at," or "barriers with."

25. **The best answer is D.** The underlined portion contains information that does not add any relevance to the sentence. It is best to omit or remove it from the sentence.

26. **The best answer is H.** This question requires you to determine the correct use of commas. A conjunctive adverb like *for example* needs to be set off with commas. That is, you should place a comma before and after the phrase, as in answer choice H.

27. **The best answer is A.** The main point of the passage is that fences can provide "privacy and security." The other answer choices are not supported by the context of the passage.

28. **The best answer is J.** Because the word *carefully* is used in the sentence and is not part of the underlined portion, you should not also use words like *cautious* and *cautiously*, or phrases like *take care*. Answer choices F, G, and H create redundancy. It is best to omit, or remove the underlined portion.

29. **The best answer is B.** The passage discusses some forms of "natural" fences, such as "evergreen trees and shrubs," and indicates that they may take some time to grow. The other answer choices simply do not make sense.

30. **The best answer is F.** The question requires you to express the idea clearly and simply. *Costfull* is

not actually a word, so eliminate answer choice G. Answer choices H and J have the same meaning as *costly* but are more complicated and should be eliminated.

PASSAGE III

31. **The best answer is D.** This question requires you to determine the correct punctuation. It is necessary to separate the items in a list with commas, so eliminate answer choices A and C. A semicolon should be followed by an independent clause, so eliminate answer choice B.

32. **The best answer is F.** The first part of the sentence offers a description of Maya Angelou. Nothing in the passage suggests that she is dead, so it is proper to use the present-tense verb *is*. Eliminate answer choice J. Since the pronoun *that* refers to the description of Maya Angelou, it is appropriate here. The word *whom* is used as a direct object, so eliminate answer choice H. Answer choice G implies a question, which is not appropriate.

33. **The best answer is B.** This question requires you to express the idea clearly and simply. Since the passage indicates that the book is about Maya Angelou's childhood, eliminate answer choice C. Eliminate answer choice D because it creates an awkward sentence. Answer choices A and B say essentially the same thing, but answer choice B is less awkward and wordy.

34. **The best answer is J.** Answer choice J creates an incomplete sentence, so it would NOT be an acceptable alternative to the underlined portion.

35. **The best answer is A.** The sentence indicates that, after a certain "traumatic incident," Maya did not speak for five years. It is important to have some explanation for her behavior. If that phrase were deleted, you would not have a clear picture of why Maya "spent the next five years in total and utter silence."

36. **The best answer is H.** The sentence describes the different things that Maya did to support herself when she was young. Deleting the word *singing* would not detract from the sentence. Also, to be grammatically correct, the word *singing* should be followed by a comma, so deleting the word *singing* would actually improve the grammar of the sentence.

37. **The best answer is B.** This question requires you to determine the correct use of commas. A good rule of thumb when it comes to commas is to use them where you would naturally pause when reading the sentence. It is not necessary to use any commas within the underlined portion. While you may be tempted to pause slightly before the word *and*, none of the answer choices includes a comma before the word *and* only.

38. **The best answer is J.** This question requires you to determine the main idea of the essay. The essay is primarily about Maya Angelou's life. The sentence that the writer is considering adding does not add any important or useful information about Maya Angelou's life, so it should not be included. Eliminate answer choices F and G. The sentence does not detract from the points regarding Angelou's difficult childhood; it is simply irrelevant.

39. **The best answer is C.** This question does not require any information about which United States president Maya Angelou read her poetry to. The best option is to end the sentence with the word *president*. Also, the word *president* would only be capitalized when used as a title: "President Bill Clinton." It is not used in that way in this sentence.

40. **The best answer is G.** You would either "listen to" or "watch." You would not watch "to," so eliminate answer choices F and J. Answer choice J also includes an unnecessary comma. You would not watch "with," so eliminate answer choice H.

41. **The best answer is B.** It is important to maintain parallel construction within the sentence. Since the canons are "deafening," the flowers must be "blossoming," answer choice B.

42. **The best answer is J.** This question tests your ability to express an idea clearly and simply. Maya Angelou is instilling the sense of wonder and joy, so that phrase should directly follow her name in the sentence. She does not "sense" the wonder and joy, so eliminate answer choice F. Answer choices G and H are awkward and should be eliminated as well.

43. **The best answer is C.** This question requires you to select the correct verb form. The sentence as it is written does not clearly indicate what Angelou has the ability to do, so eliminate answer choice A. You would not say that someone "has the ability for" or "has the ability with," so eliminate answer choices B and D. Answer choice C clearly indicates Angelou's ability to do something.

44. **The best answer is F.** The sentence does not specify one particular listener, but, instead, refers to anyone who listens to Maya Angelou. Eliminate answer choice G. Answer choice H is

wordy and awkward, and should also be eliminated. If you omit, or remove, the underlined portion, the relative pronoun *that* becomes ambiguous.

45. The best answer is D. This question requires you to determine the main idea of the essay. While the essay mentions that Maya Angelou had a difficult childhood, it in no way focuses on southern poverty, so eliminate answer choices A and B. The main focus of the passage is Maya Angelou's life, answer choice D.

PASSAGE IV

46. The best answer is F. This question tests your ability to express an idea clearly and simply. It does not make sense that "visiting ... every summer" would be the highlight of "my summer visits," so eliminate answer choice H. Answer choices G and J are redundant and should be eliminated as well.

47. The best answer is B. This question requires you to determine the correct use of commas and other punctuation. A good rule of thumb when it comes to commas is to use them where you would naturally pause when reading the sentence. It is not necessary to use any form of punctuation within the underlined portion. Because the adverbial clause *to the nearest shopping center* directly follows the verbal, you should not use a comma.

48. The best answer is G. Because this essay is a reflection of past events, you should use the past-tense verb *seemed*; eliminate answer choices F, H, and J. In addition, answer choice J is incorrect because it creates an incomplete sentence.

49. The best answer is C. Sentence 4 introduces the idea that the writer's mother would receive the fabric. Sentence 5 then indicates that much of the material would be turned into the writer's school clothes. It makes the most sense to place the new sentence between Sentences 4 and 5.

50. The best answer is H. The preposition *because* implies that one thing happened as the result of another. In this sentence, the result of the writer spending most of her time with her grandmother is that she really remembers the "brief moments" that she shared with her grandfather. The other answer choices are not supported by the context of the essay.

51. The best answer is D. A sentence is composed of two main parts: a subject and a verb. Answer choice D is NOT acceptable because it lacks a verb.

52. The best answer is F. The writer indicates that her grandfather "always seemed to be in-and-out, but mostly out." This suggests that he was gone much of the time. The other answer choices are not supported by the context of the essay.

53. The best answer is B. Since the subject includes two items, the chair *and* ottoman, it is a plural subject. Therefore, you must use the plural verb *were*. Eliminate answer choice A. Also, this action takes place in the past, so a past-tense form of the verb should be used. Eliminate answer choices H and J because they do not include a past-tense verb.

54. The best answer is F. This question tests your ability to express an idea clearly and simply. The sentence makes it clear that, when the writer's grandfather was away on a fishing trip, the chair and ottoman were still forbidden. While answer choice H could work, it is too wordy and awkward, and is, therefore, not the best choice.

55. The best answer is C. This question requires you to express an idea clearly and simply. Answer choice C clearly identifies the writer as the child who thought that her grandfather seemed like a small man. The sentence as it is written implies that Grandpa is the child, so eliminate answer choice A. Eliminate answer choice D for the same reason. Answer choice B is very awkward and should also be eliminated.

56. The best answer is H. This question requires you to express an idea clearly and simply. Since a "king," by definition is "royal," you do not need to use both words in the same sentence. Eliminate answer choices F and J. It is not correct to say "a royalty," so eliminate answer choice G.

57. The best answer is B. This sentence is expressing the idea that the writer's grandfather could typically be found in his workshop when he was not out fishing. It does not make sense that her grandfather would be in his workshop when he *was* fishing, so eliminate answer choices A, C, and D.

58. The best answer is F. In order to maintain parallel construction within this sentence, the verbs should match. Since the writer says that her grandfather "would invite" her to the garage, you should say that he "would show" her how to tie the fishing lure together, answer choice F. Eliminate answer choice G because it creates a run-on sentence. Answer choices H and J are awkward and should be eliminated.

59. **The best answer is C.** In the underlined portion, it is unclear to whom or what the pronoun *they* refers. To create clarity within the sentence, it is necessary to identify who moved out of the city. It does not make sense that the "lone summer visits" moved anywhere, but the pronoun *they* is ambiguous, so it is best to eliminate answer choices A and B. Eliminate answer choice D because it contains the singular pronoun *it*.

60. **The best answer is H.** This question requires you to determine the main idea of the essay. The essay is primarily about the writer's experiences at her grandparents' house. It does not mention the relationship that her grandparents had with each other, so eliminate answer choices F and G. While it is true that the writer spent more time with her grandmother, this is off-topic and does not effectively answer the question.

PASSAGE V

61. **The best answer is D.** This question requires you to recognize redundancy. Because *jointly*, *with each other*, and *together* all have the same meaning, it is not necessary to use more than one of them in the sentence. Eliminate answer choices A, B, and C because they are redundant.

62. **The best answer is H.** The passage includes information about the importance of the electric motor, so the most appropriate word choice would be *important*. The other answer choices are not supported by the context of the passage.

63. **The best answer is A.** This question requires you to express an idea clearly and simply. The verb *separate* is directly modified by the phrase *more efficiently*. Therefore, the sentence is best written as it is written. The other answer choices are awkward.

64. **The best answer is H.** This question requires you to express an idea clearly and simply. The idea being expressed in the sentence is that Thomas Davenport was so intrigued by the electromagnet, he convinced his brother to raise the money to purchase one.

65. **The best answer is A.** This question requires you to determine the correct use of commas and other punctuation. Because the phrase *who witnessed much of their work* is extra information in the sentence, it is considered a nonrestrictive clause (you could remove the phrase from the sentence without changing the meaning of the

sentence), and must be set off by commas. In other words, there must be a comma at the beginning and at the end of the phrase, as in answer choice A. Answer choice B incorrectly uses a semicolon.

66. **The best answer is G.** The proper past-tense form of the verb *wind* is *wound*, not *winded* or *wounded*. Eliminate answer choices F and J. Since *wire* is a singular noun, you should eliminate answer choice H because it includes the plural verb *have been*.

67. **The best answer is D.** This question requires you to determine the correct use of commas and other punctuation. A good rule of thumb when it comes to commas is to use them where you would naturally pause when reading the sentence. There is a natural pause after *dress*, so answer choice D is best. Also, you should use a comma to separate main clauses in a sentence when you use a coordinating conjunction such as *and*.

68. **The best answer is G.** This question requires you to express an idea clearly and simply. Since the previous sentence states that the strips of silk were torn from Emily's wedding dress, it is not necessary to repeat that statement in this sentence.

69. **The best answer is C.** The underlined portion refers to the electromagnet, and how it could be "used" to spin a wheel. It does not make sense that the electromagnet would be "weary," so eliminate answer choice D. The word *utilized* means *used*, but answer choice B is missing the helping verb *to*.

70. **The best answer is F.** The passage refers to only one wheel, so eliminate answer choice G. Since *commence* and *start* have the same meaning, it is not necessary to use them both in the same sentence. Eliminate answer choice H. Answer choice J contains unnecessary commas, so it should be eliminated as well.

71. **The best answer is D.** The passage indicates that they performed the action in the past, so you must use the past-tense verb *tried*. Eliminate answer choices A and C because they do not contain a past-tense verb. The phrase *would of* is never correct, so eliminate answer choice B.

72. **The best answer is H.** Sentence 2 states that Thomas "grew very frustrated." It makes sense that something would cause that frustration.

Sentence 1 does not include any information that would suggest a reason for Thomas's frustration, so eliminate answer choice F. The best place for Sentence 2 is between Sentences 5 and 6, because Sentence 2 makes it clear what they "tried" in Sentence 6.

73. **The best answer is C.** First, determine the topic of the paragraph. Information in the paragraph indicates that Thomas "finally received a patent," so it would make sense that a sentence introducing this paragraph would include some mention of patents. Only answer choice C does so.

74. **The best answer is G.** This sentence begins with a prepositional phrase, which must be set off from the rest of the sentence with a comma. The sentence as it is written does not include any punctuation, so eliminate answer choice F. Answer choices H and J imply that the electric motor was greatly excited, which doesn't make sense.

75. **The best answer is D.** The underlined portion indicates that Davenport's electric motors are in current use all over the world. This best supports answer choice D. The other answer choices are not supported by the essay.

Mathematics Test Explanations

1. **The correct answer is D.** According to information in the problem, a vehicle must be *at most* 1,500 pounds to cross the bridge. This means that a vehicle can weigh 1,500 pounds, but it cannot weigh more than 1,500 pounds. Express this mathematically as follows: weight $(w) \leq 1,500$, answer choice D.

2. **The correct answer is H.** This problem requires you to find the number into which 2, 6, and 9 all go. Eliminate answer choice G, because 17 is an odd number and cannot be a multiple of 2. Next, because you are asked to find the smallest multiple, try the remaining answer choices in order from smallest to largest:

   (1) 9 does not go into 12, so eliminate answer choice F.

   (2) $2 \times 9 = 18$, and $6 \times 3 = 18$, so 18 is the smallest positive integer that is a multiple of 2, 6, and 9. Answer choice H is correct.

3. **The correct answer is A.** Anytime that you have zero in the denominator, the expression is undefined. Therefore, the only number that CANNOT be zero is u, which is in the denominator.

4. **The correct answer is H.** The first step in solving this problem is to calculate the percentage of residents who DO have a white house. Set up a proportion:

   (1) 648 is to 2,160 as x% is to 100%

   (2) $\dfrac{648}{2,160} = \dfrac{x}{100}$

   Cross-multiply and solve for x:
   (3) $2,160x = 64,800$

   (4) $x = 30$

   30% of the residents have a white house. Therefore, 100% − 30%, or 70% of the residents DO NOT have a white house, answer choice H.

5. **The correct answer is D.** To solve this problem, substitute −1 for q and 3 for s wherever those variables appear in the expression:

   (1) $\dfrac{(q - s)}{3q} =$

   (2) $\dfrac{(-1 - 3)}{3(-1)} =$

   (3) $\dfrac{-4}{-3} = \dfrac{4}{3}$, answer choice D.

6. **The correct answer is K.** To put this equation into the proper form, isolate y on the left side of the equation, as follows:

   (1) $\dfrac{1}{4}y - 3x = 5$

   (2) $\dfrac{1}{4}y = 3x + 5$

   (3) $4\left(\dfrac{1}{4}y\right) = 4(3x) + 4(5)$

   (4) $y = 12x + 20$, answer choice K.

7. **The correct answer is B.** Line s is a transversal that cuts the parallel lines, p and q. When a transversal cuts 2 parallel lines, all corresponding angles created have the same measurement. $\angle m$ corresponds with $\angle n$, because they are alternate interior angles, so they have the same measurement. Since you are given that $m + n = 230°$, both $\angle m$ and $\angle n$ must equal $230° \div 2$, or $115°$. There are $180°$ in a straight line. Therefore, if $\angle m$ is $115°$, then angle o must be $180° - 115°$, or $65°$, answer choice B.

8. **The correct answer is J.** You are given the equation for the volume of a cylinder, and you are given the lengths of the 2 variables. Simply plug these values into the equation and solve:

   (1) Volume $= \pi r^2 h$

   (2) Volume $= \pi\,(4)^2(5)$

   (3) Volume $= \pi\,(16)(5)$

   (4) Volume $= \pi 80$, or 80π, answer choice J.

9. **The correct answer is C.** The absolute value of a number is the numerical value of a real number without regard to its sign. In order to solve this problem, you must first substitute the number 7 for the x in $|4 - x|$, so that you get $|4 - 7|$. Then, perform the operation within the vertical lines, so that you get $|-3|$. Since you must disregard the negative sign in order to determine absolute value, you know that the absolute value of $|-3|$, is 3, answer choice C.

10. **The correct answer is K.** The first step in solving this problem is to recognize that the angles adjacent to the 110° and 135° angles are complementary to 110° and 135°. This means that, when added together, 110° and the angle adjacent to it must equal 180°, and 135° and the angle adjacent to it must equal 180°. So, the angle adjacent to 110° must equal 70°, and the angle adjacent to 135° must equal 45°. Fill in the measurements on the diagram as shown:

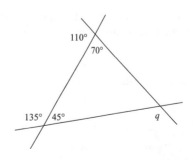

The sum of the interior angles of any triangle is $180°$. So, $70° + 45° +$ the measure of the third angle $= 180°$. Solve for the measure of the third angle

(1) $70 + 45 + x = 180$

(2) $115 + x = 180$

(3) $x = 65$

The angle adjacent to angle q is $65°$, which means that angle q must be $180° - 65°$, or $115°$, answer choice K.

11. **The correct answer is D.** Use the FOIL method to solve this equation. Multiply the First terms, then the Outside terms, then the Inside terms, then the Last terms, as follows:

(1) $(\sqrt{2} - 6)(\sqrt{2} - 6) =$

(2) First terms: $(\sqrt{2})(\sqrt{2}) = 2$

(3) Outside terms: $(\sqrt{2})(-4) = -4\sqrt{2}$

(4) Inside terms: $(\sqrt{2})(-6) = -6\sqrt{2}$

(5) Last terms: $(-6)(-4) = 24$

Now, add like terms together

(6) $2 + 24 + (-4\sqrt{2}) + (-6\sqrt{2})$

(7) $26 - 10\sqrt{2}$, answer choice D.

12. **The correct answer is G.** Use the FOIL method to solve this equation. Multiply the First terms, then the Outside terms, then the Inside terms, then the Last terms, as follows:

(1) $(x - 3y)^2 = (x - 3y)(x - 3y)$

(2) First terms: $(x)(x) = x^2$

(3) Outside terms: $(x)(-3y) = -3xy$

(4) Inside terms: $(-3y)(x) = -3xy$

(5) Last terms: $(-3y)(-3y) = 9y^2$

Now, add like terms together

(6) $x^2 + (-3xy) + (-3xy) + 9y^2$

(7) $x^2 + (-6xy) + 9y^2$, answer choice G.

13. **The correct answer is C.** The first step in solving this problem is to distribute the 3, as follows:

(1) $3(x + 3y) = 3x + 9y$

Now, you can add the like terms:

(2) $x - 4y + 3x + 9y =$

(3) $x + 3x + (-4y + 9y) =$

(4) $4x + 5y$, answer choice C.

14. **The correct answer is J.** In order to solve this problem, you must put the equations into the standard form, $y = mx + b$. The equation in the problem is equivalent to $y = \dfrac{-x}{8} + \dfrac{3}{8}$ Convert the answer choices into the standard form:

(1) $3x + 11y = 6$; $11y = -3x + 6$; $y = \dfrac{-3}{11}x + \dfrac{6}{11}$

(2) $2x + 10y = 5$; $10y = -2x + 5$;

$y = \dfrac{-2}{10}x + \dfrac{5}{10}$; $y = \dfrac{-1}{5} + 2$

(3) $3x + y = 8$; $y = -3x + \dfrac{8}{3}$.

(4) $3x + 2y = 9$; $24y = -3x + 9$; $y = \dfrac{-3x}{24} + \dfrac{9}{24}$;

$y = \dfrac{-1}{8}x + \dfrac{3}{8}$

Answer choice J, when simplified, is the same equation as the one given in the problem, so this choice is correct.

15. **The correct answer is B.** To solve this problem, set up an equation. The combined age is 24, which means that Anne's age plus Kyle's age equals 24.

(1) $\text{Anne} + \text{Kyle} = 24$

(2) $\text{Anne} = 3(\text{Kyle})$

(3) $3(\text{Kyle}) + \text{Kyle} = 24$

(4) $4(\text{Kyle}) = 24$

(5) $\text{Kyle} = \dfrac{24}{4} = 6$.

Anne is 6×3, or 18 years old, answer choice B.

16. **The correct answer is H.** Lines $\overline{PQ}$ and $\overline{ST}$ are 2 parallel lines cut by transversals. This means that the angles created have special relationships. For example, opposite interior angles are congruent, that is, they have the same measurement. So, angle P is congruent to angle T, which means that the measure of angle T must also be $65°$, answer choice H.

17. **The correct answer is E.** If you have 4 choices of meats, 3 choices of vegetables, and 5 choices of desserts, then you have $(4)(3)(5) = 60$ meal options. For every meat choice, you have 3 vegetable choices. Given 4 meat choices, you have $(4)(3) = 12$ meat and vegetable choices. For every meat and vegetable combination, you have 5 dessert choices. Given 12 meat and vegetable choices, you have $(12)(5) = 60$ meal options.

18. **The correct answer is G.** Solve for a by isolating a on the left side of the equation. Be careful to line up the decimal points:

(1) $0.2a + 1.8 = a - 2.2$

(2) $0.2a - a = -2.2 - 1.8$

a is equivalent to $1.0a$; $1.0 - 0.2 = .8$.

(3) $-0.8a = -4.0$

(4) $a = -\dfrac{-4.0}{-0.8} = 5$, answer choice G

19. **The correct answer is A.** The best way to solve this problem is to plug the answer choices in for x and solve until you get a negative number. Since the question asks you for the smallest integer, start with the smallest answer choice:

(1) $-\sqrt{8} + 2 = -\sqrt{4} \cdot \sqrt{2} + 2 = -2\sqrt{2} + 2$

(2) $-2(1.41) + 2 = -2.82 + 2 = -0.82$

The smallest integer, x, that will result in a negative value is 2, answer choice A.

20. **The correct answer is H.** The first step in solving this problem is to calculate the total number of vehicles at the dealership:

(1) $265 + 435 = 700$.

Now, calculate the percentage that are trucks (NOT cars):

(2) 435 trucks is to 700 total vehicles as $x\%$ is to 100%.

(3) $\dfrac{435}{700} = \dfrac{x}{100}$

(4) $700x = 43,500$

(5) $x = 62.14$

Approximately 62% of the vehicles at the dealership are NOT cars, answer choice H.

21. **The correct answer is B.** The formula for the area of a circle is πr^2. Since the area is given as 49π, r^2 must equal 49, and r must equal 7. The diameter is equal to twice the radius, so the diameter equals 2(7), or 14, answer choice B.

22. **The correct answer is H.** The first step in solving this problem is to recognize that the figure is made up of a right triangle and a rectangle. Calculate the area of each separate figure, then add the results to get the area of the entire figure:

(1) Area of a triangle $= \dfrac{1}{2}(bh)$

(2) Area $= \dfrac{1}{2}(3 \cdot 4)$

(3) Area $= \dfrac{1}{2}(12) = 6$

The area of the triangle is 6.

(4) Area of a rectangle $= l \cdot w$

(5) Area $= 7 \cdot 4 = 28$

The area of the rectangle is 28. Therefore, the area of the figure shown is $6 + 28$, or 34, answer choice H.

23. **The correct answer is D.** The question asks you to reduce the equation into simpler terms. Since there are 3 variables, a, b, and c, begin simplifying the a's first, then the b's, and finally the c's. When multiplying like coefficients with exponents, add the exponents. When dividing like coefficients with exponents, subtract the exponents.

(1) $\dfrac{3a^2 b^{-4} c^2}{2^{-2} a c^{-2}} = \dfrac{3ab^{-4} c^2}{2^{-2} c^{-2}}$; $b^{-4} = \dfrac{1}{b^4}$

(2) $\dfrac{3ab^{-4} c^2}{2^{-2} c^{-2}} = \dfrac{3ac^2}{2^{-2} b^4 c^{-2}}$; $2^{-2} = \dfrac{1}{4}$

(3) $\dfrac{3ac^2}{\frac{1}{4} b^4 c^{-2}} = \dfrac{3ac^4}{\frac{1}{4} b^4}$

(4) $\dfrac{3ac^4}{\frac{1}{4} b^4} = \dfrac{4(3ac^4)}{1\ b^4} = \dfrac{12ac^4}{b^4}$, answer choice D.

24. **The correct answer is J.** Solve this problem by plugging the value given for P into the equation. You are given that the monthly payment, P is $233.00:

(1) $P = \dfrac{C}{240} - 0.007P + 35$

(2) $233 = \dfrac{C}{240} - 0.007(233) + 35$

Now, solve for C, the cost of the car:

(3) $233 = \dfrac{C}{240} - 1.631 + 35$

(4) $233 = \dfrac{C}{240} + 33.369$

(5) $233 - 33.369 = \dfrac{C}{240}$

(6) $199.631(240) = C$

(7) $47,911.44 = C$. This can be rounded down to $47,911; answer choice J.

25. **The correct answer is D.** The first step in solving this problem is to rearrange the terms and set the equation equal to 0:

(1) $3x^2 - 4x = 0$

The next step is to factor the common value, x, from each of the terms:

(2) $x(3x - 4) = 0$

(3) $x = 0$, and $3x - 4 = 0$; solve for x.

(4) $3x = 4$

(5) $x = \dfrac{4}{3}$

Therefore, the solutions for x are 0 or $\dfrac{4}{3}$, answer choice D.

26. **The correct answer is K.** The slope of a line measures the steepness of a line, and can be calculated by using the following formula: $\dfrac{y_1 - y_2}{x_1 - x_2}$ Two points on the line are given: $(3, -8)$ and $(4, 7)$. The y values are -8 and 7, so the change in y is $-8 - 7$, or -15. The x values are 3 and 4, so the change in x is $3 - 4$, or -1. The slope is -15 over -1, or 15, answer choice K.

27. **The correct answer is B.** A circle centered at (a,b) with a radius r, has the equation $(x-a)^2 + (y-b)^2 = r^2$. Plug the information given in the question into the equation:

    (1) $(x-2)^2 + (y-(-7))^2 = 5^2$

    (2) $(x-2)^2 + (y+7)^2 = 25$, answer choice B.

28. **The correct answer is H.** The key to solving this problem is to recognize that $8x^2 - 8x - 6$ can be factored, as follows:

    (1) $8x^2 - 8x - 6 =$

    (2) $(2x-3)(4x+2)$

    So, $(2x-3)(4x-2) = (ax-3)(4x-a)$. Therefore, a must equal 2, answer choice H.

29. **The correct answer is A.** The slope-intercept form of a line is $y = mx + b$, where m is the slope and b is the y-intercept. By definition, a line perpendicular to any given line will have a slope equal to the negative reciprocal of the given line. Since the slope of the given line is $-\left(\dfrac{1}{4}\right)$, the slope of a line perpendicular to the given line will have a slope of 4. Eliminate answer choices B, D, and E, because they do not have a slope of 4. You are given that another point on the line is $(0, -5)$. This means, that when $x = 0$, $y = -5$; by definition, therefore, -5 is the y-intercept. So the slope-intercept form of the line in the question is $y = 4x - 5$, answer choice A.

30. **The correct answer is K.** To solve this problem, set up a proportion showing the relationship between the quantity of flour and the number of cookies.

    (1) 24 cookies is to 60 cookies as 2 cups of flour is to x cups of flour.

    (2) $\dfrac{24}{60} = \dfrac{2}{x}$; solve for x

    (3) $24x = 120$

    (4) $x = 5$, answer choice K.

31. **The correct answer is D.** The best way to solve this problem is to plug in the answer choices for the first p-value and solve the equation. Start with the answer choice in the middle, answer choice C. Since you are multiplying by a decimal, if plugging answer choice C into the equation yields a result that is too small, you can eliminate any answer choices that are greater than answer choice C:

    (1) $0.1(800 + 1,800) =$

    (2) $0.1(2,600) = 260$; 260 is smaller than 800.

Now you can eliminate answer choices A, B, and C. Try answer choice D:

(3) $0.1(200 + 1,800) = 200$; $200 = 200$, so answer choice D is correct.

32. **The correct answer is F.** The formula of a circle is $(x-a)^2 + (y-b)^2 = r^2$, where (a,b) is the center of the circle, and r is the radius. The diagram shows 1 edge of the circle at $(6,0)$, and the other at $(0,0)$. The midpoint between 0 and 6 is 3, so the radius is 3 and the center of the circle is at point $(3,0)$. Plug these values into the formula for a and b and the radius, 3, for r:

    (1) $(x-3)^2 + (y-0)^2 = 3^2$

    (2) $(x-3)^2 + y^2 = 9$, answer choice F.

33. **The correct answer is B.** To find the solution for the given inequality, isolate x on the left side of the inequality:

    (1) $x + 2(5 - x) \le 2x + 3$

    (2) $x + 10 - 2x \le 2x + 3$

    (3) $-x + 10 \le 2x + 3$

    (4) $-3x \le -7$

Now, you need to divide both sides of the inequality by -3; remember to reverse the inequality sign:

    (5) $x \ge \dfrac{7}{3}$, answer choice B.

34. **The correct answer is G.** Use the Pythagorean Theorem to solve this problem: $a^2 + b^2 = c^2$, where c is the hypotenuse:

    (1) $8^2 + b^2 = 10^2$

    (2) $64 + b^2 = 100$

    (3) $b^2 = 36$

    (4) $b = 6$, answer choice G.

35. **The correct answer is B.** The formula for the area of a parallelogram is base × height. You will need to calculate the height by applying the Pythagorean Theorem: $a^2 + b^2 = c^2$. The unshaded region is a right triangle, so plug the given values into the Pythagorean Theorem:

    (1) $3^2 + b^2 = 5^2$

    (2) $9 + b^2 = 25$

    (3) $b^2 = 16$

    (4) $b = 4$

The height of the parallelogram is 4. The base is given as 8, so the area of the parallelogram is

4×8, or 32. Now, calculate the area of the unshaded triangle and subtract it from the total area of the parallelogram. The area of a triangle is $\frac{1}{2}(bh)$, where b is the base, and h is the height:

(1) $\frac{1}{2}(3 \times 4) =$

(2) $\frac{1}{2}(12) = 6$

$32 - 6 = 26$, answer choice B.

36. **The correct answer is K.** This problem requires you to solve for x. Isolate x on the left side of the equation:

(1) $\frac{3}{4}x - \frac{3}{8} = \frac{1}{4} + \frac{5}{8}x$

(2) $\frac{3}{4}x - \frac{5}{8}x = \frac{1}{4} + \frac{3}{8}$

Now, find the lowest common denominator so that you can add and subtract the fractions. Since both 4 and 8 go into 8, 8 is the lowest common denominator:

(3) $\frac{3}{4}x = \frac{6}{8}x; \frac{1}{4} = \frac{2}{8}$

(4) $\frac{6}{8}x - \frac{5}{8}x = \frac{2}{8} + \frac{3}{8}$

(5) $\frac{1}{8}x = \frac{5}{8}$

(6) $x = 8\left(\frac{5}{8}\right)$

(7) $x = 5$, answer choice K.

37. **The correct answer is D.** By definition, an isosceles triangle has 2 sides of equal length and the hypotenuse is equal to $\sqrt{2}$ times the length of either of the sides. Therefore, the smaller isosceles triangle with a hypotenuse of $2\sqrt{2}$ cm has 2 sides with lengths both equal to 2 cm. To answer this question, you must recognize that similar triangles have the same shape and the same proportions. The smaller triangle has lengths of 2, 2, and $2\sqrt{2}$. You are given that the larger, similar triangle has a perimeter 2 times the perimeter of the smaller triangle. Therefore, each side in the larger triangle must be 2 times the length of the corresponding side in the smaller triangle. Since the 2 equal sides of the smaller triangle are each 2 cm, the 2 equal sides of the larger triangle are each 4 cm, answer choice D.

38. **The correct answer is G.** To solve this problem, you must calculate the area of the parallelogram and the area of the triangle, then add the results. The area of a parallelogram is equivalent to the base times the height. The area of a triangle is equivalent to $\frac{1}{2}(bh)$, where b is the base and h is the height. You will need to use the Pythagorean

Theorem to calculate the height, which will be the same for both the parallelogram and the triangle.

(1) $a^2 + b^2 = c^2$

(2) $6^2 + b^2 = 10^2$

(3) $36 + b^2 = 100$

(4) $b^2 = 64$

(5) $b = 8$

Now, plug the appropriate values into the equations:

(6) Parallelogram $= (b)(h) = (13)(8) = 104$.

(7) Triangle $= \frac{1}{2}(b)(h) = \frac{1}{2}(6)(8) = \frac{1}{2}(48) = 24$.

(8) $104 + 24 = 128$, answer choice G.

39. **The correct answer is C.** By definition, the sine of any acute angle is calculated by dividing the length of the side opposite the acute angle by the hypotenuse ($\sin = \frac{\text{opp}}{\text{hyp}}$). The length of the side opposite angle a is 3, and the length of the hypotenuse is 5. Therefore, $\sin a = \frac{3}{5}$, answer choice C.

40. **The correct answer is H.** The first step in solving this problem is to solve each element of the equation for x.

(1) $(x + m) = 0$

(2) $x = -m$

(3) $(x + n) = 0$

(4) $x = -n$

Now, substitute the value of the solutions given in the equation for x in order to get the values for m and n:

(5) $x = -m; -3 = -m$, so $m = 3$

(6) $x = -n; 5 = -n$, so $n = -5$

Now add m (3) to n (-5):

(7) $3 + -5 = -2$, answer choice H.

41. **The correct answer is D.** The slope-intercept form of the equation for a line is $y = mx + b$, where m is the slope and b is the y-intercept. You can determine the slope of the line with the 2 points given in the question: $(-2, -1)$ and $(2, 2)$. By definition, the slope is equal to $\frac{y_1 - y_2}{x_1 - x_2}$:

(1) $\frac{-1 - 2}{-2 - 2} = \frac{-3}{-4} = \frac{3}{4}$

The slope of the line is $\frac{3}{4}$. Use this value as m and 1 of the 2 points given in the question as

x and y in the equation for a line. Solve for b:

(2) $2 = \frac{3}{4}(2) + b$

(3) $2 = \frac{3}{2} + b$

(4) $b = \frac{1}{2}$

The equation of this line is $y = \frac{3}{4}x + \frac{1}{2}$. The question asks you to determine what the value of x is when $y = 5$, so substitute 5 for y in the equation of the line and solve for x:

(1) $5 = \frac{3}{4}x + \frac{1}{2}$

(2) $4\frac{1}{2} = \frac{3}{4}x$

(3) $x = 6$

When $y = 5$, $x = 6$, answer choice D.

42. **The correct answer is F.** By definition, the tangent of any acute angle is the $\frac{\sin}{\cos}$. The sin B is given as $\frac{7}{17}$ and the cos B is given as $\frac{10}{17}$. Therefore, $\tan B = \frac{7}{17} \div \frac{10}{17}$. To divide fractions, multiply the numerator by the reciprocal of the denominator:

(1) $\frac{7}{17} \cdot \frac{17}{10}$; the 17s will cancel each other out, so the tangent of $B = \frac{7}{10}$, answer choice F.

43. **The correct answer is A.** The first step in solving this problem is to recognize that you are looking for the equation of a line in the slope-intercept form, $y = mx + b$, where m is the slope and b is the y-intercept. Since the line shown intersects the y-axis at 5, the y-intercept must be 5. Eliminate answer choices C, D, and E. Since the line shown has a positive slope, answer choice A must be correct. You can calculate the slope as the change in y-values over the change in x-values:

(1) $\frac{5-0}{0-(-3)} = \frac{5}{3}$, answer choice A.

44. **The correct answer is G.** The area of a square is calculated by squaring the length of a side. If the diagonal is 8 centimeters, the length of each side must be less than 8 centimeters, so eliminate answer choice A. When you draw the diagonal, you create 2 identical right isosceles triangles, with the diagonal as the hypotenuse. The sides of these triangles have the following relationship:

(1) The legs are congruent, or equal.

(2) The hypotenuse is $\sqrt{2}$ times the length of either leg.

Since you know the hypotenuse is 8, each leg must be equal to $\frac{8}{\sqrt{2}}$. Square this value to find

the area of square $SPQR$:

(3) $\left(\frac{8}{\sqrt{2}}\right)\left(\frac{8}{\sqrt{2}}\right) = \frac{64}{2} = 32$, answer choice G.

45. **The correct answer is B.** The circumference of a circle is equivalent to $2\pi r$. Since the circumference is given as 7π, 7 must equal $2r$, so r is $\frac{7}{2}$, answer choice B.

46. **The correct answer is H.** The volume of a cube is calculated by multiplying the length by the width by the height ($l \cdot w \cdot h$). You are given that each side has a length of 5 centimeters, so the volume would be equivalent to $5 \cdot 5 \cdot 5$, or 5^3, answer choice H.

47. **The correct answer is E.** This problem requires you to find the values of x that make $3x^2 + 4x - 15$ positive. Set up the inequality $3x^2 + 4x - 15 > 0$. First, solve this as if there was an equal sign.

(1) $3x^2 + 4x - 15 = 0$

(2) $(3x - 5)(x + 3) = 0$

(3) $x = \frac{5}{3}$ and -3

These number tell you when $3x^2 + 4x - 15$ is equal to 0. Since answer choices A, B, C, and D do not reference both of these numbers, they can be eliminated. To make sure that answer choice E is correct, pick a number that is greater than $\frac{5}{3}$, like 2. Plug 2 into the expressions and see if it yields a positive result. Pick another number that is less than -3, like -4. Plug -4 into the expression and see if it yields a positive result. Since both do, answer choice E is correct.

48. **The correct answer is F.** By definition, in a perfect square trinomial the first and last terms are perfect squares, and the middle term is twice the product of the square roots of the first and last terms. Eliminate answer choices G and J because the last terms are not perfect squares. Eliminate choice H because the first term is not a perfect square. Look at the middle term in answer choices F and K; $12 = 2(2 \cdot 3)$, so answer choice F is a perfect square trinomial: $4x^2 + 12x + 9 = (2x + 3)(2x + 3)$

49. **The correct answer is E.** By definition, a rational number can be expressed as a ratio of 2 integers. Whole numbers are rational numbers, as are fractions and most decimal numbers. Since you are given that both p and q are negative integers, all of the operations represented by the roman numerals will result in rational numbers. Negative numbers can be rational; pick numbers

that solve the equation given to check this theory:

(1) $p = 2q$

(2) $-6 = 2(-3)$; $p = -6$ and $q = -3$

Now try the given operations using these values:

(3) $p + 2q = -6 + -3 = -9$; this is a rational number.

(4) $\dfrac{p}{q} = \dfrac{-6}{-3} = 2$; this is a rational number.

(5) $\dfrac{q}{p} = \dfrac{-3}{-6} = \dfrac{1}{2}$; this is a rational number.

50. **The correct answer is J.** To solve this problem, make x minutes the time that it took Marcia to get to Alan's house. On the way home, Marcia went 2 times as fast as she did going to Alan's house, which means that it took her $\dfrac{1}{2}$ the time, or $\dfrac{1}{2}x$ minutes. The total number of minutes that Marcia biked is equal to x minutes $+\left(\dfrac{1}{2}\right)x$ minutes:

(1) $x + \dfrac{1}{2}x$

To add the fractions together, you must convert x into like terms:

(2) $\dfrac{2}{2}x + \dfrac{1}{2}x = \dfrac{3}{2}x$, answer choice J.

51. **The correct answer is D.** Since the 2 lines are parallel, the 2 triangles are similar and share the same constant ratio. The smaller triangle has 1 side with a length of 2 centimeters (cm), and the larger triangle has 2 sides with a length of 8 cm. The legs of the triangles have a ratio of 2:8, which can be reduced to 1:4. This means that the length of the base of the smaller triangle is also 2. Since the area of the smaller triangle is 10 cm^2, the height of the smaller triangle must be 10:

(1) $\dfrac{1}{2}$(base)(height) $= \dfrac{1}{2}(2)(10) = 10$

The height of the larger triangle must be 40 cm because of the ratio of 1:4. So, the area of the larger triangle is $\frac{1}{2}(8)(40) = 160$ cm^2, answer choice D.

52. **The correct answer is K.** To find the measure of an interior angle of a regular octagon, first we need to calculate the sum of all interior angles of a regular octagon. To find the sum of the interior angles of a regular octagon, first choose a vertex

and draw as many diagonals as you can from that 1 vertex.

As you can see, there were 5 diagonals that formed 6 triangles. Each triangle has 180°, so the sum of the interior angles of a regular octagon is 6(180°), or 1,080°. Since all of the angles are the same, each interior is angle is $\dfrac{1,080°}{8} = 135°$, or answer choice K.

53. **The correct answer is D.** The best way to solve this problem is to set up a table indicating the time period in years, and the number of both CDs and videogames purchased during the years given. The consumption rate is the same, so, based on information in the problem, you can fill in the table as follows:

Time Period	CDs	Videogames
1995	5	2
1996	6	4
1997	7	6
1998	8	8
1999	9	10

Teenagers bought the same average number of CDs and videogames in 1998, answer choice D.

54. **The correct answer is K.** The first step in answering this question is to set $x^2 - 15b^2 = 2xb$ equal to 0:

(1) $x^2 - 2xb - 15b^2 = 0$

The next step is to factor the equation and set each group equal to 0 in order to solve for x:

(2) $(x + 3b)(x - 5b) = 0$

(3) $x + 3b = 0$, so $x = -3b$

(4) $x - 5b = 0$, so $x = 5b$

The 2 solutions for x are $-3b$ or $5b$, answer choice K.

55. **The correct answer is E.** This question tests your ability to recognize and apply the distributive

property. According to the distributive property, for any numbers a, b, and c, $c(a+b)=ca+cb$. According to the distributive property, then, $a(b+c)=$

(1) $ab+ac$ is equivalent to $ca+ba$, so Roman Numeral I is correct; eliminate answer choices B and C.

(2) $ab+ac$, so Roman Numeral II is correct; eliminate answer choice A.

(3) $(b+c)a$, so Roman Numeral III is also correct, eliminate answer choice D.

Since all of the operations are equivalent to $a(b+c)$, answer choice E is correct.

56. **The correct answer is F.** By definition, the tangent of any angle is the $\dfrac{\sin}{\cos}$. Therefore,

$\dfrac{(\tan x)}{(\sin x \cos x)}$, simplified as $(\tan x) \cdot \dfrac{1}{\sin x \cos x}$, is equal to $\dfrac{\sin}{\cos} \cdot \dfrac{1}{\sin x \cos x}$ Multiply the fractions, first canceling the $\sin x$ from the numerator and denominator:

(1) $\dfrac{1}{\cos^2 x}$, answer choice F.

57. **The correct answer is C.** The absolute value is always positive, so in order for the absolute value of x^3 to equal $-x^3$, x must be either a negative number, or 0, answer choice C. If you cube a negative number, the result is always positive. So, if x were equal to -1, for example, the absolute value of x^3 would be $(-1)(-1)(-1)$, or 1. The value of $-x^3$ would also be 1, because $-(-1)^3$ is equivalent to 1^3. Zero is an option as well, since 0 is neither negative nor positive, and 0 raised to any power is still 0.

58. **The correct answer is F.** The best way to solve this problem is to plug in the answer choices for c, and factor the equation:

(1) $3x^2+2x-1=0$

(2) $(3x-1)(x+1)=0$

(3) $3x-1=0$; $3x=1$; $x=\dfrac{1}{3}$

(4) $x+1=0$; $x=-1$

Answer choice F gives you 2 real solutions for x. Testing the other answer choices will yield 2 distinct complex roots, not real roots.

59. **The correct answer is B.** You are given that angle QPR and angle PRS are right triangles; you are also given the lengths of diagonal PR (12), and side PS (20). Draw a diagram to help visualize the problem:

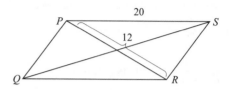

You should now see that you have the length of 1 side of the right triangle PRS (12), and the length of the hypotenuse (20). Use the Pythagorean Theorem to calculate the length of the remaining side:

(1) $a^2+b^2=c^2$

(2) $12^2+b^2=20^2$

(3) $144+b^2=400$

(4) $b^2=256$

(5) $b=16$

The length of RS is 16, answer choice B.

60. **The correct answer is K.** Before you answer the question, notice that the ramp forms a triangle with sides s and x, and a hypotenuse of an unknown length that represents the length of the ramp. The slope of the ramp can be defined in the same way the slope of a line is defined: $\dfrac{\text{change in } y}{\text{change in } x}$. In this instance, the change in y is the vertical length, or height of the triangle, and the change in x is the horizontal length, or base, of the triangle. If the slope of the ramp is t, then:

(1) $t=\dfrac{\text{change in } y}{\text{change in } x}=\dfrac{s}{x}$

(2) $x=\dfrac{s}{t}$

Now that you have a value for x, you can use the Pythagorean Theorem, $a^2+b^2=c^2$ to solve for the length of the ramp (or the hypotenuse), c:

(1) $(\text{length of the ramp})^2=s^2+\left(\dfrac{s}{t}\right)^2$

(2) length of the ramp $=\sqrt{s^2+\left(\dfrac{s}{t}\right)^2}$, answer choice K.

Reading Test Explanations

PASSAGE I

1. **The best answer is B.** Paragraph 2 states that the narrator "had fancied it was down nearer the Circus," which suggests that he is not sure where the Magic Shop is, and had only "imagined" its location. The other answer choices are not supported by the context of the passage.

2. **The best answer is H.** It is clear in the passage that the narrator is not certain where the Magic Shop is located, answer choice H.

3. **The best answer is A.** The first paragraph indicates that the narrator "had seen the Magic Shop from afar several times; I had passed it once or twice"; this suggests that he first learned of the Magic Shop when he had passed by it before, answer choice A. The other answer choices are not supported by details in the passage.

4. **The best answer is J.** The context in which that statement was made suggests that Gip was a polite child, answer choice J. The passage indicates that Gip "inherits his mother's breeding," but not that he was worried about his mother, so eliminate answer choice F. The other answer choices are not supported by the passage.

5. **The best answer is A.** Paragraph 4 indicates that the narrator found the clerk's action "unexpected," which means the same as "surprising." This best supports answer choice A.

6. **The best answer is F.** Based on the last two paragraphs, Gip's reaction to the shopman's trick can best be described as quietly astonished. Gip does not speak either during or after the trick, and after taking the glass balls he "resumed [the narrator's] reassuring finger, and nerved himself for the next event." The other answer choices are not supported by the passage.

7. **The best answer is D.** During his discussion with the shopman, the narrator indicates that he is looking for something "amusing" to purchase for his son. This best supports answer choice D.

8. **The best answer is J.** The passage indicates that Gip is excited about entering the Magic Shop. He "hauled [the narrator] by my finger right up to the window" and went on to describe each of the items in the window. The other answer choices are not supported by the passage.

9. **The best answer is A.** Paragraph 4 suggests that the narrator and his son were surprised to find the shopman suddenly behind the counter; "and so with a start we were aware of him." It is likely that this surprise caused them to stop laughing together, since this is what they were doing just before the surprise. The other answer choices are not supported by the passage.

10. **The best answer is J.** The last sentence in the passage states that Gip "nerved himself for the next event." This suggests that, although the may have been a bit uncertain, he was ready to see the next trick, answer choice J.

PASSAGE II

11. **The best answer is D.** The passage focuses on the difficulties that Alaska and her inhabitants encountered on the way to achieving statehood. In fact, according to the passage, it "took almost 100 years from beginning to end." This best supports answer choice D.

12. **The best answer is G.** The word *enigma* refers to a riddle, or anything that is puzzling. Since, according to Paragraph 1, the author doesn't know a lot about Alaska (at least as compared to Hawaii) it makes sense that *enigma* would mean "mystery," answer choice G.

13. **The best answer is A.** Paragraph 1 states that the author was "a ten-year-old girl" when Alaska became a state. The paragraph goes on to state that "nearly fifty years later,... Alaska remains an enigma." It is safe to conclude, then, that the author must be almost sixty years old, answer choice A.

14. **The best answer is H.** The passage states that "Alaska and the nearby Aleutian Island chain were threatened by their proximity to Japan." This suggests that the Aleutian Islands must be fairly close to Japan, answer choice H.

15. **The best answer is B.** The passage emphasizes Alaska's struggle for statehood. You can infer that the reason the author posed the question is to introduce the main topic of the passage and follow it up with supporting information.

16. **The best answer is H.** While the author does offer some personal information, she does not make an emotional appeal, nor does she describe her childhood. Eliminate answer choice F. It is made clear in the passage that the author has never visited Alaska, so eliminate answer choice G. The bulk of the passage contains historical background information on Alaska's progression to statehood, which best supports answer choice H.

17. **The best answer is C.** The statement that "Alaska's own natural wealth was being stripped for the benefit of a handful of outside entrepreneurs" suggests that Alaskans were not reaping the benefits of their own land's resources, answer choice C.

18. **The best answer is F.** Paragraph 4 states that "the bombing of Pearl Harbor ... propelled Congress to provide Alaska with billions of dollars in defense spending," which suggests that Congress was motivated to give Alaska money due to the onset of World War II.

19. **The best answer is D.** The only reason that the author contrasts Alaska and Hawaii throughout the passage is to emphasize her personal impressions of each state, answer choice D. The other answer choices are not supported by the passage.

20. **The best answer is F.** The final sentence in Paragraph 4 states that "Alaska finally gained its statehood on January 3, 1959, due primarily to growing and organized public and political pressure." This best supports answer choice F.

PASSAGE III

21. **The best answer is B.** The main focus of the passage is on vocal training and technique. Statements like "it is a very great mistake for any girl to begin serious training" before the age of twenty, and "the voice, even more than the hands, needs a kind of exhaustive technical drill," suggesting that the author has very strong opinions about voice training, answer choice B.

22. **The best answer is F.** The passage states that "the feminine voice ... is hardly settled" until the age of twenty. It is likely that the narrator believed it was better for her voice to wait until age twenty to begin her voice training, answer choice F.

23. **The best answer is D.** The second and third paragraphs stress the importance of vocal exercises in developing a well-trained voice. In the second paragraph the narrator states that "in the case of the voice, the instrument has to be developed and sometimes made by study." She goes on to say early in the third paragraph that some vocal exercises "are marvelously beneficial when intelligently studied." The other answer choices are not supported by details in the passage.

24. **The best answer is F.** It makes sense that the narrator made that claim to indicate that some

types of music are better for the human voice than other types. This would suggest that she understands different types of music, answer choice F. The other answer choices are not supported by the passage.

25. **The best answer is C.** The first sentence of the paragraph states that "when the student has her voice under complete control, it is safe to take up the lyric repertoire of Mendelssohn, Old English songs, etc." Earlier in the passage the narrator expresses the importance of waiting until the voice is settled, and then developing the voice. This best supports answer choice C.

26. **The best answer is G.** It is reasonable to infer that the narrator suggests getting advice from a native French coach because the French language can be difficult to learn. This best supports answer choice G.

27. **The best answer is D.** Throughout the passage the narrator, Alma Gluck, offers her personal experience and opinions relating to learning to sing. It makes sense that her purpose is to inform her audience. This best supports answer choice D.

28. **The best answer is H.** When Gluck claims that in America "we are rich in the quantity of songs rather than in the quality," she means that there are many songs, but perhaps many of them are not well-composed. This best supports answer choice H.

29. **The best answer is B.** The tone of the initial few sentences in Paragraph 7 is negative, suggesting that *iniquitous* will have a negative connotation. It is clear that the narrator does not agree with the statement "art for art's sake," so you can eliminate answer choices A and C. Answer choice B has a negative connotation, and best fits the context of the paragraph.

30. **The best answer is H.** Gluck states in the last paragraph that "the bird sings ... because it is her natural characteristic," and that this is also the reason a "real artist" works. This best supports answer choice H.

PASSAGE IV

31. **The best answer is B.** Throughout the passage the author discusses several options for eradicating EAB disease. The author also indicates that some of these options have not been proven (insecticide treatment), while others can be costly (cutting down and destroying infested trees).

This suggests that the author believes EAB disease can possibly be controlled or eradicated, but it may take a lot of time and money. Answer choice B is best supported by information in the passage.

32. **The best answer is J.** The passage indicates that the EAB is native to Asia, which means that it occurs naturally in Asia, answer choice J. The other answer choices are not supported by the passage.

33. **The best answer is C.** Paragraph 1 states that "transporting firewood in certain areas of Michigan and Ohio is a federal crime, punishable by a whopping four thousand dollar fine." The other answer choices are not supported by details in the passage.

34. **The best answer is J.** The primary focus of the first paragraph is the destruction of millions of trees and the infestation of "over 5,000 square miles of Michigan and Canadian land," which suggests that the main worry expressed is the decimation (extensive destruction) of ash trees in North America, answer choice J.

35. **The best answer is A.** Clearly the author is interested in the study of EAB disease. In addition, the author expresses a concern for the spread of the disease, as well as for the quantity of time and money that most likely will be needed to study EAB disease. The other answer choices are not supported by details in the passage.

36. **The best answer is J.** According to the passage, *Agrilus planipennis* is the scientific name for the Emerald Ash Borer beetle, answer choice J.

37. **The best answer is A.** The passage states that infested trees are being "cut down and destroyed, along with the beetle colonies, or galleries." The other answer choices are not supported by the passage.

38. **The best answer is H.** The passage clearly states that the EAB beetle is native to Asia, answer choice H.

39. **The best answer is D.** Paragraph 2 states that "the adults settle high within the tree's canopy." The "canopy" refers to the upper branches of the ash tree, answer choice D.

40. **The best answer is G.** According to the passage, "identification of infested trees is taking place in all susceptible areas," and that "identified trees are being cut down and destroyed." While insecticide spray is being considered as a method of control, the passage does not indicate that it is currently being used. Eliminate answer choice H. The other answer choices are not supported by details in the passage.

SCIENCE REASONING TEST EXPLANATIONS

PASSAGE I

1. **The correct answer is C.** To answer this question, look at the list of drawbacks for each drug-delivery system. According to Table 1, in the Pressure drug-delivery system, "food taken with the capsule may alter the pressure enough to disintegrate the capsule in the stomach."

2. **The correct answer is H.** The passage states that "new research has targeted the colon as an ideal environment for drug absorption to treat certain illnesses." This suggests that the intended target in these experiments is the colon. According to the results of Experiment 2 (found in Table 3) the tablet with the "B" outer coating and the "1" inner coating reached the colon in the shortest amount of time. Therefore, answer choice H is correct.

3. **The correct answer is B.** The results of Experiment 1 are shown in Table 2. Both Group I and Group II included tablets with Tracer A. But, the tablets in each group had different coatings. Therefore, it is most likely that the coating would have a greater impact on either gastric emptying time or colonic arrival; eliminate answer choices A and D. Since the target is the same for all groups (the colon) the drug's target destination will not be affected; eliminate answer choice C. You can see that with Coating 2, the colonic arrival time is faster than with Coating 1, which best supports answer choice B.

4. **The correct answer is J.** According to the results of both experiments, across all groups, the time that remained standard, or constant, was the gastric emptying time, answer choice J.

5. **The correct answer is D.** Table 1 provides details about each drug-delivery system. When you locate Time-dependent delivery, you see that the mechanics of the delivery include an inner barrier that delays release, answer choice D. The other answer choices are not associated with time-dependent delivery.

PASSAGE II

6. **The correct answer is J.** To answer this question you need to consider the data in both Table 1 and Table 2. According to Table 2, the source rock basalt results in either schist or amphibolite. Table 1 indicates that schist is a foliated rock, and amphibolite is a nonfoliated rock. Therefore, the metamorphic results of basalt can be either foliated or nonfoliated.

7. **The correct answer is C.** Look at Table 2 and find marble in the second column. The source rock is listed directly to the left, in the first column. Based on Table 2, limestone is the source rock for marble.

8. **The correct answer is F.** Figure 1 indicates that, at low levels of metamorphic intensity there is little to no foliation. As metamorphic intensity increases, so does foliation. This best supports answer choice F.

9. **The correct answer is B.** According to Figure 1, shale is at the far left of the metamorphic intensity scale. This corresponds to a low level of intensity. Schist forms at a higher level of metamorphic intensity, as shown in Figure 1. This data best supports answer choice B.

10. **The correct answer is F.** According to Table 2, rhyolite is the source rock for schist. This means that, at a certain level of intensity, rhyolite becomes schist. Schist is the source rock for gneiss. It would be logical to conclude that levels of metamorphic intensity increase as one type of rock changes into another, as Figure 1 indicates. Figure 1 also shows that, as metamorphic activity increases, foliation increases. This information best supports answer choice F.

11. **The correct answer is C.** To answer this question, first find schist in Column 2 (Result) of Table 2. It appears 3 times, and is the result of 3 different source rocks: slate, rhyolite, and basalt, answer choice C.

PASSAGE III

12. **The correct answer is H.** The results of Experiment 1 are shown in Table 1. According to these results, the fast dissolution time was recorded when the tablet was in fine-powder form, dissolved in HCl, answer choice H.

13. **The correct answer is A.** According to the passage, the tablets were only dissolved in water in Experiment 2, whereas, both water and HCl were used as solvents in Experiment 1. This best supports answer choice A.

14. **The correct answer is J.** Based on Table 1, the dissolution time was always faster when the tablet was crushed, answer choice J. The other answer choices are not supported by the passage.

15. **The correct answer is B.** The temperature was varied in Experiment 2, so look at Table 2 first to answer this question. At 80°, it took 12 seconds for a whole tablet to dissolve. According to Experiment 1, crushing the tablet resulted in faster dissolution times. Therefore, you can conclude that the dissolution time would be faster than 12 seconds, answer choice B.

16. **The correct answer is J.** The results of Experiment 1 reveal that crushing the tablet increases the dissolution rate, as does dissolving the tablet in HCl. Eliminate answer choices G and H. Table 2 indicates that lower temperatures result in slower dissolution times. This best supports answer choice J.

17. **The correct answer is A.** The results of Experiment 1 indicate that crushing the tablet increases the dissolution rate, so eliminate answer choices B and C. According to Table 2, lower temperatures result in slower dissolution times, so dissolving a whole tablet in 10°C water would be slower than dissolving a whole tablet in 80°C water.

PASSAGE IV

18. **The correct answer is F.** The passage states that the average starting length of the rats in each group was 10 cm. Beginning with answer choice F, calculate the difference between the starting length and the average length after 6 weeks for each group.

    (1) Group 6: $18.25 - 10.00 = 8.25\,cm$

    (2) Group 2: $18.00 - 10.00 = 8.00\,cm$

    (3) Group 7: $14.25 - 10.00 = 4.25\,cm$

    (4) Group 4: $17.00 - 10.00 = 7.00\,cm$

    The rats in Group 6 increased the most in average length, answer choice F.

19. **The correct answer is A.** The passage states that the average starting weight of the rats in each group was 30 grams. Find the corresponding group on Table 2 for each feed-type listed, and calculate the difference between the starting weight and the average weight after 6 weeks for each group.

    (1) Feed M = Group 5: $52 - 30 = 22\,g$

    (2) Feed N = Group 6: $49 - 30 = 19\,g$

    (3) Feed O = Group 7: $42 - 30 = 12\,g$

    (4) Feed P = Group 8: $44 - 30 = 14\,g$

    Feed M resulted in the greatest weight gain, answer choice A.

20. **The correct answer is J.** The passage states that the rats in each group weighed an average of 30 grams at the start of the experiments. Starting with answer choice F, calculate the difference between the starting weight and the average weight after 6 weeks for all groups:

    (1) Group 1: $50 - 30 = 20\,g$

    (2) Group 3: $43 - 13 = 13\,g$

    (3) Group 5: $52 - 30 = 22\,g$

    (4) Group 7: $42 - 30 = 12\,g$

    The rats in Group 7 gained the least amount of weight, answer choice J.

21. **The correct answer is C.** According to the question, Group 9 would receive Feed M (the same as Group 5) and a vitamin supplement (like Group 6). According to Table 1 and the information in the passage, the rats in Group 6 had a greater average length than did Group 5 after 6 weeks. Therefore, if Group 9 is fed vitamin supplements, the rats will most likely have a greater average length than the rats in Group 5, answer choice C.

22. **The correct answer is J.** The best way to answer this question is to examine each of the answer choices, and eliminate those that are not supported by the data in Table 2. Group 7 is the control group. Group 6 was fed Feed N. It is not true that the rats in Group 6 were twice as long as the rats in Group 7, so eliminate answer choice F. Group 5 was fed Feed M. It is not true that the rats in Group 5 weighed 3 times more than the rats in Group 7, so eliminate answer choice G. Group 8 was fed Feed P; rats in this group did not have the greatest average length, so eliminate answer choice H. Answer choice J is correct, because it is true that the rats in Group 7 are similar in both weight and length to the rats in Group 8.

PASSAGE V

23. **The correct answer is D.** According to Table 2, granite is phaneritic in texture. Table 1 indicates that phaneritic rocks cool slowly, and Figure 1 indicates that phaneritic rocks have coarse

grains. This information best supports answer choice D.

24. The correct answer is H. According to Table 2, both rhyolite and andesite are aphanitic in texture. Table 1 indicates that aphanitic rocks cool "quickly but more slowly than glassy textured rocks," answer choice H.

25. The correct answer is A. Figure 1 indicates that phaneritic rocks have a slower cooling rate and coarser grain size than either glassy or aphanitic rocks. According to Table 1, the grains in phaneritic rocks can be seen without a microscope, so they are larger than the grains of both glassy and aphanitic rocks. This information best supports answer choice A.

26. The correct answer is G. To answer this question, look at the cooling characteristics listed in Table 1. Glassy rock "cools rapidly and above the temperature for crystals to form." This information best supports answer choice G.

27. The correct answer is C. Table 1 indicates that aphanitic rocks cool quickly. Table 2 lists rhyolite, andesite, and basalt as aphanitic rocks. The other answer choices are not supported by information in the passage.

28. The correct answer is G. According to Table 1, rocks with interlocking grains that can be seen without a microscope are classified as phaneritic rocks. The cooling characteristics of phaneritic rocks indicate that the rocks "cool very slowly at a uniform rate," answer choice G.

PASSAGE VI

29. The correct answer is B. The passage states that the sun has a mass of 1. Therefore, star type B, with a mass of 18, has a mass 18 times that of the sun.

30. The correct answer is J. To answer this question, find the column for surface temperature in Table 1. Stars with a surface temperature less than 3,500 K are red in color, answer choice J.

31. The correct answer is A. The giant stars shown in Figure 1 have a surface temperature ranging from about 5,000 K to about 2,500 K. According to Table 1, stars at these temperatures will range from orange to red, answer choice A.

32. The correct answer is H. This question requires you to look at both Figure 1 and Table 1. The main sequence stars in Figure 1 have a temperature range from about 20,000 K down to about 2,500 K. According to Table 1, star type O has a surface temperature that ranges from 28,000 K to 60,000 K. Star type O, therefore, is NOT a main sequence star.

33. The correct answer is B. To answer this question, look at Figure 1. A star with a temperature of 15,000 K and a luminosity of 10^{-4} would most likely be a white dwarf, answer choice B.

PASSAGE VII

34. The correct answer G. To answer this question look at both Table 1 and Table 2. The data presented in each table indicate that, at 40% relative humidity, Litter C absorbs water faster than either Litter A and Litter B.

35. The correct answer is D. According to Table 1, at 80% relative humidity, Litter B absorbs water in about 9 hours. It makes sense that at a higher relative humidity level, it would take longer to absorb water, so answer choice D is correct.

36. The correct answer is F. To answer this question, compare the answer choices with the data presented in Table 1. Based on Table 1, Litter A took 16 hours to absorb water at a relative humidity level of 80%, while it took 9 hours for Litter B to absorb water, and 5 hours for Litter C to absorb water at a relative humidity level of 80%. This information best supports answer choice F.

37. The correct answer is C. In Experiment 1, the relative humidity levels were varied from 40% to 80%, while in Experiment 2, the relative humidity level was held constant at 40%. The other answer choices are not supported by the passage.

38. The correct answer is F. According to the results of both experiments, adding baking soda to the litter decreased the absorption time for Litter A only, answer choice F.

39. The correct answer is D. It makes sense that decreasing the quantity of water added to all of the litter types would also decrease the absorption time. The other answer choices are not supported by the passage.

40. The correct answer is H. The results of the experiments indicate that the different litter types had different absorption rates. This best supports answer choice H. The other answer choices are not supported by the results of the experiments.

▰▰▰ ANSWER SHEET

ACT PRACTICE TEST 4
Answer Sheet

ENGLISH

1 (A) (B) (C) (D)	21 (A) (B) (C) (D)	41 (A) (B) (C) (D)	61 (A) (B) (C) (D)
2 (F) (G) (H) (J)	22 (F) (G) (H) (J)	42 (F) (G) (H) (J)	62 (F) (G) (H) (J)
3 (A) (B) (C) (D)	23 (A) (B) (C) (D)	43 (A) (B) (C) (D)	63 (A) (B) (C) (D)
4 (F) (G) (H) (J)	24 (F) (G) (H) (J)	44 (F) (G) (H) (J)	64 (F) (G) (H) (J)
5 (A) (B) (C) (D)	25 (A) (B) (C) (D)	45 (A) (B) (C) (D)	65 (A) (B) (C) (D)
6 (F) (G) (H) (J)	26 (F) (G) (H) (J)	46 (F) (G) (H) (J)	66 (F) (G) (H) (J)
7 (A) (B) (C) (D)	27 (A) (B) (C) (D)	47 (A) (B) (C) (D)	67 (A) (B) (C) (D)
8 (F) (G) (H) (J)	28 (F) (G) (H) (J)	48 (F) (G) (H) (J)	68 (F) (G) (H) (J)
9 (A) (B) (C) (D)	29 (A) (B) (C) (D)	49 (A) (B) (C) (D)	69 (A) (B) (C) (D)
10 (F) (G) (H) (J)	30 (F) (G) (H) (J)	50 (F) (G) (H) (J)	70 (F) (G) (H) (J)
11 (A) (B) (C) (D)	31 (A) (B) (C) (D)	51 (A) (B) (C) (D)	71 (A) (B) (C) (D)
12 (F) (G) (H) (J)	32 (F) (G) (H) (J)	52 (F) (G) (H) (J)	72 (F) (G) (H) (J)
13 (A) (B) (C) (D)	33 (A) (B) (C) (D)	53 (A) (B) (C) (D)	73 (A) (B) (C) (D)
14 (F) (G) (H) (J)	34 (F) (G) (H) (J)	54 (F) (G) (H) (J)	74 (F) (G) (H) (J)
15 (A) (B) (C) (D)	35 (A) (B) (C) (D)	55 (A) (B) (C) (D)	75 (A) (B) (C) (D)
16 (F) (G) (H) (J)	36 (F) (G) (H) (J)	56 (F) (G) (H) (J)	
17 (A) (B) (C) (D)	37 (A) (B) (C) (D)	57 (A) (B) (C) (D)	
18 (F) (G) (H) (J)	38 (F) (G) (H) (J)	58 (F) (G) (H) (J)	
19 (A) (B) (C) (D)	39 (A) (B) (C) (D)	59 (A) (B) (C) (D)	
20 (F) (G) (H) (J)	40 (F) (G) (H) (J)	60 (F) (G) (H) (J)	

MATH

1 (A) (B) (C) (D) (E)	16 (F) (G) (H) (J) (K)	31 (A) (B) (C) (D) (E)	46 (F) (G) (H) (J) (K)
2 (F) (G) (H) (J) (K)	17 (A) (B) (C) (D) (E)	32 (F) (G) (H) (J) (K)	47 (A) (B) (C) (D) (E)
3 (A) (B) (C) (D) (E)	18 (F) (G) (H) (J) (K)	33 (A) (B) (C) (D) (E)	48 (F) (G) (H) (J) (K)
4 (F) (G) (H) (J) (K)	19 (A) (B) (C) (D) (E)	34 (F) (G) (H) (J) (K)	49 (A) (B) (C) (D) (E)
5 (A) (B) (C) (D) (E)	20 (F) (G) (H) (J) (K)	35 (A) (B) (C) (D) (E)	50 (F) (G) (H) (J) (K)
6 (F) (G) (H) (J) (K)	21 (A) (B) (C) (D) (E)	36 (F) (G) (H) (J) (K)	51 (A) (B) (C) (D) (E)
7 (A) (B) (C) (D) (E)	22 (F) (G) (H) (J) (K)	37 (A) (B) (C) (D) (E)	52 (F) (G) (H) (J) (K)
8 (F) (G) (H) (J) (K)	23 (A) (B) (C) (D) (E)	38 (F) (G) (H) (J) (K)	53 (A) (B) (C) (D) (E)
9 (A) (B) (C) (D) (E)	24 (F) (G) (H) (J) (K)	39 (A) (B) (C) (D) (E)	54 (F) (G) (H) (J) (K)
10 (F) (G) (H) (J) (K)	25 (A) (B) (C) (D) (E)	40 (F) (G) (H) (J) (K)	55 (A) (B) (C) (D) (E)
11 (A) (B) (C) (D) (E)	26 (F) (G) (H) (J) (K)	41 (A) (B) (C) (D) (E)	56 (F) (G) (H) (J) (K)
12 (F) (G) (H) (J) (K)	27 (A) (B) (C) (D) (E)	42 (F) (G) (H) (J) (K)	57 (A) (B) (C) (D) (E)
13 (A) (B) (C) (D) (E)	28 (F) (G) (H) (J) (K)	43 (A) (B) (C) (D) (E)	58 (F) (G) (H) (J) (K)
14 (F) (G) (H) (J) (K)	29 (A) (B) (C) (D) (E)	44 (F) (G) (H) (J) (K)	59 (A) (B) (C) (D) (E)
15 (A) (B) (C) (D) (E)	30 (F) (G) (H) (J) (K)	45 (A) (B) (C) (D) (E)	60 (F) (G) (H) (J) (K)

READING

1 Ⓐ Ⓑ Ⓒ Ⓓ	11 Ⓐ Ⓑ Ⓒ Ⓓ	21 Ⓐ Ⓑ Ⓒ Ⓓ	31 Ⓐ Ⓑ Ⓒ Ⓓ
2 Ⓕ Ⓖ Ⓗ Ⓙ	12 Ⓕ Ⓖ Ⓗ Ⓙ	22 Ⓕ Ⓖ Ⓗ Ⓙ	32 Ⓕ Ⓖ Ⓗ Ⓙ
3 Ⓐ Ⓑ Ⓒ Ⓓ	13 Ⓐ Ⓑ Ⓒ Ⓓ	23 Ⓐ Ⓑ Ⓒ Ⓓ	33 Ⓐ Ⓑ Ⓒ Ⓓ
4 Ⓕ Ⓖ Ⓗ Ⓙ	14 Ⓕ Ⓖ Ⓗ Ⓙ	24 Ⓕ Ⓖ Ⓗ Ⓙ	34 Ⓕ Ⓖ Ⓗ Ⓙ
5 Ⓐ Ⓑ Ⓒ Ⓓ	15 Ⓐ Ⓑ Ⓒ Ⓓ	25 Ⓐ Ⓑ Ⓒ Ⓓ	35 Ⓐ Ⓑ Ⓒ Ⓓ
6 Ⓕ Ⓖ Ⓗ Ⓙ	16 Ⓕ Ⓖ Ⓗ Ⓙ	26 Ⓕ Ⓖ Ⓗ Ⓙ	36 Ⓕ Ⓖ Ⓗ Ⓙ
7 Ⓐ Ⓑ Ⓒ Ⓓ	17 Ⓐ Ⓑ Ⓒ Ⓓ	27 Ⓐ Ⓑ Ⓒ Ⓓ	37 Ⓐ Ⓑ Ⓒ Ⓓ
8 Ⓕ Ⓖ Ⓗ Ⓙ	18 Ⓕ Ⓖ Ⓗ Ⓙ	28 Ⓕ Ⓖ Ⓗ Ⓙ	38 Ⓕ Ⓖ Ⓗ Ⓙ
9 Ⓐ Ⓑ Ⓒ Ⓓ	19 Ⓐ Ⓑ Ⓒ Ⓓ	29 Ⓐ Ⓑ Ⓒ Ⓓ	39 Ⓐ Ⓑ Ⓒ Ⓓ
10 Ⓕ Ⓖ Ⓗ Ⓙ	20 Ⓕ Ⓖ Ⓗ Ⓙ	30 Ⓕ Ⓖ Ⓗ Ⓙ	40 Ⓕ Ⓖ Ⓗ Ⓙ

SCIENCE

1 Ⓐ Ⓑ Ⓒ Ⓓ	11 Ⓐ Ⓑ Ⓒ Ⓓ	21 Ⓐ Ⓑ Ⓒ Ⓓ	31 Ⓐ Ⓑ Ⓒ Ⓓ
2 Ⓕ Ⓖ Ⓗ Ⓙ	12 Ⓕ Ⓖ Ⓗ Ⓙ	22 Ⓕ Ⓖ Ⓗ Ⓙ	32 Ⓕ Ⓖ Ⓗ Ⓙ
3 Ⓐ Ⓑ Ⓒ Ⓓ	13 Ⓐ Ⓑ Ⓒ Ⓓ	23 Ⓐ Ⓑ Ⓒ Ⓓ	33 Ⓐ Ⓑ Ⓒ Ⓓ
4 Ⓕ Ⓖ Ⓗ Ⓙ	14 Ⓕ Ⓖ Ⓗ Ⓙ	24 Ⓕ Ⓖ Ⓗ Ⓙ	34 Ⓕ Ⓖ Ⓗ Ⓙ
5 Ⓐ Ⓑ Ⓒ Ⓓ	15 Ⓐ Ⓑ Ⓒ Ⓓ	25 Ⓐ Ⓑ Ⓒ Ⓓ	35 Ⓐ Ⓑ Ⓒ Ⓓ
6 Ⓕ Ⓖ Ⓗ Ⓙ	16 Ⓕ Ⓖ Ⓗ Ⓙ	26 Ⓕ Ⓖ Ⓗ Ⓙ	36 Ⓕ Ⓖ Ⓗ Ⓙ
7 Ⓐ Ⓑ Ⓒ Ⓓ	17 Ⓐ Ⓑ Ⓒ Ⓓ	27 Ⓐ Ⓑ Ⓒ Ⓓ	37 Ⓐ Ⓑ Ⓒ Ⓓ
8 Ⓕ Ⓖ Ⓗ Ⓙ	18 Ⓕ Ⓖ Ⓗ Ⓙ	28 Ⓕ Ⓖ Ⓗ Ⓙ	38 Ⓕ Ⓖ Ⓗ Ⓙ
9 Ⓐ Ⓑ Ⓒ Ⓓ	19 Ⓐ Ⓑ Ⓒ Ⓓ	29 Ⓐ Ⓑ Ⓒ Ⓓ	39 Ⓐ Ⓑ Ⓒ Ⓓ
10 Ⓕ Ⓖ Ⓗ Ⓙ	20 Ⓕ Ⓖ Ⓗ Ⓙ	30 Ⓕ Ⓖ Ⓗ Ⓙ	40 Ⓕ Ⓖ Ⓗ Ⓙ

RAW SCORES	SCALE SCORES	DATE TAKEN:
ENGLISH _____	ENGLISH _____	
MATH _____	MATH _____	ENGLISH/WRITING _____
READING _____	READING _____	
SCIENCE _____	SCIENCE _____	**COMPOSITE SCORE**

1 ■ ■ ■ ■ ■ ■ ■ ■ 1

ENGLISH TEST

45 Minutes – 75 Questions

DIRECTIONS: In the passages that follow, some words and phrases are underlined and numbered. In the answer column, you will find alternatives for the words and phrases that are underlined. Choose the alternative that you think is best and fill in the corresponding bubble on your answer sheet. If you think that the original version is best, choose "NO CHANGE," which will always be either answer choice A or F. You will also find questions about a particular section of the passage, or about the entire passage. These questions will be identified by either an underlined portion or by a number in a box. Look for the answer that clearly expresses the idea, is consistent with the style and tone of the passage, and makes the correct use of standard written English. Read the passage through once before answering the questions. For some questions, you should read beyond the indicated portion before you answer.

PASSAGE I

> The following paragraphs may or may not be in the most logical order. You may be asked questions about the logical order of the paragraphs, as well as where to place sentences logically within any given paragraph.

Rubber Cement

[1]

[1] The next time you <u>should see</u> one of those huge
                          ¹

cement trucks moving down the <u>road take</u> a closer look.
                                    ²
[2] You may find that the truck is labeled "rubber

cement" as opposed to "concrete." [3] I can remember

using rubber cement in grade school, the kind with the

little brush attached to the underside of the jar's lid. ③

[1] Of course, these huge rubber cement trucks are not

making deliveries of glue to the local elementary schools

for students to use at their desks. [2] <u>In fact</u>, they may be
                                           ⁴
on their way to a high school's athletic facilities, to pour

out a thick layer of rubber cement for a tennis or

1. **A.** NO CHANGE
   B. might see
   C. ought to see
   D. see

2. **F.** NO CHANGE
   G. road, take
   H. road; take
   J. road — take

3. At this point, the writer would like to extend the discussion of her personal experience with rubber cement. Which of the following sentences (assuming all are true), if added here, would most successfully achieve this effect?
   A. We decided to have our driveway paved with rubber cement instead of concrete.
   B. I remember that I found it difficult to keep the glue from dripping all over the place.
   C. We also used paste in elementary school.
   D. Today, glue sticks make it much easier to do craft projects.

4. **F.** NO CHANGE
   G. However,
   H. And yet,
   J. Nevertheless,

GO ON TO THE NEXT PAGE.

1 ■ ■ ■ ■ ■ ■ ■ ■ 1

basketball court. [3] Rubber cement surfaces are also being used on athletic tracks.

[2]

⑤ [1] Experts are finding that the pliability of a rubber cement surface adds to the comfort level of

walkers and runners. [2] It provides a bit of a bounce
    ―6―

in addition to the solid hardness of concrete. [3] This
―7―
bounciness also tends to cause less injury to the leg joints, such as knees, shins, and ankles. [4] A rubber cement surface also helps athletes to reduce the dangers of falling and is easier to smooth out than traditional cement.
        ―8―

[3]

[1] Many consumers are taking into consideration
    ―――――――――――――――――――――
                      9

cement for their patios and driveways. [2] Cities are also
         ―10―
considering its use for sidewalks. [3] Another

advantage, of rubber cement surfacing is the ease of
―――――――11
repairing it. [4] Unlike other surfaces, cracks or etchings

can be more easily taken out of rubber cement by using a
――――――――――――――――――
             12
blowtorch. [5] Some regions of the country experience

5. Which of the following sentences (assuming all are true), if added here, would best introduce the new subject of Paragraph 2?
   A. There are many reasons why rubber cement is winning out over other traditional surfacing materials.
   B. Use of athletic tracks is increasing.
   C. Rubber cement is still useful as an adhesive.
   D. Rubber cement trucks are often even larger than traditional cement trucks.

6. F. NO CHANGE
   G. It will
   H. They
   J. The surface

7. A. NO CHANGE
   B. as opposed to
   C. for
   D. because of

8. F. NO CHANGE
   G. are easier
   H. is made easier
   J. are to be easier

9. A. NO CHANGE
   B. Taking into consideration are many consumers
   C. Many consumers are choosing
   D. Considering many consumers choose

10. F. NO CHANGE
    G. there
    H. they're
    J. those

11. A. NO CHANGE
    B. advantage of
    C. advantage;
    D. advantage:

12. F. NO CHANGE
    G. are most easily removed out of
    H. can be removed or taken easily out of
    J. are easily removed from

GO ON TO THE NEXT PAGE.

weather conditions that are less conducive to the
                    ‾‾‾‾‾‾‾‾‾
                        13

durability as rubber cement surfacing.
          ‾‾
          14

13. **A.** NO CHANGE
    B. that have fewer
    C. that are few
    D. that is less

14. **F.** NO CHANGE
    G. with
    H. to
    J. of

Question 15 asks about the passage as a whole.

---

15. In reviewing notes, the writer discovers that the following information has been left out of the essay:

    > For example, regions of the country that receive a great deal of sunshine may experience problems with rubber cement surfaces, such as cracking, yellowing, and peeling.

    If added to the essay, the sentence would most logically be placed after Sentence:
    A. 3 in Paragraph 3.
    B. 5 in Paragraph 3.
    C. 2 in Paragraph 2.
    D. 3 in Paragraph 1.

PASSAGE II

Rosalind Franklin

Nearly every student of science learns about James Watson and Francis Crick, the scientists who discovered the structure of DNA, but probably not as many have learned about other scientists whose work was important
                                                                   ‾‾‾‾‾‾‾‾‾‾‾‾
                                                                        16
to make their discovery.

16. The writer wants to emphasize that Watson and Crick did not arrive at their conclusions about DNA alone. Which choice does that best?
    F. NO CHANGE
    G. they realized for Watson and Crick
    H. Watson and Crick relied upon
    J. was accurate

[17] Franklin graduated from Cambridge in 1941 and then began work on her doctorate.

17. Which of the following sentences, if inserted here, would best connect the idea that Rosalind Franklin was one of the scientists whose work is referred to in the first paragraph?
    A. Rosalind Franklin was a pioneering and brilliant scientist.
    B. Rosalind Franklin was one of the most well known female scientists of her time.
    C. One of these lesser-known scientists was Rosalind Franklin.
    D. Watson and Crick used the work of a prominent scientist named Rosalind Franklin to make their discovery.

This advanced degree focused on, using coal and
‾‾‾‾‾‾‾‾‾‾‾‾‾‾‾‾‾‾‾‾‾‾‾‾‾‾‾‾‾‾‾‾‾‾‾‾‾‾‾
               18
charcoal efficiently, which was very important during

18. **F.** NO CHANGE
    G. This advanced degree, focused on using
    H. This advanced degree, on using her research
    J. Her research focused on using

GO ON TO THE NEXT PAGE.

1 ■ ■ ■ ■ ■ ■ ■ ■ **1**

World War II. After earning her Ph.D., Franklin spent
some time in France, and there she would learn x-ray
——————————————————————
19
diffraction techniques that later became essential to for
——————————————————————————————
19
her work on DNA. She decided to return to England to
——————
19

19. A. NO CHANGE
    B. France, learning x-ray diffraction techniques that later became essential to her work on DNA.
    C. France, and learned complicated and esoteric x-ray diffraction techniques that later became absolutely critical for her work on DNA as well as forever changing the landscape of modern science.
    D. France learning a lot of things that would be useful later.

further her scientific career, and she accepting an offer to
                                       —————
                                        20
work with a team of scientists studying DNA at King's

20. F. NO CHANGE
    G. accepted
    H. was accepting
    J. accepted to

College in the early 1950s! At this time,
                   ————————
                     21

21. A. NO CHANGE
    B. 1950s: at
    C. 1950s. At
    D. 1950s at

there were a race among scientists to find the structure of
——————
22
DNA. The leader of Franklin's team assigned her to

22. F. NO CHANGE
    G. there would be
    H. is
    J. there was

work with a graduate student — Maurice Wilkins, on a
                      —————————————————————
                                23
DNA project. Either due to a miscommunication or to
bad management on the part of the team leader,
Wilkins thought that Franklin was there to assist him,
——————————————————————————————————
24
while Franklin correctly assumed they were equals.
——————————————————————————————
24

23. A. NO CHANGE
    B. student — Maurice Wilkins — on
    C. student Maurice Wilkins on
    D. student Maurice Wilkins, on

24. Given that all of them are true, which choice most specifically illustrates the result of the miscommunication?
    F. NO CHANGE
    G. Wilkins and Franklin continued to have problems with their work relationship.
    H. Wilkins and Franklin were still excellent scientists.
    J. Wilkins and Franklin were able to work together on DNA anyway.

    Despite the tension between Wilkins and herself,
Franklin still performed meticulous research on

DNA. This was not easy being a woman in a
——————————————————————
25
man's world. She utilized x-ray diffraction technology
—————————
25
to photograph DNA strands. One of these photographs

25. A. NO CHANGE
    B. DNA.
    C. DNA — This was not easy being a woman in a man's world!
    D. DNA, which all scientists would probably do as well.

is what ultimately gave them the definitive edge in the
                           ————
                            26
DNA race. Wilkins showed the photograph to Watson

26. F. NO CHANGE
    G. Wilkins
    H. Watson and Crick
    J. the DNA strands

GO ON TO THE NEXT PAGE.

without <u>Franklins'</u> permission, and Watson realized it was
₂₇

a crucial piece of the puzzle in their search <u>to uncover</u> the
₂₈
structure of DNA. Very soon thereafter, Watson and

Crick published the now-famous article revealing the

structure of DNA.

It was only in later years that the full truth about

Franklin's contribution <u>come</u> to light; unfortunately,
₂₉
much of the credit came after her death at the age of

thirty-seven. ▢30

27. **A.** NO CHANGE
    B. Franklins's
    C. Franklins
    D. Franklin's

28. **F.** NO CHANGE
    G. recovering
    H. covering for
    J. where they would uncover

29. **A.** NO CHANGE
    B. had come
    C. was coming
    D. came

30. The writer wants the final sentence of the last
    paragraph to reflect the main idea of the whole
    essay. Given that all of the following sentences are
    true, which one, if inserted here, would do that best?
    F. Soon after the DNA incident, Franklin left
    King's College and continued to perform other
    work and research at Birkbeck College.
    G. The DNA race was an exciting time in the history
    of science.
    H. Although she is most famous for her role in the
    discovery of the structure of DNA, Franklin
    contributed much to the body of science both
    before and after the DNA incident.
    J. The discovery of the structure of DNA proved to
    be a crucial scientific breakthrough, and Watson,
    Crick, and Wilkins were later awarded the Nobel
    Prize for their work.

PASSAGE III

Family Remodel

We had managed to raise a family of five children in

our <u>home,</u> mostly by moving the master bedroom to the
₃₁
finished basement. At the time, the move made

<u>sense, the</u> kids had the upstairs (ground level) and
₃₂
we had a nice big room downstairs.

<u>As our youngest child neared high school graduation,</u>
₃₃
the time came to consider moving back upstairs. At this

point, however, a move back into the original master

31. Which choice would most precisely sharpen the focus
    of this paragraph?
    A. NO CHANGE
    B. brick home
    C. three-bedroom ranch home
    D. ranch home

32. **F.** NO CHANGE
    G. sense, and the kids
    H. sense the kids
    J. sense; the kids

33. Which choice best specifies the basis on which the
    writer was ready to move back upstairs?
    A. NO CHANGE
    B. While the children were young,
    C. As the bedrooms filled up,
    D. When guests would come for a visit,

GO ON TO THE NEXT PAGE.

1 ■ ■ ■ ■ ■ ■ ■ ■ **1**

bedroom would have reduced <u>the space</u> by over half; in
₃₄

fact, our bedroom furniture <u>would even</u> fit up there! Add
₃₅
to that a hopeful future with grandchildren, and we came
to the conclusion that it was time to expand our little
ranch. Due to the limited size of our lot, <u>the only way to</u>
₃₆
<u>go was up.</u>
₃₆

We began formulating our building plans,

<u>and including</u> cathedral ceilings, an open second-floor
₃₇
walkway, a huge master bedroom, a good-sized

office, and a nursery. The concepts and ideas <u>flowed</u>
₃₈
endlessly from our creative imaginations.

The first sign that our major remodeling project
would have its ups and downs was when the contractor
announced his bottom-line price to cover all those
wondrous plans; it became <u>immediately clear right away</u>
₃₉
that a scale-back was necessary. For the sake of
maintaining our enthusiasm for the project, my husband
and I sat right down and began discussing those items <u>that</u>
₄₀
could easily give

<u>up; some of them</u> now actually seemed grandiose and
₄₁
silly. After managing to reduce the contractor's original

bid by a significant <u>amount we</u> now had a feasible plan
₄₂
and work soon began.

A major remodeling job is fraught with intense
emotion. <u>Nevertheless,</u> these absolute strangers who
₄₃
have begun invading your home quickly become like
members of your family. They regularly use your

34. **F.** NO CHANGE
    G. its space
    H. our space
    J. their space

35. **A.** NO CHANGE
    B. would have even
    C. wouldn't of even
    D. wouldn't even

36. **F.** NO CHANGE
    G. our house was so small.
    H. all of the children would soon be gone.
    J. OMIT the underlined portion

37. **A.** NO CHANGE
    B. which included
    C. by inclusion of
    D. so included

38. **F.** NO CHANGE
    G. had flows
    H. had been flowing
    J. flow

39. **A.** NO CHANGE
    B. right away immediately clear
    C. immediately clear instantly
    D. immediately clear

40. **F.** NO CHANGE
    G. they
    H. I
    J. we

41. **A.** NO CHANGE
    B. up, so some of them
    C. up, some of them
    D. OMIT the underlined portion

42. **F.** NO CHANGE
    G. amount, then we
    H. amount, we
    J. amount because we

43. **A.** NO CHANGE
    B. Before,
    C. Once,
    D. Suddenly,

GO ON TO THE NEXT PAGE.

1 ■ ■ ■ ■ ■ ■ ■ ■ 1

bathroom facilities, observe you in your

bathrobe and spend entire days with you for the next
          44

several months. And, just as with family, your emotions

range from hating these people to not being able to

live without them.

　　Be prepared for a lot of change if you

should ever want to decide to remodel your home in a
          45

major way. Just as with each of our children as he or she

left home, we were elated to see our beloved workers leave

when the project was finished, but we mourned their loss

for a solid two months afterward.

PASSAGE IV

"Weathering" the Climate

　　Visitors to the United States need to take care when
                                      46

describing the United States and its climate to family and

friends. Because of the vast size of the United States, and

the huge differences in temperatures and weather
            47

patterns across the regions, it is not appropriate or
   47

accurate to describe the whole countrys climate as
                         48

anything but diverse. It is clear that climate varies

drastically depending

on where you are. ▣49

44. F. NO CHANGE
　　G. bathrobe, and spend
　　H. bathrobe; and spend
　　J. bathrobe. And spend

45. A. NO CHANGE
　　B. should
　　C. should ever have to decide
　　D. decide

46. F. NO CHANGE
　　G. need to care
　　H. need to make observations
　　J. need to be descriptive

47. A. NO CHANGE
　　B. temperature differences and weather patterns
　　C. differing weather patterns and temperature differences
　　D. difference in temperature weather patterns

48. F. NO CHANGE
　　G. country's
　　H. whole
　　J. OMIT the underlined portion

49. The writer would like to link the information already presented about climate to her personal experiences regarding weather diversity. Assuming all are true, which of the following sentences best achieves this effect?
　　A. I have spoken to people across the country about variations in climate, and they agree that the United States is very large.
　　B. I have lived in the Northwest most of my life, and, while I enjoy the mild winters, the abundance of rainfall in the summer is quite tiresome.
　　C. I have seen people struggle through bad weather conditions, and often suggest that they relocate.
　　D. Many people enjoy the different climates that exist in the United States.

GO ON TO THE NEXT PAGE.

1 ■ ■ ■ ■ ■ ■ ■ ■ 1

Two of my sisters live in the <u>Southwest, one in</u>
                              ⎯⎯⎯⎯
                               50
Phoenix, Arizona, and the other in Las Vegas,

Nevada. <u>Both of these</u> cities
        ⎯⎯⎯⎯⎯⎯⎯
            51

<u>are known</u> for their constant
⎯⎯⎯⎯⎯⎯
   52

<u>sunshine, and soaring</u> summer temperatures. To both my
⎯⎯⎯⎯⎯⎯⎯⎯⎯⎯⎯
        53
sisters, a "partly cloudy" weather report generally

signifies <u>a few light, puffy clouds here and there.</u>
          ⎯⎯⎯⎯⎯⎯⎯⎯⎯⎯⎯⎯⎯⎯⎯⎯⎯⎯⎯⎯⎯⎯⎯⎯
                          54
"Mostly cloudy" still allows for the sun to peek out

almost all day long. Local newspapers and meteorologists

are constantly challenged to come up with new phrases to

describe yet another sunny day. Basically, the only real

topic of conversation regarding the weather in either

Phoenix or Las Vegas is the monsoon <u>season; which is a</u>
                                     ⎯⎯⎯⎯⎯⎯⎯⎯⎯⎯⎯⎯⎯
                                             55
two to three-week period of on and off rain. One of my

sisters loves to go to her vacation home on the Pacific

Ocean, because "they have weather there; a nice fog

<u>rolling in</u> every morning."
⎯⎯⎯⎯⎯⎯
   56
    By contrast, many northern U.S. inhabitants are

ecstatic when the sun pokes through the constant clouds,

even if for only a few moments in a twenty-four-hour

period. A "mostly cloudy" description means there will be

a thick, heavy layer of grayish cloud cover and no sun

visible for the entire day. A verdict of "cloudy" means

that this condition will probably continue for at least a

solid three-day period.

50. **F.** NO CHANGE
     G. Southwest one in
     H. Southwest: one in
     J. Southwest. One in

51. **A.** NO CHANGE
     B. Both
     C. Some of these
     D. OMIT the underlined portion.

52. **F.** NO CHANGE
     G. is known
     H. were known
     J. have been known

53. **A.** NO CHANGE
     B. sunshine and, soaring
     C. sunshine and soaring
     D. sunshine and soaring,

54. **F.** NO CHANGE
     G. here and there, a few light, puffy clouds.
     H. light, puffy clouds, here and there, a few.
     J. a few, here and there, light, puffy clouds.

55. **A.** NO CHANGE
     B. season. A
     C. season, which is a
     D. season a

56. **F.** NO CHANGE
     G. rolled in
     H. rolls in
     J. is rolling in

GO ON TO THE NEXT PAGE.

[57] Surviving days and months of bad weather truly

does build character; first, <u>you come out</u> a stronger,
₅₈
tougher person whose survival skills have been tested.

Second, you can <u>great enhanced</u> your vocabulary as you
₅₉
attempt to find at least one positive description of the

weather each day. This winter, the positives on my list

include "crystalline," "deafeningly silent," and "rugged."

I may make it through this winter after all!

PASSAGE V

The following paragraphs may or may not be in the
most logical order. You may be asked questions
about the logical order of the paragraphs, as well as
where to place sentences logically within any given
paragraph.

Trip to Turkey

[1]

I was incredibly jet-lagged from the long plane flight

I had just <u>been enduring</u>, but that could scarcely dampen
₆₁
my enthusiasm for arriving in Istanbul, Turkey. Our tour

guide knew that we would be hungry and would like to

57. Which of the following choices, if inserted here,
provides the most effective introductory sentence to
the essay's concluding paragraph?
   A. Good weather can often enhance your mood.
   B. It is healthier to live in areas of predominant
sunshine and warm temperatures.
   C. A poor climate can be extremely detrimental to
human survival.
   D. There are advantages to living in more severe
climates.

58.   **F.** NO CHANGE
   G. you come to be
   H. you get to be
   J. you become

59.   **A.** NO CHANGE
   B. greatly enhance
   C. enhanced great
   D. enhance its greatness

Question 60 asks about the passage as whole.

60. Suppose the writer had been assigned to write a brief
essay illustrating all of the differences in climate
across the entire country. Would this essay fulfill the
assignment?
   F. Yes, because the essay focuses on climate
differences between some regions of the country.
   G. Yes, because the writer has had personal experience living in the Northwest.
   H. No, because the essay limits its comparison to the
Southwest and the Northwest.
   J. No, because the essay is primarily focused on
descriptive words for different weather conditions.

61.   **A.** NO CHANGE
   B. happened to endure
   C. finished enduring
   D. endured

GO ON TO THE NEXT PAGE.

1 ■ ■ ■ ■ ■ ■ ■ ■ **1**

relax. So he took us to a restaurant in a tourist area.
We sat down on rugs around a low table, and were

served the very popular Turkish drink "chai,"(tea) and
delicious Turkish food. We enjoyed a traditional Turkish
band and were surprised to see a local woman get up and
begin to dance!

[2]

Because of the copious amounts of *chai* I drank at the
restaurant, I was still able to easily fall asleep as soon as
we got back to the hotel. I woke up the next day ready to
experience this major cosmopolitan city. As we walked, I
was struck by how the city was similar to large American
cities in many ways, yet it was also very different.
For example, people rushing about in business clothes
talking on their cell phones was a common sight.

Regardless, nearly as common was the sight of vendors
walking around balancing huge platters full of little
cups of *chai.*

[3]

The first stop on our tour was the world-famous
Hagia Sophia. Being that I had studied a bit of its
history on the Internet, I knew that it had been a
church for nearly 1,000 years, and then a mosque
for over 500 years. The photos I had looked at on the

62. **F.** NO CHANGE
    G. relax; so
    H. relax, so
    J. relax — so

63. **A.** NO CHANGE
    B. *"chai"* (tea)
    C. *"chai;"* tea
    D. *"chai"*: (tea)

64. **F.** NO CHANGE
    G. Despite
    H. In lieu of
    J. However,

65. **A.** NO CHANGE
    B. People rushing about talking on their cell phones was a common sight in their business clothes, for example.
    C. For example, rushing about wearing business clothes, people were a common sight talking on their cell phones.
    D. Talking on their cell phones, for example, people were a common sight rushing about in business clothes.

66. **F.** NO CHANGE
    G. By the way,
    H. Nonetheless,
    J. Yet

67. **A.** NO CHANGE
    B. I knew that it had been a church for nearly 1,000 years, and then a mosque for over 500 years; I had studied a bit of its history on the Internet.
    C. I knew that it had been a church for nearly 1,000 years because I had studied a bit of its history on the Internet, and then a mosque for over 500 years.
    D. I had studied a bit of its history on the Internet, and knew that it had been a church for nearly 1,000 years and then a mosque for over 500 years.

GO ON TO THE NEXT PAGE.

Internet did not compare to the <u>actual sights that</u>
₆₈
<u>were on the inside of this magnificent building.</u>
₆₈

The central dome soared high above us. <u>Near</u> every
₆₉
surface was covered in beautiful Turkish designs. Ancient
mosaics spoke of superb craftsmanship from an era so
different from our own. ⊡70

[4]

[1] After leaving the Hagia Sophia, we headed to the
"Grand Bazaar." [2] It is a huge, covered market, where
thousands of vendors sell jewelry, spices, rugs,

<u>alabaster; and,</u> various other Turkish crafts. [3] As
₇₁
I walked through the Bazaar, I was

<u>held captive because of</u> the merchants calling out in
₇₂
German, French, Spanish, English, and Japanese, trying
to appeal to as many tourists as possible. [4] As we headed
back to the hotel, I relished the memories of a day full of
exotic cultural experiences. ⊡73

68. F. NO CHANGE
G. magnificent building and the actual sights.
H. actual sight of this magnificent building.
J. the magnificent inside of the actual sight of this building.

69. A. NO CHANGE
B. (Begin new paragraph) Near
C. (Do NOT begin new paragraph) On near
D. (Do NOT begin new paragraph) Nearly

70. At this point, the writer would like to convey a sense of wonder about the Hagia Sophia. Which of the following sentences, if added here, would most effectively accomplish this?
F. I couldn't help but wish that modern buildings could be as breathtaking as the Hagia Sophia.
G. The restaurant where we ate the night before couldn't compare to the Hagia Sophia!
H. It was simply hard to comprehend that this place was constructed nearly 1,500 years ago.
J. It occurred to me that perhaps I should take a course in architecture next semester, in order to learn more about the Hagia Sophia.

71. A. NO CHANGE
B. alabaster;
C. alabaster, and
D. alabaster — and

72. F. NO CHANGE
G. captivated by
H. a captive of many of
J. in captivity of

73. The writer would like to add the following sentence to the final paragraph:

After almost two overwhelming hours in the Bazaar, our tour group was ready to rest.
Where is the best place to put it?

A. After Sentence 1.
B. After Sentence 2.
C. After Sentence 3.
D. After Sentence 4.

Questions 74 and 75 ask about the essay as a whole.

74. The writer is considering adding the following sentence to the essay in order to emphasize her interest in the blending of cultures:

It was intriguing to observe firsthand some of the effects of cross-cultural exchange.

If added, this new sentence would best be placed:
F. at the end of Paragraph 1
G. at the end of Paragraph 2
H. at the end of Paragraph 3
J. at the beginning of Paragraph 4

GO ON TO THE NEXT PAGE.

1 ■ ■ ■ ■ ■ ■ ■ ■ **1**

75. Suppose the writer had been assigned to write a short essay in an art history class about the Hagia Sophia. Would this essay successfully fulfill that assignment?
   A. Yes, because the essay describes several of the key artistic features of the Hagia Sophia.
   B. Yes, because the essay is scholarly in form.
   C. No, because the essay makes a brief mention of the religious history of the Hagia Sophia.
   D. No, because the essay is focused on a description of a visit to Istanbul.

END OF THE ENGLISH TEST
STOP! IF YOU HAVE TIME LEFT OVER, CHECK YOUR WORK ON THIS SECTION ONLY.

2  **2**

MATHEMATICS TEST

60 Minutes – 60 Questions

DIRECTIONS: Solve each of the problems in the time allowed, then fill in the corresponding bubble on your answer sheet. Do not spend too much time on any one problem; skip the more difficult problems and go back to them later. You may use a calculator on this test. For this test you should assume that figures are NOT necessarily drawn to scale, that all geometric figures lie in a plane, and that the word *line* is used to indicate a straight line.

1. Amanda ate lunch at a restaurant, where her bill was $27.60. She tipped 15%. What was the amount of Amanda's tip?
  A. $4.14
  B. $12.60
  C. $15.00
  D. $23.46
  E. $31.74

2. What is the fourth term of the arithmetic sequence 3, 7, 11, ___, 19?
  F. 5
  G. 9
  H. 12
  J. 13
  K. 15

3. A library contains 1,274 books. Of these books, 524 are paperback. Approximately what percentage of the books at the library are paperback?
  A. 37.4%
  B. 41.1%
  C. 52.4%
  D. 58.8%
  E. 74.8%

4. If $5x + 4 = 7(x-2)$, then $x = ?$
  F. 4
  G. 5
  H. 7
  J. 9
  K. 18

5. What is the least common denominator when adding the fractions $\frac{f}{3}$, $\frac{g}{4}$, $\frac{h}{8}$, and $\frac{j}{12}$?

  A. 24
  B. 48
  C. 64
  D. 96
  E. 288

6. If $x = -4$, then $21 - 3(x - 2) = ?$
  F. 3
  G. 11
  H. 15
  J. 27
  K. 39

DO YOUR FIGURING HERE.

GO ON TO THE NEXT PAGE.

2   **2**

7. What is the value of $x^2y + 2x - 3y$ if $x = -4$ and $y = 2$?
   A. −9
   B. 0
   C. 18
   D. 30
   E. 32

8. Randall is scheduling his classes for next term. He has a choice of 3 different science classes, 4 different math classes, and 5 different humanities classes. How many different class schedules can Randall create if he must take 1 science class, 1 math class, and 1 humanities class?
   F. 14
   G. 23
   H. 30
   J. 45
   K. 60

9. Michelle expects to get 85% of the questions correct on her 120-question math test. If Michelle gets 10 more questions correct than she expects, approximately what percentage of questions will she get correct on the test?
   A. 75%
   B. 80%
   C. 93%
   D. 95%
   E. 100%

10. Which of the following represents the inequality shown on the number graph below?

   F. $x > -1$
   G. $x < -1$
   H. $x = -1$
   J. $x \leq -1$
   K. $x \geq -1$

11. Which of the following figures is NOT a parallelogram?

   A.

   B.

   C.

   D.

   E.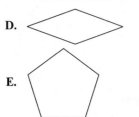

DO YOUR FIGURING HERE.

GO ON TO THE NEXT PAGE.

2   **2**

12. What is the area of a circle with a circumference of 8π?
- **F.** 2π
- **G.** 4π
- **H.** 8π
- **J.** 16π
- **K.** 32π

DO YOUR FIGURING HERE.

13. What is the smallest integer that divides evenly into 36 and 72, but not into 21?
- **A.** 3
- **B.** 4
- **C.** 5
- **D.** 6
- **E.** 8

14. What is the value of $f(3)$ if $f(x) = x^3 - 3x + 3$?
- **F.** 3
- **G.** 6
- **H.** 12
- **J.** 21
- **K.** 27

15. Of 36 students in the Chess Club, 14 are new members. If 1 of the 36 students is chosen at random to design the club logo, what is the probability that the student chosen will be a new member?
- **A.** $\dfrac{1}{36}$
- **B.** $\dfrac{1}{14}$
- **C.** $\dfrac{7}{18}$
- **D.** $\dfrac{18}{25}$
- **E.** $\dfrac{7}{25}$

16. If the hypotenuse of a right triangle measures 10 cm and 1 of the legs measures 8 cm, what is the length, in centimeters, of the third leg of the triangle?
- **F.** 6
- **G.** $4\sqrt{41}$
- **H.** $\sqrt{10}$
- **J.** $2\sqrt{2}$
- **K.** 9

17. In the standard (x,y) coordinate plane, what is the y-intercept of the line $\dfrac{1}{5}y = x - \dfrac{1}{5}$
- **A.** 5
- **B.** 1
- **C.** $\dfrac{1}{5}$
- **D.** $-\dfrac{1}{5}$
- **E.** -1

GO ON TO THE NEXT PAGE.

2   △ △ **2**

18. For all x, $\sqrt{[(x+2)(x-2)]}$ is equivalent to:
   F. $x^2 - 4$
   G. $x - 2$
   H. $\sqrt{(x^2 - 4)}$
   J. $|x^2 - 2|$
   K. $x + 2$

DO YOUR FIGURING HERE.

19. If the area of a rectangle is equal to $9w^2 - 1$ and the width is equal to $3w + 1$, which of the following is an expression of the length of the rectangle?
   A. $\dfrac{(9w^2 - 1)}{(3w - 1)}$
   B. $3w - 1$
   C. $\dfrac{(3w + 1)}{(9w^2 - 1)}$
   D. $3w + 1$
   E. $9w^2 + 3w$

20. A family uses $1\frac{1}{5}$ gallons of milk each week. How many weeks will 6 gallons of milk last?
   F. 4.8
   G. 5.0
   H. 6.0
   J. 7.2
   K. 8.0

21. Which of the following is a polynomial factor of $3x^2 + 3x - 18$?
   A. $(3x + 3)$
   B. $3(x + 6)$
   C. $(x + 3)$
   D. $(x - 3)$
   E. $3x(x + 2)$

22. What is the sum of the 2 solutions of the equation $x^2 + 7x - 18 = 0$?
   F. 9
   G. 7
   H. 2
   J. 0
   K. -7

23. If the lengths of the sides of one triangle are 2 inches, 5 inches, and 7 inches respectively, and the shortest leg of a similar triangle is 4 inches, what is the perimeter of the second triangle, in inches?
   A. 14
   B. 18
   C. 28
   D. 36
   E. 56

GO ON TO THE NEXT PAGE.

2 △ △ △ △ △ △ △ **2**

24. If tan angle P is $\frac{6}{8}$, then sin angle P is $=$?

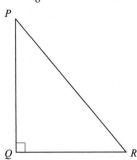

DO YOUR FIGURING HERE.

F. $\frac{8}{6}$

G. $\frac{10}{6}$

H. $\frac{10}{8}$

J. $\frac{8}{10}$

K. $\frac{6}{10}$

25. Which of the following is equivalent to $\frac{(4x - \sqrt{2})}{\sqrt{2}}$?

A. $4\sqrt{2x} - 2\sqrt{2}$

B. $2\sqrt{2x}$

C. $\frac{x - 2}{2}$

D. $4\sqrt{2} - 2x$

E. $2x\sqrt{2} - 1$

26. Allen makes a fixed amount of money for every calendar that he sells. If Allen makes $84.00 when he sells 24 calendars, how much would he make if he sold 10 more calendars?

F. $119.00

G. $108.00

H. $94.00

J. $74.00

K. $49.00

27. What is the sum of 0.375 and $\frac{1}{4}$?

A. 0.0125

B. 0.093

C. 0.40

D. 0.625

E. 1.5

GO ON TO THE NEXT PAGE.

2   **2**

28. Which of the following is an obtuse triangle?

DO YOUR FIGURING HERE.

F.

G.

H.

J.

K.

29. $\dfrac{(1.181 + 0.019)}{[3(1.155) - 5(0.533)]} = ?$

   A. 0.80
   B. 0.96
   C. 1.20
   D. 1.33
   E. 1.50

30. If $22 - 2(3 + x) = (x + 4)$, then $x = ?$
   F. 3
   G. 4
   H. 6
   J. 9
   K. 10

31. The following sketch shows a parking lot. What is the total surface area of the parking lot in square feet?

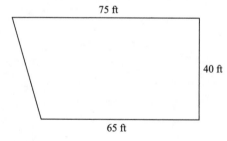

75 ft

40 ft

65 ft

   A. 2,600
   B. 2,800
   C. 3,000
   D. 3,400
   E. 5,525

GO ON TO THE NEXT PAGE.

2   **2**

32. What is the slope of the line that is parallel to the line with the equation $4y - 3x = 8$?

   F. 2

   G. $\dfrac{3}{4}$

   H. $\dfrac{1}{2}$

   J. $-\dfrac{4}{3}$

   K. $-\dfrac{8}{3}$

DO YOUR FIGURING HERE.

33. In the standard (x,y) coordinate plane, what is the midpoint of the line segment that has end points $(-2,-1)$ and $(3,4)$?

   A. $\left(\dfrac{1}{2},\dfrac{5}{2}\right)$

   B. $\left(\dfrac{1}{2},2\right)$

   C. $\left(\dfrac{1}{2},\dfrac{3}{2}\right)$

   D. $(1, 3)$

   E. $(5, 5)$

34. In the standard (x,y) coordinate plane, the line $-2y = x - 9$ has a y-intercept of:

   F. -9

   G. $-\dfrac{9}{2}$

   H. -2

   J. $\dfrac{9}{2}$

   K. 9

35. If $a = bc - 2$ and $b \neq 0$, which of the following equations expresses c in terms of b and a?

   A. $c = \dfrac{b - 2}{a}$

   B. $c = \dfrac{a}{2b}$

   C. $c = \dfrac{b}{a - 2}$

   D. $c = \dfrac{a}{b + 2}$

   E. $c = \dfrac{a + 2}{b}$

GO ON TO THE NEXT PAGE.

2   **2**

36. *PQR* and *PQS* are right triangles. If the sine of angle *QPR* is $\frac{6}{10}$ and the tan of angle *PSQ* is $\frac{8}{10}$, what is the length of $\overline{PS}$?

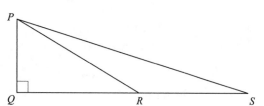

    F. 60
    G. 36
    H. $8\sqrt{10}$
    J. $2\sqrt{41}$
    K. $2\sqrt{10}$

37. The solution set of $\sqrt{(x+1)} < 4$ is the set of all real numbers *x* such that:
    A. $x < 16$
    B. $x < 15$
    C. $x > 4$
    D. $x > 3$
    E. $x = 4$

38. Which of the following conditions of the equation $(x-1)^2 - (2x-3)$ will make the solution negative?
    F. $x < 2$
    G. $x \geq -2$
    H. $x > 2$
    J. $x < -2$
    K. $x \leq 2$

39. In the standard (x,y) coordinate plane, if the *x*-coordinate of each point on a line is 3 less than twice its *y*-coordinate, what is the *y*-intercept of the line?
    A. 3
    B. $\frac{3}{2}$
    C. 1
    D. $-\frac{1}{2}$
    E. $-\frac{3}{2}$

40. A triangle has sides of length 1.5 feet and 7 feet. Which of the following CANNOT be the length of the third side, in feet?
      I. 4.5
      II. 6
      III. 9

    F. I only
    G. I and II only
    H. I and III only
    J. II and III only
    K. I, II, and III only

GO ON TO THE NEXT PAGE.

2 △ △ △ △ △ △ △ △ **2**

41. The lengths of the sides of a right triangle are shown in the figure below. What is the sine of the larger of the unknown angles?

DO YOUR FIGURING HERE.

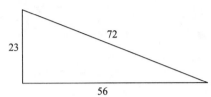

   A. $\dfrac{23}{72}$

   B. $\dfrac{72}{56}$

   C. $\dfrac{23}{56}$

   D. $\dfrac{56}{72}$

   E. $\dfrac{56}{23}$

42. How many different solutions are there for the equation $2x - 4 = (x + 3)^2$
   F. 0
   G. 1
   H. 2
   J. 3
   K. 4

43. In the figure below, an equilateral triangle ABC is circumscribed by a circle with a radius of 3 inches. What is the length of arc AC?

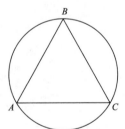

   A. $\dfrac{1}{3}\pi$

   B. $\dfrac{1}{2}\pi$

   C. π

   D. 3π

   E. 6π

44. If $(x + 3)$ is a factor of $x^2 - 17x - b$, what is the value of b?
   F. 3
   G. 17
   H. 20
   J. 34
   K. 60

GO ON TO THE NEXT PAGE.

45. Which of the following are the solutions to $x^2 + \frac{5}{4}x = 0$?

  A. 1 and $\frac{4}{5}$

  B. 0 and $\frac{5}{4}$

  C. -1 and $-\frac{4}{5}$

  D. $-\frac{5}{4}$ and $\frac{4}{5}$

  E. 0 and $-\frac{5}{4}$

46. A sound wave travels at approximately 761.18 miles per hour at sea level. About how many miles will a sound wave travel at sea level in 4 hours?

  F. 3.04×10^3
  G. 3.04×10^5
  H. 3.04×10^6
  J. 7.61×10^4
  K. 19.03×10^4

47. The sides of a triangle are 5, 12, and 13 inches long. What is the measure of the angle between the shortest side and the longest side?

  A. $15°$
  B. $30°$
  C. $45°$
  D. $60°$
  E. $90°$

48. In the figure below, the lengths of the sides are given in inches. What is the total area of pentagon *RSTUV*, in square inches?

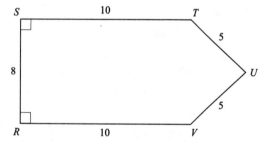

  F. 38
  G. 50
  H. 80
  J. 92
  K. 106

49. In the standard (x,y) coordinate plane, what is the equation of a circle with a center at $(4,3)$ that passes through point $(0,3)$?

  A. $(x-4)^2 + (y-3)^2 = 16$
  B. $(x-3)^2 + (y-3)^2 = 16$
  C. $(x-4)^2 + (y-3)^2 = 9$
  D. $(x+4)^2 - (y+3)^2 = 16$
  E. $(x+4)^2 + (y+3)^2 = 9$

DO YOUR FIGURING HERE.

GO ON TO THE NEXT PAGE.

2   **2**

DO YOUR FIGURING HERE.

50. In the standard (x,y) coordinate plane, at which point do the lines $y = -\frac{1}{2}x + 5$ and $y = 2x - 10$ intersect?

 F. The lines do not intersect.
 G. (2,6)
 H. (6,3)
 J. (6,2)
 K. (2,−1)

51. What is 0.3333... written as a fraction?

 A. $\frac{1}{3}$
 B. $\frac{3}{6}$
 C. $\frac{3}{5}$
 D. $\frac{2}{3}$
 E. $\frac{3}{4}$

52. For which values of x will $5(x+2) \geq 2(5+x)$?
 F. $x > 5$
 G. $x \geq 2$
 H. $x \geq \frac{20}{3}$
 J. $x < \frac{3}{20}$
 K. $x < 5$

53. If $x = 3a + 7$ and $y = 6 + a$, which of the following expresses y in terms of x?
 A. $y = 6x + 21$
 B. $y = 4x + 13$
 C. $y = 2x - 1$
 D. $y = \frac{6x}{21}$
 E. $y = \frac{11 + x}{3}$

54. *ABCD* is a trapezoid that is bisected by line $\overline{PQ}$, which is parallel to lines $\overline{AB}$ and $\overline{DC}$. If the length of line $\overline{DP}$ is 5 units, the length of line $\overline{PA}$ is 7 units, and the length of line $\overline{AB}$ is 21 units, what is the length of $\overline{PQ}$?

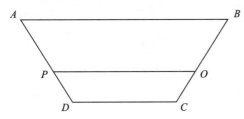

 F. 15
 G. 14
 H. 16
 J. 12
 K. 19

GO ON TO THE NEXT PAGE.

55. What is the corresponding acute angle to a 110° angle?

A. 20°
B. 30°
C. 40°
D. 70°
E. 90°

DO YOUR FIGURING HERE.

56. In the figure below, sin α =?

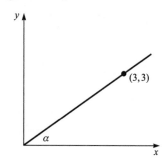

F. $\dfrac{1}{3}$

G. $\dfrac{3}{3\sqrt{2}}$

H. 1

J. $\dfrac{3\sqrt{2}}{3}$

K. $\dfrac{3\sqrt{2}}{1}$

57. For all real integers, which of the following is *always* an odd number?

    I. x^3
    II. $x+1$
    III. $2x+1$

A. I only
B. II only
C. III only
D. I and II only
E. II and III only

58. Jenny has an empty container and puts in 4 red chips. She now wants to put in enough white chips so that the probability of drawing a red chip at random from the container is $\dfrac{1}{5}$. How many white chips should she put in?

F. 1
G. 5
H. 9
J. 16
K. 20

GO ON TO THE NEXT PAGE.

2 △ △ △ △ △ △ △ △ **2**

59. A wheel 37 inches in diameter rolls along a line. How many inches does the wheel roll along the line in 20 revolutions?

  A. 18.5π
  B. 370
  C. 740
  D. 370π
  E. 740π

60. For any real number a, the equation $|x - a| = 9$. On a number line, how far apart are the 2 solutions for x?

  F. a
  G. $9 + a$
  H. $9a$
  J. 18
  K. $3\sqrt{a}$

DO YOUR FIGURING HERE.

END OF THE MATH TEST
STOP! IF YOU HAVE TIME LEFT OVER, CHECK YOUR WORK ON THIS SECTION ONLY.

3 ███████████████████████████████ **3**

READING TEST

35 Minutes – 40 Questions

DIRECTIONS: This test includes four passages, each followed by ten questions. Read the passage and choose the best answer to each question. After you have selected your answer, fill in the corresponding bubble on your answer sheet. You should refer to the passages as often as necessary when answering the questions.

Passage I

PROSE FICTION: *This passage is adapted from "Paul Prescott's Charge" by Horatio Alger, published in 1865.*

"HANNAH!"

The speaker was a tall, pompous-looking man, whose age appeared to verge close upon fifty. He was sitting bolt upright in a high-backed chair and looked
5 as if it would be quite impossible to deviate from his position of unbending rigidity.

Squire Benjamin Newcome, as he was called, in the right of his position as Justice of the Peace, Chairman of the Selectmen, and wealthiest resident
10 of Wrenville, was a man of rule and measure. He was measured in his walk, measured in his utterance, and measured in all his transactions. He might be called a dignified machine. He had a very exalted conception of his own position, and the respect which he felt to
15 be his due, not only from his own household, but from all who approached him. If the President of the United States had called upon him, Squire Newcome would very probably have felt that he himself was the party who conferred distinction, and not received it.
20 Squire Newcome was a widower. His wife, who was as different from him as could well be conceived, did not live long after marriage. She was chilled to death, as it was thought, by the dignified iceberg of whose establishment she had become a part. She had
25 left, however, a child, who had now grown to be a boy of twelve. This boy was a thorn in the side of his father, who had endeavored in vain to mould him according to his idea of propriety. But Ben was gifted with a spirit of fun, sometimes running into mischief,
30 which was constantly bursting out in new directions, in spite of his father's numerous and rather prosy lectures.

"Han-nah!" again called Squire Newcome, sepa- rating the two syllables by a pause of deliberation,
35 and strongly accenting the last syllable — a habit of his with all proper names. Hannah was the Irish servant of all work, who was just then engaged in mixing up bread in the room adjoining, which was the kitchen.

Feeling a natural reluctance to appear before her
40 employer with her hands covered with dough, she hastily washed them. All this, however, took time, and before she responded to the first summons, the second "Han-nah!" delivered with a little sharp emphasis, had been uttered. At length she appeared
45 at the door of the sitting-room.

"Han-nah!" said Squire Newcome, fixing his cold gray eye upon her, "when you hear my voice a calling you, it is your duty to answer the summons IMMEJIATELY."
50 I have endeavored to represent the Squire's pronunciation of the last word.

"So I would have come IMMEJOUSLY," said Hannah, displaying a most reprehensible ignorance, "but me hands were all covered with flour."
55 "That makes no difference," interrupted the Squire. "Flour is an accidental circumstance."

"What's that?" thought Hannah, opening her eyes in amazement.

"And should not be allowed to interpose an
60 obstacle to an IMMEJIATE answer to my summons."

"Sir," said Hannah, who guessed at the meaning though she did not understand the words, "you wouldn't have me dirty the door-handle with me
65 doughy hands?"

"That could easily be remedied by ablution."

"There ain't any ablution in the house," said the mystified Hannah.

"I mean," Squire Newcome condescended to
70 explain, "the application of water — in short, washing."

"Shure," said Hannah, as light broke in upon her mind, "I never knew that was what they called it before."
75 "Is Ben-ja-min at home?"

"Yes, sir. He was out playin' in the yard a minute ago. I guess you can see him from the winder."

So saying she stepped forward, and looking out, all at once gave a shrill scream, and rushed from the
80 room, leaving her employer in his bolt-upright attitude gazing after her with as much astonishment as he was capable of.

GO ON TO THE NEXT PAGE.

3 ████████████████████████████████ **3**

1. The passage suggests that one of the concerns Squire Newcome had about his son was that:
   A. the boy lacked a sense of humor.
   B. the boy was too pompous.
   C. the boy was undisciplined.
   D. the boy received gifts from his servant.

2. Information in the passage as a whole best supports which of the following statements about Squire Newcome?
   F. Squire Newcome was well liked both within the community and within his own household.
   G. Squire Newcome thought very highly of himself and his position within the community.
   H. Squire Newcome was overjoyed by his son's sense of humor and adventure.
   J. Squire Newcome showed great respect for the servants that he employed.

3. The passage indicates that Hannah was delayed in answering Squire Newcome's calls because:
   A. she intentionally ignored them.
   B. she had to wash her hands.
   C. she had to finish baking the bread.
   D. she was looking for Benjamin.

4. As she is presented in the passage, Hannah can best be described as:
   F. hardworking and uneducated.
   G. well educated and cultured.
   H. condescending and pompous.
   J. uneducated and lazy.

5. It is implied in the third paragraph (lines 20–32) that Squire Newcome's wife died because:
   A. the house in which they lived was too cold.
   B. she stepped on a thorn shortly after she was married and was poisoned.
   C. childbirth was too difficult.
   D. her husband cared more about his position than he did about her.

6. As it is used in the passage (line 13) the word *exalted* most nearly means:
   F. elevated.
   G. extended.
   H. humble.
   J. ordinary.

7. It can be inferred from the last paragraph (lines 78–82) that:
   A. Squire Newcome was very astonished by Hannah's attitude and subsequent behavior.
   B. Hannah was frightened by something that Squire Newcome had said.
   C. Hannah was greatly alarmed by something that she saw when she looked out the window.
   D. Benjamin was not allowed to play out in the yard under any circumstances.

8. In the fourth paragraph (lines 33–38) the phrase "a habit of his with all proper names" contributes to the passage's depiction of Squire Newcome as someone who is:
   F. mischievous and happy.
   G. rigid and formal.
   H. ignorant and distinguished.
   J. wealthy and solemn.

9. The passage indicates that Hannah's remark "So I would have come IMMEJOUSLY" is an attempt to:
   A. disrespect her employer.
   B. intentionally mispronounce a word.
   C. copy her employer's language.
   D. show her employer that she is more intelligent than he is.

10. It can be reasonably inferred that Ben's attitude toward his father was one of:
    F. great admiration.
    G. disdain.
    H. deep respect.
    J. indifference.

GO ON TO THE NEXT PAGE.

3 ███████████████████████████████████ **3**

Passage II
Social Science: *Marcus Garvey, Man of Action*

Marcus Garvey wrote in his book *Philosophy and Opinions*, "Where is the black man's government? Where is his king and his kingdom? Where is his president, his country and his ambassador, his army,
5   his navy, his men of big affairs?" These questions posed by Garvey clearly enumerated his goals and dreams. Garvey was a famous Black-Nationalist leader, poet, writer, orator, businessman, entrepreneur, political candidate, and philosopher. His fiery
10   speeches and strong opinions made him many enemies, but his beliefs and achievements continue to make him a prominent figure in American history. To fully understand where Garvey's anger and radical agenda stemmed from, the social environment
15   of early 1900s must be examined. World War I had ended. Many African American soldiers had fought in the war and died for their country. However, when the surviving African American soldiers returned to the United States, they still found themselves facing
20   discrimination and prejudice. There was an enormous amount of racial tension in America. Bloody incidents like the East St. Louis race riots and the Red Summer broke out across the country. Despite these tense conditions, the Negro Era began to
25   emerge and The Harlem Renaissance started to gain national recognition. It was amidst these changes that Garvey came to America and began a movement that would forever change American society.
Garvey had many bold ideas for African
30   Americans. He admired the Black Power and Black Pride movements. He also greatly supported the legendary "Back to Africa" movement known as Black Nationalism. He wanted to colonize Africa and make a new homeland in Libya for all displaced
35   Africans. Garvey believed that the races could never mix and live together in harmony. Garvey despised integration and believed African Americans should own their own businesses, have their own churches, and live in separate nations from other races.
40   Garvey's platform, entitled "Negro World," had eight main goals. These lofty aspirations encouraged pride and autonomy for black people around the world.
Garvey's radical ideas were far from universally
45   popular. Garvey's most powerful enemies came from his controversial stance against the National Association for the Advancement of Colored People and the peaceful civil rights movement. Garvey argued that the NAACP only supported and helped certain
50   members of the African American population. His harsh comments against the peaceful NAACP and the civil rights movement turned many important people against him. In addition, Garvey's refusal to accept mainstream America's help or support made
55   many people angry.
Despite his overly simplistic philosophy and blunt behavior, Garvey did many things to inspire his race. He organized the Universal Negro Improvement Association (UNIA) in Harlem and
60   started many African American–owned businesses and industries. The UNIA was very impressive. It had a thousand divisions around the world, with thousands of members. Garvey also organized a thirty-one-day conclave in Madison Square Garden,
65   which resulted in the Back to Africa movement and the Declaration of Black Rights. Garvey even wrote poems and books that provided encouragement and praise for the African race.
Garvey's life was a notable one. He came from
70   Jamaica as an immigrant without connections, friends, or money. Garvey went on to create a small empire. Although his plan for a colony in Africa was mostly a failure, his ability to instill pride in his race was remarkable. In a period of history
75   where African Americans were continually told that they were inferior, Garvey reminded them that success and happiness were possible.
Although Garvey did some imprudent things in his career, it must be remembered that he devoted
80   his life to a cause he believed in. Garvey's views never wavered even when he was harshly criticized. Today, there is a United Negro Improvement Association that promotes many of the same values that Garvey preached back in the 1920s.
85   Marcus Garvey is dead, but his pride and goals live on in today's dreamers, and his writing continues to inspire leaders around the world.

11. According to the passage, Marcus Garvey was all of the following EXCEPT:
   A. a painter.
   B. a writer.
   C. an orator.
   D. a philosopher.

12. From the information given in the passage, the work of Marcus Garvey can best be summarized as being about:
   F. becoming an important literary figure.
   G. political and social change.
   H. attacking prominent African American organizations.
   J. inciting race riots in East St. Louis.

13. According to the information presented in the passage, which of the following best describes the relationship between Marcus Garvey and the NAACP?
   A. A partnership, because both groups had the same goals and strategies.
   B. Competitive, because African Americans were equally divided in support of these two rivals.
   C. Antagonistic, because of Garvey's opinion of the NAACP.
   D. Indifferent, because Garvey and the NAACP were interested in different aspects of African American life.

GO ON TO THE NEXT PAGE.

3 ████████████████████████████ **3**

14. According to the passage, African Americans in the early 1900s were angry because:
    F. many of them had died in World War I.
    G. there were race riots in East St. Louis and other cities in America.
    H. despite having fought for America in World War I, they were still subject to unfair treatment.
    J. they felt that the NAACP and W.E.B. Dubois only fought for the interests of certain groups of African Americans.

18. According to the passage, all of these things were occurring around the time Marcus Garvey came to America EXCEPT:
    F. riots in East St. Louis.
    G. the Negro Era.
    H. the Harlem Renaissance.
    J. the Back to Africa Movement.

15. As it is used in line 41, the word *lofty* mostly closely means:
    A. lengthy.
    B. upper-class.
    C. idealistic.
    D. superior.

19. According to the passage, all of the following words could be used to describe Marcus Garvey EXCEPT:
    A. direct.
    B. ambitious.
    C. timid.
    D. multifaceted.

16. As it is depicted in the passage, the UNIA can best be described as:
    F. secretive and selective.
    G. diverse and international.
    H. controversial and discriminatory.
    J. inactive and poorly organized.

20. According to the passage, which of the following is true of the UNIA?
    F. The UNIA ceased to exist after Marcus Garvey died and reemerged during the late twentieth century.
    G. The UNIA had almost one hundred divisions around the world.
    H. The UNIA was criticized by the NAACP and W.E.B. Dubois.
    J. The UNIA had thousands of members.

17. It can be inferred that the word *empire*, as it is used in the fifth paragraph, primarily refers to Garvey's:
    A. plan to create a colony in Libya.
    B. feelings about the NAACP's status in America.
    C. achievements in many areas of society.
    D. creation of the UNIA.

GO ON TO THE NEXT PAGE.

3 ████████████████████████████████████ **3**

Passage III

Humanities: *Surviving the Great Depression: One Woman's Courage*

How did people in the 1930s manage to survive the Great Depression when unemployment rose, land and homes were repossessed, and proud women and men had to stand in long lines to receive
5 government aid to feed their families? The freedom to work, to provide for a family, and to live the American Dream did not exist during what my Grandmother remembers as the most devastating time in her life. Imagine, if you can, an entire family
10 standing in the yard watching, after a police officer and banker told them that they were homeless because they could not make their mortgage payments. To get some idea of what things were like, listen to the stories of the Great Depression's survi-
15 vors and read the works of American authors, like John Steinbeck, who hoped to immortalize this brave generation.

In the early 1920s, life had never been better in America. The stock market was booming, people
20 were becoming fabulously wealthy, and carefree flappers danced the night away listening to a new wave of music fresh from Harlem. However, all of this changed when the stock market crashed in 1929. Overnight, millionaires became paupers and
25 the whole nation began to crumble. In 1932, my grandmother was fifteen years old. Within three years of the stock market crashing, her family had lost their car, farm, and dreams.

My grandmother helped patch and resew the
30 only two dresses she owned. After her family was forced to move into town, she cleaned a rich woman's house for twenty-five cents a week to help feed her eight brothers and sisters. During these hardships, my grandmother managed to finish high
35 school. She knew that an education could one day allow her to have a job that did not involve scrubbing or mopping.

During her teenage years, my grandmother did not spend her time giggling with friends at slumber
40 parties or going to the movies. Her day began early in the morning as she caught the streetcar and rode it to school. After school was out for the day, my grandmother rushed home to clean the rich woman's house. When she was done, there was still homework
45 and helping around her own house. There was never a moment for her to rest or be carefree. The secret dreams and fantasies so common of teenage girls today were absent from my grandmother's life as she focused on earning money to continue her education
50 and to help her family.

But what, you will ask, did my hardworking grandmother have to show for her sacrifices and struggle?

Her reward came in her late twenties when a shy
55 car salesman looked beyond her work-roughened hands and tired face and saw the woman of his dreams. After they were married, my grandmother cared for him and their two children through good times and bad. When my grandfather suffered a
60 stroke, my grandmother learned to drive at the age of sixty and faithfully shuttled him back and forth between endless doctors' appointments and hospital

visits. The grace, determination, and work ethic she had acquired in her teenage years during the Great
65 Depression served her well as she faced the many challenges of married life.

During my teenage years, I went in search of my grandmother's past. She was always so stern and hardworking. There was nothing frivolous or extra-
70 vagant about her. She was a frugal and thrifty woman who used coupons, recycled plastic margarine containers, and drove a fifteen-year-old Chevy. Her social life revolved around her many church activities, where she was known among the
75 congregation as the most virtuous and pious of women. My grandmother also busied herself with numerous charitable activities and always managed to spare both time and money to help those less fortunate than she was.
80 Although my grandmother never did move back to a farm, the seeds of goodness and virtue she planted in the big city sprouted and flourished. With strength, determination, and a spirit that refused to be muzzled, my grandmother, and all of the other
85 survivors of the Great Depression, showed the next generations of Americans what it really takes to achieve the American Dream.

21. The passage suggests that the narrator's grandmother, as a young girl, was different than most teenage girls because:
A. most teenage girls do not work, while the narrator's grandmother did.
B. the narrator's grandmother did not attend school like most teenage girls because of the Great Depression.
C. the narrator's grandmother did not have time to spend doing some of the activities that modern teenage girls enjoy.
D. most teenage girls seem to be callous about the needs of their families and concentrate solely on their own dreams and fantasies.

22. It can be reasonably inferred from the sixth paragraph that the narrator's grandmother:
F. was often bitter because of her struggle to raise two children and care for a sick husband.
G. was willing to learn new things if she needed to in order to help her family.
H. married the shy car salesman in order to have comfort and security.
J. had more difficulties as an adult than she did as a teenager during the Great Depression.

23. The passage primarily emphasizes the idea that the narrator's grandmother:
A. was braver and more hardworking than subsequent generations of women.
B. was poor and forced to work hard her whole life in order for her family to survive.
C. was involved in charity work and church activities because of her own hardships and poverty.
D. was a woman who used the character traits developed earlier in her life to overcome challenges in adulthood.

GO ON TO THE NEXT PAGE.

3   **3**

24. As it is used in line 84, the word *muzzled* most nearly means:
 F. sustained.
 G. nurtured.
 H. suppressed.
 J. matured.

25. The passage begins by asking a question that the rest of the passage:
 A. investigates.
 B. modifies.
 C. disregards.
 D. reiterates.

26. In the context of the passage, the phrase "with strength, determination, and a spirit that refused to be muzzled, my grandmother, and all of the other survivors of the Great Depression, showed the next generations of Americans what it really takes to achieve the American Dream" suggests that:
 F. without surviving a crisis like the Great Depression, the American Dream is unlikely to be achieved.
 G. despite facing poverty and hardship, everyone will achieve the American Dream.
 H. the American Dream can be achieved by emulating the qualities of the narrator's grandmother and other Great Depression survivors.
 J. it is unlikely that people before the Great Depression truly achieved the American Dream.

27. It can reasonably be inferred from the passage that the narrator uses the example of her grandmother learning to drive a car at age sixty to:
 A. illustrate the bravery and determination of the narrator in the face of adversity.
 B. show that her grandmother's bravery was undiminished throughout her life.
 C. prove that only through hardship will people conquer their fears and learn new skills.
 D. show that the narrator's grandmother used her hard-won education to earn more money later in life.

28. The passage indicates that all of these are true of the narrator's grandmother EXCEPT:
 F. she was involved in activities outside of her home during adulthood.
 G. she planted and grew seeds in a garden at her city home.
 H. she was not prone to excess or a lavish lifestyle.
 J. she was devoted to her family and the less fortunate.

29. The narrator indicates that life in the early 1920s:
 A. had no effect on her grandmother because her grandmother was too young to remember that time period.
 B. caused her grandmother to reject the lavish and extravagant lifestyle of the early 1920s.
 C. could be compared to her grandmother's early childhood that was carefree and marked by wealth.
 D. was associated with the wealth and lightheartedness that became foreign to her grandmother in the 1930s.

30. It can reasonably be inferred from the passage's last sentence that when the author thinks of her grandmother, the memory of her grandmother's life makes her feel:
 F. pained over the loss of a loved one.
 G. proud of her grandmother's accomplishments and character.
 H. eager to have the same experiences that her grandmother did.
 J. anxious that today's society is not dedicated to the same principles of discipline and hard work.

GO ON TO THE NEXT PAGE.

3 ███████████████████████████████████████ **3**

Passage IV
Natural Science: *El Niño*

El Niño is the name given to a periodic disturbance of the normal ocean and atmospheric system in the tropical Pacific that causes severe weather disturbances around the world. In ordinary
5 years, the trade winds blow west across the tropical Pacific. These trade winds then build up warm surface water in the west Pacific. This results in Indonesia having a sea surface about a half meter higher than Ecuador.
10 The surface temperature of the ocean is about eight degrees higher in the west. An upwelling of cold water from deeper levels leads to cooler temperatures near South America. This cold water is full of nutrients that are essential for maintaining
15 the marine ecosystems and fishing industries of the region.

During El Niño years, the trade winds become more calm in the central and western Pacific. This reduction in air movement leads to fewer tempera-
20 ture changes in the deep waters of the eastern Pacific Ocean, and greater temperature changes in the deep waters of the western Pacific Ocean. This change decreases the ability of upwelling to cool the surface water. By reducing the upwelling, the supply of
25 cooler water to the euphotic zone (the surface layer of the ocean) is greatly decreased. This results in warmer sea surface temperature and a severe decline in the population of organisms such as phyto-plankton. This reduction of lower-food-chain organ-
30 isms harms the higher levels of the food chain, including fish. During El Niño, the easterly trade winds weaken. Rain follows the warm water east-ward. This rain causes flooding in Peru and drought in Australia and its neighbors.
35 Professionals define El Niño as including con-tinual heavy precipitation near parts of the equator, with excessively warm ocean surface temperatures that reach from the International Date Line to the South American coast. El Niños occur on an
40 average of every four to five years. El Niños can last up to a year and a half, often dramatically affecting global weather and climate. The initial sign of an impending El Niño is unusually warm water in the tropical Pacific Ocean. This provides more rising
45 warm air, which can change the air pressure patterns.

Some common impacts on the United States include fewer tropical storms in the Atlantic region; a dry monsoon around Mexico, Arizona, and New
50 Mexico; an especially dry fall and winter around Oregon and Washington; an extremely wet winter in the Gulf Coast; and a warmer-than-average fall and winter in many Midwestern States.

Industries directly affected by weather or climate
55 compose almost 10 percent of the Gross Domestic Product (GDP) in the United States. Weather and climate also impact insurance industries, services, retail and wholesale trade, and manufacturing. Nearly 25 percent of the GDP may be directly or
60 indirectly affected by weather and climate.

Unusual weather can lead to both gains and losses in different regions and industries. For instance, department store sales went up by 5 to 15 percent during an El Niño winter in the Midwest.
65 However, snowmobile and ski sales were down dras-tically during that same period. During an El Niño year, the ski industry was unusually profitable in the West, but the unusually warm Midwest saw a decrease in skiing. Households and businesses
70 saved two to seven billion dollars in heating costs during an El Niño year while the energy industry lost money from sales.

El Niños can cause severe economic loss when storms ravage property or crops fail. These losses
75 are not usually offset by other gains and are also largely unpreventable. An average El Niño results in agricultural losses of almost two billion dollars worldwide. In recent years, El Niños have caused damages reaching almost three billion dollars
80 worldwide.

Within the agriculture industry, many things can be adjusted to reduce susceptibility to El Niño weather conditions. The water industry and hydro-electric power companies can make storage and
85 production decisions that take into account the large rainfall of El Niño years. The natural gas and fuel industries can adjust their production and distribu-tion levels to decrease losses when warm El Niño winter conditions are expected. Homeowners and
90 the public can also make appropriate plans to safeguard their homes or offices against dangerous storms.

31. The suggestions made in the last paragraph are used in this passage to support the idea that:
   A. the effects of El Niño can be completely elimi-nated by taking specific precautions.
   B. El Niños are predictable and therefore pose less of a danger than other weather occurrences.
   C. El Niños can cause many problems to different industries, but some precautions may help alle-viate some of the hardship caused by the effects of this phenomenon.
   D. Any attempts to prepare for El Niños are useless because it is impossible to gauge how long a particular El Niño will last.

32. The author refers to the affects of El Niño on the GDP primarily to underscore the idea that:
   F. El Niños merely harm very specific weather-sensitive industries, like fishing and skiing.
   G. steps need to be taken to ensure that El Niños do not occur because they cause severe economic hardship.
   H. El Niño weather affects a wide range of busi-nesses and industries, and it can harm the overall economic health of a region.
   J. all negative effects of El Niño weather are compensated for in other economic gains.

GO ON TO THE NEXT PAGE.

3 ■■■ **3**

33. The passage suggests that:
   A. the decrease of phytoplankton and similar creatures may affect the fishing industry.
   B. phytoplankton are not essential to maintaining marine ecosystems.
   C. once phytoplankton populations decrease, they will only reemerge during subsequent El Niño episodes.
   D. phytoplankton prefer the warmer sea temperatures that an El Niño year can bring to their region.

34. As it is used in Paragraph 1, the word *disturbances* refers to all of these mentioned in the passage EXCEPT:
   F. flooding in certain regions.
   G. excess rainfall in the Gulf Coast.
   H. unusual drought near and in Mexico
   J. decrease in temperatures and snowfall in the Midwest.

35. The author's main purpose in Paragraph 7 is to show:
   A. El Niños wreak havoc on all industries across America.
   B. El Niños can harm some industries or groups while benefiting others.
   C. the effects of El Niño are not positive ones because they cause unusual weather changes.
   D. the GDP is not always an accurate way to measure a region's economic health.? >

36. The author of the passage makes it clear that, when attempting to reduce the effects of El Niños, it is necessary:
   F. to accurately predict when an El Niño will occur.
   G. to stop production of fuel and gas.
   H. for hydroelectric power to increase.
   J. for some industries to make adjustments.

37. The last paragraph suggests the author's main reason for advising industries and groups to take precautions is:
   A. that it is very possible for all industries to benefit in some way from El Niño if they take the proper precautionary measures.
   B. some industries may be able to reduce the harmful effects of El Niño by paying attention to predictions about when an El Niño is going to occur.
   C. some industries that take precautions may actually help decrease the length of an El Niño episode.
   D. only the industries discussed are able to prepare for El Niño years.

38. The description of an El Niño given in the first paragraph does all of the following EXCEPT:
   F. provide information on sea levels in Indonesia and Ecuador.
   G. explain the behavior of trade winds during non-El Niño years.
   H. explain a consequence of abnormal trade wind activity.
   J. indicate what El Niño is.

39. As it is used in line 74, the word *ravage* most nearly means:
   A. to offset a gain or loss.
   B. to severely damage or injure.
   C. to lose meaning or essential features.
   D. to reconstruct or rebuild.

40. The passage states that El Niños:
   F. occur roughly every year and a half and last about four to five months.
   G. occur approximately every four to five years and never last for more than one year.
   H. occur about every four to five years and last up to a year and a half.
   J. occur roughly every four to six years and normally last about two years.

END OF THE READING TEST
STOP! IF YOU HAVE TIME LEFT OVER, CHECK YOUR WORK ON THIS SECTION ONLY.

4 ◯ ◯ ◯ ◯ ◯ ◯ ◯ ◯ 4

SCIENCE REASONING TEST

35 Minutes — 40 Questions

DIRECTIONS: There are seven passages in this test. Each passage is followed by several questions. You should refer to the passages as often as necessary in order to choose the best answer to each question. Once you have selected your answer, fill in the corresponding bubble on your answer sheet. You may NOT use a calculator on this test.

Passage I

The Earth's lithosphere, or crust, consists of tectonic plates that move. It is believed that at one point in the past, all of the continents were one large landmass. Over time, the plates shifted to form the continents as we know them today. There is not a consensus in the scientific community about why the tectonic plates move. Two scientists discuss their viewpoints.

Scientist 1

The tectonic plates are constantly moving, causing earthquakes and volcanic eruptions. A large burst of energy along with this movement is what created the separate continents on the Earth. The tectonic plates move as a result of convection currents within the fluid, lower layer of the Earth's crust, the asthenosphere. The plates rest on top of this hot, plastic substance of the mantle. The asthenosphere moves in a circular motion, causing the plates to collide with each other on all sides. This circular motion is evidenced by the multiple locations along each plate's boundary where earthquakes and volcanic eruptions occur.

Scientist 2

The tectonic plates only move with sudden bursts of lithospheric motion. Otherwise they are stationary. The creation of the individual continents is the first evidence of this theory. There was originally one large landmass. A sudden burst of energy caused the plates to move apart and form the continents. Since that time there has not been much movement. The little movement that does occur releases small bursts of energy in only one direction along a fault line. This is apparent when looking at historical data and the fact that there are certain areas that are more affected by earthquakes than others.

1. Which of the following phrases best describes the main point that the 2 scientists have in common?
   A. The movement of the tectonic plates created the continents.
   B. The tectonic plates are constantly moving.
   C. The tectonic plates are not linked to earthquake activity.
   D. The movement of the tectonic plates is circular in nature.

2. You can infer from Scientist 1's viewpoint that which of the following could cause an earthquake?
   F. A volcanic eruption
   G. Tectonic plate collision
   H. A small burst of energy
   J. Stationary fault lines

3. Scientist 1's viewpoint indicates that the material in the asthenosphere is:
   A. liquid.
   B. solid.
   C. gaseous.
   D. stationary.

4. Which of the following statements best describes how Scientist 2 would explain the occurrence of many small earthquakes?
   F. Constant tectonic plate movement creates large bursts of energy along the plates' boundaries.
   G. Convection currents within the asthenosphere move the tectonic plates against each other.
   H. Volcanic eruptions along the fault lines move in only one direction.
   J. Limited tectonic plate movement releases small bursts of energy along the fault line.

GO ON TO THE NEXT PAGE.

4 ○ ○ ○ ○ ○ ○ ○ ○ ○ **4**

5. According to the passage, the lower layer of the Earth's crust is called the:
   A. continental shift.
   B. asthenosphere.
   C. fault line.
   D. lithosphere.

6. Which of the following statements would both scientists most likely use to explain the creation of the continents? The tectonic plates experienced:
   F. a large burst of energy.
   G. little movement.
   H. many small energy bursts.
   J. slow, gradual motion.

7. Scientist 1's viewpoint would be *weakened* by which of the following statements about tectonic plates, if true?
   A. The tectonic plates rest on the rigid upper crust.
   B. The tectonic plates experience constant motion.
   C. The tectonic plates cause multiple earthquakes.
   D. The tectonic plates experience large bursts of motion.

GO ON TO THE NEXT PAGE.

4 ◯ ◯ ◯ ◯ ◯ ◯ ◯ ◯ ◯ **4**

Passage II

Fire is the result of a chemical reaction between oxygen and a fuel, such as wood or gasoline, that has been heated to its ignition temperature (the temperature that a fuel must reach before combustion can begin). Once a fuel has been heated, it begins thermal degradation. Thermal degradation is a process by which materials in the fuel are broken down into several by-products. Wood, for example, breaks down into charred wood, ash, and a volatile gas (smoke). The actual burning of wood will begin once the volatile gas has reached a high enough temperature. In this case, the volatile gas must reach approximately 260°C before the wood will actually begin to burn.

A study was conducted to investigate the use of flame retardants in treating plywood samples to reduce the risk of fire damage. Flame retardants reduce fire damage by interfering with the combustive actions of fuels. In order to work, the flame retardant must suppress or slow down the combustion process. Flame retardants can be used to suppress combustion at many different stages in the process. This study focused on protective coatings that act as an insulator to protect against fire damage during the beginning stages of combustion: thermal degradation and heat transfer.

Blocks of untreated pine plywood were tested at various temperatures in a controlled environment. Three different types of fire retardant, inorganic salts were used to treat several other identical blocks of pine plywood that were tested at the same temperatures as the untreated plywood. The percentage loss of mass was recorded for both the untreated and treated plywood samples after being exposed to various temperatures, as shown in Figure 1 below.

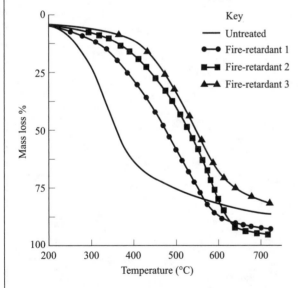

Figure 1

8. At 175°C, wood begins to break down into char and smoke. According to the passage, this is called:
   F. the combustion phase.
   G. thermal degradation.
   H. the ignition temperature.
   J. the insulation point.

9. According to the passage, flame-retardant protective coating on wood is used to:
   A. protect against the breakdown of the materials in the wood.
   B. transform the volatile gases released into non-combustible material.
   C. protect against the heat transferred during the final stages of combustion.
   D. destroy any ash that was produced during combustion.

10. According to Figure 1, the untreated wood loses mass most quickly:
    F. between 200° and 260°C.
    G. between 260° and 400°C.
    H. between 400° and 600°C.
    J. between 600° and 700°C.

11. Which of the following is true of the plywood treated with Fire retardant 3, as compared to the other samples of plywood used in the study?
    A. Fire retardant 3 suppresses combustion more effectively than either Fire retardant 1 or Fire retardant 2.
    B. Fire retardant 3 only protects from the loss of mass at lower temperatures.
    C. Fire retardant 3 is the least effective at temperatures above 600°C.
    D. Fire retardant 3 is more effective than untreated wood, but less effective than Fire retardant 2.

12. According to the passage, at which temperature do Fire retardant 1 and Fire retardant 2 experience the same percent of mass loss?
    F. 250°C
    G. 425°C
    H. 550°C
    J. 625°C

GO ON TO THE NEXT PAGE.

4 ◯ ◯ ◯ ◯ ◯ ◯ ◯ ◯ ◯ **4**

Passage III

All scientists agree that carbon dioxide is used by trees during photosynthesis. Trees and other plants that undergo photosynthesis are often called carbon sinks because they absorb large amounts of carbon dioxide present in the atmosphere. It seems logical that planting more trees and cutting down fewer trees would be the best solution to removing excess carbon dioxide from the atmosphere. Excess carbon dioxide in the atmosphere is blamed for the greenhouse effect that may be leading to global climate change.

Two scientists present their views on tree planting and tree preservation as a solution to eliminating excess carbon dioxide in the atmosphere.

Scientist 1

Planting new trees and preserving existing trees is not a good long-term solution to eliminate excess carbon dioxide in the atmosphere. As the world's population increases, forestland is needed to grow food and raise livestock. In addition, planting more trees or preserving trees may give people the impression that no other measures are needed to reduce carbon dioxide emissions. Car pooling, conservation of electricity, and creation of cars that do not emit carbon dioxide are necessary for long-term reduction of carbon dioxide in the atmosphere. Furthermore, dead and decomposing trees emit carbon dioxide. Forest fires and droughts are just two forces that kill off large numbers of trees and cause a rapid release of carbon dioxide into the atmosphere. In addition, planting trees also accelerates climate change in snow-covered areas by reducing the amount of sunlight energy that is directed back into space.

Scientist 2

Planting and preserving trees is a great long-term solution for reducing the levels of carbon dioxide in the atmosphere. Planting and preserving trees can help reduce the destruction of the world's forests and protect bio-diversity. Trees and forests are the largest carbon sinks known to man. In fact, 458 tons of carbon dioxide are absorbed and stored in one hectare of mature forests. Although some carbon dioxide is released when the leaves decompose, planting or preserving trees is still an effective means by which to greatly reduce the carbon dioxide levels in the atmosphere.

13. If Scientist 1 is correct, which of the following generalizations about carbon dioxide levels is most accurate?
- **A.** Tree planting is the only known way to decrease the levels of carbon dioxide in the atmosphere.
- **B.** Young forests do not store as much carbon dioxide as older forests.
- **C.** It will not be possible to both reduce carbon dioxide levels and feed the growing population.
- **D.** It will take more than 1 measure to effectively reduce carbon dioxide levels in the atmosphere in the long run.

14. There have been periods of increased carbon dioxide levels in the atmosphere during hot, dry summers. Scientist 1 would probably explain this by saying that:
- **F.** hot and dry summers often lead to droughts and forest fires that kill large numbers of trees. These dying trees release stored carbon dioxide into the air.
- **G.** hot and dry summers most likely accelerate climate change because leaves grow smaller and create less shade. This leads to the ground absorbing more sunlight than usual.
- **H.** trees planted during hot and dry summers are less likely to flourish. They will grow to be smaller than normal and absorb less carbon dioxide.
- **J.** cool and wet weather allows trees to absorb more carbon dioxide because there is more carbon dioxide present in the atmosphere.

15. In 2004, people reported that they believed the number one way to reduce carbon dioxide levels in the atmosphere was to plant or preserve trees. According to Scientist 2, what other benefits could new and preserved forest areas provide?
- **A.** Increased economic stability for people who harvest trees for furniture and lumber
- **B.** Increased climate change as the trees absorb carbon dioxide from the atmosphere
- **C.** Reduction in the destruction of forest areas and protection of biodiversity
- **D.** Increased interest in decreasing the levels of carbon dioxide in the atmosphere

16. Which of the following is NOT mentioned by Scientist 1?
- **F.** Car pooling
- **G.** Forest fires
- **H.** Solar power
- **J.** Livestock

17. According to the information presented in the passage, Scientists 1 and 2 disagree on:
- **A.** whether car pooling can reduce carbon dioxide levels in the atmosphere more than conservation of electricity will.
- **B.** whether planting and preserving trees is a good long-term solution to reducing the levels of carbon dioxide in the atmosphere.
- **C.** whether decomposing trees and leaves release carbon dioxide.
- **D.** whether excess carbon dioxide can lead to global climate change.

GO ON TO THE NEXT PAGE.

4 ◯ ◯ ◯ ◯ ◯ ◯ ◯ ◯ ◯ **4**

18. An increase in newly planted trees in snow-covered areas has not accelerated climate change. How might Scientist 1 account for this?

  F. The newly planted trees have not yet grown large enough to reduce the amount of sunlight energy directed back into space.

  G. The newly planted trees are not absorbing as much carbon dioxide as mature trees.

  H. The newly planted trees are not compensating for other practices that are increasing the carbon dioxide levels in the atmosphere.

  J. There has been an overall reduction in carbon dioxide levels from droughts and forest fires.

19. Which of the following findings, if true, would weaken the arguments of Scientist 2?

  A. Cities that encourage car pooling have lower levels of carbon dioxide in their atmospheres than cities that do not encourage carpooling.

  B. Decomposing leaves reemit 99% of the carbon dioxide that a tree absorbs.

  C. Sales of cars that emit less carbon dioxide are rapidly growing in areas with snow-covered terrain.

  D. Planting trees in areas that receive little or no snow has not been found to accelerate climate change.

GO ON TO THE NEXT PAGE.

4 ○ ○ ○ ○ ○ ○ ○ ○ ○ **4**

Passage IV

The color of a leaf results from an interaction of different pigments (colored substances) produced by the plant. The main pigment classes responsible for leaf color are *porphyrins*, *carotenoids*, and *flavonoids*. The leaf color that we see depends on the amount and types of the pigments that are present.

The primary porphyrin in leaves is a green pigment called *chlorophyll*. Chlorophyll is produced in response to sunlight. As the seasons change and the amount of sunlight decreases, less chlorophyll is produced by the leaves, and the leaves appear less green. Chlorophyll is broken down at a constant rate, so green leaf color will gradually fade as chlorophyll production slows or stops.

Light is not needed in order for a plant to produce carotenoids; therefore, these pigments are always present in a living plant. One of the flavonoids, *anthocyanin*, provides a natural sunscreen for plants.

Chlorophyll masks the other pigment colors, so when it is present, leaves will appear green. Anthocyanins, in turn, mask carotenoids. As summer turns to autumn, decreasing light levels cause chlorophyll production to slow. At the same time, anthocyanin production in leaves increases. Leaves containing primarily anthocyanins will appear red. Leaves with large amounts of both anthocyanins and carotenoids will appear orange. Leaves with carotenoids but little or no anthocyanins will appear yellow.

Table 1 shows the three main pigment classes, the compounds that make up the pigments, and the leaf colors that they produce.

Table 1		
Pigment class	Compound type	Resulting colors
Porphyrin	Chlorophyll	Green
Carotenoid	Carotene and lycopene	Yellow, orange, red
Flavonoid	Xanthophyll	Yellow
	Flavone	Yellow
	Flavonol	Yellow
	Anthocyanin	Red, blue, purple

20. According to the passage, chlorophyll production:
    F. increases the amount of carotenoids.
    G. is dependent upon sunlight.
    H. slows down in the summer.
    J. decreases the amount of pigment.

21. Based on Table 1, the presence of which of the following compounds results in yellow leaves?
    A. Lycopene only
    B. Chlorophyll only
    C. Lycopene and anthocyanin
    D. Lycopene, flavone, and carotene

22. Is the statement "decreased light levels have little to no effect on color changes in leaves" supported by information presented in the passage, and why?
    F. Yes, because light is not needed for a plant to produce flavonol, which causes leaves to change from green to yellow.
    G. Yes, because chlorophyll breaks down at a constant rate.
    H. No, because chlorophyll is produced in response to sunlight, and decreasing light levels slow chlorophyll production.
    J. No, because anthocyanin provides a natural sunscreen for plants.

23. According to the passage, leaves with more anthocyanins than carotenoids will:
    A. retain their green color.
    B. appear red.
    C. appear yellow.
    D. not produce chlorophyll.

24. According to the passage, of the three main pigment classes, which has the most color variety?
    F. Porphyrin
    G. Chlorophyll
    H. Flavonoid
    J. Carotenoid

GO ON TO THE NEXT PAGE.

4 ◯ ◯ ◯ ◯ ◯ ◯ ◯ ◯ 4

Passage V

The meerkat is a member of the mongoose family that lives on the African grasslands. Unlike other mongooses, meerkats live in large social communities of up to 30 members. These groups are called "mobs" or "gangs." Often at sunrise, all of the members of a gang will gather together, stand up, and turn their bellies to the sun, soaking up the sunlight.

In addition to being social, meerkats are very territorial, and they will fiercely defend their homes against other meerkat gangs, as well as against all other intruders. Meerkat "sentries" can often be seen scanning the horizon for predators, standing up on their hind legs and using their tails for balance. When a predator or other intruder appears, a sentry will make an alarm call, alerting the other members of its gang to possible danger. Known meerkat predators include eagles and jackals.

Meerkats feed on small mammals, birds, and reptiles, as well as eggs and the roots of some plants. Scorpions are considered a special treat for meerkats; the scorpion's stinger is quickly bitten off before the rest of the animal is consumed. It is thought that meerkats use specialized vocalizations to alert the gang to the presence of food, as well.

Zoologists have been studying meerkat alarm calls to determine whether they have special meanings. A gang of meerkats was observed for several days. The observer noted the type of call that was made, the time of day that the call was made, and the possible reason for the alarm call (approaching predator, etc.) The aggregate results of these observations are presented in Table 1 below.

Table 1		
Meerkat alarm call	Time of day	Possible alarm call cue
One quick "chirp"	Sunset or sunrise only	None observed
Series of repeating quick "chirps"	Throughout the day	Individual meerkat from another gang; small group of meerkats from another gang
Constant loud "chattering"	Throughout the day	Jackal, eagle, large snake
Three quick "chirps" followed by a short pause and three more "chirps"	Throughout the day	Meerkat from the sentry's gang

25. Based on Table 1, when a meerkat sentry begins to chatter constantly, it is most likely signaling:
   A. the end of the day.
   B. the approach of a meerkat from another gang.
   C. the approach of a predator.
   D. the presence of a food source.

26. Meerkats have been called the "Solar Panel of the Animal World." The most likely reason for this is:
   F. the meerkats' natural habitat on the African grasslands.
   G. the meerkats' habit of soaking up the morning sun.
   H. the meerkats' ability to make specialized alarm calls.
   J. the meerkats' ability to stand up on their hind legs.

27. According to the passage, as compared to other mongooses, meerkats:
   A. eat small mammals and birds.
   B. live in Africa.
   C. do not live in large social groups.
   D. live in large social groups.

28. Which of the following statements is most consistent with the results shown in Table 1?
   F. Meerkats vocalize for reasons other than to warn each other of possible danger.
   G. Meerkats will only vocalize when predators are close by.
   H. Meerkats have specialized alarm calls for each type of predator.
   J. Meerkats will not vocalize if a member of a rival gang approaches.

GO ON TO THE NEXT PAGE.

4 ○ ○ ○ ○ ○ ○ ○ ○ ○ **4**

29. Which of the following assumptions about meerkat alarm calls was made before the observations were noted?

   A. None of the meerkats in rival gangs would be able to hear the alarm calls made by the sentries.

   B. All of the meerkats in a certain gang will recognize and understand the different alarm calls made by the sentries.

   C. Only the alarm calls made after sunrise would be considered important.

   D. Meerkat predators may be able to mimic the alarm calls made by the sentries.

30. Which of the following, if it had occurred, would NOT support the theory that meerkat alarm calls have special meanings?

   F. The sentries repeated the same alarm call to indicate the presence of both predators and members of rival gangs.

   G. The sentries varied the alarm calls depending on what type of predator was approaching.

   H. Different alarm calls were made depending on the direction from which the predator was approaching.

   J. The sentries altered the alarm call to indicate the proximity of the approaching rival gang.

GO ON TO THE NEXT PAGE.

4 ◯ ◯ ◯ ◯ ◯ ◯ ◯ ◯ **4**

Passage VI

The oceans of the world contain millions of creatures and animals, and more are being discovered each day. Every animal found in the ocean has special characteristics that define its living conditions, or, more specifically, the different zones of the ocean in which each animal will best survive. Figure 1 shows the different zones of the ocean, beginning at the surface and continuing to the sea floor, which can extend as far as 11,000 meters (m) in some locations.

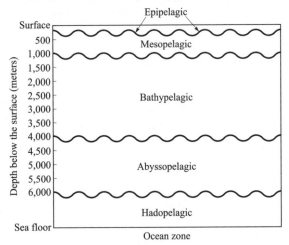

Figure 1

In the midwater zone (200 m–2,000 m) of the ocean, many fish must adapt to the scarce food supply. The debris that falls from more shallow waters and the other animals that live there make up the available food supply. Most of these animals have relatively low levels of protein in their muscles, making them very weak. Most likely, these characteristics are adaptations to the low-energy environment. To compensate, the animals have unique mechanisms to ensure survival even though feedings are infrequent: mouths that expand to two times the size of their bodies, large stomachs, and large teeth to maximize the size of prey that they can consume, as well as large eyes and photophores, or organs that produce light, which make it possible to survive in an environment of little to no light. Table 1 shows several animals that live at various depths of the ocean. Although most animals generally stay within a certain range of depths, some are found in much deeper zones.

Table 1		
Animal	Found at depths (m)	Max depth (m)
Snipe Eel	40–550	2,000
Crested Bigscale	600–2,100	3,200
Eelpout	2,500–5,000	5,000
Cuskeel	1,975–5,200	5,200
Stout Blacksmelt	225–1,400	6,700

Some midwater species are vertical migrators that travel up to 1,500 feet each day. At night, they travel closer to the surface (at the uppermost part of their range of depth) to feed in areas where more food is available, and then travel back down during the day (to the lowermost part of their range of depth). These creatures travel at night to reduce the chances of being seen and preyed upon.

31. Based on information in the passage, which of the following is the most likely reason for the expandable mouth of a midwater species? The expandable mouth is used:
    A. to catch and consume available prey that may be larger in size.
    B. to absorb more carbon dioxide from the deep-sea waters.
    C. to make use of the sensory pores inside the mouth.
    D. to communicate with other animals.

32. According to the passage, the midwater zone includes which of the following ocean zones?
    F. Epipelagic and mesopelagic
    G. Mesopelagic and bathypelagic
    H. Bathypelagic and abyssopelagic
    J. Abyssopelagic and hadopelagic

33. According to the passage, the snipe eel may be found in which zones of the ocean?
    A. Eepipelagic only
    B. Epipelagic and mesopelagic
    C. Mesopelagic only
    D. Epipelagic, mesopelagic, and bathypelagic

34. According to the passage, if eelpouts are vertical migrators, at which depth might they travel to at night?
    F. 225 m below the surface.
    G. 1,400 m below the surface.
    H. 2,500 m below the surface.
    J. 5,000 m below the surface.

35. The worldwide average temperature of the ocean from the surface down to 400 m below the surface is 22°C. From 400 to 800 m, the temperature drops drastically, and the temperatures range from 0°C to 4°C from this point down to the sea floor. According to Table 1 and the information given, which of the following animals would best survive at any temperature from the surface to the deep sea?
    A. Cuskeel
    B. Crested Bigscale
    C. Stout Blacksmelt
    D. Eelpout

GO ON TO THE NEXT PAGE.

4 ◯ ◯ ◯ ◯ ◯ ◯ ◯ ◯ **4**

Passage VII

When 2 female snakes encounter each other, there is often a threat display. The dominant snake usually forces the submissive snake to coil. A biologist conducted 2 experiments to determine the rank in aggression in female snakes. In the experiments described below, 5 adult female snakes were placed together in a cage and their interactions were observed and recorded.

Experiment 1

To determine what factors might affect aggressiveness, the biologists recorded the sequence in which the snakes were placed in the cage, their length, their ages, and the number of hisses each snake made during the experiment. In addition, the snakes were ranked according to their aggressiveness toward one another, from most aggressive (1) to least aggressive (5). The results are shown in Table 1.

		Table 1			
Snake	Sequence	Length (cm)	Age in years	Number of hisses	Aggression (rank)
A	1st	50	3	26	2
B	2nd	30	5	10	5
C	3rd	40	2	31	1
D	4th	60	4	20	3
E	5th	20	1	17	4

Experiment 2

The snakes were placed back into the cage in the same sequence as in Experiment 1. The results of all aggressive encounters between pairs of snakes were recorded. A snake was declared a "winner" if it forced the other snake, the "loser," to coil. Table 2 shows the results of the interactions between the snakes. There were no draws, or *ties*, observed.

Table 2					
Winning snake	A	B	C	D	E
A	–	20	10	20	20
B	0	–	0	5	10
C	15	30	–	20	25
D	15	25	5	–	20
E	0	20	5	15	–

Table 3 summarizes the results of all the encounters for each snake.

	Table 3		
Snake	Wins	Losses	Encounters
A	70	30	100
B	15	95	110
C	90	15	105
D	65	60	125
E	35	75	110

36. Which of the following generalizations about the relationship between snake length and rank is consistent with the experimental results?
   F. The longest snake will be the most dominant.
   G. The longest snake will be the most submissive.
   H. Length has no effect on rank.
   J. The shortest snake will be the most dominant.

37. It was suggested that the more dominant a female snake was, the safer her eggs were. Accordingly, one would predict, based on win-loss records, that the snake with the safest eggs would be:
   A. Snake B
   B. Snake D
   C. Snake C
   D. Snake A

38. A sixth snake, whose length was 55 centimeters and whose age was 3 years was added to the experimental cage. It was observed that the snake hissed a total of 21 times during the experiment. Based on the results of Experiment 1, what would be the rank of the sixth snake in terms of its aggressiveness?
   F. 2
   G. 3
   H. 4
   J. 5

39. According to the results of Experiments 1 and 2, which of the following factors is (are) related to the number of hisses the snake will make?
   I. Age
   II. Length
   III. Aggressiveness

   A. I and II only
   B. I and III only
   C. II only
   D. III only

40. One can conclude from the results of Experiment 2 that snake C and snake A had a total of how many encounters with each other?
   F. 15
   G. 20
   H. 25
   J. 40

END OF THE SCIENCE REASONING TEST
STOP! IF YOU HAVE TIME LEFT OVER, CHECK YOUR WORK ON THIS SECTION ONLY.

5  **5**

WRITING TEST

DIRECTIONS: This test is designed to assess your writing skills. You have thirty (30) minutes to plan and write an essay based on the stimulus provided. Be sure to take a position on the issue and support your position using logical reasoning and relevant examples. Organize your ideas in a focused and logical way, and use the English language to clearly and effectively express your position.

When you have finished writing, refer to the Scoring Rubrics discussed in Chapter 7 to estimate your score.

Note: On the actual ACT you will receive approximately 2.5 pages of scratch paper on which to develop your essay, and approximately 4 pages of notebook paper on which to write your essay. We recommend that you limit yourself to this number of pages when you write your practice essays.

Essay Prompt

Some high schools require physical education for all of their students. Some teachers and parents think that this requirement helps to develop good health habits for students that will stay with them for the rest of their lives. Other teachers and parents think that high schools should not require physical education for high school students since the students are already very busy and could use the time for more important courses. In your opinion, should high schools require students to complete physical education requirements?

In your essay, take a position on this question. You may write about one of the points of view mentioned above, or you may give another point of view on this issue. Use specific examples and reasons for your position.

English Test

1. D	21. C	41. A	61. D
2. G	22. J	42. H	62. H
3. B	23. B	43. A	63. B
4. F	24. F	44. G	64. G
5. A	25. B	45. D	65. A
6. J	26. H	46. F	66. J
7. B	27. D	47. A	67. D
8. F	28. F	48. J	68. H
9. C	29. D	49. B	69. D
10. F	30. H	50. H	70. F
11. B	31. C	51. B	71. C
12. J	32. J	52. F	72. G
13. A	33. A	53. C	73. C
14. J	34. H	54. F	74. G
15. B	35. D	55. C	75. D
16. H	36. F	56. H	
17. C	37. B	57. D	
18. J	38. F	58. J	
19. B	39. D	59. B	
20. G	40. J	60. H	

Mathematics Test

1. A	21. C	41. D
2. K	22. K	42. H
3. B	23. C	43. C
4. J	24. K	44. K
5. A	25. E	45. E
6. K	26. F	46. F
7. C	27. D	47. D
8. K	28. H	48. J
9. C	29. E	49. A
10. K	30. G	50. J
11. E	31. B	51. A
12. J	32. G	52. H
13. B	33. C	53. E
14. J	34. J	54. F
15. C	35. E	55. D
16. F	36. J	56. G
17. E	37. B	57. C
18. H	38. K	58. J
19. B	39. B	59. E
20. G	40. F	60. J

Reading Test

1. C	21. C
2. G	22. G
3. B	23. D
4. F	24. H
5. D	25. A
6. F	26. H
7. C	27. B
8. G	28. G
9. C	29. D
10. J	30. G
11. A	31. C
12. G	32. H
13. C	33. A
14. H	34. J
15. C	35. B
16. G	36. J
17. C	37. B
18. J	38. H
19. C	39. B
20. J	40. H

Science Reasoning Test

1. A	21. D
2. G	22. H
3. A	23. B
4. J	24. H
5. B	25. C
6. F	26. G
7. A	27. D
8. G	28. F
9. A	29. B
10. G	30. F
11. A	31. A
12. J	32. G
13. D	33. D
14. F	34. H
15. C	35. C
16. H	36. H
17. B	37. C
18. F	38. F
19. B	39. D
20. G	40. H

SCORING GUIDE

Your final reported score is your COMPOSITE SCORE. Your COMPOSITE SCORE is the average of all of your SCALED SCORES.

Your SCALED SCORES for the four multiple-choice sections are derived from the Scoring Table on the next page. Use your RAW SCORE, or the number of questions that you answered correctly for each section, to determine your SCALED SCORE. If you got a RAW SCORE of 60 on the English test, for example, you correctly answered 60 out of 75 questions.

Step 1 Determine your RAW SCORE for each of the four multiple-choice sections:

English   _____

Mathematics   _____

Reading   _____

Science Reasoning   _____

The following Raw Score Table shows the total possible points for each section.

RAW SCORE TABLE	
KNOWLEDGE AND SKILL AREAS	**RAW SCORES**
ENGLISH	75
MATHEMATICS	60
READING	40
SCIENCE REASONING	40
WRITING	12

Multiple-Choice Scoring Worksheet

Step 2 Determine your SCALED SCORE for each of the four multiple-choice sections using the following Scoring Worksheet. Each SCALED SCORE should be rounded to the nearest number according to normal rules. For example, $31.2 \approx 31$ and $31.5 \approx 32$. If you answered 61 questions correctly on the English section, for example, your SCALED SCORE would be 28.

English

$\underline{\hspace{3cm}} \times 36 = \underline{\hspace{3cm}} \div 75 = \underline{\hspace{3cm}}$
RAW SCORE

$\underline{\hspace{1cm}} - 2$ (*correction factor)

$\underline{\hspace{6cm}}$
SCALED SCORE

Mathematics

$\underline{\hspace{3cm}} \times 36 = \underline{\hspace{3cm}} \div 60 = \underline{\hspace{3cm}}$
RAW SCORE

$\underline{\hspace{1cm}} + 1$ (*correction factor)

$\underline{\hspace{6cm}}$
SCALED SCORE

Reading

$\underline{\hspace{3cm}} \times 36 = \underline{\hspace{3cm}} \div 40 = \underline{\hspace{3cm}}$
RAW SCORE

$\underline{\hspace{1cm}} + 2$ (*correction factor)

$\underline{\hspace{6cm}}$
SCALED SCORE

Science Reasoning

$\underline{\hspace{3cm}} \times 36 = \underline{\hspace{3cm}} \div 40 = \underline{\hspace{3cm}}$
RAW SCORE

$\underline{\hspace{1cm}} + 1.5$ (*correction factor)

$\underline{\hspace{6cm}}$
SCALED SCORE

*The correction factor is an approximation based on the average from several recent ACT tests. It is most valid for scores in the middle 50% (approximately 16–24 scaled composite score) of the scoring range.

The scores are all approximate. Actual ACT scoring scales vary from one administration to the next based upon several factors.

If you take the optional Writing Test, you will need to combine your English and Writing scores to obtain your final COMPOSITE SCORE. Refer to Chapter 7 for guidelines on scoring your Writing Test Essay. Once you have determined a score for your essay out of 12 possible points, you will need to determine your ENGLISH/WRITING SCALED SCORE, using both your ENGLISH SCALED SCORE and your WRITING TEST SCORE. The combination of the two scores will give you an ENGLISH/WRITING SCALED SCORE, from 1 to 36, that will be used to determine your COMPOSITE SCORE mentioned earlier.

Using the English/Writing Scoring Table, find your ENGLISH SCALED SCORE on the left or right hand side of the table and your WRITING TEST SCORE on the top of the table. Follow your ENGLISH SCALED SCORE over and your WRITING TEST SCORE down until the two columns meet at a number. This number is your ENGLISH/WRITING SCALED SCORE and will be used to determine your COMPOSITE SCORE.

Step 3 Determine your ENGLISH/WRITING SCALED SCORE using the English/Writing Scoring Table on the following page:

English $\underline{\hspace{3cm}}$

Writing $\underline{\hspace{3cm}}$

English/Writing $\underline{\hspace{3cm}}$

ENGLISH/WRITING SCORING TABLE

ENGLISH SCALED SCORE	WRITING TEST SCORE											ENGLISH SCALED SCORE
	2	3	4	5	6	7	8	9	10	11	12	
36	26	27	28	29	30	31	32	33	34	32	36	36
35	26	27	28	29	30	31	31	32	33	34	35	35
34	25	26	27	28	29	30	31	32	33	34	35	34
33	24	25	26	27	28	29	30	31	32	33	34	33
32	24	25	25	26	27	28	29	30	31	32	33	32
31	23	24	25	26	27	28	29	30	30	31	32	31
30	22	23	24	25	26	27	28	29	30	31	32	30
29	21	22	23	24	25	26	27	28	29	30	31	29
28	21	22	23	24	24	25	26	27	28	29	30	28
27	20	21	22	23	24	25	26	27	28	28	29	27
26	19	20	21	22	23	24	25	26	27	28	29	26
25	18	19	20	21	22	23	24	25	26	27	28	25
24	18	19	20	21	22	23	23	24	25	26	27	24
23	17	18	19	20	21	22	23	24	25	26	27	23
22	16	17	18	19	20	21	22	23	24	25	26	22
21	16	17	17	18	19	20	21	22	23	24	25	21
20	15	16	17	18	19	20	21	21	22	23	24	20
19	14	15	16	17	18	19	20	21	22	23	24	19
18	13	14	15	16	17	18	19	20	21	22	23	18
17	13	14	15	16	16	17	18	19	20	21	22	17
16	12	13	14	15	16	17	18	19	20	20	21	16
15	11	12	13	14	15	16	17	18	19	20	21	15
14	10	11	12	13	14	15	16	17	18	19	20	14
13	10	11	12	13	14	14	15	16	17	18	19	13
12	9	10	11	12	13	14	15	16	17	18	19	12
11	8	9	10	11	12	13	14	15	16	17	18	11
10	8	9	9	10	11	12	13	14	15	16	17	10
9	7	8	9	10	11	12	13	13	14	15	16	9
8	6	7	8	9	10	11	12	13	14	15	16	8
7	5	6	7	8	9	10	11	12	13	14	15	7
6	5	6	7	7	8	9	10	11	12	13	14	6
5	4	5	6	7	8	9	10	11	12	12	13	5
4	3	4	5	6	7	8	9	10	11	12	13	4
3	2	3	4	5	6	7	8	9	10	11	12	3
2	2	3	4	5	6	6	7	8	9	10	11	2
1	1	2	3	4	5	6	7	8	9	10	11	1

Step 4 Determine your COMPOSITE SCORE by finding the sum of all your SCALED SCORES for each of the four sections: English only (if you do not choose to take the optional Writing Test) *or* English/Writing (if you choose to take the optional Writing Test), Mathematics, Reading, and Science Reasoning, and divide by 4 to find the average. Round your COMPOSITE SCORE according to normal rules. For example, $31.2 \approx 31$ and $31.5 \approx 32$.

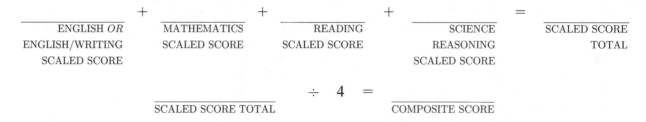

_____ + _____ + _____ + _____ = _____

ENGLISH *OR*   MATHEMATICS   READING   SCIENCE   SCALED SCORE
ENGLISH/WRITING   SCALED SCORE   SCALED SCORE   REASONING   TOTAL
SCALED SCORE   SCALED SCORE

_____ ÷ 4 = _____

SCALED SCORE TOTAL   COMPOSITE SCORE

ANSWERS AND EXPLANATIONS

English Test Explanations
PASSAGE I

1. **The best answer is D.** The author of the passage wants you to look more closely at a certain kind of truck "the next time" you see one. The other answer choices are all conditional and awkward. Answer choice D is the most concise.

2. **The best answer is G.** This question requires you to determine the correct punctuation for the underlined portion. A comma is necessary here to indicate a break between the main clause of the sentence and the first descriptive clause. Answer choice H incorrectly uses a semicolon, and answer choice J incorrectly uses a dash.

3. **The best answer is B.** Since the question asks for the answer that extends the discussion of the writer's personal experience with rubber cement, answer choice B is the only real possibility here. The other choices either discuss other subjects or are not necessarily about the writer's experiences.

4. **The best answer is F.** The sentence is correct as it is written. Since the other answer choices all indicate contrast, they must all be incorrect. There can be only one correct answer.

5. **The best answer is A.** The new subject of Paragraph 2 is the various uses to which rubber cement can be put. Answer choice A effectively introduces this topic. The other answer choices are either focused on narrow details or irrelevant information, and they should be eliminated.

6. **The best answer is J.** The other answer choices all include pronouns with unclear antecedents. Answer choice J is the only selection that provides a clear subject for the sentence.

7. **The best answer is B.** This sentence seeks to point out a contrast. Answer choice B, "as opposed to," is the only selection that does this. The other answer choices are either signals of continuation or signals of conclusion.

8. **The best answer is F.** The word *surface* is singular and, therefore, you should use the singular form of the verb *is* to keep the sentence construction parallel. The other answer choices are appropriate for plural subjects.

9. **The best answer is C.** This question tests your ability to express an idea clearly and simply. Answer choice C is the shortest and most concise selection. The other answer choices are excessively wordy and awkward. Answer choice B is in the passive voice, and answer choice D is nonsensical.

10. **The best answer is F.** ACT questions often reward test takers who understand the differences between homonyms such as *they're*, *there*, and *their*. In this case, the sentence demands the plural possessive form. Answer choice F is correct here because *their* is the plural possessive form.

11. **The best answer is B.** This question requires you to determine the correct use of commas. A good rule of thumb when it comes to commas is to use them where you would naturally pause when reading the sentence. It is not necessary to use any commas within the underlined portion. All of the other answer choices are incorrectly punctuated. Eliminate answer choice C, because a semicolon links two independent clauses and the phrase a*nother advantage* cannot stand on its own.

12. **The best answer is J.** The sentence is incorrect as written because it implies that cracks can be taken out of other surfaces with a blowtorch. Answer choices G and H are incorrect because they are awkwardly phrased and cumbersome.

13. **The best answer is A.** The sentence is correct as written. The plural form of the verb is required because the subject of the sentence is *regions*, which is plural. The word *conditions* in this case does not refer to something that is divisible and countable. Therefore, *few* and *fewer* are inappropriate.

14. **The best answer is J.** The phrase *durability of* is idiomatic, or accepted through common usage. The other answer choices would form phrases that are not commonly accepted or are simply incorrect when applied to an adjective like *durability*.

15. **The best answer is B.** The new sentence gives a specific example of conditions that are experienced in some parts of the country and may

create problems with rubber cement surfaces. It makes the most sense to place this sentence after Sentence 5 in Paragraph 3. Clear writing often involves placing specific examples immediately after general statements as illustrations.

PASSAGE II

16. **The best answer is H.** It is important to use Watson and Crick's names again at this point to avoid having an unclear antecedent for the pronoun *their* in *their discovery* at the end of the sentence. Answer choice G is awkward and does not make sense. Only answer choice H completes the sentence so that it is clear and concise.

17. **The best answer is C.** Answer choice C ties the introduction of Rosalind Franklin to the ideas that precede it. The other choices either add irrelevant information or are needlessly redundant, and should be eliminated.

18. **The best answer is J.** This question tests your ability to express an idea clearly and simply. Answer choices F, G, and H all refer to "this advanced degree," apparently referring back to the "doctorate" mentioned in the previous sentence. The main idea of the sentence and the paragraph is that Dr. Franklin's research was of benefit during World War II. This best supports answer choice J.

19. **The best answer is B.** This question tests your ability to express an idea clearly and simply. Answer choices A and C are too wordy. Answer choice D is too general. Only answer choice B makes the point of the sentence without using unnecessary language.

20. **The best answer is G.** The sentence is in past tense since the verb *decided* is used previously. Note that *decided* is not part of the underlined portion; therefore, the sentence will remain in the past tense. The only two answer choices that are in the past tense are G and J. Answer choice J is not idiomatic. In other words, it is not in a commonly accepted form. Therefore, only answer choice G remains as a possible answer.

21. **The best answer is C.** An exclamation point is clearly not appropriate here. So, answer choice A must be eliminated. Answer choice B is incorrect since it misuses a colon. Eliminate answer choice D because it creates a run-on sentence.

22. **The best answer is J.** As it is written, the sentence contains an error in number. *Race* is singular, so you need the singular form of the verb. Answer

choices G and H are in the wrong tense. The sentence is in the past tense. Only answer choice J is both singular and in the past tense.

23. **The best answer is B.** The ACT sometimes uses dashes (hyphens) in pairs to set off parenthetical material. In this case, the student's name, Maurice Wilkins, adds further information to the sentence but is not essential to the structure of the sentence.

24. **The best answer is F.** The sentence is appropriate and correct as written. Each of the other answer choices contains irrelevant information.

25. **The best answer is B.** This question tests your ability to express an idea clearly and simply. The information following the period in the underlined portion does not contribute anything meaningful to the essay. Therefore, it should not be included. It is best to end the sentence after *DNA*.

26. **The best answer is H.** It is not clear to whom or what the pronoun *them* refers. In order to maintain clarity in the sentence, it is best to identify who received "the definitive edge in the DNA race." You know it was not Wilkins — also, Wilkins is a singular noun, so the plural pronoun *them* is not appropriate — which means you should eliminate answer choice G. It does not make sense that the DNA strands received the "definitive edge" so eliminate answer choice J.

27. **The best answer is D.** The first step in answering this question is to recognize that Franklin is one person and that the "permission" is hers. You should, therefore, use the singular possessive "s." Eliminate answer choices A and C. Answer choice B includes an extra *s*, which doesn't make sense.

28. **The best answer is F.** This question tests your ability to express an idea clearly and simply. The passage indicates that Watson and Crick were trying to find the structure of DNA. The word *recovering* suggests that the structure was found, but then lost. Eliminate answer choice G. Eliminate answer choice H because it does not make sense. Answer choice J is awkward and wordy, so it should be eliminated as well.

29. **The best answer is D.** The action took place in the past, so you should use the simple past-tense verb *came*. The verb *had come* is a past participle, which suggests passive voice. This is not consistent with the structure of the sentence, so eliminate answer choice B. Eliminate answer

choices A and C because they do not include a past-tense verb.

30. **The best answer is H.** This question requires you to determine the main idea of the last paragraph. The paragraph consists of one sentence that discusses Franklin's contribution to the discovery of the structure of DNA. It would make sense to insert a sentence that includes additional information about both Franklin and the discovery of the structure of DNA. Only answer choice H does this. The other answer choices are either too broad or irrelevant.

PASSAGE III

31. **The best answer is C.** The best way to sharpen the focus of the first paragraph would be to include a better description of the home in which the writer raised her family. The first sentence implies that it was difficult to raise five children in the home, primarily because it was too small. The phrase *three-bedroom ranch home* is a better, more detailed description of the home. Since the size of the home is what is important, the fact that it was a "brick home" is irrelevant. Eliminate answer choice B. Answer choices A and D are too broad.

32. **The best answer is J.** This question requires you to identify the correct punctuation for the underlined portion. This sentence contains two independent clauses, which should be separated with some sort of punctuation. Eliminate answer choice H. Answer choice G is wordy and awkward, so it should be eliminated as well. You should not use a comma to separate independent clauses in a sentence; this is called a comma splice. Therefore, eliminate answer choice F. It is correct to use a semicolon to separate two independent clauses that relate to each other.

33. **The best answer is A.** The context of the passage implies that, because the kids no longer needed the master bedroom, it was time for the writer and her husband to move back upstairs. The sentence is correct as it is written, because it best identifies the reason behind the writer's decision to move back upstairs. The other answer choices are not supported by the context of the passage.

34. **The best answer is H.** This question tests your ability to express an idea clearly and simply. In the sentence as it is written, there is no clear sense of which space is being discussed. The context of the passage indicates that the writer's

space will be reduced if she and her husband move from their current bedroom (in the basement) back into the master bedroom. Therefore, you should use the possessive plural pronoun *our*. The other answer choices contain ambiguous pronouns.

35. **The best answer is D.** The context of the passage implies that the space in the master bedroom is too small, so it makes sense that the writer's furniture would *not* fit. Eliminate answer choices A and B because they suggest that the furniture *would* fit. You should never say "wouldn't of," so eliminate answer choice C. Many people confuse the correct phrase *wouldn't have* with the incorrect phrase *wouldn't of.*

36. **The best answer is F.** The paragraph discusses the topic of the house being too small and the need to expand. The phrase *the only way to go was up* indicates that the ranch home most likely would have to be turned into a two-story home. Answer choices G and H do not make sense based on the context of the paragraph. If you omit, or remove, the underlined portion, the sentence will lack a verb. The phrase *the only way to go was up* indicates that the ranch home would most likely have to be turned into a two-story home, which is supported by the context of the passage.

37. **The best answer is B.** The underlined portion introduces some of the plans that the writer had for the expansion of her home. The sentence as it is written is incomplete, so eliminate answer choice A. Answer choice B does not clearly indicate that the plans included the items that follow. It does not make sense that the writer would "formulate" her plans "by including" the items listed, so eliminate answer choice B. Likewise, answer choice D should be eliminated because the conjunction *so* is not correct.

38. **The best answer is F.** In order to maintain parallel construction within the paragraph, the verb forms must match. The past-tense verb *began* was used earlier in the paragraph, so you should use the past-tense verb *flowed* here. Eliminate the other answer choices because they do not include a past-tense verb form.

39. **The best answer is D.** This question requires you to express the idea clearly and simply. Because *right away*, *instantly*, and *immediately* all have the same meaning, it is not necessary to use more than one of them in the sentence. Eliminate answer choices A, B, and C because they are redundant.

40. **The best answer is J.** The sentence makes it clear that both the writer and her husband are discussing the remodeling project ("our enthusiasm"). Therefore, you should use the plural pronoun *we*.

41. **The best answer is A.** A semicolon is used to separate two independent clauses within a sentence, so the sentence is correct as it is written. You should not use a comma to separate main clauses; this is called a comma splice. Eliminate answer choice C. Omitting, or removing, the underlined portion creates an awkward sentence, so eliminate answer choice D.

42. **The best answer is H.** This question requires you to punctuate the underlined portion correctly. The sentence begins with a prepositional phrase, so a comma should be used to separate the first part of the sentence from the last part of the sentence, as in answer choice H. The addition of the transition words *then* and *because* does not help with the clarity of the sentence, so eliminate answer choices G and J.

43. **The best answer is A.** The sentence preceding the underlined portion indicates a problem that could result from beginning a remodeling project. The passage goes on to describe something good that results from remodeling your home. The transition word *nevertheless* suggests this contrast. The words *before*, *once*, and *suddenly* indicate a passage of time that is not clearly implied in the paragraph, so eliminate answer choices B, C, and D.

44. **The best answer is G.** This question requires you to punctuate the underlined portion correctly. You should separate the items in a list with commas. Both a semicolon and a period should be followed by an independent clause. Eliminate answer choices H and J because they create incomplete sentences.

45. **The best answer is D.** This question requires you to express the idea clearly and simply. The sentence as it is written is awkward and wordy, so eliminate answer choice A. Eliminate answer choice C for the same reason. Answer choice B deletes the verb, which creates an incomplete sentence.

PASSAGE IV

46. **The best answer is F.** This question requires you to express the idea clearly and simply. The implication in the paragraph is that visitors can sometimes give inaccurate descriptions of the climate in the United States, if they only visit one region. So, it makes sense that the writer would advise them to "take care" in their descriptions. Answer choices H and J are redundant and should be eliminated.

47. **The best answer is A.** This question requires you to express the idea clearly and simply. "Temperatures" and "weather patterns" are two distinct things. The sentence as it is written makes this clear. Answer choice B suggests that the "weather patterns," not the "differences in weather patterns," are huge. This does not make sense, so eliminate answer choice B. Answer choice D should be eliminated because the phrase *temperature weather patterns is* not correct.

48. **The best answer is J.** This question requires you to express the idea clearly and simply. The word *countrys* is not correct, so eliminate answer choice F. If you only include the word *whole*, the sentence loses its meaning, so eliminate answer choice H. Since the sentence already mentions the United States, you can omit, or remove, the underlined portion and the sentence still makes sense.

49. **The best answer is B.** The question requires you to select the sentence that links information already presented with information about the writer's personal experiences. Eliminate answer choices A, C, and D because they discuss other people, not the writer. Answer choice B is the only selection that introduces a personal experience of the writer.

50. **The best answer is H.** This question requires you to punctuate the underlined portion correctly. Use a colon to introduce items in a list: "one in Phoenix, Arizona, and the other in Las Vegas, Nevada." You should not use a comma to separate main clauses in a sentence; this is called a comma splice. Eliminate answer choice F. Eliminate answer choice G because it creates a run-on sentence, and eliminate answer choice J because it creates an incomplete sentence.

51. **The best answer is B.** This question requires you to express the idea clearly and simply. Since *both* and *both of these cities* express the same idea, you should select the more simple choice. The phrase *some of these* does not make sense, because the paragraph only mentions two cities. Eliminate answer choice C. Omitting the underlined portion changes the meaning of the sentence, so eliminate answer choice D.

52. The best answer is F. Because there are two cities mentioned in the sentence, you should use the plural verb *are*. Eliminate answer choice G. Also, this action is currently taking place — the cities are currently known for sunshine and high temperatures, so the verb form must be present tense. Eliminate answer choices H and J because they do not include simple present tense verbs.

53. The best answer is C. This question requires you to punctuate the underlined portion correctly. The phrase *constant sunshine and soaring summer temperatures* is an adjective phrase describing the cities. You do not need to separate the elements of that phrase with a comma. No punctuation is necessary.

54. The best answer is F. This question requires you to express the idea clearly and simply. The direct object of the verb *signifies* is the noun *clouds*. For the sake of clarity, the direct object of a verb should directly follow the verb. Eliminate answer choices G and J. Answer choice H is awkward, so it should also be eliminated.

55. The best answer is C. This question requires you to punctuate the underlined portion correctly. The relative pronoun *which* should be preceded by a comma, not a semicolon, so eliminate answer choice A. Eliminate answer choice B because it creates an incomplete sentence, and eliminate answer choice D because it creates a run-on sentence.

56. The best answer is H. The idea being expressed in this quotation is that the "fog" is considered "weather." The word *rolling* implies that something should follow that is caused by the action of rolling. This is not the case here, so eliminate answer choices F and J. To maintain parallel construction within the quote, the verb forms must match. Since *they have weather* is present tense, it makes sense to say the "fog rolls" in, present tense.

57. The best answer is D. This question requires you to determine the topic of the paragraph. Since the paragraph is a discussion of enduring severe weather, it makes sense that the introductory paragraph would mention some aspect of living in severe weather conditions. Eliminate answer choices A and B, which include information on good weather conditions. The paragraph discusses some character-building aspects of good weather. Eliminate answer choice C because it is too negative.

58. The best answer is J. This question requires you to express the idea clearly and simply.

The sentence as it is written does not make clear what "you come out" of, so eliminate answer choice F. Answer choices G and H do not follow the pattern of the sentence. Only answer choice J clearly indicates that, by surviving bad weather conditions, you become a stronger person.

59. The best answer is B. This question requires you to express the idea clearly and simply. The idea being expressed here is that surviving severe weather conditions can enhance your vocabulary. Eliminate answer choices A and C because they include the past-tense word *enhanced*. The adverb *greatly* is used to describe the verb *enhance*; this is the best selection.

60. The best answer is H. This question requires you to determine the main idea of the passage. Because the passage focuses on only two regions of the United States, it would not fulfill the assignment. Eliminate answer choices F and G. Eliminate answer choice J because the primary focus of the passage is not the descriptive words for different weather conditions.

PASSAGE IV

61. The best answer is D. This question requires you to express the idea clearly and simply. To maintain parallel construction within the sentence, you should use the past-tense verb *endured*. The other answer choices either do not use the past tense, or they are awkward.

62. The best answer is H. This question requires you to punctuate the underlined portion correctly. It is necessary to separate the prepositional phrase *so he took us to a restaurant in a tourist area* from the rest of the sentence with a comma. The underlined portion as it is written creates an incomplete sentence, so eliminate answer choice F. A semicolon should be followed by an independent clause, so eliminate answer choice G.

63. The best answer is B. This question requires you to punctuate the underlined portion correctly. The information in parentheses does not need to be set off with any additional punctuation, so answer choice B is correct.

64. The best answer is G. The connecting word *despite* indicates that, even though the writer drank copious, or large, amounts of tea, she was still able to fall asleep. This makes the most sense based on the context of the paragraph. It does not make sense that drinking a lot of tea would cause the writer to fall asleep, so eliminate answer choice F. The other answer choices also do not make sense based on the context of the paragraph.

65. **The best answer is A.** This question requires you to express the idea clearly and simply. The writer is providing an example of how the city was similar to American cities. It makes the most sense that the sentence would begin with the connection phrase, *for example*. Eliminate answer choices B and D. Answer choice C is awkward, and does not really make clear who is doing what.

66. **The best answer is J.** This question requires you to express the idea clearly and simply. Here, the writer is expressing the idea that, while the city is similar to American cities, it is also different. The preposition *yet* suggests a contrast and is the best selection.

67. **The best answer is D.** This question requires you to express the idea clearly and simply. The point of the underlined portion is that the writer performed an action (studied a bit of its history on the Internet) and that is how she obtained her information (it had been a church for nearly 1,000 years and then a mosque for over 500 years). The other answer choices are awkward and confusing.

68. **The best answer is H.** This question requires you to express the idea clearly and simply. The idea being expressed here is that the photographs could not compare the real thing, or the "actual sight." Eliminate answer choices F, G, and J, because they are wordy and confusing.

69. **The best answer is D.** It is not necessary to begin a new paragraph, because this sentence directly relates to the sentence preceding it. Eliminate answer choice B. The writer is trying to express the idea that almost, or "nearly," every surface of the central dome was covered in beautiful designs.

70. **The best answer is F.** The best way to convey a sense of wonder is to use words such as

breathtaking, as answer choice F does. The other answer choices are not effective.

71. **The best answer is C.** This question requires you to punctuate the underlined portion correctly. It is necessary to separate items in a list with a comma. Also, you need the coordinating conjunction *and* because it introduces the last item on the list. A semicolon should be followed by an independent clause, so eliminate answer choice A. You need the coordinating conjunction *and* because it introduces the last item on the list.

72. **The best answer is G.** This question requires you to express the idea clearly and simply. It does not make sense that the writer was "held captive by" or was "a captive" of the merchants, so eliminate answer choices F and H. Likewise, she was not "in captivity" so eliminate answer choice J.

73. **The best answer is C.** The last sentence (Sentence 4) of the paragraph indicates that the tour group was heading back to the hotel. It would make sense that the sentence before the last sentence would include a reason for the group to head back to the hotel. The new sentence does just that, so it should be placed between Sentence 3 and Sentence 4.

74. **The best answer is G.** Paragraph 2 includes a discussion of the similarities and differences between Istanbul and American cities. This implies the "cross-cultural exchange" mentioned in the new sentence. The new sentence would be inappropriate placed in any other paragraph.

75. **The best answer is D.** This question requires you to determine the main idea of the passage. The passage mentions the Hagia Sophia, but the focus of the passage is the writer's visit to Istanbul. Eliminate answer choices A and B. Because, as already mentioned, the main focus of the passage is a description of a visit to Istanbul, answer choice D is correct.

Mathematics Test Explanations

1. **The correct answer is A.** To solve this problem, calculate 15% of $27.60. Multiply $27.60 by 0.15, the decimal equivalent of 15%:

   $27.60(0.15) = $4.14, answer choice A.

   You should eliminate answer choice E, because it is greater than the total amount of her bill.

2. **The correct answer is K.** By definition, an arithmetic sequence has a constant that is added to the previous number to get the next number, and so on. The first step in solving this problem is to calculate the constant in the sequence. To find the constant, find the difference between each of the terms. The difference between 3 and 7 is 4, and the difference between 7 and 11 is 4. Since the difference in the terms is 4, the missing number must be 15, answer choice K.

3. **The correct answer is B.** This problem requires you to determine the percent of 1,274 that is equivalent to 524. Set up a proportion, as follows:

   (1) 524 books is to 1,274 books as x% is to 100%

   (2) $\frac{524}{1,274} = \frac{x}{100}$; solve for x

   (3) $1,274x = 52,400$

   (4) $x = 41.13$, or approximately 41.1%, answer choice B.

4. **The correct answer is J.** This problem requires you to solve for x. Isolate x on the left side of the equation:

   (1) $5x + 4 = 7(x - 2)$

   (2) $5x + 4 = 7x - 14$

   (3) $-2x = -18$

   (4) $x = 9$, answer choice J.

5. **The correct answer is A.** The first step in finding the least common denominator is to calculate the least common multiple of the fractions given. In other words, what is the smallest number into which all of the denominators will divide evenly? The denominators are 3, 4, 8, and 12. The smallest number into which all of those numbers divide evenly is 24. Therefore, the least (smallest) common denominator is 24, answer choice A.

6. **The correct answer is K.** The best way to solve this problem is to substitute -4 for x where it appears in the equation, and solve the equation. Remember to keep track of the negative signs!

   (1) $21 - 3(-4 - 2)$

   (2) $21 - 3(-6)$

   (3) $21 - (-18)$

   (4) $21 + 18 = 39$, answer choice K.

7. **The correct answer is C.** To solve this problem, substitute -4 for x and 2 for y wherever they appear in the equation, and solve the equation. Remember to keep track of the negative signs!

   (1) $x^2y + 2y - 3$

   (2) $(-4)^2(2) + 2(-4) - 3(2) =$

   (3) $16(2) + -8 - 6$

   (4) $32 - 8 - 6 =$

   (5) $26 - 6 = 18$, answer choice C.

8. **The correct answer is K.** To answer this question, you need to multiply the number of choices of science, math, and humanities classes together to determine the total number of combinations. The question states that there are 3 science class choices, 4 math class choices, and 5 humanities class choices:

   If you have 3 choices of science classes, 4 choices of math classes, and 5 choices humanities classes, then you have $(3)(4)(5) = 60$ total class options. For every science class choice, you have 4 math class choices. Given 4 math class choices, you have $(3)(4) = 12$ science and math class choices. For every science and math class combination, you have 5 humanities class choices. Given 12 math and science class choices, you have $(12)(5) = 60$ total class options.

   $3 \cdot 4 \cdot 5 = 60$, answer choice K.

9. **The correct answer is C.** The first step in solving this problem is to calculate 85% of 120. Multiply 120 by 0.85, the decimal equivalent of 85%:

   (1) $120 \cdot 0.85 = 102$

   Michelle expects to get 102 questions correct. If she gets 10 more questions correct, she will get 112 questions correct on the test. Calculate the percent of 120 that is equivalent to 112. Set up a proportion, as follows:

   (2) 112 is to 120 as x% is to 100%

   (3) $\frac{112}{120} = \frac{x}{100}$; solve for x

   (4) $120x = 11,200$

   (5) $x = 93.33$%, or 93%, answer choice C.

10. **The correct answer is K.** Since the circle is filled in, that means -1 will be included. Eliminate answer choices F and G because they don't include the value -1. Any movement to the right

on the number line means that the values are getting larger. So, the inequality should include -1, and all numbers greater than -1, answer choice K.

11. **The correct answer is E.** By definition, a parallelogram is a quadrilateral (has 4 sides) with opposite sides that are parallel and congruent. Answer choice E is a pentagon, which has 5 sides and is not a parallelogram.

12. **The correct answer is J.** The circumference of a circle is calculated by using the formula $2\pi r$. You are given that the circumference is 8π, so $2r$ must be equal to 8, and r must be equal to 4. The area of a circle is calculated by using the formula πr^2. Substitute 4 for r:

(1) $\pi r^2 =$

(2) $\pi(4)^2 = \pi 16$, or 16π, answer choice J.

13. **The correct answer is B.** Since the question asks you to find the smallest integer that divides evenly into 36 and 72, but not into 21, try the answer choices in order from smallest to greatest:

(1) Answer choice A: The integer 3 divides evenly into 36 ($3 \times 12 = 36$), 72 ($3 \times 24 = 72$), and 21 ($3 \times 7 = 21$), so eliminate answer choice A.

(2) Answer choice B: The integer 4 divides evenly into 36 ($4 \times 9 = 36$) and 72 ($4 \times 18 = 72$). However, 4 does not divide evenly into 21, so answer choice B is the correct answer.

Answer choices C, D, and E can be eliminated because they are greater than 4.

14. **The correct answer is J.** $f(x)$ is function notation that means "f of x" and indicates that you should solve the equation by substituting a number for x. The question states that x is 3. To solve this problem, substitute 3 for x wherever it appears in the expression.

(1) $f(3) = 3^3 - 3(3) + 3$

(2) $f(3) = 27 - 9 + 3$

(3) $f(3) = 21$, answer choice J.

15. **The correct answer is C.** Since 14 of the members are new and there are a total of 36 members, the probability, or chance, that the member chosen to design the logo is a new member is $\frac{14}{36}$, which can be reduced to $\frac{7}{18}$, answer choice C.

16. **The correct answer is F.** To solve this problem, use the Pythagorean Theorem, which says that $a^2 + b^2 = c^2$, where c is the hypotenuse.

(1) $8^2 + b^2 = 10^2$

(2) $64 + b^2 = 100$

(3) $b^2 = 36$

(4) $b = 6$, answer choice F.

17. **The correct answer is E.** The first step in solving this problem is to put the equation in the slope-intercept form of a line, $y = mx + b$, where b is the y-intercept.

(1) $\frac{1}{5}y = x - \frac{1}{5}$

(2) $y = 5x - 1$

The y-intercept is -1, answer choice E.

18. **The correct answer is H.** The best way to solve this problem is to perform the operation under the square root sign, using the FOIL method:

(1) $(x + 2)(x - 2)$

(2) Multiply the first terms: $(x)(x) = x^2$

(3) Multiply the outside terms: $(x)(-2) = -2x$

(4) Multiply the inside terms: $(x)(2) = 2x$

(5) Multiply the last terms: $(2)(-2) = -4$

   Now, add the like terms.

(6) $x^2 + -2x + 2x - 4 = x^2 - 4$

This value should be under the square root sign, answer choice H.

19. **The correct answer is B.** The area of a rectangle is calculated by multiplying the length by the width. You are given that the area is $9w^2 - 1$ and the width is $3w + 1$. Plug these values into the formula Area $=$ (length) (width).

(1) $9w^2 - 1 = \text{length}(3w + 1)$

(2) $\frac{9w^2 - 1}{3w + 1} = \text{length}$

(3) Factoring $9w^2 - 1$ gives you $(3w + 1)(3w - 1)$

Canceling the $(3w + 1)$ from the numerator and denominator leaves you with $3w - 1$, answer choice B.

20. **The correct answer is G.** To solve this problem, set up a ratio:

(1) $1\frac{1}{5}$ gallons is to 6 gallons as 1 week is to x weeks.

First, since the answer choices are given as decimals, convert $\frac{1}{5}$ into its decimal equivalent.

(2) $\frac{1}{5}$ is equivalent to 0.20

(3) $\dfrac{1.20 \text{ gallons}}{6.0 \text{ gallons}} = \dfrac{1}{x}$; solve for x

(4) $1.2x = 6.0$

(5) $x = 5.0$, answer choice G.

21. **The correct answer is C.** To solve this problem you need to factor $3x^2 + 3x - 18$.

(1) $3x^2 + 3x - 18 = 0$

(2) $3(x^2 + x - 6) = 0$

(3) $3(x + \underline{\hspace{1em}})(x - \underline{\hspace{1em}}) = 0$

Find 2 numbers that, when added together give you 1, and that when multiplied together give you -6. The only numbers that will work are 3 and -2.

(3) $3(x + 3)(x - 2)$ are all factors of $3x^2 + 3x - 18$, but only $(x + 3)$, answer choice C, appears as an option.

22. **The correct answer is K.** To find the sum of the 2 solutions, you must first find the 2 solutions. Solutions to equations are found by factoring. Factoring a number means taking the number apart to find its factors. Create 2 solution sets as follows:

(1) $(x + \underline{\hspace{1em}})(x - \underline{\hspace{1em}})$

Because the last value in the equation is negative (-18), you know that the solution sets will be "x plus some number" and "x minus some number." Next, find 2 numbers that, when multiplied together give you -18, and when added together give you 7. These 2 numbers will fill in the blanks in your solution sets. The only numbers that work are 9 and -2. So, your solution sets become $(x + 9)$ and $(x - 2)$. To find the solutions, set each of those sets equal to zero, and solve for x:

(2) $(x + 9) = 0$

(3) $(x - 2) = 2$

The sum of 2 and -9 is -7, so answer choice K is correct.

23. **The correct answer is C.** Since the 2 triangles are similar, the ratio of the sides is the same. So, if the shortest leg on the smaller triangle is 2 and the shortest leg on the larger triangle is 4, then the lengths of the other 2 sides of the larger triangle are twice the lengths of the sides of the smaller triangle. So, the lengths of the larger

triangle are 4, 10 $(2 \cdot 5)$, and 14 $(2 \cdot 7)$. To find the perimeter, add the lengths of all of the sides.

$4 + 10 + 14 = 28$, answer choice C.

24. **The correct answer is K.** The tangent of any acute angle is calculated by dividing the length of the side opposite the acute angle by the length side adjacent to the acute angle $\left(\tan = \dfrac{\text{opp}}{\text{adj}}\right)$. The sine of any acute angle is calculated by dividing the length of the side opposite to the acute angle by the hypotenuse $\left(\sin = \dfrac{\text{opp}}{\text{hyp}}\right)$ This means that the length of the side opposite angle P is 6, and the length of the side adjacent to angle P is 8. Use the Pythagorean Theorem to calculate the length of the hypotenuse.

(1) $a^2 + b^2 = c^2$

(2) $8^2 + 6^2 = c^2$

(3) $64 + 36 = c^2$

(4) $100 = c^2$, $c = 10$.

The sine of angle P, then, is $\dfrac{6}{10}$, answer choice K.

25. **The correct answer is E.** The question asks you to reduce the equation into simpler terms. First, remove $\sqrt{2}$ from the denominator by multiplying the numerator and denominator by $\sqrt{2}$:

(1) $\dfrac{(4x - \sqrt{2})}{\sqrt{2}} \times \dfrac{\sqrt{2}}{\sqrt{2}}$

(2) $\dfrac{\sqrt{2}(4x - \sqrt{2})}{\sqrt{2}(\sqrt{2})} =$

Distribute $\sqrt{2}$ as follows:

(3) $\dfrac{4x\sqrt{2} - 2}{2}$

Now, factor out the 2:

(4) $\dfrac{4x\sqrt{2} - 2}{2} = \dfrac{2(2x\sqrt{2} - 1)}{2}$

The 2s will cancel each other out to leave you with $2x\sqrt{2} - 1$, answer choice E.

26. **The correct answer is F.** To solve this problem, set up a proportion. $84.00 is to x as 24 calendars is to $(24 + 10)$ calendars.

(1) $\dfrac{84}{x} = \dfrac{24}{34}$; solve for x

(2) $24x = 2,856$

(3) $x = 119$

Allen would make $119.00, answer choice F.

27. **The correct answer is D.** Since the answer choices are all decimals, convert $\frac{1}{4}$ into its decimal equivalent, which is 0.25. Now add 0.25 to 0.375, remembering to align the decimal points:

$$\begin{array}{r} 0.375 \\ +0.25 \\ \hline 0.625 \end{array}$$, answer choice D.

28. **The correct answer is H.** An obtuse triangle has 1 angle that is greater than 90°. All of the angles in the triangles shown in answer choices F and K are less than 90°, so eliminate these choices. Answer choices G and J are right triangles, so one of the angles in each triangle is equal to 90°, and the other two angles are less that 90°. This leaves answer choice H, which is an obtuse triangle.

29. **The correct answer is E.** To solve this problem, perform the operations inside the parentheses and brackets.

(1) $(1.181 + 0.019) = 1.2$

(2) $[3(1.155) - 5(.533)] =$

(3) $3.465 - 2.665 = 0.8$

Now you are left with $\frac{1.2}{0.8}$. Divide 1.2 by 0.8 $(1.2 \div 0.8)$ to get 1.5, answer choice E.

30. **The correct answer is G.** This problem requires you to perform the operations in the correct order and then solve for x.

(1) $22 - 2(3 + x) = (x + 4)$

(2) $22 - (6 + 2x) = (x + 4)$

(3) $22 - 6 - 2x = x + 4$

(4) $16 - 4 = x + 2x$

(5) $12 = 3x$

(6) $4 = x$, answer choice G.

31. **The correct answer is B.** To calculate the surface area of the figure shown, break it down into a rectangle and a right triangle, as shown below.

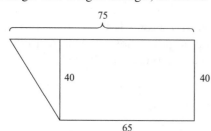

Calculate the area of the rectangle $(l \cdot w)$:

(1) $65 \cdot 40 = 2,600$

Because the length of the top side is 75, and the length of the bottom side is 65, the length of the short side, or base, of the triangle must be 10. Calculate the area of the triangle $\left(\frac{1}{2}\right)(b)(h)$, where b is the base, and h is the height:

(2) $\frac{1}{2}(10)(40) =$

(3) $\frac{1}{2}(400) = 200$

Now, add the area of the rectangle (2,600) to the area of the triangle (200) to get a total surface area of 2,800, answer choice B.

32. **The correct answer is G.** The first step in solving this problem is to put the given equation into the slope-intercept form, $y = mx + b$, where m is the slope.

(1) $4y - 3x = 8$

(2) $4y = 3x + 8$

(3) $y = \frac{3}{4}x + 2$

The slope of this line is $\frac{3}{4}$. By definition, parallel lines have the same slope, so answer choice G is correct.

33. **The correct answer is C.** If you are given 2 points on a line, you can find the midpoint by applying the following formula: $\frac{(x_1 + x_2)}{2}$ and $\frac{(y_1 + y_2)}{2}$ Plug in the given points, $(-2, -1)$ and $(3, 4)$ and solve:

(1) $\frac{(-2 + 3)}{2}$ and $\frac{(-1 + 4)}{2}$

(2) $\frac{1}{2}$ and $\frac{3}{2}$

The midpoint of the line segment is $\left(\frac{1}{2}, \frac{3}{2}\right)$, answer choice C.

34. **The correct answer is J.** The first step in solving this problem is to put the equation given into the slope-intercept form, $y = mx + b$, where b is the y-intercept.

(1) $-2y = x - 9$

(2) $y = \frac{-x}{2} + \frac{9}{2}$, or $\frac{-1}{2}x + \frac{9}{2}$

The y-intercept is $\frac{9}{2}$, answer choice J.

35. **The correct answer is E.** The question asks you to solve for c, so isolate c on the left side of the equation:

(1) $a = bc - 2$

(2) $a - bc = -2$

(3) $-bc = -a - 2$

(4) $bc = a + 2$

(5) $c = \dfrac{a+2}{b}$, answer choice E

36. **The correct answer is J.** The tangent of any acute angle is calculated by dividing the length of the side opposite the acute angle by the length side adjacent to the acute angle $\left(\tan = \dfrac{\text{opp}}{\text{adj}}\right)$. The sine of any acute angle is calculated by dividing the length of the side opposite to the acute angle by the hypotenuse $\left(\sin = \dfrac{\text{opp}}{\text{hyp}}\right)$. This means that the length of the side opposite angle P, QR, is equal to 6, and the length of the hypotenuse, PR, is equal to 10. This also means that the length of the side opposite angle S, PQ, is 8, and the length of the side adjacent to angle S, QS, is 10. Draw a diagram to keep track of the lengths of the sides:

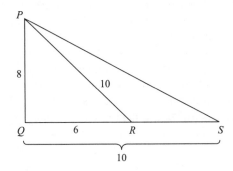

Now, use the Pythagorean Theorem to calculate the length of side PS.

(1) $a^2 + b^2 = c^2$

(2) $8^2 + 10^2 = c^2$

(3) $64 + 100 = c^2$

(4) $164 = c^2$

(5) $\sqrt{164} = c$

(6) $\sqrt{4 \cdot 41} = c$

(7) $2\sqrt{41} = c$, answer choice J.

37. **The correct answer is B.** Because 4 is the square root of 16, the quantity $(x + 1)$ must be less than 16. Set up the inequality and solve for x:

(1) $x + 1 < 16$

(2) $x < 15$

Two answer choices contain this, so which is correct? Remember that the value under the square root sign must always be positive for the number to be real.

(3) So, $x + 1 > 0$

(4) $x > -1$, answer choice B.

38. **The correct answer is K.** If the solution is negative, it must be less than 0. Set up an inequality to reflect this:

(1) $(x - 1)^2 - (2x - 3) < 0$

The next step is to expand the inequality and combine like terms:

(2) $x^2 - 2x + 1 - (2x - 3) < 0$

(3) $x^2 - 4x + 4 < 0$

The final steps are to factor the equation on the left side of the inequality and solve for x:

(4) $(x - 2)(x - 2) < 0$

(5) $(x - 2)^2 < 0$

Since any value squared can never be negative, there is no solution, answer choice K.

39. **The correct answer is B.** If the x-coordinate is 3 less than twice the y-coordinate, then $x = 2y - 3$. Put this equation into the slope-intercept form of a line, $y = mx + b$, where m is the slope, and b is the y-intercept.

(1) $x = 2y - 3$

(2) $-2y = -x - 3$

(3) $y = \dfrac{1}{2}x + \dfrac{3}{2}$

The y-intercept is $\dfrac{3}{2}$, answer choice B.

40. **The correct answer is F.** By definition, the sum of the lengths of any 2 sides of a triangle is greater than the length of the third side. Since $4.5 + 1.5 = 6$, 4.5 CANNOT be the length of the third side. The other options will always yield a result that meets the criteria of the definition.

41. **The correct answer is D.** By definition, the longer side will be opposite the larger angle. So, the angle opposite the side with a length of 56 is the larger of the unknown angles. (The measure of the angle opposite the hypotenuse is 90°.) The sine of any acute angle is calculated by dividing the length of the side opposite to the acute angle by the hypotenuse $\left(\sin = \dfrac{\text{opp}}{\text{hyp}}\right)$. This means that the sine of the larger of the unknown angles is $\dfrac{56}{72}$, answer choice D.

42. The correct answer is H. The first step in answering this question is to put the equation in the quadratic form.

(1) $2x - 4 = (x + 3)(x + 3)$

(2) $2x - 4 = x^2 + 6x + 9$

(3) $0 = x^2 + 4x + 13$

By definition, an equation in the quadratic form has 2 solutions, answer choice H.

43. The correct answer is C. Since the triangle is circumscribed inside the circle, arc AC has the same ratio to the circumference of the circle as the interior triangle angle has to the total number of degrees in a circle:

(1) $\dfrac{\text{arc } AC}{\text{circumference}} = \dfrac{\text{interior angle}}{\text{degrees of circle}}$

To answer the problem, you need to determine the values of each of the ratios above. The circumference of a circle is $2\pi r$, where r is the radius. In this problem, the circle has a radius of 3, so the circumference of the circle is 6π. The triangle inside the circle is an equilateral triangle, which means that all the sides are the same length and all the angles are $60°$ angles. There are $360°$ in a circle. Use these values in the ratio above and solve for the length of arc AC:

(2) $\dfrac{\text{arc } AC}{6\pi} = \dfrac{60°}{360°}$

(3) $\dfrac{\text{arc } AC}{6\pi} = \dfrac{1}{6}$

(4) $6 \text{ arc } AC = 6\pi$

(5) $\text{arc } AC = \pi$

The length of arc AC is π, answer choice C.

44. The correct answer is K. If $(x + 3)$ is a factor of $x^2 - 17x + b$, there must be another factor $(x - a)$, where $(x + 3)(x - a) = x^2 - 17x + b$. The value of a must be a number that when added to 3 gives you -17 and when multiplied by 3 gives you b. 20 is the only value for a that yields -17 when added to 3. Therefore, b must be equal to $20 \cdot 3$, or 60, answer choice K.

45. The correct answer is E. To answer this question, you need to factor the equation and set each group equal to 0:

(1) $x^2 + \dfrac{5}{4}x = 0$

(2) $x\left(x + \dfrac{5}{4}\right) = 0$

(3) $x = 0$, and

(4) $x + \dfrac{5}{4} = 0$

(5) $x = -\dfrac{5}{4}$

The solutions to this equation are $x = 0$ and $x = -\dfrac{5}{4}$, answer choice E.

46. The correct answer is F. The first step in solving this problem is to multiply 761.18 by 4.

(1) $761.18 \times 4 = 3,044.72$

Next, to find the correct scientific notation, count the number of places that the decimal point moves from 3,044.72, to 3.04.

(2) $\begin{array}{cccc} 3 & 0 & 4 & 4.72 \to 3.04 \\ \underline{|\quad|\quad|\quad|} \\ 3 & 2 & 1 \end{array}$

The decimal point moved 3 places to the left, so 3,044.72 is approximately equal to 3.04×10^3, answer choice F.

47. The correct answer is D. The triangle described is a special right triangle, where the measures of the angles are $90°$, $60°$, and $30°$. Since the shortest side is opposite the smallest angle, and the hypotenuse is the longest side, the angle adjacent to both the shortest side and the hypotenuse must be $60°$, answer choice D. Test this by drawing a diagram:

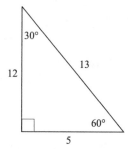

48. The correct answer is J. The best way to solve this problem is to divide the pentagon into a triangle and a rectangle, as shown below:

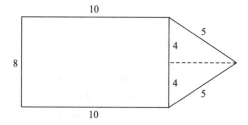

Calculate the area of the rectangle ($l \cdot w$):

$10 \cdot 8 = 80$

Since the pentagon will have a larger area than the rectangle, eliminate answer choices F, G, and H. The area of the triangle is calculated by using the formula $\dfrac{1}{2}(b)(h)$, where b is the base and h is the height. You know that the base is 8. Determine the height by using the Pythagorean Theorem, which says that $a^2 + b^2 = c^2$, where c is the hypotenuse.

(1) $a^2 + b^2 = c^2$

(2) $4^2 + b^2 = 5^2$

(3) $16 + b^2 = 25$

(4) $b^2 = 9$

(5) $b = 3$

The area of the triangle is $\frac{1}{2}(8)(3)$ or $\frac{1}{2}(24)$, which is 12. Add this to the area of the rectangle (80 + 12) to get 92, answer choice J.

49. **The correct answer is A.** The formula for a circle is $(x - a)^2 + (y - b)^2 = r^2$, where (a,b) is the center of the circle and r is the radius of the circle. The first step is to determine the radius of the circle. The question gives you the center of the circle as (4,3) and another point on the circle as (0,3). Since the y is constant, these 2 points form a straight line from the center to the edge of the circle, or the radius. Point (0,3) is 4 units away from (4,3) on the x-axis, so the radius is 4. Use the points given for the center of the circle, (4,3), and the radius in the formula:

(1) $(x - 4)^2 + (y - 3)^2 = 4^2$

(2) $(x - 4)^2 + (y - 3)^2 = 16$, answer choice A.

50. **The correct answer is J.** To determine the point where the 2 lines intersect, you need to find the values of x and y that make the equations equal to each other. Set the equations equal to each other and solve for x first:

(1) $2x - 10 = -\frac{1}{2}x + 5$

(2) $2\frac{1}{2}x - 10 = 5$

(3) $2\frac{1}{2}x = 15$

(4) $x = 6$

Now that you know the value of $x = 6$, plug 6 into 1 of the equations to solve for y:

(5) $y = -\frac{1}{2}(6) + 5$

(6) $y = -3 + 5$

(7) $y = 2$

The point where the 2 lines intersect is (6,2), answer choice J.

51. **The correct answer is A.** You may recognize that the repeating decimal $0.3\overline{33}$ is equivalent to $\frac{1}{3}$,

answer choice A. If you didn't, the best way to solve this problem is to divide the numerators by the denominators in each of the answer choices, until the result is 0.333.

$$1 \div 3 = 0.3\overline{33}, \text{ answer choice A.}$$

52. **The correct answer is H.** To answer this question, solve the inequality for x. Isolate x on the left side of the inequality.

(1) $5(x - 2) \geq 2(5 + x)$

(2) $5x - 10 \geq 10 + 2x$

(3) $3x \geq 20$

(4) $x \geq \frac{20}{3}$, answer choice H.

53. **The correct answer is E.** The first step in solving this problem is to solve $x = 3a + 7$ for a.

(1) $x = 3a + 7$

(2) $x - 7 = 3a$

(3) $\frac{x - 7}{3} = a$

Now you can substitute $\frac{x - 7}{3}$ for a in the second equation, and solve for y:

(4) $y = 6 + a$

(5) $y = 6 + \frac{(x - 7)}{3}$

(6) $y = \frac{18}{3} + \frac{x - 7}{3}$

(7) $y = \frac{18 + x - 7}{3}$

(8) $y = \frac{11 + x}{3}$, answer choice E.

54. **The correct answer is F.** In a trapezoid, the bases are parallel, so $\overline{AB} \| \overline{DC}$. You are given that $\overline{PQ} \| \overline{AB} \| \overline{DC}$. By definition, the ratio of the length of $\overline{DP}$ to the length of $\overline{PA}$ is the same as the ratio of $\overline{PQ}$ to $\overline{AB}$. In other words:

(1) $\frac{DP}{PA} = \frac{PQ}{AB}$

Plug in the lengths that are given and solve for PQ:

(2) $\frac{5}{7} = \frac{\overline{PQ}}{21}$

(3) $25 \times \frac{5}{7} = \overline{PQ}$

(4) $3 \times 5 = \overline{PQ}$

(5) $15 = \overline{PQ}$, answer choice F.

55. **The correct answer is D.** By definition, the sum of corresponding angles is 180°. Therefore, the corresponding acute angle to a 110° angle must be 70°, answer choice D.

56. The correct answer is G. The sine of any acute angle is calculated by dividing the length of the side opposite to the acute angle by the hypotenuse $\left(\sin = \dfrac{\text{adj}}{\text{hyp}}\right)$. It may help you to draw a diagram to solve this problem:

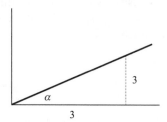

Use the Pythagorean Theorem to calculate the length of the hypotenuse.

(1) $a^2 + b^2 = c$

(2) $3^2 + 3^2 = c^2$

(3) $9 + 9 = c^2$

(4) $18 = c^2$

(5) $\sqrt{18} = c$; $\sqrt{9}\sqrt{2} = c$; $3\sqrt{2} = c$

So, the sine of angle α is $\dfrac{3}{3\sqrt{2}}$, answer choice G.

57. The correct answer is C. Integers can be even or odd, and positive or negative. Pick real numbers to substitute into the expressions in each roman numeral, then eliminate any roman numerals that do not always yield an odd number.

(1) x^3: substitute 1, 2, −1, and −2 for x:

(2) $1^3 = 1$; $2^3 = 8$, which is not an odd number, so stop here and eliminate answer choices A and D.

(3) $x + 1$; substitute 1, 2, −1, and −2 for x:

(4) $1 + 1 = 2$, which is not an odd number, so stop here and eliminate answer choices B and E.

This means that answer choice C must be correct. Whenever you multiply any integer by 2, the result will be even; when you then add 1, the result will always be odd.

58. The correct answer is J. Probability refers to the likelihood of something happening. How many white chips should Jenny put into the container so that she is likely to draw a red chip on every fifth draw? Try the answer choices.

(1) If she puts in 1 white chip, then the probability of drawing a red chip is 4 (red chips) out of 5 (total chips). Eliminate answer choice F.

(2) If she puts in 5 white chips, then the probability of drawing a red chip is 4 (red chips) out of 9 (total chips). Eliminate answer choice G.

(3) If she puts in 9 white chips, then the probability of drawing a red chip is 4 (red chips) out of 13 (total chips). Eliminate answer choice H.

(4) If she puts in 16 white chips, then the probability of drawing a red chip is 4 (red chips) out of 20 (total chips), which is equivalent to 1 out of 5, or $\dfrac{1}{5}$. She should add 16 white chips, answer choice J.

59. The correct answer is E. When a wheel makes 1 revolution that means that it goes completely around 1 time. The distance 1 time around a wheel is equal to the wheel's circumference. A wheel is a circle, so the formula for the circumference of a wheel is $C = 2\pi r$. If the diameter of the wheel is 37, then 1 time around, or 1 revolution of the wheel is equal to 37, which is equal to $2r$. So, the circumference of the wheel is $2r\pi$, or, 37π. Since the wheel made 20 revolutions, multiply 20 by 37π to get 740π, answer choice E.

60. The correct answer is J. The absolute value of a number is indicated by placing that number inside 2 vertical lines. For example, the absolute value of 10 is written as follows: |10|. Absolute value can be defined as the numerical value of a real number without regard to its sign. This means that the absolute value of 10, |10|, is the same as the absolute value of −10, |−10|, in that they both equal 10. If the absolute value of x − a = 9, then x + a must also equal 9. These equations are represented on the number line as follows:

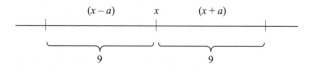

So, the distance apart on the number line is $9 + 9$, or 18, answer choice J.

Reading Test Explanations

PASSAGE I

1. **The best answer is C.** The passage states that Squire Newcome's son "was a thorn in the side of his father, who had endeavoured in vain to mould him according to his idea of propriety." This suggests that Squire Newcome had some trouble disciplining his son, which best supports answer choice C. The other answer choices are not supported by the passage.

2. **The best answer is G.** The second paragraph states that Squire Newcome had "a very exalted conception of his own position, and the respect which he felt to be his due, not only from his own household, but from all who approached him." This statement, along with other information in the passage, best supports answer choice G.

3. **The best answer is B.** According to the passage, Hannah felt "a natural reluctance to appear before her employer with her hands covered with dough, so she hastily washed them." This took time, however, so she was delayed. The other answer choices are not supported by the passage.

4. **The best answer is F.** The conversation between Hannah and Squire Newcome suggests that Hannah was not very well educated, so eliminate answer choice G. The words *condescending* and *pompous* can be used to describe Squire Newcome, not Hannah, so eliminate answer choice H. Nothing in the passage suggests that Hannah was lazy, so eliminate answer choice J.

5. **The best answer is D.** The third paragraph states that Squire Newcome's wife "did not live long after marriage." The paragraph goes on to suggest that the reason for this is that she found her husband and her marriage to be cold. Based on the description of Squire Newcome, you can infer that this coldness was the result of his preoccupation with his position in the community, and that he cared more about that relationship than he did about his marriage. The other answer choices are not supported by the passage.

6. **The best answer is F.** The context of the passage makes it clear that Squire Newcome thought very highly of himself, so it makes sense that he would have an "exalted," or "elevated" conception of his own position. The other answer choices are not supported by the context of the passage.

7. **The best answer is C.** According to the last paragraph, Hannah stepped toward the window, looked out, and immediately "gave a shrill scream." This suggests that she was greatly alarmed or surprised by something that she saw. The other answer choices are not supported by the passage.

8. **The best answer is G.** Squire Newcome is depicted in the passage as being rigid, as mentioned in the first paragraph, and dignified, as mentioned in the second paragraph. The statement supports this depiction by suggesting another way in which the Squire is rigid and dignified, or formal. While Squire Newcome may be wealthy and solemn, the phrase does not contribute to this depiction of him. The other answer choices are not supported by the passage.

9. **The best answer is C.** The passage indicates that Squire Newcome's use of the word *IMMEJIATELY* is an attempt to place importance and emphasis on the word *immediately*. It is clear that Hannah did not recognize that attempt, and simply copied her employer's use of the language. The other answer choices are not supported by the passage.

10. **The best answer is J.** According to the passage, it was more important to Ben to have fun than to listen to his father. The passage states that Ben "was constantly bursting out in new directions, in spite of his father's numerous and rather prosy lectures." This best supports the idea that Ben was *indifferent* to his father's instructions on how he was to behave. There is nothing in the passage to indicate that Ben felt "great admiration" or "deep respect" for his father. So eliminate answer choices F and H. *Disdain* means "hatred" or "contempt," which are too strong based on the context of the passage. So eliminate answer choice G.

PASSAGE II

11. **The best answer is A**. The passage states, "Garvey was a famous Black-Nationalist leader, poet, writer, orator, businessman, entrepreneur, political candidate, and philosopher." There is no mention of him being a painter.

12. **The best answer is G.** The passage mentions Garvey's work to advance African Americans both politically and socially. An example of Garvey's work for social advancement is his organization of "the Universal Negro Improvement Association in Harlem" and "many African American–owned businesses and industries". An example of Garvey's work for political advancement is his organization of

"a thirty-one-day conclave in Madison Square Garden, which resulted in the Back to Africa Movement and the Declaration of Black Rights."

13. **The best answer is C.** The passage states, "Garvey's most powerful enemies came from his controversial stance against the National Association for the Advancement of Colored People and the peaceful civil rights movement. Garvey argued that the NAACP only supported and helped certain members of the African American population. Garvey's harsh comments against the peaceful NAACP and the civil rights movement turned many important people against him." This best supports answer choice C.

14. **The best answer is H.** The passage states, "World War I had ended. Many African American soldiers had fought in the war and died for their country. However, when the surviving African American soldiers returned to the United States, they still found themselves facing discrimination and prejudice." This best supports answer choice H.

15. **The best answer is C.** The word "lofty" is often used to indicate that a person has "high," or idealistic goals. The context of the paragraph best supports answer choice C.

16. **The best answer is G.** The passage states, "The UNIA was very impressive. It had a thousand divisions around the world, with thousands of members." This best supports answer choice G.

17. **The best answer is C.** The passage states that Garvey achieved success in literary, financial, political, social, and academic fields. This far-reaching influence allowed Garvey to control many aspects of those fields because he was so successful.

18. **The best answer is J.** The passage states that the following events were occurring when Garvey arrived in America: "Bloody incidents like the East St. Louis's *race riots* and the Red Summer broke out across the country. Despite these tense conditions, the *Negro Era* began to emerge and *The Harlem Renaissance* started to gain national recognition." Garvey himself started the Back to Africa Movement.

19. **The best answer is C.** Garvey's behavior was described as "blunt" and he had "bold ideas." He would not be described as "timid." He was also very ambitious and successful in many areas.

20. **The best answer is J.** The passage states, "The UNIA was very impressive. It had a thousand divisions around the world, with thousands of members." The other answer choices are not supported by details in the passage.

PASSAGE III

21. **The best answer is C.** The passage states that "during her teenage years, my grandmother did not spend her time giggling with friends at slumber parties or going to the movies." In addition, the passage reveals, "The secret dreams and fantasies so common of teenage girls today were absent from my grandmother's life as she focused on earning money to continue her education and to help her family." This best supports answer choice C.

22. **The best answer is G.** The passage states, "When my grandfather suffered a stroke, my grandmother learned to drive at the age of sixty and faithfully shuttled him back and forth between endless doctor's appointments and hospital visits." Therefore, we know that the grandmother learned to drive late in life in order to take her husband to doctor's appointments. This best supports answer choice G.

23. **The best answer is D.** The passage states, "The grace, determination, and work ethic she had acquired in her teenage years during the Great Depression served her well as she faced the many challenges of married life." The beginning of the passage talks about how and why the grandmother acquired her personality traits. The rest of the paragraph speaks about how the grandmother used these personality traits throughout her life.

24. **The best answer is H.** Based on the context of the paragraph, *muzzled* is another word for *suppressed*. The narrator is telling us that her grandmother's spirit prevailed and would not be suppressed even though the grandmother faced great hardship throughout her life. The other answer choices are not supported by the passage.

25. **The best answer is A.** The passage begins by asking the question, "How did people in the 1930s manage to survive the Great Depression when unemployment rose, land and homes were repossessed, and proud women and men had to stand in long lines to receive government aid to feed their families?" The rest of the passage explains how one woman survived the Great

Depression and used what she learned during that period to succeed in life. This best supports answer choice A.

26. **The best answer is H.** Strength, determination, and spirit were qualities that the narrator's grandmother and her fellow survivors had. The narrator suggests that having these qualities was what helped the "Great Depression generation" achieve the American Dream, and also that having these qualities could help others achieve their dreams.

27. **The best answer is B.** The narrator is pointing out that it took bravery and determination to learn how to drive so late in life, and that her grandmother's bravery had not diminished over the years.

28. **The best answer is G.** The passage states, "Although my grandmother never did move back to a farm, the seeds of goodness and virtue she planted in the big city sprouted and flourished." These seeds were not planted in a garden at a city home. These seeds were a metaphor for the grandmother's ability to grow and spread goodness and virtue during her life.

29. **The best answer is D.** The passage states, "In the early 1920s, life had never been better in America. The stock market was booming, people were becoming fabulously wealthy, and carefree flappers danced the night away listening to a new wave of music fresh from Harlem. However, all of this changed when the stock market crashed in 1929. Overnight, millionaires became paupers and the whole nation began to crumble. In 1932, my grandmother was fifteen years old. Within three years of the stock market crashing, her family had lost their car, farm, and dreams." The narrator is pointing out that the wealth and lightheartedness of the 1920s is in sharp contrast to the hardships of the 1930s.

30. **The best answer is G.** The narrator expresses pride in her grandmother and her grandmother's accomplishments by telling about the trials and adversities that her grandmother overcame throughout her life. The narrator also speaks about her grandmother's strong work ethic, goodness, and strength. This best supports answer choice G.

PASSAGE IV

31. **The best answer is C.** The end of the passage details the problems El Niño might cause certain industries, but it also gives advice about how the different industries can help prevent some of the disastrous effects. For instance the passage states, "The natural gas and fuel industries can adjust their production and distribution to decrease losses when warm El Niño winter conditions are expected." This best supports answer choice C.

32. **The best answer is H.** The passage states, "Industries directly affected by weather or climate compose almost 10 percent of the Gross Domestic Product (GDP) in the United States. Weather and climate also impact insurance industries, services, retail and wholesale trade, and manufacturing. Nearly 25 percent of the GDP may be directly or indirectly somehow affected by weather and climate." These statements inform the reader that almost all of the industries can be impacted by El Niño and that a significant percent of the GDP could be affected.

33. **The best answer is A.** The passage suggests that, because phytoplankton are among the organisms harmed when the upwelling decreases the supply of cooler water to the euphotic zone, the fish that eat phytoplankton would see a decrease in their food supply. This would in turn, harm the fishing industry. The other answer choices are not supported by the passage.

34. **The best answer is J.** The passage states that "some common impacts on the United States include fewer tropical storms in the Atlantic region; a dry monsoon around Mexico, Arizona, and New Mexico; an especially dry fall and winter around Oregon and Washington; an extremely wet winter in the Gulf Coast; and a warmer-than-average fall and winter in many Midwestern States."

35. **The best answer is B.** Paragraph 7 indicates that department store sales went up during an El Niño, but sales of skis went down. Therefore, some industries benefit from El Niño, but some are harmed. The main idea of this passage is to emphasize that not all industries are necessarily harmed by El Niño weather.

36. **The best answer is J.** The passage states, "The water industry and hydroelectric power companies can make storage and production decisions that take into account the large rainfall of El Niño years. The natural gas and fuel industries can adjust their production and distribution levels to decrease losses when warm El Niño winter conditions are expected." This supports answer choice J.

37. **The best answer is B.** The last paragraph does not guarantee that industries will gain from El Niño weather. Instead, it suggests ways for certain industries to help decrease their losses. The passage does not state that taking the precautions suggested will actually change the weather, nor does the passage state that only the industries mentioned are able to prepare for El Niño weather.

38. **The best answer is H.** The first paragraph compares the sea levels of Indonesia and Ecuador, explains the behavior of trade winds during normal, or "non-El Niño" years, and indicates what El Niño is. It does not explain a consequence of abnormal trade wind activity.

39. **The best answer is B.** The word *ravage* is used in this passage to describe the damage that storms cause to crops and property. The other answer choices are not supported by the passage.

40. **The best answer is H.** The passage states that "El Niños occur on an average of every four to five years. El Niños can last up to a year and a half."

Science Reasoning Test Explanations

PASSAGE I

1. **The correct answer is A.** Both scientists directly state that the movement of tectonic plates created the continents. None of the other answer choices are supported by information the passage.

2. **The correct answer is G.** Scientist 1 states that circular motion of the asthenosphere causes "the plates to collide with each other." The passage goes on to say that earthquakes occur in the same location as the circular motion, implying that where circular motion occurs, earthquakes also occur. The other answer choices are not supported by the passage.

3. **The correct answer is A.** The passage states that tectonic plates move "within the fluid, lower layer of Earth's crust, the asthenosphere." This best supports answer choice A.

4. **The correct answer is J.** Scientist 2 states that, since the formation of the continents, there has been little movement of the tectonic plates. The movement that does occur is released in "small bursts ... along a fault line." It is also "apparent in the fact that there are certain areas that are more affected by earthquakes than others." In other words, Scientist 2 claims that the small bursts of energy that occur on fault lines cause earthquakes, answer choice J. The other answer choices are not supported by the passage.

5. **The correct answer B.** The passage directly states that the "fluid, lower layer of the Earth's crust" is the asthenosphere, answer choice B.

6. **The correct answer is F.** Scientist 1 states that a "large burst of energy ... is what created the separate continents." Scientist 2 states that the continents were formed from "a sudden burst of energy" and that now only "small bursts of energy" occur, causing earthquakes. You can assume from this statement that Scientist 2 believes that a large burst of energy must have caused the separation of the continents. The other answer choices are contradictory to the statements made by both scientists.

7. **The correct answer is A.** Scientist 1 states that the "tectonic plates are constantly moving." Therefore, if the tectonic plates did not move, Scientist 1's viewpoint would be weakened. If the tectonic plates rested on the "rigid, upper crust," they would not be "constantly moving."

PASSAGE II

8. **The correct answer is G.** The passage states that the breakdown of wood into charred wood, ash, and volatile gas occurs during thermal degradation, answer choice G. While the ignition temperature must be reached before thermal degradation can begin, the ignition temperature is not the process in which the breakdown of wood occurs, so you can eliminate answer choice H. The other answer choices are not supported by information in the passage.

9. **The correct answer is A.** According to the passage, the study focused on protective coating that "acts as an insulator to protect against fire damage during ... thermal degradation." Thermal degradation is the process in which the materials of a fuel (wood) break down into several by-products, including char and smoke. The other answer choices are not supported by information in the passage.

10. **The correct answer is G.** The question requires you to look at the line that represents untreated wood in Figure 1 and find the part of the line where a small increase in Temperature results in the largest decrease in Mass Loss %. This part of the line will represent the temperatures at which the untreated wood lost the greatest percent of mass. As you can see in Figure 1, the line that represents untreated wood slowly declines at first (between 200° and 260°C), rapidly declines at temperatures between 260° and 400°C, and levels off to a more gradual decrease in mass after 400°. Therefore, the greatest amount of mass is lost between 260° and 400°C, answer choice G.

11. **The correct answer is A.** Figure 1 shows the amount of mass that is lost as the temperature that the plywood was exposed to is increased. At each of the temperatures tested, Fire retardant 3 consistently had the greatest amount of mass remaining. According to the passage, a fire retardant is more effective when it reduces the amount of damage caused by combustion. Therefore, Fire retardant 3 is most effective at suppressing combustion. The other answer choices are not supported by the passage.

12. **The correct answer is J.** To answer this question, you must find the point on Figure 1 where the line representing Fire retardant 1 meets the line representing Fire retardant 2. This point represents the moment when both fire retardant wood samples (1 and 2) experience the same percent of mass loss. Once you have found the point where the two lines meet, follow it down to determine

the temperature at this point. According to Figure 1, the 2 lines meet at approximately 625°C, answer choice J.

PASSAGE III

13. **The correct answer is D.** Scientist 1 claims that "planting more trees or preserving trees…" "is not a good long-term solution" and "may give people the impression that no other measures are needed to reduce carbon dioxide emissions." Scientist 1 goes on to list many ways in which carbon dioxide emissions can be reduced. Based on this information, answer choice D is best. Answer choices A, B, and C can be eliminated because they are not supported by the passage.

14. **The correct answer is F.** The question requires you to determine what might cause increased carbon dioxide levels during a hot, dry summer. Common sense tells you that hot, dry summers are related to the occurrence of drought and forest fires. The passage states that forest fires and droughts rapidly increase carbon dioxide levels. Based on this information, you can assume that answer choice F is correct. The remaining answer choices cannot be supported by information in the passage.

15. **The correct answer is C.** Scientist 2 directly states that planting and preserving trees "can help reduce the destruction of the world's forests and protect biodiversity." The other answer choices are not supported by the passage.

16. **The correct answer is H.** All of the other answer choices are mentioned in the passage. While "sunlight energy" is mentioned, it is not the same thing as "solar power," which is usable power, usually heat or electricity that is created from the sun's radiation.

17. **The correct answer is B.** According to the passage, Scientist 1 believes that planting and preserving trees is "not a good long-term solution" and Scientist 2 believes that it is a "great long-term solution" to reducing the levels of carbon dioxide in the atmosphere. This best supports answer choice B.

18. **The correct answer is F.** Scientist 1 claims that "planting trees … accelerates climate change in snow-covered areas by reducing the amount of sunlight energy that is directed back into space." You can assume that this occurs because the leaves and branches reduce the amount of sunlight that can be reflected off the snow. If it is found that newly planted trees in snow-covered areas have not accelerated climate change, then Scientist 1 would most likely say that the leaves and branches were not large enough to block sunlight and cause a change in climate.

19. **The correct answer is B.** Scientist 2 says that "although some carbon dioxide is released when the leaves decompose, planting or preserving trees is still an effective means by which to greatly reduce the carbon dioxide levels in the atmosphere." If most of the carbon dioxide was emitted when a plant decomposed, planting or preserving trees would not be a great way to help reduce the carbon dioxide levels.

PASSAGE IV

20. **The correct answer is G.** The passage states that "chlorophyll is produced in response to sunlight," which best supports answer choice G. The other answer choices are not supported by details in the passage.

21. **The correct answer is D.** To answer this question, locate yellow in the Resulting Colors column of Table 1. Next, move to the left to see which compound type corresponds with yellow. The information in Table 1 indicates that the presence of lycopene, flavone, and carotene will result in yellow leaves.

22. **The correct answer is H.** The first step in answering this question is to answer either yes or no. It is clear in the passage that light levels do affect color change, so eliminate answer choices F and G. The passage states that "chlorophyll is produced in response to sunlight" and "decreasing light levels cause chlorophyll production to slow." Chlorophyll is responsible for the green color of leaves; answer choice H is correct.

23. **The correct answer is B.** The passage states that leaves "containing primarily anthocyanins will appear red," answer choice B.

24. **The correct answer is H.** To answer this question, look at Table 1, and find the column for Pigment Class. You will see that Porphyrin yields only green leaves, so eliminate answer choice F. Chlorophyll is not a Pigment Class—it is a Compound Type—so eliminate answer choice G. Based on Table 2, Flavonoid yields yellow, red, blue, and purple, so it has the most color variety.

PASSAGE V

25. The correct answer is C. According to the passage, meerkat predators include eagles and jackals. Table 1 indicates that a constant loud chattering is produced when the sentry sees a jackal, eagle, or a large snake. This information best supports answer choice C.

26. The correct answer is G. The passage states that meerkats "will gather together, stand up, and turn their bellies to the sun, soaking up the sunlight." Since a solar panel also soaks up the sunlight, it makes sense that meerkats would be called the "Solar Panel of the Animal World" due to their habit of soaking up the morning sun, answer choice G.

27. The correct answer is D. The passage states that "unlike other mongooses, meerkats live in large social communities," answer choice D.

28. The correct answer is F. The results shown in Table 1 indicate that meerkat sentries will make one quick "chirp" at sunrise and sunset, when no possible alarm cue is observed. This suggests that meerkats vocalize for other reasons, and not just to warn each other of danger. The other answer choices are not supported by the results shown in Table 1.

29. The correct answer is B. The observers must have assumed that the meerkats would recognize and understand what the different alarm calls meant, otherwise the study would have been pointless.

30. The correct answer is F. The theory that alarm calls have special meanings would NOT be supported if the same alarm call was made to indicate more than one thing. The other answer choices all indicate different alarm calls being made to signal specific events, which, if they had occurred, would support the theory.

PASSAGE VI

31. The correct answer is A. According to the passage, the animals have "mouths that expand two times the size of their bodies . . . to maximize the size of prey that they can consume." This best supports answer choice A.

32. The correct answer is G. The passage states that the midwater zone extends from 200 m to 2,000 m. According to Figure 1, this range includes the mesopelagic zone (that extends from 200 m to 1,000 m) and a portion of the

bathypelagic zone (that extends from 1,000 m to 4,000 m).

33. The correct answer is D. To answer this question, look at Table 1. The table shows that the Snipe Eel can be found in the ocean from depths of 40 to 550 m and at a maximum of 2,000 m. Now look at Figure 1. Since the Snipe Eel can be found anywhere between 40 and 2,000 m, determine which of the ocean zones fall within this range: a portion of the epipelagic zone, the entire mesopelagic zone, and a portion of the bathypelagic, answer choice D.

34. The correct answer is H. The passage states that vertical migrators travel toward the surface at night, to "the uppermost part of their range of depth." According to Table 1, the Eelpout is found at depths ranging from 2,500 m to 5,000 m. The uppermost part of this range is 2,500 m, so that depth is most likely where the Eelpouts would travel up to at night, if they were vertical migrators.

35. The correct answer is C. The question requires you to determine which species could survive at the broad range of temperatures that exist from the ocean's surface down to the sea floor. The temperature of the ocean water depends on the depth. The Stout Blacksmelt is normally found in depths of 225 m to 1,400 m, but it can also be found at depths of 6,700 m. This is the broadest range of any of the species listed, so answer choice C is correct.

PASSAGE VII

36. The correct answer is H. The best approach to solving this problem is process of elimination. All of the answer choices refer to snake length, so look at Table 1. Snake D is the longest snake, but it ranks 3rd in aggression, so eliminate answer choice F. By the same token, eliminate answer choice G. It does not appear that length has any effect on rank, so answer choice H is correct.

37. The correct answer is C. Table 3 shows win-loss records for all of the snakes. You can logically conclude that the more dominant snake would have more wins. Therefore, the snake with the most wins would also have the safest eggs. According to Table 3, Snake C had the most wins.

38. The correct answer is F. To solve this problem, compare the values given with the values listed in Table 1. Based on those values, the 6th snake is most similar to Snake A, which had an aggression rank of 2. This best supports answer choice F.

39. **The correct answer is D.** To solve this problem, look at each roman numeral and decide if it answers the question. According to Table 2, there is not a direct relationship between age and the number of hisses. Therefore, roman numeral I does not meet the requirements stated in the question. Eliminate answer choices A and B, because they include roman numeral I. Table 1 also indicates that length is not directly related to the number of hisses. So, eliminate answer choice C, which leaves you with answer choice D.

40. **The correct answer is H.** The results of Experiment 2 are shown in Table 2. When Snake A encountered Snake C, Snake A won 10 times, and Snake C won 15 times. Therefore, they must have had a total of 25 encounters with each other, answer choice H.

PART V

APPENDIXES

APPENDIX 1
WHAT'S NEXT?

Once you have successfully tackled the ACT exam, you will still need to deal with the rest of the admissions process. This chapter is meant to provide some useful hints and suggestions to help you to make the best decisions about what colleges and programs to apply to, as well as how to maximize your chances of getting into the college and program of your choice.

CHOOSING THE BEST COLLEGE OR UNIVERSITY FOR YOU

There are many resources out there that include lists of the "best" schools. The truth is that there may be several "best" schools for you as an individual and you may not be a good fit for any of the so-called top schools that appear on those lists. There are positive and negative features of all colleges, and the final decision is up to you and your parents. Our goal here is to provide some food for thought as you make your decision. The following are some factors to consider when choosing a school. As you will see, there are many areas where the factors overlap.

Size

The largest university campuses are in the 35,000 to 50,000 student range. They are small cities unto themselves with their own fire departments and police forces and their own streets and power plants. At the other end of the spectrum are small colleges with just a few hundred students, which are smaller than many high schools. Of course, there are campuses of every size in between.

It is possible to make some generalizations about large versus small campuses. Large campuses tend to have more interesting activities and a wider variety of resources such as libraries and museums. There will be people from all walks of life and from many different places in the world. Large campuses are just more exciting for students than most smaller schools are. On the negative side, large campuses typically have terrible parking problems. One large Midwestern school takes in over one million dollars every year just in parking ticket fines. There also can be more serious crime issues with large schools. Predators of every sort are sometimes drawn to places where there are many young people who may be less vigilant about personal security and theft prevention than they should be. Another negative is the fact that many students at large schools find that it is increasingly difficult to graduate within the traditional four years. Graduation times for a first bachelor's degree are closer to five years than four at many schools. This means one extra year of tuition, and room and board expenses, and one fewer year of making money working in your chosen field.

Location

Many students want to stay close to the support system of their parents' homes. They like the idea of visiting on weekends and of short travel times back and forth. Other students like the idea of striking out on their own and becoming self-reliant. One of the negatives of being far away can be the expense and inconvenience of travel during holiday breaks and other time off. Also, there is the issue of residency to consider. At most state-supported colleges and universities, nonresidents pay a much higher rate for tuition than do residents. The difference in cost can make a state school just as expensive as any private school.

Climate is another factor that falls within the general topic of location. If you are used to surf and sun, think twice before you enroll at a school where summer is defined as "three months of bad sledding."

Another way to look at location is to realize that there are three general types of campuses: rural, suburban, and urban. Each has its own advantages and disadvantages, which you should carefully consider before selecting a campus where you will probably be spending much of your early adulthood.

Money

Several financial factors need to be considered. For some students, at some campuses, tuition is not the most important financial factor to consider. Housing is. There are some college towns where a student can expect to pay an amount each month for housing and parking that is equal to his or her parents' house payment back home. In many such places, it is simply cost prohibitive for a student to own a car. In fact, some campuses are so short on parking that they actually forbid undergraduates from having cars on campus. Make sure that you can afford the rent at the college that you select so that you don't end up living on toast sandwiches, oatmeal, and ramen noodles for four years.

There is also the issue of financial aid, which is a significant question for many students. Make sure that you contact the financial aid office at all of the schools that you are seriously considering to find out about loans, scholarships, and grants that might be available. Do not assume that your family is too well off for you to qualify for aid. Some scholarships are not need-based and can be awarded to students based solely on other factors such as academic performance or standardized test scores.

Reputation

A school's reputation is the most subjective factor to consider. Some schools are so famous that everyone has heard of them. Many more are known only to specialists in a specific field or industry or to people in a certain geographic area. Maybe one of this latter group of schools is just the place for you. Although there may be some correlation between the school you attend and your starting pay or the opportunities that are available to you right after graduation, those correlations tend to break down as time progresses and you build a career and resume of your own.

The reputation of an institution can be affected by factors that are completely nonrelated to what you will experience as a student. For example, schools that win big national athletic championships tend to be well known; many people assume that they are academically superior to other schools, even though there may be no connection at all between those two aspects of a university.

Resources

If you plan to study physics, you should probably look for a school that has some advanced physics equipment. If you want to study large-animal veterinary medicine, you should probably look for a school that has a farm where you can care for horses and cows. This may seem like common sense. But, as Voltaire pointed out, "Common sense isn't." We have seen many students who were disappointed by the actual facilities available for their chosen majors at various campuses.

Athletics

There are two major aspects to athletics at the college level: participation and observation. Do you want a school where you can be an athlete or a fan? Are there scholarship dollars available for your sport? Is your sport a varsity sport or a club sport at the schools in which you are interested? Does your sport even exist at all of the colleges on your list? If you are interested in being a fan, the good news is that even the big powerhouse athletic departments are good about setting aside a fair number of tickets just for students.

Instructors

Some schools, usually the larger ones, have a high proportion of classes that are taught by graduate students, usually called TAs (Teaching Assistants) or GAs (Graduate Assistants). Like most college professors, they probably have had little or no instruction on how to be a teacher. They are underpaid and often sleep deprived. Some of them have a tenuous grasp of the English language. But, there are also some gems. Some of these people are bound to be among the best teachers that you have ever had. However, some students and their families feel that it is worth going out of their way to be certain that they have access to professors and that the class sizes are manageable. Some classes at some colleges can have hundreds of students in a large, amphitheatre-like lecture hall. There isn't much opportunity for meaningful interaction in a situation like that.

Some professors are famous. You may decide that it is worth going out of your way just to sit in a large crowd being lectured to by a particular person of note in his or her chosen field. Some students are, frankly, more comfortable in an environment where it is easy to blend in and they don't have to worry about being called on to answer in class.

Many professors and instructors are focused on delivering quality education to their students, and some colleges go out of their way to arrange for frequent and high-quality interaction between students and instructors.

Social Environment

Everyone is aware that part of the college experience is social interaction. Some schools are single-sex and some are co-ed. Some dorms are segregated by sex also. The male-female ratio can vary from one school to the next. Some schools have reputations for being "party schools." Some schools that are not known as "party schools" actually have some issues with things getting out of control from time to time.

Generally, smaller schools tend to be more socially homogeneous. Students tend to act, dress, and think more like one another. Larger schools tend to consist of a wider variety of perspectives and subcultures. Your comfort level with the social circumstances at your school can have an impact on your college success. Think about your personal social needs carefully when choosing a college.

Diversity

Diversity usually means racial diversity to most people. There are other aspects to diversity at college also: diversity of opinion, socioeconomic background, gender, majors, and countries of origin. All of these are factors on many college campuses. Some students feel that they will learn best in an environment where they are surrounded by people more like themselves. Others are interested in experiencing more diversity and learning from people with different backgrounds.

Overall, the best way to get the true picture of most of these factors is to visit the campuses about which you are serious. You can do some preliminary research on the World Wide Web, but you should remember that Web sites set up by the schools are essentially sales brochures. They have a significant financial interest in getting you to attend. You should be a wise consumer and take some of the sales pitches that you receive with a grain of salt. In fact, it is not a bad idea to try to meet some "real" students if you do a campus visit. Chances are that the school will match you up with a "campus guide," who is a student with training in salesmanship. He or she will tell you about all of the wonderful aspects of life on campus. You probably won't hear any complaints from your campus guide. It might be worth getting out on campus on your own for a while.

APPLYING TO COLLEGE

The general rule of thumb is that you should get all of your application materials into the colleges to which you are applying by the holiday break of your senior year. This means that you will have to have all of your personal statements finished, your applications filled out, your letters of recommendation and resume sent in, and your test scores available to the admissions departments by New Year's Day if you want to be ahead of most of the applicants, some of whom will often actually wait until near the final deadlines to turn in their applications.

Don't "shotgun" your applications; be selective when choosing colleges. Many applications contain a question asking you to list all other colleges to which you are applying. The admissions office will review the answer to this question in order to gauge how realistic you are and whether you actually think that you have a shot at their school.

A good average number of schools to which to apply is about five. Choose one or two "backup" schools that you will attend only if something goes horribly wrong with your applications to your other choices. Two or three should be the schools that are realistic choices for you in terms of your GPA, ACT score, and other factors. One or two should be "reach" or "stretch" schools that might be long shots but where you have some chance at getting in and you will certainly attend if you are selected.

Applications

Applications are usually available as paper documents or as online forms on the schools' Web sites. They vary in length (from two to ten pages, usually three or four pages) and in the type of information that they request. Fees and deadlines also vary. Don't send in an application too early. Candid discussions with admissions professionals reveal that they appreciate promptness and neatness and don't mind a reasonable amount of follow-up. What they do NOT like is sloppiness, an apparent inability to follow directions (sending a five-page personal statement when there is a two-page limit), aggressive and/ or annoying follow-up, last-minute applications, or applications that come in before the department is ready for the year's avalanche of incoming documents.

If you call an admissions department with a specific question or two, be focused. Write down your question ahead of time and keep your call polite, professional, and short. Do not expect anyone in the department to tell you that you can get in or definitely cannot get in. They have a procedure for making those decisions and they simply cannot make exceptions. You should listen for "code words" when you talk to admissions professionals. If they say, "we recommend…" they mean, "Do it." If they say, "we discourage…" they mean, "Don't do it."

Personal Statements

Many schools require you to write an essay or two. Some schools are very general in their requirements. They simply ask you to write an essay explaining why you would be a valuable addition to the school. Other institutions give very specific assignments. You should follow the directions and guidance that they give. Don't write on a topic of your own choosing. Don't go over the page limits given. Don't turn in more essays than requested. Do make sure that the essays that you turn in are your own work. There is nothing wrong with asking a family member, teacher, or other professional for a little guidance and editing assistance. However, if you actually let someone else write your statements for you, it will be fairly simple for an experienced admissions professional to spot your fraud.

The best way to come up with a solid personal statement is to start early. Brainstorm a bit at the beginning of the process. List all of the topics and points that you want to include. Create a few different outlines. Get input from friends, family, teachers, and other professionals. Then do first drafts of the two or three best ideas. Put them aside for a week or two, then take them back out and read them again. We all have a tendency to fall in love with our own ideas and our own writing at first. If the idea still looks solid when you review it days later, it is probably worth finishing. Plan to go through several drafts and to get feedback from people that you trust along the way. The personal statement is usually your only chance to get the admissions committee to see you as a human being rather than just a set of numbers or a resume.

The best personal statements are more than just mere resume information. They are also more than just the all-too-common "kiss up" letter. You should definitely avoid the standard format of "You guys are soooo cool! [Here are some details that I looked up to prove it.] And, I'm cool too! [Here are some wonderful things about me.] Therefore, let me in!"

Instead, you should try to tell a story about yourself that illustrates a positive characteristic about which you want the admissions committee to know. A narrative format with a beginning, a middle, and a conclusion is far more effective than simply pasting in some information about the school that you probably learned from its Web site and that they probably already know. If the story illustrates something unique about you, or a hardship that you have overcome, that is fine. But make sure that you avoid the whiny tone that turns readers off. There is a big difference between explaining a legitimate reason for a temporary dip in your Grade Point Average and trying to gain admission through sympathy for your plight. The latter almost never works.

Letters of Recommendation

Most colleges have some famous alumni. They are not likely to be overly impressed if you get a recommendation letter from someone who is famous or powerful, unless that person actually knows you well and can honestly praise you effusively and in great detail. Be careful about the choice of people you ask to recommend you. Make sure that they are people who know you well and can speak about your academic strengths and/or strength of character. Give them plenty of time and don't be afraid to follow up to be certain that your letters are ready or went out to the schools on time. Provide them with a pre-addressed, stamped envelope if the letter is to be sent via U.S. Mail. Offer to provide them with a copy of your resume, or work that you did in their class, or a list of bullet points that you hope that they will include in your letter.

Be sensitive to "code words" in this situation also. If you hear, "I'm not sure that I'd be the best person for this," or, "I'm not 100% comfortable..." or, "Maybe you should ask someone who knows you better," run, don't walk, to find someone else to write your letter. If you persist, some folks are too polite to refuse outright but they may end up doing something that is fairly well known in the admissions game, called "damning with faint praise." If a letter of recommendation is lukewarm in its descriptions of your abilities and positive attributes, the admissions committee reads it as saying, "I couldn't get out of this gracefully but I can't really recommend this candidate wholeheartedly."

Resume

You may not have ever had a reason to put together a resume before. Most colleges will either ask you for one or accept one if you include it with your application. There are many great sources of information regarding how to format your resume. The best advice is to keep it simple and straightforward. Don't play games with fonts, colors, and so on. Just lay out the information in an easy-to-read format so that the busy person who will be looking at it can quickly find what he or she needs. Don't include information that might be construed as negative. For instance, if you volunteered for a political candidate, you might think twice about putting that information on your resume for application purposes. The people reading your resume might have political ideals that are directly opposed to "your" candidate and they might let their feelings about politics start to influence their decisions about your application.

SUGGESTED HIGH SCHOOL COURSES

We are including a discussion of the courses that you should probably take to help with your ACT score and to help you get ready for college. Not surprisingly, most of the courses that help with ACT preparation also help with college preparation. Actual course names vary by high school so we are listing the course content that you should try to get in if there is still time.

Mathematics: Algebra, Geometry, Trigonometry, Precalculus

Basic, intermediate, and some advanced algebra concepts will be tested on the ACT. There won't be any geometry proofs, but, there will be plenty of circles and triangles and at least one diagram that will include two parallel lines crossed by a transversal. There won't be any more than four trigonometry questions, so it is probably not worth taking a whole trigonometry course just to do better on the ACT. But, it will probably come in handy as preparation for college math. Similarly, precalculus will help with a very limited number of ACT math problems but is an important part of a College Prep curriculum.

English: Writing/Composition courses

Reading and discussing literature can be an enlightening experience and is certainly part of a good education. However, the English courses that help most with the ACT are the ones that focus on writing skills. Creative Writing course instructors can sometimes be too easy on mechanics and clarity of expression. The more rigorous the course, the better it will prepare you for the ACT and for college-level work.

Science: Biology, Chemistry, Physics

The Science Reasoning Test does not test your memory of the concepts that you learn in high school science courses. It does, however, assume that you have some background knowledge and a clear understanding of how scientific experiments and studies are conducted. If you have written up a few lab reports of your own, you will have a much easier time reading and understanding the information on the Science Reasoning Test.

Languages: Latin, Spanish, Italian, French

Most English vocabulary comes from Latin. If you study Latin, or one of the modern versions of Latin that is spoken today, you'll have a much easier time with English vocabulary. It is also true that many native English-speaking students learn much more about English grammar by studying a foreign language than those students who take only English courses.

Good Luck!

If you have followed our advice and worked through all of the material in this book, you should give yourself a hearty "Well done!" and remember that you have put in plenty of effort to ensure your ACT success. Thanks for letting us help you get ready for the ACT. Good luck with your exam and with college!

ACT VOCABULARY LIST

All of these words have been used on past ACTs. Some of them are included because former students asked about them. Some are included here because they have been selected by experienced ACT instructors as representative of the vocabulary level that is expected on the ACT.

Abound: to be well supplied; to have great quantities

Absence: being away or lacking something; inattentiveness

Absurd: extremely ridiculous or completely lacking reason

Abundance: having considerably more than is necessary or adequate; more than plenty

Acceleration: the rate of change of velocity

Accommodate: to adapt or adjust in a way that makes someone else comfortable; to make room

Accusation: a statement blaming someone for a crime or error

Acrid: harsh or bitter taste or smell

Acute: (n.) an angle that is less than 90 degrees; a triangle with angles that are all less than 90 degrees; (adj.) sharp; quick and precise; intense

Adapt: to change or modify to suit a particular purpose

Adjacent: in the nearest position; next to

Adolescence: the stage of development between puberty and maturity

Aerobic respiration: the breakdown of glucose in the body of an animal to supply muscles with oxygen

Aerosol: solid or liquid particles suspended in gas

Aesthetic: appeals to the senses because it is beautiful

Affiliation: a connection between groups of people, organizations, or establishments

Agility: the quality of being quick and nimble

Agronomist: a soil management and field-crop production expert

Alienate: to isolate oneself from others or another person from oneself

Align: to adjust parts so that they fit together correctly, usually in a straight line

Alkalinity: having a pH greater than 7 (contrast with *basic* which is having a pH less than 7)

Allegiance: loyalty to a person, group, country, or cause

Altitude: elevation above a level of reference, usually given in feet above sea level

Ambiguous: unclear or capable of having more than one meaning

Amino acids: organic compounds that link together to form proteins

Ample: a more-than-sufficient amount; roomy

Analogous: items that are similar and comparable in some way; serving a similar function

Analogy: a comparison of similarities between two or more things

Anatomical: related to the structure of an organism

Ancestral: relating to or inherited from an ancestor

Anew: starting again in a new or different way

Anomaly: something that is different from the norm

Anticipate: to look forward to or to expect

Antigen: a substance such as a toxin or enzyme capable of eliciting an immune response

Antitoxin: an antibody created for and capable of neutralizing a toxin

Apathy: lack of any emotion or concern

Aperture: an opening or hole, usually in an optical instrument, such as a camera, that limits the amount of light passing through a lens

Apocalypse: great or total devastation; approximating the end of the world

Apparatus: a group of materials or devices used for a specific purpose

Appealing: attractive or inviting; the act of making a request for a decision or help

Arisen: the state of being up after sitting or lying

Aristocratic: having the qualities of the elite, ruling class

Articulate: (v.) to clearly explain; (n.) the quality of being able to speak clearly

Aspect: a certain part of something; the side of an object that faces in a certain direction

Assert: to demonstrate power; to defend a statement as true

Assumption: something believed to be true without proof; unsupported evidence

Asteroid: small celestial bodies that revolve around the sun, with diameters between a few and several hundred kilometers

Asthenosphere: the lower layer of the Earth's crust

Astonishing: amazing or bewildering

Atrium:	an area of a building, usually a courtyard, that is skylighted or open to the sky and that often contains plants
Bacteria:	single-celled microorganisms
Banish:	to force to leave; to exile
Banyan:	East Indian tree that has aerial shoots growing down into the soil and forming additional trunks; loose jacket worn in India
Basalt:	solidified lava; a dense, dark, gray fine-grained igneous rock
Bemoan:	to express grief; to deplore
Beneficiary:	recipient of benefits, for example, funds or property from an insurance policy or will
Binge:	a duration of excessive and uncontrolled self-indulgence
Biomass:	total mass of all the living matter within a given area
Biosynthesis:	the production of a chemical compound within the body
Boiling point:	the temperature a liquid must be to change states from liquid to gas
Brood:	(v.) to dwell over past misfortune; (n.) a group of offspring
Buoyant:	tending to float; lighthearted
Bureaucrat:	an official in government; a term usually used in an insulting manner
By-products:	sometimes unexpected products made in the process of making something else
Calamity:	horrible event that results in extreme loss
Calligraphy:	beautiful handwriting
Capacity:	maximum amount that an object or area can hold; mental ability
Capillary:	a very slim tube; one of a network of extremely small blood vessels
Carbohydrate:	sugars and starches that serve as a major energy source for animals
Catalogue:	a systematic list of things, such as books in a library or items for sale at a store
Catalyst:	an agent that causes or speeds up a chemical reaction
Celestial:	relating to the sky; divine or heavenly
Celsius:	a temperature scale in which the freezing point of water is 0 degrees and the boiling point is 100 degrees under normal atmospheric conditions
Cerebral edema:	brain swelling
Cesarean:	relating to the medical procedure of surgical abdominal birth, referred to as a *cesarean section*
Chaos:	a state of complete disarray
Characteristics:	distinguishing attributes or qualities of a person or thing

Chlorophyll: a green pigment produced in response to sunlight during photosynthesis

Cholesterol: a soft, waxy compound found in the body and in the food we eat

Chronology: a list of events arranged by time of occurrence

Circumscribe: to enclose a shape with lines or curves, so that every vertex of the enclosed object touches part of the enclosing configuration

Coherent: the quality of being logical and clear

Cohesiveness: the quality of sticking together

Coincidental: occurring by chance

Collinear: passing through or lying on the same straight line

Colloid: a gelatinous material

Comet: a celestial body, having an elongated, curved vapor tail, which is seen only in that part of its orbit that is relatively close to the sun

Commendable: worthy of praise

Common difference: the equal distance between one number in an arithmetic sequence and the next (for example, the common difference between 4, 6, and 8 is 2.)

Common ratio: the ratio of one term and the next in a geometric sequence (for example, the common ratio between 2, 4, and 8 is $\frac{4}{2}$ and $\frac{8}{4}$, or 2.)

Comparison: a description of similarities or differences between two things

Compatriot: someone from one's own country; a colleague

Competence: the quality of having adequate skill, knowledge, and experience

Compose: to form by placing parts or elements together; to bring oneself to a state of calm

Comprehensive: all-inclusive

Compressibility: the ease with which pressure can alter the volume of matter

Concede: to admit or reluctantly yield; to surrender

Concentration: the amount of one substance contained within another; intense mental effort or focus

Concentric: having a common center

Concerto: composition for an orchestra and one or more solo instruments, typically in three movements

Concoct: to prepare by mixing ingredients together; devise a plan

Condense: to become more compact; to change from a vapor to a liquid

Conducive: tending to cause or bring about

Congruent: corresponding; equal in length or measure

Conjure: to bring to mind; to produce as if by magic

Conscience: the mental sense that guides moral decisions

Consecutive:	uninterrupted sequence
Consent:	(n.) permission; (v.) to agree to
Consequence:	result of an action
Conservatory:	a fine arts school; a greenhouse of plants aesthetically arranged
Constant:	the quality of being unchanging; marked by firm resolution or loyalty
Constituency:	a group of citizens who have the power to elect an official; an electoral district
Contemplate:	to carefully consider
Contemporaries:	people or things of the same time era or age
Contemporary:	singular form of *contemporaries*; current, modern
Context:	text or spoken words that surround a word or passage and help determine meaning; circumstances that surround an event
Contradict:	to assert the opposite
Contrive:	to clearly plan; to cleverly devise
Controversial:	characterized by dispute or controversy
Cordial:	sincere; courteous
Correlate:	to have corresponding characteristics
Cos:	abbreviation of cosine
Cosine:	In a right triangle, the ratio of the length of the side adjacent to the acute angle divided by the hypotenuse ($\cos = \dfrac{adj.}{hyp}$)
Credulity:	a tendency to trust too easily
Crimson:	a deep red color
Criterion:	requirements on which judgment can be based
Crucial:	extremely important
Cryopreservation:	preservation (as of cells) by very low temperatures
Cube:	a term raised to the third power; a regular solid having six congruent faces
Cubic inch:	the volume of a cube with edges that all measure one inch
Cuisine:	the food prepared by a style of cooking, for example, "Italian cuisine"
Cylindrical:	having the shape of a cylinder, or a solid with circular ends and straight sides
Decipher:	to interpret the meaning, usually of a code or hard-to-read handwriting
Decompose:	to disintegrate into components
De-emphasize:	to minimize the importance

Defection:	withdrawing one's support; to escape or become a traitor
Deform:	to disfigure; to ruin the shape of an object
Degree:	one in a series of steps in a process or scale; a unit of measurement
Delegate:	(v.) to transfer responsibilities to another; (n.) a personal representative
Deliberate:	(adj.) carefully planned out; (v.) to consider carefully
Delve:	to deeply and thoroughly search
Demean:	to reduce in worth
Demise:	the end of existence
Demur:	to express opposition
Derive:	to infer certain knowledge; to trace the origin or development of something
Descend:	to come from a particular origin; to move down from a higher point
Descendant:	a person, animal, or plant that can be traced back to a certain origin; future or subsequent generations
Deter:	to prevent from taking a particular course of action
Determinant:	the difference between multiplied terms in a matrix
Deviation:	a divergence from a certain path; in mathematics: the difference, especially the absolute difference, between one number in a set and the mean of the set
Devise:	(v.) to design or create; often confused with the noun *device*, which means "tool that fulfills a certain purpose"
Diagonal:	a line segment joining two nonadjacent vertices of a polygon or solid (polyhedron)
Diffusion time:	the time that it takes for a material to spread from one area to another
Diligent:	continuously putting in great effort
Dilute:	to weaken the strength of a solution
Diminish:	to make smaller, decrease, or lessen
Directly proportional:	increasing or decreasing together or with the same ratio
Disavow:	to deny knowledge of, responsibility for, or association with
Discern:	to differentiate or distinguish; to perceive
Discomforting:	embarrassing
Disconcerting:	unsettling
Discriminatory:	showing a bias
Disdainful:	scornful and sneering
Dispel:	to rid one's mind of; to drive out

Disperse:	to scatter or spread out everywhere
Disquieting:	lacking peace of mind; mental unrest
Dissolution:	the process of dissolving or disintegrating
Dissolve:	to pass into or and become part of; to terminate
Distinct:	easily distinguishable from others
Dominant:	the most prominent; exuding authority
Dowry:	in certain cultures, the money, goods, and so on, that a woman brings to a marriage
Drag force:	the force that resists or slows down motion through a medium such as air
Drastic:	extreme
Durable goods:	in economics, goods that are not depleted with use, such as household appliances and cars
Durable:	resistant to wear
Ecology:	the field of science that concentrates on relationships between organisms and their environments
Elaborate:	(adj.) rich with detail and well developed; (v.) to expand on the idea of something
Electorate:	the body of all of the people who possess the right to vote
Eloquent:	very clear and precise; quality of being skilled in clear and precise speech
Emanant:	something such as a gas or odor coming forth and off of a source
Embalm:	to maintain a dead body by treating it with chemical preservatives
Embittered:	possessing bitter feelings
Embrace:	to enclose in one's arms; become accepting of other ideas or people
Emigration:	leaving one country and traveling to live in another
Emissions:	things that are discharged (often gases into the air)
Emit:	to release particular things such as liquid, heat, gases
Empowered:	possessing the necessary abilities for a particular task; given power or authority
Emulate:	to follow an admirable example; imitate
Emulsion:	a state in which one liquid is suspended in another because the liquids will not dissolve in one another
Endorsement:	a guarantee to support; a signature on a document such as a check
Endow:	to give a positive trait; to provide monetary funds by donation
Endpoints:	what defines the beginning and end-of-line segment
Endure:	to continue despite difficulty; to tolerate

Enormity:	traditionally, the term has meant a horrible wrong; today, it commonly means "of tremendous size"
Enrich:	to improve
Enshrine:	to enclose in a shrine or place of devotion
Entangle:	to twist and tie up in a complicated manner
Enumerate:	to state things in a list
Envision:	to picture a mental image
Eon:	duration of time, so long it cannot be measured
Epic:	(n.) widely celebrated literary work that has survived a long period of time; (adj.) very impressive and extraordinary
Epicanthic fold:	a fold of skin of the upper eyelid that only partly covers the eye's inner corner
Equilibrium:	a state of balance
Erosion:	the wearing away of an object by outside forces, like wind or water
Error:	a mistake; the difference between a computed value and the correct value
Escapist:	one who mentally leaves the real world for a world of fantasy
Essence:	important characteristics that help differentiate something; the key element of an idea; something spiritual; a scent
Essential:	(adj.) the quality of being indispensable or necessary
Essentially:	at the very core
Establish:	to create a foundation
Ethical:	in line with what is right and wrong
Ethnicity:	cultural and racial association
Evaporate:	to draw away moisture and convert into vapor
Exceed:	to go far beyond a limit; excel
Exceptional:	rare due to uncommonly great qualities
Exhibit:	(v.) to display; (n.) something that is displayed; (n.) a piece of evidence submitted to a court during a trial
Expatriate:	(v.) to banish someone; (v.) to move from one's native land; (n.) one who lives in a foreign country
Experimental variables:	elements of an experiment that are changed (distinguished from *constants*, which are held the same in order to produce significant results)
Expertise:	skill or knowledge in a certain area
Exquisite:	characterized by great beauty and intricacy
Extensive:	detailed and far-reaching
Extinct:	no longer existing

Extrapolate:	to guess by inferring from known information
Extravagant:	lavish beyond the norm
Exultant:	gleeful because of success
Fahrenheit:	a temperature scale that measures the boiling point of water at 212 degrees and the freezing point at 32 degrees
Feign:	to fabricate or deceive
Fermentation:	the chemical process of breaking down an organic substance into simpler substances such as the fermentation of sugar to alcohol
Fickle:	constantly changing one's mind
Fjord:	an inlet lined by steep slopes that is long, narrow, and deep
Fledgling:	technically, a young bird that has just acquired feathers; also used to describe an inexperienced newcomer
Flourish:	(v.) to plentifully abound; (v.) to thrive; (n.) a dramatic gesture; (n.) a written embellishment
Foil:	(n.) a character whose traits exemplify the opposite traits of another character when they are compared; (v.) to prevent an action, often by ruining a plan; (n.) a weapon used in the sport of fencing
Foliation:	the alternating layers of different mineral compositions within solid rocks
Forecast:	to predict future events, such as the weather
Foresee:	to know beforehand
Foreshadow:	to suggest or hint at future occurrences
Forgo:	to refrain from doing something previously planned
Formalize:	to make something official or valid
Franchise:	a right given to an individual or group to operate a branch of a business and sell the business's products; the right to vote
Frenzied:	in a temporary crazed state
Friction:	the force resistant to motion
Frivolous:	unnecessary and silly
Gable:	the triangular section of a wall that fills the space between the two slopes of a roof
Galvanism:	a direct electrical current produced by chemical reactions
Gas:	a fluid (as air) that is not independent in shape or volume but tends to expand
Gas chromatograph:	a device used to detect the composition of an unknown material
Gastric emptying:	the movement from the stomach to the small intestine, and finally into the colon
Gaudy:	tastelessly flashy

Glacial: relating to a glacier; callous and cold; extremely slow

Glib: doing something with ease and slickness, but lacking sincerity

Gravity: the force of attraction between two bodies of mass

Gypsum: a yellowish-white mineral used to make plaster

Haggle: to bargain in an annoying manner; to harass

Halitosis: the condition of having breath with a foul odor

Harbinger: a sign that foreshadows upcoming events

Herbivorous: a plant-eating organism

Hindu: (adj.) relating to the religion of Hinduism, which originated in India; (n.) a person who practices Hinduism

Hoist: to lift up

Homeric epic: a classic Greek tale of heroism written by the ninth-century Greek author Homer

Hue: color

Humidity: a measure of how damp the air is

Hydraulic: operated by using water or fluid pressure

Hydrogen bonding: the chemical bonding of a hydrogen atom with another electro-negative atom

Hypotenuse: the longest side of a right-angle triangle, which is always the side opposite of the right angle

Ideological: relating to the fundamental ideas of an individual or group

Idiosyncrasy: a peculiar characteristic

Igneous rock: rocks that are formed by the cooling and solidification of molten magma

Ignition temperature: the temperature that a fuel must reach before combustion can begin

Immerse: to completely submerge

Imminent: close to happening; impending

Imply: to indirectly suggest, often confused with *infer*, which means "to conclude"

Improvise: to do or perform without preparation; to create something only from readily available materials.

Inalienable: impossible to take away

Inauguration: a formal initiation or induction

Incarcerate: to imprison

Incinerate: to set fire to and burn something until it is reduced to ashes

Inclined: (v.) disposed to a certain path of thought; (adj.) sloping angle

Inconstant: not following a pattern; varying

Incorporate:	to bring two things or certain aspects of two things together
Indifference:	total lack of concern or interest
Indigenous:	native to or naturally existing in a certain area
Indignation:	anger due to unfairness
Indulge:	to freely partake in; to yield to the wish or desire of oneself or others
Inevitable:	bound to happen; unavoidable
Inexhaustible:	plentiful; impossible to use up completely
Inexplicable:	impossible to give the reason for; unexplainable
Infer:	to deduce from evidence, often confused with *imply*
Infirmary:	a small hospital, often in an institution, used to provide care for the sick
Infrared:	light energy having a wavelength below the visible range; it is experienced as heat
Infuse:	for one substance to penetrate into another (for example, steak infused with garlic flavor)
Ingenious:	brilliant and clever
Inherent:	naturally occurring, permanent element or attribute
Inscribe:	to write or engrave words on a surface; to write one's name on something
Insinuate:	to subtly imply
Institute:	(v.) to enact or establish; (n.) an organization
Institution:	an establishment; a pillar of society (for example, the institution of marriage)
Interior angle:	an angle inside of a shape (that is, all of the interior angles in a triangle add up to 180 degrees)
Intern:	one who is confined during wartime against his or her will; a student or recent graduate working as an apprentice in a certain professional field
Interpret:	to translate or explain a concept
Interpretation:	a personal explanation for another's creation, such as a play or poem
Interstitial:	(n.) fluid outside of cells; (adj.) occupying the small spaces between objects; (adj.) occurring during the short time periods between events
Intracellular:	fluid in cells
Intricacy:	a detail of something complex
Invaluable:	priceless
Involuntary:	an action done without one's consent or free will

Irony:	use of words to express a meaning that is the opposite of the real meaning; similar to and often confused with *sarcasm*, which means "words used to insult or scorn"
Irreconcilable:	impossible to adjust or compromise
Irrelevant:	not relevant or pertinent; outside the scope of a discussion or argument
Irrevocable:	impossible to reverse
Isosceles triangle:	a triangle with two congruent sides and two congruent angles
Isotopes:	two or more atoms with an identical atomic number and differing electrical charges
Juxtaposition:	an act of placing things next to each other, usually for comparing or contrasting
Kelvin:	a unit of temperature where $0\,K$ is absolute zero, the freezing point of water is $273\,K$, and the boiling point of water is $373\,K$
Languish:	to become weak; to become disenchanted
Lavish:	(adj.) elaborate and luxurious; (v.) to freely and boundlessly bestow
Law of Sines:	the relationship among the angles and the sides of a triangle (the sine of the angles is equal to the lengths of the sides)
Least common denominator (LCD):	the smallest number (other than 0) that is a multiple of a set of denominators (for example, the LCD of $\frac{1}{4}$ and $\frac{1}{6}$ is 12)
Least common multiple (LCM):	the smallest number (other than 0) that is a multiple of a set of numbers (for example, the LCM of 6 and 9 is 18)
Liberally:	done in a manner that is generous (for example, liberally applying sunscreen)
Limbo:	a precarious state; in Roman Catholicism, the otherworldly place for unbaptized but good people
Linear:	relating to a line
Lipid:	an oily/waxy organic compound that cannot be dissolved in water
Liquid:	(n.) neither a solid nor a gas; (adj.) flowing freely
Lithosphere:	the outer part of the earth that includes the crust and upper mantle
Log:	abbreviation of *logarithm*. Logarithms are used to indicate exponents of certain numbers called bases. By definition, $\log_a b = c$ if $a^c = b$, (for example, $\log_x 36 = 2$ if $x^2 = 36$. In this case, $x = 6$.)
Lumbering:	lethargically walking around with clumsiness
Macrophages:	protective cells
Manifest:	(adj.) clearly recognizable; (v.) to make clear; (n.) a list of transported goods or passengers used for recordkeeping
Manometer:	a device that measures the pressure of liquids and gases

Marine:	(adj.) relating to the sea; (n.) a member of the U.S. Marine Corps
Matrix:	rows and columns of elements arranged in a rectangle
Mean – (also: *arithmetic mean***):**	average. Found by adding all the terms in a set and dividing by the number of terms.
Median:	the middle value in a set of ordered numbers
Mediocre:	lacking any special qualities, even inferior
Melancholy:	glumness; deep contemplative thought
Melting point:	the temperature at which a solid softens into a liquid
Mere:	small; (adv. merely) nothing more
Mesosphere:	a layer of the atmosphere fifty to eighty kilometers above the earth's surface
Metamorphism:	the process of altering solid rocks by changing its temperature, pressure, and chemistry
Meteorite:	a meteor that reaches the surface of the earth before it is entirely vaporized
Meticulous:	devoting a high amount of attention to detail
Microorganisms:	an organism of microscopic or very small size
Midpoint:	the point that divides a line segment into two equal segments
Minuscule:	extremely small; unimportant
Mole:	a unit of measurement for the molecular weight of a substance
Molecular weight:	the weight of all of the atoms in a molecule
Molten:	turned to liquid because of heat
Moral:	(adj.) based on standards of good and bad; (n.) a rule of proper behavior
Morale:	mental well-being; mood
Mortar:	a bowl in which substances are ground; a mixture, usually cement and water, used to bond bricks or stones; a military weapon similar to portable artillery
Mutability:	the ability to transform
Nanometer:	one billionth of a meter
Negligible:	meaningless and insignificant
Neural:	relating to the nervous system
Neurological:	relating to neurology, the study of the nervous system
Newton:	the amount of force needed to accelerate a one-kilogram mass at a rate of one meter per second, per second
Nostalgia:	sentimental yearning for the past
Notion:	a belief, sometimes without much conviction

Numerous:	existing in great numbers of units or persons
Oblong:	deviating from a square, circular, or spherical form by being slightly longer in one area
Obtuse:	an angle that is larger than a right angle
Offal:	wasted trimmings of an animal carcass; trash or rubbish
Onus:	a burden of responsibility
Opus:	a creative composition, usually musical
Oracle:	a shrine devoted to a future-telling deity or the deity himself; a prophet
Organic matter:	matter that is derived from living organisms
Organism:	a living thing, either plant or animal
Overt:	obvious and clearly shown
Paradox:	a statement that seems contradictory but is actually true
Paragon:	an example of excellence
Parallel:	lines in the same plane that do not intersect each other; in a coordinate plane, noncollinear lines or segments having the same slope as one another
Parallelogram:	a quadrilateral (a figure that has four sides) with opposite sides that are parallel and congruent
Parenthetical:	an explanatory statement that is set off by parentheses
Pathetic:	deserves pity or sympathy
Peculiarity:	unusual quality or characteristic
Pendulum:	a device that is suspended in such a way to allow it to swing back and forth using gravity
Perceive:	the act of becoming aware of something, usually through the senses
Percolate:	to slowly pass through a porous substance
Perfunctorily:	in a manner that suggests little interest or attention; a routine duty
Perimeter:	the distance around a figure
Periphery:	the outermost boundary of an area
Perpendicular:	lines that intersect and form 90-degree angles
pH:	a scale that measures how acidic or basic a substance is on a scale of 0 to 14. Lower numbers indicate an increasing acidity and higher numbers indicate increasing basicity
Phantom:	exists only in the mind (an illusion); a ghost
Phenomenon:	an event or circumstance that is significant or extraordinary
Photophores:	organs that produce light
Photosynthesis:	the process by which plants turn carbon dioxide and water into energy with the aid of sunlight

Pigmentation:	coloration
Plagiarism:	an act of fraud consisting of copying another's work and pretending that it is original
Point-slope formula:	the formula used to calculate the slope of a line: $\dfrac{(y_1 - y_2)}{(x_1 - x_2)}$
Positive slope:	a line that slants upward (from left to right) because of the positive sign of its slope
Pow-wow:	a meeting or gathering
Preceding:	coming before
Precipitate:	to cause something to happen very suddenly
Precipitation:	the quality or state that causes vapor to condense and fall
Predominant:	having superior strength, paramount
Preliminary:	precedes or comes prior to
Prerequisite:	required beforehand
Prestigious:	having honor or respect from others
Prevail:	to triumph or come out on top
Prevalent:	commonly used or occurring
Prime number:	a positive integer that can only be evenly divided by 1 and itself
Primordial:	happening first or very early
Protagonist:	the main character of a story or tale
Protein:	a compound that consists of amino acids and plays various structural, mechanical, and nutritional roles within organisms
Prototype:	an original form of something
Protract:	to lengthen or prolong
Prowess:	great skill in something
Pseudoscience:	irrational or unfounded beliefs masquerading as science (for example, astrology)
Psychologizing:	explaining something in psychological terms
Pyrotechnics:	a display of fireworks
Quadrant:	one part of a larger object that has been divided into four parts
Quadratic equation:	an equation in the form of $ax^2 + bx + c = 0$, where $a \neq 0$, and has only two solutions for x
Quasi:	resembles to some degree
Quintessential:	considered the perfect form
Radian:	a unit of angle measure within a circle
Radiate:	to emit energy or light that extends from a single source
Radii:	the plural form of radius

Radioactive decay:	a natural process by which an atom of a radioactive isotope spontaneously decays into another element
Radius:	a line segment with endpoints at the center of the circle and on the perimeter of the circle, equal to one-half the length of the diameter
Rapid:	moving very quickly
Rapt:	being completely occupied by, or focused on, something
Ratio:	a comparison between two quantities (for example, the ratio of girls to boys in the class is 1:2)
Real number line:	an infinite line of real numbers represented on a one-dimensional graph
Real numbers:	numbers that can be associated with points on a number line
Recount:	to describe the facts or details of a past event; to retell a story or repeat testimony
Rectangular:	having the shape of a rectangle (a parallelogram with four right angles)
Recurrent:	taking place over and over
Redeem:	to pay off a debt or fulfill an obligation; to make good
Redirect:	to alter the course or direction
Rediscover:	to learn about or see something as though for the first time
Regular hexagon:	a six-sided figure with congruent sides and angles
Relevant:	logically connected; pertinent
Reluctant:	unwilling and resistant
Reparation:	compensation given to make amends
Resonate:	to produce vibrations
Respectively:	in the order given
Retention:	the ability to hold things in or retain
Rifling:	(v.) to search through, looking for something to steal; (n.) the spiral grooves on the inside of a gun barrel
Rift:	a split or a break
Rotate vs. Revolve:	rotate: to turn about a fixed point; revolve: to turn on an axis
Rudimentary:	very basic or not fully developed
Sacrilege:	to misuse something that is sacred
Sanctuary:	a sacred place; a refuge
Saplings:	young trees
Saturation:	a state of being completely full or soaked
Sauropod:	a type of plant-eating dinosaur, for example, the brontosaur

Scientific inquiry:	based on experiment and observation and the application of the Scientific Method
Scrutiny:	very close examination
Sediment:	solid materials that sink to the bottom of a liquid
Seedling:	a young plant grown from seed
Seminal:	forms the basis for future development; at the beginning; original
Simultaneously:	happening or existing at the same time
Skepticism:	an attitude of doubt or disbelief
Social rituals:	specific manners and behaviors that are observed by members of a community
Solace:	comfort; safety
Solid:	neither gas nor liquid; of the same or coherent texture
Solute:	a dissolved substance
Solution:	a mixture of two or more substances
Solution set:	the set of values that make an equation true
Sovereign:	(adj.) having supreme power; (n.) ruler or king
Span:	distance between two things
Specific gravity:	the ratio of the weight of one substance to the weight of another substance
Speculators:	people who form theories based on uncertain evidence; those who purchase something with the hope of reselling it later at a profit
Sphere:	a solid, round figure where all points on the surface are the same distance from the center (for example, a basketball)
Spleen:	a vascular, ductless organ that is located in the left abdominal region close to the stomach
Stagnant:	not moving or changing; stale
Standard (x, y) coordinate plane:	a plane that is formed by a horizontal x-axis and a vertical y-axis that meet at point $(0,0)$ (also known as the *Cartesian Coordinate Plane*)
Steerage passenger:	someone who rides in the least expensive section of a ship
Straddle:	having one leg on each side of something
Stratosphere:	a layer of the atmosphere between the troposphere and mesosphere
Subcontractor:	someone who agrees to perform one part of a larger commitment or contract
Subjective:	depending on a person's attitudes or opinions
Subsequent:	to come next or later
Subtropical:	near the tropical areas of the world; extremely humid and hot climate
Sucrose:	a simple sugar

Summary: (n.) a statement that has condensed a larger body of work; (adj.) without trial

Supercooled: below freezing but remaining liquid

Suspensions: the state of a substance when its particles are combined together but have not been dissolved in a fluid or solid

Sustenance: things that provide nourishment for survival

Synchronized: occurring at the same time and at the same rate

Synthesis: combining separate elements to form a whole

Synthetic polymer: a human-made, repeating chain of atoms

Tenet: a belief that is held to be true by a certain group

Terrestrial: relating to dry land as opposed to water; relating to the Earth as opposed to other planets

Territorial: the protective behavior that is displayed when an animal is defending its area

Thermal degradation: a process of combustion where materials in a fuel are broken down into several by-products

Thermosphere: the outermost layer of the atmosphere

Toxins: poisons

Transcend: to go above and beyond; to rise above

Translucent: allowing light to pass through but clouded or frosted in such a way that objects on the other side are not clearly visible; often confused with *transparent,* which means "clear"

Transversal: a line that cuts through two or more lines

Trapezoid: a quadrilateral (a figure with four sides) with only two parallel lines

Treason: a betrayal of loyalty

Triannual: lasting three years or occurring every three years

Tropical Area: an area near the equator that has a frost-free climate with high temperatures that can support year-round vegetation

Troposphere: the lowest part of the earth's atmosphere

Tyranny: absolute power exercised by an oppressive ruler

Ultraviolet: invisible rays of light with wavelengths above the visible spectrum

Unemotional: devoid of sentiment or emotion

Uniform: (adj.) continuing to be the same or consistent; (n.) identical clothing worn by members of a certain group

Unilaterally: performed in a one-sided manner

Unparalleled: without an equal or comparison

Unprecedented: having no previous example

Unsolicited: unwanted

Vapor pressure: the pressure exerted by a vapor

Vaporize: to change into a cloud of diffused matter

Various: of differing kinds

Velocity: speed of motion

Vertical migrators: marine species that travel toward the surface of the ocean to feed

Vertices: the plural form of vertex, which is a point of intersection

Vindication: the act of clearing someone or something from blame

Virtually: in almost all instances; simulated as by a computer

Virus: organism that causes infection

Viscosity: a fluid's resistance to flow

Visionary: (adj.) characterized by dreams or illusions; (n.) a person with vision or foresight

Voltage: a measure of the energy of an electric current

Wavelength: the distance between repeating peaks or crests of waves

x-intercept: the point where a line on a graph crosses the x-axis

y-intercept: the point where a line on a graph crosses the y-axis